KT-477-286

Ukrai...

Lviv & Western Ukraine p108
Kyiv p42
Central Ukraine p90
The Carpathians p142
Eastern Ukraine p204
Southern Ukraine p173
Crimea p193

95100000182271

PLAN YOUR TRIP

ON THE ROAD

EFESENKO / SHUTTERSTOCK ©

FOOD STALL, KYIV P42

OLEKSIY MAKSYMENKO / GETTY IMAGES ©

PYROHIV MUSEUM OF FOLK ARCHITECTURE, KYIV P60

SERGIY TROFIMOV PHOTOGRAPHY / GETTY IMAGES ©

Contents

CARPATHIAN MOUNTAINS
P142

UNDERSTAND

SURVIVAL GUIDE

SPECIAL FEATURES

Welcome to Ukraine

Big, diverse and largely undiscovered, Ukraine is one of Europe's last genuine travel frontiers, a nation rich in colourful tradition, warm-hearted people and off-the-map experiences.

Big & Diverse

Ukraine is big. In fact it's Europe's biggest country (not counting Russia, which isn't entirely in Europe) and packs a lot of diversity into its borders. You can be clambering around the Carpathians in search of Hutsul festivities, sipping Eastern Europe's best coffee in sophisticated Lviv and partying on the beach in Odesa all in a few days. Ukrainians are also a diverse crowd: from the wired sophisticates of Kyiv's business quarters to the Gogolesque farmers in Poltava, the Hungarian-speaking bus drivers of Uzhhorod to the Crimean Tatar cafe owners just about everywhere.

Hospitable Hosts

Despite their often glum reticence and initial distrust of strangers, travellers to the country quickly find that Ukrainians are, when given the chance, one of Europe's most open and hospitable people. Break down that reserve and you'll soon be slurping *borshch* in someone's Soviet-era kitchen, listening to a fellow train passenger's life story or being taken on an impromptu tour of a town's sights by the guy you asked for directions. Much social interaction takes place around Ukraine's hearty food, always brought out in belt-stretching quantities. Learn a bit of Ukrainian and you double the effect.

Living History

As we have now all sadly realised, history didn't end around 1989, and that's doubly true in Ukraine. Having only appeared on the map in 1991, the country has managed two revolutions and a Russian invasion already, and fighting in the Donbas is ongoing. History ancient and recent is all around you in this vast land, whether it be among the Gothic churches of Lviv, the Stalinist facades of Kyiv, the remnants of the once-animated Jewish culture of west Ukraine or the ubiquitous Soviet high-rises.

Outdoor Fun

A diverse landscape obviously throws up a whole bunch of outdoorsy activities – from mountain biking and hill walking in the Carpathians to bird spotting in the Danube Delta, from cycling along the Dnipro in Kyiv to water sports in the Black Sea. But if the idea of burning calories on hill and wave has you fleeing for the sofa, rest assured that most Ukrainians have never tried any of the above, but love nothing more than wandering their country's vast forests, foraging for berries and mushrooms or picnicking by a meandering river.

Why I Love Ukraine

by Marc Di Duca, Writer

Is it the feeling of being elsewhere but still in Europe, the bizarre Soviet legacy, the country's raw history, the unexpected travel experiences, the locals' openness or the stories tall and true of life under communism? Or is it the star-dusted nights in Myrhorod, the *Nutcracker* at the opera house in snow-bound Kyiv, empty churches on rainy autumn Wednesdays in Lviv or the endless train journeys across the steppe in the company of Gogol? I suppose it's all the above and volumes more that have me returning to this magical Slavic hinterland time and again.

For more about our writers, see p288

Above: Kyevo-Pecherska Lavra (p56), Kyiv

Ukraine

BELARUS
POLAND
MOLDOVA
ROMANIA
Uman
Wander Uman's spectacular landscaped park (p95)
Chornobyl
Tour the exclusion zone and ghost town (p30)
Lviv
Join the crowds on the city's central piazza (p110)
The Carpathians
Bike and hike Ukraine's relaxing uplands (p142)
Kamyanets-Podilsky
Wander this town atop a rock island (p100)
Kolomyya
An engaging base for Carpathian exploration (p150)
Odesa
Beach parties by the Black Sea (p174)
Danube Delta
Bird spotting and watery vistas (p191)
Babrujsk
Brest
Pinsk
Home
Novy Yarylovichy
Makrany
Shatsky National Park
Lublin
Okopy Nowe
Kovel
Sarni
VOLYN REGION
RIVNE REGION
Ovruch
Chornobyl
Korosten
POLISSYA
Kyivske Reservoir
Lutsk
Rivne
Korets
Novohrad Volynsky
Chervonohrad
Dubno
Rzeszów
Zhovkva
Kremenets
Shepetivka
Zhulyany Airport
Shehyni
Lviv
Olesko
Pochayiv
Zhytomyr
LVIV REGION
Berdychiv
Bila Tserkva
Drohobych
Ternopil
Stry
Khmelnytsky
TERNOPIL REGION
Vyšné Nemecké
Vinnytsya
Ivano-Frankivsk
Chortkiv
Uzhhorod
Nemyriv
Mukacheve
Yaremche
Kamyanets-Podilsky
PODILLYA
Carpathian NP
Kolomyya
Mogyliv-Podilsky
Uman
Tatariv
Kosiv
Khotyn
Yasinya
Bukovel
Rakhiv
Chernivtsi
Briceni
Siret
Pervomaysk
Balta
Duba
Cluj-Napoca
Chişinău
Berezivka
Tylihulsky lyman
Tiraspol
Kuchurhan
Odesa
Chornomorsk
Sibiu
Bilhorod-Dnistrovsky
Dnistrovsk lyman
Lake Sasyk
Bolhrad
oz Kytay
oz Katlabukh
oz Kahul
Izmayil
Vylkovo
Brăila
oz Yalpuh
Dunaysky NP
Piteşti
Black Sea (Karadeniz)
Bucharest
29°E
30°E
31°E

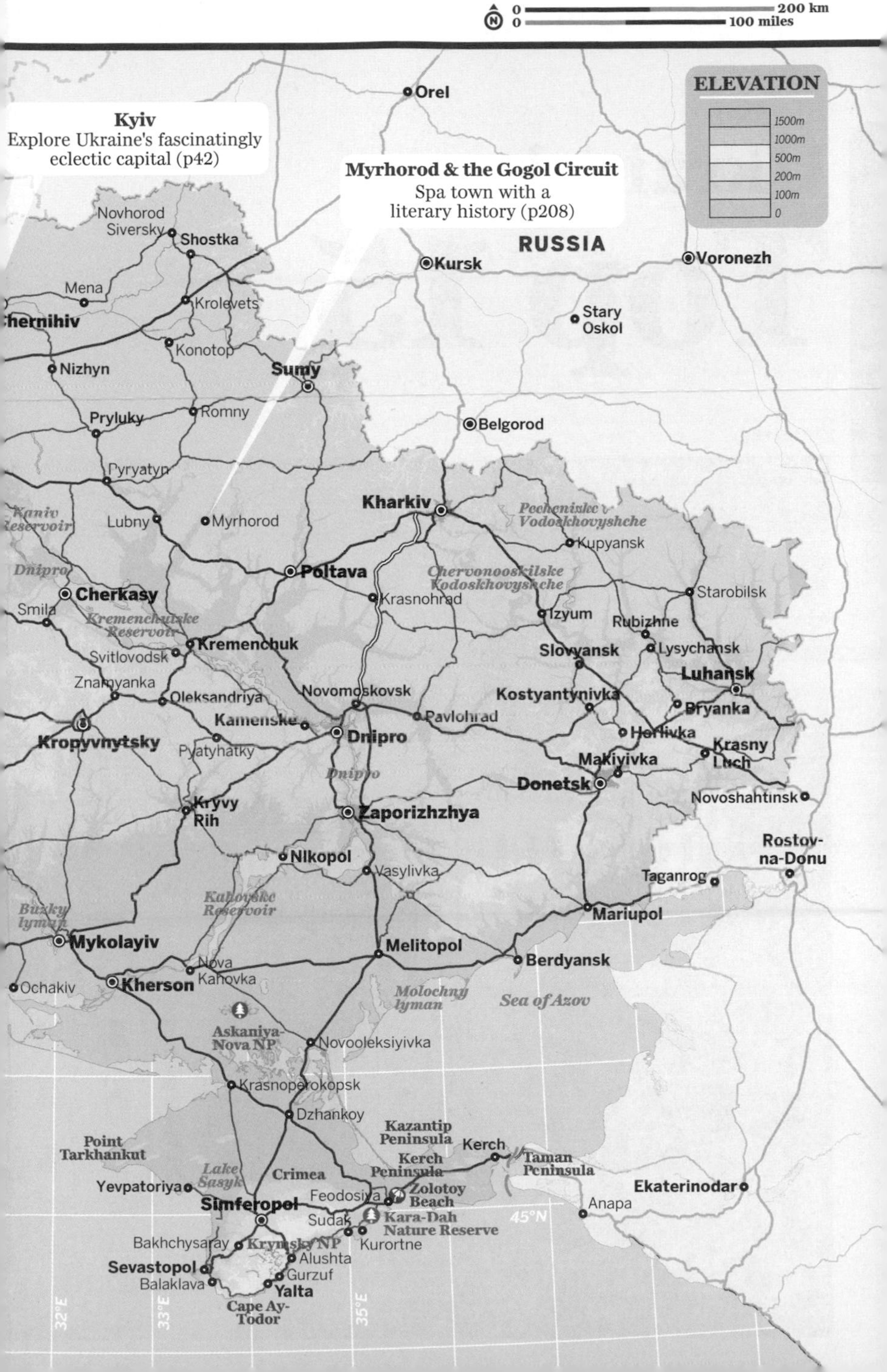

0 200 km
0 100 miles

Kyiv
Explore Ukraine's fascinatingly eclectic capital (p42)

Myrhorod & the Gogol Circuit
Spa town with a literary history (p208)

ELEVATION
1500m
1000m
500m
200m
100m
0

Orel
RUSSIA
Kursk
Voronezh
Novhorod Siversky
Shostka
Mena
Krolevets
Chernihiv
Stary Oskol
Konotop
Nizhyn
Sumy
Romny
Pryluky
Belgorod
Pyryatyn
Kharkiv
Kaniv Reservoir
Lubny
Myrhorod
Pechenizke Vodoskhovyshche
Kupyansk
Dnipro
Poltava
Chervonooskilske Vodoskhovyshche
Cherkasy
Krasnohrad
Starobilsk
Smila
Kremenchutske Reservoir
Izyum
Rubizhne
Kremenchuk
Lysychansk
Slovyansk
Svitlovodsk
Luhansk
Znamyanka
Novomoskovsk
Kostyantynivka
Oleksandriya
Bryanka
Pavlohrad
Kamenske
Horlivka
Kropyvnytsky
Dnipro
Krasny Luch
Pyatyhatky
Makiyivka
Dnipro
Donetsk
Novoshahtinsk
Kryvy Rih
Zaporizhzhya
Rostov-na-Donu
Nikopol
Vasylivka
Taganrog
Kakhovske Reservoir
Buzky lyman
Mariupol
Mykolayiv
Melitopol
Berdyansk
Nova Kahovka
Ochakiv
Kherson
Molochny lyman
Sea of Azov
Askaniya-Nova NP
Novooleksiyivka
Krasnoperokopsk
Dzhankoy
Kazantip Peninsula
Point Tarkhankut
Kerch
Kerch Peninsula
Taman Peninsula
Lake Sasyk
Crimea
Ekaterinodar
Yevpatoriya
Feodosiya
Zolotoy Beach
Simferopol
Kara-Dah Nature Reserve
Anapa
Sudak
45°N
Bakhchysaray
Krymsky NP
Kurortne
Alushta
Sevastopol
Gurzuf
Balaklava
Yalta
Cape Ay-Todor
32°E
33°E
35°E

Ukraine's Top 15

1

Andriyivsky Uzviz, Kyiv

1 The apostle Andrew is said to have climbed this steep ascent (p52) to erect a cross and prophesy the rise of Kyiv. Today it's the haunt of artists, who install their canvases on this cobbled Montmartre-like street, which – in true decadent style – Kyivites call 'Andrew's Descent'. Packed with souvenir stands selling all sorts of junk, the *uzviz* has heaps of Bohemian charm and is great for people-watching. Here Russian writer Mikhail Bulgakov wrote *The White Guard*, perhaps the best novel about Kyiv and its people; his house is now a museum.

Carpathian Landscapes

2 By and large, Ukraine is as flat as a topographically challenged *blin* (pancake), which makes its bumpy bits all the more special. Ukraine's slice of the Carpathian arc barely reaches over 2000m, but its soothing wooded slopes, rough stony trails, flower-filled upland pastures and wide, snaking valleys make this prime hiking, biking and skiing territory. Needless to say, the Carpathians (p142) are home to Ukraine's highest peak, Mt Hoverla (pictured below), a fairly easy trek from nearby villages, as well as the Hutsuls, the country's most colourful ethnic group.

ART_JAZZ / SHUTTERSTOCK ©

2

SYNERGYDESIGN / SHUTTERSTOCK ©

3

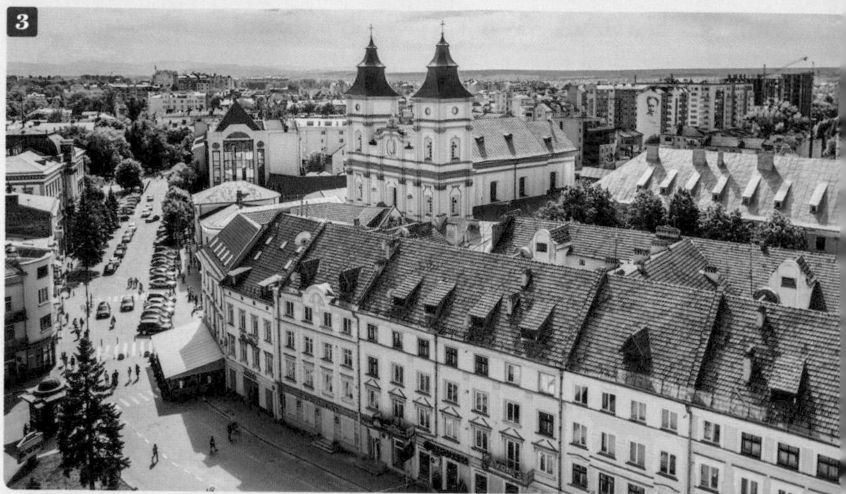

4

Ivano-Frankivsk

3 This once off-limits city (p144) may not entirely live up to its nickname 'Little Lviv', but its historic centre is one of Ukraine's most pleasant, especially in the summer when buskers entertain the evening *corso* (promenade) and cafe tables scatter across pretty squares. Like Lviv, I-F is centred around its *ratusha*, an unusual, star-shaped structure with a climbable tower. When you tire of the city's architectural grandeur, its friendly locals and some of west Ukraine's best food, this is also your northern gateway to the Carpathians.

Danube Delta Biosphere Reserve

4 This reserve (p191) is Europe's largest wetland, located in a huge delta in Ukraine's far southwest where the Danube dumps water and silt into the Black Sea. Few make it to this far-flung wedge of fertile Ukrainian territory (few Ukrainians have been there), but those who do are rewarded with some astoundingly beautiful scenery, colourful birdlife, memorable days out on the water and serene evenings in drowsy Vylkovo, fancifully nicknamed the 'Ukrainian Venice' thanks to its network of canals.

Colourful Markets

5 In the market for a 5L jar of gherkins, a Lada gearbox, a kilo of pig fat or a bottle of fake-brand perfume? You'll probably find them all, plus almost everything else under the sun, at Ukraine's amazing bazaars. They're the best spots to source seasonal fruit and veg, and if you're looking to pack a picnic, these are the places to get supplies. Towns large and small have sprawling markets, but the biggest and best can be found in Chernivtsi (p155), Odesa (p188) and Kyiv (p42).

Top: Bessarabsky Rynok (p81), Kyiv

Kamyanets-Podilsky

6 There are few more eye-pleasing spots in Ukraine than this Podillyan town (p100), ringed by the dramatic gorge of the Smotrych River. A stroll from the new bridge takes you through the cobbled quarters of this once-divided community, past beautifully renovated churches, crumbling palaces and forgotten pieces of the once beefy defences, to the town's impossibly picturesque fortress (pictured above), surely a highlight of any visit to Ukraine. And the best thing? Outside high season you may have the place entirely to yourself.

Lviv's Historical Centre

7 Lviv (p110) is the beating cultural heart of Ukraine and the city most geared up to accept foreign visitors. Its bustling centre is the main square, pl Rynok, in the middle of which rises the huge *ratusha* (town hall). In the shadow of its tall tower mill, clutches of selfie-stick-toting tourists, quick-footed locals and rattling Soviet-era trams somehow squeeze through the crowds. Head in any direction and you will quickly stumble upon a magnificent, aromatic church: each one, it seems, belonging to a different denomination.

Kyevo-Pecherska Lavra, Kyiv

8 Descend into catacombs to see mummies of much-revered saints on an excursion to the holy of holies for all eastern Slavs. Founded as a cave monastery in 1051, the *lavra* (p56) is packed with golden-domed churches, baroque edifices and orchards. Religious ceremonies take place in lavishly decorated, icon-filled interiors, accompanied by exquisite choir singing and attended by flocks of pilgrims and monks. Obscure museums in the grounds are dedicated to Scythian gold, micro-miniatures and decorative arts.

7

WITOLD SKRYPCZAK / ALAMY STOCK PHOTO ©

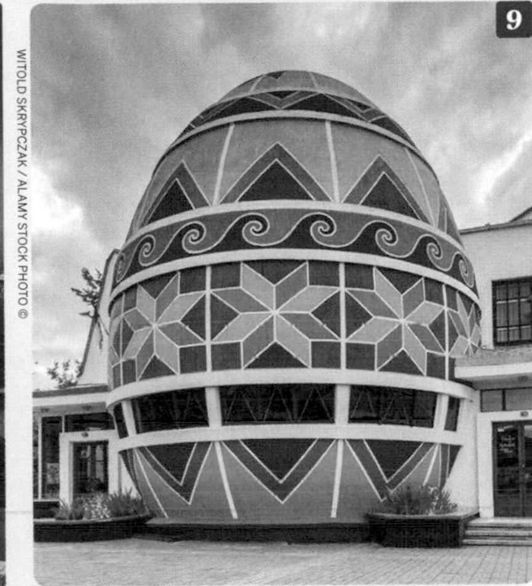

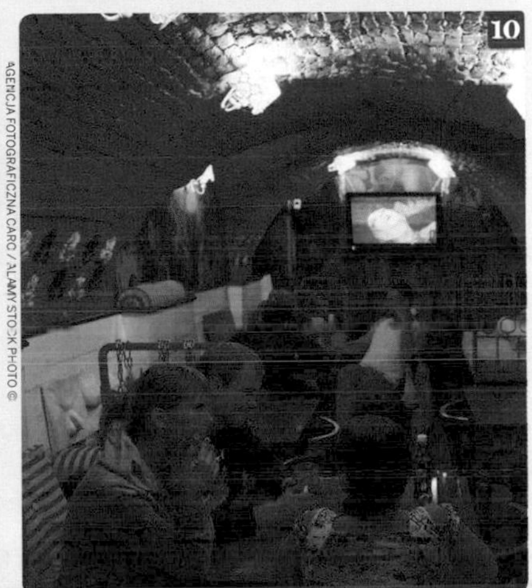

AGENCJA FOTOGRAFICZNA CARO / ALAMY STOCK PHOTO ©

Kolomyya

9 With its traveller-friendly places to stay, two fascinating museums and effortless access to the surrounding forested hills, Kolomyya (p150) is one of the best bases from which to scale the heights of the Carpathians. The town's central Pysanky Museum, housed in a giant Easter egg (pictured top right), is the obvious highlight, but aimless wandering also bears fruit in the shape of some twirling Art Nouveau architecture from the town's Austro-Hungarian days. It also boasts one of the country's best ethnographical museums examining the woolly culture of the local Hutsuls.

Lviv's Food Culture

10 Coffee, chocolate, gingerbread, strudel, cherry liqueur, beer – Lviv (p110) seems to have a festival dedicated to every naughty pleasure, but you don't have to turn up on a red letter day to satisfy your sweet tooth. Ukraine's gastronomic capital has Eastern Europe's best coffee year-round, drunk central European style in cosy cafes. Lviv chocolate is a national phenomenon, as is the local beer – once a favourite in the Kremlin. The city's theme restaurants are also giving way to authentic local cuisine, one of Eastern Europe's most diverse. Above: Masoch Cafe (p128)

Myrhorod & the Gogol Circuit

11 One of the East's most worthwhile stops, the spa town of Myrhorod (p208) will be forever associated with Nikolai Gogol, who was born in a nearby village and who set many of his early tales in and around the town. Take the waters in the Soviet-era tap house and stroll in the pretty spa park before boarding village buses (or hiring a car) to explore the Gogol circuit, a rare tourist route taking in many of the surrounding sights with a Gogol association.

Odesa's Nightlife

12 By day Odesa's (p185) museums, parks, beaches and, of course, the celebrated Potemkin Steps provide ample distraction, but it's at night that the city really comes alive. With its imaginatively styled dance temples and chill-out zones just steps from the Black Sea, Arkadia Beach is the place to strut and pose until the wee summer hours. But Odesa also has a stomping alternative scene, with several hip venues serving up cool ales to the sound of guitar-happy indie bands and local DJs.

ULANA SWITUCHA / ALAMY STOCK PHOTO ©

ALEX SKELLY / GETTY IMAGES ©

Sofiyivka Park, Uman

13 Forget boxes of chocolates, bouquets of roses or even diamond rings – how about wowing your loved one with a gift measuring 150 hectares, replete with grottoes, water features and an entire town's worth of architectural follies? That was the grandiose way one 18th-century Polish magnate chose to express adoration for his wife, Sofia. The legacy of his devotion is this amazing landscaped park (p95) intended to resemble the countryside of Sofia's native land. Her response – an affair with his son.

Pyrohiv Museum of Folk Architecture, Kyiv

14 You can safely claim you've seen all of Ukraine after a visit to Pyrohiv (p60) – a large chunk of countryside just outside Kyiv filled with traditional wooden architecture representing all parts of the country, east and west. Whole churches, windmills, shops and houses were brought here from their original villages, providing a wonderful backdrop for folk festivals, which frequently take place on the grounds. Here, Transcarpathia is walking distance from the Poltava region, although it might require a bit of footwork.

Visiting Chornobyl

15 Touring the site (p30) of the world's worst nuclear accident may not be everyone's idea of a great day out, but this perfectly safe trip is a real eye-opener. Two hours north of Kyiv, guided tours take you into the exclusion zone and as near to the reactor as you can go. However, it's the moving stories of evacuation and the sacrifices made by those sent in to stem the flow of radiation that will live in the memory, as will Pripyat, the model Soviet settlement turned eerie Cold War ghost town.

Need to Know

For more information, see Survival Guide (p255)

Currency

Hryvnya (uah)

Language

Ukrainian and Russian

Money

ATMs are widespread, even in small towns.

Visas

Generally not needed for stays of up to 90 days.

Mobile Phones

Local SIM cards can be used in European and Australian phones. US and other phones aren't compatible; consider a cheap Ukrainian mobile.

Time

East European Time (GMT/UTC plus two hours)

When to Go

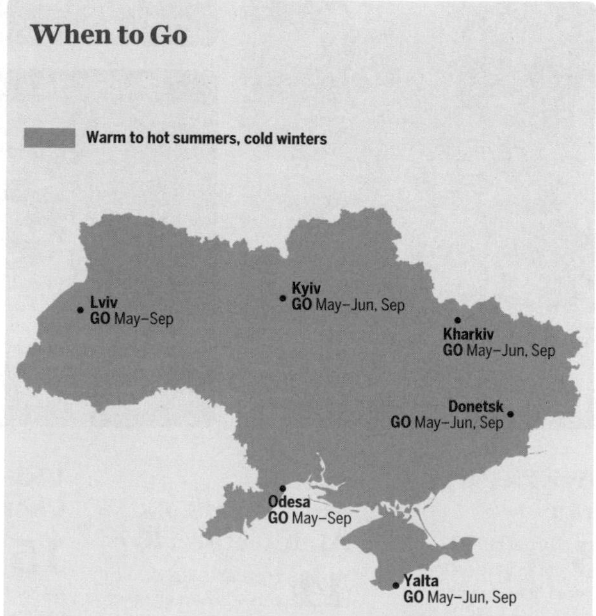

High Season (Jul–Aug)

➡ Expect stifling heat and humidity as well as heavy thunderstorms.

➡ Accommodation rates rise in Odesa but fall in the Carpathians.

➡ Cities empty as people head for the coast and their country cottages.

Shoulder (May–Jun & Sep–Oct)

➡ Travel now to dodge the extreme temperatures of summer or winter.

➡ Spring can be chilly, but it's a pleasant time to be in blossoming Kyiv.

➡ Visit Odesa in autumn and avoid the summer crowds.

Low Season (Nov–Apr)

➡ Expect temperatures well below zero, heavy snowfalls and hard frosts.

➡ The Carpathians skiing season runs November to March.

➡ Book ahead for New Year and early January.

Useful Websites

Lonely Planet (www.lonelyplanet.com/ukraine) Destination information, hotel bookings, traveller forum and more.

Brama (www.brama.com) The most useful Ukraine gateway site.

Ukraine.com (www.ukraine.com) Portal featuring news and lots of background info.

Ukraine Encyclopedia (www.encyclopediaofukraine.com) One of the largest sources of info on Ukraine.

Travel to Ukraine (www.traveltoukraine.org) Official state tourism website.

Kyiv Post (www.kyivpost.com) Daily news, political and cultural commentary.

Important Numbers

When calling within a city, leave off the city code.

Ukraine country code	☎38
International access code	☎00
General emergency number	☎112

Exchange Rates

Australia	A$1	21uah
Canada	C$1	21.50uah
Europe	€1	31.50uah
Japan	¥100	24uah
New Zealand	NZ$1	19uah
Poland	1zł	7uah
Russia	R10	4.50uah
UK	UK£1	34uah
US	US$1	26uah

For current exchange rates see www.xe.com.

Daily Costs

Budget: Less than 500uah

- 100km of bus travel: 130uah
- Cafeteria-style meal: from 80uah
- Dorm beds: 100–250uah

Midrange: 500–2000uah

- Double room with breakfast in a good hotel: 800–1500uah
- Three-course dinner in a restaurant with waiters: from 400uah
- 100km of travel by express train: 100uah

Top end: More than 2000uah

- Double room in a comfortable, European standard hotel: from 2000uah
- Meal in a top restaurant: from 700uah
- English-speaking guide and driver per day: 500–1000uah

Arriving in Ukraine

Boryspil International Airport, Kyiv (p84) Regular round-the-clock bus services leave from outside the terminal to the main train station. Taxis cost 650uah to the city centre (around 40 minutes).

Lviv International Airport (p133) Take trolleybus 9 to the university or bus 48 to the corner of vul Doroshenka and pr Svobody. Taxis cost around 100uah to the city centre.

Odesa International Airport (p188) Trolleybus 14 runs to the city centre between 7am and 7pm. Taking a taxi here is not recommended.

Getting Around

Public transport in Ukraine is very cheap and commendably efficient. It's also slow and, in the summer months, overcrowded.

Train Cheap but slow, especially the old-school overnight services. New express trains, which travel by day, connect Kyiv with Ukraine's biggest cities. Ukrainian Railways (www.uz.gov.ua) has an online timetable and you can book tickets on the web.

Bus Very cheap, with regular services, but sometimes packed to bursting and unbearably hot in summer. Handy when there is no convenient train and/or for shorter trips. Detailed bus timetables can be found at www.bus.com.ua.

Car For daring individuals this is a good and fun way to travel around Ukraine, if you don't mind dire road quality and maniac drivers.

Air Domestic flights are convenient for travelling across the country but tend to be a bit pricey.

For much more on **getting around**, see p266

First Time Ukraine

For more information, see Survival Guide (p255)

Checklist

➡ Arrange appropriate medical insurance

➡ Check airline baggage restrictions (especially budget airlines)

➡ If not from the EU or North America, check whether you need a visa

➡ Make sure your passport is valid for the duration of your stay

➡ Stock up on any medicines you may need

➡ Check your country's travel advice if heading to Ukraine's east

What to Pack

➡ Good walking shoes or trail shoes

➡ Mosquito spray or cream

➡ Penknife

➡ Small day pack with concealed zips

➡ Hand sanitiser

➡ Travel sink plug

➡ Sewing kit for emergency repairs

➡ Flip-flops (thongs) or slippers for train journeys

➡ Ample supply of patience and good humour

Top Tips for Your Trip

➡ Avoid travelling in the oven-hot summer months if you're planning to stay in cities or move around by bus.

➡ Book accommodation well in advance in Odesa from June to August; in Kyiv in late December, early January and early May; and in the Carpathians in early spring as well as the height of summer.

➡ Make sure you have comprehensive medical insurance.

➡ Try to learn the Ukrainian Cyrillic alphabet before you go.

➡ In east Ukraine, avoid conversations with strangers about the war with Russia, Crimea and the downing of flight MH17.

➡ Eat in self-service canteens – they are cheap and the food is excellent.

➡ In cities, use the public transport rather than taxis.

What to Wear

Summer and winter present the greatest challenges when it comes to clothing. In summer only the lightest of apparel will do, as temperatures soar. In winter you'll want plenty of layers to protect you from guaranteed subzero temperatures.

Ukrainians are pretty laid-back about formal attire – there are few situations where you'd be required to dress up. For clubbing in Kyiv, Lviv or Odesa you might need to look the part to get past face control.

For city touring, comfortable clothing is best; for hikes in the Carpathians make sure you have the right gear, at least proper hiking boots, waterproofs and a hat.

Sleeping

Booking a bed a long time ahead is only necessary during the summer in Lviv and Odesa and across the country in early January and early May. The Carpathians are normally busy at the height of summer and to a lesser extent during the skiing season.

Money

ATMs are widespread, even in small towns. Credit cards are accepted at most hotels and restaurants.

For more information, see p259.

Bargaining

Haggling is not common in Ukraine and probably shouldn't be attempted. The only time we would recommend it is if you know you are being overcharged at a market.

Tipping

Tipping is rare in Ukraine, with most people rounding restaurant and taxi bills up to the nearest 10 or 50uah. Adding an extra 10% to a check would be met with bewilderment in many eateries.

Etiquette

Ukrainians are pretty relaxed about foreigners making the odd faux pas, but there are a few dos and don'ts you should know about to avoid embarrassment.

➡ Always remove your shoes when entering someone's house – slippers will be provided.

➡ Bring a small gift when invited to someone's home.

➡ Saying the odd *dobry den* (hello), *do pobachenya* (goodbye) and *dyakuju* (thanks) goes a long way.

➡ Women should cover their heads in Orthodox churches.

➡ On public transport, give up your seat to those with children.

➡ Avoid declaring constantly how cheap Ukraine is for you – it ain't for most locals.

➡ Be wary of talking to strangers about the war with Russia and the occupation of Crimea.

Eating

Ukraine's cuisine is a hearty blend of Russian, European and Caucasian fare, with many a local dish featuring on menus. Quality has improved immensely in recent years as Ukrainians demand the same standards as in Europe. Eating out is still relatively cheap for foreign visitors, though prices are on the rise. Lviv is the unrivalled foodie capital of Ukraine with the most variety and the most pleasant European-style restaurants serving local food.

What's New

Kyiv's Murals

Since the Maidan revolution, gigantic murals painted by Ukrainian and international artists have appeared on multistorey blocks across the capital, some becoming tourist attractions in their own right.

Lviv's Beer Attractions

Lviv's brewery museum has been given a complete makeover, turning it into a world-class experience. However, the city's legendary beer is being given a run for its money by the new Pravda Beer Theatre right on pl Rynok. (p114) (p129)

'Decommunisation'

Finally, finally… After almost three decades of independence, Ukraine is ridding itself of all those Lenin statues, Red Army Streets and squares named after obscure Hungarian revolutionaries. Kharkiv and Dnipro are changing every other street name, the latter having been renamed itself. (p213) (p219)

Odesa's Green Theatre

A child of Maidan revolution, the revived open-air stage at Shevchenko Park has become a magnet for Odesa intellectuals who flock here for concerts of Ukrainian and Russian bands, film screenings and literary evenings. (p186)

Phaeton Museum of Machinery

A huge hangar in Zaporizhya contains a new and lovingly arranged exhibition of civilian and military vehicles. Highlights include Soviet government limousines and many examples of the Zaporozhets, the Morris Minor of the USSR. (p223)

Trains, Planes & Automobiles

Infrastructure is the watchword these days in Ukraine as the country tries to modernise its long-neglected transport networks. New roads, express trains to Poland and possibly direct Ryanair connections to European cities are just some of the improvements so far.

Kukhnya

The best recent addition to the food scene in Transcarpathia is this gourmet dining spot in Uzhhorod. European favourites are crafted using fresh, local produce. (p163)

Odesa Food Scene

Odesa's Tsimes street food market, City Food Market and Green Theatre food court are putting Odesa firmly on the foodie map in a way no other Ukrainian city has achieved. (p183) (p184)

Lvivska Maysternya Pryanykiv

Lviv has finally revived its gingerbread tradition and this new shop-cafe-workshop is the place to find out what it's all about. Buy, eat or make your own, the choice is yours. (p131)

Grassroots Kyiv

Out of the ashes of war in the east, a counterculture movement has arisen in Kyiv. It's driven by art and music and epitomised by alternative venues like Skvorechnik, Closer and Donetsk transplant Izolyatsia. (p61) (p75) (p55)

For more recommendations and reviews, see lonelyplanet.com/ukraine

If You Like...

Churches

Stalin did his levelling best to destroy Ukraine's stock of wonderful churches, but somehow many survived.

Kyevo-Pecherska Lavra This gathering of golden domes is Ukraine's holiest site. (p56)

Carpathian wooden churches Ukraine's timber places of worship are part of Unesco's list of World Heritage Sites. (p142)

St Sophia's Cathedral Kyiv's most atmospheric place of worship. (p50)

St Andrew's Church Many a 19th-century aristocratic wedding took place in this magnificent chunk of baroque architecture. (p52)

Chernihiv The town's collection of exquisite church buildings has earned it Unesco recognition. (p205)

Pochayiv This golden-domed huddle of churches and monastery buildings can be seen for miles around. (p137)

Folk Culture

Traditional folk culture has boomed since independence, with new festivals and events added to an ever-growing calendar.

Pyrohiv Museum of Folk Architecture This is the best open-air museum in the country highlighting local crafts and customs. (p60)

Hutsul Celebrations Hutsul festivals, weddings and red-letter days are the best times to see the culture of the Carpathians' Hutsul people in all its woolly glory. (p149)

Pysanky Museum This unique museum dedicated to egg decoration is itself housed in a giant Easter Egg. (p151)

Kosiv craft market Ukraine's biggest traditional craft market is the place to pick up genuine handmade souvenirs. (p153)

Jewish Sites

Cemeteries, former synagogues, 19th-century *shetls* (villages) and tombs can be found across Ukraine, but the holocaust left few Jews to tend to them.

Uman The tomb of Rabbi Nachman draws thousands of pilgrims at Jewish New Year. (p95)

Berdychiv The highlight here is the tomb of Levi Yitzhak set amid toppling, Hebrew-inscribed graves. (p93)

Lviv The city centre is dotted with reminders of a once vibrant Jewish community. (p111)

Dnipro Check out eastern Ukraine's best Jewish museum. (p219)

Museums

Many of Ukraine's museums are threadbare, underfunded affairs; however, there are some notable exceptions.

Lvivarnya A tour of Lviv's revamped 21st-century brewery museum ends with the all-important tasting session. (p114)

Museum of Hutsul Folk Art This excellent Kolomyya museum is dedicated to the woolly culture of the Carpathian-dwelling Hutsuls. (p150)

Museum of One Street Relates the story of Kyiv's Andriyivsky uzviz in a delightful jumble of knick-knacks. (p53)

Chornobyl Museum Tells the horrific story of the world's worst nuclear disaster. (p53)

Korolyov Cosmonaut Museum A blast off from the Soviet space program past. (p92)

Outdoor Activities

Ukraine's moody mountains and forests mean there's no shortage of activity for those looking to get out in the wilds.

Carpathian National Nature Park Marked trails lead hikers and bikers through Ukraine's largest national park. (p147)

Mt Hoverla A hike up Ukraine's highest peak is not as strenuous as it might sound. (p148)

Bukovel The country's top ski resort can be found in the heart of the Carpathian Mountains. (p148)

Chornohora Ridge Mountaineering in the peaks here requires a guide and forward planning. (p148)

Yaremche This Carpathian resort village is the best place to pick up guides and join tours. (p148)

Soviet Architecture

Ukraine's taxi-hailing Lenin statues are now mostly a thing of the past, but its brutish war memorials, plinthed tanks and megalomaniac Soviet buildings would take a lot of dynamite to erase.

Kyiv metro Some of Kyiv's metro stations are proof that the Soviets did sometimes create things of ornate beauty. (p42)

Rodina Mat This 62m-tall titanium goddess wields sword and shield high above the Dnipro River. (p56)

Friendship of Nations Monument A huge Soviet realist monument under a tin rainbow in Kyiv. (p47)

Derzhprom This megalomaniac's dream in concrete even manages to dominate the world's second-largest square. (p214)

Top: Museum of One Street (p53), Kyiv

Bottom: Yaremche (p148), Carpathian National Nature Park

Month by Month

TOP EVENTS

Carnival Humorina, April

Ivan Kupala, July

Zakhidfest, August

Lviv Coffee Festival, September

New Year's Eve, December

January

Winter bites cold in January and you'll have to wrap up pretty snugly to do any sightseeing. However, this is a great time to snap on skis in the Carpathian Mountains.

Old New Year's Eve

Not only do Ukrainians get to celebrate two Christmases (Catholic and Orthodox), they also get two stabs at New Year – according to the Julian Calendar, Orthodox New Year falls on 13 January.

Epiphany

Across Ukraine during 18–19 January, deranged individuals can be seen leaping into icy rivers to celebrate the arrival of Christianity in Kyivan Rus. Kyiv sees the biggest event with scores of men braving the numbing waters of the Dnipro River.

Orthodox Christmas

Only revived nationally since independence, Ukrainians celebrate Orthodox Christmas according to the old Julian Calendar on 7 January. On Christmas Eve families gather for the 12-course meal of Svyata Vecherya (Holy Supper).

February

The ski season is in full swing in the Carpathians, the late winter sun often creating a wonderland of snow and ice. Late February can bring a slight thaw turning cities into lakes of slush.

March

There's usually little sign of spring in March, with temperatures hovering around zero and occasional snow falls. The Carpathian skiing season begins to wind up mid-month.

April

Things begin to warm up along the southern coast, but inland you'll still need those chunky Hutsul woollen socks. Visit Kyiv at the end of the month when thousands of chestnut trees begin to bloom.

Carnival Humorina

Odesa's biggest annual fiesta is a one-day street parade on 1 April. Floats, music, dancing and lots of food flood the streets to celebrate the city's status as Ukrainian capital of humour.

Orthodox Easter

Falling two weeks after Catholic Easter, colourful Orthodox *paskha* arrives in April two years out of three. This is more of a religious festival than in the West, with churchgoers taking baskets of *pysanky* (painted eggs) and specially baked loaves to be blessed by priests.

May

Ukraine is most definitely a shoulder-season destination and May is the

first of those shoulders. Colour returns to the snow-bleached land, the last river ice fades and the first seedlings nudge through Ukraine's black soil.

Kamyanets-Podilsky Days

Mid-May sees street parties, concerts, choirs, parades, exhibitions and sporting events take over the rock-island town of Kamyanets-Podilsky.

Kyiv Day

A colourful spring celebration and festival in honour of the capital city held on the last weekend of May. The day of fun events comes to an end around 10pm with a huge firework display over the Dnipro.

Lviv City Day

Early May is the time to be in Lviv when the city celebrates its 'day' as well as a number of other festivals that take place to coincide with the long May holidays.

June

Comfortable temperatures continue across the steppe but things begin to heat up on the coast. Along with September, this is one of the most pleasant months to travel, before the worst of the heat arrives.

July

Alas, most visitors arrive in the hottest months of the year when travel becomes a sweaty ordeal. Give the big cities a wide berth at this time of year and head for the cooler Carpathians.

Ivan Kupala

An exhilarating pagan celebration of midsummer involving fire jumping, maypole dancing, fortune-telling, wreath floating and strong overtones of sex. Celebrated 7 July, head for the countryside for the real heathen deal.

Odesa Film Festival

Established in 2010, the Odesa Film Festival (www.oiff.com.ua) has arguably become Ukraine's top film event. Cannes it ain't, but the competition still attracts a long list of international filmmakers. The closing ceremony takes place against the grand backdrop of the Opera and Ballet Theatre.

Taras Bulba Festival

Each July rock fans swell the population of little Dubno to enjoy one of the better known music festivals in the country. Attracts big names and fans from across Ukraine.

August

Crowded and super-heated, Odesa is the place to avoid during August. Colossal sunflower fields are a gobsmacking sight across Ukraine's agricultural heartlands this month, and by the end the harvest is in full swing.

Bandershtat

One of the biggest rock festivals held in Ukraine, Bandershtat (www.bandershtat.org.ua) has a nationalist flavour and is held just outside the town of Lutsk. Some of the biggest names in Ukrainian rock take part.

Independence Day

On the 24th, cities across the land lay on festivals and parades with performances and special events. But the place to be is Kyiv's maydan Nezalezhnosti (Independence Sq), which bops to an evening pop concert followed by a mega firework show.

Koktebel Jazz

A fugitive from the occupied Crimea, one of Ukraine's two top jazz festivals is now held in Chornomorsk, near Odesa, which has an even nicer beach than Crimea's Koktebel. Expect top Ukrainian and international musicians to perform before a crowd dressed in little more than swimsuits.

Sorochynsky Yarmarok

Farmers and tourists gather for five days of festivities at this famous village fair, famously described by Gogol. Folksy musical acts accompany top Ukrainian politicians (often the president) as they admire the country's fattest pumpkins, sweetest watermelons and tenderest *salo* (raw pig fat).

Zakhidfest

'Westfest' (www.zaxidfest.com) is held in the village of Rodatychi near Lviv in late August and has become one of the top Ukrainian annual music festivals. Over three days, anyone who's anyone on the Ukrainian music scene performs on four stages to big crowds.

September

Temperatures mellow out, people return to the cities and everyday life resumes in the hazy light of Ukrainian autumn. By far the best time to travel and to gorge on Ukraine's legendary fruit and veg.

Gogolfest

The biggest festival of the autumn in Kyiv, Gogolfest takes place at various venues across the capital. The week-long festival includes art, theatre, music, cinema, workshops and kid's events.

Lviv Coffee Festival

Disciples of the bean should go west to Ukraine's caffeine capital for the country's only coffee festival (www.coffeefest.lviv.ua). Highlights of the three-day event include the presentation of an award for 'Lviv coffeehouse of the year', various concerts and coffee-themed tours.

Rakhiv Bryndza Festival

One of the Carpathians' top culinary events, this cheese festival sees thousands descend on little Rakhiv to try and to buy. Held at the town's amphitheatre, it attracts an international contingent from Moldova and Slovakia.

October

The comfortable temperatures give way to chilly days, falling leaves and the first frosts. Ukrainians head out to their country cottages and gardens to wind up the season and lock up for the long winter.

Kyiv International Film Festival Molodist

Late October sees Kyiv host this superb film festival (www.molodist.com), a great opportunity to check out new cinematic talent from Ukraine and other countries. Running for over four decades, it's recognised as one of Eastern Europe's top film events.

Lviv Chocolate Festival

One of Ukraine's most enjoyable food bashes, Lviv's celebration of chocolate (www.shokolad.lviv.ua) is a chance to gorge on the city's Belgian-style toothrotter. Also involves lots of amazing chocolate sculptures and side events.

November

Autumn is over quickly leaving November cold and often damp. This is the best month to come to Ukraine if you like your destinations tourist-free.

December

End-of-year commercialism is yet to take off in a big way here, so if you're looking to flee the Christmas shopping blues, decidedly un-festive and very chilly Ukraine could be the antidote.

Catholic Christmas

On 25 December Catholic Ukrainians celebrate the first of two Christmases the country marks every year. However, for most people, especially in the predominantly Orthodox and Russian-speaking areas, this is just an ordinary working day.

New Year's Eve

This is by far the biggest bash of the year and if you think you've seen it all on New Year's Eve, you haven't been to Kyiv. Needless to say, gallons of *horilka* (vodka) and cheap bubbly are involved.

Itineraries

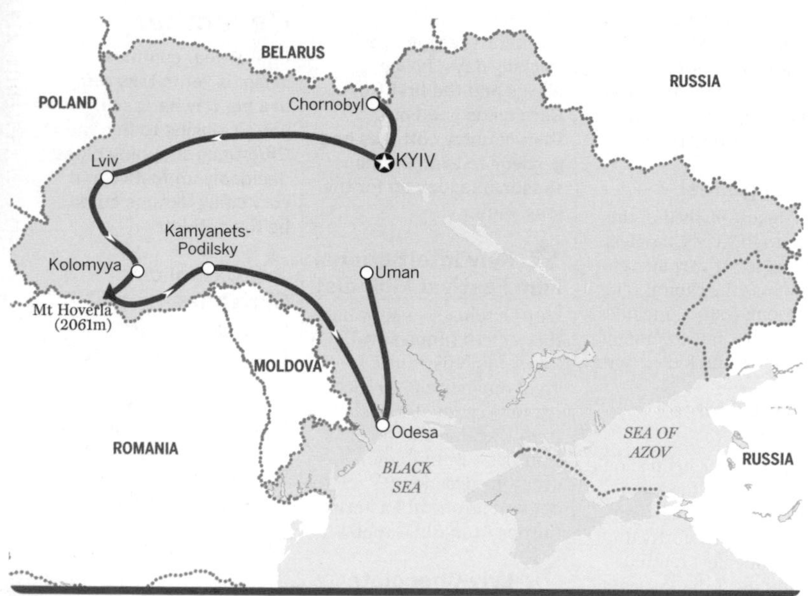

Essential Ukraine

This exhilarating sweep though Ukraine's must-sees takes you from the bustling national capital to the tranquility of Uman's Sofiyivka Park via the central European delights of Lviv.

The quintessential Ukrainian experience starts in **Kyiv**, the cradle of Slavic civilisation. Three days are just enough to absorb the mix of gold-domed Orthodox churches, monumental Stalinist architecture and raucous nightlife. An easily organised guided tour can take you to **Chornobyl** to see the sarcophagus now in place over the reactor and the ghost town of Pripyat. Back in Kyiv, catch an overnight sleeper train to the former Habsburg city of **Lviv**. With its Italianate buildings and Austrian-style cafes, it's a cosy contrast to the Soviet capital.

From there it's a simple ride south to **Kolomyya**, a great base from which to explore the Carpathian Mountains and perhaps climb Mt Hoverla. A short journey from here brings you to dramatic **Kamyanets-Podilsky**, where the medieval Old Town perches atop a tall rock in the middle of a river loop. Next head to **Odesa**, famous for the Potemkin Steps and weekend clubbing at Arkadia Beach. On your way back to Kyiv, stop off in **Uman** to see the exquisite Sofiyivka Park.

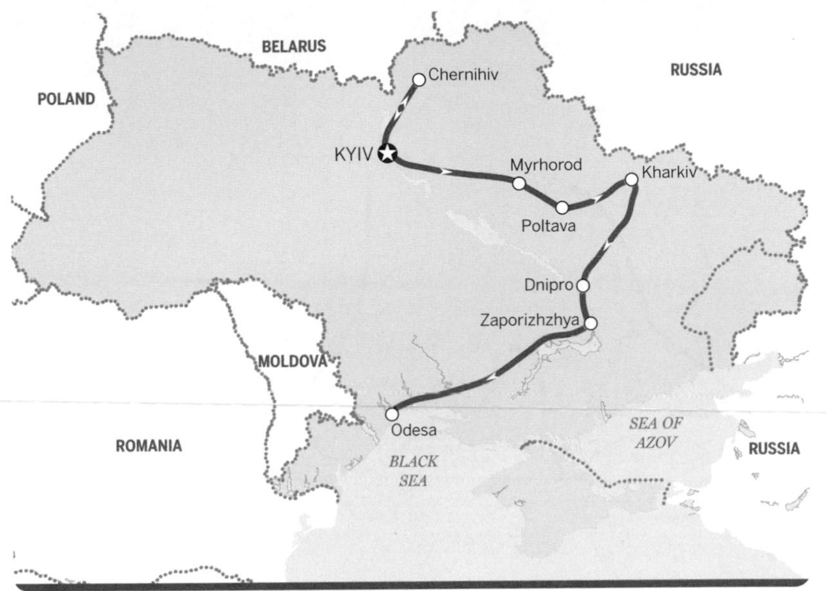

Kyiv to the Black Sea

East Ukraine isn't on many itineraries these days but the war with Russia is confined to a small area in the far east, leaving the rest of the region undisturbed. This 10-day journey takes in the best of the East, including spa towns, the Black Sea coast and several big cities.

This venture into the less-frequented east begins with a quick jump north from **Kyiv** to atmospheric **Chernihiv**, with its amazing Unesco-listed collection of monasteries and cathedrals. Most make this a day trip from the capital, but staying the night gives more time to appreciate the wonderful collection of ancient church buildings.

Unless you're up for slow and complicated train journeys, backtrack to the capital and board an express train heading east – first stop, the spa town of **Myrhorod**, where you can take the waters and wander the spa park by the sluggish River Khorol. Gogol was born nearby, and the town and surrounding area feature in many of his tales. Get off the beaten track in these parts by spending a couple of days on the Gogol Circuit, which visits many sites associated with the author. Local guesthouses can put you up for a few hryvnya.

Reboard the express for the short trip to **Poltava**, a pleasant, park-dotted place. Designed as a kind of mini St Petersburg, this grand city contrasts with the surrounding bucolic scenery and is well worth half a day's exploration. The final stop of the express is **Kharkiv**, a huge student city. Essential viewing here is the world's second-largest city square, which is dominated by the mammoth, Stalinist-era Derzhprom building.

From Kharkiv it's a smooth roll south to another of Ukraine's eastern megacities – **Dnipro** – still a major centre for Ukraine's rocket and aviation industries (so be careful what you aim your camera at!). Take a stroll by the Dnipro River before continuing south to **Zaporizhzhya**, an ugly industrial city but also the location of Khortytsya Island, where Ukrainian Cossacks once gathered at the *sich* (fort). This is the best place in the country to learn about the Cossacks, their way of life and their influence on the country's history.

Your final stop is the seaside city of **Odesa**, a lively port frequented by both bucket-and-spade holidaymakers and hardcore clubbers who flock to its beachside nightclubs. Kyiv is six hours by express coach or an overnight train journey.

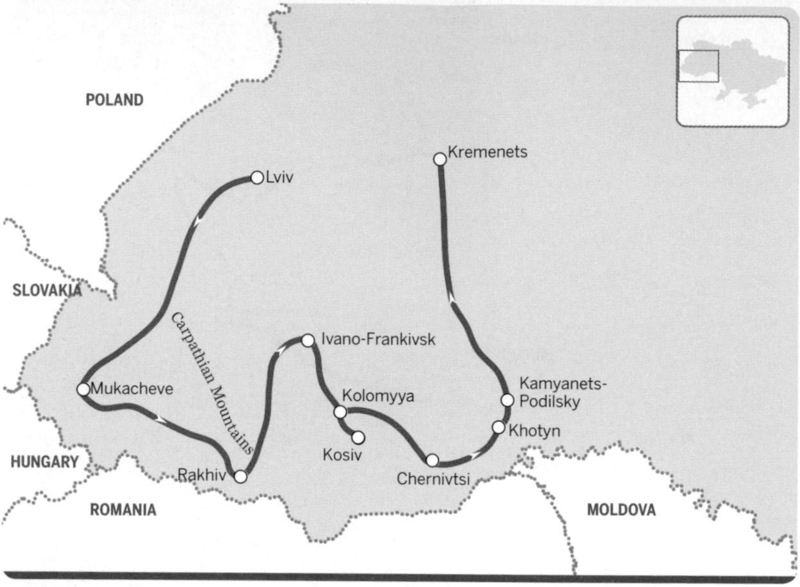

POLAND
Kremenets
Lviv
SLOVAKIA
Carpathian Mountains
Ivano-Frankivsk
Mukacheve
Kamyanets-Podilsky
Kolomyya
Khotyn
Kosiv
HUNGARY
Rakhiv
Chernivtsi
ROMANIA
MOLDOVA

Lviv & the Carpathians

A trip through West Ukraine highlights the country at its folksy best, from the coffee shops of Lviv to a trio of castles with long and turbulent histories. In between rise the wooded slopes of the Carpathian Mountains, home to the colourful Hutsuls.

Launch your loop around Ukraine's far west in **Lviv**, a now quite touristy eastern outpost of central Europe with a strong cafe culture and some gobsmacking architecture that make it one of Ukraine's top stops for any visitor. Outside the city centre the Lychakivske Cemetery is a must-see. The city also has some of the country's best dining and the most celebrated beer in Ukraine, the subject of a modern new museum.

Hop on board a slow train south to low-key **Mukacheve**, where one of Ukraine's most dramatic hilltop castles awaits. From here it's into soothingly forested mountain country, the Carpathians to be exact. Ukraine's wedge of the Carpathian arc is etched with long broad valleys, and a great place to start your exploration is **Rakhiv**. Here you can have your first brush with Hutsul culture and head off into the hills for some exhilarating hiking and biking, before picking your way north along the newly paved road linking resort villages, ski centres and hiking bases en route. Eventually buses will deliver you to the up-and-coming city of **Ivano-Frankivsk**; with its cafes, squares and relaxed vibe, it's the only city in Ukraine that comes near Lviv for atmosphere.

After that head south and call a halt at quaint **Kolomyya**, a superb launch pad for more hikes. The town also has two intriguing museums, including the famous Pysanky Museum housed in a giant Easter egg. A side trip to **Kosiv** provides more Hutsul culture. Consider short stops at energetic **Chernivtsi**, to visit the psychedelic university building, and the spectacular **Khotyn** fortress on the banks of the wide Dnister River, before you next unpack your bags in the show-stopping island town of **Kamyanets-Podilsky**. One of Ukraine's must-see attractions, the town is as historically fascinating as it is dramatically situated in a loop of the Smotrych River.

From K-P, a long bus ride across giant fields of sunflowers and sugar beet via off-the-beaten-track Ternopil delivers you to picturesque **Kremenets**, another town boasting a superb fortress as well as an eerie Cossack cemetery.

Top: Kyevo-Pecherska Lavra (p56), Kyiv

Bottom: Palanok Castle (p163), Mukacheve

Plan Your Trip

Visiting Chornobyl

Advance Planning

Chornobyl is located 110km north of Kyiv city centre as the crow flies, around two hours' drive.

You can only realistically visit Chornobyl as part of a guided tour from Kyiv (US$80 to US$110 per person for a day tour, considerably more for two-day tours).

To join a tour you must be over 18 years of age (no children are allowed into the exclusion zones).

Day tours leave Kyiv early morning, returning in the early evening.

On multiple-day trips you can sleep in the town of Chornobyl near the outer limits of the exclusion zone.

You can visit any time of year; however, as most of the tour takes place outdoors, warmer months are better.

The world's most unlikely tourist attraction, one of dark tourism's most sinister day's out, a moving journey back to the days of the Soviet Union and the most thought-provoking nine hours you'll spend in Ukraine – few fail to be stirred, scared and/or angered by a tour to Chornobyl, apocalyptic site of the world's worst nuclear accident.

The Accident

In perhaps the blackest of ironies in history, the world's worst nuclear catastrophe was the result of an unnecessary safety test. On the night of 25 April 1986, reactor No. 4 at the Chornobyl power plant was due to be shut down for regular maintenance. Workers decided to use the opportunity to see if, in the event of a shutdown, enough electricity remained in the grid to power the reactor core cooling systems, and turned off the emergency cooling mechanism. For various reasons, including a design flaw, operational errors and flouted safety procedures, the result was a power surge, a steam explosion and a full-blown nuclear explosion. At 1.26am on 26 April 1986, the reactor blew its 500-tonne top and spewed tonnes of radioactive material mainly over Belarus and Ukraine. Some material also wafted over Sweden, whose scientists were the first to alert the world.

The Tour

The day begins at a meeting point in central Kyiv. Passports are checked, and Geiger counters hired. Then it's into the minibus for the two-hour drive to the exclusion zone.

Having arrived at the **Dytyatky checkpoint** (30km from the reactor), papers and passports are rechecked and the official guide joins the group. The guides really know their stuff, and where to find hotspots caused by buried bits of radioactive something – which send the Geiger counter readout soaring.

After the 10km checkpoint (more checks), itineraries vary from agency to agency, but all trips include a stop near **reactor No. 4** and its impressive new silo, and a stroll around the eerie ghost town of **Pripyat.**

As of 2017, reactor No. 4 is completely covered by the soaring €1.5 billion New Safe Confinement shelter. It is absolutely gargantuan: 108m tall, 250m long and 159m wide. The shelter is designed to be leak-proof for 100 years.

At the end of your tour, simple radiation checks are carried out as you once again pass through the two checkpoints. You'll likely be in a pensive mood by that point. Whether it be the plight of the 'liquidators', the nonchalance of the Soviet authorities, the tragedy of Pripyat, or the sheer scale of money spent on containing the disaster, Chornobyl will not leave you unmoved.

Is it Dangerous?

Is it dangerous? The simple answer is – no. Well, not unless you go wandering off into undergrowth for too long, bring back a few Soviet-era souvenirs from Pripyat, or feast on forest berries and mushrooms (all activities strictly forbidden, by the way). By all accounts you are exposed to twice the amount of radiation on a trans-Atlantic flight than you are during an entire day at Chornobyl. If you're worried about radiation, hire a Geiger counter from your tour agency.

DOS AND DON'TS

➡ Do remember your passport – you won't be allowed on the bus without it.

➡ Do wear clothes that cover most of your body – no shorts, T-shirts or sandals (gloves, hat or gas mask not required!).

➡ Do not sit on the ground or let personal items touch the ground, especially in contaminated zones.

➡ Do not enter any buildings without the permission of your guide.

➡ Don't take photos of anything you're told not to by the guides, especially around checkpoints.

➡ Don't pocket 'souvenirs' from the buildings in Pripyat – much of the junk strewn around the place is radioactive.

Tour Agencies

Agencies should provide transfers to the exclusion zone, transport around it, an English-speaking guide, and the necessary permits and insurance as a minimum. Some charge extra for lunch and most will rent you a Geiger counter for US$6 to US$10 a day. Recommended companies for Chornobyl trips:

SoloEast Travel (p65) Long-running and very reliable Kyiv-based operator with a sensible online-booking and credit-card payment scheme. They also offer comfortable accommodation in a woodsy **cottage** (www.chernobylhotel.com) just outside the exclusion zone.

Go2Chernobyl (☎044-337 1737; www.go2chernobyl.com; vul Kirova 38A, Chornobyl town) Responsive and responsible operator; has some of the best prices.

Chornobyl Tour (p65) Broad set of tours up to seven days' duration. Online booking and payment.

New Logic (p65) Large, professionally run agency; has been in the business awhile; service less personalised.

Plan Your Trip

Outdoor Activities

Best for Hiking

Best Bases

Yaremche, Rakhiv, Kolomyya, Ivano-Frankivsk

Best time to Go

Late spring/early summer (May and June) or early autumn (September to mid-October)

Best Time to Avoid

High summer (July to August) and depths of winter (December to February)

Best Maps

Kartohrafiya series – widely available from outdoor gear shops, tourist offices and book shops

Best Hikes

Hoverla, Chornohora Ridge

Best Kit

Very sturdy boots, reliable compass, waterproofs, food and water, mobile phone

Best Places to Find a Guide

Kolomiyya, Yaremche

Best Hiking off the Beaten Track

Forests north of Kyiv, Dnister Gorge, Shatsky Lakes, Podilski Tovtry National Park

With its brooding mountains, Black Sea coast, thick forests and wide rivers, Ukraine boasts some commendably wild environments for outdoor activities, from hiking the Carpathians to birdspotting in the Danube Delta, skiing in Bukovel and cycling through the sunflower fields.

Hiking

Pulling on boots and donning a backpack is probably the most popular outdoor activity in Ukraine among locals and tourists alike. Crimea offers excellent walks but with the peninsula firmly off limits, Ukraine's slice of the Carpathian Mountains is where most of the action takes place these days. The Carpathian National Nature Park (CNNP) provides a (virtually) unspoilt backdrop to many an outing – walks can be anything from linear hikes lasting several days to there-and-back day walks from a base such as Rakhiv or Yaremche. Hiking in the Carpathians is usually best done in the company of locals and there is no shortage of guides and tours, official and unofficial, in the area.

If you do strike out on your own, a word of warning: hiking 'trails' criss-cross the Carpathians, but may not be as well-marked as you are used to. Maps show trails clearly, but marking can sometimes be badly executed or missing altogether. However, the trail to Ukraine's highest

Chornohora Ridge (p148), Carpathian National Nature Park

peak, Mt Hoverla (2061m), is well marked, as is the continuing journey along the Chornohora Ridge.

There are few risks involved when hiking in the Carpathians but you should be aware of a few issues. Bears do live in these parts but most stay well away from anywhere hikers may wander. A greater risk than bears is the weather – most walkers who get into any kind of difficulty do so when the weather changes – make sure you have warm clothes and emergency food. Very occasionally you may come across areas fenced off for the enjoyment of some government honcho or businessman – these are often patrolled by quite unpleasant security guards with dogs.

Cycling

Two decades ago the only bikes you might have see in Ukraine were rickety old Soviet-era bone-shakers ridden by grandmas on their way to market. Times have certainly changed and now two-wheelers are the latest craze, especially mountain bikes. Some hire centres have even appeared, most notably in Yaremche and Kyiv, and a lot of hotels and guesthouses in the Carpathians have bikes you can borrow. The mountainous southwest is obviously the best place to get into the saddle, but maps showing cycling trails are rare. For this reason you may be better off joining a tour if you want to really get off-road. Away from the mountains Ukraine is pretty flat, which lends itself to idle peddling. Roads away from towns are usually pretty quiet.

Urban cycling here is only for the hardened cyclist – locking handlebars with Ukraine's deranged drivers is not our idea of fun. However, some cycle paths are appearing – Kyiv is adding them and Lviv has a few, although they are often blocked by pedestrians, parked cars and even kiosks. Always wear a helmet and don't expect drivers to know you are there.

A project called Bikeland was started around a decade ago, the aim of which was to mark trails and generally assist cyclists in enjoying the country. This may be revived in coming years.

TOUR AGENCIES

The following outfits will get you active in Ukraine:

Active Ukraine (www.activeukraine.com) West-based agency specialising in hiking and cycling, mainly in the Carpathians.

Aero-Kiev (www.aero-kiev.com) Paragliding outfit based in Kyiv.

Green Ukraine (www.green-ukraine.com) Superb, professionally run outfit offering a range of Carpathian tours.

Gutsulandia (www.gutsulandia.com) Agency running extreme outdoor activities in the Carpathians.

JC Travel (www.enjoy-ukraine.com) Kyiv-based agency that can organise any outdoor activity you can think up just about anywhere in the country.

Karpaty Travel (www.karpaty-travel.com.ua) Agency organising all kinds of outdoor adventures and tours in the Carpathians.

Outdoor Ukraine (www.outdoorukraine.com) Arranges hiking tours in Ukraine's outdoor hot spots.

Velokosiv (www.velokosiv.if.ua) Bike trips into the Carpathian Mountains.

Skiiing

Skiing in Ukraine is all about one resort, the glitzy, professionally run Bukovel (p148), to the southwest of Yaremche in the Carpathian Mountains. It's by far the country's biggest and best with 60km of trails and lots of other activities such as skating, snow-tubing, dog-sled trips and jeep tours. There's a full hire service so no need to drag your gear to Ukraine; prices are reasonable, but the place gets packed out in ski season, which runs from December to March.

Away from Bukovel's smooth facilities, Ukraine has another 120km of ski slopes, almost all in the Carpathians. There are several slopes around Slavske, the resort at Makovytsya; Mizhhirya has seen improvement and there's some good skiing at Krasiya. For more information on Ukraine's lesser-known slopes and lifts, see www.skiresort.info.

Water Sports

Flat as a млинець (pancake), Ukraine abounds with lakes and rivers where locals cool off in the hot summers. Locals know where it's safe to swim, so do as they do. Sometimes they even take the plunge through a hole in the ice at Epiphany. Boats can sometimes be hired (in Myrhorod and Ternopil, for instance). Otherwise the main water sports hotspots are along the Black Sea coast, most notably in Odesa although Crimea has a much better location. The peninsula also has the best beaches but with these offline for the forseeable future, Odesa is the place to head for a tan.

Wildlife-watching & Birdwatching

The Danube Delta in the country's far southwest and the weird-and-wonderful safari at Askaniya Nova provide the best opportunities for those looking to spot Ukraine's rarer species. The Carpathians are also teeming with wildlife and one beautiful sight you are certain to notice from bus windows is Ukraine's stork population that builds its huge nests atop telegraph poles.

Top: Beach (p178), Odesa

Bottom: Kingfisher, Danube Delta Biosphere Reserve (p191)

RYZHKOV SERGEY / SHUTTERSTOCK ©

Plan Your Trip

Travel with Children

It may not be everyone's idea of a family holiday destination, but anyone who's actually taken children to Ukraine will tell you that not only is it possible, it can also be fun. Indeed, over the summer an army of expat children descend on babysitting country grannies to enjoy Ukraine's fruit, farm animals, swimmable lakes and cheap entertainment.

Best Regions for Kids

With its Slavic seaside fun, Crimea was once one of the best places to holiday with young ones, but a visit to the Russian-occupied peninsula is certainly not recommended today.

Kyiv

Naturally the capital has the most facilities and indoor entertainment for children, including puppet theatres and aquaparks.

Eastern Ukraine

With its pools, beaches, paddle boats and playgrounds, the spa town of Myrhorod is an enjoyable base for children.

Odesa & Southern Ukraine

Odesa's beaches are an obvious attraction for young and old.

The Carpathians

Time among the cool forests and tumbling rivers is the perfect antidote to all those electronic devices.

Ukraine for Kids

Ukraine can be a truly fascinating place for the under 10s: a summer holiday here is a never-ending pageant of farm animals, sandy river beaches, late nights under the Milky Way and bags and bags of bargain fruit. Get it right and Ukraine might be one of your kid's fondest childhood memories.

Ukraine is Fun

Aquaparks and lakes, puppet theatres and quirky museums, playgrounds and rowboats, new friends and funny fauna – Ukraine can be entertaining and educational to boot. Kids love water and when the temperature rises, there's no better place to be than by a beach. Puppet theatres may not hold everyone's attention, but some kids love them; more inquisitive minds will be fed by some stimulating museums. And animals are everywhere – go salamander spotting in the Carpathians or feed goats on the steppe, but avoid Ukraine's stray dog population.

Dining with Kids

If your offspring are addicted to sugary junk, Ukraine provides the opportunity to get them eating some real food. The Ukrainian menu of fresh fruit and vegetables, milk products, meat and grains is the ideal diet for growing kiddies. And when it comes to sweet stuff, Ukraine has plenty of that too.

Great places to eat are self-service canteens where kids can see what they are getting. Midrange restaurants focusing on casual dining are pretty child-friendly these days, especially newer establishments. However, special kids' menus are rare. For the tiniest visitors, breastfeeding in public is perfectly acceptable.

Getting Around

Airless minivans and grimy bus stations are not places you'll want to spend quality family time, so train is the way to go. However, sleeper trains present their own challenges. Even if there are only three of you travelling, make sure you book a whole four-berth compartment. Children up to five can sleep with their parents on one bunk. Take lots of food and an arsenal of games to play. In cities, the metro is usually fine. Slings are always better than prams in Ukraine.

Children's Highlights

Beaches

Odesa's Beaches (p175) Bucket and spade fun on Ukraine's Black Sea coast.

Hydropark, Kyiv (p64) Quiet, forest-backed beaches in central Kyiv.

Myrhorod Excellent paid beach next to the sluggish River Khorol.

Museums

Pysanky Museum, Kolomyya (p151) A museum inside an Easter egg – what larks!

Pyrohiv, Kyiv (p60) Clambering around timber houses straight from a fairytale.

Korolyov Cosmonaut Museum, Zhytomyr (p92) Space-obssessed lads and lasses will love this Soviet astronautics museum.

Castles

Kamyanets-Podilsky Fortress (p101) Ukraine's finest fortress with ample kids attractions.

Palanok Castle, Mukacheve (p163) Scramble round the arcaded courtyards of Transcarpathia's top castle.

Khotyn Fortress (p159) Another medieval hulk to get imaginations racing.

Treats

Roshen (nationwide) The president's Willy Wonka–style chocolate shops are found across the nation.

Lviv Chocolate Festival (p123) The best kid-oriented festival on the calendar.

Lvivska Maysternya Shokoladu, Lviv (p129) This temple to chocolate will have tots drooling.

Planning

Accommodation

- Stay in apartments – you'll have access to a kitchen and probably a full-size bathroom.
- Few hotels have been built with children in mind, but the higher up the hotel food chain, the better things get.

What to Pack

Ukraine's supermarkets stock everything you need for babies and children. However, there are some things you might want to pack:

- hand sanitiser
- children's sun cream
- nappies (expensive in Ukraine)
- mosquito-repellent spray/cream
- medication your child needs (note its Latin name)

Regions at a Glance

Kyiv

Architecture
History
Walks

Eclectic Cityscape

Early medieval monasteries, Polish-influenced baroque, Russian Art Nouveau, Stalinist bombast, drab Soviet constructivism and post-Soviet kitsch – Kyiv's architecture is a charmingly incongruous cocktail of epochs and styles.

Kyivan Rus

One of those places 'where it all started', Kyiv is the cradle of all things Russian, Ukrainian and Belarusian. While visiting St Sophia's Cathedral or Kyevo-Pecherska Lavra, you'll be stepping on stones that remember the arrival of the Viking princes and Greek bishops who shaped East Slavic civilisation.

Riverside Promenade

You might feel as if you are flying above the mind-bogglingly wide Dnipro when you observe it from the hilly right bank. Here, a chain of parks forms a long green belt separating Kyiv's centre from the river.

p42

Central Ukraine

Architecture
Jewish Heritage
Museums

Architectural Landscape

Central Ukraine boasts one of the country's most spectacular castles at Kamyanets-Podilsky, but there are many other fortresses and mansions. Zhytomyr flaunts a stern Soviet style, while Uman wows with its romantically landscaped Sofiyivka Park.

Jewish Sites

The Nazis and post-Soviet emigration emptied Central Ukraine's cities of Jews, but many a crooked, Hebrew-inscribed gravestone and cracked synagogue remain. The region is also the birthplace of Hasidism, its founders' tombs attracting a stream of pilgrims every year.

Quirky Museums

What do an embalmed doctor, a real nuclear missile launch site and assorted junk from the space race have in common? Well, Central Ukraine has a museum dedicated to them all – surely the oddest collection in the country.

p90

Lviv & Western Ukraine

Architecture
Coffee
Castles

Architectural Style

From the handsome austerity of Gothic churches to box-ugly Soviet apartment blocks, Lviv is a textbook of European architectural styles from the last seven centuries. Echoes of the past can be found in towns and villages across the region.

Cafe Culture

Lviv has a distinct Central European coffeehouse tradition that sets it firmly apart from the rest of Ukraine. One of the city's delights is visiting its many intimate, bean-perfumed coffeehouses, sampling the country's best doses of Arabica.

Castles & Fortresses

No other region in Ukraine possesses such a large number of castles, fortresses, chateaux and mansions. When they ruled the roost, the Polish nobility converted many crumbling medieval castles into noble baroque residences. In a strange way their current shabby state just adds to the magic.

p108

The Carpathians

Outdoor Fun
Food
Landscapes

Boot & Bike

The mountains have become a mecca for more adventurous outdoorsy types with routes for both knobbly tyre and treaded boot criss-crossing the forested ranges. Cycling and hiking trails have been marked out in places, but on the whole the going is delightfully rough and uncharted.

Carpathian Menu

The mountain-dwelling Hutsuls have a traditional diet dominated by the ingredients they fish, pluck and forage from the Carpathians' bountiful rivers and forests. But star of the food show in these parts is the delicious local cheese, made in special huts high up in the mountains.

Forested Mountainscape

Only Crimea can rival the Carpathians for mountain vistas and peak-top views. Carpeted in thick forest, the Carpathians are generally more soothing than dramatic, but some of the views out across the valleys are spectacular.

p142

Southern Ukraine

Beaches
Nightlife
Wildlife

Black Sea Fun

The Black Sea's sand-fringed shores attract once-a-year holidaymakers from across the former USSR, who tan until crisp before wallowing in the tepid waters. Not the cleanest beaches in the world, but the further out of the city you go, the better they get.

Seaside Clubbing

Odesa's nightlife comes a close second to the capital's, with bars, clubs and music venues to suit every taste and hairstyle. The blingy beachside megaclubs attract the glitterati for nights of see-and-be-seen clubbing, but the city centre hides more low-key spots for an alternative crowd.

Ukrainian Safari

Southern Ukraine is a magnet for wildlife spotters with two unique areas teeming with winged and hooved critters. Go on safari around the Askaniya Nova Reserve, where zebras, camels and Przewalski horses roam free, or venture into the Danube Delta.

p173

Crimea

Battlefields
Palaces
Mountains

Crimean War

The Crimean War was fought on some of the world's most picturesque battlefields. While the landscape here remembers Florence Nightingale and the Charge of the Light Brigade, there's also a turquoise sea, while Balaklava is more about seafood than dodgy head gear.

Royal Retreats

Russian aristocrats squandered fortunes here on the whimsical creations of fin de siècle architects. These monuments of imperial decadence dot the Crimean coast, surrounded by lush parks and memories of the last Romanovs.

Stunning Landscapes

A chain of plateaus with near-vertical slopes looms above the Black Sea, which is almost always a stunning shade of sapphire. Looking like cream topping on a cake, their limestone hats hide ancient cave cities and bizarrely eroded forms. Spring transforms them into flower-filled Oriental tapestries.

p193

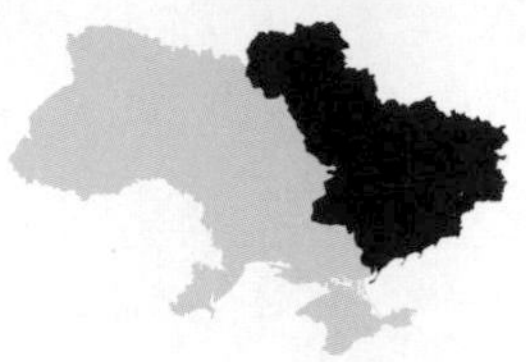

Eastern Ukraine

Cossacks
Gogol Country
Village Life

Cossack Stronghold

Wondering about the Cossacks? Spend a day on the island of Khortytsya in Zaporizhzhya, the site of their main stronghold known as the Sich. History aside, the place is beautiful with its rocky cliffs and rapids and Dniproges dam looming in the distance.

Gogol's Myrhorod

The spa town of Myrhorod and the surrounding countryside is the place to get acquainted with Nikolai Gogol, who was born in these parts. Sip the town's mineral springs before setting out on a Gogol-themed driving tour of the area.

Northern Countryside

The seldom-visited north is Ukrainian to the core, complete with sunflowers, pumpkins and timeless villages. Tourist infrastructure is embryonic here, and transport decidedly second world, so you'll be among the few rare visitors to discover it.

p204

On the Road

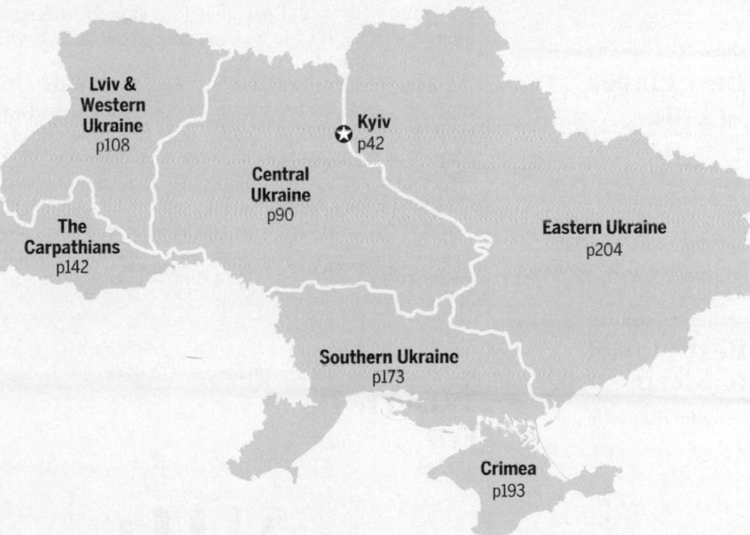

Lviv & Western Ukraine
p108
Kyiv
p42
Central Ukraine
p90
The Carpathians
p142
Eastern Ukraine
p204
Southern Ukraine
p173
Crimea
p193

Kyiv Київ

044 / POP 2.9 MILLION

Includes ➡

Best Places to Eat

- ➡ Shoti (p74)
- ➡ Osteria Pantagruel (p73)
- ➡ Imbir (p72)
- ➡ Under Wonder (p72)
- ➡ Tsarske Selo (p75)

Best Places to Sleep

- ➡ Dream House Hostel (p67)
- ➡ Sunflower B&B Hotel (p66)
- ➡ 11 Mirrors (p67)
- ➡ Hotel Ukraine (p66)
- ➡ Golden Gate Inn (p66)

Why Go?

In the beginning there was Kyiv. Long before Ukraine and Russia existed, the city's inhabitants were already striding up and down the green hills, idling hot afternoons away on the Dnipro River and promenading along Khreshchatyk – then a stream, now the main avenue. From here, East Slavic civilisation spread all the way to Alaska.

Today, history continues to unfold. As revolution has come and gone, and as war in the east smoulders, Ukraine's capital has rebelled yet again, only this time culturally. A creative wave has swept over the city, embodied by urban art, vintage cafes and 24-hour parties. Seemingly overnight, Kyiv has become hip.

It's also cheap. You can eat at superb restaurants and drink at hidden cocktail bars for a fraction of what they would cost in the West. Kyiv's time is clearly now – or until the next revolution rolls around.

When to Go

Kyiv

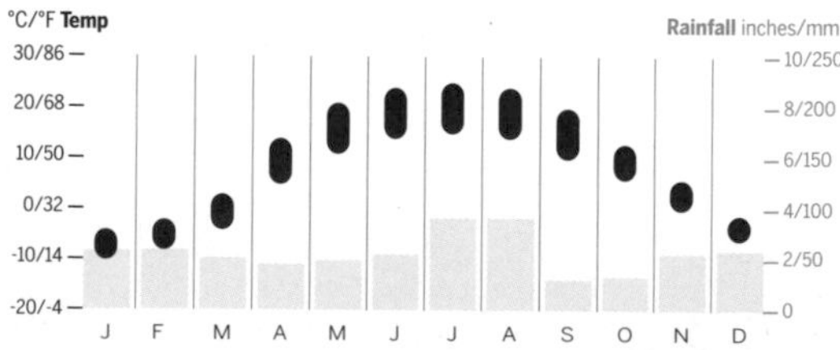

Jan Party on New Year's night, then repent at an Orthodox Christmas service a week later.

May Frolic in Kyiv's two botanical gardens, where just about every tree is blossoming.

Jul Witness ancient rites and enjoy great music during the Ivan Kupala festival.

History

Legend has it that four Slavic siblings founded Kyiv. The eldest, Kyi, gave the city its name. The names of brothers Shchek and Khoriv and sister Lybid now appear in its topography. An iconic statue of the four siblings – the Foundation of Kyiv Monument (Пам'ятник засновникам Києва) – stands on the banks of the Dnipro River.

Four hundred years later the city really started to prosper, after Vikings from Novgorod took control. Circa 864 Novgorod warlords Askold and Dir settled in Kyiv after a failed raid on Constantinople. Novgorod's new prince Oleh journeyed to Kyiv in 882, dispatched the two Vikings and declared himself ruler. This was the beginning of Kyivan Rus ('Rus' being the Slavic name for the red-haired Scandinavians). The city thrived on river trade, sending furs, honey and slaves to pay for luxury goods from Constantinople. Within 100 years its empire stretched from the Volga to the Danube and to Novgorod.

In 989 Kyivan prince Volodymyr decided to forge a closer alliance with Constantinople, marrying the emperor's daughter and adopting Orthodox Christianity. Kyiv's pagan idols were destroyed and its people driven into the Dnipro for a mass baptism.

Under Volodymyr's son, Yaroslav the Wise (1017–54), Kyiv became a cultural and political centre in the Byzantine mould. St Sophia's Cathedral was built to proclaim the glory of both God and city. However, by the 12th century, Kyiv's economic star had begun to wane, with power shifting to northeast principalities (near today's Moscow).

In 1240 Mongol raiders sacked Kyiv. Citizens fled or took refuge wherever they could, including the roof of the Desyatynna Church, which collapsed under the weight.

The city shrank to the riverside district of Podil, which remained its centre for centuries. Only when Ukraine formally passed into Russian hands at the end of the 18th century did Kyiv again grow in importance. The city went through an enormous boom at the turn of the 20th century, when it was essentially the third imperial capital after St Petersburg and Moscow. Many new mansions were erected at this time, including the remarkable House of Chimeras.

During the chaos following the Bolshevik Revolution, Kyiv was the site of frequent battles between Red and White Russian forces, Ukrainian nationalists, and German and Polish armies. Author Mikhail Bulgakov captured the era's uncertainty in his first novel, *The White Guard*. The home in which he wrote this book is now a museum.

In August 1941 German troops captured Kyiv and more than half a million Soviet soldiers were imprisoned or killed. The city suffered terribly. Germans massacred about 100,000 at Babyn Yar and 80% of the city's inhabitants were homeless by the time the Red Army retook Kyiv on 6 November 1943.

The postwar years saw rapid industrialisation and the construction of unsightly suburbs. During the late 1980s nationalistic and democratic movements from western Ukraine began to catch on in the capital. Throughout the presidency of Leonid Kuchma, Kyiv and its young population increasingly became a base of opposition politics. During the Orange Revolution of 2004, activists from around Ukraine poured into the capital to demonstrate on maydan Nezalezhnosti (Independence Sq) and outside the parliament building.

History was repeated during Euromaidan protests in the winter of 2013–14, only this time events took a much nastier turn. More than a hundred people died in clashes between riot troops and pro-Western protesters that led to the ousting of president Yanukovych. The city's residents displayed outstanding stamina and solidarity – filling sacks with ice and snow to build barricades, bringing food to antigovernment militiamen, throwing petrol bombs at the police and dragging the injured from the battlefield under a shower of bullets.

Sights

City Centre

★Maydan Nezalezhnosti SQUARE

(майдан Незалежності; Independence Sq; Map p48; M Maydan Nezalezhnosti) Be it celebration or revolution, whenever Ukrainians want to get together – and they often do – 'Maydan' is the nation's meeting point. The square saw pro-independence protests in the 1990s and the Orange Revolution in 2004. But all of that was eclipsed by the Euromaidan Revolution in 2013–14, when the square was transformed into an urban guerrilla camp besieged by government forces. In peaceful times, Maydan is more about festiveness than feistiness, with weekend concerts and a popular nightly fountain show.

All streets in the centre seem to spill into maydan Nezalezhnosti, and with them spills a cross-section of Kyiv life: vendors selling

Kyiv Highlights

❶ Kyevo-Pecherska Lavra (p56) Admiring the beauty of Orthodox ritual and meeting the mummies of the famous caves.

❷ Maydan Nezalezhnosti (p43) Standing on the hallowed central square where duelling revolutions changed Ukrainian history.

❸ Bar-hopping (p75) Joining the hipster masses to explore Kyiv's electric bar scene.

❹ St Sophia's Cathedral (p50) Being mesmerised by 1000-years-old frescoes in this ancient church where Yaroslav the Wise once roamed.

❺ Andriyivsky uzviz (p52) Stepping on the rugged cobblestones and

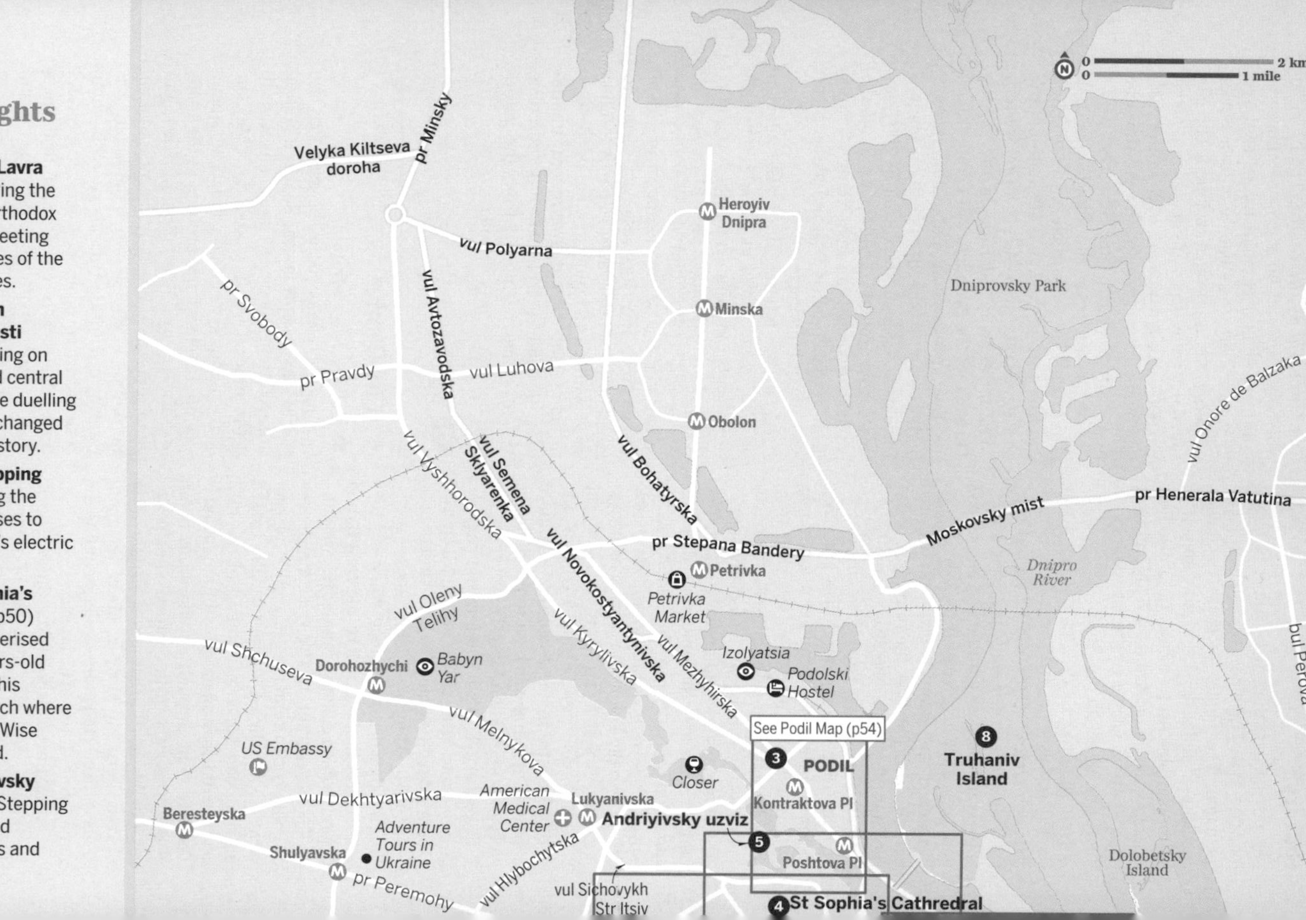

inhaling the Parisian air of this postcard-friendly descent.

6 Pyrohiv Museum of Folk Architecture (p60) Exploring all of Ukraine in one day at this country-fried treat.

7 Khreshchatyk (p46) Promenading on Kyiv's central street – a quintessential experience.

8 Trukhaniv Island (p64) Sunbathing in view of the Lavra, cycling or banging drums at Skvorechnik.

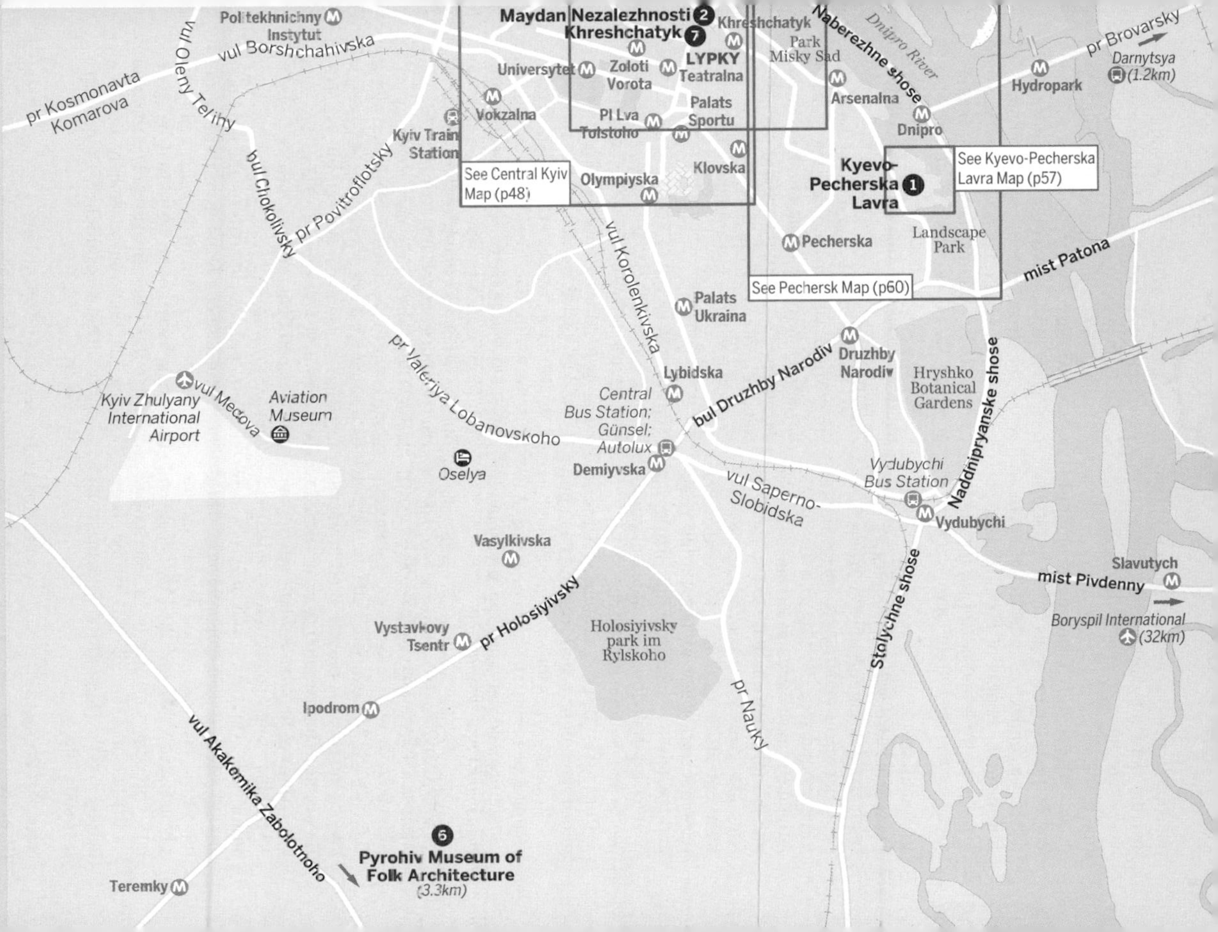

Maydan Nezalezhnosti 2
Khreshchatyk 7
Khreshchatyk
LYPKY
Universytet
Zoloti Vorota
Teatralna
Palats Sportu
Pl Lva Tolstoho
Vokzalna
Kyiv Train Station
See Central Kyiv Map (p48)
Olympiyska
Klovska
Park Misky Sad
Arsenalna
Naberezhne shose
Dnipro River
Dnipro
Hydropark
pr Brovarsky
Darnytsya (1.2km)
Kyevo-Pecherska Lavra 1
See Kyevo-Pechersk Lavra Map (p57)
Pecherska
Landscape Park
See Pechersk Map (p60)
mist Patona
Politekhnichny Instytut
vul Borshchahivska
vul Oleny Teliny
pr Kosmonavta Komarova
bul Chokolivsky
pr Povitroflotsky
vul Korolenkivska
Palats Ukraina
Lybidska
Druzhby Narodiv
bul Druzhby Narodiv
Hryshko Botanical Gardens
Naddniprуanske shose
Central Bus Station; Günsel; Autolux
Demiyvska
pr Valeriya Lobanovskoho
Kyiv Zhulyany International Airport
vul Medova
Aviation Museum
Oselya
Vydubychi Bus Station
Vydubychi
vul Saperno-Slobidska
Vasylkivska
Slavutych
mist Pivdenny
Boryspil International (32km)
Stolychne shose
Vystavkovy Tsentr
pr Holosiyivsky
Holosiyivsky park im Rylskoho
pr Nauky
Ipodrom
vul Akakemika Zabolotnoho
6 Pyrohiv Museum of Folk Architecture (3.3km)
Teremky

food and souvenirs; teenagers carousing under the watchful gaze of winged-angel statues; skate rats and snake charmers, lovers and bums.

Yet the echo of revolution is omnipresent. Makeshift memorials on vul Instytutska serve as a sombre reminder of those slain in Euromaidan. Images of burning tyres and army tents from that fateful winter will forever linger in the Ukrainian conscience.

Khreshchatyk STREET

(Хрещатик; Map p48; Ⓜ Khreshchatyk) Kyiv's main drag is named after a river, which these days runs underneath, enclosed in an underground pipe. Getting gussied up and strolling Khreshchatyk is Kyivans' number one pastime. Don't hesitate to join them for a few laps, pausing occasionally at one of the many streetside cafes and kiosks that line the boulevard. It's at its best during weekends, when the section south of maydan Nezalezhnosti is closed to traffic and various events and contests take place.

During WWII the retreating Soviet army mined the buildings here, turning them into deadly booby traps for any German soldiers setting foot inside. Most places exploded or caught fire, and were subsequently rebuilt in the current Stalinesque style.

St Volodymyr's Cathedral CHURCH

(Map p48; bul Tarasa Shevchenka 20; Ⓜ Universytet) Although not one of Kyiv's most important churches, St Volodymyr's Cathedral arguably has the prettiest interior. Built in the late 19th century to mark 900 years of Orthodox Christianity in the city, its yellow exterior and seven blue domes conform to standard Byzantine style. However, inside it breaks new ground with art nouveau influences. Huge murals, flecked with golden accents, include a painting of Volodymyr the Great's baptism into Orthodox Christianity in Chersonesus (now Khersones) and of Kyiv's citizens being herded into the Dnipro River for a mass baptism soon afterwards.

House of Chimeras NOTABLE BUILDING

(Map p48; vul Bankova 10; ⏲ by tour only; Ⓜ Khreshchatyk) Many of the 'chimeras' that adorn the awning of Kyiv's weirdest building are depictions of architect Władysław Horodecki's hunting trophies – antelope, rhinos (!!), crocodiles, etc. He kept many prototypes inside – in the stuffed form. The house and the street on which it's located are closed off, but the **Museum of History of Kyiv** (vul Bohdana Khmelnytskoho 7) arranges group tours on some Saturdays (75uah per person). Otherwise you can stand on pl Ivana Franka to ogle it from afar.

Built at the start of the 20th century, this was Horodecki's private house but is now owned by the presidential administration across the street. The 'chimeras' were meant not only to decorate, but also to advertise the revolutionary building material – concrete, of which Horodecki was a huge fan. Many locals say that the house is best admired at night, when spooky creatures seem ready to come alive and jump down from the roof.

To join a tour, go to room 412 of the Museum of History of Kyiv and put your name on the list. A few tour companies can get you on the museum's list, but they charge 400uah to 500uah to do so. If you do enter, about the first thing you'll see is a fireplace shaped as an octopus.

Khanenko Museum of Arts MUSEUM

(Музей Ханенків; Map p48; www.khanenkomuseum.kiev.ua; vul Tereshchenkivska 15 (Western Art) & 17 (Eastern Art); adult/student 40/22uah per wing or 60/40uah for both wings, free 1st Wed of month; ⏲ 10.30am-5.30pm Wed-Sun; Ⓜ Pl Lva Tolstoho) This museum's 'Western Art' wing houses Kyiv's most impressive collection of European paintings, with Bosch, Velázquez and Rubens among the many masters represented. The 19th-century house, with its frescoed ceilings and intricately carved woodwork, alone is worth the price of admission. All the better that it's packed with priceless antique furniture, ancient Greek sculptures, porcelain ceramics and dazzling paintings, such as a version of Hieronymus Bosch's *Temptation of St Anthony*.

The museum's climax is on the top floor: four rare religious icons from the 6th and 7th centuries. Even if icons aren't your thing, it's hard not to be moved by these primitive Byzantine treasures. The separate 'Eastern Art' wing, in an equally stunning mansion (1878), has Buddhist, Chinese and Islamic art.

Fomin Botanical Gardens GARDENS

(Map p48; vul Tarasa Shevchenka; Ⓜ Universytet) FREE Lying behind the Universytet metro station building, the landscaped gardens are best visited in spring when just about everything there is blooming.

A short walk to the left from the entrance, you'll find a leaning apron-clad bronze figure wielding something that looks like a bow. This strange-looking monument is dedicated to the professors and students who died defending Kyiv in WWII. Students cynically call it 'monument to the deceased botanist' – 'botanist' being the Russian slang word for nerd.

★ **PinchukArtCentre** GALLERY

(Map p48; http://pinchukartcentre.org; Arena Entertainment Complex, vul Baseyna 2A; ⌚noon-9pm Tue-Sun; Ⓜ Pl Lva Tolstoho, Teatralna) FREE The rotating exhibits at this world-class gallery feature elite names in the world of European contemporary art and design, all financed by billionaire mogul Viktor Pinchuk. Works by world giants like Antony Gormley, Damian Hirst and Ai Weiwei have exhibited here. Don't miss the view of Kyiv's roofs from the excellent coffee shop on the top floor. The oligarch-style security at the door and inside the gallery can be a little off-putting, but you may regard them as modern art objects. English-speaking guides are on the ready in each room to answer any questions you have about the exhibits.

Kyiv National Museum of Russian Art MUSEUM

(Map p48; www.kmrm.com.ua; vul Tereshchenkivska 9; adult/student 50/15uah; ⌚11am-6pm Tue-Wed & Fri-Sun; Ⓜ Pl Lva Tolstoho) With 2000 paintings, only a fraction of which are on display at any one time, this museum, set in an impressive tsar-era mansion, has the largest collection of Russian artwork outside Moscow and St Petersburg. There's lots of Repin and Shishkin, plus a Rerikh or two. The permanent collection is on the 2nd floor, while the ground floor hosts rotating exhibits.

National Art Museum MUSEUM, GALLERY

(Національний художній музей України; Map p48; http://namu.kiev.ua; vul Hrushevskoho 6; adult/student 40/20uah; ⌚10am-6pm Wed, Thu & Sun, 12-8pm Fri, 11am-7pm Sat; Ⓜ Maydan Nezalezhnosti) In a historic building designed by Władysław Horodecki, this long-running museum has a wide-ranging collection of Ukrainian paintings spanning the eras, including a notable collection of Ukrainian avant garde from the early 20th century. In recent years it has become well known for its professionally curated exhibitions, with each opening an important event in Kyiv contemporary art circles. This is where the art and treasures rescued from former President Viktor Yanukovych's Mezhyhirya estate (p64) were first exhibited. Also here, in the permanent collection, are some works by the polymath national poet, Taras Shevchenko. It's worth popping into the **bookstore** after your visit.

Taras Shevchenko Memorial House Museum MUSEUM

(Літературно-меморіальний будинок-музей Тараса Шевченка; Map p48; prov Tarasa Shevchenka 8A; adult/student 15/10uah; ⌚10am-6pm Sat-Thu; Ⓜ Maydan Nezalezhnosti) A beautifully restored, 19th-century wooden house where the man who dominates the Ukrainian literary pantheon once lived. You can see drawings he made on ethnological expeditions of Ukraine, which inspired his nationalism. Do have a stroll around the attractive grounds and gardens at the back.

Water Museum MUSEUM

(Музей води; Map p48; vul Hrushevskoho 1V; tour adult/child 50/40; ⌚10am-5pm, to 6pm Sat & Sun; 👪; Ⓜ Maydan Nezalezhnosti) The Dutch funded the launch of this museum inside a 1980s water pump, but it now operates independently. On the obligatory 45-minute tour (in English by request), you're taken on a walk through a rainwater collector, allowed to sit on a giant toilet or stand inside a bubble, and introduced to a yellow fish called Vasily. Good for children.

National Museum of Literature of Ukraine MUSEUM

(Map p48; http://museumlit.org.ua; vul Bohdana Khmelnytskoho 11; adult/student 20/15uah; ⌚9am-5pm Mon-Fri, 10am-6pm Sat; Ⓜ Teatralna) A must for aficionados of Ukrainian literature, this museum is housed in the former main building of the Pavlo Galagan Collegium, built in 1871. It presents the history of Ukrainian literature from the 9th century until the modern times. The highlight is the splendid, well-preserved **Collegium library** from the 19th century. There's also a replica of the Church of St Paul, where famous Ukrainian writer Ivan Franko married Olga Horuzhinska in May 1886.

Chocolate House MUSEUM

(Map p48; vul Shovkovychna 17; 30uah, photos 40uah; ⌚10am-6pm Tue-Wed & Fri-Sun; Ⓜ Khreshchatyk) This distinctive neo-Renaissance mansion in Kyiv's wealthy Lypky district, built in 1901, is notable for its lavish interiors. There's a small sculpture display inside, but mostly it's about viewing the palatial rooms with their meticulously carved Moorish ceilings and chandeliers.

Friendship of Nations Monument MONUMENT

(Map p48; Ⓜ Maydan Nezalezhnosti) This is a giant metal parabola celebrating the 1654

Central Kyiv

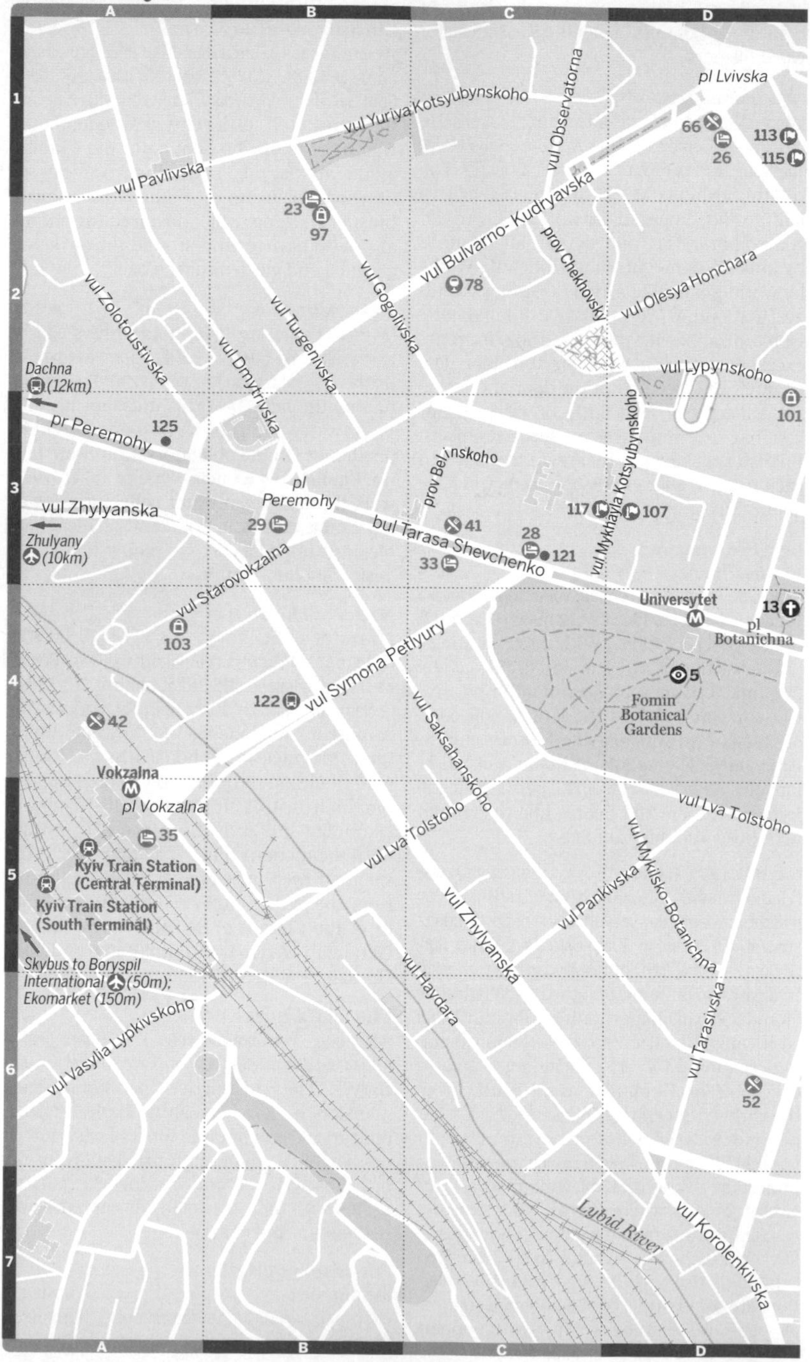

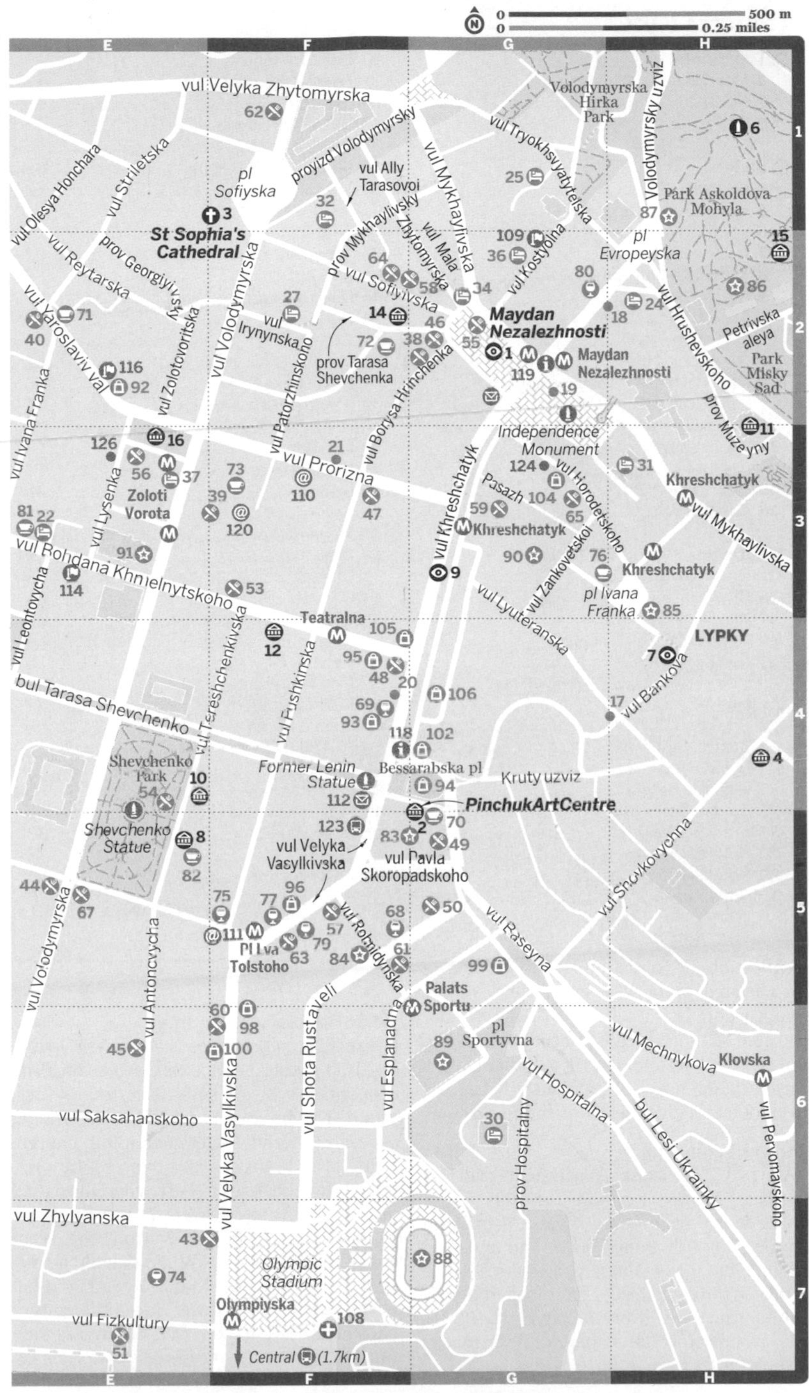
0 500 m
0 0.25 miles
vul Velyka Zhytomyrska
Volodymyrska Hirka Park
Volodymyrsky uzviz
proyizd Volodymyrsky
vul Tryokhsvyatytelska
pl Sofiyska
St Sophia's Cathedral
vul Ally Tarasovoi
vul Mykhaylivska
Park Askoldova Mohyla
pl Evropeyska
vul Kostyolna
vul Mala Zhytomyrska
vul Sofiyivska
prov Mykhaylivsky
Maydan Nezalezhnosti
vul Hrushevskoho
Petrivska aleya
Park Misky Sad
prov Tarasa Shevchenka
vul Irynynska
vul Borysa Hrinchenka
Independence Monument
prov Muzeyny
vul Prorizna
Zoloti Vorota
vul Horodetskoho
Pasazh
Khreshchatyk
vul Mykhaylivska
vul Khreshchatyk
vul Zankovetskoi
pl Ivana Franka
vul Lyuteranska
LYPKY
vul Bohdana Khmelnytskoho
Teatralna
vul Bankova
bul Tarasa Shevchenko
vul Pushkinska
vul Tereshchenkivska
Shevchenko Park
Former Lenin Statue
Bessarabska pl
Kruty uzviz
PinchukArtCentre
Shevchenko Statue
vul Velyka Vasylkivska
vul Pavla Skoropadskoho
vul Shovkovychna
vul Rohnidynska
Pl Lva Tolstoho
vul Raseyna
Palats Sportu
pl Sportyvna
vul Mechnykova
Klovska
vul Hospitalna
bul Lesi Ukrainky
vul Pervomayskoho
vul Saksahanskoho
vul Shota Rustaveli
vul Esplanadna
prov Hospitalny
vul Zhylyanska
Olympic Stadium
Olympiyska
vul Fizkultury
Central (1.7km)
vul Olesya Honchara
vul Striletska
vul Reytarska
prov Georgiyivsky
vul Yaroslaviv Val
vul Zolotovoritska
vul Volodymyrska
vul Patorzhinskoho
vul Ivana Franka
vul Lysenka
vul Leontovycha
vul Antonovycha
E
F
G
H
1
2
3
4
5
6
7

Central Kyiv

Top Sights
1 Maydan Nezalezhnosti G2
2 PinchukArtCentre G5
3 St Sophia's Cathedral F1

Sights
4 Chocolate House H4
5 Fomin Botanical Gardens D4
6 Friendship of Nations Monument H1
7 House of Chimeras H4
8 Khanenko Museum of Arts E5
9 Khreshchatyk G3
10 Kyiv National Museum of Russian Art E4
11 National Art Museum H3
12 National Museum of Literature of Ukraine F4
13 St Volodymyr's Cathedral D4
14 Taras Shevchenko Memorial House Museum F2
15 Water Museum H2
16 Zoloti Vorota E3

Activities, Courses & Tours
17 Chervona Ruta H4
18 City Sightseeing Kyiv H2
19 Kiev Walking Tours G2
20 New Logic F4
21 SoloEast Travel F3

Sleeping
22 11 Mirrors E3
23 Central Station Hostel B2
24 Dnipro Hotel H2
25 Gintama Hotel G1
26 Golden Gate Inn D1
27 Hotel Bontiak F2
28 Hotel Express C3
29 Hotel Lybid B3
30 Hotel Rus G6
31 Hotel Ukraine H3
32 Hyatt Regency Kyiv F1
33 Ibis C3
34 Kozatskiy Hotel G2
35 Service Centre A5
36 Sunflower B&B Hotel G2
37 Veselka Hostel E3

Eating
38 Arbequina G2
39 Barkas F3
40 Bulochnaya Yaroslavna E2
41 Dio Long C3
42 Ekomarket A4
43 Imbir E7
44 Khinkalnya Gogi E5
45 Klyukva i Bryukva E6
46 Krym G2
47 Kupidon F3
48 Kyivska Perepichka F4
49 Le Silpo G5
50 Linas Caffe G5
51 Megamarket E7
52 Musafir D6
53 Oliv'e F3
54 O'Panas Blyny Stand E4
55 Ostannya Barikada G2
56 Osteria Pantagruel E3
57 Pervak F5
58 Pizza Veterano G2
59 Puzata Khata G3
60 Puzata Khata F6
61 Pyrizhkova Titka Klara F5
62 Spotykach F1
63 Under Wonder F5
64 Walter's F2
65 Wolkonsky G3
66 Zheltok D1
67 Zheltok E5

'unification' of Russia and Ukraine. It's on an elevated plaza with great views of the Dnipro and Kyiv's left (east) bank. Under the arch is a social-realist statue of a Ukrainian (on the left) and a burlier Russian, arms raised in solidarity. Miraculously it has not been defaced, given tensions in the east.

Former Lenin Statue STATUE
(Map p48; vul Tarasa Shevchenka; M Pl Lva Tolstoho) At the terminus of vul Tarasa Shevchenka once stood Kyiv's last Lenin statue, famously pulled down and smashed to bits by Euromaidan protesters in late 2013. Until his demise, Lenin looked across thundering vul Khreshchatyk (p46) to the wonderfully atmospheric Bessarabsky Rynok (p81).

Old Town

★St Sophia's Cathedral CHURCH
(Map p48; pl Sofiyska; grounds/cathedral/bell tower 20/80/40uah; ⏲cathedral & museums 10am-6pm, grounds & bell tower 9am-7pm; M Zoloti Vorota) The interior is the most astounding aspect of Kyiv's oldest standing church. Many of the mosaics and frescoes are original, dating back to 1017–31, when the cathedral was built to celebrate Prince Yaroslav's victory in protecting Kyiv from the Pechenegs (tribal raiders). While equally attractive, the building's gold domes and 76m-tall wedding-cake bell tower are 18th-century baroque additions. It's well worth climbing the bell tower for a bird's-eye view of the cathedral and 360-degree panoramas of Kyiv.

Drinking & Nightlife
68 Alchemist Bar F5
Banka .... (see 67)
69 Barman Dictat F4
70 Chashka G5
71 Honey E2
72 Kaffa F2
73 Kharms F3
74 Lift E7
75 Mur Mur F5
76 Na Stanislavskogo G3
77 Old Bar F5
78 Palata No.6 .... C2
Paliturka Coffee & Books .... (see 93)
79 Parovoz F5
80 Pivna Duma G2
81 Repriza E3
82 Squat 17b Yard Cafe E5

Entertainment
83 Arena City F5
84 Bel Etage F5
85 Ivan Franko National Academic Drama Theatre H3
86 Kyiv Academic Puppet Theatre H2
87 National Philharmonic H1
88 Olympic Stadium G7
89 Palats Sportu G6
90 Pomada G3
91 Taras Shevchenko National Opera Theatre E3

Shopping
92 482 .... E2
93 Art Store Podval F4
94 Bessarabsky Rynok G4
95 Bukva F4
96 Caramel Manufactory F5
97 Diskultura B2
98 Dobro Store F6
99 Gulliver G5
100 Imbir Healthy Shop F6
101 Laska D3
102 Roshen G4
103 Roshen A4
104 Ruta G3
105 TsUM F4
106 Vsi. Svoi G4

Information
Australian Consulate .... (see 109)
107 Belarusian Embassy D3
108 Boris F7
109 Canadian Embassy G2
110 Central Library F3
111 Chasopys F5
112 DHL International F4
113 French Embassy D1
Georgian Embassy .... (see 33)
114 German Embassy E3
115 Hungarian Embassy D1
116 Polish Embassy E2
117 Romanian Embassy C3
118 Tour Info Kiev F4
119 Tour Info Kiev G2
120 Tsiferblat F3

Transport
121 Advance Train Ticket Office C3
122 Avtostantsiya Kyiv B4
123 Bessarabska Pl Bus Stop F5
124 Kiy Avia G3
125 Kiy Avia A3
126 Ukraine International Airlines E3

Named after the great Hagia Sofia in Istanbul, St Sophia's Byzantine architecture announced the new religious and political authority of Kyiv. It was a centre of learning and culture, housing the first school and library in Kyivan Rus. Adjacent to the Royal Palace, it was also where coronations and other royal ceremonies were staged, treaties signed and foreign dignitaries received.

Each mosaic and fresco had its allotted position according to Byzantine decorative schemes, turning the church into a giant 3D symbol of the Orthodox world order. There are explanations in English of individual mosaics, but the one that immediately strikes you is the 6m-high **Virgin Orans** dominating the central apse. The Virgin Orans is a peculiarly Orthodox concept of the Virgin as a symbol of the earthly church interceding for the salvation of humanity. Having survived this long, this particular Orans is now thought indestructible by Orthodox believers. (Unesco was slightly less certain, adding the cathedral to its World Heritage list in 1990.)

Less obvious, but worth seeking out, are two secular **group portraits of Yaroslav and family**, one on either side of the central nave. Prince Yaroslav himself was buried here, but his remains are believed to have been smuggled into the US by a collaborationist priest, who left Kyiv with the retreating German army during WWII. The Ukrainian government is engaged in negotiations about their return. The prince's empty tomb can be found on the ground floor, in the far-left corner from the main entrance.

Other highlights of the cathedral include the cast-iron tile floors, which date from the 18th century; a model depicting Kyiv at the time of the Kyivan Rus; and art galleries upstairs containing ancient icons and fragments of original frescoes rescued from nearby St Michael's Golden-Domed Monastery before the Soviets demolished it in 1937.

Additional **museums** on the cathedral grounds are of little interest. Just before the bell tower lies the ornate tomb of Kyiv Patriarch Volodymyr Romanyuk. Religious disputes prevented him from being buried within the complex. In front of the cathedral complex on pl Sofiyska is a **statue** of Cossack hero Bohdan Khmelnytsky.

★ St Michael's Golden-Domed Monastery MONASTERY
(Михайлівський Золотоверхий монастир; Map p54; www.archangel.kiev.ua; vul Tryokhsvyatytelska 6; ⌚territory 8am-7pm; Ⓜ Poshtova Pl) Looking from St Sophia's past the Bohdan Khmelnytsky statue, it's impossible to ignore the gold-domed blue church at the other end of proyizd Volodymyrsky. This is St Michael's, named after Kyiv's patron saint. As the impossibly shiny cupolas imply, this is a fresh (2001) copy of the original (1108), which was torn down by the Soviets in 1937. The church's fascinating history is explained in great detail (in Ukrainian and English placards) in a **museum** (14uah; ⌚10am-7pm Tue-Sun) in the monastery's bell tower.

Heading around the left of the church to the rear, you'll find the quaint **funicular** (tickets 4uah; ⌚9am-10pm) that runs down a steep hillside to the river terminal in the mercantile district of Podil. Although in summer trees partially obscure your view, this is still the most fun public-transport ride in town.

Zoloti Vorota HISTORIC BUILDING
(Golden Gate; Map p48; vul Volodymyrska; adult/student 40/15uah; ⌚10am-6pm Mon-Thu, to 8am Fri-Sun; Ⓜ Zoloti Vorota) Part of Kyiv's fortifications during the rule of Yaroslav the Wise, the famous Zoloti Vorota was erected in 1037. Modelled on Constantinople's Golden Gate, it was the was the main entrance into the ancient city, with ramparts stretching out from both sides. However, the gate was largely destroyed in the 1240 Mongol sacking of Kyiv, so what you see today is a 1982 reconstruction, although chunks of the original gate have been preserved inside.

Also inside, English placards detail the history of the Golden Gate, and there are a few old artefacts, such as the original 10th-century seal of Grand Prince Sviatoslav the Brave. You can climb up to the top of the 29m pavilion.

The statue to the side of Zoloti Vorota is of Yaroslav the Wise, although people call it 'monument to the Kyiv cake' – you'll understand why when you see it.

Andriyivsky Uzviz

According to legend, a man walked up the hill here, erected a cross and prophesied, 'A great city will stand on this spot.' That man was the Apostle Andrew, hence the name of Kyiv's quaintest thoroughfare, **Andriyivsky uzviz** (Андріївський узвіз; Map p54; Ⓜ Kontraktova Pl), which translates as Andrew's descent. It's a steep, cobbled affair with a vaguely Montparnasse feel as it winds its way up from Kontraktova pl to vul Volodymyrska. Along the length of 'the uzviz' you'll find cafes, art galleries and vendors selling all manner of souvenir and kitsch.

An interesting cluster of modern urban art can be found near the top of Andriyivsky uzviz, along **Peyzazhna aleya**, which starts at the National Museum of Ukrainian History and skirts around a large ravine offering great views of the city.

St Andrew's Church CHURCH
(Map p54; Andriyivsky uzviz; platform 10uah; Ⓜ Kontraktova Pl) The gold-and-blue baroque masterpiece that dominates the view as you walk up Andriyivsky uzviz was built in 1754 by Italian architect Bartolomeo Rastrelli, who also designed the Winter Palace in St Petersburg. It's a magnificent interpretation of the traditional Ukrainian five-domed, cross-shaped church. Unfortunately the interior has been closed for years, but you can climb the steps to the platform around its base for terrific views of Podil and the Dnipro River.

National Museum of Ukrainian History MUSEUM
(Національний музей історії України; Map p54; ☎044-278 4864; vul Volodymyrska 2; adult/student 50/30uah, excursion 240uah; ⌚10am-6pm Mon-Fri, 11am-7.30pm Sat & Sun; Ⓜ Kontraktova Pl) Located more or less at the spot where history began for Kyiv, this huge museum has been fully modernised in recent years and represents a fantastic stroll through all stages of Ukraine's past, from the Stone Age to the ongoing war with Russia in the east. Displays are in chronological order, and while not all are in English, each room has an English placard describing the period of history covered within.

Some of the most interesting displays are on the top floor, where Ukraine's modern revolutions and the war with Russia are covered through poignant photos, press clippings and war-battered signs and other objects. Expect more such exhibits to be added as history unfolds. Highlights from more distant epochs include an excellent collection of medieval armour, a fantastic diorama of Kyiv at the time of the Kyivan Rus, and a gilded carriage given to Rafael Zaborovsky, metropolitan of Kyiv in the 18th century, by the daughter of Peter the Great.

Bulgakov Museum MUSEUM
(Музей Булгакова; Map p54; ☎044-425 3188; www.bulgakov.org.ua; Andriyivsky uzviz 13; adult/student 40/25uah, tour per group 100uah; ⏲10am-6pm Tue & Thu-Sun, noon-6pm Mon; Ⓜ Kontraktova Pl) The much-loved author of *The Master and Margarita* lived in this house between 1906 and 1919 – long before writing his most famous book. The house became the model for the Turbin family home in *The White Guard,* Bulgakov's first full-length novel, published in 1925 and still the best book to read about Kyiv. The museum can only be visited on a scheduled tour, so drop by or call a day or so in advance to put your name on the list.

The museum consists mainly of old Bulgakov family photos and memorabilia in barren, white washed rooms. Tours take in some Bulgakov family history and revisit scenes from *The White Guard*, so it's advisable to read the book before visiting. Tours are generally in Ukrainian or Russian, but can be done in English with some advance warning. They happen every 30 minutes or so; the last one is at 5.15pm.

Museum of One Street MUSEUM
(Музей однієї вулиці; Map p54; www.onestreet.kiev.ua; Andriyivsky uzviz 2B; adult/student 50/30uah, tour in English 100uah; ⏲noon-7pm; Ⓜ Kontraktova Pl) This museum lays out individual histories of Andriyivsky uzviz buildings. The sheer jumble-sale eclecticism of the collection – showcasing the lives of, among others, a rabbi (Podil was Kyiv's Jewish district between the wars), a Syrian-born Orientalist, a circus-performing couple, and a certain family named Bulgakov – exudes bags of charm. Definitely spring for the guided tour in English as everything is in Ukrainian.

Desyatynna Church Ruins RUINS
(Десятинна церква; Map p54; vul Volodymyrska; Ⓜ Zoloti Vorota) Prince Volodymyr ordered the Desyatynna Church built in 989 and devoted 10% of his income to it, hence the name (*desyatyn* means 'one-tenth'). The church collapsed under the weight of the people who took refuge on its roof during the Mongol sacking of Kyiv in 1240. It was rebuilt in the 19th century, but later was destroyed once again, this time by the Soviets. The ruins of the church are in a park near the National Museum of Ukrainian History.

Ministry of Foreign Affairs LANDMARK
(Міністерство закордонних справ; Map p54; pl Mykhaylivska 1; Ⓜ Poshtova Pl) The Ministry of Foreign Affairs was built by the Soviets on the site of the Tryokhsvyatytelska Church, one of Kyiv's holiest edifices, destroyed by Stalin in 1934. The sheer size of the building was undoubtedly meant as an additional slap in the face to the church.

Podil

The funicular and Andriyivsky uzviz both lead down to this riverside mercantile quarter, an appealing grid of streets lined with quaint lanterns and eclectic turn-of-the-20th-century buildings. Dating back to the earliest settlements, the area grew quickly around the port. Podil was last rebuilt in 1811 after a devastating fire and emerged largely unscathed from WWII. Today it's a buzzing bar and restaurant district.

Chornobyl Museum MUSEUM
(Map p54; www.chornobylmuseum.kiev.ua; prov Khoryva 1; 10uah, audio guide 50uah; ⏲10am-6pm Mon-Sat; Ⓜ Kontraktova Pl) It's hard to convey the full horror of the world's worst nuclear accident, but the Chornobyl Museum makes a valiant attempt. It is not so much a museum as a shrine to all the firemen, soldiers, engineers, peasants and whole villages that perished in the aftermath of the explosion of Chornobyl power plant reactor No. 4, on 26 April 1986. The exhibits are predominantly in Russian and Ukrainian, but 100-minute audio guides are available in English and several other languages.

The audio guides are hard to come by, so get there early if you want one. The signs above the stairs as you enter represent the 'ghost' cities evacuated from the Chornobyl area in the wake of the disaster. Among the highlights once you're inside are touch screens, funded by the Japanese government after Fukushima, that profile every village evacuated and every person who died as a result of the Chornobyl disaster. There's a multimedia time-lapse diorama that dramatically recreates the explosion of reactor No. 4 and the subsequent addition of

Podil

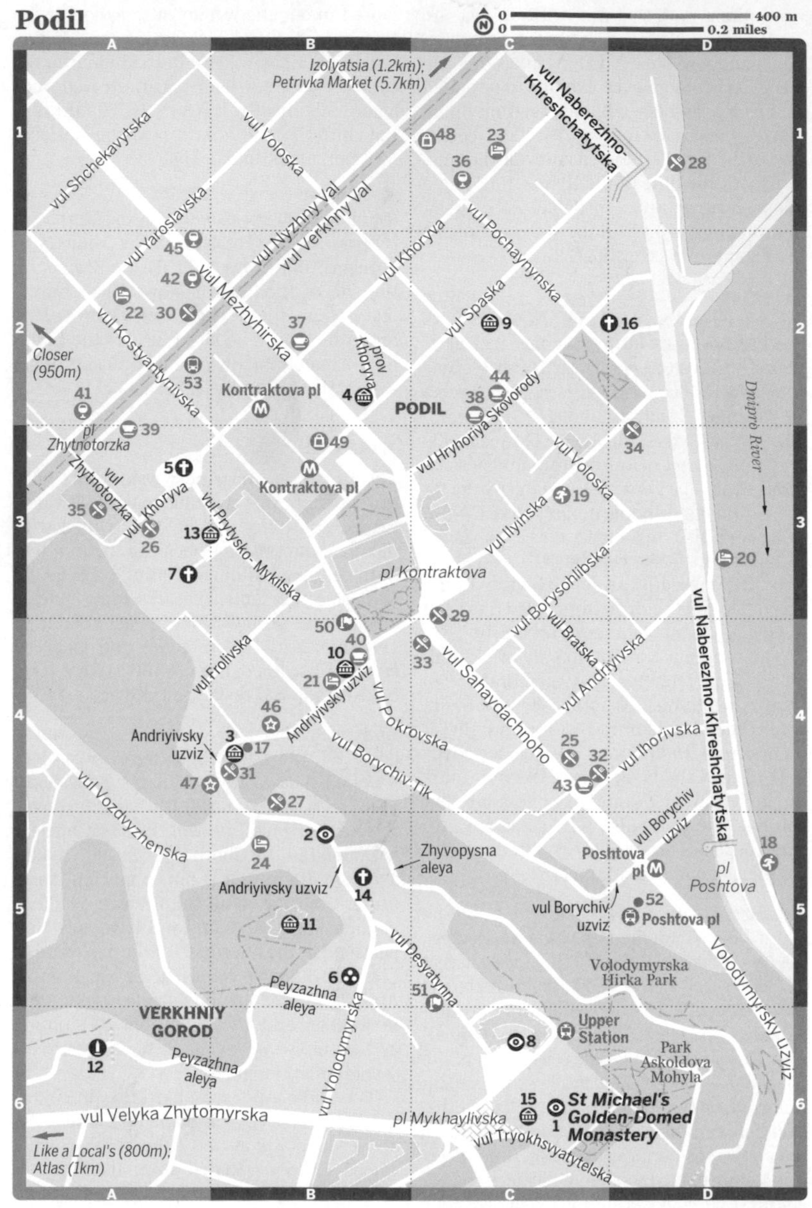

sarcophagi over the years. Front pages of the *New York Times* and *Philadelphia Inquirer* from the days immediately following the accident are on display, and there are distressing photos of the sorts of deformities – in animals and humans – the accident caused.

Florivsky Monastery CONVENT

(Флорівський жіночий монастир; Map p54; vul Prytytsko Mykilska; grounds 6am-10pm; M Kontraktova Pl) This 15th-century women's convent remained open during the communist era. Pass through the bell tower to

Podil

Top Sights
1 St Michael's Golden-Domed Monastery ... C6

Sights
2 Andriyivsky Uzviz ... B5
3 Bulgakov Museum ... B4
4 Chornobyl Museum ... B2
5 Church of Mykola Prytysk ... A3
6 Desyatynna Church Ruins ... B5
7 Florivsky Monastery ... A3
8 Ministry of Foreign Affairs ... C6
9 Museum of Hetmanship ... C2
10 Museum of One Street ... B4
11 National Museum of Ukrainian History ... B5
12 Peyzazhna aleya ... A6
13 Pharmacy Museum ... A3
14 St Andrew's Church ... B5
15 St Michael's Monastery Museum ... C6
16 St Nicholas Naberezhny ... D2

Activities, Courses & Tours
17 Chornobyl Tour ... B4
18 Dnipro River Boats ... D5
19 Tour2Chernobyl ... C3
veliki.ua ... (see 21)

Sleeping
20 Bohdan Khmelnitsky Boatel ... D3
21 Dream House Hostel ... D4
22 Kyiv Art Hostel ... A2
23 Mackintosh Hotel ... C1
24 Vozdvyzhensky Hotel ... B5

Eating
25 Alaverdy ... C4
26 Harbuzyk ... A3
27 Kanapa ... B4
28 Khutorets na Dnipri ... D1
29 Puzata Khata ... C3
30 Pyrizhkova Titka Klara ... A2
31 Svitlytsya ... B4
32 Tsymes ... C4
33 Varenichnaya Katyusha ... C4
34 Vero Vero ... D3
35 Zhytny Rynok ... A3

Drinking & Nightlife
36 Amigos Bar ... C1
Druzi Cafe ... (see 21)
37 Espressoholic ... B2
38 Kaffa ... C2
39 London ... A3
40 Lviv Handmade Chocolate ... B4
41 Pink Freud ... A2
42 Podil East India Company ... A2
43 Repriza ... C4
44 Vagabond ... C2
45 Wood You Like Bar ... A2

Entertainment
46 Koleso Theatre ... B4
47 Theatre on Podol ... A4

Shopping
48 Etnodim ... C1
49 Ye Bookstore ... B3

Information
50 Dutch Embassy ... B4
51 UK Embassy ... C5

Transport
52 Funicular ... D5
53 Kontraktova Pl Bus Stop ... A2

the peaceful grounds, which contain several attractive churches surrounded by well-manicured gardens.

Izolyatsia ARTS CENTRE
(ІЗОЛЯЦІЯ; Izone; ☎050 477 2620; http://izolyatsia.org/en; vul Naberezhno-Luhova 8; ⊙10am-8pm; Ⓜ Tarasa Shevchenka) FREE Izolyatsia is a self-described platform for cultural initiatives and contemporary culture occupying an old shipyard in north Podil. Originally from Donetsk, it's a refugee of the war in the east. The galleries here showcase top-notch international and local artistic talent. All manner of workshops, discussions and presentations take place on any given day, and on weekends you might find concerts, flea markets or full-blown festivals in their sprawling outdoor courtyard.

Workshops are held through the affiliated **Izone** coworking space (www.izone.ua), a wonderfully creative environment in its own right (drop-in rate 160uah per day).

Izolyatsia takes its name from the abandoned insulation materials factory in Donetsk where it was formerly located. They moved to Kyiv soon after rebels seized the Donetsk space in June 2014.

Pharmacy Museum MUSEUM
(Аптека-музей; Map p54; vul Prytytsko Mykilska 7; adult/student 30/25uah; ⊙9am-5pm; Ⓜ Kontraktova Pl) This museum is set in the premises of an early-19th-century German pharmacy. There are separate rooms dedicated to alchemy and witchcraft – all quite interesting, even if nothing is in English.

Church of Mykola Prytysk CHURCH

(Церква Миколи Притиска; Map p54; vul Khoryva 5A; Ⓜ Kontraktova Pl) The Church of Mykola Prytysk survived the 1811 fire that destroyed much of Podil. This Ukrainian Orthodox church is the oldest structure in the district (1631) and is surrounded by several pastel-coloured brick buildings exhibiting the eclectic style in vogue in Kyiv at the end of the 19th century.

Museum of Hetmanship MUSEUM

(Map p54; www.en.getman-museum.kiev.ua; vul Spaska 16B; adult/student 15/5uah; ⏲10am-5pm Sat-Thu; Ⓜ Kontraktova Pl) This small museum is devoted to Ukrainian *hetmans*, the military commanders of the Ukrainian Cossack State. Set in a stone house built at the beginning of the 18th century, it has several expositions dedicated to the life of the most famous *hetmans*, Ivan Mazepa, Pylyp Orlyk and Pavlo Skoropadsky. All sections include information in English.

St Nicholas Naberezhny CHURCH

(Церква Миколи Набережного; Map p54; vul Grygoria Skovorody 12; Ⓜ Kontraktova Pl) Church lovers will find several attractive and historic specimens in Podil, including this 1863 church near the river, which is dedicated to sailors and others journeying along the river to do business. Consider coming here if you are taking a cruise of the Dnipro.

Pechersk & Around

Any day and in any weather, Arsenalna metro station in Pechersk discharges a steady flow of tourists and pilgrims moving along vul Ivana Mazepy towards pl Slavy. Their main magnet is the Kyevo-Pecherska Lavra – the holiest of holy sites in Ukraine and beyond – but you can continue south past the Lavra to a bevy of other worthwhile attractions around here, such as Rodina Mat and the Hryshko Botanical Gardens (p62).

★ **Kyevo-Pecherska Lavra** MONASTERY

(Києво-Печерська лавра; Caves Monastery; Map p60; ☎044-406 6375; http://kplavra.kiev.ua; vul Lavrska 9; upper/lower Lavra 25uah/free; ⏲9am-7pm Apr-Sep, 9am-6pm Oct-Mar, caves 8.30am-4.30pm; Ⓜ Arsenalna) Tourists and Orthodox pilgrims alike flock to the Lavra, set on 28 hectares of grassy hills above the Dnipro River in Pechersk. It's easy to see why tourists come: the monastery's cluster of gold-domed churches is a feast for the eyes, the hoard of Scythian gold rivals that of the Hermitage, and the underground labyrinths lined with mummified monks are exotic and intriguing. For pilgrims, the rationale is much simpler: to them, this is the holiest ground in the country.

A *lavra* is a senior monastery, while *pecherska* means 'of the caves'. The Greek St Antony founded this *lavra* in 1051, after Orthodoxy was adopted as Kyivan Rus' official religion. He and his follower Feodosy progressively dug out a series of catacombs, where they and other reclusive monks worshipped, studied and lived. When they died their bodies were naturally preserved, without embalming, by the caves' cool temperature and dry atmosphere. The mummies survive even today, confirmation for believers that these were true holy men.

The monastery prospered above ground as well. The Dormition Cathedral was built from 1073 to 1089 as Kyiv's second great Byzantine-inspired church, and the monastery became Kyivan Rus' intellectual centre, producing chronicles and icons and training builders and artists.

Wrecked by the Tatars in 1240, the Lavra went through a series of revivals and disastrous fires before being mostly rebuilt, with its prevailing baroque influences, in the 18th century. It was made a museum in 1926 but was partly returned to the Ukrainian Orthodox Church (Moscow Patriarchate) in 1988.

See p58 for details on visiting the Lavra.

Rodina Mat MEMORIAL

(Батьківщина-мати; Defence of the Motherland; Map p60; vul Lavrska 24; lower/top platform 50/200uah; ⏲10am-4pm; 🚌24, Ⓜ Arsenalna, 🚎38) As you journey into Kyiv from the airport, at some point a giant statue of a female warrior will loom up on the horizon and make you ask, 'What the hell is that?' It's Rodina Mat – literally 'Nation's Mother'. Inaugurated by Soviet leader Leonid Brezhnev in 1981, it was the second and last Nation's Mother monument erected in the USSR. Today it houses the excellent Great Patriotic War Museum in its base, and has a pair of viewing platforms.

The top platform is all the way up at the top of her shield at 91m, but it's subject to weather-related closures and long lines, as the elevator can only accommodate two visitors at at time. There's a lower platform at 36.6m, served by a separate, larger elevator.

Although initially designed by the same artist as the iconic Rodina Mat in Volgograd, this version completely lacked its sister's appeal and became a subject of ridicule, especially when the communist authorities reduced the size of the sword so that it doesn't rise over the cupolas of Kyevo-Pecherska Lavra. Even if you don't like such Soviet pomposity, don't say too much; you'd be taking on a titanium woman carrying 12 tonnes of shield and sword.

The grounds around Rodina Mat are popular for strolling and contain a number of intriguing relics of the communist era, including an eternal flame in memory of WWII victims; various old tanks, helicopters and anti-aircraft guns; and a veritable garden of Soviet realist sculpture in and around the underpass leading towards the Lavra.

Rodina Mat is an easy stroll from the Lavra, or take bus 24 or trolleybus 38 from the stop opposite Arsenalna metro.

Holodomor Victims Memorial MEMORIAL
(Map p60; vul Ivana Mazepy 15A; adult/student 16/9uah; Ⓜ Arsenalna) FREE At the far end of Vichnoy Slavy Park, which is centred around a Soviet-era war memorial, you will find a shrine from an entirely different epoch. Former President Viktor Yushchenko's pet project, this monument and museum is dedicated to almost four million victims of the famine artificially induced by Stalin's policy of collectivisation in 1932–33. Inside, touch screens take you through this dark period of Ukrainian history, and massive bound books contain some of the names of those who died. Placards parrot bloodthirsty quotes from Bolshevik leaders, such as Lenin's 'We should resolve the Cossack issue by the means of their full extermination; all assets and property to be confiscated.'

Great Patriotic War Museum MUSEUM
(National Museum of the History of Ukraine in the Second World War; Map p60; www.warmuseum.kiev.ua; vul Lavrska 24; adult/student 20/5uah, audioguide/excursion in English 50/100uah; ⏲10am-6pm Mon-Fri, 11am-7pm Sat & Sun; Ⓜ Arsenalna) Located at the base of the towering Rodina Mat, this museum was built belatedly in 1981 to honour Kyiv's defenders during the Great Patriotic War (as WWII is known in these parts). While the focus is still on

Kyevo-Pecherska Lavra

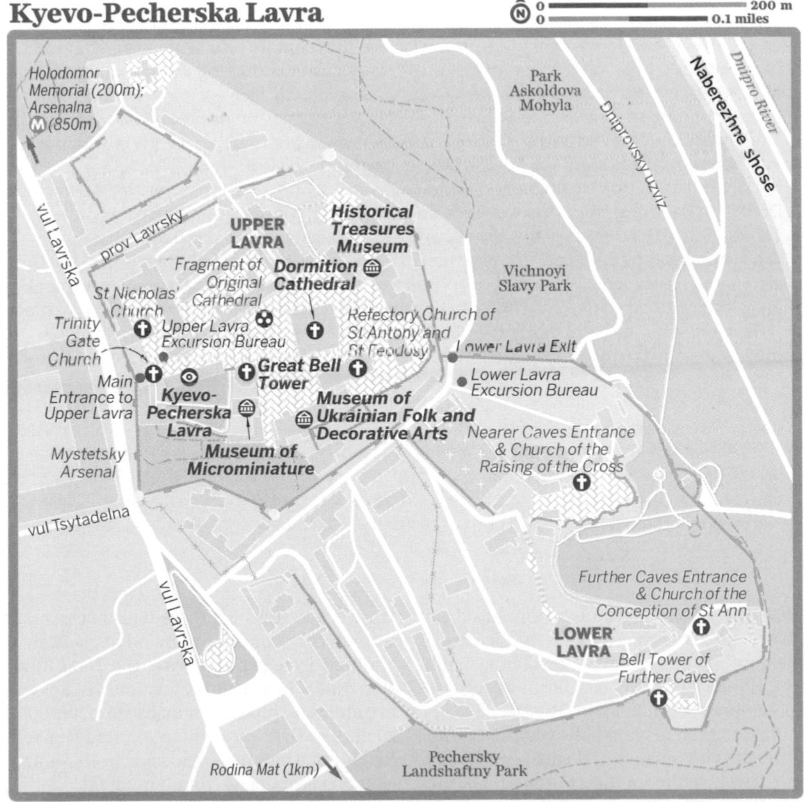

VISITING THE LAVRA

Kyevo-Pecherska Lavra is a pleasant 1.3km walk from Arsenalna metro, or take any trolleybus (No 38 works) or marshrutka heading south from the bus stop opposite the metro station on vul Ivana Mazepy.

The complex is divided into the upper lavra (owned by the government and Kyiv Patriarchate) and lower lavra (which belongs to the Moscow Patriarchate and contains the caves). You will need at least half a day to get a decent introduction to both halves. Try to avoid the Lavra on weekends, when the whole complex gets extremely busy and the caves in particular can be uncomfortably crowded. If you must go then, visit early and head for the caves first.

Entrance to the upper lavra is free from 6am to 9am, and for a couple of hours after closing (until sunset). Admission to the upper lavra allows access to the churches, but several museums on-site charge additional fees. The **Upper Lavra Excursion Bureau**, just to the left past the main entrance to the upper lavra, guides two-hour private tours in various languages (800uah), or you can join a group tour in Ukrainian for 80uah. Book in advance during peak periods.

Entrance to the lower lavra and the caves is free. To enter the caves, women must wear a headscarf and either a skirt that extends below their knees or, at a pinch, trousers. For men, shorts and tank tops are forbidden. Don't worry too much if you show up in the wrong threads – they supply proper coverings at the cave entrances. Private excursions of the lower lavra and caves in English (from 280uah, one hour) are run out of the **Lower Lavra Excursion Bureau** (Екскурсійне бюро нижньої лаври), located near the exit from the upper lavra.

Upper Lavra

The main entrance to the upper lavra is through the striking **Trinity Gate Church** (Троїцька надбрамна церква; Troitska Nadbramna Tserkva), a well-preserved piece of early-12th-century Rus architecture. Rebuilt in the 18th century, it once doubled as a watchtower and as part of the monastery fortifications. It's well worth going inside to observe its rich frescoes and lavish gilded altar. To access the church, turn left immediately after entering through the main gate. Also in this northwest section of the grounds is the small, late-17th-century **St Nicholas' Church** (Церква святого Миколая), its unique blue dome adorned with golden stars. It's now an administrative building.

Back out on the main path, walk straight past a clutch of 200-year-old chestnut trees to Dormition Cathedral (Успенський собор; Uspensky Sobor) with its seven gleaming domes. This is a year-2000 replica of the famous and sacred original, which was blown up during WWII – probably by Soviet partisans, although pro-Russian historians still blame it on the Nazis. There's a daily service at 9am, but you are free to enter the church anytime. The big rock in the square between the cathedral and the bell tower is a fragment of the original cathedral.

Towering over the cathedral is the 96.5m tall **Great Bell Tower** (Дзвіниця). Climbing the 174 steps to the top (adult/student 25/50uah) is an essential experience, with unparalleled views of Kyiv your reward.

Beneath the Great Bell Tower on the south side, the **Museum of Microminiature** (Музей мікромініатюр;www.microart.kiev.ua; adult/student 50/25uah; ⏲9am-1pm & 2-7pm Wed-Mon) provides something even for atheists within this holiest of holies – and, boy, is it popular! Possibly the most orderly queues in unruly Kyiv form in front of Russian artist Nikolai Siadristy's tiny creations. The world's smallest book (with some verses of Shevchenko, a balalaika with strings one-fortieth the width of a human hair and a flea fitted with golden horseshoes are

WWII, the huge foyer out front has been turned into a shrine of sorts to victims of the war in the east, with revolving exhibits telling the story of Ukraine's all-too-contemporary conflict with Russia.

Behind that, 12 giant halls walk the visitor through every nuance and stage of WWII, a war that killed more than 8 million Ukrainians. A walk through these halls is essential to understanding the tremendous suffering endured by Ukraine during the Nazi invasion and subsequent occupation. It's a sombre and sometimes even macabre exhibition, such as in Hall No. 6 where you find yourself looking at a pair of gloves made from human skin and soap made from human fat.

just some of his works of whimsy. Each is so small that microscopes are needed to view them, but you can occupy yourself with the brief English explanations while you wait.

The cluster of buildings just south of the Assumption Cathedral includes the excellent **Museum of Ukrainian Folk Decorative Arts** (Музей українського народного декоративного мистецтва; adult/student 40/20uah; ⏰10am-6pm, closed Tue & last day of month), which boasts a vast collection of clothes, carpets, jewellery, ceramics and other beautiful items produced by generations of Ukrainian craftspeople. Nearby is the **Refectory Church of St Antony & St Feodosy** (Трапезна церква), sporting the monastery's most famous gold-striped dome (1885–1905). The main domed space is slightly reminiscent of Istanbul's Hagia Sophia, with its ring of small narrow windows along the base of the drum. The interior is beautifully painted with biblical scenes, saints and art nouveau patterns. The generously frescoed refectory (Трапезна палата) attached to the church is a sight in itself.

The **Historical Treasures Museum** (Музей історичних коштовностей України; adult/student 50/30uah; ⏰10am-5.45pm, closed Mon & last Fri of month), behind the Dormition Cathedral, has an astounding collection of precious stones and metal found or made in Ukraine. The highlight is the fabulous hoard of gold jewellery worked for the Scythians by Greek Black Sea colonists. Much of the treasures come from a handful of circa 4th-century-BC burial mounds in the Dnipropetrovsk, Zaporizhzhya and Kherson regions.

Lower Lavra

To get to the Lower Lavra from the Upper Lavra, follow the path behind the Dormition Cathedral and head downhill under the flying buttress. The entrance to the **Nearer Caves** (Вхід у Ближні печери) is inside the **Church of the Raising of the Cross** (Хрестовоздвиженська церква; 1700). Before the stairs head downwards, there's a table selling candles to light your way through the dark passages. The use of cameras is forbidden in the caves.

Underground, the mummified monks' bodies, in glass cases, are clothed; you only see the occasional protruding toe or finger. The bodies are believed to have healing powers and pilgrims will bow to kiss the feet of one or the hand of another.

The coffins are arranged in niches in the tunnels, underground dining hall and three **subterranean churches**. Antony, the monastery's founder, and Nestor the Chronicler are just two of the 123 bodies down here. Students consider the latter their patron saint and leave candles near his mummy to have luck at exams. Another notable monk lying here is Ioann the Long-Sufferer, who fought the sin of womanising by half-burying himself in the ground every year for the duration of Lent. As a result, his sinning lower half completely decayed, while his saintly upper half remained intact. Would it be accurate to call him a half-saint?

The **Further Caves** were the original caves built by Antony and Feodosy. Their entrance is in the **Church of the Conception of St Ann** (Аннозачатіївська церква; 1679), reached from the Nearer Caves by a viaduct. This cave system is also lined with ornamented mummified monks and contains three underground churches. Uphill from the Church of the Conception of St Ann is the seven-domed **Church of the Nativity of the Virgin** (Церква Різдва Пресвятої Богородиці; 1696). Rising to the right is the unusual high-baroque **Bell Tower of Further Caves** (Дзвіниця на Дальніх печерах; 1761).

From the Further Caves it's a long walk back up the hill to the **main entrance** on vul Lavrska, or you can exit (or enter) at the nearby **lower entrance**. There may be taxis waiting at the lower entrance, or you can walk 1.5km north along busy Naberezhne shose to the Dnipro metro station.

Displays are mainly in Ukrainian, but English placards summarise the highlights in each hall.

The museum was recently renamed the National Museum of the History of Ukraine in the Second World War; not surprisingly, the name has yet to catch on.

Mystetsky Arsenal GALLERY

(Мистецький арсенал; Map p60; ☎044 288 5225; http://artarsenal.in.ua; vul Lavrska 10-12; 60uah; ⏰11am-8pm Tue-Sun; Ⓜ Arsenalna) Once a storage for gunpowder and harnesses, these days it is a playground for visionary curators – each exhibition becomes an event of national importance. Eclecticism rules –

exhibitions feature both new and old art. Unfortunately, the place often closes for months on end in the interim periods between exhibitions. Check its website to see what's on during your visit.

Ivan Honchar Museum MUSEUM, GALLERY

(Map p60; https://honchar.org.ua; vul Lavrska 19; adult/student 30/10uah; 10am-6pm; M Arsenalna) This Pechersk-based facility is more than a museum, it's a crucible for preserving Ukrainian folk culture in the 21st century. In addition to permanent ethnographic exhibits of clothing, textiles, musical instruments, *pysanky* (decorative Easter eggs) and the like, they hold bold exhibitions that blend modern and traditional art and/or fashion, plus run well-regarded workshops on costume design, folk art and national song.

Outside the City Centre

Pyrohiv Museum of Folk Architecture MUSEUM

(http://pirogovo.org.ua; vul Akademika Tronko; adult/child 40/20uah; houses 10am-6pm Thu-Tue, box office to 5pm, grounds to at least 9.30pm; marshrutka 496) Some 300 traditional structures, some dating back to the 16th century, have been transplanted form various parts

Pechersk

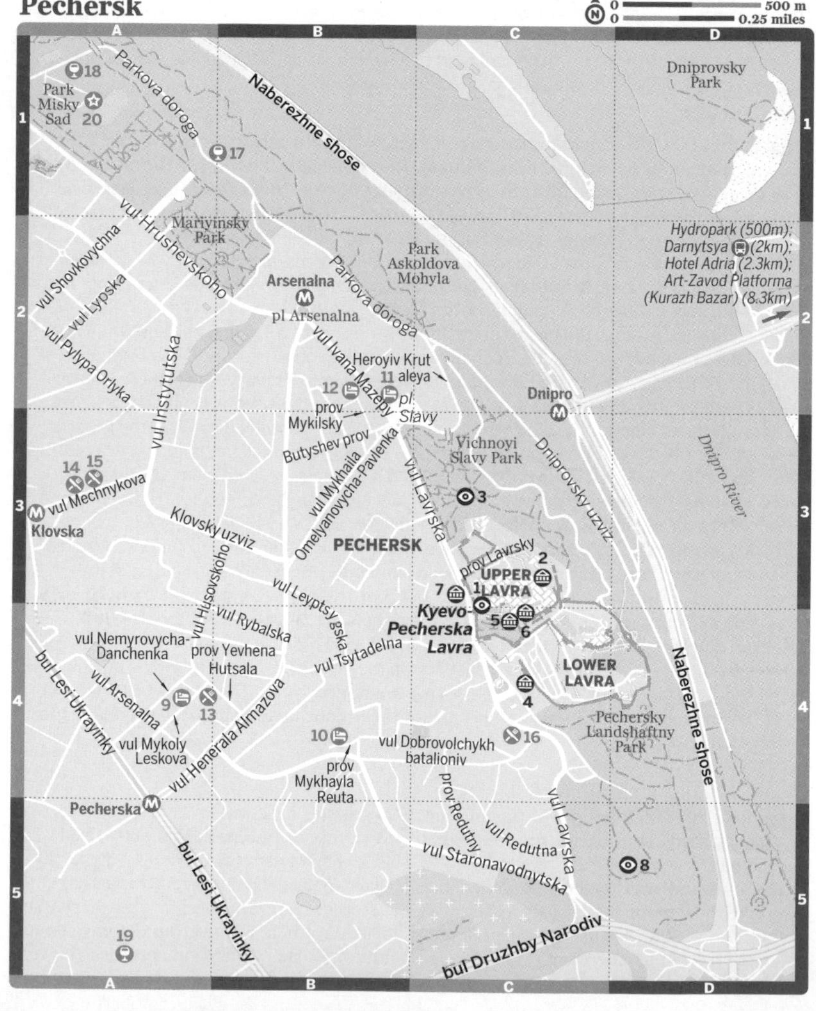

of Ukraine to this open-air folk museum. On weekends in the warm months, medieval-themed events and contests take place and the entire compound assumes a festive atmosphere, with much singing, dancing and eating going on. It's about 12km south of central Kyiv; *marshrutka* 496 from Lukyanivska metro station takes you right to the entrance.

In the summer workers enact different village roles, carving wood, making pottery, doing embroidery, and driving horses and carts. Other activities include a zipline (100uah), horse riding and archery. There is a cluster of outdoor eateries at the centre of the action that serve wonderful *shashlyk* and all manner of traditional Ukrainian food and drink. Ukrainian musicians play on weekends.

The quaint 17th- to 20th-century wooden churches, cottages, farmsteads and windmills are divided into seven 'villages' representing regional areas of Ukraine. In just one long afternoon you can visit the architecture of eastern, western and southern Ukraine. It's always fun, especially so if you visit during a festival. Pyrohovo hosts several, the biggest of which is the countrywide Ivan Kupala festival (p65).

★ Skvorechnik CULTURAL CENTRE

(Скворечник; Birdhouse; www.facebook.com/skvorechnikcafe; Trukhaniv Island; Ⓜ Poshtova Pl)
It's hard to characterise this beachfront hippie haven on Trukhaniv Island. It derives its name from the smattering of raised wooden chill-out huts that dot the grounds. While you can rent these out, Skvorechnik is about much more than birdhouses. It's like a mini Burning Man festival – an alcohol-free zone of singalongs, yoga, zen meditation, massage, dreamcatcher-making classes – well, you get the idea. Of course there's also a **beach** and a busy **vegetarian cafe** keeping people fed and fuelled.

Regular talks and parties are centred on green topics and earth-friendly themes. You can rent a couple of the birdhouses overnight, including one that is winterised, and there's talk of them officially launching a hostel here (it would instantly become Kyiv's quirkiest place to stay).

Babyn Yar MEMORIAL

(vul Oleny Telihy; 24hr; Ⓜ Dorohozhychi) FREE
On 29 September 1941, Nazi troops rounded up Kyiv's 34,000-strong Jewish population, marched them to the Babyn Yar ravine and massacred them. Victims were shot and buried in the ravine, some of them still alive. Today the site is a sobering memorial marked by a poignant menorah.

The Nazis would kill many more Jews and non-Jews here in subsequent years. The entire story is told through an open-air alley of placards, in Ukrainian and English, near the northeast park entrance on vul Oleny Telihy.

The site has been mired in controversy over the years. Because of their own anti-Semitism, it took decades for the Soviets to recognise the Babyn Yar tragedy before they finally erected a monument in 1976. The monument, a nonsectarian creation comprised of choking figures, infuriated the Jewish community. It made no mention of Jews, only of 'Soviet victims of fascism', and was located well south of the ravine where the atrocities occurred.

It wasn't until after the Soviet Union collapsed that the Jewish community was given permission to erect their menorah near

Pechersk

Top Sights
1 Kyevo-Pecherska Lavra C3

Sights
Great Patriotic War Museum .... (see 8)
2 Historical Treasures Museum C3
3 Holodomor Victims Memorial C3
4 Ivan Honchar Museum C4
5 Museum of Microminiature C4
6 Museum of Ukrainian Folk Decorative Arts C4
7 Mystetsky Arsenal C3
8 Rodina Mat D5

Sleeping
9 Asteri A4
10 Black Sea B4
11 Hotel Salute B2
12 Sherborne Guest House B2

Eating
13 Barsuk A4
14 Good Wine A3
15 Shoti A3
16 Tsarske Selo C4

Drinking & Nightlife
17 Chi B1
18 Hangover Bar A1
19 Open Space A5

Entertainment
20 Lobanovsky Dynamo Stadium A1

the actual killing site. From the menorah, several paths lead to points overlooking the ravine itself.

The Nazis ultimately turned this entire area into the Syrets concentration camp, killing thousands more people of all ethnic, religious and political backgrounds. The total number of people buried here is estimated at 100,000. Close to a dozen monuments commemorating various groups targeted by the Nazis – among them Russian Orthodox priests, Ukrainian nationalists, Romany people and female Ukrainian slave labourers who were shipped to Germany – are scattered around the unkempt park.

The controversial Soviet monument is in an adjacent park south of Dorohozhychi metro and vul Melnykova.

Vydubytsky Monastery MONASTERY

(Видубицький монастир; vul Vydubytska 40) Few churches appear more frozen in time than those of the Vydubytsky Monastery, nestled into a hill beneath the Hryshko Botanical Gardens (p62). If you found the crowds at the Lavra a little too much to bear, you should not hesitate to come here, although noise from the adjacent highway spoils the atmosphere somewhat near the entrance and the main **St Michael's Church**, which dates to the 11th century.

Aviation Museum MUSEUM

(Музей авіації; http://aviamuseum.com.ua; vul Medova 1; adult/student 50/20uah, photo 10uah; ⌚10am-7pm Wed-Sun, to 5pm winter) Located at the far side of Zhulyany airfield, this open-air museum displays dozens of Soviet aircraft designed to carry people or tanks, land on ice or water, drop bombs or engage in dogfights. You can climb aboard a few of the planes and helicopters. It's about a 1.5km walk or taxi ride along vul Medova from Zhulyany Airport.

Hryshko Botanical Gardens PARK

(Ботанічний сад імені Гришка; vul Tymiryazevska 1; adult/student 40/20uah; ⌚8.30am-9pm; marshrutka 62k, 🚎14, 62) The long, steep hill running along the Dnipro River from Olympic Stadium and Mariyinsky Palace to Rodina Mat continues south for several kilometres, eventually becoming these lovely botanical gardens. The 130 hectares here are fastidiously manicured and criss-crossed by a network of paths leading to hidden viewpoints and churches frozen in time. To get here, take *marshrutka* 62k or trolleybus 14 from Pecherska metro station, or trolleybus 62 from the Kontraktova Pl stop in Podil. There's a second

City Walk
Eras & Chimeras

START MAYDAN NEZALEZHNOSTI
END BESSARABSKY RYNOK
LENGTH 6KM; THREE HOURS

Set out from **1 maydan Nezalezhnosti** (p43), walking south along cobbled vul Horodetskoho to **2 pl Ivana Franka**, with tsar-era buildings like the Ivan Franko Drama Theatre and the Kyivenergo Headquarters at pl Ivana Franka 5. Up on the hill behind the square you'll spot Władysław Horodecki's bizarre House of Chimeras.

Retreat from pl Ivana Franka to vul Zankovetskoyi and walk left to vul Lyuteranska. Glance to the right and spot the elaborate art nouveau façade of **3 vul Lyuteranska 6**, an apartment house built in 1905. Then head left up the hill, past **4 St Catherine's Lutheran Church**, to another art nouveau masterpiece, the **5 Weeping Widow House** at vul Lyuteranska 23. It is best seen when it rains and water is dripping down the cheeks of the sad female face on the facade.

Continue straight and take a left at the next corner onto vul Shovkovychna. Many of Kyiv's aristocrats built mansions in this area, known as Lypky, at the turn of the 20th century. Examples include the neo-Gothic mansion at **6 vul Shovkovychna 19** and, next door, the brown-coloured **7 Chocolate House** (p47) . Head inside if you like to view its elaborate Moorish and rococo interiors.

From Chocolate House, follow vul Shovkovychna until it terminates at the **8 Verkhovna Rada** (Parliament Building). Cross the street and walk through Park Misky Sad to the right of the Verkhovna Rada. The blue baroque building on your left is **9 Mariyinsky Palace**, based on a design by Italian architect Bartolomeo Rastrelli, who built St Andrew's Church and much of St Petersburg. A former Kyiv residence of the Russian royals, it is now used for official ceremonies attended by the Ukrainian president.

Behind the palace, follow a path leading northwest through the park. Eventually you'll spy **10 Dynamo Stadium**, just before crossing the high **11 Devil's Bridge** adorned with hundreds of locks left by newlywed couples who defiantly ignore the

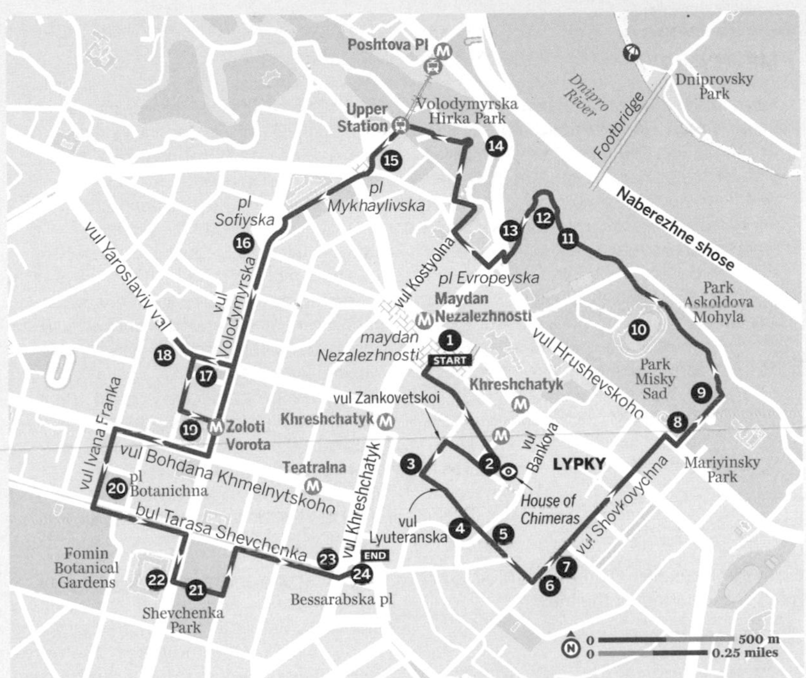

bridge's name. Continue past two beloved Kyiv statues – the Love Story Monument, about an Italian WWII POW and a Ukrainian nurse reunited in 2004 after 60 years apart; and Monument to the Frog, which locals rub for good luck. Eventually you'll come to a giant, dull, metal parabola. It is part of the ⓬ **Friendship of Nations Monument** (p47) celebrating the 1654 'unification' of Russia and Ukraine. Under the arch is a social realist statue of a Ukrainian (on the left) and a burlier Russian, arms raised in solidarity. Miraculously it has not been defaced, given tensions in the east.

Descend the hill via a path leading by the ⓭ **National Philharmonic** (p79), and cross pl Evropeyska. On the other side, follow vul Tryokhsvyatytelska uphill, turning right into Volodymyrska Hirka Park beyond the intersection of vul Kostyolna. All trails in here lead to the viewpoint looking down on the ⓮ **statue of Volodymyr the Great** – who brought Christianity to the eastern Slavs in 989 – and out across the Dnipro and the monolithic suburbs beyond.

Continue round the elevated riverbank, past a children's playground to the blue-and-gold ⓯ **St Michael's Monastery**. From pl Mykhaylivska you can see the tall bell tower and gold domes of ⓰ **St Sophia's Cathedral** (p50), which you should now head towards. After exploring St Sophia's, head south along vul Volodymyrska until you hit ⓱ **Zoloti Vorota** (p52). Make a quick detour to the Gothic ⓲ **Karaite Kenasa** (1900) at vul Yaroslaviv Val 5/7, built by Władysław Horodecki. Karaites are a small Crimean ethnic group who have preserved a peculiar religion mixing Judaism and Turkic paganism. Having lost a massive cupola in the Soviet period, the temple is now home to the House of Actors.

Back on vul Volodymirska walk towards ⓳ **Taras Shevchenko National Opera Theatre** (p79) before turning right into vul Bohdana Khmelnytskoho and, two blocks later, left onto vul Ivana Franka. At the end of this road on the left stands ⓴ **St Volodymyr's Cathedral**.

Turning left, you're on bul Tarasa Shevchenka, named after the Ukrainian national poet, Taras Shevchenko. On the right is his ㉑ **statue** in Shevchenka Park. A quick detour will give you a look at ㉒ **Kyiv University**.

At the end of the street once stood Kyiv's last ㉓ **Lenin statue**, pulled down and smashed by Euromaidan protesters in 2013. Until his demise, Lenin looked across thundering vul Khreshchatyk to the wonderfully atmospheric ㉔ **Bessarabsky Rynok** (p81).

WORTH A TRIP

MEZHYHIRYA

Kyiv's newest tourist attraction is **Mezhyhirya** (☎050 664 0080; www.mnp.org.ua; vul Ivana Franka 19, Novi Petrivtsi; adult/child 120/50uah; ⏲8am-9.30pm May-Sep, 8am to dark Oct-Apr; 🚌397), the estate that once 'belonged' to ex-president and wannabe Ukrainian dictator, Viktor Yanukovych, famously ousted in the Euromaidan Revolution of 2014. A wander through the opulent grounds – totalling 137 hectares and costing hundreds of millions of dollars to create – gives visitors an idea of just how corrupt the Yanukovych regime had become. Now a national park, the estate is built around Yanukovych's personal dacha (country house), a 620 sq m pinewood behemoth.

Other shocking highlights include a zoo, horse stables, tennis courts, a golf course, a rare-breed dog kennel and a museum of exotic cars. A general admission ticket gets you access to most of the compound, including the zoo. Entering the dacha can only be done on a special pre-arranged tour – see the park's website for details.

The adult admission price is reduced to 50uah before 9am or after 7pm, and to 40uah all day on Tuesday.Mezhyhirya is about 15km north of Kyiv. Bus 397 goes right to the park, via Vyshhorod centre, from either Petrivka (15uah, 50 minutes) or Heroyiv Dnipra (35 minutes) metro stations. Departures are every hour on the hour from Petrivka.

If you have spare time to wander around Vyshhorod, you'll find a few attractive churches and, south of Mezhyhirya, yachties and fishers frolicking on the Kyiv Sea.

entrance near the Vydubytsky Monastery (p62) at the bottom of the hill.

Activities

Trukhaniv Island BEACH

(Ⓜ Poshtova Pl) The island opposite Podil on the Dnipro is accessible via the **Parkovy footbridge** – an experience in its own right, full of life and colour. In the summer brave souls bungee off the bridge for 200uah (we do not vouch for the safety of this!). Trukhaniv is criss-crossed by forested roads and paths – a great place for cycling. There's a long sandy and usually uncrowded beach facing the city. Skvorechnik (p61) is here, and on the extreme southeast tip there's a **nude beach**, from where you can shuttle over to Hydropark (p64) by boat.

Hydropark BEACH

(Ⓜ Hydropark) The main recreational zone on the Dnipro islands, Hydropark deafens people arriving by metro with pop music blasted from dozens of bars near the entrance. Venture deeper into the park, however, and you'll find Kyivans in their element. There's an old-school outdoor gym, sports zones, *shashlyk* stands and all manner of beach, be it gay or straight, clothed or nude. There are also stunning views over to the Kyevo-Pecherska Lavra (p56) on the Dnipro's opposite (right) bank.

Dnipro River Boats CRUISE

(Map p54; cruises 150-200uah; ⏲10am-11pm, every 20 min May-Aug, when full Apr & Sep-Oct; Ⓜ Poshtova Pl) These one- to 1½-hour cruises are highly recommended. Loud pop music blasts on some boats, but it's all part of the experience. The night 'disco' cruises can turn into rowdy affairs. Didn't think you'd get caught dead dancing to Russian pop? Think again. Cruises leave when full from several piers behind the Richnoy Vokzal (River Port) in Podil. The port itself is shuttered up, but the promenade out front is a bustling outdoor cafe zone, perfect for grabbing a drink or a bite before or after your cruise.

Tour2Chernobyl TRAVEL AGENCY

(Map p54; ☎096 785 4363; www.tour2chernobyl.com; vul Illinska 12; ⏲9am-6pm Mon-Fri; Ⓜ Kontraktova Pl) A good choice for one- or two-day Chornobyl tours.

veliki.ua CYCLING

(Map p54; www.veliki.ua; Andriyivsky uzviz 2D; per hr/day 50/300uah; Ⓜ Universytet) With its long green belt along the river, forested islands and wide sidewalks, Kyiv is a good place for cycling. This bicycle-rental coop runs several outlets around Kyiv, but this location at Dream House Hostel is by far the most convenient.

Tours

★ **JC Travel** TOURS

(☎068 920 5397; www.enjoy-ukraine.com) One of the best new Kyiv-based tour companies offering tours of all kinds to any region of Ukraine you wish to visit and any activity you can think of when you get there. Also arranges multiday tours to Moldova and Belarus.

★Kiev Walking Tours WALKING
(Map p48; ☎093 006 1217; www.kievwalkingtours.com.ua; cnr vul Khreshchatyk & vul Institutska; ⊙free tours 11am & 3pm daily Mar-Oct, Sat & Sun only Nov-Feb; Ⓜ Maydan Nezalezhnosti) If you're in the market for a guided walking tour or a translator for the day, this is your best choice. Free two-hour walking tours in English kick off every day from the Founders of Kyiv Monument on maydan Nezalezhnosti. Just show up and walk. These are a great way to learn a little about the city and some central sights. Additionally they offer an excellent range of **paid tours**, all fairly priced.

The 11pm free tour takes in mainly historical sites, while the 3pm tour explores Soviet sites. A small tip for these is appreciated.

Chornobyl Tour TOURS
(Map p54; ☎044-221 1986; www.chornobyl-tour.com; Andriyivsky uzviz 11; ⊙10am-6pm) Broad set of tours up to 7 days' duration. Online booking and payment.

BeInside TOURS
(https://beinsideukraine.com) Good guides and a great range of tours, including unique food, drink and cultural tours, a mural-art walk and a fashion tour. They do all the standard tours as well, including Chornobyl.

Adventure Tours in Ukraine ADVENTURE SPORTS
(☎066 588 0507; www.adventuretours.in.ua; pr Peremohy 44) For the seriously adventurous, these guys run a range of aerial tours – including joyrides in helicopters, ultralights, balloons and various planes – plus tank rides and the usual shooting-range and Chornobyl tours.

Chervona Ruta CRUISE
(Червона Рута; Map p48; ☎044-253 6909; www.ruta-cruise.com; vul Lyuteranska 24; Ⓜ Khreshchatyk) The best port of call if you're interested in Dnipro River and Black Sea cruises. The standard cruise is one week from Kyiv to Odesa. Some cruises go into the Danube delta, and there are other trips around Kyiv (check the website).

SoloEast Travel TOURS
(Map p48; ☎044-279 3505; www.tourkiev.com; vul Prorizna 10, office 105; ⊙9am-6pm Mon-Fri, 10am-2pm Sat; Ⓜ Khreshchatyk) Led by a Ukrainian-husband-and-Canadian-wife team, this is probably the most helpful, friendly tour company in Kyiv, with reliable Chornobyl tours, a sensible payment scheme and a host of alternative excursions on offer. Enter around the back.

They can book also good **apartments** and have a rustic **cottage** for rent five minutes outside the Chornobyl exclusion zone.

Interesniy Kiev WALKING
(Mysterious Kiev; ☎044-364 5112; www.interesniy.kiev.ua) This company hooks you up with tour guides offering all sorts of walks around the city, including some tours of some of Kyiv's lesser-visited and unusual sights.

New Logic TOURS
(Map p48; ☎044-206 2200; www.newlogic.ua; vul Khreshchatyk 42A; ⊙9am-6pm Mon-Fri; Ⓜ Teatralna) A giant travel agency that specialises in Chornobyl tours for individual tourists looking to join groups.

City Sightseeing Kyiv BUS
(Map p48; www.visitkyiv.travel/locations/city_sightseeing_kyiv; vul Khreshchatyk 7/11; tour 300uah; ⊙hourly 11am-7pm; Ⓜ Maydan Nezalezhnosti) These 1½-hour hop-on, hop-off, double-decker bus tours are a great way to see lots of Kyiv at once. Tours kick off on vul Khreshchatyk near the Dnipro Hotel and stop briefly at most of the big sights – including the Lavra, Bessarabsky Rynok, Zoloti Vorota and St Sophia's Cathedral. You can linger at any site and just hop back on the next bus. Purchase tickets on the website or at any Tour Info Kiev (p84) kiosk, or just show up at the starting point for tour time.

Festivals & Events

Kyiv Days FIESTA
(⊙May) This celebration of spring brings musicians and street performers to Andriyivsky uzviz (p52), maydan Nezalezhnosti (p43) and other streets of the capital on the last weekend of May. Coincides with the **Kyiv Marathon**.

Ivan Kupala CULTURAL
(Іван Купала; ⊙6 Jul (or nearest weekend)) On the night of this pagan fest, crowds pour into Pyrohiv Museum of Folk Architecture (p60) to sing and dance, consume tons of food and – most importantly – jump over fire with their beloved ones.

Kraina Mriy Festival MUSIC
(www.krainamriy.com; ⊙Jan, Jul) VV frontman Oleh Skrypka organises a three-day festival of ethnic music from Ukraine and elsewhere in July during the countrywide Ivan Kupala festival. Over the last few years the same festival has also taken place in January around Orthodox Christmas.

Gogolfest ART
(www.gogolfest.org.ua; ⌚ early Sep) Taking place at several venues around Kyiv, this is a lively festival of modern theatre, music, cinema, architecture and all imaginable kinds of art dedicated to writer Nikolai Gogol.

Epiphany RELIGIOUS
(⌚ Jan) Scores of the faithful leap into the Dnipro River in Hydropark (p64) and elsewhere to celebrate the baptism of Christ.

Ostrov Festival DANCE
(www.qievdance.com; ⌚ late Jun-early Jul) Seriously fun three-day electronica festival held in the open air on Trukhaniv Island (p64). Draws top international DJ talent.

Kyiv International Film Festival Molodist FILM
(www.molodist.com; ⌚ end Oct) An annual event that takes place during the last week of October.

Ulichnaya Eda FOOD & DRINK
(Art Zavod Platforma, vul Bilomorska 1a) Runs monthly themed street-food festivals, plus an annual October beer festival and two 'White Nights' festivals of electronic music and dance (in early June and early September). The venue is the **Art-Zavod Platforma** (http://artzavodplatforma.com), a giant events space occupying a former silk factory on the left bank.

Baptism of Rus RELIGIOUS
(⌚ 12 Aug) Kyivans plunge into the Dnipro River, just as they did in 988 AD on the orders of Prince Volodymyr, who decided that his land should join the Christian world.

Sleeping

Thanks to the currency collapse of 2014, Kyiv suddenly has a nice range of midrange options, to complement a lovely hostel scene at the budget end, and a clutch of long-standing luxury properties at the high end. Reasonably valued boutique hotels are few and far between, however. Midrange properties tend to be large, renovated Soviet jobs.

City Centre

Veselka Hostel HOSTEL $
(Map p48; ☎093 426 5999; www.keytogates.com.ua; vul Volodymyrska 42A; dm 160-220uah, d 650-850uah; ❄ 📶; Ⓜ Zoloti Vorota) Locations don't get much better than around the corner from Zoloti Vorota (p52) in the very centre of the city. Throw in sharp dorm rooms, bright doubles, fair prices and arguably Kyiv's most stylish common/kitchen area, and you have a real winner. It's not a particularly social hostel, but if you prefer peace over people look no further.

★ **Sunflower B&B Hotel** B&B $$
(Map p48; ☎044-279 3846; www.sunflowerhotel.kiev.ua; vul Kostyolna 9/41; s 1400-1600uah, d 1650-1850uah; ❄ @ 📶; Ⓜ Maydan Nezalezhnosti) Just off maydan Nezalezhnosti but well hidden from noisy traffic and crowds, this B&B (and definitely not hotel) seems to have been designed by a super-tidy granny. The airy, light-coloured rooms have a retro feel and there are extras like umbrellas and a shoe-polishing machine that you wouldn't expect. Continental breakfast is served in your room.

★ **Hotel Ukraine** HOTEL $$
(Готель Україна; Map p48; ☎044-278 2804; www.ukraine-hotel.kiev.ua; vul Instytutska 4; incl breakfast s €42-55, d €54-70 ste €115-165; ❄ 📶; Ⓜ Maydan Nezalezhnosti) This Stalin-era giant presiding over maydan Nezalezhnosti offers solid value smack dab in the centre of town. Short on comforts, big on atmosphere, its 368 rooms have glorious views and air-con to protect you from natural and political heat should further revolutions arise just outside. A big Ukrainian buffet breakfast is part of the package.

★ **Golden Gate Inn** HOTEL $$
(Map p48; ☎068 687 8171; www.kievgoldengateinn.com; vul Yaroslaviv Val 33A; d 900-1500uah; ❄ 📶; Ⓜ Zoloti Vorota) Golden Gate is a functional, anti-Soviet hotel with decent-sized rooms just a short walk from the centre of the old town. The clean rooms have microwaves and mini-refrigerators – nice amenities at these reasonable prices. The cheapest rooms are at the basement level. There's no on-site restaurant but you can order breakfast to your room for just 100uah.

Hotel Rus HOTEL $$
(Готель Русь; Map p48; ☎044-256 4000; www.hotelrus.phnr.com; vul Hospitalna 4; incl breakfast s/d from 1350/1570uah, ste 2800-5500uah; ❄ @ 📶; Ⓜ Palats Sportu) Perched above Olympic Stadium, it is a mammoth, 450-room, Soviet-era highrise transformed into a professionally run establishment. It's a bit of an uphill grind to walk here, but it's perfect if you're in town for a football match.

It's also convenient for the bars and restaurants around vul Shota Rustavelli.

Kozatskiy Hotel HOTEL $$

(Map p48; ☎044-279 4914; www.kozatskiy.kiev.ua; vul Mykhaylivska 1/3; s/d from 1115/1385uah, ste 1665-2280; ❄📶; Ⓜ Maydan Nezalezhnosti) If location were all that mattered, the Kozatskiy would be Kyiv's top hotel. It's smack dab on maydan Nezalezhnosti. The once-musty rooms have come a long way and boast new furniture such as full-length mirrors, wardrobes and desks, albeit with bland office-style carpeting and only half-renovated bathrooms. Still, it's excellent value.

Dnipro Hotel HOTEL $$

(Map p48; ☎044-254 6777; vul Khreshchatyk 1/2; incl breakfast s 1350-1500uah, d 1400-1600uah; Ⓜ Maydan Nezalezhnosti) The giant Dnipro basically anchors the northeast end of vul Khreshchatyk, so as a location play it's hard to beat. Add in decently renovated Soviet rooms and a good buffet breakfast, and you could do a lot worse.

Hotel Greguar HOTEL $$$

(Грегуар; ☎044-498 9790; www.greguar.com.ua; vul Velyka Vasylkivska 67/7; studio 3500-4500uah, ste 5600-7500uah; ❄📶; Ⓜ Olympiyska) What makes this hotel different is a kitchenette in each of the large comfortable rooms. It's not like Kyiv has any shortage of good inexpensive food, but should you need to cater for yourself – here is a perfect choice. The attached **Gregoire French Bakery** is a fine breakfast option.

Gintama Hotel HOTEL $$$

(Map p48; ☎044-278 5092; www.gintama.com.ua; vul Tryokhsvyatytelska 9; incl breakfast s/d 2000/2600uah, ste 2900-3300uah; ❄📶; Ⓜ Maydan Nezalezhnosti) This friendly family-run hotel has smallish rooms individually decorated in a formal, traditional style if you're into that sort of thing. Think opulent wallpaper and satiny curtains, albeit with fewer florals than some properties of this ilk. Location is great – quiet and just a three-minute walk from maydan Nezalezhnosti. There's a sauna with a small pool attached.

Old Town

Hyatt Regency Kyiv HOTEL $$$

(Map p48; ☎044-581 1234; http://kiev.regency.hyatt.com; vul Ally Tarasovoi 5; r incl breakfast weekday/weekend from €390/330; P❄📶🏊; Ⓜ Maydan Nezalezhnosti) Other Ukrainian hotels can only dream of having the Hyatt's view of duelling 11th-century churches. Inside, everything is just as perfect, from the fabulous gym and the spacious and eminently comfortable rooms, to its popular rooftop **Bar on 8 and Grill Asia** restaurant. Western leaders tend to stay here and we've never heard them complain.

11 Mirrors LUXURY HOTEL $$$

(Map p48; ☎044-581 1111; www.11mirrors-hotel.com; vul Bohdana Khmelnytskoho 34A; incl breakfast d €230-455, ste €645-765; ❄📶; Ⓜ Zoloti Vorota) If you want to admire the cupola of St Volodymyr's Cathedral from your bathtub through a one-way transparent wall or perhaps share a sumptous buffet breakfast with boxing champions the Klitschko brothers, who are associated with the business, here is your chic place to stay. The better the view, the more expensive the room.

Rates are slightly cheaper at weekends. The sumptuous breakfast is available for nonguests for 400uah.

Hotel Bontiak BOUTIQUE HOTEL $$$

(Map p48; ☎044-284 0475; www.bontiak.com; vul Irynynska 5; incl breakfast s 2500, d 2980-3390uah; ❄@📶; Ⓜ Zoloti Vorota) Tucked in a quiet courtyard a five-minute walk from maydan Nezalezhnosti, this cosy boutique hotel is built into Kyiv's hilly landscape, which is why the reception is located at the top floor. The stylishly minimalist rooms are generously sized and well equipped, and breakfast is served in your room.

Andriyivsky Uzviz & Podil

★ **Dream House Hostel** HOSTEL $

(Map p54; ☎095 703 2979; www.dream-family.com; Andriyivsky uzviz 2D; dm/s/d without bathroom from 240/560/900uah, d with bathroom 1030-1350uah; ❄@📶; Ⓜ Kontraktova Pl) Kyiv's most happening hostel is this gleaming 100-bed affair superbly located at the bottom of Andriyivsky uzviz. An attached cafe-bar (p78), a basement kitchen, a laundry room, key cards, bike hire, and daily events and tours make this a comfortable and engaging base from which to explore the capital. The expert, English-speaking staff are a great source of tourist information, and they run fun tours to Chornobyl and other excursions out of Kyiv.

Kyiv Art Hostel HOSTEL $

(Map p54; ☎063 457 7589; vul Kostyantynivska 20/14; dm 270uah, d without bathroom 550-600uah; ❄📶; Ⓜ Kontraktova Pl) Owner Valentin, an artist, has created a masterpiece in his Podil apartment. It consists of a single dorm room with six double-wide beds, and two small private rooms (shoot for the pricier one, best described as a boutique cave). A concert-quality stereo playing suitably vintage jazz invigorates the living room and kitchen, which are stuffed with wistful bric-a-brac and antique furniture.

You'll very much feel at home here, and there's free coffee and tea to boot.

Podolski Hostel HOSTEL $
(☎068 567 7833; www.podolskihostel.com.ua; vul Nabarezhno-Luhova 7; dm 100-180uah, s/d 350/500; 📶; Ⓜ Tarasa Shevchenka) This simple but clean hostel in residential neighbourhood in north Podil is good value, although you'll want to request a room facing the courtyard, as highway-facing rooms are very noisy. Air-conditioning in the private rooms costs 50uah extra. It's convenient to the Izolyatsia arts centre (p55) and a short walk to the metro.

Bohdan Khmelnitsky Boatel HOUSEBOAT $
(Map p54; ☎063 578 0190; www.3317000.com; vul Naberezhno-Khreshchatytska, moorage 5; r 300-600uah; ❄📶; Ⓜ Kontraktova Pl) The grand dame of the Dnipro River fleet, this paddle boat built in Budapest in 1954 is now based in Podil and offers budget accommodation when it's not out on the odd river tour. The cabin rooms are tiny and stuffy – hey, it's a ship – but have a certain charm with darkwood panelling and diminutive bathrooms.

Mackintosh Hotel HOTEL $$
(Map p54; ☎044-463 5999; www.mackintosh.com.ua; vul Khoryva 49A; incl breakfast s 1290, d 1940-2200uah, ste 3000uah; ❄📶; Ⓜ Kontraktova Pl) If the big Soviet hotels aren't for you and the boutique hotels too pricey, this new 26-room property in Podil is an excellent middle-ground choice. Rooms are Scandinavian-style and spiffy, sky-toned and outfitted with comfortable beds, full-length mirrors, night stands and anything else you might need. Friendly service and an elegant lobby bar top it off.

Vozdvyzhensky Hotel BOUTIQUE HOTEL $$$
(Готель Воздвиженський; Map p54; ☎044-531 9900; www.vozd-hotel.com; vul Vozdvyzhenska 60; incl breakfast economy s €119, std s/d €139/194; ❄@📶; Ⓜ Kontraktova Pl) Tucked away in a nook just off Andriyivsky uzviz, the Vozdvyzhensky is one of Kyiv's few true boutique hotels. The 29 rooms are all individually designed and boast fine art. The hotel highlight is the rooftop summer terrace, which has views overlooking Podil. Our main gripes are the small standard rooms and the difficulty pronouncing 'Vozdvyzhensky'.

Train Station Area

Central Station Hostel HOSTEL $
(Map p48; ☎093 758 7468; www.kievcentralstation.com; vul Gogolivska 25, apt 11; dm 200-350uah; Ⓜ Vokzalna) This popular hostel is a good choice if you're looking to meet other travellers and perhaps have a pub crawl, often led by the Brazilian owner. It occupies two floors of a high-rise next to the historic 'Cat House', a 1.5km walk from both the centre and the train station.

The dorms are nice enough, if overpriced for Kyiv, but the common areas can get overcrowded. The remote location and lack of signage make it a poor choice for walk-ins, so book ahead.

LOSE OR DIE

During WWII, when Kyiv was occupied by Nazi Germany, the members of the talented Dynamo football team were challenged to a public match with a team of German soldiers. The Ukrainians formed a team called Start and, despite physical weakness brought on by the occupation, they were soon ahead in their first match. At half-time, German officers came into the dressing room and commanded them to let up. Nevertheless, Start continued to play hard, and before the game finished the referee blew the whistle and called it off (with a score of 4–1).

The Germans reshuffled their players, and Start was offered another chance to lose. Instead they won. Next, Start was pitted against a Hungarian team – and won again. Finally, the enraged Germans challenged Start to a match against their finest, undefeated team, Flakelf. When the 'Übermensch' of Flakelf lost, the Nazis gave up – and proceeded to arrest most of the Start players, several of whom were executed at Babyn Yar (p61).

A monument to the 'Death Match' stands outside Dynamo Stadium (p81) in Kyiv. Their story inspired the movie *Victory*, starring Sylvester Stallone and soccer legend Pele. Andy Dougan's *Dynamo: Defending the Honour of Kiev* (2001) is a readable, well-researched account of the incident.

Hotel Express HOTEL $$

(Готель Експрес; Map p48; ☎044-234 2113; www.expresskiev.com; bul Tarasa Shevchenka 38/40; s/d from 1100/1350uah; ❄@; ⓂUniversytet) The Soviet-style Express has a mix of renovated and unrefurbished rooms. The cheapest have tiny beds and lack showers, but at least have air-conditioning. Prices increase proportionally as amenities and coats of paint are added. Prices go down by about 100uah during weekends and in July/August.

Service Centre HOSTEL $$

(Сервісний центр; Map p48; ☎044-465 2080; pl Vokzalna 2; dm 140-240uah, d 540uah, ste 670uah; ❄; ⓂVokzalna) These resting rooms in the southeast corner of the train station make a great choice if you are arriving late or departing early by train. The comfortable doubles and spacious suites are superb value. Head to the right as you exit the Central Terminal.You can also opt for a dorm-style arrangement here or in separate 'parenting rooms', for women and children only, in the South terminal.

Hotel Lybid HOTEL $$

(Готель Либідь; Map p48; ☎044-597 9007; www.lybid-hotel.phnr.com; pl Peremohy 1; s 890-1180uah, d 1040-1350uah, ste 2070-3340uah; ❄@📶; ⓂUniversytet) Lybid hails from the same Soviet architectural incubator as many other hotels in Kyiv. Rooms have seen varying degrees of renovation, but retain cheap furniture, bland office carpeting and tiny old TVs. On the plus side, service is friendly and the location is convenient to the train station (just a five-minute walk). Book directly on their website for the best deals.

Ibis HOTEL $$$

(Map p48; ☎044-591 2222; www.ibis.com; bul Tarasa Shevchenka 25; d weekend/weekday from 1650/1990uah; ❄📶; ⓂUniversytet) Yes, it is a predictable chain hotel, but it is sparkling clean and about the best value you can get for under €80 a night – and the most comfortable bed, too! Otherwise, it is Ibis – with minimalistically designed, slightly cramped rooms and no minibar. The buffet breakfast costs 240uah extra.

Pechersk & Around

Sherborne Guest House APARTMENT $$

(Map p60; ☎044-280 2315; www.sherbornehotel.com.ua; prov Mykilsky 9, 1st entrance; apt from 1600uah; ❄📶; ⓂArsenalna) An apartment hotel in Pechersk, this is very salubrious both inside and out, with 12 spacious apartments where you can cook for yourself and go about your business unhindered. There's speedy wi-fi and you can avail of various business services in their office. Book well in advance, as this place is justifiably popular.

Hotel Salute HOTEL $$

(Готель Салют; Map p60; ☎044-494 1420; www.salutehotel.kiev.ua; vul Ivana Mazepy 11B; s/d from 1250/1500uah; ⊖❄@📶; ⓂArsenalna) Perhaps a small step down from the best Soviet business hotels, the Salute nonetheless scores serious style points for its design. It's affectionately dubbed 'the grenade', with rooms that adhere to its unorthodox barrel shape. It does have some surprising benefits, like smiling receptionists and a 24-hour business centre.

Black Sea HOTEL $$

(Чорне море; Map p60; ☎044-364 1054; www.bs-hotel.com.ua; vul Leyptsygska 16A; s/d incl breakfast from 1365/1525uah; ❄📶; ⓂPecherska) A bit of a last resort if you need to be in Pechersk, where accommodation pickings are slim. It occupies the ground floor of an otherwise abandoned high-rise on an unpopulated side street. If you want peace and quiet, look no further, but look elsewhere if service or style are factors.

Asteri HOTEL $$$

(Map p60; ☎044-300 1050; http://asteri.kiev.ua; vul Mykoly Leskova 4; s/d/ste 1750/2100/2900uah; ⓂPecherska) With breakfast served on the rooftop of a highrise building, most of which is occupied by tax collectors (oops), this new hotel is good value for money in Pechersk. The only complaint is that the receptionist can be hard to find when you need her most.

Outside the City Centre

Oselya BOUTIQUE HOTEL $$

(Оселя; ☎050 380 7756; www.oselya.in.ua; vul Kamenyariv 11; s/d from 1500/1600uah; ❄@📶) Inconveniently located around 5km south of the city centre, roughly between Zhulyany Airport and the Central bus station, this friendly seven-room family-run hotel has immaculately kept rooms in period style and receives encouraging reviews from travellers. The location feels almost rural, and you'll need to arrange a pickup from Lybidska metro station to find it, or grab a cab.

Hotel Adria HOTEL $$

(Готель Адрія; ☎044-568 4457; www.eurohotel.com.ua; vul Raisy Okipnoi 2; s/d from 640/750uah; ❄@; ⓂLivoberezhna) This Polish outfit occupies

APARTMENTS

Despite the recent drop in hotel prices, apartments still tend to be better value than hotels and indeed there are some real gems out there. You can use any online consolidator, but for more personalised service you might try a local agency. Booking is best done online or via phone or text message, as only a few firms have offices. All of these local agencies accept credit cards:

Absolut (☎044-541 1740; www.hotelservice.kiev.ua; apt from 1000uah) Slightly more upscale, with reasonable, if not great, service.

Best Kiev Apartment (☎067 506 1875; www.bestkievapartment.com; apt from 900uah) Smartly renovated apartments.

Rentguru (☎050 240 2581; www.rentguru.com.ua/en; apt from 550uah) Some good deals, but properties tend to be further from centre.

Teren Plus (☎044-289 3949; www.teren.kiev.ua; apt from 650uah) Tried and true.

Uarent (☎067 403 6030; www.uarent.com; apt from 600uah) Apartments in prime locations for average price.

several floors of the lower-quality Hotel Tourist on the left (east) bank of the Dnipro near Livoberezhna metro station. This area is getting trendier thanks to its proximity to Rusanivka Island, an up-and-coming quay area with cafes, bars and restaurants with plenty of open-terrace seating, plus a locally famous fountain show. Breakfast costs 132uah extra.

Bratislava Hotel HOTEL $$
(☎044-537 3975; www.bratislava.com.ua/en; vul Andriya Malyshka 1; s/d from 900/1050uah; ❄📶; Ⓜ Darnytsa) In an old-school Soviet high rise on the left bank, Bratislava caters to business travellers, offering plenty of services and smartly renovated rooms. Nothing too fancy, you'll just pay a lot less than for a similar hotel in the centre. It's a five-minute walk to Darnytsya metro station and a 10-minute taxi ride to trendy Rusanivka Island.

Eating

Kyiv has arrived as a foodie destination, with a seemingly unlimited supply of high-quality restaurants. Nor are they expensive, as even the best restaurants cost about one-third of what you would expect to pay in Western Europe. For penny pinchers there are some great local eating options, often taking the form of *stolovayas* (cafeterias) offering a smorgasbord of national cuisine.

Maydan & Khreshchatyk Area

★**Kyivska Perepichka** PIES $
(Київська перепічка; Map p48; vul Bohdana Khmelnytskoho 3; perepichka 12uah; ⏲8.30am-9pm Mon-Sat, 10am-9pm Sun; Ⓜ Teatralna) A perpetually long queue moves with lightning speed towards a window where two women hand out pieces of fried dough enclosing a mouthwatering sausage. The place became a local institution long before the first 'hot dog' hit town. An essential Kyiv experience.

Krym TATAR $
(Крим; Map p48; prov Tarasa Shevchenka 1; dishes 25-80; ⏲9am-11pm, to 1am Fri & Sat; ❄📶; Ⓜ Maydan Nezalezhnosti) Krym also goes by 'Qirim' and occupies several spaces around maydan Nezalezhnosti, including a well-placed summer terrace. Tasty and wildly affordable Crimean specialities such as a delicious Tatar salad infused with crispy fried potato flakes (mix it yourself), *manty* (dumplings) and *shurpa* (meat soup). Homemade flatbread and Georgian wine also offered.

Kupidon UKRAINIAN $
(Купідон; Map p48; vul Pushkinska 1-3/5; mains 50-100uah; ⏲10am-11pm, to midnight Fri & Sat; ❄📶; Ⓜ Khreshchatyk) Cupid is a great Lviv-styled cellar *knaypa* (pub) abutting a secondhand bookshop. The culinary highlights are the domestic sausages and the eclectic, potato-based, Galician and Hutsul meals-in-a-jar, but other Ukrainian staples are well represented. They also serve fine beer snacks to accompany marvellously cheap (25uah) pints of Lvivske.

Puzata Khata CAFETERIA $
(Пузата Хата; Map p48; vul Khreshchatyk 15/4; dishes 20-30uah; ⏲8am-11pm; ❄📶; Ⓜ Khreshchatyk) The Khreshchatyk branch of this wildly popular chain of *stolovayas* is located just off the glamorous Pasazh shopping arcade.

Oliv'e CAFETERIA $

(Олів'є; Map p48; vul Bohdana Khmelnytskoho 16-22; dishes 25-35uah; 8am-10pm; ; Teatralna) Named after the ubiquitous Russian salad, this modern *stolovaya* (cafeteria) is a great place in the centre of town to fill up cheaply on Slavic specialities like chicken Kiev, lulya kebab and *borshch*. The food is absolutely fresh despite being pre-prepared, and it's hugely popular with locals.

Linas Caffe MIDDLE EASTERN $$

(Map p48; vul Shota Rustaveli 8; mains 80-200uah; 9am-1am; ; Palats Sportu) A lively falafel embassy in the land of *borshch*. Lamb *kapsa* (shoulder with wild rice, good for two) and *shashlyk* (kebab) are the specialities; burgers are also locally famous. Plenty of sidewalk seating or sit inside where members of the local Lebanese community play backgammon and smoke *kalyan* (hookahs).

Arbequina SPANISH, SEAFOOD $$

(Map p48; 096 401 7444; vul Borysa Hrinchenka 4; mains 100-150uah; 9am-11pm; ; Maydan Nezalezhnosti) Barcelona meets Odesa in this miniature restaurant a few steps from maydan Nezalezhnosti. Food is mostly Spanish – think *paella* and *fideua* – but the chef successfully experiments with Black Sea fish and Eastern European staples, which results in most unusual combinations. Excellent value.

Pizza Veterano PIZZA $$

(Map p48; 096 725 0202; vul Sofiyivska 8; pizzas 100-200uah; 11am-11pm; ; Maydan Nezalezhnosti) This centrally located pizzeria is entirely owned and operated by veterans of the war in the east. More than a great story, it actually has really good pizza. There's indoor and outdoor seating, plenty of military hardware (think bullets under glass-top tables), and nationalist-leaning posters on the walls. Some profits go toward supporting war-veteran causes.

Himalaya INDIAN $$

(Гімалая; 044 289 2345; www.himalaya.com.ua; vul Velyka Vasylkivska 80; mains 100-200uah; 11.30am-11.30pm; ; Olympiyska) In business since 1997, Himalaya is the best place to get your curry fix in Kyiv. It somehow has gotten both better and cheaper with age. The Indian food is spicier than you'd expect in these parts and there are many veggie options.

★ **Ostannya Barikada** UKRAINIAN $$$

(Last Barricade; Map p48; 068 907 1991; maydan Nezalezhnosti 1; mains 150-400uah; 11am-midnight; ; Maydan Nezalezhnosti) Hidden in a 'secret bunker' under maydan Nezalezhnosti, this is both a nationalist shrine and one of Kyiv's best restaurants. Everything – from the cheeses and *horilka* (vodka) to the craft beer and steaks – is 100% homegrown. Ukraine's three modern revolutions are eulogised everywhere. Getting in is a quest, but as poet Taras Shevchenko said, 'Fight and you'll win.' Start by pushing 'ОБ' on the Globus mall (west wing) elevator. Once you're in you get a free tour of the place.

Walter's ITALIAN $$$

(Map p48; 050 469 8629; vul Sofiyvska 10; mains 150-350uah; 12am-11.30pm; ; Maydan Nezalezhnosti) Owner Walter has made this simple eatery near the maydan a home-away-from-home for expats from the Apennines – a sure sign that nothing can go terribly wrong with your pizza or North Italian meat dishes, which dominate the menu. There are also a few good options for vegetarians.

Wolkonsky CAFE $$$

(Волконський; Map p48; vul Zankovetskoi 2; mains 150-300uah; 8am-10pm; ; Khreshchatyk) This pricey French-owned cafe offers a chance to mingle with oligarchs, politicians and their dressed-to-kill partners. There's a full raw/vegan menu, including pasta made from zucchini, in addition to a main menu of sandwiches, salads and steaks. Good desserts, too, and a prime patio abutting a pleasant park on central vul Horodetskoho.

Pl Lva Tolstoho & Olympic Stadium Area

Pyrizhkova Titka Klara BAKERY $

(Map p48; vul Rohnidynska 1; pies 12-18uah; 8:30am-9pm Mon-Sun; ; Palats Sportu) This little bakery specialises in delicious pies with various fillings, all hand-rolled and freshly baked on premises – you can watch the bakers work their magic behind a big glass pane. Also a good choice for a spot of coffee or tea. Several locations around town, including in Podil (p73).

Khinkalnya Gogi GEORGIAN $

(Хінкальня Гогі; Map p48; 063 079 9102; www.gogi.com.ua; vul Lva Tolstoho 13; dumplings 15uah, mains 55-145uah; 11am-11pm; ; Pl Lva Tolstoho) Wildly popular Gogi serves four varieties of *khinkali* (dumplings) in addition to the full complement of Georgian staples and soups, like *chakapuli* (lamb stew with dry white wine). The staff is pleasant and the white-brick-walled interior pleasing. It's sensational value.

Puzata Khata CAFETERIA **$**

(Пузата Хата; Map p48; vul Velyka Vasylkivska 40; dishes 20-30uah; ⏲8am-11pm; ❄📶; Ⓜ Pl Lva Tolstoho) Here at the central branch of the excellent and wildly popular upscale *stolovaya* chain, you'll find a whole range of traditional Ukrainian cuisine.

★ **Musafir** TATAR **$$**

(Мусафір; Map p48; ☎099 409 4686; www.musafir.com.ua; vul Saksahanskoho 57; mains 85-125uah; ⏲10am-10pm; 📶) One of Bakhchysaray's best restaurants, Musafir relocated to Kyiv in 2015. The unmistakable scent of Crimean cooking wafts from the kitchen, where a *plov* (pilaf) master conjures a magic stew in the *kazan* (traditional wrought-iron bowl). Apart from the usual Tatar dishes, they make excellent *yantyk* (pie-like pastry) and Turkish coffee. The latter is served with lumps of sugar that you're expected to put straight in your mouth, rather than your cup.

Imbir VEGETARIAN **$$**

(Имбирь; Map p48; ☎044-407 0494; www.imbir.ua; vul Zhylyanska 7; mains 90-125uah; ⏲8am-11pm; ❄📶🖉; Ⓜ Olimpiyska) 'Ginger' is a delightfully earthy cafe filled with books, Zen-inspired music and the scent of jasmine. The Asian and European menu is all-vegetarian, including plenty of vegan and raw options, and there's a cosy patio if you prefer to dine in the open air. Great smoothies and lassies as well. They also run the Imbir health-food store (p82) nearby on vul Velyka Vasylkivska.

Pervak UKRAINIAN **$$**

(Первак; Map p48; ☎044 235 0952; vul Rohnidynska 2; mains 150-250uah; ⏲11am-midnight, to 2am Fri & Sat; 📶; Ⓜ Pl Lva Tolstoho) This place masterfully re-creates old Kyiv (c 1900) without falling into the schmaltz trap that dogs many a Ukrainian-theme restaurant. The chefs boldly prepare original takes on Ukrainian classics, which are then adroitly delivered to tables by waitresses in frilly, cleavage-baring country outfits. There's folksy live music and black-and-white silent movies playing on old Soviet TVs.

Rambutan CAFE **$$**

(vul Velyka Vasylkivska 82; dishes 100-200uah; ⏲10am-10pm Mon-Sun; ❄📶🖉; Ⓜ Olimpiyska) 🍃 This beautifully designed cafe brims with exotic fruits and healthy vibes. Fuel up with a protein-laced power bowl, mango and couscous salad or cottage cheese pancakes for breakfast. Saddle up to the smoothie bar or take a table on the street. Alcoholic cocktails on offer as well.

Klyukva i Bryukva UKRAINIAN **$$**

(Клюква і Брюква; Map p48; ☎096 500 5097; vul Antonovycha 16; mains 120-230uah; ⏲noon-midnight; ❄📶) 🍃 Foodies will love this farm-to-table restaurant for its seasonal menu and locally sourced ingredients. Classic dishes are incorporated with different but complementary tastes, like sweet and salty, hence the name, 'Cranberry and Rutabaga'. Lounge in the overstuffed chairs and admire paintings from local artists.

Artwork is rotated regularly with a gallery-opening-type party. Check the Facebook page (Klukva&Brukva) for dates.

Zheltok AMERICAN **$$**

(Желток; Map p48; Yaroslaviv Val 37/1; mains 100-200uah; ⏲8am-11pm; ❄📶; Ⓜ Zoloti Vorota) The closest you'll find in Kyiv to an American diner. Think large bowls of salad, burgers, hot dogs, fluffy pancakes and full English breakfasts. The pride of the place are the ice-cream sundaes. Full cocktail menu available. Another branch in the centre near **Shevchenka Park** (Желток; Map p48; vul Lva Tolstoho 11; mains 100-200uah; ⏲8am-11pm; ❄📶; Ⓜ Pl Lva Tolstoho).

Under Wonder INTERNATIONAL **$$$**

(Map p48; ☎044-234 2181; www.underwonder.com.ua; vul Velyka Vasylkivska 21; mains 175-500uah; ⏲24hr; ❄📶; Ⓜ Pl Lva Tolstoho) The food here is some kind of magic: salmon carpaccio, *bistecca alla fiorentina*, ravioli nero with salmon and a nice rack of New Zealand lamb – certainly not what most would expect from a round-the-clock establishment in Europe's east. Great ambience and good wine list too, plus prime people-watching on the sidewalk terrace.

Old Town

Bulochnaya Yaroslavna PIES **$**

(Булочна Ярославна; Map p48; vul Yaroslaviv Val 13; pies 10-15uah; ⏲9am-8pm Mon-Sat; Ⓜ Zoloti Vorota) This veteran institution with stand-up tables serves awesome pies with a variety of fillings – from jam to meat – and coffee. There's also an adjoining cafe with reasonably priced rabbit and other delicacies, but mainly people come for the pies.

O'Panas Blyny Stand UKRAINIAN **$**

(Млинцевий кіоск Опанас; Map p48; Shevchenka Park; blyny 12-22uah; ⏲9am-8pm; Ⓜ Pl Lva

WHERE THE STREETS HAVE TWO NAMES

The names of many Kyiv streets were officially changed soon after Independence in 1991, with very Russian and very Soviet monikers like vul Krasnoarmeyskaya (Red Army St) giving way to Ukrainian names.

For almost 25 years, most of Kyiv happily pretended that the new names did not exist. Then Euromaidan happened in 2014. With Russia annexing Crimea and stirring up trouble in the east, Kyiv redoubled its efforts to purge street names of any Russian or Soviet connotations. Dozens more streets were renamed, and street signs abruptly changed to reflect the new names.

This time the trend has caught on, at least in Kyiv. You'll still hear the old Russian names used by many cabbies and other old-timers, but more and more people are using the new names – such as Velyka Vasylkivska in the case of the street formerly known as Red Army St. We use the new names exclusively, but we wouldn't rule out another round of name changes in the future.

Tolstoho) The capital's best *blyny* (pancakes) come from a shack in front of the otherwise unspectacular Ukrainian restaurant, O'Panas, in the heart of Shevchenka Park. *Varenyky* also available.

★Spotykach UKRAINIAN **$$**

(Спотикач; Map p48; ☎044-586 4095; vul Volodymyrska 16; mains 125-250uah; ⊙11am-midnight; ❄📶; M Zoloti Vorota) Spotykach shed its retro-Soviet theme in 2014 and adopted a Ukraininan revolutionary theme, with pictures of Taras Shevchenko and Bohdan Khelmytsky (and Che Guevara) replacing Lenin. They do highly original takes on Ukrainian classics, including yellow-and-blue *varenyky* – the ultimate nationalist expression – and a *borshch* popsicle.

Spotykach itself is vodka-based liquor made with different flavours, from blackcurrant to horseradish, and takes its name from the Russian for 'stumble' – an effect it might have on the uninitiated.

Dio Long CHINESE **$$**

(Діо Лонг; Map p48; ☎044 331 0710; bul Tarasa Shevchenka 46B; mains 100-200uah; ⊙11am-11pm; ❄📶; M Universytet) Beijing duck comes in all shapes and sizes in this Chinese-expat getaway hiding in a courtyard off bul Tarasa Shevchenka.

★Osteria Pantagruel ITALIAN **$$$**

(Остерія Пантагрюель; Map p48; ☎044 278 8142; vul Lysenka 1; mains 200-350uah; ⊙11am-11pm; ❄📶; M Zoloti Vorota) Kyiv's best Italian restaurant has been around seemingly forever, churning out legendary homemade pasta and risotto in a whitewashed cellar smack next to Zoloti Vorota. The warm months see tables and chairs spill onto the square out the front – the perfect place for a beer on a summer evening, with a separate menu of cheaper Ukrainian fare and burgers.

The bronze cat across the road is a monument to Pantyusha, who once lived in the restaurant.

Barkas SEAFOOD **$$$**

(Баркас; Map p48; ☎044-569 5642; vul Volodymyrska 49A; mains 200-600uah; ⊙11am-11pm; 📶; M Zoloti Vorota) Fresh from the Black Sea is the fish and fresh from Sevastopol is this Crimean transplant. Favourites include the sterlet (a small sturgeon) and Black Sea mussels, and there are suggested wine pairings on the menu. Be careful as many prices are per 100g. The restaurant is hidden in the courtyard of a business centre.

Andriyivsky Uzviz & Podil

★Puzata Khata CAFETERIA **$**

(Пузата Хата; Map p54; vul Sahaydachnoho 24; dishes 20-30uah; ⊙8am-11pm; ❄📶; M Kontraktova Pl) An upscale *stolovaya*, 'Hut of the Pot Belly' is an excellent place for budget travellers to sample traditional Ukrainian cuisine. There are plenty of soups and salads, cheap veggie options, delicious pastries and even a full bar. Nothing is in English but you can just point at what you want.

There are many additional outlets, including on Khreshchatyk (p70) and near pl Lva Tolstoho.

Pyrizhkova Titka Klara BAKERY **$**

(Map p54; vul Nyzhniy Val 33; pies 12-18uah; ⊙8.30am-9pm; 📶; M Kontraktova Pl) Delicious little spot for fresh-baked *pyrizhky* (pies), with several locations around town, including near Palats Sportu (p71).

Svitlytsya UKRAINIAN $

(Map p54; Andriyivsky uzviz 136; snacks 50-100uah; ⌚11am-10pm; ❄📶; Ⓜ Kontraktova Pl) A great snack stop occupying a supremely cosy wood house next to the Bulgakov Museum (p53), specialising in extra-thin *bliny* (pancakes) topped with cheese, eggs and other goodies. Their *deruny* (potato pancakes) also make a good snack and there are some heavier, meatier items on the menu as well.

Alaverdy GEORGIAN $

(Алаверди; Map p54; ☎ 044-425 0156; vul Sahaydachnoho 12; mains 75-100uah; ⌚11am-midnight; ❄📶; Ⓜ Poshtova Pl) This long-running basement restaurant in a courtyard off Podil's vul Sahaydachnoho does reliable *khachapuri*, *khinkali* (dumplings), *chanakhi* (lamb stew) and other Georgian faves. Warm up with baked *suluguni* (cheese) and a glass of saperavi (a Georgian red wine) on the summer terrace.

Harbuzyk UKRAINIAN $

(Гарбузик; Little Pumpkin; Map p54; vul Khoryva 2V; mains 50-150uah; ⌚11am-11pm; 📶; Ⓜ Kontraktova Pl) This fun if slightly hokey eatery offers a great introduction to Ukrainian food without breaking the bank. Pumpkin is not just in the name, it's all over the menu – from the *varenyky* to the *banosh* (Hutsul polenta-like dish) to fresh pumpkin juice. Wash it down with *horilka* (vodka) – pure and pumpkin-free. Set lunch served between 11am and 5pm is a great deal at 79uah.

Varenichnaya Katyusha EASTERN EUROPEAN $

(Варенична Катюша; Map p54; vul Sahaydachnoho 41; mains 45-100uah; ⌚24hr; 📶; Ⓜ Poshtova Pl) This popular chain serves food from around the former Soviet Union, be it Ukrainian, Russian, Central Asian, Caucasian – you name it. But the *pelmeni* (Russian dumplings) and *varenyky* (Ukrainian dumplngs), with all imaginable fillings, are the specialities. Conveniently for Podil party animals, it provides fodder round the clock.

Tsymes JEWISH $$

(Цимес; Map p54; ☎ 044-428 7579; vul Sahaydachnoho 10/5; mains 85-180uah; ⌚11am-11pm; ❄📶; Ⓜ Poshtova Pl) Tucked into a vaulted cellar with green walls and Chagall-style frescoes, this place has a unique menu of Jewish dishes from all over Ukraine. The bill is a laugh – if only in the sense that it comes with a random Jewish joke, although the three-course business lunch (weekdays only) is also laughably cheap at 86uah.

★ **Kanapa** UKRAINIAN $$$

(Канапа; Map p54; ☎ 044-425 4548; Andriyivsky uzviz 19A; mains 150-250uah; ⌚10am-midnight; 📶; Ⓜ Kontraktova Pl) 🍃 Sneak away from the busy *uzviz* into this beautiful old wooden house with sliding-glass doors overlooking a lush ravine out back. Kanapa serves modern cuisine largely made from its own farm's produce. Traditional it is not: green *borshch* is made of nettles and chicken Kiev is not chicken but pheasant. Ukrainian mussels, caviar and pâté are other specialities. It's a good place for an affordable and highly original breakfast (10am to noon). Newly opened sister cafe **Kanapka** across the street focuses on lighter meals and wine.

Khutorets na Dnipri UKRAINIAN $$$

(Хуторець на Дніпрі; Map p54; ☎ 067 209 1444; vul Naberezhno-Khreshchatytska; mains 200-300uah; ⌚11am-midnight; ❄📶; Ⓜ Kontraktova Pl) For a memorable dining experience on the Dnipro River, visit this elegant restaurant in a stationary boat. The view alone is worth the visit but the menu is also impressive. They offer all the classics, plus seven different types of *salo* (cured lard), Black Sea fish and 80 different types of Ukrainian vodka. Make sure you ask to see the 'Vodka Room'!

Vero Vero ITALIAN $$$

(Map p54; ☎ 067 214 1818; vul Illinska 18; mains 200-400uah; ⌚8am-midnight; ❄📶👪; Ⓜ Kontraktova Pl) In addition to being the most kid-friendly restaurant in town, Vero Vero serves some of the best Italian food in Italy-obsessed Kyiv, highlighted by its mozzarella menu. Summer is best, when tables are set around a venerable fountain in the park opposite the restaurant proper. A trampoline keeps the kiddies busy while the grown-ups sample an ample selection of global wines.

Pechersk & Lypky

★ **Shoti** GEORGIAN $$$

(Шоті; Map p60; ☎ 044 339 9399; vul Mechnykova 9; mains 150-350uah; ⌚noon-11pm; ❄📶; Ⓜ Klovska) This is modern Georgian cuisine at its finest. Try the fork-whipped egg-and-butter *khachapuri* (cheese bread) and a shoulder of lamb or charcoal-grilled catfish, all served with fresh, complimentary, Shoti flat bread. Huge racks of the finest Georgian wines, professionally decanted, tempt oenophiles. Sit outside on the broad veranda, or settle into the restaurant proper with its meticulously scuffed wood floor.

Tsarske Selo UKRAINIAN $$$

(Царське Село; Map p60; ☎044-280 3066; vul Lavrska 22; mains 150-300uah; ⏱9am-1am; ❄📶; Ⓜ Arsenalna) This is Kyiv's quintessential theme restaurant, decorated in rustic 18th-century style and filled with tour groups from the nearby Lavra. Ukrainian staples are superbly done, but the most famous dish is the dessert of *salo* (cured lard) in chocolate. Despite being a tad overdone, it's easily the best restaurant in Pechersk.

Barsuk INTERNATIONAL $$$

(Барсук; Map p60; prov Kutuzova 3A; mains 150-350uah; ⏱8am-11pm; ❄📶; Ⓜ Pecherska) Tucked away in a small lane opposite Pechersky market, the Badger set several trends when it opened in 2010 – namely, gastropub, organic food and open-view kitchen. Renowned local chef Dima Borisov has since done bigger and better things (including Ostannya Barikada (p71)), but his flagship remains a top pick in Pechersk, especially for lunch.

Good Wine INTERNATIONAL $$$

(Map p60; vul Mechnykova 9; mains 200-750uah; ⏱8am-11pm Sun-Thu, 10am-11pm Fri & Sat; ❄📶; Ⓜ Klovska) This is much more than the best **wine shop** in increasingly wine-happy Kyiv. On the premises you'll also find an upscale **grocery store**, a top **pizzeria** (Napule) and a handful of **cafes** – most notably trendy Lucky Vinoteque, which has some of the most exciting contemporary fusion fare in town. Try Lucky's sturgeon or the truffle burger with marbled beef.

Self-catering

Zhytny Rynok MARKET $

(Житній ринок; Map p54; vul Zhytnotorzka; ⏱7am-7pm Tue-Sun, 7am-2pm Mon) It's been here in Podil since the times of the Vikings (though not the current Soviet structure). Like any Ukrainian market, it is always rich in seasonal fruit and vegetables.

Megamarket SUPERMARKET $

(Мегамаркет; Map p48; vul Antonovycha 50; ⏱8am-11pm; Ⓜ Olympiyska) A little outside the city centre, but worth it for self-caterers who seek size and selection.

Ekomarket SUPERMARKET $

(Екомаркет; Map p48; Vokzalna pl 1; ⏱24hr; Ⓜ Vokzalna) Convenient for stocking up on food before a train journey.

Le Silpo SUPERMARKET $$

(Ле Сільпо; Map p48; basement, Mandarin Plaza Shopping Centre, vul Baseyna 4; mains 300-400uah; ⏱24hr; Ⓜ Pl Lva Tolstoho) An upscale supermarket with imported foods, pre-prepared meals and a clutch of expensive cafes where chefs do creative things with all of that premium produce.

Drinking & Nightlife

Dark basement establishments – now blissfully smoke free thanks to the nationwide smoking ban – dominate the bar scene in Kyiv until late spring, when the drinking masses move outside to summer terraces and rooftops lounges. There's an up-and-coming club-and-electronica scene, including some noteworthy open-air summer raves, as Kyiv takes its cues from Berlin.

Kyiv has officially gone coffee crazy; there's a coffee shop, truck, or kiosk seemingly on every corner. There are also some seriously cool, often vintage-styled cafes serving third-wave coffee for more discerning drinkers.

★ **Alchemist Bar** COCKTAIL BAR

(Map p48; vul Shota Rustaveli 12; ⏱noon-3am, to 5am Fri & Sat; 📶; Ⓜ Palats Sportu) Kyiv's best bar is set in an intimate basement space on vibrant vul Shota Rustaveli. No pretensions, no strict *feiskontrol* (face control), just an eclectic mix of fun-loving patrons chasing good music, good drinks and good conversation. Most nights see truly excellent bands play, after which DJs take over and many people start dancing near the bar.

It can get crowded on Fridays and Saturdays so come early to avoid a wait.

★ **Closer** CLUB

(☎067 658 8951; www.facebook.com/closerkiev; vul Nyzhnoyurkivska 31; cover 200-300uah; ⏱midnight-noon Fri & Sat; 📶; Ⓜ Tarasa Shevchenka) More than just a nightclub, Closer is a bohemian *tour-de-force* that epitomises Kyiv's emergence as a hub of creativity and counterculture. Heavily influenced by Berlin's community of 24hr party people, Closer throws weekend raves that last well into the following afternoon. There are spaces to fit all moods, including three dance halls, a chill-out garden, and a mini–outdoor amphitheatre. There's even a **vintage clothing shop** on premises should you feel the need for a 4am buying spree. Sporadic weekday events include superb jazz nights roughly every other Thursday – check the Facebook page for the schedule.

★ **Pink Freud** COCKTAIL BAR

(Map p54; ☎050 991 9818; www.facebook.com/pinkfreudkyiv; vul Nyzhniy Val 19; ⏱6pm-1am, to 2.30am Fri & Sat; ; MKontraktova Pl) Pink Freud reckons it can cure you with quality cocktails. They may be right: their talented mixologists have created an original drink for every mood and taste. The food is equally cathartic – think spare ribs, boutique sandwiches and sinful desserts – and they employ talented solo musicians (guitar, sax, piano) most weeknights. DJs take over at weekends. It's set in the courtyard of a historic house (winterised in the frigid months).

★Kharms CAFE
(Map p48; vul Volodymyrska 45A; 10am-10pm Mon-Sun; ; MZoloti Vorota) This indie cafe at the back of the House of Scientists has a creative atmosphere, excellent coffee and a strong wi-fi connection – a perfect spot to plant with a laptop on rainy days. It also sells vinyl and books, including some English-language titles and Moleskine notebooks.

★Na Stanislavskogo CAFE
(Map p48; vul Stanislavskoho 3; 10am-11pm; ; MKhreshchatyk) Billing itself as a 'theatre cafe' (due to its proximity to the playhouses on nearby pl Ivana Franka), this place is an arty delight. It's all scuffed-leather furniture, recycled wood, antique trinkets and soothing jazz. The chalkboard menu of light bites is in Ukrainian, but you can point to desserts such as carrot cake and handmade chocolate, accompanied by Turkish coffee.

★Mur Mur LOUNGE
(Map p48; 044 234 7788; vul Pushkinska 42/4; noon-2am; MPl Lva Tolstoho) Mur Mur has been pushing the envelope of cutting-edge design in Kyiv for two decades – first as Concord restaurant, and now in its latest incarnation as a sumptuous rooftop lounge. Two large terraces – one winterised – offer outstanding views, while inside gorgeous people kick back in vintage-style furniture, expensive cocktails in hand and extravagant fusion fare on plate.

The sound system is Kyiv's best and name DJs take over the stacks at weekends.

Espressoholic CAFE
(Map p54; vul Khoryva 25; 8am-10pm; MKontraktova Pl) A tiny but immensely popular coffee shop in Podil with high-quality caffeinated beverages, friendly baristas and low prices. The action spills out into the street, often blending with the crowd from a neighbouring bar and pizzeria to form a mini-block party. It's a great spot to mingle with locals.

Parovoz COCKTAIL BAR
(Map p48; www.parovoz.bar; vul Velyka Vasylkivska 19; noon-2am, to 3am Fri & Sat; MLva Tolstoho) Hidden in the basement of the Kyiv Cinema, this is Kyiv's original speakeasy and a legend among Kyiv's bars. Whereas the bartenders at most top cocktail bars in Kyiv are men, many here are women. And they can sure sling a drink: cocktails at Parovoz are handcrafted works of art. Excellent food as well.

Mokhnaty Khmil CRAFT BEER
(Мохнатий Хміль; Woolly Hops; vul Velyka Vasylkivska 126; 4pm-1am; ; MPalats Ukraina) You gotta love a place called 'Woolly Hops.' The selection of IPAs at this basement place is more wonderful than woolly, but we're not complaining. There's a bar lined with solid wooden keg taps, and a 400ml glass of local craft beer costs just 45uah to 65uah. It's a local place, with local people and local bar snacks.

Pivna Duma MICROBREWERY
(Пивна Дума; Beer Parliament; Map p48; vul Khreshchatyk 10; noon-midnight; MMaydan Nezalezhnosti) A brewpub smack dab in the middle of town? Works for us. They produce a crisp pilsner, an aggressive wheat bock (6.2% alcohol), and seasonal specialities, all at about 55uah a glass. They also have wine, steaks and sausages, and table-football (beat the bartender for free beer!). A few other branches around town.

Squat 17b Yard Cafe CAFE
(Map p48; vul Tereshchenkivska 17B; 11am-11pm, closed winter; ; MPl Lva Tolstoho) Run by squatters living upstairs at the same address. It was once large enough to host live bands, but much of their space was reclaimed in 2017 and the open-air coffeeshop reduced to a narrow strip. Still, it retains a decidedly bohemian vibe, with Louis Armstrong on the soundtrack, excellent coffee, pies and mildly alcoholic cider.

It's at the back left of the courtyard behind the Khanenko Museum of Arts (p46).

Lift CLUB
(Map p48; 093 044 5091; vul Velyka Vasylkivska 72A, enter on vul Antonovycha 43; 11pm-6am; MOlympiyska) Probably the best and most 'clubby' of Kyiv's growing repertoire of gay clubs, it gets quite packed on weekends and attracts a mostly gay clientele but also a fair amount of straight revellers. Tuesdays and Thursdays are for drag shows or karaoke nights. Weekends are for DJs. It's on the 4th floor of a high-rise building.

Vagabond CAFE

(Map p54; www.facebook.com/vagabondvintagecoffeecorner; vul Hryhoriya Skovorody 7; ⌚9am-10.30pm; 📶; Ⓜ Kontraktova Pl) This little bohemian hangout near Kyiv Mohyla Academy holds nightly events that might include poetry readings, storytelling or live music on the sidewalk outside. Coffee by day, cocktails by night, and a small, all-vegetarian food menu. It's owned by a couple of self-styled global nomads, one Russian and one American.

Podil East India Company BAR

(Map p54; vul Mezhyhirska 9; ⌚11am-2am; 📶; Ⓜ Kontraktova Pl) As the name implies, this American-owned place in the heart of Podil's bar district offers drinks as well as food with an Oriental twist. It's American owned but inspired by the likes of Maugham and Kipling. At the back is an intimate room where couples speak in hushed tones.

Paliturka Coffee & Books CAFE

(Map p48; vul Khreshchatyk 46A; ⌚8am-9pm Mon-Fri, 10am-11pm Fri & Sat; 📶; Ⓜ Teatralna) An excellent find hidden in a courtyard off Khreshchyk, Paliturka has good tunes and a boho vibe, in addition to fine coffee. Plenty of spaces to chat or hover over a laptop, plus some outside seating. It's attached to eclectic Art Store Podval (p81).

Hangover Bar CLUB

(Map p60; ☎044-536 3200; Petrivska aleya; ⌚noon-1am, to 5am Fri & Sat; 📶; Ⓜ Maydan Nezalezhnosti) With an open-air dance floor packed with beautiful bodies, this is Kyiv's top summer nightclub. The action is, predictably, centred on weekend nights; at other times it's a self-styled **American restaurant** pumping out groovy electronic beats. Tends to draw a younger crowd.

Amigos Bar BAR

(Map p54; vul Pochaynynska 24, Podil; ⌚11am-2.30am; 📶; Ⓜ Kontraktova Pl) A bar for real bar flies, Amigos is a laid-back place with friendly bartenders and big variety of original and classic drinks. It's significantly cheaper than some of Kyiv's fancier cocktail bars, but you don't give up anything in quality.

Barman Dictat COCKTAIL BAR

(Бармен Диктат; Map p48; vul Khreshchatyk 44b; ⌚6pm-3am, to 6am Sat & Sun; 📶; Ⓜ Teatralna) This is a huge, open basement space with one of the longest bars we've ever seen, backed by Kyiv's most impressive wall of booze. It's has plenty of exposed brick and industrial piping, and a stage at the back for live jazz and other tunes. Formerly expat playground Art Club 44, it's still popular with foreigners.

It's hidden in a courtyard behind vul Khreshchatyk 44 (take the first door on the left and walk down).

Old Bar CRAFT BEER

(Map p48; vul Velyka Vasylkivska 20a; ⌚4pm-midnight; Ⓜ Pl Lva Tolstoho) Ukraine is grain country, so no surprise you can find good craft beer. There are 180 types of bottled beer here and more than 25 on tap – many of them local. At around 50uah a pint, it's astounding value for quality ales. The warm and welcoming courtyard terrace is preferred, or head underground. The hearty Teutonic fare on

HIPSTER KYIV

Open co-working spaces are all the rage in Kyiv these days. Often called 'anti-cafes' or '*khipstery*' (hipster) cafes, the best ones are a cross between a really cool internet cafe and an artfully designed coffee shop, offering free coffee, high-speed wi-fi and a creative environment. Some hold community events such as acoustic concerts and poetry readings. One of the best, albeit a little out of the way, is **Izone** at the Izolyatsia (p55) arts centre. Others include the following:

Chasopys (Часопис; Map p48; ☎044-591 2535; www.chasopys.ua; vul Lva Tolstoho 3; per hr/day 45/179; ⌚8am-1.30am, to 3pm Sun; Ⓜ pl Lva Tolstoho) A super-comfortable environment where you can surf the web using your own gadget or one of the local notebooks. There are many nooks and crannies that you can choose, depending on whether you want to be close to other people or left completely alone.

Tsiferblat (Циферблат; Map p48; ☎063 745 4434; http://kiev.ziferblat.net/en; vul Volodymyrska 49A; per hr/day 42/132uah; ⌚9am-11pm Mon-Fri, 11am-11pm Sat & Sun; Ⓜ Zoloti Vorota) Kyiv's original open space is more artsy and less businesslike than others. Attracts younger people, hosts an English club and holds a Saturday movie night. To find it, enter the courtyard of the new business centre, walk past Barkas restaurant and then down one level.

the menu is a holdout from the previous German owner – Kyiv bar legend Erik.

Like a Local's WINE BAR
(26 Sichovykh Striltsiv; ⏲4-11pm, to 1am Fri & Sat; 📶; 🚌Pl Lvivska) Ukraine has some good wine-growing areas in the south and in the west, and this welcoming little space is *the* place to sample them. Plenty of dry varietals from the likes of Odesa, Southern Bessarabia and Uzhhorod. You can taste before you buy. A glass of *vino* costs 50uah to 70uah and light bites and homegrown cheeses are available.

Kaffa COFFEE
(Каффа; Map p54; vul Hryhoriya Skovorody 5; ⏲9am-10pm; 📶; Ⓜ Kontraktova Pl) The Podil branch of the long-running Africa-themed, coffee shop. The original is just off maydan Nezalezhnosti.

London CAFE
(Map p54; vul Verkhniy Val 18; ⏲10am-10pm; 📶; Ⓜ Kontraktova Pl) Enter through a door in the form of a red telephone box to find yourself in this classy UK-inspired cafe. Siphon, aeropress and pour-over brews are available for coffee fanatics, plus some single-origin beans. The small food selection includes fresh quiche and delicious desserts.

Wood You Like Bar BAR
(Map p54; vul. Mezhyhirska 24; ⏲9am-last customer Sun-Thu, from 1pm Sat & Sun; 📶; Ⓜ Kontraktova Pl) This is an intimate, welcoming place serving great cocktails at reasonable prices. Try the killer Old Fashioned with Plantation rum (69% ABV) or the Tanqueray-based Fitzgerald. Wine by the glass (60uah to 80uah) also available, and coffee and cakes in the morning.

Lviv Handmade Chocolate CAFE
(Львівська Майстерня Шоколаду; Map p54; Andriyivsky uzviz 2B; ⏲10am-10pm; 📶; Ⓜ Kontraktova Pl) A de rigueur stop after descending Andriyivsky uzviz, this dessert-cafe specialises in rich melted-chocolate concoctions from Lviv – Ukraine's unofficial chocolate capital. With high ceilings, jazz and a delightful old world ambience, it's a good place for a coffee or to buy a box of hand-crafted chocolate for any sweet-toothed loved ones back home.

Druzi Cafe CAFE
(Map p54; Andriyivsky uzviz 2D; ⏲8am-midnight; 📶; Ⓜ Kontraktova Pl) This bar/cafe spills into a courtyard near the origin of Andriyivsky uzviz. Choose between coffee, refreshing lemonades and competently mixed cocktails. It is attached to Dream House Hostel (p67), so it's always full of young foreign and ex-Soviet travellers, who engage in table games and long drinking sessions. The food menu includes burgers, salads and fajitas.

Kaffa COFFEE
(Каффа; Map p48; prov Tarasa Shevchenka 3; ⏲10am-10pm; 📶; Ⓜ Maydan Nezalezhnosti) Around for years, Kaffa still serves the most heart-pumping, rich-tasting brew in town. Coffees and teas from all over the world are served in a pot sufficient for two or three punters in a whitewashed African-inspired interior – all ethnic masks, beads and leather. Another branch in Podil.

Chi CLUB
(Map p60; ☎044-466 2013; Parkova doroga 16A; ⏲11pm-4am Sun-Thu, to 6am Fri & Sat) Aptly named Chi is Kyiv's top playground for the chichi set. Expect plenty of attitude from the staff and strict *feiskontrol* (face control), so dress the part. On the plus side, it draws top-notch DJ talent at weekends and there are lots and lots of beautiful people. It's a restaurant by day/evening, but it's much more notable as a nightclub.

Open Space GAY
(Map p60; ☎068 697 2781; www.ospace.club; vul Yevhena Konovaltsa 44A; 50uah; ⏲11pm-7am Fri & Sat, 9am-2am Sun; Ⓜ Pecherska) This is a men-only 'cruising bar', which basically means that just about anything goes. Private lockers, variety shows and regular theme parties announced via their Facebook page. It's a bit tricky to find – see the website for detailed walking directions from the Pecherska metro stop.

Honey CAFE
(Map p48; vul Yaroslaviv Val 20; ⏲8am-10pm; 📶; Ⓜ Zoloti Vorota) Set over two spacious levels on trendy vul Yaroslaviv Val, Honey is a cafe and patisserie that offers a variety of desserts including 15 different types of traditional French macaroons. The menu also includes healthy sandwiches, salads, soups and a great breakfast selection.

Chashka CAFE
(Чашка; Map p48; vul Velyka Vasylkivska 1; ⏲8am-11pm; 📶; Ⓜ Teatralna) A very friendly cafe serving breakfasts and lattes with rather experimental local flavours – such as *uzvar* (dried-pear drink) and *khalva* (Turkish sweet) – it kind of works, but regular coffee is also available.

Banka BAR

(Банка; Map p48; ☎098 988 7988; www.bankabar.com.ua; vul Lva Tolstoho 11; shots/cocktails 20/40uah; ⏲noon-1am; Ⓜ Pl Lva Tolstoho) Loosely based on Andy Warhol's *32 Campbell Soup Cans*, this underground place has cans on the wall and serves all drinks out of cans or jars (*banka* means both in Ukrainian). Cocktails are invigorating and prices very competitive. Naturally, no draught beer, only canned. The outdoor terrace works until 10pm in the warm months.

Palata No.6 BAR

(Ward No.6; Map p48; vul Bulvarno-Kudryavska 31A; ⏲11am-2am; 📶; Ⓜ Universytet) For a healthy dose of insanity sneak into this well-hidden bar named after Anton Chekhov's tale about life in a madhouse. Dressed in doctors' white robes, stern-looking waiters nurse you vodka poured into your glass through a giant pyramid of test tubes – ask for the '*pyramida*'. Or try the 'helmet', involving absinthe, a helmet and flames.

Repriza CAFE

(Реприза; Map p54; vul Sahaydachnoho 10; ⏲9am-9pm Mon-Sat; Ⓜ Poshtova Pl) This spacious, long-running cafe has a small selection of snacks, including quiche and spinach turnovers, and decent coffee in the heart of Podil's main drag. Another branch on **Bohdana Khmelnytskoho** (Реприза; Map p48; vul Bohdana Khmelnytskoho 40/25; ⏲8am-9pm; Ⓜ Zoloti Vorota).

☆ Entertainment

Advance tickets and schedules are available at individual theatres or at any Tour Info Kiev (p84) kiosk in the centre. Some venues, including the National Opera Theatre and the Philharmonic, have an online booking option. Check the Entertainment Guide of the *Kyiv Post* newspaper or *Kiev Check-In* magazine for the latest arts and entertainment listings.

Rock

Palats Sportu CONCERT VENUE

(Палац Спорту; Sports Palace; Map p48; ☎044-246 7405; http://spalace.com.ua; pl Sportyvna 1; Ⓜ Palats Sportu) One of the main venues for rock concerts. It also hosts Ukraine's international basketball and hockey games.

Palats Ukraina CONCERT VENUE

(Палац Україна; Ukraine Palace; ☎044-247 2476; vul Velyka Vasylkivska 103; Ⓜ Palats Ukraina) A main venue for rock concerts.

Live Music

Bel Etage LIVE MUSIC

(Map p48; ☎067 171 1616; www.etage.kiev.ua; vul Shota Rustaveli 16A; 📶; Ⓜ Pl Lva Tolstoho) Definitely check the website to see what's going on here, as they draw some really top-notch international music talent, especially jazz and blues. In the summer the action often takes place on the rooftop, filling the streets below with heavenly sounds. It doubles as a well-regarded, French-influenced cafe.

Atlas CONCERT VENUE

(Атлас; ☎067 155 2255; www.facebook.com/atlas37; vul Sichovykh Striltsiv 37-41; tickets 250-2000uah; 🚌 Pl Lvivska) This industrial-style multi-storey venue, complete with roof terrace, caters to all musical tastes from techno to heavy metal with a sprinkling of theatre and poetry readings. The best of the best in Ukrainian and foreign music gravitate here these days.

Classical Music & Theatre

Tickets to the performing arts are significantly cheaper than in the West – typically less than 100uah for a decent seat. Theatre performances tend to be in Ukrainian, but taking in an opera or ballet at the National Opera Theatre is still a worthwhile experience.

★ Taras Shevchenko National Opera Theatre OPERA

(Map p48; ☎044-235 2606; www.opera.com.ua; vul Volodymyrska 50; tickets 20-500uah; ⏲box office 11am-5.30pm; shows 7pm; closed mid-Jun–Aug; Ⓜ Zoloti Vorota) Performances at this lavish theatre (opened 1901) are grandiose affairs, but tickets are cheap. True disciples of Ukrainian culture should not miss a performance of *Zaporozhets za Dunaem* (Zaporizhzhyans Beyond the Danube), a sort of operatic, purely Ukrainian version of *Fiddler on the Roof*. It was during a performance here in 1911 that young terrorist Dmitry Bogrov shot progressive Russian prime minister Pyotr Stolypin, which many believe predetermined Russia's plunge into revolutionary chaos.

★ National Philharmonic LIVE MUSIC

(Map p48; ☎044-278 1697; www.filarmonia.com.ua; Volodymyrsky uzviz 2; tickets from 70uah; ⏲shows 7pm; Ⓜ Maydan Nezalezhnosti) Originally the Kyiv Merchants' Assembly headquarters, this beautiful building is now home to the national orchestra, plus many other musical treats. The season for the national orchestra is mid-June to mid-September, but the theatre remains open for a variety of smaller summer concerts.

House of Organ & Chamber Music CONCERT VENUE
(Національний будинок органної та камерної музики; ☎044-528 8452; www.organhall.kiev.ua; vul Velyka Vasylkivska 77; tickets from 20uah; ⊙shows 7.30pm, closed Jul-Aug; Ⓜ Palats Ukraina) Beautiful concerts housed in neo-Gothic St Nicholas' Cathedral, built by Władysław Horodecki in 1909.

Dakh Theatre THEATRE
(☎044-529 4062; http://dax.com.ua; vul Velyka Vasylkivska 136; ⊙shows 7pm or 8pm; Ⓜ Lybidska) Simply the coolest thing that's happening on Ukrainian theatre stage. Look out for perfomances involving *The Dakh Daughters* – a 15-strong 'singing siren' collective which took YouTube by storm with the mock Gothic 'Donbass Roses' clip.

Ivan Franko National Academic Drama Theatre THEATRE
(Map p48; ☎044-279 5991; http://ft.org.ua; pl Ivana Franka 3; ⊙closed Jul-Aug; Ⓜ Khreshchatyk) Kyiv's most respected theatre. Shows are in Ukrainian, so may be of little interest to foreign travellers, but it's worth stopping by for a glimpse of the beautiful building, which dates to 1898.

Kyiv Academic Puppet Theatre PUPPET THEATRE
(Київський академічний театр ляльок; Map p48; ☎044-599 4687; www.akadempuppet.kiev.ua; vul Hrushevskoho 1A; tickets 30-100uah; Ⓜ Maydan Nezalezhnosti) In addition to being a beautiful building (both inside and out) for adults to admire, the puppet theatre is a hit for kids of all ages and languages.

Theatre on Podol THEATRE
(Театр на Подолі | Kyiv Academic Drama Theatre; Map p54; ☎044-332 2217; www.theatreonpodol.com; Andriyivsky uzviz 20B; tickets 90-200uah; ⊙shows 7pm, closed July to mid-September; Ⓜ Kontraktova Pl) The best of Ukrainian and Russian drama, both classic and contemporary, is shown here, although shows are in Ukrainian. The theatre building was controversially rebuilt in a modernist style in 2016, drawing a firestorm of criticism on social media. Preservationists were outraged that it dwarfs and contrasts with the surrounding structures on historic Andriyivsky uzviz.

Koleso Theatre THEATRE
(Театр Колесо; Map p54; ☎044-425 0422; http://teatr-koleso.kiev.ua; Andriyivsky uzviz 8A; Ⓜ Kontraktova Pl) Performances at the semi-avant-garde 'Wheel' involve much song and dance, so understanding the language is not quite so essential.

Sport

Olympic Stadium SPECTATOR SPORT
(Олімпійський стадіон; Map p48; www.nsc-olimpiyskiy.com.ua; vul Velyka Vasylkivska 55; Ⓜ Olympiyska) Kyiv's main football arena was completely rebuilt for the Euro 2012 football (soccer) tournament. Today it's the home stadium for Dynamo Kyiv and hosts most of

GAY & LESBIAN KYIV

Kyiv was considerably homophobic in the two decades following the collapse of the Soviet Union, but that has changed in the 'teens as Ukraine has pivoted toward Europe. The nascent counterculture movement that has sprung out of Euromaidan and the war with Russia in the east has contributed to this softening of attitudes toward gay people. International events like the gay-friendly Eurovision Song Contest in 2017 have also helped.

Several new gay bars and clubs have sprung up in recent years, and the annual summer gay pride march has gone off without major incidents in recent years. The city's summer raves and festivals are all very gay-friendly, as are grassrootsy, bohemian initiatives like Closer (p75), Izolyatsia (p55) and Skvorechnik (p61), and indeed most bars and clubs. Other gay-friendly places are Hydropark (p64) and Trukhaniv Island (p64).

But don't be fooled into thinking that this free-spirited attitude has swept over the masses. Old attitudes and biases die hard. Away from the above-mentioned oases of tolerance, it's best to refrain even from mild public displays of affection, such as holding hands. Like all of Ukraine, Kyiv has small pockets of right-wing intolerance, and acts of violence against homosexuals are not unheard of.

LGBT Portal (www.lgbt.org.ua) is the definitive guide to all things gay and lesbian in Ukraine. **KyivPride** (http://kyivpride.org) is an NGO supporting LGBT rights and hosts the annual pride march, as well as the annual KyivPride week, and has a map on its website of LGBT-friendly places in Kyiv.

Ukraine's international matches, as well as the occasional big-name concert. Out front is a **shop** selling good-quality Dynamo swag, and a one-room **Klitschko Museum** (free admission) dedicated to accomplishments of Ukraine's famous boxing brothers.

Lobanovsky Dynamo Stadium SPECTATOR SPORT

(Map p60; vul Hrushevskoho 3; tickets from 75uah; Ⓜ Maydan Nezalezhnosti) Named after legendary Ukrainian coach Valeriy Lobanovsky (1939–2002), this is the home of Dynamo Kyiv, although they play most of their games in Olympic Stadium these days. There's a **Dynamo Kyiv museum** and a statue of a young Lobanovsky out front, and out on vul Hrushevskoho there's a memorial to the famous Death Match (p68).

Nightclubs

Pomada GAY

(Помада; Lipstick; Map p48; ☎044-279 5552; www.pomada-club.com.ua; vul Zankovetskoi 6; admission varies; ⏲11pm-6am; Ⓜ Khreshchatyk) You know Kyiv's come a long way when we can actually publish the names of gay clubs (they used to all be underground). This is a lively and centrally located place with a small stage for drag shows and the like.

Arena City CLUB

(Арена Сіті; Map p48; vul Baseyna 2A; admission varies; ⏲24hr; Ⓜ Pl Lva Tolstoho) Not a single club, but rather a collection of bars, brewpubs and nightclubs of all stripes – and we mean *all* stripes. Not the most wholesome of places, but one of the few places in town where you'll find some action any night of the week.

Shopping

You'll find more than a dozen shops selling reasonably priced national costumes, textiles and other souvenirs in the **maydan Nezalezhnosti underpass**. Quality tends to be better at speciality shops, however. Andriyivsky uzviz (p52) is the top spot for touristy stuff like *matryoshka* dolls, fur hats, kitschy art, Dynamo Kyiv kit and Soviet posters and coins. Definitely bring home a bottle of *horilka* (vodka), available at any foodstore.

★ **Kurazh Bazar** MARKET

(Кураж Базар; http://kurazhbazar.com.ua; Art-Zavod Platforma, vul Bilomorska 1A; 70uah; Ⓜ Lisova) Kurazh Bazar is a fantastic monthly weekend flea market on Kyiv's left (east) bank. You'll find some 400 vendors selling all manner of new and used clothes, antiques and bric-a-brac, in addition to plenty of street food, street performers, kids' activities and live music on a large central stage. The venue, **Art-Zavod Platforma** (http://artzavodplatforma.com/en), is an attraction in its own right.

Occupying a gigantic former silk factory, it's a multi-use creative zone with galleries, music and fashion studios, co-working spaces and cafes. It hosts various special events, including the Ulichnaya Eda (p66) street-food and 'White Nights' music festivals, and is open seven days a week.

★ **Vsi. Svoi** CLOTHING

(Всі. Свої; Map p48; vul Khreschatyk 27; ⏲10am-10pm; Ⓜ Khreshchatyk) The 'biggest store selling Ukrainian brands in the world' (as it markets itself) is strategically set on the central bul Khreshchatyk. Set over four floors, it carries a huge selection of all things Ukrainian-made. The collection of modern national designs, including shirts by Etnodim (p82), is particularly impressive, and there are great T-shirts, plus handbags and jewellery.

★ **Bessarabsky Rynok** MARKET

(Бессарабський ринок; Map p48; Bessarabska pl; ⏲8am-10pm; Ⓜ Teatralna) Kyiv's beautiful, light-filled, central market, built in 1910–12 for traders coming to Kyiv from Bessarabia, is not to be missed. The arrangements of colourful fruit, vegetables and flowers are nothing less than works of art. This is a great place to buy caviar and Ukraine trademark *salo* (cured lard), among other culinary souvenirs.

Laska CLOTHING

(Map p48; http://laskastore.com; vul Lypynskoho 3; ⏲10am-9pm; Ⓜ Universytet) Laska is a charity shop that sells both secondhand items and new clothing by Ukrainian designers. There are lovely notebooks, leather wallets and purses, and very stylish backpacks and messenger bags. It also has a **laundry** and a cosy **bar** where you can sip a drink while listening to vinyl records.

Art Store Podval GIFTS & SOUVENIRS

(Basement; Map p48; vul Khreshchatyk 46A; ⏲11am-8pm; Ⓜ Teatralna) This is an apparel and crafts store where everything sold is of 100% Ukrainian origin. Most notable is the clothing, including some highly original national designs, but there are also notebooks, cards, fragrant soaps and even some spreads and other food products. Upstairs is a hip cafe, Paliturka (p77).

Ruta CLOTHING

(Map p48; www.rutashik.com; vul Horodetskoho 4; ⌚11am-8pm Mon-Fri, to 6pm Sat & Sun; Ⓜ Maydan Nezalezhnosti) Some beautiful national-style threads here. The style is best described as high-end folk fashion, with high-end prices to match.

Etnodim CLOTHING

(Map p54; vul Verhniy Val 58/28; ⌚10am-8pm Mon-Fri, 11am-7pm Sat & Sun; Ⓜ Kontraktova Pl) This small showroom in Podil has a great collection of clothing that incorporates Ukrainian national motifs and modern fashion trends. It's the perfect place to buy a *vyshyvanka* (traditional Ukrainian embroidered shirt) or a pair of stylish made-in-Ukraine shoes.

You'll also find traditional Ukrainian belts and *motanka* dolls, embroidered towels and flower crowns here.

Diskultura MUSIC

(Map p48; vul Gogolivska 27; ⌚noon-9pm; Ⓜ Universytet) A paradise for vinyl lovers, Diskultura boasts one of the biggest collections of both used and new vinyl records in Ukraine. Set in a basement of a residential building, this little record store has an authentic underground atmosphere perfect for choosing the right tunes.

482 CLOTHING

(Map p48; vul Yaroslaviv Val 10; ⌚8am-8pm Mon-Fri, 10am-9pm Sat & Sun; Ⓜ Zoloti Vorota) A small showroom that sells midrange-priced smart-casual clothes by Ukrainian designers, including good T-shirts, plus leather wallets and handbags. The '482' in the name stands for the first three digits of the barcode used for products coming from Ukraine.

Kartografia MAPS

(vul Velyka Vasylkivska 69; ⌚11am-7pm Mon-Fri; Ⓜ Olympiyska) A paradise for map wonks, this place stocks every conceivable map related to Ukraine plus many other places of the world and the universe.

Dobro Store GIFTS & SOUVENIRS

(Map p48; vul Velyka Vasylkivska 29/31; ⌚11am-7pm Mon-Fri, noon-6pm Sat & Sun; Ⓜ pl Lva Tolstoho) Dobro sells 'only high-quality gifts that are made in Ukraine by awesome people'. We could never improve on that description, but will add that the highlights are the home-grown bags and other leather products, the quirky stuffed animals and the stationery.

Imbir Healthy Shop FOOD & DRINKS

(Map p48; vul Velyka Vasylkivska 42; ⌚8am-10pm; Ⓜ pl Lva Tolstoho) A great health-food store where you can find plenty of raw, gluten-free and vegan products as well as natural cosmetics and creams. Much of their stock is made in Ukraine and it can help you find yoga sessions.

TsUM DEPARTMENT STORE

(Map p48; http://tsum.ua; vul Khreshchatyk 38; ⌚10am-10pm Mon-Sun; 📶; Ⓜ Teatralna) Set in an impressive 1939 rationalist building in the very heart of Khreshchatyk, TsUM has undergone an extreme transformation in recent years, from Soviet-style department store to gleaming luxury shopping centre populated by chichi coffee shops. It had much more appeal before they destroyed the art deco interior, but it's still an icon.

Ye Bookstore BOOKS

(Map p54; vul Spaska 5; ⌚9am-9pm Mon-Sun; Ⓜ Kontraktova Pl) Part of a bookstore chain with an excellent selection of books, helpful staff, daily presentations and cosy atmosphere. Ye is also one of the best places in Kyiv for foreign-language books, especially in English but also French, German and Polish.

Bukva BOOKS

(Map p48; vul Bohdana Khmelnytskoho 36; ⌚10am-10pm; Ⓜ Teatralna) This centrally located bookstore is well stocked with maps, coffee-table books and travel guides on Ukraine and beyond. You can also enjoy a cup of coffee or a smoothie in a **cafe** on the 2nd floor.

Gulliver SHOPPING CENTRE

(Map p48; pl Sportyvna 1; ⌚10am-10pm; Ⓜ Palats Sportu) A big shopping mall set in one of Kyiv's skyscrapers with a nice selection of fashion brands combined with a cinema, large grocery store, bowling alleys and an extensive food court.

Roshen FOOD

(Рошен; Map p48; vul Khreshchatyk 29; ⌚8am-10pm; Ⓜ Khreshchatyk) On the sweet-tooth front, there is nothing more symbolic than *Kyivsky tort*, a nutty, layered sponge cake sold in circular cardboard cartons. Its main producer has a chain of immaculate shops, including this flagship on Kyiv's main drag. It's filled to the top shelf with all kinds of sweets, especially chocolate.

Another outlet (p84) can be found near the train station on vul Starovokzalna 21.

Petrivka Market MARKET

(Ринок Петрівка; vul Verbova; ⏲8am-6pm; Ⓜ Petrivka) Locals call it the 'book market' but the vast array of junk you can get here isn't limited to books. It's also Kyiv's main receptacle of DVDs, CDs and software of questionable legitimacy. It's located just outside Petrivka metro station.

Caramel Manufactory FOOD

(Майстерня карамелі; Map p48; vul Velyka Vasylkivska 18; ⏲10am-9pm; Ⓜ Lva Tolstoho) At this confectionery you can taste and buy many variations of handmade caramel and observe the caramel-making process. A great place to go with children.

KYIV FOR CHILDREN

Kyiv is a happening city for kids, although diversions are concentrated in the warm months.

Front and center are the flea market Kurazh Bazar (p81) and the food festival Ulichnaya Eda (p66), both of which take place monthly at the wonderful Art-Zavod Platforma events venue on the left bank. Both events have designated areas for family-focused activities.

Among the museums, Pyrohiv Museum of Folk Architecture (p60) is at the top of the list, with acres of rolling fields for kids to romp around in. There are craft workshops, a zipline, bicycle rental and, on weekends, activities such as archery or pottery making. A little outside of town is Mezhyhirya Estate (p64), the former presidential compound with a zoo, barnyard animals, and beautiful paved trails for bicycles or Segways.

In the city centre, you'll find creative playgrounds galore along Peyzazhna aleya (p52), while near the top of the funicular, in Volodymyrska Hirka park, there are little pedal carts for rent, an airslide, a trampoline and a sand box. Shevchenka Park has similar activities, plus pony rides on some weekends. More pony rides can sometimes be found in Park Askoldova Mohyla, near the Friendship of Nations Monument (p47). In the same park you'll find the child-friendly Water Museum (p47) and the Puppet Theatre (p80). At all of the above, your kids will find plenty of local playmates!

The Dnipro River islands yield a few fun things, though we don't recommend letting your kids swim in the mighty river, both for safety and sanitary reasons. Hydropark (p64) has an old-school amusement park. The footbridge to Trukhaniv Island (p64) is a fun jaunt. Once on the other side, head to Skvorechnik (p61), where there's always music or some such colourful event or activity going on.

At the very centre of the city, vul Khreshchatyk (p46) is closed off to vehicles and turns into a giant playground at weekends with kids' activities galore. Maydan Nezalezhnosti (p43) is a happening place with a colourful nightly dancing fountain that your children will love.

For food, Ostannya Barikada (p71), hidden beneath the fountain on maydan Nezalezhnosti, is relatively fun and child-friendly. Or head down to Podil and drink wine at Vero Vero (p74) while the kids play around the fountain and bounce on their trampoline.

For shoppers, the Roshen (p82) confectionary shops are colourful and fun (plus have lots of candy).

Practicalities

- Kyiv is experiencing a mini–baby boom, which means more and more restaurants and public places have changing tables and high chairs. But they remain the exception rather than the rule.
- There is a slew of children's shops in the Globus Mall under maydan Nezalezhnosti.
- Nappies are readily available in supermarkets.
- Ubers and taxis do not supply child seats so bring your own.
- Sidewalks are wide and generally pram-friendly, at least in the centre around vul Khreshchatyk.

Roshen FOOD
(Рошен; Map p48; vul Starovokzalna 21; ⌚9am-8pm; Ⓜ Vokzalna) This branch of the famous Ukrainian confectionery near the train station has a huge model train set on premises, making it a good stop for those with kids in tow. Chocolates, cookies and iconic *Kyivsky tort* (cake).

Information

INTERNET ACCESS

Virtually all cafes, restaurants and hotels have wi-fi, and speeds are generally very good. Wi-fi networks tend to be open (no password required) so poaching wi-fi connections is easy.

3G internet access provided by the major cellphone providers costs almost nothing, coverage is excellent and speeds fast.

Open co-working spaces (p77) are a good option if you need extended time on the laptop.

Central Library (Центральна бібліотека; Map p48; vul Prorizna 15; ⌚noon-7pm Mon-Sat; 📶; Ⓜ Zoloti Vorota) Free internet on quality computers is available on the air-conditioned ground floor here. Or plop your notebook down on a table and take advantage of free wi-fi.

Central Post Office (p84) Offers internet access (18uah per hour) and printing services.

MEDICAL SERVICES

American Medical Center (☎emergency hotline 044-490 7600; http://amcenters.com; vul Berdychivska 1; ⌚24hr; Ⓜ Lukyanivska) Western-run medical centre with English-speaking doctors.

Boris (Борис; Map p48; ☎044-502 8040, 24hr emergency 044-238 0000; www.boris.kiev.ua; vul Velyka Vasylkivska 55A; ⌚24hr; Ⓜ Olympiyska) Respected local clinic next to Olympic Stadium with modern facilities, some English-speaking doctors and 24hr emergency care.

MONEY

Both ATMs and exchange booths signposted 'обмін валют' *(obmin valyut)* are ubiquitous. Rates offered by exchange booths in hotels are not necessarily worse. Larger banks will cash travellers cheques and give cash advances on credit cards.

POST

Central Post Office (Map p48; www.ukrposhta.com; vul Khreshchatyk 22; ⌚8am-9pm, to 7pm Sun; Ⓜ Maydan Nezalezhnosti)

DHL International (Map p48; ☎044-490 2600; www.dhl.com.ua; vul Velyka Vasylkivska 2; ⌚9am-8pm Mon-Fri, 9am-2pm Sat; Ⓜ Pl Lva Tolstoho)

TOURIST INFORMATION

Tour Info Kiev (www.tourinfo.kiev.ua) The city runs about a dozen of these booths, including at **maydan Nezalezhnosti** (Map p48; cnr vul Khreshchatyk & vul Instytutska; ⌚9am-7pm, to 5.30pm Sun) and near **Bessarabska Rynok** (Map p48; cnr vul Khreshchatyk & vul Baseyna; ⌚9am-7pm, to 5.30pm Fri), and at both airports. They are of moderate usefulness, but are usually staffed by an English speaker who can answer simple questions and distribute free maps and brochures. For a small commission they also sell theatre and concert tickets as well as bus and train tickets. For more details, see www.visitkyiv.travel.

Getting There & Away

AIR

Boryspil International Airport

Most international flights use Kyiv's **main airport** (☎044-364 4505; www.kbp.aero), about 35km east of the city. The airport has a good website listing airlines and flight schedules. Most flights of the national carrier, **Ukraine International Airlines** (Map p48; ☎044-581 5050; www.flyuia.com; vul Lysenka 4; ⌚8am-7.30pm, to 5.30pm Sun; Ⓜ Maydan Nezalezhnosti), use this airport.

Kyiv Zhulyany International Airport

This small, modern **airport** (☎044-585 0211; www.airport.kiev.ua; vul Medova 2; 🚎9, marshrutka 302, 368, 805) is much more convenient to the centre. It serves domestic flights and a growing number of international flights, including flights by budget carrier **Wizz Air**.

BOAT

Chervona Ruta (p65) is your port of call if you're interested in Dnipro River and Black Sea cruises. The standard cruise is one week from Kyiv to Odesa. Some cruises go into the Danube delta, and there are other trips around Kyiv (check the website).

BUS

There are a half-dozen bus terminals, but the most useful for both domestic and international long-distance trips is the **Central bus station** (Tsentralny Avtovokzal; ☎044-525 5774; pl Moskovska 3; 🚎1, 12), near Demiivska metro station – look out for McDonald's as you exit.

Vydubychi bus station (Автостанція Видубичі; ☎044-524 7426; Zaliznychne shose 10; Ⓜ Vydubychi) is another useful bus station with lots of long-distance domestic and international trips, especially heading southbound. This is also the station to use for Kaniv.

Buses for Zhytomyr and Berdychiv leave from several points, including the central bus station and the **Dachna bus station** (pr Peremohi 142; Ⓜ Zhytomyrska).

Autolux (☎ 044-594 9500; www.autolux.ua; Central Bus Station; ⏰ 6.30am-9pm) and Turkish-owned **Günsel** (☎ 044-525 4505; www.gunsel.com.ua; Central Bus Station), both based at the central station, run the most comfortable buses, including wildly popular express services to Odesa (315uah, six hours, several daily) from both the central bus station and Vydubychi bus station. Many trips go via, or continue to, Boryspil International Airport.

Online booking is possible through bus-company websites or through **InBus** (www.inbus.ua), or buy tickets in person at the bus station of departure, Boryspil airport, or Tour Info Kiev kiosks.

MARSHRUTKA

Many destinations in Central and Western Ukraine can be reached by private *marshrutky* (fixed-route minibuses), which take the form of 15-seat vans or somewhat larger minibuses.

The largest *marshrutka* station – **Avtostantsiya Kyiv** (Map p48; vul Symona Petlyury 32; Ⓜ Vokzalna) – is out toward the main road from the train station. From here, vehicles leave for Odesa (380uah, six hours, hourly), Rivne (200uah, 4½ hours, hourly), Ternopil (250uah, seven hours, hourly), Uman (120uah, three hours, hourly), Vinnytsya (150uah, 3½ hours, four daily) and Zhytomyr (80uah, two hours, frequent). There's a daily trip at 1pm to Chernivtsi (350uah, eight hours) via Kamyanets-Podilsky (300uah, six hours).

For Chernihiv, *marshrutky* leave from a lot near Lisova metro station (100uah, 1¾ hours, every 15 minutes).

Kharkivska metro station is the point of departure for *marshrutky* to Pereyaslav-Khmelnytsky (50uah, one hour, every 20 minutes) and Cherkasy (80uah, 2½ hours).

TRAIN

You can get pretty much everywhere in the country from Kyiv's modern **train station** (Central Terminal; Map p48; ☎ 044-309 7005; pl Vokzalna 2; Ⓜ Vokzalna), conveniently located near the city centre at Vokzalna metro station. A taxi to the centre should cost 50-100uah.

'Intercity' trains serve many regional centres. These usually have airplane-style seating and are significantly faster than regular passenger (sleeper) trains.

Summer sees additional trains added to Odesa and other summer resort areas on the Black Sea.

The #20 and #21 ticket booths at the main, central terminal usually have an English speaker. For last-minute ticket purchases, use the express booth immediately to the right as you enter the central terminal; it usually has no line.

You can also buy tickets in the newer, adjacent **South Terminal** (Південний вокзал | Pivdenniy Vokzal; Map p48; vul Polzunova), or at the **advance train ticket office** (Map p48; bul Tarasa Shevchenka 38/40; ⏰ 8am-8pm; Ⓜ Universytet), a 1.5km walk from the station, next to Hotel Express. You can purchase tickets for a commission from **Kiy Avia** at **vul Horodetskoho** (Map p48; ☎ 044-490 4901; www.kiyavia.com; vul Horodetskoho 4; ⏰ 8am-9pm, to 6pm Sun; Ⓜ Maydan Nezalezhnosti) or **pl Peremohy** (Map p48; ☎ 044-490 4901; www.kiyavia.com; pr Peremohy 2; ⏰ 8am-9pm, to 6pm Sun; Ⓜ Vokzalna), or from Tour Info Kiev kiosks.

On the 2nd floor of the station's main terminal there's a comfortable air-conditioned **waiting lounge** with wi-fi (40uah per hour). Walk up and

POPULAR TRAINS FROM KYIV

DESTINATION	TYPE	PRICE PLATSKART/ KUPE (UAH)	DURATION (HR)	FREQUENCY
Chernivtsi	Passenger	115/185	11½	8.05pm
Ivano-Frankivsk	Passenger	from 115/260	9-12½	3-5 daily
Ivano-Frankivsk	Intercity	275	8	2.09pm
Kamyanets-Podilsky	Passenger	from 100/150	7½-8½	2-3 daily
Kharkiv	Passenger	from 115/275	7-10	4-7 daily
Kharkiv	Intercity	260	4¾	4 daily
Lviv	Passenger	from 135/240	6½-11	frequent
Lviv	Intercity	300	5	3 daily
Odesa	Passenger	from 150/350	9-14	2-4 daily
Odesa	Intercity		7	4.35pm
Uzhhorod	Passenger	from 150/225	12½-16	2-4 daily

to the left. You can also wait in comfort in the **Service Centre** (p69; 50uah per hour).

Bag storage (25uah per day per piece) is available in the basement of the central terminal.

Getting Around

TO/FROM THE AIRPORT

For Boryspil International Airport, there is a convenient, round-the-clock **Skybus** service (90uah, 45 minutes to one hour) to/from vul Polzunova outside Kyiv train station's South Terminal (p85). Departures are every 20 minutes during the day, less frequent at night. You can also pick this up at Kharkivska metro station on the left bank (50uah, 20 minutes) – a nice time-saver during rush hour. Metred taxis into town (about 40 minutes) from the airport cost around 450uah if arranged at the airport taxi desk, but freelance drivers can sometimes be bargained down to 350uah or 400uah.

To reach Kyiv Zhulyany International Airport you can take trolleybus 9 from the **Bessarabska Pl** (Map p48; vul Velyka Vasylkivska) stop in the centre, or marshrutka 302 from the **Kontraktova Pl** (Map p54; cnr vul Nizhny Val & vul Kostyantynivska) stop. Marshrutka 368 or 805 go to/from the stop outside the South train terminal (Pivdenniy Vokzal), where you can transfer to the metro at Vokzalna. A taxi to the centre should only cost about 100uah (five to 15 minutes).

PUBLIC TRANSPORT

Although often crowded, Kyiv's metro is clean, efficient, reliable and easy to use. It is also the world's deepest, requiring escalator rides of seven to eight minutes! Trains run frequently between around 6am and midnight on all three lines. Blue *zhetony* (plastic tokens) costing 5uah (good for one ride) are sold by cashiers, or you can buy a plastic card that can be topped up at any station.

Buses, trolleybuses, trams and many quicker *marshrutky* (minibuses) serve most routes. Tickets for buses, trams and trolleybuses cost 4uah and are sold at street kiosks or directly from the driver/conductor. *Marshrutky* rides usually cost 6uah.

Kyiv Metro

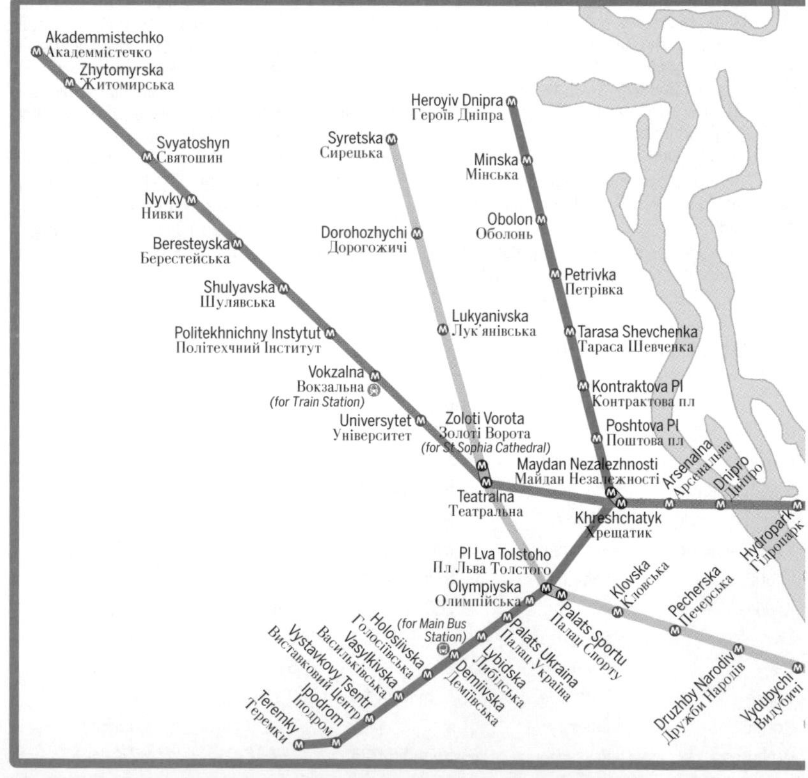

TAXI

Taxi prices in Kyiv are cheap by world standards. Expect to pay 50uah for short (less than 3km) trips within central Kyiv.

Locals prefer booking taxis by phone – they arrive fast and you know the price in advance. Uber is extremely popular in Kyiv if you have it on your smartphone. Otherwise, ask your hotel reception or anyone else for assistance in dialing a metred taxi service such as the reliable **Taxi Ekspres** (http://express-taxi.ua, 044-239 1515).

If you flag a taxi or a private car in the street – as people still do – always agree on the price before getting in, unless the car is an official metered taxi. Taking standing taxis from outside hotels, as well as train and bus stations, inevitably incurs a much higher price.

For Boryspil airport (p84), it's better to order a taxi by phone.

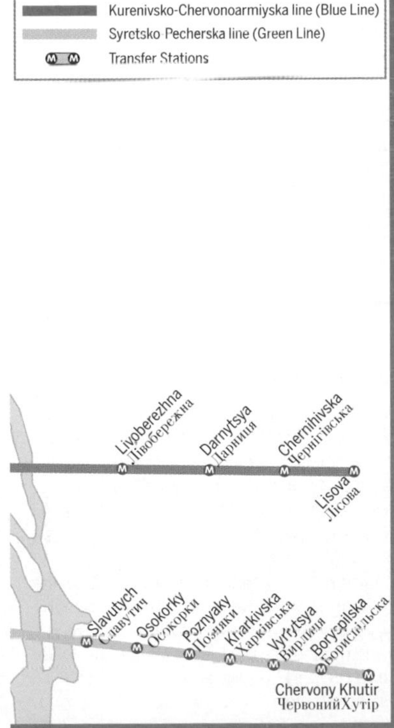

AROUND KYIV

Camping, *shashlyking* (BBQ-ing) and mushroom picking are popular in the forests of Polissya that roll northwest and northeast out of Kyiv along the Desna and Teteriv Rivers. Further north is Chornobyl, which has become one of the country's top tourism attractions in recent years. South of Kyiv the Dnipro divides fertile plains, creating stunning sunsets and panoramas such as those found at Taras Shevchenko's grave site in Kaniv.

Bus or *marshrutka* are generally the way to roll when heading into Kyiv's suburbs and beyond. Services are frequent and cheap. However, travelling between outlying towns often requires a trip back to Kyiv, so consider renting a car if you want to visit more than one destination in a day.

Visiting Chornobyl, for all intents and purposes, requires an organised tour.

Bila Tserkva

☎04563 / POP 200,000

Some 80km south of Kyiv, the drowsy town of Bila Tserkva is an easy and rewarding day trip out of the capital, especially for those who appreciate a little faded aristocratic splendour and a chance to picnic. The town's main claim to fame is Dendropark Oleksandriya (p87), the largest landscaped park in Ukraine and perfect for a bike ride.

The park is about 5km northwest of central **pl Soborny** along pleasant, tree-lined bul Oleksandriysky. A five-minute walk north from pl Soborny is the town's former epicentre, **Torgova pl**, where you can wander the now semi-deserted early-19th-century **covered market** (Torgovy Ryad).

History

Founded by Yaroslav the Wise in 1032 as Yuriev, the town's main claim to historical fame is that Cossack *hetman* (chieftain) Bohdan Khmelnytsky signed the Treaty of Bila Tserkva with the Polish-Lithuanian Commonwealth here in 1651 after defeat in the battle of Bila Tserkva. In the 18th century the estate was owned by the influential Polish Branicki family, who created most of the town's places of interest.

Sights

Dendropark Oleksandriya PARK

(Дендропарк Олександрія; entrance on bul Oleksandriysky; adult/student 20/10uah; ⏲8am-9pm;

(🚎1, 4) Bila Tserkva's wonderful Dendropark Oleksandriya is Ukraine's largest landscaped park. It's much bigger than Uman's more-heralded Sofiyivka Park, but it is not as nicely manicured and draws far fewer visitors. The park is dotted with glades, bridges, cafes, gazebos, ponds and pieces of sculpture. It's a lot of territory to cover on foot, so consider hiring a bicycle outside the entrance (per hr/day 35/100uah). Pick up a map of the park and the town at the park entrance (15uah).

The park derives its name from Aleksandra von Engelhardt, Potemkin's niece and wife of Poland's Crown Hetman (head of the Polish army) Ksawery Branicki, who in the mid-18th century commissioned French garden architects to create this 200ha chunk of greenery.

There is ample opportunity for getting lost and picnicking with the locals among the park's quietly overgrown woods and crumbling architecture. Where Polish silk dresses once rustled and aristocratic canes crunched on gravel paths, now headscarved babushkas march entrusted grandchildren on health walks and couples smooch on park benches, but the style and romantic megalomania of the Polish nobility still shines through in faded lustre.

To get here, board trolleybus 1 or 4 anywhere along bul Oleksandriysky (4uah).

Spaso-Preobrazhensky Cathedral CHURCH
(vul Gagarina) A beeswax candle's throw from pl Soborny is the Spaso-Preobrazhensky Cathedral, which has a much more atmospheric interior than the rather plain 1830s exterior might suggest. The complex is surrounded by attractive **gardens** and there's a **statue** of Taras Shevchenko off to the south side.

Sleeping

Ros HOTEL $
(Рось; ☎04563-664 27; bul Oleksandriysky 94; std s/d 140/260uah, deluxe 300uah) You're in for the Soviet experience here, not the creature comforts. The barely renovated rooms are stuck in the '70s, but at these prices you can't complain. Beds are better than you'd expect and the 'deluxe' rooms even come with full-size bathtubs. One semifunctional lift serves the nine creaky floors. It's roughly opposite Dendropark Oleksandriya's entrance (p87).

City Park Hotel HOTEL $$
(☎04563-015 75; www.citypark-hotels.com; vul Yaroslava Mydroho 14; s/d incl breakfast from 1160/1305uah; ❄📶) Each room here is sleek and modern with attractive orange panelling, slate-grey paint, large plasma TVs, clean carpets and smooth lines. Bathrooms are boutique-style, with vessel sinks. There's a 45uah business lunch in the **cafe**, and they hand out maps and some tourism brochures. Overall, fine value.

Eating

Kav'yarnya na Soborny CAFE $$
(Кав'ярня на Соборній; ☎04563-917 72; pl Soborna 1/1; mains 50-150uah; ⏰9am-11pm; ❄📶) Bila Tserkva's most upscale eatery has a summer terrace right on central pl Soborny and an elegant interior. The menu has pictures to point at but no English. Among the choices are *myaso po frantsuzsky* (French-style

WORTH A TRIP

MID-DNIPRO MUSEUM OF FOLK ARCHITECTURE & LIFE

This brilliant outdoor museum in Pereyaslav-Khmelnytsky, 90km southeast of Kyiv, has around 70 heritage wooden buildings brought here from nearby villages and clustered tightly on 32 hectares of forested land. Some of them have been turned into little thematic museums; the more interesting ones cost an additional 10uah. Highlights are the charmingly retro-Soviet Bread Museum; the childhood house of leading Yiddish writer Sholem Aleichem, who was born in Pereyaslav; and the Space Museum, which occupies a wooden village church.

To get here from Kyiv catch one of the buses or *marshrutky* that depart every 20 to 40 minutes from outside Kharkivska, Borispilska or Chernihivska metro stations (all 50uah, 1¼ hours). You'll be dropped of at the bus station at the main intersection in town. From here you can walk easily enough, about 2km, to the museum's back entrance. Otherwise take a taxi (75uah) via an 8km roundabout route to the park's main entrance. You can then exit through the back gate and find your way into town.

cutlet – a Soviet staple), salmon in cream sauce and *pelmeni* (Russian dumplings).

The **adjoining hotel** has a few rooms, though they are not the best value.

Getting There & Away

The stop for *marshrutky* to/from Kyiv (50uah, 1¼ hours) is 100m south of central pl Soborny on vul Knyazya Volodymyra. The last trip back to Kyiv is at 8pm. There are several departure points in Kyiv, including Lybidska and Vasylkivska metro stations.

Kaniv Канів

☎04736 / POP 25,000

When Taras Shevchenko, Ukraine's national poet, died in 1861, his famous poem 'Zapovit' (Testament) requested his fellow countryfolk bury him on a hill overlooking the great Dnipro River where, after rising up and liberating the land, they could 'freely, and with good intent, speak quietly of him'.

Kaniv, 162km down the Dnipro from Kyiv, is the spot they chose. In 1925 the steep and scenic bluff overlooking the river, **Tarasova Hora**, was designated a State Cultural Preserve. Today the shrine is accessible via a long and steep staircase. On top you'll find the poet's tomb crowned with a tremendous statue of the man himself.

There is an observation point in front of the statue with breathtaking views of the Dnipro. Behind the grave is the huge and surprisingly glitzy **Taras Shevchenko Museum** (Музей Тараса Шевченка; www.shevchenko-museum.com.ua; 20uah; ⏲9.30am-5pm Tue-Sun, closed last Fri of month), which features interactive touchscreens, glass cases of first editions and big-print engravings of the moustachioed one.

Sleeping

Stary Kaniv HOTEL $

(☎04736-354 38; vul Lenina 17; r 250-350uah, ste 500uah; ❄📶) The best hotel in the centre of town is in a classic salmon-toned tsar-era building. It's a remarkable value, especially the suites, which have air-con, cable TV and bidets. For this price? Count us in. Just 11 clean rooms and an appealing dungeon-style **restaurant** that gets loud at weekends.

Knyazha Hora HOTEL $$

(☎04736-315 88; www.knyazhahora.com; vul Dniprovska 1; r 1000-1500uah, ste 2000uah; ❄📶) The fancy, 13-room Knyazhya Hora is down by the river just 1km before Tarasova Hora. It offers immaculate, European-standard facilities and a contemporary **restaurant** (mains 150uah to 300uah) festooned with modern art.

Getting There & Away

Kaniv is just about doable as a long day trip from Kyiv. Buses (90uah, 3½ hours, at least hourly) depart from the capital's Vydubychi bus station (p84).

There's a 6.30am *marshrutka* to Pereyaslav-Khmelnytsky (60uah, 1½ hours), a very pleasant 50km ride across the giant Kaniv dam on the Dnipro and on through Van Gogh–like sunflower- and haystack-filled landscapes.

Getting Around

Tarasova Hora is about 7km (35uah by taxi) south of the bus station, which is in the centre of town.

Central Ukraine
Центральна Україна

POP 5.5 MILLION

Includes ➡

Best Places to Eat

➡ Buba (p92)
➡ Blomanzhe (p106)
➡ Tamero (p99)
➡ Pan Kaban (p96)
➡ Front (p106)

Best Places to Stay

➡ Kleopatra (p105)
➡ Vin Hostel (p98)
➡ Hotel France (p98)
➡ Reikartz Zhytomyr (p92)
➡ Bilya Richky (p104)

Why Go?

Layered with dark fertile soil, Ukraine's breadbasket heartlands are split between forested Polissya to the north and the endless agricultural flatlands of Podillya to the south. Life isn't complicated in these parts; people work the land and fish the streams and, when it's time to relax, they head to the woods or, in winter, the *banya* (bathhouse). Some say this region epitomises the 'real Ukraine' and, frankly, it would be hard to argue with that.

The highlights include a clutch of fortresses, a missile museum, two seriously elaborate fountains, and the show-stopping island town of Kamyanets-Podilsky. In the 19th century the region was the heart of Catherine the Great's Jewish Pale of Settlement, birthplace of both Hasidism and the Jewish shtetl. The Nazis obliterated most traces of Jewish culture, although a few old Jewish cemeteries and synagogues remain.

When to Go

Zhytomyr

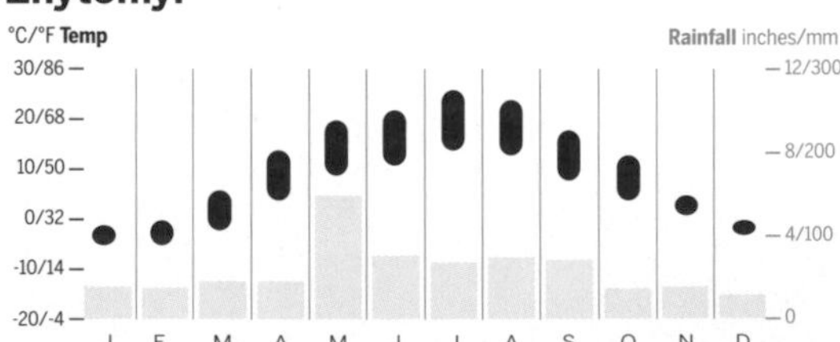

Aug Gaze in awe at Central Ukraine's humongous sunflower fields in full bloom.

Sep Pick mushrooms and berries in the vast forests of Polissya.

May The most festive time to visit Kamyanets-Podilsky and its famous fortress.

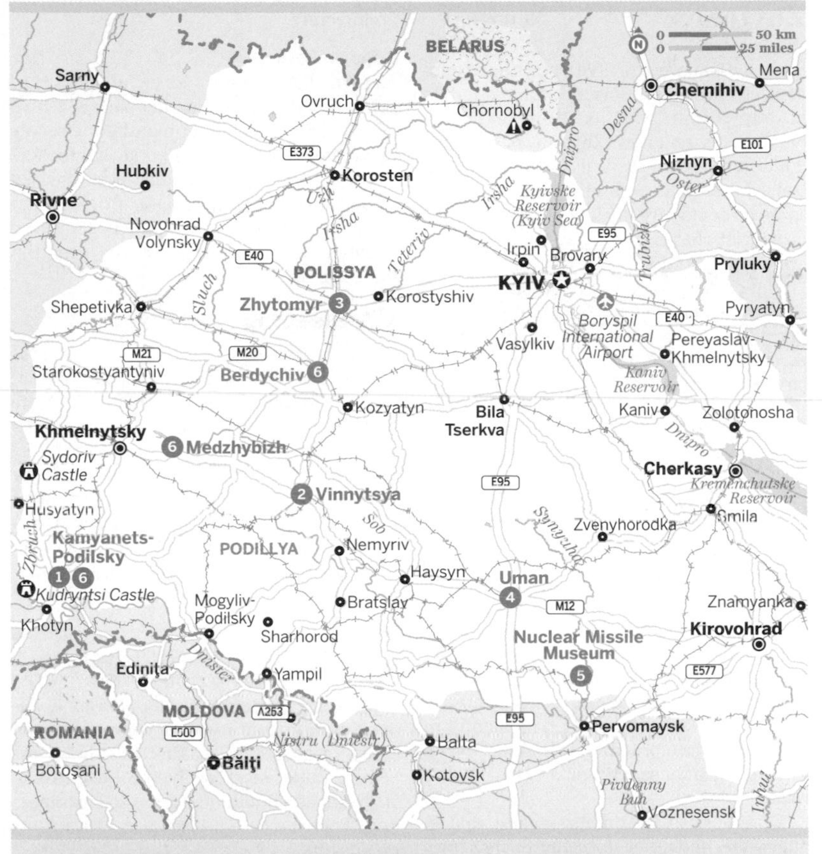

Central Ukraine Highlights

❶ **Kamyanets-Podilsky** (p100) Laying photographic siege to the medieval island town and its dramatic fortress.

❷ **Vinnytsya** (p96) Enjoying its range of quirky attractions, such as Ukraine's most spectacular water feature.

❸ **Zhytomyr** (p92) Stepping back to the days of the USSR in the Korolyov Cosmonaut Museum, a classic celebration of Soviet space successes.

❹ **Uman** (p95) Taking in its elaborate dancing fountain show and strolling peaceful Sofiyivka Park.

❺ **Nuclear Missile Museum** (p94) Descending 45m underground in an old Soviet cylinder to the point where the push of a button could have ended the world.

❻ **Fortresses** (p93) Chasing old castles in Berdychiv, Medzhybyzh and Kamyanets-Podilsky.

POLISSYA

The woodsy, river-sliced region radiating out of Kyiv in all directions is known as Polissya. The bulk of the region lies north of the capital, extending into Belarus, and sees none of the tourist traffic of southern and western Ukraine. Those who do make it here are usually campers, mountain bikers, rock climbers, mushroom pickers, canoeists and the odd hunter. If you don't fit one of those categories, you might enjoy taking in Zhytomyr's Soviet-era small-town charm or exploring the rich Jewish history of Berdychiv, both west of Kyiv.

Zhytomyr Житомир

0412 / POP 267,350

Some 140km west of Kyiv, no other right-bank city evokes the Soviet Union more than Zhytomyr. Even with its Lenin and Marx monuments removed, Zhytomyr's plinthed tank and wreathed war memorials, old trolleybuses and a fascinatingly nostalgic space museum give it a kind of time-warped provincial charm that makes it just worth leaving Kyiv to see.

The centre of town is pl Peremohy, next to the towering yellow Ukrainian Orthodox **Transfiguration Church**. Just south of pl Peremohy is pl Soborno, one of Ukraine's largest traffic circles.

Sights

Korolyov Cosmonaut Museum MUSEUM
(Музей космонавтики ім. С. П. Корольова; 0412-472 627; www.cosmosmuseum.info; vul Dmytrivska 5; adult/student 20/10uah, photos 10uah, excursion in English 120uah; 10am-1pm & 2-5.15pm Tue-Sun) Named after acclaimed Soviet rocket engineer and local lad Sergei Korolyov, this surprisingly well-curated museum is famous across the former Soviet Union. Suitably space-aged music plays and fake stars glimmer as you walk around a dark hall packed with assorted mementos of the Soviet space program, including several satellites, a lunar ranger and an actual Soyuz rocket.

More amusing exhibits include black-and-white photos of dogs the Soviets propelled into space, sachets and tubes of real space food (cottage cheese, mashed potato!), and a section on the Soviet space shuttle that literally never got off the ground. All in all, not bad for a country that struggled to produce reliable combustion engines and functional plumbing.

The house where Korolyov was born, now a museum (same hours) dedicated to his life, is directly across the street from the museum, but is of little interest to foreign visitors.

To reach the museum, from pl Soborna head along vul Velika Berdychivska for two blocks until you reach vul Ivana Franka. Turn left here and continue for 400m until you see the museum on your right.

St Sophia's Church CHURCH
(vul Kafedralna) With its distinctive ochre-and-white exterior, double clock towers and lavish interior, this small church dating from 1746 is a must-see for fans of baroque architecture.

Gagarin Park PARK
Flanking the Teteriv River about 1.5km south of the city centre, this park is a hive of activity in the summer months and serves up great views of the river gorge and the forest beyond, accessible via the Berdychivsky bridge over the gorge. You can descend to the river and hire little paddle boats in the summer. There's a TU-104 plane near the park entrance.

Sleeping

Reikartz Zhytomyr HOTEL $$
(0412-558 910; www.reikartz.com; maydan Zamkovy 5/8; incl breakfast s/d from 600/880uah, ste 1680uah;) A member of the slick, home-grown Reikartz opertion, the Zhtomyr version does not disappoint, with perfectly appointed rooms in soothingly coordinated fabrics and woods, luscious linens, pin-clean bathrooms and amiable, English-speaking staff. Upgrading to a suite nets significantly more space and is highly recommended.

Hotel Ukraina HOTEL $$
(Готель Україна; 0412-472 999; vul Kyivska 3; s/d/ste incl breakfast 400/700/1000uah;) All the rooms here have undergone de-Sovietisation, and some of them even have shiny plasma TVs, making this hotel excellent value – especially the businesslike singles (the doubles are a tad too flamboyant). There's a decent **Georgian restaurant** downstairs.

Eating

Chas Poyisty CAFETERIA $
(Час Поїсти; pl Peremohy 3; dishes 20-40uah; 9am-10pm) When it's 'time to eat' (a translation of the name), join the feeding frenzy at this cheap, quick and painless self-service canteen just across from the mounted tank on pl Peremohy. Serves all the usual favourites from across the ex-USSR, plus decent coffees and beers.

★ **Buba** GEORGIAN $$
(Буба; 098 482 0089; vul Kyivska 10; 60-120uah; 11am-11pm;) It's almost worth a special trip from Kyiv to dine here – it's as good as most Georgian restaurants in the capital and a third the price. The classic Caucasian stews and *khachapuri* (cheese bread) are well represented, only with modern twists.

The English menu and an English-speaking waiter or two are rarities in these parts.

Schultz BEER HALL **$$**
(www.schulz.ua; vul Peremohy 1; mains 75-125uah; ⏲11am-midnight; ❄📶) This underground Ukrainian interpretation of a Czech microbrewery, with exposed beer vats, serves several varieties of home brew, including a commendable wheat beer and dark ale, plus good bar snacks and meaty meals.

Getting There & Away

The simplest way to make Zhytomyr a day trip from Kyiv is to take a (virtually) nonstop *marshrutka* (fixed-price minibus; 40uah, 1½ hours) from Zhytomyrska metro station. These drop you off and pick you up at pl Peremohy next to the mounted tank.

Use the bus station, a short trolleybus ride from the city centre, for buses to Berdychiv (30uah, one hour) or to Kyiv's central bus station or Avtostantsiya Kyiv (p85; 80uah, two hours).

Berdychiv Бердичів

☎04143 / POP 76,700

You'd never guess today that this sleepy town on the southern edge of Polissya was once an important intellectual centre and hotbed of Jewish culture. At the turn of the 19th century, Berdychiv's population was more than 80% Jewish. The Nazis took care of that, murdering just about every one of the city's 39,000 Jews and burying them in mass graves on the town's outskirts.

These days Berdychiv's Jewish community numbers only several hundred, but the city remains an important pilgrimage site for followers of revered Hasidic master Levi Yitzhak (1740–1810), who is buried in the town's remarkable Jewish cemetery. Berdychiv also has links to two great 19th-century literary figures: Joseph Conrad was born in Berdychiv (1857), and Honoré de Balzac (of all people) was married to Polish noblewoman Ewelina Hańska (1850) in the rose-tinted, neoclassical **St Barbara Church** (vul Yevropeyska 25), which bears a brass plaque celebrating the event.

Sights

Jewish Cemetery CEMETERY
(vul Zhytomyrska) FREE Levi Yitzhak's mausoleum is in Berdychiv's huge Jewish Cemetery. For decades, with the exception of Yitzhak's mausoleum, the cemetery was overgrown and neglected, but these days it's well tended to by a Stakhanovite team of weed-whacker-wielding caretakers. What will strike you is the odd, boot-like shape of the tombstones, most of which bear barely legible Hebrew inscriptions and lie hideously askew or flat on the ground – evoking images, all too common in this region – of humans toppled en masse by Nazi bullets.

Joseph Conrad Museum MUSEUM
(Soborna pl; ⏲10am-6pm Tue-Fri, 9am-6pm Sat, 9am-2pm Sun) FREE Józef Teodor Konrad Korzeniowski was born in 1957 to noble Polish parents in Berdychiv, then part of the Russian empire, and spent the first four years of his life in the immediate area. This little museum within Berdychiv Fortress, funded by the Polish government, documents every detail of the young Korzeniowski's life, in these parts and beyond, through a series of wonderful multimedia touch screens and exhibits.

Berdychiv Fortress MONASTERY
(http://karmel.org.ua; Soborna pl; ⏲territory 7am-9pm) FREE The impressive brick-walled complex hogging the horizon as you approach Berdychiv from Khmelnytsky is widely known as the *fortetsya* (fortress),

BERDYCHIV'S KILLING FIELDS

Those who are interested can try to hunt down some **mass burial sites** that lie outside the town. At such sites the Nazis typically shot their victims in the back of the head and let their slumped bodies fall into pre-dug pits.

The easiest to find is about 3km west of the Berdychiv Fortress on the highway to Khmilnyk. A memorial on the right side of the highway commemorates the 18,640 'Soviet citizens' killed here in September 1941 – like all Soviet Holocaust monuments, it makes no mention of Jews. The memorial is just past a crosswalk and just before the sign indicating that you are leaving Berdychiv.

The actual burial site, marked by a plaque with Hebrew writing, is hidden under a clump of low-lying trees about 250m into the cow pasture behind the Soviet plaque.

but it's actually a Carmelite (Roman Catholic) monastery. The towering **Church of Our Lady**, which lords over the complex, dates to the 17th century. It's well worth going inside to check out its beautiful interior, dominated by the soaring central nave. The monastery's fortress-like defensive walls and towers were built in the late 18th century.

Sleeping & Eating

Berdychiv is best visited as a day trip from, or en route to, Vinnytsya or Zhytomyr. If you do want to stay the night, there are a few places to bed down.

Berdychiv's culinary scene is less than dynamic, to put it politely, but there are a few OK cafes in the centre, or try the hotel restaurants.

Deja Vu HOTEL **$$**
(Дежа Вю; 04143-400 55; www.hotel-dejavu.com; vul Vinnytska 3B; s/d/tr/ste 420/700/800/1050uah;) Deja Vu purports to be fancier than it is – witness the incredibly overdone **restaurant** – yet it remains Berd-

WORTH A TRIP

MUSEUM OF STRATEGIC MISSILE FORCES

It's not easy to find, but deep in Ukraine's agricultural heartland, 25km north of Pervomaysk, lies one of Ukraine's coolest museums. The **Museum of Strategic Missile Forces** (Музей ракетних військ стратегічного призначення; Nuclear Mission Museum; 05161-732 18; www.rvsp.net.ua; Pervomaysk District; adult/student incl tour in Ukrainian 80/20uah, photos 20uah, tour in English per group US$15; 10am-5pm), better known as the Nuclear Missile Museum, was formerly a nuclear-missile launch facility. The highlight is the journey taking you 12 storeys underground in a Brezhnev-era elevator to the control room (extra 200uah).

Here you can sit at the desk of doom, pretend to take that fateful call on an old Soviet phone, and press the button that once would have ended civilisation as we know it. These days it sets off lights and alarms, but thankfully no missiles are launched. The facility housed 10 missiles, each of which lay hidden in subterranean silos near the control room, with an additional 75 missiles or so floating around the region and administered by this facility.

On the grounds of the museum are four huge decommissioned intercontinental ballistic missiles (ICBM), including a 75ft SS-18 Satan rocket, the Soviets' largest ICBM (it's an import from Baikanor, Kazakhstan). Many more rockets and pieces of military hardware are scattered around the grounds. The excellent museum proper documents milestones of the Cold War and post-Cold War eras, including the decommissioning of this facility with US assistance.

To get the most out of this intriguing museum, book a tour in English with Pervomaysk guide Elena Smerichevskaya (contact her on 095 200 7578 or elena-smerichevskaya@yandex.ru). Elena can also arrange transport from Kyiv (about 3000uah round-trip for a car or minivan) or Odesa. Tour agencies in Kyiv charge much more both for transport and for Elena's services.

Keep in mind that the museum is a very long day trip from Kyiv – up to 3½ hours each way. It's better to visit the museum from Uman or when travelling between Odesa and Kyiv. Sleeping in Pervomaysk is also an option. The best hotels are **Hostinny Dvir** (05161-557 31; www.hotel-pervomaysk.com.ua; vul Hrushevskoho 58, Pervomaysk; s/d from 300/500uah;) in the centre of town, and the slightly fancier **Postoyaiy Dvir** (Bogopol Hotel; 066 264 3690; hotel-bogopol@yandex.ua; vul Bohopilska 96, Pervomaysk; d/tr from 330/560uah;), about 2km west of the centre on the road to the museum.

To get to the museum from Kyiv take the daily comfortable Günsel bus at 9.45am (return trip at 3.05pm) or any Mykolayiv- or Kherson-bound public bus from the Central bus station (p84) in Kyiv (250uah, five hours) and have them drop you off at the museum access road, from where it's a 1.5km walk. A taxi to the museum from Pervomaysk costs 100uah one-way, and there are a few daily buses that pass by the access road.

ychiv's nicest hotel by a wide margin. Each room has a wardrobe, big bathroom and ultra-slim flat-screen TV. Most receptionists speak English and there's a **sports bar** on premises (open from 1pm).

We'd like to see them ditch the reservation charge (100uah to 300uah, depending on room category).

Melanzh CAFE $

(vul Yevropeyska 10; mains 50-125uah; ⏲10am-11pm; ❄📶) This modern and central cafe opposite St Nicholas Church is about as good as it gets. There's no English menu, but there are pictures so you can point to what you want, which might include salmon steak or a Caesar salad. The squat toilet is a reminder that you are deep in the provinces.

Getting There & Away

Buses head this way from Zhytomyr (30uah, one hour) every half-hour, terminating at Berdychiv's Central bus station. However, the station is a long way from anywhere so ask to be dropped off in the town centre. There are buses or *marshrutky* at least every hour to Vinnytsya (54uah, 1¾ hours) and Kyiv (112uah, 2½ hours).

PODILLYA

Uman Умань

☎04744 / POP 85,500

All roads in Ukraine seem to pass through this central hub, home of relentlessly idyllic Sofiyivka Park and the final resting place of the revered Hasidic Rabbi Nachman of Bratslav. Beyond these highlights and a buzzy new fountain, there's not much else happening, but it's a good place to break up the long journey between Kyiv and Odesa.

Sights

Sofiyivka Park PARK

(☎04744-407 39; www.sofiyivka.org.ua; vul Sadova; adult/child 40/25uah, tour in English 660uah; ⏲7am-10pm) Sofia Pototsky was a legendary beauty, and Uman's stunning park is her husband Count Felix's monument to her physical perfection. Having bought Sofia for two million zloty from her former husband (she had been sold into slavery at an early age by her parents), the Polish count set to landscaping this 150-hectare site with grottoes, lakes, waterfalls, fountains, pavilions and 500 species of tree. The result, completed in 1802, was Ukraine's answer to Versailles.

A map available at the park entrance (10uah) highlights 60 points of interest within the park, many bearing sentimental names like Island of Love and Grotto of Venus. The marble sculptures are replicas of those that graced the park in Pototsky's time. Some of the originals are safe-kept in the atrium of the Hotel Sofiyivka (p96) near the park entrance. As it turns out, Sofia broke Felix's heart before he died, having an affair with his son.

The park is about a 10-minute walk from central Uman, down vul Sadova. Services in the park, including the ticket booth, run only from 9am until 6pm (until 8pm on Fridays and Saturdays). At other times, entrance to the park is free.

Uman Fountain FOUNTAIN

(vul Nezalezhnosti; ⏲9pm-10.30pm) FREE Move over, Vinnytsya (p97): there's a new fountain in the 'hood. Uman's is not as gigantic or as hyped as the one that illuminates the Pivdenny Buh to the west, but it is more original – a sound, light and water show that presents dramatic Ukrainian-themed vignettes via hologram in a wall of spray. The Friday, Saturday and Sunday shows are the ones to see; weekday shows are watered down, so to speak. By necessity it shuts down in the cold months.

Rabbi Nachman's Tomb TOMB

(vul Pushkina) Rabbi Nachman (1772–1810) was the 18th-century sage who founded the Breslov branch of Hasidism. Tens of thousands of Jewish pilgrims flock to Uman every Jewish New Year (Rosh Hashana), but at any time of year you'll find devout Jewish devotees praying at his grave site, home to the **Breslov World Center**. To visit, head towards Sofiyivka Park from the centre and about halfway down vul Sadova, turn right onto vul Pushkina and proceed 600m.

Sleeping & Eating

Most Uman residents rent out their flats to pilgrims for Rosh Hashana. Forget about visiting during that time. If you want to see the spectacle, do so as a day trip.

PILGRIMS FLOCK TO CENTRAL UKRAINE

Ever since the death of Rabbi Nachman (1772–1810), Jewish pilgrims have flocked to his graveside in Uman every Rosh Hashana (Jewish New Year) to pay homage to this 18th-century sage who founded the Breslov branch of Hasidism.

The rabbi was born in Medzhybizh, made his name in Bratslav (Breslov), near Vinnytsya, and died of tuberculosis in Uman at the young age of 38. On his deathbed, Nachman promised his followers that he would save and protect anyone who came to pray beside his tomb. Today up to 40,000 Jews answer his call at Rosh Hashana, and at any time of year you'll find a handful of devout worshippers – male and female – praying at his grave site.

Pilgrimages also take place to the grave of the Baal Shem Tov (Besht), Rabbi Nachman's grandfather and the founder of Hasidism, in Medzhybizh; to Levi Yitzhak's grave in Berdychiv; and to Bratslav.

Hotel Uman HOTEL **$**

(Готель Умань; ☎04744-46 999; www.hotel-uman.com.ua; vul Nebesnoi Sotni 7; economy/standard r 240/420uah, ste from 720uah;) You would expect much, much worse for these prices. The rooms are well attended to by Stakhanovite maids and the location is as central as it gets. One of Ukraine's true bargains, although it is worth springing for a standard room.

Hotel Sofiyivka HOTEL **$**

(Готель Софіївка; ☎04744-335 27; vul Sadova 53; d/ste 350/550uah) The best thing about this place is the atrium that doubles as a museum of 18th-century marble sculpture. The sculptures of Plato, Alexander the Great and others were the originals from Sofiyivka Park (p95). Unfortunately it all goes downhill from there – think barely renovated Soviet fare – but is nonetheless good value if you want to be right next to the park.

Pan Kaban UKRAINIAN **$**

(Пан Кабан; ☎063 807 7854; vul Nebesnoi Sotni 4; mains 60-100uah;) The best all-around option in Uman, with a faux-country interior and a broad and busy summer terrace. It's English-challenged, so dial up *shashlyk* (kebabs) or point to something on the pizza picture menu. Groups of three should order the *Khosper Nabir* – a collection of grilled meat, veggies and *lavash* (flat bread) on a bread board.

Nightly live synthesiser music incurs a 20uah per person surcharge.

Bel Canto ITALIAN **$**

(vul Sadova 20; mains 60-120uah; 10am-11pm;) This Italian place sits halfway between the centre and Sofiyivka Park, serving the best pizzas in town along with soups, well-presented salads and some Ukrainian dishes.

Getting There & Away

Uman is located 210km south of Kyiv and 280km north of Odesa. Autolux (www.autolux.ua) and Günsel (www.gunsel.com.ua) buses to Odesa pass through Uman and are the most comfortable way to go, but these generally drop you off on the highway, requiring a 4km taxi ride into town. One Günsel bus terminates at Uman's **bus station** (Автовокзал; vul Kyivska), 2km north of the centre.

Marshrutky to/from the capital's Avtostantsiya Kyiv drop off and pick up passengers right in the centre of town at vul Nebesnoi Sotni 8 (120uah, three hours, hourly).

Regular old public buses to Kyiv, Vinnytsya (110uah, 3½ hours) and Odesa (175 to 200uah, five hours) depart every one to two hours from the bus station, and there are two night buses to Kamyanets-Podilsky (200uah, seven hours).

Vinnytsya Вінниця

☎0432 / POP 372,700

Straddling a kink in the Pivdenny Buh River, Vinnytsya is a city that's come on in leaps and bounds in recent years. Commendably digestible museums, great-value hotels, a tourist office and quaint little trams (bought secondhand from Zurich) make this one of the more user-friendly regional centres in Ukraine.

The city plays host to the embalmed body of a renowned Russian doctor, a notorious Hitler bunker and a celebrity dancing fountain, but its true appeal lies in its city centre, where several churches, a park and a pleasant pedestrian street compete for your attention.

Sights

★ Avtomotovelofototeleradio Museum
MUSEUM

(Автомотовелофототелерадио Музей; vul Soborna 1; adult/student 30/20uah; ⏲11am-8pm) Big name for a small museum but worthwhile for anyone with a wistful soft spot for the days of Soviet mass production. This octagonal building near the main bridge over the river (on the city-centre side) houses some wonderful Soviet classic cars (Trabant, Zaporozhets, Moskvich, Lada), as well as clunky old Soviet TVs, radios, gramophones, cameras and other assorted junk.

Roshen Fountain
FOUNTAIN

(Фонтан Рошен; www.roshen.com; nab Roshen; ⏲shows 9pm Apr-Oct) FREE Ukraine's original big-time spray show (since 2011), the Roshen Fountain lights up the Pivdenny Buh River every night in the mild months. Built by the Roshen chocolate company next to its shiny new factory (billionaire owner Petro Poroshenko, Ukraine's Willy Wonka before he became president, was brought up in Vinnytsya), it's the biggest floating fountain in Europe. It features lasers, holograms and dozens of water jets – a truly amazing spectacle when in full *son-et-lumière* mode.

Crowds pack Vinnytsia Quay to watch the free spectacle – show up early if you want a good seat. Vinnytsya's biggest water feature warms up and flexes its muscles during the day, but it's well worth sticking around until 9pm to see the full one-hour spectacle – which happens every night but is bigger and bolder on weekends.

Vinnytsya's fountain has started a trend, with similarly grand fountain shows opening in Uman (p95) and on maydan Nezalezhnosti in Kyiv in recent years.

Pirogov Church-Mausoleum
TOMB

(Церква-некрополь Пирогова; www.pirogov.com.ua; vul Pyrogova 195; adult/student incl tour 30/15uah; ⏲9am-5.30pm Tue-Thu, 10am-6.30pm Fri-Sun; 🚌7, marshrutka 29) The second-most famous embalmed corpse in the former Soviet Union (after Lenin in Moscow) rests in the basement of a chapel in the suburb of Pyrohove about 7km southwest of central Vinnytsya. Nikolai Pirogov was a Russian medical pioneer who invented a type of cast as well as a revolutionary anaesthesia technique. His wife had him embalmed and laid to rest here in 1881. Without question one of Ukraine's oddest sites.

Visiting the body requires a tour and you may have to wait around for a few minutes until a few more people show up. The body is said to be much better preserved than Lenin's younger corpse.

Maydan Nezalezhnosti
MONUMENT

(vul Soborna) Vinnytsya's epicentre is maydan Nezalezhnosti (Independence Sq), where major demonstrations and meetings take place. A rather inconspicuous **monument** on its western side honours the Orange Revolution in 2004, when major protests took place here.

War Veterans Museum
MUSEUM

(Музей пам'яті воїнів Вінниччини; vul Ovodova 20; adult/student 10/5uah; ⏲10am-6pm Tue-Sun) The red-brick clock tower on pedestrian vul Ovodova houses an interesting museum where you'll find tributes to the 167 young local men who made the ultimate sacrifice in the Soviet-Afghan War.

Pirogov Garden-Museum
MUSEUM

(Музей-Садиба Пирогова; vul Pyrogova 155; adult/student 50/25uah; ⏲9am-5.30pm Tue-Thu, 10am-6.30pm Fri-Sun; 🚌7, marshrutka 29) About 1.5km before you get to the chapel containing Pirogov's body, you can see his house, now a museum. It's actually more interesting than you'd expect, and not just because of the Soviet character of the place (the Soviets claimed Pirogov as a hero many years after his death, because his inventions saved countless lives in the world wars). The doctor's anatomical sketches are also quite interesting, and one room remains unchanged from the surgeon's era.

Regional Museum
MUSEUM

(Краєзнавчий музей; vul Soborna 19; adult/student 20/10uah; ⏲10am-6pm Tue-Sun) This large and diverse museum is well worth an hour or two for its interesting archaeological artefacts, bug-eyed taxidermy and large WWII exhibition with Soviet propaganda posters galore. Other highlights include a 30,000-year-old mammoth skeleton, pieces of Scythian gold ornament and some Scythian-era stone figures.

Immediately next to it is the **Regional Art Museum**, which has a few gems such as a Malevich and a Repin and – somewhat shockingly – English-speaking staff to show you around.

WEHRWOLF

Between May 1942 and July 1943, Adolf Hitler paid several visits (accounts vary) to his regional military headquarters in a vast bunker 8km north Vinnytsya. Code-named Wehrwolf, it was a top-secret facility under the protection of the Fuhrer's personal escort battalion. The Germans blew the whole place up on their retreat in 1944, and for decades it lay derelict. Now it has been turned into a fantastic walking museum, where informative signboards guide you through this disturbing period of history.

At its peak the Wehrwolf complex consisted of three bunkers and 20 standing structures, complete with swimming pool, movie theatre and casino. The Germans grew 800 trees here – the forest that remains today – to hide the place, and surrounded the compound with anti-aircraft positions.

More than 4000 people worked on building the ambitious facility, among them Ukrainian and German civilians, German troops and prisoners of war. Hitler reportedly ordered all of them executed, ostensibly because he was worried that they would spill the beans about the bunker's location.

There's not much to see of the bunkers themselves, which consist mainly of tangled, semi-submerged heaps of concrete and steel reinforcing rods. The attraction is the walk and the whiff of history. There's an enclosed museum wing near the entrance with rare pictures of the complex being built and disturbing photos of Nazi atrocities. It's worth springing for the audio guide.

To get here take bus 138 bound for Stryzhavka and alight at the 'Camping' (Kemping) stop. It's a 1km walk from the highway to the entrance. Or take a taxi (about 150uah return).

Sleeping

★Vin Hostel HOSTEL $

(☎0432-507 316; www.vinhostel.com.ua; vul Soborna 46A; dm 150uah; ❄📶) The Vin is everything you'd want in a hostel: beautiful bunk beds with personal sockets and lights; a big, bright kitchen and common area outfitted with bean-bag chairs, a long laptop-friendly desk and a massive TV. Oh yeah, and an absolutely perfect central location on pedestrian vul Ovodova.

★Hotel France HOTEL $$

(☎0432-558 888; www.hotelfrance.com.ua; vul Soborna 34; incl breakfast s 1000uah, d1200-1400uah, ste 2000-3000uah; ❄@📶) Such a fine hotel, really, and at this price? You'll almost feel guilty paying so little. While on the small side, rooms include all amenities and the beds are downy nests. They also have about the best service in central Ukraine, with smiling, fluent English-speaking staff. There's a big buffet breakfast spread in the adjoining Mount Blanc restaurant.

Park Hotel HOTEL $$

(Парк Готель; ☎0432-675 844; vul Hrushevskoho 28; incl breakfast r 600-900uah, ste 1250uah; 🚭❄📶) While not fancy, the 15 rooms at this small hotel above a **pizza place** represent good value, and the location near the water tower on central Yevropeyska pl is primo. The decor is a touch over the top (giraffe-print carpets, lime-green curtains) but everything is well maintained and spotless. Staff speak little English.

Vinnytsya Hotel HOTEL $$

(Вінниця Готель; ☎0432-610 332; vul Soborna 69; incl breakfast s/d 590/790uah, ste 1120uah; 📶) A member of the once prestigious Savoy group, the Vinnytsya at 50 rooms is downright intimate for a former Soviet hotel. Rooms have high ceilings and are clean and comfortable, if cheaply renovated and tacky. But overall it's a good value, especially with breakfast thrown in.

Eating

There's a good **Silpo supermarket** (Сільпо; Sky Park shopping centre, vul Ovodova; ⏰8am-11pm) buried deep within the unexpectedly upmarket Sky Park shopping centre.

★Biblioteka Cafe CAFE $

(Бібліотека; vul Ovodova 32; mains 40-100uah; ⏰9.30am-11pm; ❄📶) This funky little cafe on Vinnytsya's central walking strip has plenty going for it: bold English and German breakfasts, scrumptious thin-crust pizza, fresh salads and a delightful summer terrace. Inside the restaurant proper, with walls plastered in book covers, a hip alternative playlist hums.

Tamero INTERNATIONAL **$$**
(☎0432-562 929; www.tamero.com.ua; vul Teatralna 24; mains 50-200uah; ⏲11am to midnight; ❄📶) Popular Tamero is a bright restaurant with a menu that leans Italian, an outdoor terrace with blankets for when it gets cool, and a unique circular design. The remarkably affordable steaks and osso buco are the highlights, but there is an impressive range of seafood, ravioli filled several ways, and of course pizzas.

They have three **rooms** available upstairs with racy photos on the wall. They are extremely comfortable and almost absurdly affordable (450uah to 700uah).

Masai Mara CAFE **$$**
(Масаї Мара; vul Hrushevskoho 70; mains 50-130uah; ⏲9am-11pm Mon-Fri, 10am-11pm Sat & Sun; ❄📶) One of a handful of places along vul Hrushevskoho in the centre, this funky coffeehouse at the gates to Vinnytsya's central park has an African theme (think cave drawings and lots of rough-hewn wood), but the menu of light meals is firmly Eurasian. The outdoor seating draws a crowd in the evenings.

Drinking & Nightlife

Lviv Handmade Chocolates CAFE
(Львівська Майстерня Шоколаду; vul Hrushevskoho 28; ⏲9am-11pm; 📶) We're not sure what local chocolate giant Roshen thinks about this national chain on its turf, but the people of Vinnytsya sure seem to appreciate its presence on central Yevropeyska pl. Trademark melted-chocolate drinks and coffee are the favourites.

Hungry Duck BAR
(vul Pyrohovo 2; ⏲2pm to 2am; 📶) Named after an old Moscow institution (though the bartenders claimed to have never heard of it), this is about as good a bar as you'll find in the centre. It's a dark bar with modern rock playing, a longish bar and booths to hide in. Not flashy but reliable.

Shopping

Roshen FOOD
(vul Soborna 22; ⏲9am-8pm) As well as selling mouthwatering slabs of chocolate and other tooth-rotting goodies, the central Vinnytsya branch of hometown chocolatier Roshen has a fun mechanical puppet show in the window.

Information

Tourist Office (☎0432-508 585; Vinnytsya Tower, vul Ovodova 20; ⏲10am-7pm) Covering Vinnytsya and all of Podillya, the tourist office can help you get to sights outside the city as well as supplying free maps and other information. Also can arrange tour guides who speak English, Polish or Italian for about 250uah per hour.

Getting There & Away

BUS

Most services leave from the **Central bus station** (Центральний Автовокзал; ☎0432-671 342; vul Kyivska 8). Destinations include the following:

Berdychiv 54uah, 1¾ hours, at least two hourly
Bratslav 47uah, 1½ hours, hourly
Kyiv 200uah, 4½ hours, 10 daily
Uman 110uah, 3½ hours, seven daily
Zhytomyr 37uah, 2¾ hours, at least two hourly

Most western destinations are better served from the **West bus station** (Західний Автовокзал; ☎0432-464 891; Khmelnytske shose 107), 5km west of the centre. Destinations include the following:

Lviv 220uah, 7¾ hours, two daily
Kamyanets-Podilsky 150uah, 4½ hours, four daily
Sharhorod 50uah, 1½ hours, every 30 to 60 minutes

TRAIN

Vinnytsya is a major stop for many east–west trains and north–south trains, including some international services.

The quickest and most comfortable way to Kyiv from the **train station** (☎0432-632 311; pl Pryvokzalna) are the twice-daily intercity trains (200uah, 2½ hours).

There are at least five services to Lviv (from 110uah, seven hours) including an intercity service (275uah, 4½ hours), and five to Odesa (from 100uah, six to seven hours), including an intercity (240uah, 4¾ hours).

There are two daily trains to Kamyanets-Podilsky (100uah, 4½ hours) and a night train to Chernivtsi (from 175uah, 8½ hours).

Getting Around

Both the bus and train stations are on the east side of the river – the central bus station is near the main bridge, while the train station is 2km east of the bridge.

From the train station, trams 1, 4 and 6, or trolleybuses 5 and 11 take you into the centre along vul Soborna.

If arriving by bus, turn left out of the Central bus station and walk 200m out to busy pr Kotsyubynskoho. From here you can walk west over the bridge into the city centre, or turn left (east), walk 400m to the nearest bus stop and take any trolleybus or tram into the centre.

Around Vinnytsya

Bratslav & Sharhorod

South of Vinnytsya are two interesting side trips to Jewish heritage sites. The village of **Bratslav**, 60km southeast of Vinnytsya, is where Rabbi Nachman lived and wrote most of his teachings before moving to Uman. Nachman's chief disciple, Nathan of Breslov, is buried in a shrine-like tomb in Bratslav's Jewish cemetery, on a hill overlooking a river. Jewish pilgrims allege that Nathan's grave has healing powers and they flock here by the score. The grave aside, it's hard to imagine a more idyllic, bucolic place than this. Locals gather to picnic and wash their horses in the river next to a partially abandoned, century-old brick hydropower plant.

Southwest of Vinnytsya is the *shtetl* town of **Sharhorod**. The *shtetl* originated in Ukraine and the one in Sharhorod is said to be the best-preserved example in the country. But sadly it's dying, as many of the rustic old houses in the Jewish quarter have been torn down in recent years. However, a few attractive old specimens still stand, as does the shuttered-up 16th-century fortress synagogue (used as a liquor factory in Soviet times). From the post office head south on vul Lenina into the Old Town. The synagogue is a little ways beyond a peach-coloured Orthodox church. The old *shtetl* emanates west from the synagogue.

Sharhorod also has a sprawling Jewish cemetery with hundreds of exquisitely carved tombstones, a few dating as far back as the 18th century. To find it, follow the lane to the right of the post office down the hill and to the left. You'll see the cemetery on a hill off in the distance and should be able to follow your nose there. A Christian shrine has been built just beneath the cemetery gates, which are marked by three large stars of David.

Both Bratslav and Sharhorod are served by frequent buses from Vinnytsya. Either can be made into a side trip en route to Kamyanets-Podilsky.

Medzhybyzh

The town of Medzhybyzh makes an excellent day trip out of Vinnytsya, 85km to the east, or a stopover en route to Lviv. It's best known as a Jewish pilgrimage site, but it also possesses delightful rural charm and a mighty 16th-century fortress.

The impressive **Medzhybyzh Fortress** (www.mezhibozh.com; vul Zamkova 1, Medzhybyzh; territory 25uah, museums 20uah; ⏲9am-5pm, to 6pm Sat & Sun) stands proudly at the confluence of the Pivdenny Buh and Buzhok Rivers. Inside its gently crumbling courtyard are an Orthodox church and a clutch of museums, including an interesting ethnography museum and a moving museum devoted to the *Holodomor* (Stalin-induced famine). You can climb up to the ramparts for scenic vistas. Outside the fortress is a statue of Ustym Karmalyuk, a Ukrainian Robin Hood and a notorious neighbourhood troublemaker in the early 19th century.

Medzhybyzh is where Hasidic master Rabbi Nachman (p96) was born and where Nachman's great-grandfather, the Baal Shem Tov, founder of Hasidic Judaism, is buried. The latter's tomb, frequented by pilgrims, is in the town's Jewish cemetery – turn right 500m beyond the fortress, just past a turquoise neoclassical building.

Any train or bus (both frequent) between Khmelnytsky and Vinnytsya will stop in Medzhybyzh.

Kamyanets-Podilsky

Кам'янець-Подільський

☎03849 / POP 100,500

Kamyanets-Podilsky is the sort of place that has writers lunging for their thesauruses in search of superlatives. Even words like 'dramatic', 'stunning' and 'breathtaking' just will not do. The town is located where a sharp loop in a river has formed a natural moat. The wide tree-lined Smotrych River canyon is 40m to 50m deep, leaving the 11th-century Old Town standing clearly apart on a tall, sheer-walled rock 'island', connected by a narrow isthmus to its impossibly picturesque fortress.

Kamyanets-Podilsky is really a tale of two cities – the noisy and slightly chaotic New Town, where the bus station and most commercial business are located, and the quieter Old Town, where all of the sights are gathered. The bulk of your time will invariably be spent in the Old Town, but the New Town has plenty of restaurants, nice parks and interesting early 20th-century Russian and Soviet architecture.

History

Named after the stone on which it sits, Kamyanets-Podilsky existed as early as the 11th century as a Kyivan Rus settlement. Like much of western Ukraine, the town spent periods under Lithuanian and Polish rule, with the latter dominating from the 15th to 17th centuries.

The Ottoman Turks were a constant threat. According to an oft-told legend, when the Turkish Sultan Osman arrived to attack the town in 1621, he asked one of his generals, 'Who has built such a mighty town?' 'Allah', came the reply, to which the Sultan responded, 'Then let Allah himself conquer it', and bid a hasty retreat. A half-century later the Ottomans would finally take the town, conquering it with a tremendous army in 1672. But they would rule only for 27 years.

After being returned to Polish rule, Kamyanets-Podilsky was conquered in 1793 by the Russians. They used its fortress as a prison for Ukrainian nationalists. In 1919 the town became the temporary capital of the short-lived Ukrainian National Republic. During WWII the Germans used the Old Town as a Jewish ghetto, where an estimated 85,000 people died. Intensive fighting and air raids destroyed some 70% of the Old Town.

Sights

★Kamyanets-Podilsky Fortress — FORTRESS

(Кам'янець-Подільська фортеця; vul Zamkova; adult/child 40/20uah; 9am-7pm, to 6pm Mon) Built of wood in the 10th to 13th centuries, then redesigned and rebuilt in stone by Italian military engineers in the 16th century, K-P's fortress is a mishmash of styles. But the overall impression is breathtaking and the view from the **Turkish Bridge** leading to the fortress would certainly make a short list of Ukraine's most iconic front-page vistas. The fortress is filled with museums and cafes, and in the summer concerts frequently take place in its vast courtyard.

The fortress is in the shape of a polygon, with nine towers of all shapes and sizes linked by a sturdy wall surrounding the courtyard.

The **New East Tower** (1544) is directly to your right as you enter the fortress and contains a well and a huge winch stretching 40m deep through the cliff to bring up water. On your right, stairs lead downwards to the debtors' hole, where locals behind in loan repayments were kept until their debt was covered. Next to the debtors' hole is the Papska (Pope's) or **Karmalyuk Tower** (1503–17), which was used as a prison. The wax figure inside is Ustym Karmalyuk, a loveable rogue who, legend has it, was so handsome that women tossed strands of hair down to him. He eventually accumulated enough hair to make a rope and escape one of his three incarcerations here between 1817 and 1823.

Walk toward the back of the courtyard and look for a white building on the right. This houses a fantastic **museum** that romps through the history of K-P and Ukraine over the last century in a jumble of nostalgia-inducing exhibits. The Euromaidan revolution is covered by a symbolic eternal flame with names and photos of victims.

Behind the fortress to the west are the remains of the largely earthen **New Fortress** (vul Zamkova).

Cathedral of Saints Peter & Paul — CHURCH

(vul Starobulvarna) The Old Town's most prominent church perfectly illustrates how the Polish and Turkish empires collided in Kamyanets-Podilsky. Built in 1580 by the Catholic Poles, the Turks took over in the late 17th century, converted it into a mosque and built a 42m-high minaret. When the town was handed back to the Poles by treaty in 1699, the Turks stipulated that the minaret could not be dismantled. So the Poles topped it with a 3.5m-tall golden statue of the Virgin Mary.

Behind the church is is a **statue of Pope John Paul II** and, about 50m beyond the pope, an **overlook** with spectacular views of the K-P fortress.

Kamyanets-Podilsky

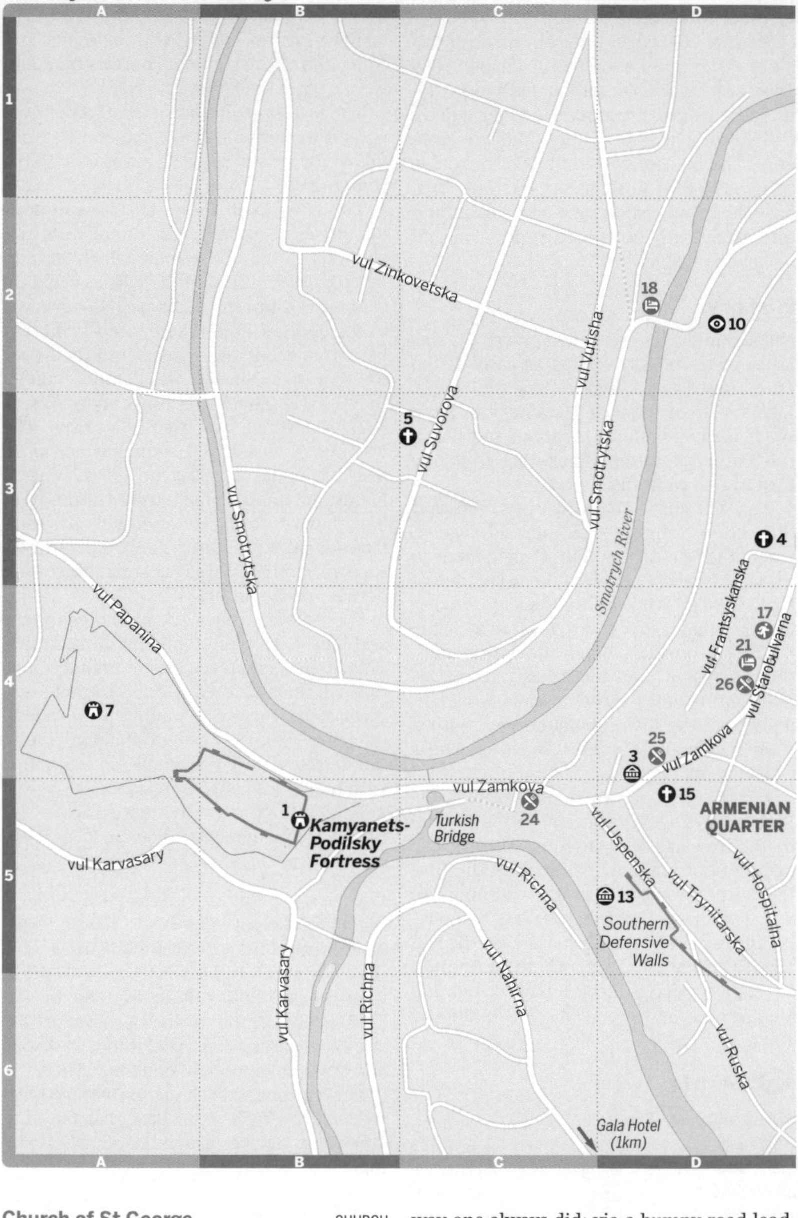

Church of St George CHURCH

(Церква Св Юрія) The historic Polish section is dominated by the 19th-century Orthodox Church of St George, with its five spires painted a brilliant azure. One gets here the way one always did: via a bumpy road leading down from the Vitryani (Windy) Gate (p105) in the northwest section of the Old Town.

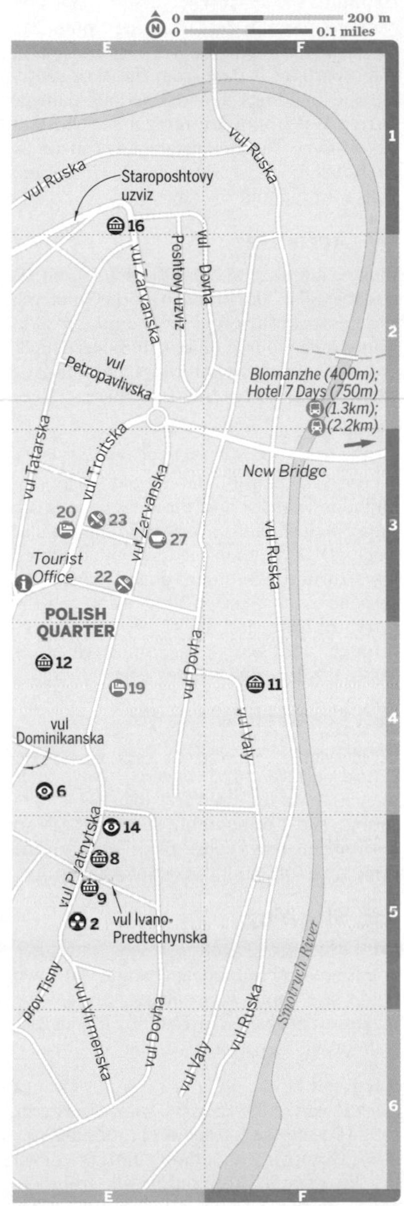

Kamyanets-Podilsky

Top Sights
1 Kamyanets-Podilsky Fortress B5

Sights
2 Armenian Church E5
3 Castles in Miniature Museum D4
4 Cathedral of Saints Peter & Paul D3
5 Church of St George C3
6 Dominican Monastery E4
7 New Fortress A4
8 Picture Gallery E5
9 Podillya Antiquities Museum E5
10 Polish Gate D2
11 Potters' Tower F4
12 Ratusha E4
13 Ruska Gate D5
14 Russian Magistrate E5
15 St Jehoshaphat's Church D5
16 Vitryani (Windy) Gate E1

Activities, Courses & Tours
17 BRDM Rides D4

Sleeping
18 Bilya Richky D2
19 Hetman E4
20 Kleopatra E3
21 Reikartz Kamyanets-Podilsky D4

Eating
22 Front E3
23 Hostynny Dvir E3
24 Kafe Pid Bramoyu C5
25 Kava Vid Politsmeystera D4
26 Nika D4

Drinking & Nightlife
27 Kav'yarnya na Zarvansky E3

Ratusha HISTORIC BUILDING
(Ратуша; pl Polsky Rynok 1; museums 35uah; ⌚9am-5pm, to 4pm Mon) Polish Market Sq is lorded over by the tall 14th-century Ratusha (Town Hall). The renovated peach-hued building now houses three modest museums. Most interesting is the **medieval justice museum** in the basement, with some displays on crude torture techniques. The other museums are devoted to coins and the Magdeburg legal system. In front of the Ratusha stands the enclosed **Armenian well** (Вірменська криниця; 1638), which looks more like a baroque chapel.

There's a decent **cafe** out front that's a great place for a cold beer on a warm day.

Podillya Antiquities Museum MUSEUM
(vul Ivano-Predtechynska 2; 10uah, tour in English 80uah; ⌚9am-5pm, to 4pm Mon) This imaginatively presented museum with English explanations takes visitors through the archaeology of Podillya in six easy steps.

You begin in a Stone Age cave and end in a courtyard of sculpted Slavic gods, passing through Trypillian, Scythian and early Slav dwellings along the way. Recent archaeological finds are scattered about the courtyard, which is overlooked by the reconstructed defensive bell tower of a 15th-century **Armenian church** (vul Virmenska), otherwise in ruins.

Slavophiles will appreciate the exhibit on the Glagolitic script (forerunner to today's Cyrillic alphabet).

Castles in Miniature Museum MUSEUM
(Музей мініатюр "Замки України"; www.castle-museum.info; vul Zamkova; adult/child 40/30uah; ⌚9am-10pm) If you don't have time to go castle-hopping around central and western Ukraine, here is your chance to see miniature models of 14 Ukrainian castles, including nearby Khotyn and Medzhybyzh castles.

St Jehoshaphat's Church CHURCH
(vul Starobulvarna) Heading towards the fortress along the main drag through the Old Town, you'll pass this baroque 18th-century Greek Catholic church (formerly St Trinity's), fronted by sculptures of two saints who appear to be boogieing on down. The interior is disappointingly plain.

Russian Magistrate NOTABLE BUILDING
(Російський магістрат; vul Pyatnytska 9) There are some interesting old buildings on vul Pyatnytska, which branches off Armenian Market Sq. The large structure with a distinctive metal dragon projecting from its facade is the old Russian Magistrate, now the headquarters of NIAZ Kamyanets (www.niazkamenec.org.ua), the body overseeing K-P's conservation area (which seems to have had limited success of late!). Closed to the public.

Picture Gallery GALLERY
(Картинна галерея; vul Pyatnytska 11; adult/student 20/10uah; ⌚9am-5pm, to 4pm Mon) The pieces on display are only a small fraction of the permanent collection, which includes some 60,000 works of art and thousands of other artefacts. They are rotated through here. Most impressive is the Great Hall, filled with 19th-century portraits and sculptures, plus some priceless original furniture from the same period. Temporary exhibitions are often worth checking out.

Dominican Monastery MONASTERY
(vul Dominikanska) You'll find the Dominican Monastery complex on vul Dominikanska; some parts of it date from the 14th century. The buildings suffered serious damage during WWII and are now under constant restoration. The monastery **Church of St Nicholas** holds services in Ukrainian and Polish throughout the day.

Activities

Bungee jumping (about 300uah per jump) is possible off a 70m bridge over the Smotrych River just southwest of town on the road to Khotyn. The tourist office (p106) has details, or just show up on Saturdays and Sundays, when it's a good bet they'll be there.

BRDM Rides CRUISE
(☎097 393 6266; www.brdm.in.ua; vul Troitska; per person 200uah) BRDM are old Soviet amphibious vehicles and these excursions are Kamyanets-Podilsky's answer to the popular Duck (DUKW) tours of the United States. It's a thrilling 1½ hours during which you descend steep Staroposhtovy uzviz via the Vitryany Gate and make several plunges through and across the Smotrych River (more thrilling when water levers are up!).

Festivals & Events

Kamyanets-Podilsky City Day FIESTA
(⌚mid-May) Features concerts, folk performances, parades, fireworks displays and, of course, acres of souvenir stalls. A **balloon festival** usually takes place around the same time (often on the same weekend).

Sleeping

K-P's hotel scene evolves slowly. New Town hotels are generally cheaper while Old Town hotels are more atmospheric (and by no means expensive!). The New Town is an easy walk or bus ride away from the Old Town.

Bilya Richky HOTEL $
(Біля Річки; ☎097 258 1734; www.hotel-kp.com.ua; vul Onufrievska 5; d 400-600uah, ste 1000uah; ❄📶) Occupying an almost rural spot down by the river, a 10-minute walk from the Polish Market Sq, this family-run hotel has just 14 timber-rich rooms and cosy dining pavilions on a babbling brook. Owners can arrange horse-riding trips, English-language tours of K-P and full board. Breakfast is a very reasonable 20uah extra.

The Polish Gate stands opposite and an anonymous chunk of the city's old defences forms part of the grounds.

Gala Hotel HOTEL $

(Гала Готель; ☎03849-383 70; www.gala-hotel.com; vul Lesi Ukrainky 84; incl breakfast s 400-580uah, d 460-740uah, apt 1100uah;) With clay tennis courts, a bowling alley and a fitness centre, this New Town hotel in an impressive neoclassical building caters to sporty types. The simple rooms are more suited for team lodging than for tourists seeking comfort, but are functional enough and most certainly cheap, and you can upgrade to an apartment with kitchenette.

It's about a 1.5km walk or taxi ride south of the New Bridge.

★Kleopatra HOTEL $$

(☎03849-906 98; www.kleopatra-kp.com; vul Troitska 2; r/ste incl breakfast from 900/1500uah;) The Kleopatra is almost unimaginable value, right in the middle of the Old Town. Even the cheapest rooms are spacious affairs with foyers, luggage racks, big flat screens, easy chairs and plush bathrobes and lines. The price includes an hour of **bowling** in their basement lanes, and there's a small indoor pool. About the only thing lagging is the service.

Reikartz Kamyanets-Podilsky HOTEL $$

(☎03849-916 35; www.reikartz.com; vul Starobulvarna 2; s/d incl breakfast from 975/1220uah;) A cushy place by K-P standards, the Reikartz occupies a former Polish palace in the thick of the Old Town. The plush emerald-green carpets and elaborate bedspreads seem tailored for the Polish *szlachta* (nobility), but rooms are on the small side. Service is tops in town, however, and there's a fitness centre and sauna.

Hetman HOTEL $$

(Гетьман; ☎03849-907 37; www.hetman-hotel.com.ua; Polsky Rynok 8; d/tr 600/700uah; @) With a great location on Polish Market Sq and easygoing staff, this atmospheric, 14-room theme hotel is a great place to lay your head. The rooms vary in style and size so check out a few, but all are plenty comfortable. The corridors are lined with paintings of Ukraine's *hetmans* (Cossack chieftains).

The **restaurant** serves five types of *borshch*.

AND THERE'S MORE...

Most visitors content themselves with a stroll from the New Bridge to the fortress and back, stopping off at a restaurant or cafe along the way. But if your legs are up to the job, there's so much more to explore in Kamyanets-Podilsky's run-down backstreets and lanes where forgotten chunks of the town's defences lurk.

Looking south from the New Bridge you can spot the 1583 **Potters' Tower** (Гончарська башта; vul Ruska), so named because it was looked after by the town's potters. Twelve of these towers once lined the bank of the gorge along the perimeter of the island; seven or eight remain today.

At the northern edge of the Old Town is the still-functioning 16th-century **Vitryani (Windy) Gate** (Вітряна брама; Staroposhtovy uzviz), where Peter the Great's hat blew off in 1711. Connected to the gate is the seven-storey stone **Kushnir (Furriers') Tower** (Кушнірська башта), a defensive structure funded by artisans who lived nearby. From the tower, Staroposhtovy uzviz turns southwest and descends steeply into the ravine down to the **Polish Gate** (Польська брама; Staroposhtovy uzviz). This gate was named after the historic Polish section of the city, which was located on the other side of the river, built around the hill dominated by the 19th-century Orthodox **Church of St George** (p102), with its five spires painted a brilliant azure.

Both the Polish Gate and the **Ruska Gate** (Руська брама; vul Ruska), on the south side of the isthmus in the old Ruthenian (Ukrainian) quarter, were built from the 16th to 17th centuries to guard the two most vulnerable entrances into the Old Town. Both gates were ingeniously fashioned with dike mechanisms that could alter the flow of the Smotrych River and flood the entrances – an impressive engineering feat for the time.

Just across the river from the fortress stands the **Khrestovozdvyzhenska Church** (Хрестовоздвиженська церква), K-P's only remaining timber temple dating from 1799.

Hotel 7 Days HOTEL $$
(☎03849-690 69; www.7dniv.ua; vul Soborna 4; incl breakfast s/d from 420/520uah, ste 1100uah; ❄📶🏊) This popular 218-room Soviet hotel in the heart of the New Town is surprisingly decent, starting with the air-conditioned, design-style lobby and the modern street-side cafe, and continuing on up to the rooms, which are tidy and bright if somewhat small and cheaply renovated. Rates include use of the large indoor swimming pool and fitness centre.

Eating

Kamyanets-Podilsky's food scene has taken strides in recent years, as several newcomers have overtaken the staid old standbys. English menus are surprisingly rare here so bone up on your Ukrainian food terms.

★Front CAFE $
(☎098 498 2817; vul Zarvanska 20; mains 35-60uah; ⏲10am-11pm; ❄📶) New in 2017, this classy eatery is in the conversation for best Old Town restaurant. Sit upstairs in the bright cafe proper with throwback murals of old Kamyanets, or downstairs in the Gothic dungeon with its vaulted ceiling. There's no English menu, unfortunately; classics like *borshch* and *varenyky* are available, or try grilled *skumbriya* (mackerel) or a *steyk* (steak).

Nika UKRAINIAN $
(Ніка; vul Starobulvarna 4; 50-90uah; ⏲8am-11pm; 📶) Probably the best restaurant in the Old Town. You can dine on the comfortable outdoor terrace (warm months only) or head upstairs to eat amid intricately carved pine wood. *Deruny*, *varenyky* and creamy Ukrainian meat dishes like *ryba u gorshchyku* (fish in a pot) highlight the menu.

Kafe Pid Bramoyu UKRAINIAN $
(Кафе під брамою; vul Zamkova 1A; mains 50-90uah; ⏲9am-midnight) Located in the 17th-century casemates near the fortress, this is the town's most characterful place to fill the hole, even if service is practically non-existent. There are a couple of dining areas, a terrace with pretty views and wait staff in folksy Ukrainian garb. The menu is a run-down of national favourites.

Kava Vid Politsmeystera CAFE $
(Кава від Поліцмейстера; vul Zamkova; mains 50-100uah; ⏲10am-11pm) This old town cafe serves *deruny* (potato pancakes), *pelmeni* (dumplings), *mamalyha* (Romanian corn mash) and Ukrainian soups, and has a summer terrace that is a good place for a beer after touring the fortress.

Blomanzhe INTERNATIONAL $$
(Бломанже; ☎096 503 0022; vul Uralska 4A; 60-150uah; ⏲11am-midnight; ❄📶) Pleasantly situated opposite a park in the New Town just over the New Bridge, Blomanzhe rolls out highly original seasonal specials infused with local fruits and vegetables. The compact main menu has a French bent – think tiger prawns with caviar. It's a fantastic deal, and sometimes a needed change from K-P's drumbeat of classic Ukrainian fare.

Hostynny Dvir UKRAINIAN $$
(Гостинний Двір; vul Troitska 1; mains 74-125uah; ⏲11am-11pm) Around for longer than anyone can remember remembering, this old favourite has a bearskin spreadeagled on one wall and crispy pizza that is its main saving grace. Service is virtually nonexistent; if you want to sit out on the summer terrace, you may have to head inside to locate the waitress.

Drinking & Nightlife

K-P isn't really a nightlife kind of place. Even the bowling alley at the Kleopatra hotel (p105) closes at 8pm. Several cafes fill the void admirably if you want have a few nightcaps. The fortress (p101) is a fine place for a beer or, when it gets chilly, mulled wine.

Kav'yarnya na Zarvansky CAFE
(Кав'ярня на Зарванській; vul Zarvanska 11; ⏲9am-11pm; 📶) They serve some of the best coffee in town, hot chocolate and deserts in atmospheric space punctuated by wicker chairs and black-and-white photos of old K-P. The tables on the sidewalk outside catch the afternoon sun and there's live acoustic guitar Thursday to Sunday from 7pm.

Information

Tourist Office (☎03849-255 33; vul Tatarska 14; ⏲10am-7pm Mon-Fri) Staff at this helpful office speak English and can get by in French and German. They sell universal museum passes, hand out free maps and other information, and can answer most questions you might have about transport schedules, etc.

Getting There & Away

Khotyn is only 30 minutes from Kamyanets-Podilsky by taxi (round-trip about 350uah). Shared taxis also shuttle between the K-P bus station and Khotyn Fortress (per person 40uah).

BUS

Kamyanets-Podilsky's **bus station** (Автовокзал; vul Knyaziv Koriatovychiv 19) is on the main drag about 800m east of the New Town centre. Keep in mind that the last trip coming back from Khotyn is at 6.30pm. Popular connections:

DESTINATION	COST (UAH)	TIME	FREQUENCY
Chernivtsi	70	2½hr	every 30-60min
Khotyn	17	45min	frequent
Kyiv	300	10hr	3 daily
Lviv	190	6hr	3 daily
Odesa	380	10hr	3 night buses
Vinnytsya	150	4½hr	4 daily

TRAIN

From Kyiv, express train 769 (120uah, 7½ hours), departing daily at 4.48pm with airplane-style seating, and sleeper train 139 (*platskart/kupe* 120/200uah, 8½ hours), departing on even days at 9.33pm, are the best options. Departures to Kyiv are at 12.54am (express) and 8.35pm (sleeper, odd days only). The daily Kyiv–Chernivtsi train also passes through K-P, albeit at ungodly hours.

Bus is better for all other destinations. The train station is 1km north of the bus station.

Getting Around

Handy bus or *marshrutka* 1 goes to the Old Town from the train station, via the bus station, New Town centre and the New Bridge.

Lviv & Western Ukraine
Львів і Західна Україна

POP 5.85 MILLION

Includes ➡

Best Places to Eat

- ➡ Baczewski (p127)
- ➡ Green (p126)
- ➡ Korona Vitovta (p140)
- ➡ Kupol (p127)
- ➡ Ratusha (p127)

Best Places to Stay

- ➡ Vintage (p125)
- ➡ Leopolis Hotel (p125)
- ➡ Old City Hostel (p124)
- ➡ Astoria (p125)
- ➡ Villa Stanislavsky (p124)

Why Go?

More quintessentially Ukrainian than the rest of the country, and distinctly more European, the west is all about its largest city, the Galician capital of Lviv. An emerging tourist magnet, the city is a truly captivating place, rich in historic architecture and with an indulgent coffee-house culture. Once off the beaten track, Lviv now welcomes tens of thousands of foreign tourists who fill the main square night and day. Away from the city centre piecemeal gentrification has made only small dents in its shabby authenticity.

The Soviets ruled for only 50 years here, making the west the most foreigner-friendly province with less surly 'no-can-do' bureaucracy than in eastern regions. People here speak Ukrainian (rather than Russian) and show greater pride in Ukrainian traditions than elsewhere.

Away from Lviv, the Carpathian Mountains are a short hop by bus, as are historic Lutsk, architecturally interesting Kremenets and the golden domes of Pochayiv Monastery.

When to Go

Lviv

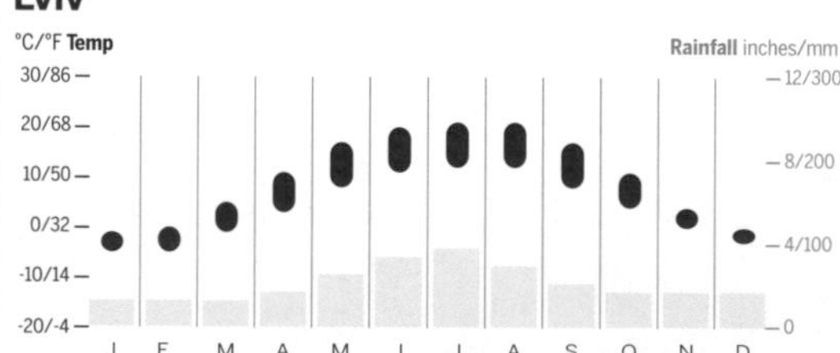

May A great time to be in Lviv with simultaneous festivals filling the early part of the month.

Aug Head for Lutsk to experience Bandershtat, one of Ukraine's top rock festivals.

Oct Visit Lviv in the atmospheric autumn when most of the tourists have left.

Lviv & Western Ukraine Highlights

1 **Lviv's historical centre** (p110) Cobble-surfing Lviv city centre packed with churches, museums and eccentric restaurants.

2 **Lychakivske Cemetery** (p110) Paying your respects to Lviv's great and good of yesteryear at the city's intriguing cemetery.

3 **Lviv's coffeehouses** (p129) Making a caffeine-and-cake halt at some of Ukraine's best cafes.

4 **Pochayiv Monastery** (p137) Joining the Orthodox faithful for a pilgrimage to find West Ukraine's most devout atmosphere.

5 **Lutsk's old quarter** (p138) Taking a turn around Lutsk's old town for a blast from western Ukraine's past.

6 **Kremenets Fortress** (p136) Heading uphill for trip-stopping views of Kremenets' many churches.

7 **Lviv's festivals** (p123) Catching a festival in Lviv – not difficult as there's something happening almost every day of the year.

History

The Mongols overrunning Kyivan Rus in 1240 never made it as far west as the powerful province of Galicia-Volynia. They did occasionally knock on its door, but the region was largely left to enjoy self-rule under King Roman Mstyslavych, his son Danylo Halytsky and his descendants.

This idyllic state was shattered in the 1340s when Polish troops invaded, but western Ukraine never lost its taste for independence. Several centuries of Polish domination saw the rise of a unique Ruthenian identity, which is the basis for much contemporary Ukrainian nationalism. Many Galician *boyars* (nobles) – often sent from Poland, Germany or Hungary – adopted the Polish language and Roman Catholicism. However, the peasants, also known as Ruthenians, remained Orthodox. They were only persuaded to join the new Ukrainian Catholic Church, also known as the Uniate Church, in 1596 (thereby acknowledging the pope's spiritual supremacy) because this church agreed to retain Orthodox forms of worship. Other Ruthenians fled southeast to set up Cossack communities.

In 1772 Galicia became part of the Habsburg Austro-Hungarian Empire and to this day western Ukrainians touchingly remember the Austrians as (relatively) liberal, tolerant rulers. In other parts of the empire separatists suffered under the Austrian yoke, but in Ukraine the Habsburgs allowed Ukrainian nationalism to re-emerge and that made them good guys in this country. Western Ukraine even enjoyed a few days' independence as the Habsburg Empire collapsed at the end of WWI, but it soon found itself again under the dreaded Polish thumb.

Following the outbreak of WWII in September 1939, things went from bad to worse in local eyes. The Red Army marched in and asserted Moscow's control over the region for the first time in history. Finally dispatching the Nazis after bloody battles during WWII, the Soviets hung around until 1991, when the USSR imploded.

Since independence, cities such as Lviv, Ternopil and Lutsk have repeatedly sent protestors to the capital when the government was deemed to be erring from the path to European civilisation. Strangely, a Ukrainian from the west is yet to hold the top job of president.

LVIV ЛЬВІВ

☎032 / POP 728,000

If you've spent time in other Ukrainian regions, Lviv will come as shock. Mysterious and architecturally lovely, this Unesco-listed city is the country's least Soviet and exudes the same authentic Central European charm as pre-tourism Prague or Kraków once did. Its quaint cobbles, bean-perfumed coffeehouses and rattling trams are a continent away from the post-Soviet badlands of the east. It's also a place where the candle of Ukrainian national identity burns brightest and where Russian is definitely a minority language.

But the secret is out, and those who foresaw that Lviv would become Ukraine's top tourist attraction are watching their prediction come true. No other city is more geared up for visitors and no other attracts so many of them. Lviv has the best range of hotels in the country, plus hostels, tour agencies, guides and English-language information abound, making this Ukraine's premier destination by a long way.

History

Lviv has had as many names as it has had rulers. It took its first name from Lev, the son of King Danylo Halytsky, who founded a hilltop fort here on present-day Castle Hill in the 13th century. When the Poles took over 100 years later, the place became known as Lwów, as it still is in Poland. Austrians called it Lemberg between the 18th and 20th centuries, and still do. The Russians, who later christened it Lvov, continue to use this historical name. Most of its names – apart from Lemberg, which has many competing origins – can be traced back to 'lion', and the city has always taken the big cat as its symbol.

Lviv had another set of unwelcome occupiers who also called the place Lemberg – the Nazis. They invaded in 1941 and they weren't driven back by the Soviets until 1944. During these three years, 136,000 people are reported to have died in Lviv's Jewish ghetto and nearly 350,000 in nearby concentration camps. The city was then swallowed up by Stalin's Soviet Union and didn't re-emerge until 1991.

The Galician capital played a major role in the movement that led to Ukrainian independence. Ukrainian nationalism and the Greek Catholic Church re-emerged here in the late 1980s, and in the early 1990s its people unanimously elected nationalist politicians and staged mass demonstrations. Lvivites played a big part in the Maydan revolution and the city now has its eyes focused firmly on Europe.

Sights

★**Lychakivsky Cemetery** CEMETERY

(Личаківський цвинтар; Map p118; ☎032 275 5415; www.lviv-lychakiv.ukrain.travel; vul Pekarska; adult/student 25/15uah; 9am-6pm Oct-Mar, to 8pm Apr-Sep; 7 tram) Don't leave town until you've seen this amazing 42ha cemetery, only a short ride on tram 7 from the centre.

This is the Père Lachaise of Eastern Europe, with the same sort of overgrown grounds and Gothic aura as the famous Parisian necropolis (but containing less-well-known people). Laid out in the late 18th century, it's packed full of western Ukraine's great and good. Pride of place goes to the grave of revered nationalist poet Ivan Franko.

Other tombs belong to Soviet gymnastics legend Viktor Chukarin, early-20th-century opera star Solomiya Krushelnytska, composer Volodymyr Ivasyuk and some 2000 Poles who died fighting Ukrainians and Bolsheviks from 1918 to 1920. There's also a memorial to the Ukrainian insurgent army (UPA), which fought for independence against both the Nazis and the Soviets, and a section for the victims of Stalin's famine in the 1930s. However, the most moving part of the cemetery contains the fresh graves of local soldiers and volunteers killed in the war with Russia in Ukraine's east, many of the plots bearing the photos of their often youthful occupants.

JEWISH LVIV

Jewish sites in Lviv may be more about what's been destroyed than what remains, but a tour through the city's rich Jewish past can still elicit a range of emotions. There were around 150,000 Jews in Lviv before WWII, not including the several thousand Jewish refugees who arrived from Germany and western Poland before the war. The Nazis murdered nearly all of them at Lviv's Janowska concentration and forced-labour camp, and at Belzec, another hideous extermination camp in present-day Poland, where, it is believed, some 600,000 people were killed and only two survived. Today Lviv's Jewish community numbers only around 2000.

Before WWII there were two Jewish districts in Lviv: a wealthy inner district around vuls Staroyevreyska (Old Jewish St), Fedorova and Ruska in the Old Town; and a larger outer district covering a vast area north and west of the Solomiya Krushelnytska Lviv Theatre of Opera and Ballet.

The late-16th-century Golden Rose Synagogue (p119) stood at the heart of the inner district before the Nazis blew it up in 1943. A wasteland for decades, the site is now occupied by a new and very moving monument to those who died. Another synagogue once stood in the open lot directly across vul Staroyevreyska.

In the outer district, you'll find the **Jewish Hospital** (Єврейська лікарня; Map p118; vul Rapporta), one of Lviv's architectural highlights. From afar this Moorish, dome-topped building looks like a mosque, but up close Jewish motifs are evident in the striking, eclectic facade. **Krakivsky Market**, right behind the hospital, was a Jewish cemetery in medieval times. Writer Sholem Aleichem lived not far away, at Kotlyarska 1, in 1906. There's a **plaque** to Aleichem on the side of the building. South of here, on vul Nalyvayka, a few old Yiddish shop signs remain. About 500m north of the Solomiya Krushelnytska Lviv Theatre of Opera and Ballet on pr Chornovola is the **Holocaust memorial** (Map p118; pr Chornovola), a vaguely cubist statue of a tormented figure looking skyward. The Lviv ghetto began here after most of the city's Jews were killed or deported to Belzec in the 'Great Action' of August 1942. Nazi hunter Simon Wiesenthal was the most famous resident of the ghetto, which was liquidated in June 1943.

The **Yanivske Cemetery** (Янівське кладовище; Map p118; vul Tarasa Shevchenka), northwest of the city centre, has a large **Jewish section** accessible from vul Yeroshenka (a side street off vul Tarasa Shevchenka). A 15-minute walk west of the cemetery are a plaque and a billboard marking the spot of the **Janowska concentration camp** (vul Vynnytsya, off vul Tarasa Shevchenka), now a prison. About 200m further west on vul Tarasa Shevchenka is **Kleparivska train station**, the last stop before Belzec on the Nazi death train. A plaque commemorates the 500,000 doomed Galician Jews who passed through here.

Artefacts of Lviv's Jewish heritage are scattered around various museums in the Old Town and the **Hesed-Arieh Jewish Centre** (Map p118; www.hesed.lviv.ua; vul Kotlyevskoho 30; ⏲9.30am-6.30pm Mon-Thu, to 3.30pm Fri) FREE has a tiny museum on Jews in Galicia. Lviv's only functioning synagogue is the attractive **Beis Aharon V'Yisrael Synagogue** (Map p118; vul Brativ Mikhnovskykh 4), built in 1924.

Central Lviv

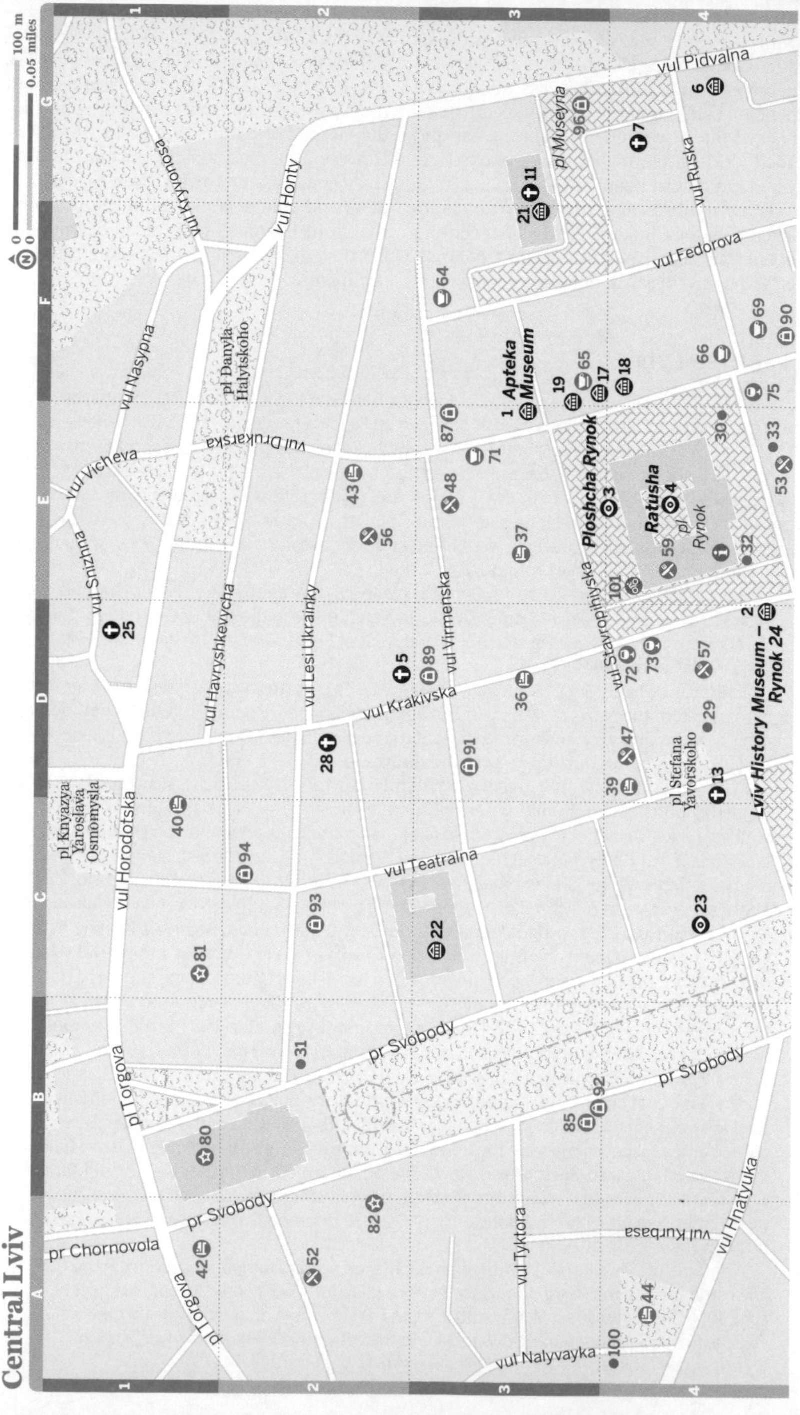

0 100 m
0 0.05 miles

A B C D E F G
1 2 3 4

pl Knyazya Yaroslava Osmomysla
vul Snizhna
vul Vicheva
vul Nasypna
vul Kryvonosa
pr Chornovola
pl Torgova
vul Horodotska
vul Havryshkevycha
pl Danyla Halytskoho
vul Drukarska
vul Honty
vul Lesi Ukrainky
pr Svobody
vul Krakivska
vul Teatralna
vul Virmenska
vul Tyktora
vul Nalyvayka
vul Kurbasa
vul Hnatyuka
vul Stavropihiyska
pl Stefana Yavorskoho
Ploshcha Rynok
Ratusha
pl Rynok
pl Museyna
vul Fedorova
vul Ruska
vul Pidvalna

1 Apteka Museum
2 Lviv History Museum – Rynok 24
3
4
5
6
7
11
13
17
18
19
21
22
23
25
28
29
30
31
32
33
36
37
39
40
42
43
44
47
48
52
53
56
57
59
64
65
66
69
71
72
73
75
80
81
82
85
87
89
90
91
92
93
94
96
100
101

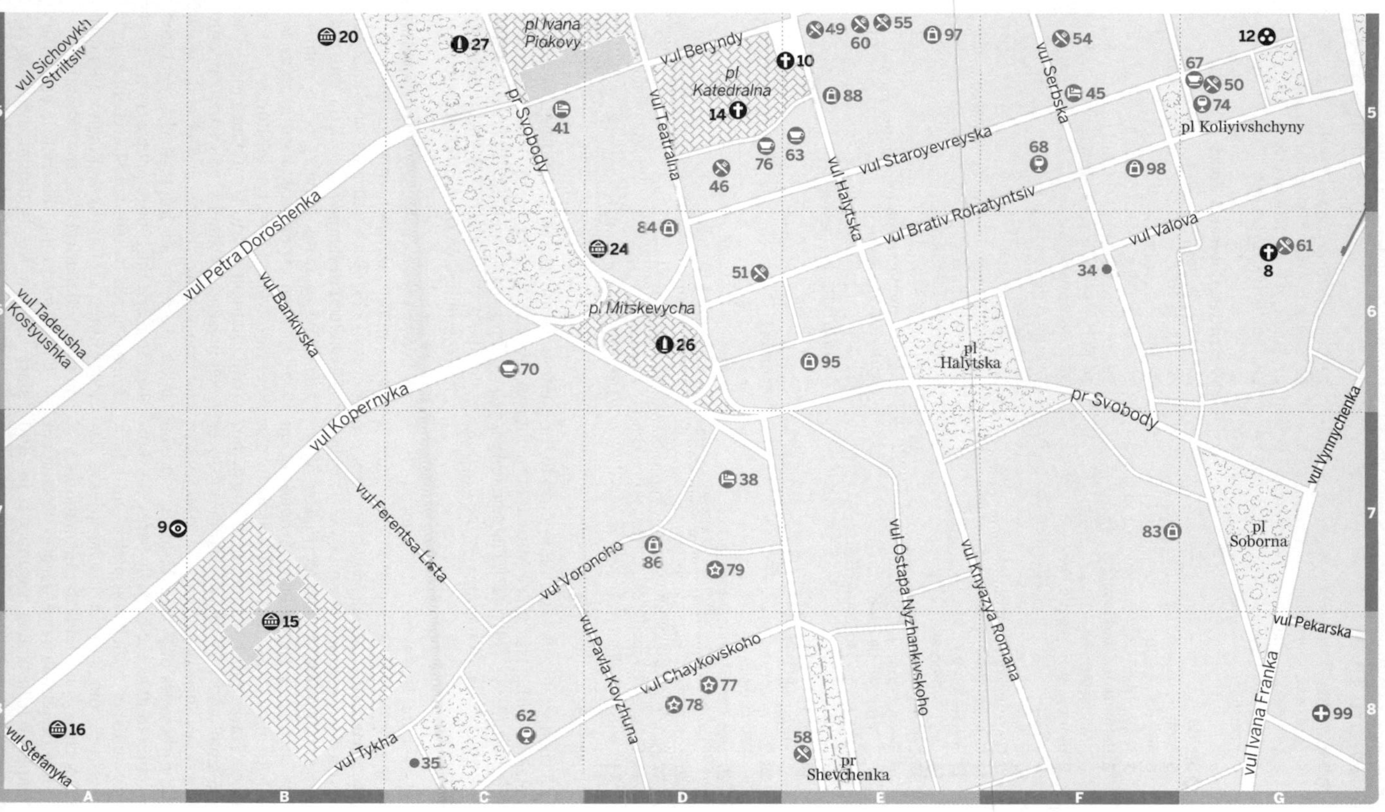
vul Sichovykh Striltsiv
pl Ivana Pidkovy
vul Beryndy
pl Katedralna
pr Svobody
vul Teatralna
vul Serbska
pl Koliyivshchyny
vul Staroyevreyska
vul Halytska
vul Brativ Rohatyntsiv
vul Valova
vul Petra Doroshenka
vul Bankivska
vul Tadeusha Kostyushka
pl Mitskevycha
pl Halytska
pr Svobody
vul Vynnychenka
vul Kopernyka
vul Ferentsa Lista
vul Voronoho
vul Ostapa Nyzhankivskoho
vul Knyazya Romana
pl Soborna
vul Pavla Kovzhuna
vul Chaykovskoho
vul Pekarska
vul Ivana Franka
vul Tykha
vul Stefanyka
pr Shevchenka
A
B
C
D
E
F
G

Central Lviv

Top Sights
- **1** Apteka Museum E3
- **2** Lviv History Museum – Rynok 24 .... D4
- **3** Ploshcha Rynok E4
- **4** Ratusha E4

Sights
- **5** Armenian Cathedral D2
- **6** Arsenal Museum G4
- **7** Assumption Church G4
- **8** Bernardine Church and Monastery G6
- **9** Birthplace of Leopold Von Sacher-Masoch A7
- **10** Boyim Chapel E5
- **11** Dominican Cathedral G3
- **12** Golden Rose Synagogue G5
- **13** Jesuit Church D4
- **14** Latin Cathedral D5
- **15** Lviv Art Gallery B8
- **16** Lviv Art Gallery – 19th-20th Century Collection A8
- **17** Lviv History Museum – Black House F3
- **18** Lviv History Museum – Kornyakt Palace F4
- **19** Lviv History Museum – Palazzo Bandinelli F3
- **20** Museum of Ethnography, Arts & Crafts B5
- **21** Museum of Religious History F3
- **22** National Museum C3
- **23** Prospekt Svobody C4
- **24** Salo Museum D6
- **25** St Mary of the Snows Church D1
- **26** Statue of Adam Mickiewicz D6
- **27** Statue of Taras Shevchenko C5
- **28** Transfiguration Church D2

Activities, Courses & Tours
- **29** Andreolli Tur D4
- **30** Chudo Tour E4
- **31** Chudo Tour Bus Tour B2
- **32** Free Walking Tour E4
- **33** Just Lviv It! E4
- **34** Kumpel Tour F6
- **35** Lviv Touristic C8

Sleeping
- **36** Dream Hostel D3
- **37** Hotel 39 .... E3
- **38** Hotel George D7
- **39** Leopolis Hotel D4
- **40** Nataliya-18 .... C1
- **41** Old City Hostel C5
- **42** Panorama Hotel A1
- **43** Reikartz Medievale E2
- **44** Rius Hotel A4
- **45** Vintage F5

Eating
- **46** Amadeus D5
- **47** Baczewski D4
- **48** Brudershaft E3
- **49** Celentano E5
- **50** Dim Lehend G5
- **51** Green D6
- **52** Krym A2

A good strategy is to combine a trip to the cemetery with a visit to the Museum of Folk Architecture and Life (p117). The cemetery is one tram stop past the stop for the open-air museum.

★ National Museum and Memorial to the Victims of Occupation MUSEUM

(Національний музей-меморіал жертв окупаційних режимів; Map p118; www.lonckoho.lviv.ua; vul Bryullova; 10am-7pm Mon-Sat, 10am-5pm Sun) FREE This infamous building on vul Bryullova was used as a prison by the Poles, Nazis and communists in turn, but the small and very moving exhibition over two floors focuses on Stalinist atrocities in the early years of WWII. Used as a prison right up to 1996, the brutally bare cells, horrific statistics posted throughout and Nazi newsreel from summer 1941 will leave few untouched. Some English explanations.

In a despicable move, disgraced president Yanukovych instigated a campaign in 2010 to stop the museum's work, even opening a criminal case against the director for violating state secret laws. Today the archives have been flung open and the truth is at last being told about the NKVD/KGB and the crimes they committed on the local populace.

★ Lvivarnya MUSEUM

(Map p118; www.lvivbeermuseum.com; vul Kleparivska 18; 60uah, tasting session extra 35uah; 10am-7pm) Revamped in 2017, the museum belonging to Lviv's brewery is an impressive, modern experience, a world away for the rickety post-Soviet repositories of the past found in many Ukrainian cities. The well-presented exhibits whet the appetite for the tasting session at the end, which takes place in an impressively renovated bar. To reach the museum, take tram 7 to St Anna Church (where vul Shevchenka peels away from vul Horodotska) then walk north along vul Kleparivska for around 600m.

The displays in the renovated cellars start right at the beginning with Egypt's beer-brewing tradition from 5000 years ago. It then traces the history of European brewing and specifically the story of the Lviv brewery from its early days as a monastical institution to the present day, via Robert Doms' purchase of the business in 1861 and the Soviet era when a batch of Lvivske was airfreighted to the Kremlin on a daily basis. Visitors emerge from the cellars into the bright, dramatically ceilinged and imaginatively illuminated copper-hued bar where they are served four types of beer in a special rack. There's English throughout.

★ Ploshcha Rynok SQUARE

(Map p112) Lviv was declared a Unesco World Heritage Site in 1998, and this old market square lies at its heart. The square was progressively rebuilt after a major fire in the early 16th century destroyed the original. Around 40 townhouses hem the square's perimeter. Most of these three- and four-storey buildings have uniform dimensions, with three windows per storey overlooking the square. This was the maximum number of windows allowed tax free, and those buildings with four or more belonged to the extremely wealthy. Pl Rynok is at its best on summer evenings when crowds of people emerge to enjoy the buskers, beer and generally good-natured atmosphere.

★ Lviv History Museum – Rynok 24 MUSEUM

(Львівський історичний музей; Map p112; www.lhm.lviv.ua; pl Rynok 24; 20uah; ⏲10am-5pm Thu-Tue) This branch of the Lviv History Museum expounds on the city's very early days starting with early cultures that inhabited Galicia and ending with the arrival of printing in the city in the 16th century.

Highlights include 2nd-century glass from the Carpathian Kurhan culture (proof the region had contact with the Romans), Scythian gold and weapons, a panorama of late 18th-century Lviv, a section on Khmelnytsky and the Cossacks, plus copies of *Apostle* (the first book printed in Ukraine (in Lviv)) and the Ostroh Bible (the first translation of the holy book into Ukrainian).

WORTH A TRIP

ZHOVKVA

If you have your own wheels, the most impressive day trip from Lviv is probably Pochayiv Monastery (p137). However, it's too difficult to visit quickly on public transport, leaving the fairly low-key historical town of Zhovkva at the top of the list. Its cluster of pastel-coloured buildings, handful of impressive churches and city-wall remnants will happily occupy you for an hour or two.

Built in the 16th century in an imitation of Italian-Renaissance style, Zhovkva was the birthplace of legendary Cossack Bohdan Khmelnytsky, who reportedly led his men through the 17th-century **Zvirynetska Gate** when liberating the town from the Poles in 1648. Ironically, however, the town's heyday was actually under the Poles, when it became the preferred residence of 17th-century King Jan III Sobiesky. Today roughly a dozen buildings – a monastery, lesser churches, a synagogue and a 'castle' that's not really a castle – cluster around the market square.

Zhovkva is 28km north of Lviv and can be reached by virtually any bus or *marshrutka* leaving bus station No. 2 (p133; 14uah, 35 minutes, several hourly).

★Ratusha NOTABLE BUILDING

(Town Hall; Map p112; www.city-adm.lviv.ua; pl Rynok 1; tower 20uah; ⏲tower 9am-9pm Apr-Oct, to 6pm Nov-Mar) The city fathers have occupied this location since the 14th century, but the present-day Italianate look dates to 1835. In a sign of openness and transparency, visitors are allowed to roam the corridors of power, but most of them do so on the arduous climb (305 steps from the 4th-floor ticket office) of the 65m-tall **tower** that looms over the Rynok. Noon is marked with a bugle call from one of the balconies on the southern side of the building.

★High Castle Hill LANDMARK

(Високий замок; Map p118; ⏲24hr) Around a 2km walk from pl Rynok, visiting the High Castle (Vysoky Zamok) on Castle Hill (Zamkova Hora) is a quintessential Lviv experience. There's little evidence of the 14th-century ruined stone fort that was Lviv's birthplace, but the summit mound sporting a mammoth Ukrainian flag thwacking in the wind offers 360-degree views of the city and the wooded hills between which it nestles.

To reach Vysoky Zamok on foot head up vul Kryvonosa from Vul Pidvalna until you reach a cafe and toilets where you should take a left. After a few minutes you will see a set of metal steps on the right. If you're feeling lazy, you can take a taxi most of the way up, approaching from the east via vul Vysoky Zamok.

★Apteka Museum MUSEUM

(Pharmacy Museum; Map p112; vul Drukarska 2; 20uah; ⏲10am-5pm) This fascinating pharmacy museum is located inside a still-functioning chemist's shop dating from 1735. Buy a ticket from the pharmacist and head down into the *pidval* (cellar) via rooms filled with still medicinally aromatic amphorae, pestles, scales, pill-processing machines and old medicines from pre-WWII Lviv. The damp and musty cellars hold exhibitions on medicinal themes.

Latin Cathedral CATHEDRAL

(Map p112; www.lwowskabazylika.org.ua; pl Katedralna 1; ⏲8.30am-5pm Mon-Sat, 2-5.30pm Sun) With various chunks dating from between 1370 and 1480, this working cathedral is one of Lviv's most impressive churches. The exterior is most definitely Gothic, while the heavily gilded interior, one of the city's highlights, has a more baroque feel, with colourfully wreathed pillars hoisting frescoed vaulting and mysterious side chapels glowing in candlelit half-light. Services are in four languages, including English.

If you walk around the outside of the cathedral, you'll eventually come to a relief of Pope John Paul II, erected to commemorate his visit to Lviv in 2001.

Lviv History Museum – Kornyakt Palace MUSEUM

(Львівський історичний музей; Map p112; www.lhm.lviv.ua; pl Rynok 6; 30uah; ⏲10am-5pm Thu-Tue) The smallest branch of the Lviv History Museum is housed in a palace, once a residence of the of Polish King Jan Sobieski III, which rises from the Renaissance Italian courtyard where arcading typical for the period is occupied by cafe and restaurant tables. Inside you can slide around in huge felt slippers on the intricately fashioned parquet floors as you admire period furniture and other antiques. It was here on 22 December

1686 that Poland and Russia signed the treaty that partitioned Ukraine.

Museum of Folk Architecture and Life MUSEUM

(Музей народної архітектури і побуту у Львові; www.lvivskansen.org; vul Chernecha Hora 1; 30uah; ⌚9am-6pm daily; 🚋7) This open-air museum displays different regional styles of farmsteads, windmills, churches and schools, which dot a huge park to the east of the city centre. Everything is pretty spread out here and a visit involves a lot of footwork. As an exhibition, it doesn't hold a candle to Kyiv's Pyrohovo Museum, but it's worth checking out if you're not heading to the capital. To get to the museum, take tram 7 from vul Pidvalna up vul Lychakivska and get off at the corner of vul Mechnykova. From the stop, walk 600m north on vul Krupyarska, following the signs.

Monument to the Victims of Soviet Crimes MONUMENT

(Map p118; vul Stepana Bandery) This grim but striking monument depicts a brutalist, angular figure breaking out from iron prison bars, with cobbles radiating out to benches around where you can sit and reflect on the crimes Lvivites suffered at the hands of the Soviets.

Prospekt Svobody STREET

(Map p112) In summer the broad pavement in the middle of this wide *prospekt* is the town's main hang-out and a hub of Lviv life, where homegrown tourists pose for photos in front of the Shevchenko statue. Locals promenade along the strip of park, kids scoot around in rented electric cars, beggars politely hassle people sitting on the many park benches and wedding parties mill around barking photo instructions. It's also the venue for an endless (apparently men-only) chess competition. At the northern end of the boulevard is the 1897–1900 Solomiya Krushelnytska Lviv Theatre of Opera and Ballet (p131). At the southern end a statue of Adam Michiewicz (p122), the Polish poet, stands in pl Mitskevycha.

Jesuit Church CHURCH

(Map p112; vul Teatralna; ⌚8am-8pm) Only reconsecrated in 2011, Lviv's impressive Jesuit church (full name – Garrison Church of Sts Peter and Paul) was used as a book repository during the Soviet years. It was the first baroque building in the city centre, erected in the early 17th century by Jesuit Italian architect Jacomo Briani. The faded baroque interior, illuminated by shafts of dust-speckled light, is busy these days as this is a military church.

St Nicholas Church CHURCH

(Map p118; vul Khmelnytskoho 28A; ⌚7am-1pm & 4-6pm) Darkly mysterious and wonderfully aromatic, this is possibly Lviv's finest church away from the tourist action. It dates back to at least 1292 and is now a Ukrainian Orthodox place of worship. Under a high dome you'll find some precious icon art, lots of embroidered towels and every wall adorned in some way.

Dominican Cathedral CHURCH

(Map p112; pl Museyna) Dominating a square to the east of pl Rynok is one of Lviv's signature sights, the large dome of the 1764 Dominican Cathedral. Inside, the typical baroque oval nave rises to a seemingly weightless unadorned dome, the entire interior sporting a restrained, austere feel, characteristic of late-baroque structures. East of the cathedral is a square where you'll see a **statue of a monk** holding a book. This is Federov, who brought printing to Ukraine in the 16th century.

Statue of Taras Shevchenko MONUMENT

(Пам'ятник Тарасу Шевченку; Map p112; pr Svobody) An enormous statue of Taras Shevchenko, Ukraine's greatest nationalist writer, rises up in the middle of pr Svobody. It was a gift to the people of Lviv from the Ukrainian diaspora in Argentina, the be whiskered poet set against a wave-shaped relief of religious folk.

Lviv History Museum – Palazzo Bandinelli MUSEUM

(Львівський історичний музей; Map p112; www.lhm.lviv.ua; pl Rynok 2; 30uah; ⌚10am-5.30pm Thu-Tue) Palazzo Bandinelli is named after an Italian merchant who bought the palace in the early 17th century. The building now houses a branch of the Lviv History Museum where you can admire the dramatic period interiors, outrageously high and chunkily carved ceilings, Florentine furniture, ceramics and tapestries.

Armenian Cathedral CHURCH

(Map p112; vul Virmenska 7) One church you should not miss is the elegant 1363 Armenian Cathedral with its ancient-feeling interior. The placid cathedral courtyard is a maze of arched passageways and squat buildings festooned with intricate Caucasian detail. Stepping into the courtyard feels like entering another era – gravestones bearing

Lviv

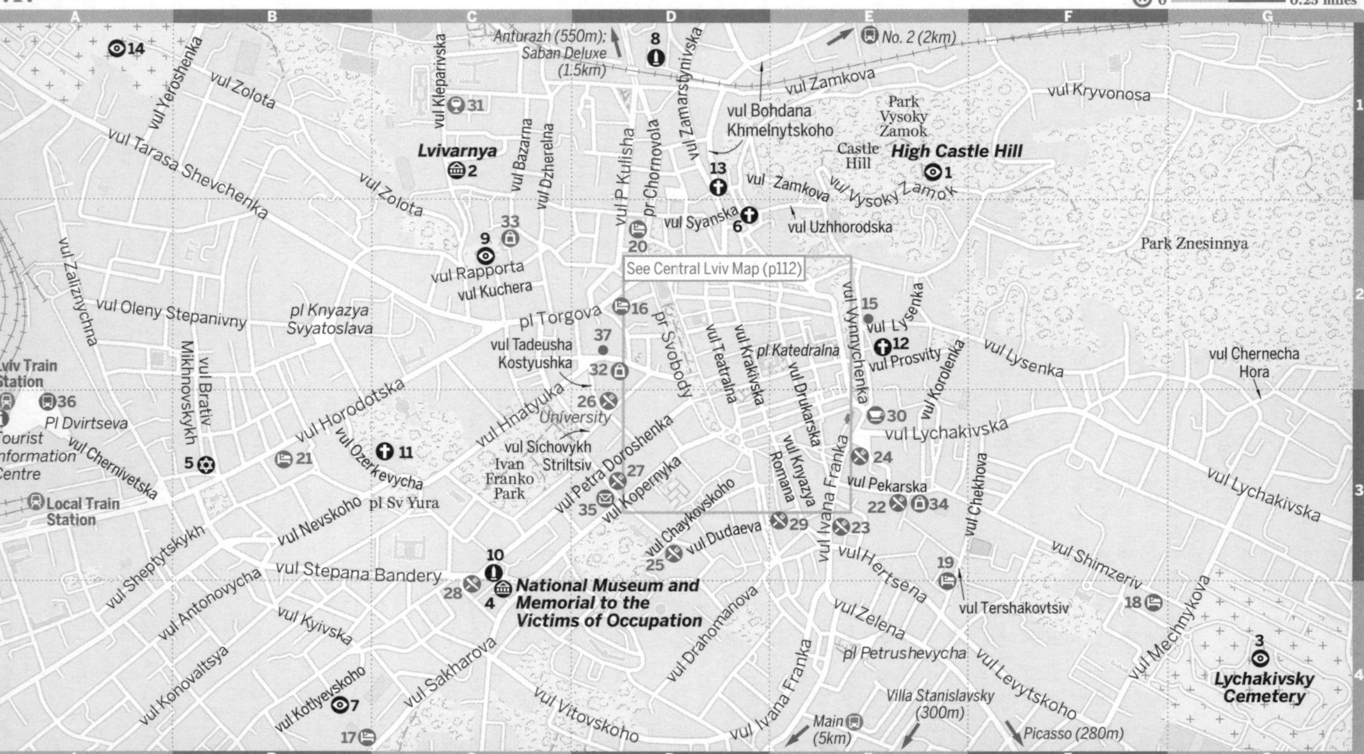
500 m
0.25 miles
Anturazh (550m); Saban Deluxe (1.5km)
No. 2 (2km)
vul Yeroshenka
vul Zolota
vul Kleparivska
vul Tarasa Shevchenka
Lvivarnya
vul Bazarna
vul Dzherelna
vul P Kulisha
pr Chornovola
vul Zamarstynivska
vul Zamkova
vul Bohdana Khmelnytskoho
Park Vysoky Zamok
Castle Hill
High Castle Hill
vul Kryvonosa
vul Zamkova
vul Vysoky Zamok
vul Syanska
vul Uzhhorodska
Park Znesinnya
vul Rapporta
vul Kuchera
See Central Lviv Map (p112)
vul Zaliznychna
vul Oleny Stepanivny
pl Knyazya Svyatoslava
pl Torgova
vul Tadeusha Kostyushka
pr Svobody
vul Teatralna
vul Krakivska
pl Katedralna
vul Drukarska
vul Vynnychenka
vul Lysenka
vul Prosvity
vul Korolenka
vul Lysenka
vul Chernecha Hora
Lviv Train Station
Pl Dvirtseva
Tourist Information Centre
vul Chernivetska
Local Train Station
vul Brativ Mikhnovskykh
vul Horodotska
vul Ozerkevycha
vul Hnatyuka
University
vul Sichovykh Striltsiv
Ivan Franko Park
vul Petra Doroshenka
vul Kopernyka
vul Knyazya Romana
vul Ivana Franka
vul Lychakivska
vul Pekarska
vul Chekhova
vul Lychakivska
vul Nevskoho
pl Sv Yura
vul Sheptytskykh
vul Stepana Bandery
vul Chaykovskoho
vul Dudaeva
vul Hertsena
vul Shimzeriv
vul Tershakovtsiv
National Museum and Memorial to the Victims of Occupation
vul Antonovycha
vul Kyivska
vul Drahomanova
vul Zelena
pl Petrushevycha
vul Mechnykova
vul Konovaltsya
vul Sakharova
vul Levytskoho
Lychakivsky Cemetery
vul Kotlyevskoho
vul Vitovskoho
vul Ivana Franka
Villa Stanislavsky (300m)
Main (5km)
Picasso (280m)

Lviv

Top Sights

1 High Castle Hill E1
2 Lvivarnya C1
3 Lychakivsky Cemetery G4
4 National Museum and Memorial to the Victims of Occupation C4

Sights

5 Beis Aharon V'Yisrael Synagogue B3
6 Church of St John the Baptist D2
7 Hesed-Arieh Jewish Centre B4
8 Holocaust Memorial D1
9 Jewish Hospital C2
10 Monument to the Victims of Soviet Crimes C3
11 St George's Cathedral C3
12 St Michael's Church E2
13 St Nicholas Church D1
14 Yanivske Cemetery A1

Activities, Courses & Tours

15 Lemberg Tour E2

Sleeping

16 Astoria D2
17 Ekotel B4
18 Eney F4
19 Eurohotel E4
20 Hotel Lviv D2
21 Reikartz Dworzec D3

Eating

22 Gamardzhoba E3
23 Harbuz E3
24 Kumpel E3
25 Kupol D3
26 Puzata Khata D3
27 Pyrizhky D3
28 Sim Porosyat C4
29 Veronika E3

Drinking & Nightlife

30 Cabinet E3
31 Robert Doms Beer House C1

Shopping

32 Gorgany.com D2
33 Krakivsky Rynok C2
34 Terra Incognita E3

Information

35 Central Post Office D3

Transport

36 Bus Station No. 8 .... A3
37 Train Ticket Office D2

inscriptions in the 54 letters of the Armenian alphabet pave the floor. Also here is a monument to the Armenian victims of genocide in Turkey. Enter at vul Krakivska 17.

Boyim Chapel CHAPEL
(Каплиця Боїмів; Map p112; pl Katedralna; 10uah; 11am-5pm Tue-Sun) The blackened facade of the burial chapel (1615), belonging to Hungarian merchant Georgi Boyim and his family, is covered in magnificent if somewhat morbid carvings. Atop the cupola is an unusual sculpture of Christ sitting with his head in one hand, pondering his sorrows. The interior is dizzying, featuring biblical reliefs with cameo appearances by members of the Boyim family. There are more images of the family patriarchs on the exterior above the door and on the wall flanking vul Halytska.

Assumption Church CHURCH
(Map p112; vul Pidvalna 9; 8am-7pm) This Ukrainian Orthodox church is easily distinguished by the 65m-high, triple-tiered Kornyakt bell tower rising beside it. The tower was named after its Greek benefactor, a merchant who was also the original owner of Kornyakt House on pl Rynok. Sadly it cannot be climbed. It's well worth going inside the church to see the beautifully gilt interior. Normally access is through the delightful **Three Saints Chapel** with its three, highly ornate minicupolas.

Golden Rose Synagogue RUINS
(Map p112; vul Staroyevreyska) The late-16th-century Golden Rose Synagogue stood at the heart of the inner district before the Nazis blew it up in 1943. A piece of wasteland for decades, the site is now occupied by a new and very moving monument to those who died in the Holocaust. Another synagogue once stood in the open lot directly across vul Staroyevreyska.

Bernardine Church and Monastery CHURCH
(Map p112; vul Vynnychenka; 7am-8pm) Lviv's most stunning baroque interior belongs to the 17th-century now **Greek Catholic Church of St Andrew**, part of the Bernadine Monastery. Populated with an army of cherubs and peppered with sunbursts, it's been painstakingly restored to its former splendour. There are usually more tourists here than worshippers, except on Sundays when mass draws the locals to prayer.

Transfiguration Church CHURCH
(Map p112; cnr vul Krakivska & vul Lesi Ukrainky; 7am-8pm) The tall copper-domed church just west of the Armenian Cathedral is the

late-17th-century, newly renovated Transfiguration Church, the first church in the city to revert to Greek Catholicism after Ukrainian independence in 1991. The bright, colourful interior is topped with a high dome lined with what look like Roman emperors. Particularly impressive during services.

Museum of Ethnography, Arts & Crafts MUSEUM
(Map p112; pr Svobody 15; 20uah; ⌚11am-5.40pm Tue-Sun) This underfunded, chaotically curated museum has a few interesting pieces of furniture, Czech glass, art nouveau posters (Mucha, Lautrec) and various 19th- and 20th-century decorative items from across Europe, the whole caboodle scattered throughout an interestingly run-down former bank. There's a large display of period clocks and the occasional well-conceived temporary exhibition.

Lviv History Museum – Black House MUSEUM
(Львівський історичний музей; Map p112; www.lhm.lviv.ua; pl Rynok 4; per section 10uah; ⌚10am-5pm Thu-Tue) Occupying the conspicuous Black House with its seemingly sooty facade, this is possibly the least interesting of the four pl Rynok branches of Lviv's history museum, unless you are particularly fired up about local coats of arms or the Ukrainian diaspora. The museum's third section looks at western Ukraine's turbulent and rather murderous 20th century, a small Soviet nostalgia section (old TVs, propaganda posters) providing light relief from Ukraine's bloody wars, resistance movements and the Holocaust. The last room examines Ukrainians in the Soviet Union's death camps and the Orange and Maydan revolutions.

St Mary of the Snows Church CHURCH
(Храм Марії Сніжної; Map p112; vul Snizhna) This seldom-visited church was founded by the German community in the 13th century as a Catholic cathedral but was given a neo-Romanesque makeover in the 19th century. Newly renovated inside, it lacks the atmosphere of Lviv's other churches.

Salo Museum GALLERY
(Map p112; pr Svobody 6/8; ⌚noon-midnight Mon-Thu, to 2am Fri-Sun) FREE For the uninitiated, *salo* is the cured pig fat (lard) that Ukrainians love to slip down with vodka and use an an ingredient in national dishes. This 'museum' is more a gallery in a restaurant where you can pay homage to *salo* at the *salo* monument and wonder at pieces of modern

City Walk Lviv's Historical Centre

START SHEVCHENKO STATUE
END DOMINICAN CATHEDRAL
LENGTH 5.3KM; TWO HOURS

Lviv's relatively compact centre makes for a pleasant walking tour that will get you to most of the major sites. This tour will take approximately two hours – three hours if the Castle Hill loop is included. It starts at the spiritual centre of modern-day Lviv, the Taras Shevchenko statue on pr Svobody, and ends at vul Virmenska in the Old Town.

With your back to the 1 **Shevchenko statue**, start walking right, glancing up at the interesting cast of stone-carved characters (one resembling New York's Statue of Liberty) on the parapet of the 2 **Museum of Ethnography, Arts & Crafts** (p120). Continue north on pr Svobody towards the 3 **Solomiya Krushelnytska Lviv Theatre of Opera & Ballet** (p131). Skirt right around the theatre, then take a right on vul Horodotska and carry on for about 250m until you reach the 4 **St Mary of the Snows Church** (p120), parts of which date to 1340. Carry on past the church up vul Snizhna then take a right into 5 **vul Chornomorska**, scene of Cold War tragedy. Vibration from Soviet tanks heading to Hungary in 1956 shook several houses to the ground, hence the gap now occupied by a children's playground. A few steps further bring you to pl Stary Rynok, where there's pleasant parkland and a few kiosks selling cheap food.

Glance up at the old buildings around pl Stary Rynok before performing a quick there-and-back movement up vul Pylnykarska to see the 6 **St Nicholas Church** (p117). Local historians claim this is Lviv's oldest church – elements of the building date back to the 13th century. Back on pl Stary Rynok head east, passing the normally closed neo-Renaissance 7 **Church of St John the Baptist** on your left, then bear right on vul Uzhhorodska. Continue uphill about 200m to the corner of vul Zamkova. From here you can easily spot the TV tower that tops 8 **Castle Hill** (p116). High Castle (Vysoky Zamok) is about a one-hour round-trip walk from here, and it's worth it for the views

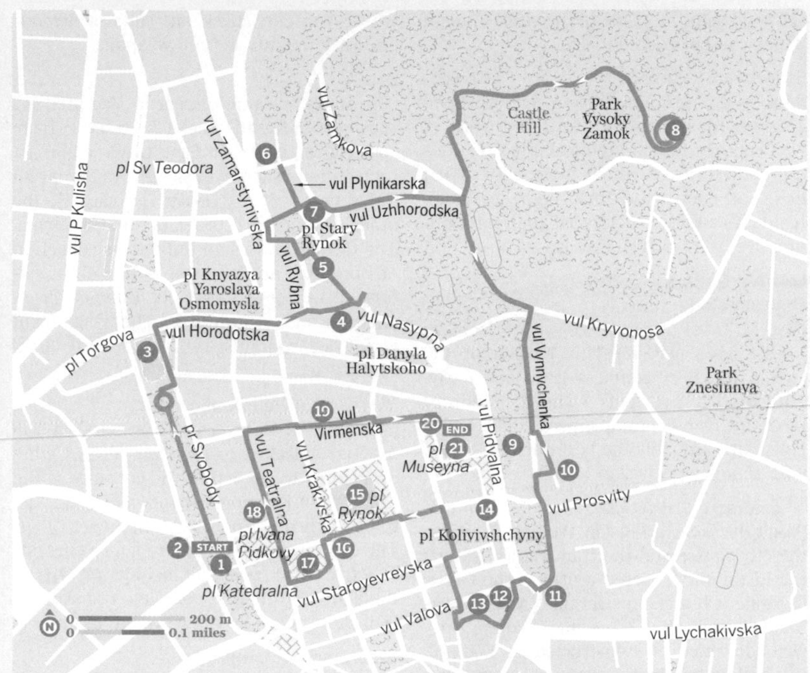

across the city. If you're not up for the climb, take a right on vul Zamkova, which leads to the Old Town.

Proceed about 300m on vul Zamkova to a three-way intersection and bear right down vul Vynnychenka. In the park on your right is the 16th-century 9 **Gunpowder Tower**, part of the old system of walls and bastions. The twin-spired church looming up the hill on your left rises the grand facade of the Greek Catholic 10 **St Michael's Church** (p122). It's worth taking a peek inside to see its striking trompe l'oeil ceiling decoration. Continue south to vul Valova at the southern end of the park.

If you need a breather, 11 **Cabinet cafe** (p130) is a fancy place for coffee. If not, backtrack about 30 paces and cross the park and tram tracks. You will see No. 20 Bapova on your left. Skirt inside the fenced sidewalk and continue along the old brick walls on your right. This is the last standing section of 12 **Lviv's medieval fortifications**. Go down the steps and duck right through the arched passageway. You are in the yard of the splendid 13 **Bernardine Church and Monastery** (p119).

Head north across the square in front of the church's entrance, cross vul Valova and continue north on vul Fedorova for about 200m until you reach vul Ruska. The 14 **Assumption Church** (p119) and its Kornyakt bell tower loom on your right. Go left on vul Ruska, keeping the 15 **Ratusha** (p116) on your right as you cross pl Rynok. Look for the black facade of 16 **Boyim Chapel** (p119), on pl Katedralna, and check inside. When you exit, head straight down the path in front of you, keeping the 17 **Latin Cathedral** (p116) on your right, and take the next right on vul Teatralna.

You're now close to where you started, walking north parallel to pr Svobody. Continue past the 18 **Jesuit Church** (p117), stopping to admire its interesting baroque and Renaissance facade. Your home stretch, vul Virmenska, is easy to spot – it's Lviv's prettiest street. Hang a right and aim for the eastern terminus of the street, where Dzyga awaits. Before you get there, pop your head into the courtyard of the 19 **Armenian Cathedral** (p117). At the 20 **Dzyga cafe** (p130), choose an outdoor table with a view of the 21 **Dominican Cathedral** (p117) and order yourself a well-deserved Lvivske beer, or a cup of Lviv's legendary coffee.

art and sculpture made of the stuff, some of which can be ordered to eat.

St Michael's Church CHURCH
(Map p118; vul Vynnychenka; ⏲6am-8pm) This grand, hilltop church is the work of 17th-century Italian architects. It was once the church of a fortified monastery which held out against the Turks and the Tatars. Inside it's a lofty, neoclassical affair with impressive trompe d'oeil ceilings.

Lviv Art Gallery – 19th–20th Century Collection GALLERY
(Map p112; vul Stefanyka; 20uah; ⏲11am-6pm Tue-Sat, noon-6pm Sun) This branch of the Lviv Art Gallery contains 19th- and early-20th-century art (plus some 21st-century pieces); this includes a superb collection of Polish art, arguably the best outside Poland with some works by Jan Matejko.

St George's Cathedral CATHEDRAL
(Map p118; pl Sv Yura 5) On the way between the city centre and the train station stands the historic and sacred centre of the Greek Catholic Church in Ukraine, which was handed back after 44 years of compulsory Orthodox control. Constructed in 1774–90, this yellow building is pleasant enough, especially since a refurbishment for the Pope's 2001 visit. However, it's perhaps not as striking as some of Lviv's less important churches. For many, the most memorable element will be the 3D icon of Christ near the far-right corner, if looking from the door. It presents Christ's face from one angle, and the image from the shroud of Turin from another.

National Museum MUSEUM
(Національний музей; Map p112; www.nm.lviv.ua; pr Svobody 20; permanent exhibitions 20uah, whole building 60uah; ⏲10am-6pm Tue-Sun) Residing in one of Lviv's grandest 19th-century palaces, this sometimes confusing museum (too many doors, ticket rippers, sections, prescribed routes) has one of the Slavic world's best collection of religious icons, most hailing from western Ukraine and eastern Poland. The earliest examples date from the 12th century and the famous Volyn School is well represented. A separate section deals with Ukrainian art of the 18th to 20th centuries including a few works by Taras Shevchenko, whose death mask can also be found here.

Arsenal Museum MUSEUM
(Музей старовинної зброї; Map p112; vul Pidvalna 5; 20uah; ⏲10am-5pm daily) The town's former arsenal (1554–56) is now a museum where you can check out suits of armour and various cannons and weapons.

Lviv Art Gallery GALLERY
(Львівська галерея мистецтв; Map p112; vul Kopernyka 15 & vul Stefanyka 3; 20uah; ⏲11am-6pm Tue-Sat, noon-6pm Sun) Lviv's main art repository has two wings – one in the lavish **Pototsky Palace** (Палац Потоцьких), the other around the corner on vul Stefanyka. The former houses an impressive collection of European art from the 14th to 18th centuries, including works by Rubens, Brueghel, Goya and Caravaggio. The wing on vul Stefanyka contains 19th- and early-20th-century art.

Museum of Religious History MUSEUM
(Map p112; pl Muzeyna 1; 20uah; ⏲10am-6pm Tue-Sun) Attached to the Dominican Cathedral (p117) to the left of the entrance is the Museum of Religious History which was actually dedicated to atheism in Soviet times. The exhibition looks at all religions currently active in Ukraine and includes an Ostroh Bible, one of the first complete translations into Old Church Slavonic printed in 1580.

Birthplace of Leopold Von Sacher-Masoch ARCHITECTURAL, CULTURAL
(Map p112; vul Kopernyka 22) Opposite the Pototsky Palace is the supposed birthplace of Leopold von Sacher-Masoch, the world's original 'masochist'. The author of *Venus in Furs* came into the world here in 1835, although he spent most of his subsequent 60 years begging to be whipped in Austria, Germany and Italy. The building cannot be accessed.

Statue of Adam Mickiewicz MONUMENT
(Map p112; pr Svobody) The statue of Poland's national poet caps the southern end of pr Svobody.

Church of St John the Baptist CHURCH
(Map p118; pl Stary Rynok) This 13th-century church was given a neo-Renaissance revamp in 1889 and has an unusual red-brick facade. Until recently it housed a book museum but it is now closed to the public.

Tours

Kumpel Tour TOURS
(Map p112; ☎098 453 5887; www.kumpel-tour.com; vul Valova 16 (enter from vul Serbska); ⏲10am-6pm Mon-Fri, to 3pm Sat) Expert Lviv historian Ihor Lylo runs the best English-language tours in town for visitors looking to get under the skin of this intriguing city.

Andreolli Tur TOURS
(Map p112; ☎067 674 2426; pl Rynok 29 (Andeolli Passage); ⊙9am-7pm Mon-Sat, to 6pm Sun; 👪) Cheap walking tours of Lviv and excursions out into the sticks (castles, Carpathians). Their 'Lviv Through Children's Eyes' is the only tour we have ever come across in Ukraine aimed specifically at kids.

Just Lviv It! TOURS
(Map p112; ☎0800 501 292; www.justlviv.it; pl Rynok 15; ⊙10am-8pm daily) Highly visible operation with an information centre on pl Rynok, its own **hostel** and tours on every Lviv theme imaginable.

Lemberg Tour TOURS
(Map p118; ☎032 276 5442; www.lemberg-tour.com.ua; vul Vynnychenka 26/1; ⊙10am-6pm Mon-Fri, to 2.30pm Sat) Quite upmarket tours with historical and cultural themes in and around Lviv. Can also **book accommodation** and transfers.

Chudo Tour RAIL
(Map p112; www.chudotour.com.ua; pl Rynok; adult/child 75/40uah; ⊙10am-8pm) Ukraine's first tourist train leaves every half hour from the right-hand side of the Ratusha on pl Rynok. The popular one-hour tour with recorded commentary takes in most of the major sights in the city centre on a 10km loop. The company also runs **themed walking tours** and a hop-on-hop-off bus.

Free Walking Tour TOURS
(Map p112; www.freewalkingtour.com; ⊙11am Wed, Fri, Sat & Sun) These free walking tours run by a Polish company cover the historical centre in 2½ hours. The starting point is outside the tourist office on pl Rynok. Tips are welcome at the end.

Chudo Tour Bus Tour BUS
(Map p112; ☎050 072 0225; www.chudotour.com.ua; pr Svobody; 110uah; ⊙9am-7pm daily) Hop-on-hop-off bus tours leaving every two hours from near the opera house. The route takes 90 minutes and in truth the only place worth doing any hopping off is the Lychakivsky Cemetery. There's an early-bird 30% discount for the 9am departure.

Lviv Touristic TOURS
(Map p112; ☎032 232 8303; www.lvivtouristic.com; pl Malanyuka 4) Tour agency offering city walks, transfers, accommodation bookings and lots more besides.

Festivals & Events

No other city in Ukraine does festivals like Lviv – even Kyiv has found itself playing catch-up and you'll find a lot of imitations of Lviv events across the country. There's something going on virtually every week of the year.

Lviv City Day FIESTA
(⊙early May) Every city has its day in Ukraine – Lviv's is in early May. Expect costumed processions, music and lots of great food.

Beer Festival BEER
(www.beerfest.lviv.ua; ⊙early May) This celebration of Lviv's hop culture is held in early May, to coincide with several other events.

LvivKlezFest MUSIC
(www.klezfest.lviv.ua; ⊙late May) This two-week Jewish music festival takes place at various outdoor venues in the city centre.

Virtuosos MUSIC
(www.philharmonia.lviv.ua; ⊙late May-early Jun) Three-week classical musical festival held at the Philharmonia (p131).

Alfa Jazz Fest MUSIC
(www.leopolisjazz.com; ⊙late Jun) Big weekend jazz bash featuring international artists.

Etnovyr CULTURAL
(www.etnovyr.org.ua; ⊙late Aug) Huge folk festival held in late August that sees tens of

LEOPOLD VON SACHER-MASOCH

Local historians regularly lock horns on the issue of where the world's original 'masochist' was born. Some claim he came into the world at vul Kopernyka 22 opposite the Pototsky Palace; others assert he must have first seen light of day in a house where the Grand Hotel now stands. Wherever the exact location may have been, the author of *Venus in Furs* was definitely born in Lviv in 1835, although he spent most of his subsequent 60 years begging to be whipped in Austria, Germany and Italy.

If you'd like to experience a light-hearted version of some of Masoch's practices, the waitresses at the Masoch Cafe (p128) will handcuff and whip you before or after a meal selected from the menu of aphrodisiacs. A bronze of Masoch himself greets 'diners' at the door.

dance and music ensembles from all over Ukraine perform in the city centre.

Coffee Festival FESTIVAL

(www.coffeefest.lviv.ua; ⌚Sep) Late September sees the city achieve a caffeine high. One of Ukraine's best festivals, held in cafes throughout the city centre.

Chocolate Festival FOOD

(www.shokolad.lviv.ua; ⌚mid-Oct) Ukraine's top chocolate festival and one of the country's choice culinary events involving chocolate sculptures, finger-licking tasting sessions and workshops.

Lviv Fashion Week FASHION

(www.lvivfashionweek.com; ⌚late Oct) One of the country's top fashion events.

Sleeping

You'd be hard pushed to find a Soviet-era hotel in this city, most having rid themselves of the pre-1991 style of hospitality. Expect to pay around twice as much in Lviv as you would elsewhere in western Ukraine. Lviv's hostel situation seems to be in constant flux, with expats setting up then selling up with alarming speed. Check that a hostel is still running before turning up without a booking.

★**Old City Hostel** HOSTEL $

(Map p112; ☎032 294 9644; www.oldcityhostel.lviv.ua; vul Beryndy 3; dm/tw from 155/550uah; @🛜) Occupying two floors of an elegantly fading tenement just steps from pl Rynok, this expertly run hostel with period features and views of the Shevchenko statue from the wraparound balcony has long since established itself as the city's best. Fluff-free dorms hold four to eight beds, shower queues are unheard of, sturdy lockers keep your stuff safe and there's a well-equipped kitchen.

Dream Hostel HOSTEL $

(Map p112; ☎032 247 1047; www.dream-hostels.com; vul Krakivska 5; dm from 145uah; 🛜) The Lviv branch of this national hostel chain sports spotless dorms with pine bunks equipped with reading lights and privacy-creating curtains. There's also a spacious lounge, a cafe and staff on hand to patiently answer all those questions they've answered a thousand times before. The location on busy Krakivska is perfect.

Ekotel HOTEL, HOSTEL $

(Екотель; Map p118; ☎032 244 3008; www.hotel-ekotel.lviv.ua; vul Sakharova 42; dm/d from 115/240uah; ❄🛜) There are no frills but plenty of smiles at this spartan but comfortable 94-bed budget hotel and hostel, 2km southwest of the city centre. To keep rates down, rooms do the absolute minimum but are clean and well maintained, though the call-centre furniture could get a touch depressing after a couple of days.

The dorms have no bunks, there's a small common room and breakfast is 35uah extra.

★**Saban Deluxe** GUESTHOUSE $$

(☎067 247 7777; www.sabandeluxe.com; vul Sinna 18; r 800-2100uah; P❄🛜) This superb guesthouse 3km north of pl Rynok is an eclectic mix of old and new, 21st century and antique, jumble sale and IKEA all rolled into one. All rooms are completely different, the owner is particularly helpful and the location isn't as inconvenient as it may seem (buses run from nearby). Full board available.

★**Villa Stanislavsky** BOUTIQUE HOTEL $$

(☎032-275 2505; www.villastanislavskyi.com.ua; vul Henerala Tarnavskoho 75; r from 1350uah; P❄🛜) This hilltop villa stands amid the splendid decay of what used to be a posh fin de siècle residential neighbourhood, 20 minutes on foot from the centre. The dark, polished wood of the stairs and furniture and the placid surroundings provide much-needed respite from the Old Town's hustle and bustle. A dedicated chess room is the cherry on the sundae.

Reikartz Dworzec HOTEL $$

(Map p118; ☎032 242 5126; www.reikartz.com; vul Horodotska 107; incl breakfast, s 800-1200uah, d1000-1650uah; ❄🛜) *Dworzec* in Polish means 'station' and it's on the way to Lviv's train terminus that you'll find another link in the Reikartz chain. Rooms are business standard, fitted out in unoffensive tones and with fully functional wi-fi and aircon. The location is good for the station and the old centre is only a short tram ride away.

Hotel 39 HOTEL $$

(Map p112; ☎032 235 7175; www.hotel39.com.ua; pl Rynok 39; s/d incl. breakfast from 1320/1420uah; 🛜) If you want good quality digs bang in the heart of the action, look no further than this superbly done-out hotel housed in the Palace Coloccini right on the Rynok. Rooms are a little cramped but furnished in reproduction antiques, and bathrooms are of the most recent vintage.

NTON HOTEL $$

(НТОН; ☎032 242 4959; www.hotelnton.lviv.ua; vul Shevchenka 154B; s/d incl breakfast from

520/750uah; ❄📶; 🚋7) Near the terminus of tram 7 in Lviv's western suburbs, this far-flung hotel on the road out to the Polish border may not seem too promising, but it is possibly Lviv's best deal. Rooms are fully renovated, spacious and well furnished, and contain little extras like kettles, sewing kits and hairdryers.

An entire *Hello!* magazine of homegrown celebs has stayed here (Ani Lorak, VIA Gra, Valery Meladze), their signed portraits lining the corridors. The breakfast is a bit 'wedding banquet' but there's enough of a choice to satisfy most tastes.

Eurohotel HOTEL **$$**
(Map p118; ☎032 275 7214; www.eurohotel.lviv.ua; vul Tershakovtsiv 6A; s/d from 1200/1300uah; ❄📶) This unexciting place is a good example of just what you can do with a surplus Soviet lumpen-hotel. The 90 bog-standard but comfortable rooms are for those who want to sleep, shower and access the web, but little else. There's a fairly decent **restaurant** on the premises.

Hotel George HOTEL **$$**
(Map p112; ☎032 232 6236; www.georgehotel.com.ua; pl Mitskevycha 1; s/d incl breakfast from 620/690; 📶) Partially renovated and still sporting lots of faded yesteryear chic, this epicentral hotel remains a travellers' favourite. A prime candidate for a showstopping five-star establishment, this gorgeous 1901 art nouveau gem has instead a mix of rooms, from threadbare bathroom-less tourist class to fairly luxurious suites. High-ceilinged period style and creaky parquet floors exist throughout though some have been victims of crass *remont*. However, communal spaces remain grandly untouched, the English-speaking staff are great and the buffet breakfast is still served in the amazing Oriental-style restaurant.

Nataliya-18 HOTEL **$$**
(Наталія-18; Map p112; ☎032 242 2068; www.natalia18.lviv.ua; pl Knyazya Yaroslava Osmomysla 7; r incl. breakfast 1450-1600uah; ❄📶) Located on the edge of the former Armenian quarter, this solid midrange choice features big bathrooms containing Ukraine' s softest, fluffiest towels. The 22 odd-shaped rooms are anchored by queen-sized beds draped in fine linens. The breakfast is cooked to order.

Hotel Lviv HOTEL **$$**
(Готель Львів; Map p118; ☎032 242 3270; www.hotel-lviv.com.ua; pr Chornovola 7; incl. breakfast s 500-1260uah, d 780-1890uah; 📶) This 1965 ugly duckling was transformed into a, well, slightly less unattractive duck in anticipation of free-spending football fans, sending standards and prices higher. Most rooms have been updated but a whiff of Soviet hotel decor still survives here and there.

★Eney DESIGN HOTEL **$$$**
(Еней; Map p118; ☎0322 768 799; www.eney.lviv.ua; vul Shimzeriv 2; d 1500-4000uah; P❄📶🏊) Conveniently located near the Lychakivsky Cemetery, this well-appointed, luxurious-feeling hotel has an impeccable reputation for service and maintenance. Rooms are imaginatively designed with big-print wallpapers, lots of cushions and crisp bathrooms, and the outdoor heated pool is the cherry on the cake.

★Astoria BOUTIQUE HOTEL **$$$**
(Map p118; ☎032 242 2701; www.astoriahotel.ua; vul Horodotska 15; r incl breakfast from 3000uah) A hotel since 1914, the Astoria was given a stylishly moody retrofit in 2013, sending it back to the monochrome world of the 1930s. The seven floors are all marble and cast iron, weighty lacquered doors and hangar-style lighting. Rooms are art-deco studies in black, white and every shade in between. Breakfast is served in the superb restaurant. The rooftop apartments have their own kitchens.

★Vintage BOUTIQUE HOTEL **$$$**
(Map p112; ☎032 235 6834; www.vintagehotel.com.ua; vul Serbska 11; s/d incl. breakfast from 1640/2550uah; ❄📶) Lviv's first real boutique hotel is a delightfully intimate 29-room place, accessed through an inconspicuous entrance in the historical centre. Rooms ooze period style with hardwood floors, polished antique-style furniture and Victorian-style wallpaper, successfully blended with flat-screen TVs and 21st-century bathrooms. You'll be looking forward all night to the breakfast, cooked to order and served in the hotel's stylish restaurant.

The genuinely friendly staff are glad to help with anything Lviv-related, plus onward travel arrangements and the like.

★Leopolis Hotel HOTEL **$$$**
(Map p112; ☎032 295 9500; www.leopolishotel.com; vul Teatralna 16; r 6260-7800uah; ❄@📶) One of the historical centre's finest places to catch some Zs. Every guest room in this 18th-century edifice is different, but all have a well-stocked minibar, elegant furniture and an Italian-marble bathroom with underfloor heating. Wheelchair-friendly

facilities, a new spa/fitness area in the cellars and a pretty decent brasserie are extras you won't find anywhere else. The Leopolis comes to you from the same designer who fashioned Tallinn's Telegraaf hotel.

Panorama Hotel HOTEL $$$

(Map p112; ☎032 225 9000; www.panorama-hotel.com.ua; pr Svobody 45; s/d incl. breakfast from 2400/2900uah; ❄📶) The Panorama has been a hotel since 1875 though it operated under a variety of names. Today the 51 vista-rich rooms are studies in crisp, 3rd-millennium style with bold fabrics contrasting with sepia and beige fittings. It's one of the few hotels that cater to both business clients and families; there's a gym, beauty salon and excursion bureau in the building.

Rius Hotel BUSINESS HOTEL $$$

(Map p112; ☎032 235 0660; www.rius-hotel.lviv.ua; vul Hnatyuka 12A; r from 2000uah; ❄📶) Modern hotel on the 6th and 7th floors of a mini high-rise aimed at business clientele, just a few minutes walk from pl Rynok. Bedrooms are done out in shades of unchallenging beige and brown and facilities include a fitness centre, a restaurant and a multipurpose conference hall.

Reikartz Medievale HOTEL $$$

(Map p112; ☎235 0890; www.reikartz.com; vul Drukarska 9; s 1200-1600uah, d 1400-1800uah; ❄📶) The Lviv link in this 100% Ukrainian chain limits the medieval theme to a few spired bedsteads, the odd tapestry and a bit of chunky furniture. There's also nothing of the Middle Ages about the huge bathrooms, crisp linens and exceptional service. More hryvnya get you a bigger room, but little else.

Eating

Lviv is more famous for cafes than restaurants, but the food scene has seen dramatic developments in recent years, with many more restaurants joining the celebration of Galicia's culinary past. The tide of whacky theme restaurants that washed ashore in the mid-2000s seems to be receding, giving way to more refined, taste- and ingredient-driven dining. Prices are slightly higher than elsewhere in Ukraine, but nowhere else will you eat this well.

★Green VEGETARIAN $

(Map p112; vul Brativ Rohatyntsiv 5; mains around 60uah; ⏲10am-9pm; 🌿) Lviv's best vegetarian eatery has a relaxing, spacious dining room where you can tuck into meat-free, vegan and raw food. In the upstairs chill-out area, kick off your shoes and lounge around on cushions as you enjoy ice cream made on the premises or a late breakfast. Also runs cookery courses and Friday is concert night. Certainly a foreigner favourite.

Sidlo GALICIAN $

(Сідло; Map p112; www.sidlo.com.ua; pl Rynok 17; mains 45-110uah; ⏲noon-midnight) Dine amid ancient columns and brick arches at this casual restaurant, whose name means 'The Saddle' (there's one out front to point you in the right direction). Ukrainian and Lviv fare dominate the menu – the Lviv *borshch* and pear strudel took our fancy but there's also *banosh* and river fish from the Carpathians.

Krym TATAR $

(Крим; Map p112; www.krim-cafe.032.ua; vul Furmanska 1; mains 30-65uah; ⏲11am-11pm daily; ❄📶) Following the occupation of Crimea, many Tatars moved their cafes to other parts of Ukraine – this bright, simple cafe serves up typically flavour-packed *plov*, *manty* (meatballs in a pasta case), *samsa* (meat pies), mutton and *shashlyk* to an oriental Crimean soundtrack. The service is pleasant and prices reasonable – the wi-fi password, 'Crimea2014' – says it all, though.

Puzata Khata CAFE $

(Пузата Хата; Map p118; www.puzatahata.com.ua; vul Sichovykh Striltsiv 12; mains around 30uah; ⏲8am-11pm daily; 📶) This supersized version of Ukraine's No. 1 restaurant chain stands out for its classy, spacious, Hutsul-themed upper floor and cheap, tasty food. This contrasts with the 21st-century basement which sports life-jacket orange seating and funky lighting.

Pyrizhky PIES $

(Пиріжки; Map p118; vul Slovatskoho 4; pyrizhky 6-8uah; ⏲8am-7pm) This blast from the Soviet past has been serving budget *pyrizhky* (pies/turnovers) here for over 50 years.

Harbuz UKRAINIAN $

(Гарбуз; Map p118; vul Ivana Franka 15; mains 40-70uah; ⏲10am-11pm; ❄📶) 'The Pumpkin' is a fun, cheap, friendly Ukrainian cafe-bar-pub way off the tourist trail offering several types of beer, a simple menu of steaks, *banosh*, river fish, *varenyky* and *deruny* (potato pancakes) amid garish decor.

Na Bambetli INTERNATIONAL $

(Map p112; pl Rynok 29, Passage Andreolli; mains around 50uah; ⏲10am-10pm; 📶) A secluded but busy spot down the Passage Andreolli just off pl Rynok, this lively place is adorned with a collection of old radios and Mucha posters and serves a simple menu of sandwiches, desserts, ice cream and, of course, coffee in several guises.

Gamardzhoba GEORGIAN $

(Гамарджоба; Map p118; vul Pekarska 24; snacks 12-25uah; ⏲10am-9pm) Nothing more than a window through which a friendly Georgian woman passes the bready-cheesy-spicey snacks the country is known for. It's all delicious and makes a great belly-filler on the run. Also very cheap coffee and other drinks.

Puzata Khata CAFE $

(Пузата Хата; Map p112; www.puzatahata.com.ua; pr Shevchenka 10; mains around 30uah; ⏲8am-11pm; ❄📶) The smaller Lviv branch of this national chain serves exactly the same food as its bigger brother but is much more cramped and stuffy in summer. However the decor is a bit more stylish and there's a pleasant brick-lined cellar where only coffee and cakes are served.

★**Ratusha** INTERNATIONAL $$

(Ратуша; Map p112; pl Rynok 1; mains 100-200uah; ⏲9am-11pm; ❄📶) For a bit of tranquil, understated elegance amid the tourist bustle of pl Rynok, head to this oh-so-central European cafe within the town hall. Order from the meat or fish menu, or just a coffee, and sit back to admire the classy high ceilings, potted palms and large ceramic stove. The big windows provide elegantly framed views of Lviv's showpiece piazza.

★**Baczewski** EASTERN EUROPEAN $$

(Ресторація Бачевських; Map p112; ☎032 224 4444; vul Shevska 8; mains 80-270; ⏲8am-midnight; 🅿) Here's how you compress your Lviv cultural studies into one evening out. Start with Jewish *forschmak* (herring pate), eased down by Ukrainian *nalyvky* (digestives) and followed by Hungarian fish soup. Proceed to Polish *pierogi* (dumplings) and finish with Viennese *Sachertorte* with Turkish coffee. An essential Lviv experience. Be sure to reserve a table for dinner at this mega-popular place.

Also serve champagne breakfast for 120uah per person. The only thing that lets Baczewski down a little is the service which can be gruff and disinterested.

★**Kupol** EUROPEAN $$

(Купол; Map p118; vul Chaykovskoho 37; mains 100-250uah; ⏲11am-9pm; 📶) One of the pre-tourism 'originals', this place is designed to feel like stepping back in time – to 1938 in particular, 'the year before civilisation ended' (ie before the Soviets rolled in). The old-world interior with its screechy parquet floors, tasselled curtains, old photos and high Austrian double doors is the perfect setting to enjoy the tasty Polish/Austrian/Ukrainian dishes. It was closed for renovation at the time of research.

WORTH A TRIP

OLESKO

Some 70km east of Lviv, Olesko boasts a French chateau-style hilltop **castle** visible for miles around. The current castle dates back to the 18th century but it was built on the site of a medieval fortress, destroyed by Tatar attacks in the 15th century. To get to Olesko, take any bus (42uah, 1½ hours, at least hourly) heading towards Brody from Lviv's bus station No. 2 (p133). Alternatively, travel agencies in Lviv organise day trips.

★**Trapezna Idey** UKRAINIAN $$

(Трапезна ідей; Map p112; ☎032-254 6155; www.idem.org.ua; vul Valova 18A; mains 50-100uah; ⏲11am-11pm) An unmarked door behind the paper-aeroplane monument leads into the bowels of a Bernardine monastery, where this lovely local-intelligentsia fave is hiding, together with a modern art gallery called the **Museum of Ideas**. People flock here for the hearty *bohrach* (a Ukrainian version of goulash) and *banosh* (Carpathian polenta with salty cottage cheese).

Dim Lehend UKRAINIAN $$

(Дім легенд; Map p112; vul Staroyevreyska 48; mains 55-140uah; ⏲11am-2am) Dedicated to the city of Lviv, there's nothing dim about the 'House of Legends'. The five floors contain a library stuffed with Lviv-themed volumes, a room showing live webcam footage of Lviv's underground river, rooms dedicated to lions and cobblestones, and another featuring the city in sounds. The menu is limited to Ukrainian staples. Excellent desserts are a bonus.

For a drink with a view, head to the top-floor terrace, where a GDR Trabant looks out across the roofs of the old town.

Mons Pius UKRAINIAN, INTERNATIONAL $$

(Map p112; www.monspius.lviv.ua; vul Lesi Ukrainky 14; mains 70-200uah; ⏲11am-11pm; ❄)

Well-regimented serving staff dart across the polished brick floors and through the intimate courtyard of this former Armenian bank, a well-established favourite on Lviv's dining scene. Meat dishes anchor the reassuringly brief menu, though there are lots of salads and a few meat-free dishes. Our only criticism are the small portions, so beef up your beef with a couple of side dishes.

Drinks include 'live' Mons Pius beer and lemonade like *babusya* (grandmother) used to make.

Celentano PIZZA $$
(Челентано; Map p112; pl Rynok 21; pizza 70-200uah, other mains 60-110uah; ⏲8am-11pm; 📶) 'Oh no!', cry those who've picked their way through Ukraine's culinary wilderness via too many Celentanos to reach Lviv's tasty delights, but the main Lviv branch of this popular national chain is a slice above its other stuck-in-the-late-1990s joints. The contemporary interior incorporates chunks of 17th-century architecture and the Apennine fare is delicious and imaginatively presented. You may have to queue for a table at popular times.

Kumpel PUB FOOD $$
(Кумпель; Map p118; vul Vynnychenka 6; mains 50-200uah; ⏲24hr; ❄📶) Centred on two huge copper brewing vats cooking up Krumpel's own beer, this superb around-the-clock microbrewery restaurant has a low-lit art deco theme. The menu is heavy on international meat-and-two-veg combos, with a few local elements included. Locals love it.

Sim Porosyat UKRAINIAN $$
(Сім поросят; Map p118; ☎032 297 5558; www.7piggies.com.ua; vul Stepana Bandery 9; mains 45-200uah; ⏲10am-10pm) Is it a museum of Ukrainian traditional village life or is it a restaurant plating up imaginatively cooked Ukrainian food? Well, the truth is, it's both and a lot of fun to boot. Take a seat among the rural knick-knacks, carved chairs and embroidered towels to enjoy dishes such as suckling pig, Transcarpathian *bohrach* soup and fried carp, served by Cossack waiters.

Lvivski Plyatsky CAFE $$
(Львівські Пляцки; Map p112; pl Rynok 13; strudel per 100g 42-55uah; ⏲8am-11pm) Sweet and savoury versions of the strudel, three types of sauce and a simple selection of drinks (this being Lviv, we'd plump for the coffee) – that's the basic idea behind this small place tucked beneath leaping Gothic vaulting on pl Rynok. The award-winning, rural-themed interior has cheese graters for lampshades and a definite fixation with the rolling pin.

Masoch Cafe CAFE $$
(Мазох-Кафе; Map p112; vul Serbska 7; 50-200uah; ⏲4pm-4am) One of Lviv's zanier eateries: a deep-pocketed bronze of Masoch himself, the local freak who lent his name to masochism, greets you at the door of this kinky 'eatery'. The menu of aphrodisiacs distracts little from the erotically themed decor and ambience – the waitresses even tie guests up, blindfold and whip them and force feed them things like lemon slices on request. It's all just a bit of fun, but not a place for the under-18s, that's for sure.

Amadeus EUROPEAN $$$
(Амадеус; Map p112; pl Katedralna 7; mains 150-400uah; ⏲10am-10pm; ❄) There's no gimmick at one of Lviv's finest dining spots where the refined interior, peaceful music and perfectly placed patio complement food that puts this place ahead of its rivals. Gourmet takes on Ukrainian dishes and international favourites cooked with imagination fill the long menu and the drinks card contains just about every beverage known to man. Very pleasant service.

Veronika INTERNATIONAL $$$
(Вероніка; Map p118; pr Shevchenka 21; mains 150-400uah; ⏲9am-11pm; ❄) This classy barrel cellar restaurant plates up the same menu as Amadeus (with a few additions) in a cool, tranquil atmosphere illuminated by Tiffany-style lamps. In addition there's a street-level *konditorei* (Central European cake shop and cafe), with criminally delicious desserts.

Brudershaft EUROPEAN $$$
(Брудершафт; Map p112; vul Virmenska 16; mains 200-300uah; ⏲noon-midnight Mon-Fri, from 9am Sat & Sun) Austro-Hungary is the theme at this friendly tavern, with Emperor Franz Joseph glowering on diners, a cache of WWI weapons against the bar, and flutters of Habsburg bureaucracy adorning the walls. This is also reflected in the menu, which is decidedly canivore-friendly and features boar and venison among more common members of the fauna world that regularly make it onto Central Europe's platters.

Masonic Restaurant EUROPEAN $$$
(Map p112; pl Rynok 14; mains before discount 300-500uah; ⏲11am-2am) Ascend to the 2nd floor and open the door of apartment 8. You'll

be accosted by an unshaven bachelor type, who eventually opens the door to reveal a fancy beamed restaurant full of Masonic symbols. Advertised as Galicia's most expensive restaurant, prices are 10 times higher than normal...so make sure you pick up a 90% discount card at Dim Lehend (p127) beforehand.

The food, by the way, is great and the beer and *kvas* (gingery, beer-like soft drink) come in crystal vases. The toilet is a candlelit Masonic throne. Ukraine's weirdest restaurant experience? Probably.

Panorama INTERNATIONAL **$$$**
(Map p112; ☎032 225 9009; www.panorama-hotel.com.ua; pr Svobody 45, Hotel Panorama; mains 150-500uah; ⏲7am-1am; ❄📶) From the top of the Panorama Hotel there are unrivalled views over pr Svobody and central Lviv. OK place for a mid-morning coffee to admire the vista but the food is overpriced and service nonchalant.

Drinking & Nightlife

Be careful: Lviv has so many lovely cafes luring you in with olde-worlde charm and the scent of arabica that disciples of the bean risk over-caffeination. The city also brews arguably Ukraine's best beer, with a fine and growing selection of watering holes. Though not big on classic clubbing, pl Rynok is a delight on warm summer nights, a troupe of buskers entertaining the corso and cafe tables tumbling out onto the cobbles.

★Pravda Beer Theatre BREWERY
(Map p112; www.pravda.beer; pl Rynok 32; ⏲10am-2am; 📶) The latest addition to Lviv's drinking scene is this dramatically industrial, multistorey beer temple right on pl Rynok. The master brewer here creates several types of beer, often given imaginative and sometimes political names such Obama Hope and Summer Lviv. Live music is provided by the brewery's very own **orchestra**, tours run throughout the day and there's a menu of good pub food.

The **shop** on the ground floor sells bottled beer and other souvenirs. Friendly, English-speaking staff are always on hand to help you choose.

★Svit Kavy CAFE
(Світ Кави; Map p112; www.svitkavy.com; pl Katedralna 6; ⏲7.45am-11pm Mon-Sat, from 8.45am Sun; 📶) Pick of the bunch on pl Katedralna, with no theme, no gimmicks, just a focus on Lviv's best coffee-making traditions (hence it's always packed with locals). Beans come from almost every continent, and if you like the drink, you can buy the unground raw ingredient in the **shop** next door.

★Pyana Vyshnya BAR
(П'яна вишня; Map p112; pl Rynok 11; ⏲10am-midnight) It's easy to find this one-drink bar – just look for the crowd of people on pl Rynok holding tiny glasses of something crimson, any time of the day. The tipple in question is the namesake, 18.5% volume, bitter-sweet cherry liqueur, sold by the crystal glass (36uah) or in bottles (200uah for 0.5L).

Made on the premises, it's left to mature for four weeks. It's madly popular and you'll have to queue to get some.

★Lvivska Maysternya Shokoladu CAFE
(Львівська майстерня шоколаду; Map p112; www.chocolate.lviv.ua; vul Serbska 3; ⏲9am-10pm) You'll find Lviv's chocolate cafes all over the country, but there's something special about the central Lviv branch where it all began. Cafe tables and serving points pack every free space in a tall townhouse on Serbska street, almost continually crammed with visitors downing slabs of cake and sublime coffees in between choosing from the huge array of chocolate goodies in the shops.

It's an unmissable spectacle, but you'd better like stairs.

★Lvivska Kopalnya Kavy CAFE
(Львівська копальня кави; Map p112; pl Rynok 10; ⏲8am-midnight Mon-Thu, to 2am Fri-Sun; 📶) Lviv is Ukraine's undisputed coffee capital, and the 'Lviv Coffee Mine' is where the stratum of arabica is excavated by local colliers from deep beneath pl Rynok. You can tour the mine or just sample the heart-pumping end product at tables as dark as the brews inside, or out on the covered courtyard.

The complex also has a coffee-themed **shop** and a section where you can purchase recently mined and milled beans.

Pyana Kachka CRAFT BEER
(П'яна качка; Map p112; pl Koliyivshchyny; ⏲11.30am-midnight) This simple pub puts the focus on great beer. The beverages in question: obscure craft ales from around Ukraine for 30 to 50uah a pint. There are also snacks to go with your beer and a friendly bunch behind the bar.

Robert Doms Beer House BEER HALL

(Хмільний Дім Роберта Домса; Map p118; www.robertdoms.lviv.ua; vul Kleparivska 18; ⌚noon-midnight) This fantastic, utterly unique beer hall is located three storeys underground in a centuries-old beer-storage vault once used by the neighbouring Lvivske brewery. It's named after the brewery's founder and features fresh Lvivske served in litre steins, plus German food and nightly live music in one of the vault's four chambers.

Pid Zolotoyu Zirkoyu CAFE

(Під Золотою Зіркою; Map p112; vul Kopernyka 1; ⌚9am-11pm) The latest addition to Lviv's cafe scene is this historical chemist's converted into a very stylish coffeehouse. The tables and bar are from liver-purple marble, the wooden pharmacy cabinets have been carefully renovated and the floor sports wonderful original tiles. The desserts and coffee are high quality but too highly priced for Ukraine.

Cafe 1 CAFE

(Map p112; pl Katedralna 1; ⌚10am-11pm) Bright and welcoming, the jumble sale of mismatched furniture, old shoes and potted plants that tumbles out onto pl Katedralna is Cafe 1, a great place for coffee and strudel. The interior is cosy and warm in winter; in summer head onto the terrace with pleasing views of the Boyim Chapel.

Medelin COFFEE

(Map p112; pl Koliyivshchyny 1; ⌚8.30am-11pm Mon-Fri, 10am-midnight Sat & Sun; 📶) This is a surprisingly untouristy coffeehouse given the location, a joint favoured by the locals for its brews from around the bean-growing world. The seats on leafy pl Koliyivshchyny are pleasant and there are cocktails when the Ukrainian sun relents.

Bierlin Lemberg PUB

(Map p112; vul Chaykovskoho 18; ⌚noon-10pm) The 17 types of mostly Ukrainian beer, the burlesque posters adorning the walls, the crude timber floor and smoky, rowdy, local-rockstar-gone-doolally atmosphere make this an entertaining spot to retox, though the service is nonchalant and the miserable cellar is a place to avoid.

Dzyga CAFE

(Дзиґа; Map p112; www.dzyga.com.ua; vul Virmenska 35; ⌚10am-midnight; 📶) This cafe–art gallery in the shadow of the Dominican Cathedral (p117) has a relaxed vibe. It's particularly popular with bohemian, alternative types but seems to attract pretty much everyone, really. The summertime outdoor seating is gathered around the city's Monument to the Smile. If it's full, there are other attractive options nearby on postcard-pretty vul Virmenska.

Pid Synoyu Plyashkoyu CAFE

(Під синьою пляшкою; Map p112; vul Ruska 4; ⌚10am-10pm) With its nostalgia for the Polish-Austrian past and its dark interior, the tiny 'Under the Blue Bottle' cafe at the back of a courtyard has a cosy, secretive atmosphere. It serves simple snacks and drinks inside and at a few tables in the cobbled courtyard. Set well back from the street along a passageway.

Cabinet CAFE

(Map p118; vul Vynnychenka 12; ⌚10am-11pm) Given a full makeover in recent years, the Cabinet has lost its ambience but is still a decent place for a coffee and cake stop. It's been done out as a cosy library with many books in English you can peruse at leisure.

Italiysky Dvorik CAFE

(Італійський дворик; Map p112; pl Rynok 6; ⌚10am-8pm) Even if you decide to skip the Lviv History Museum, it's worth popping in for a coffee in its aptly named inner courtyard with its Renaissance arcading.

Music Lab BAR

(Map p112; vul Brativ Rohatyntsiv 27; ⌚24hr) Low-beat rock *knaypa* (Lviv pub) where you can drink several kinds of beer and listen to (often) live music.

Livy Bereh PUB

(Map p112; pr Svobody 28; ⌚11am-2am) Buried deep beneath the Solomiya Krushelnytska Lviv Theatre of Opera and Ballet (p131), the latest incarnation of 'Left Bank' is as a pub-museum with beer and live music. The name refers to Lviv's underground river which flows under the building, glassed in and crossed by wooden footbridges at the entrance. The wonky walls and crooked door frames date back to when this was a theme restaurant.

Pyalnya BAR

(Map p112; pl Rynok 31; ⌚7am-11pm) All drinks are 20uah, all food (from 2pm) 40uah, at this popular, high-ceilinged, rather industrial drinking spot on pl Rynok. Soups, *pelmeni* (Russian ravioli), pigs' ears and *varenyky* are the highlights of the menu, but it's really the cheap booze punters line up for.

Poshta CAFE
(Пошта; Map p112; vul Drukarska 3; 10am-midnight) Post is the theme of this cafe with a huge collection of old postboxes, postcards, stamps and other postal paraphenalia adorning the walls. You can even make your own postcard of Lviv to send. The food is an unimaginative mix of salads and pastas and the staff let the place down a bit.

☆ Entertainment

Advance tickets for most of Lviv's venues are sold at the **Teatralni Kasy** (Theatre Box Office; Map p112; pr Svobody 37; 10am-5pm Mon-Sat).

Theatre & Live Music

Solomiya Krushelnytska Lviv Theatre of Opera and Ballet THEATRE
(Map p112; 032 255 4960; www.opera.lviv.ua; pr Svobody 28) For an evening of high culture, and to enjoy the ornate building, take in a performance at this Lviv institution. Closes for most of July and August.

Philharmonia CLASSICAL MUSIC
(Map p112; 032 235 8136; www.philharmonia.lviv.ua; vul Chaykovskoho 7) If classical music is your thing, let yourself be wooed by the sweet strains of Lviv's regional philharmonic orchestra. Things are very quiet here from July through to mid-September.

Teatr Zankovetskoy THEATRE
(Театр ім. Марії Заньковецької; Map p112; 032 235 5583; www.zankovetska.com.ua; vul Lesi Ukrayinky 1) Built on the site of Lviv's erstwhile city defences, Lviv's second theatre was the third-largest building in central Lviv when completed in the mid-19th century. Today it hosts a mix of operettas and plays in Ukrainian only.

Kult LIVE MUSIC
(Map p112; www.kult.lviv.ua; vul Chaykovskoho 7; noon-2am) This superb basement venue next to the Philarmonia reverberates with live Ukrainian rock music every night of the week.

Nightclubs

Picasso CLUB
(www.picasso.lviv.ua; vul Zelena 88; from 10pm) Lviv's most atmospheric club, inside a former theatre, has consistently good DJs and a festive crowd paying proper homage to them.

Rafinad People CLUB
(Map p112; www.rafinad-club.com; vul Rudanskoho 1; from 10pm) If you can get past the face control (no sports shoes, please), this is possibly Lviv's classiest mainstream club, with something happening every night of the week.

Anturazh DANCE
(067 105 8181; www.anturazh-club.com.ua; vul Chornovola 59; 6pm-5am) Hardcore nightclub with strict face control and dress code and a crowd of local footballers, businesspeople and the odd tourist who sneaked in. Some student and '90s nights.

Shopping

Lviv is one of the best places in Ukraine to spend your hryvnyas with lots of souvenir shops, market stalls, bookstores and embroidery boutiques to choose from. Prices are slightly higher than in other western Ukrainian cities, but choice is also greater and the retail experience pleasanter.

★Lvivska Maysternya Shokoladu CHOCOLATE
(Львівська майстерня шоколаду; Map p112; www.chocolate.lviv.ua; vul Serbska 3; 9am-10pm) A chocoholic's dream, nothing quite prepares you for this branch of Lviv's most famous franchise export. Over several floors of a seemingly endlessly vertical old townhouse, you'll find countless cafe tables interspersed with displays offering great slabs of Belgian-style chockie and all kinds of creations (animals, hearts, pralines) in milk and dark versions that will have you drooling.

A dream come true for fans of the 1970s Willy Wonka films. And don't worry if you don't manage to make it here – LMS has shop-cafes in 25 other Ukrainian cities, plus Baku and Kraków.

★Lvivska Maysternya Pryanykiv FOOD
(Львівська майстерня пряників; Map p112; vul Krakivska 14; 10am-10pm) This award-winning gingerbread shop is a must-see, even if you are on a sugar-free diet. The delicious toothrotters are decorated in everything from Ukrainian tridents and embroidery motifs to *The Simpsons* and funny farm animals. You can also enjoy a gingerbread treat together with a cup of Lviv coffee in the cafe, or create your own in a special **workshop**.

★Etno-Halereya CLOTHING

(Етно-Галерея; Map p112; pr Svobody 27, Opera Passage, 4th fl; 10am-8pm Mon-Sat, from 11am Sun) If you are in the market for some traditional Ukrainian folk costume and have rather a large budget, this vintage emporium sells the real thing with exquisitely crafted *vyshyvanky* (embroidered tunics), *ruchnyky* (ornamental towels) and jewellery, all from the last century, going for thousands of hryvnya. There's also a small **museum** (admission 30uah) with more valuable pieces.

Mamyna Svitlytsya CLOTHING

(Мамина світлиця; Map p112; vul Virmenska 12; 10am-7pm Mon-Sat, 11am-4pm Sun) This friendly souvenir shop sources Carpathian ceramics and embroidery direct from producers, meaning you get the real deal for a lower price. The range of Kosiv ceramics is particularly impressive.

Second-hand Book Market BOOKS

(Map p112; pl Museyna; dawn-dusk daily) Gathered aptly around the statue of Ukraine's first printer, Fedorov, this been-here-forever second-hand book market offers an eclectic range of reading matter, from *Kobzar* in original to *Mein Kampf*, Polish cookbooks to the complete works of Ivan Franko, all laid out on Soviet-era folding beds.

Outdoor Arts & Crafts Market MARKET

(Map p112; cnr vul Lesi Ukrainky & vul Teatralna; daylight hours) Located opposite the Zankovetska Theatre, this quite large market is the place to head if you are in the market for some Putin toilet roll, hairy Carpathian rugs, Soviet and prewar junk, *pysanky* (patterned eggs), woodcrafts and lots of dubious art.

Knyharnya Ye BOOKS

(Книгарня Є; Map p112; www.book-ye.com.ua; vul Halytska 9; 9am-9pm daily) Part of a chain, this excellent bookstore is of interest to foreign visitors thanks to its maps (Carpathians, other Ukrainian cities), better-than-average range of postcards, Lviv-themed guides in English and impressive coffee-table books on all things western Ukraine.

Roshen CHOCOLATE

(Map p112; www.roshen.ua; vul Valova 4; 8am-10pm Mon-Fri, from 9am Sat & Sun) The Lviv branch of president Poroshenko's signature chocolate shop is a carbon copy of all the others across Ukraine, complete with clockwork window display, large pick 'n' mix sweet section and powerful air-con.

Krakivsky Rynok MARKET

(Краківський ринок; Map p118; vul Bazarna; 6am-9pm Mon-Sat) Fans of outdoor markets will enjoy this real, bustling Soviet-style *rynok* (market) with all the fresh fruit, raw meat and cheap junk that entails.

Radist CLOTHING

(Радість; Map p112; vul Teatralna 24; 9am-7pm Mon-Fri, to 5pm Sat) Beautiful traditionally embroidered clothes made in Lviv and sold for realistic prices. Staff speak no English but are helpful and friendly.

Opera Passage MALL

(Map p112; www.operapassage.com; pr Svobody 27; 10am-8pm Mon-Fri, from 11am Sat & Sun) Elite-brand shopping mall housing a tranquil **cafe** and a better-than-average **supermarket** in the basement.

Iconart Gallery ARTS & CRAFTS

(Map p112; www.iconart.com.ua; vul Virmenska 26; 11am-7pm Tue-Sat, from noon Sun) Small shop and adjoining gallery specialising in high-quality modern twists on sacral art, including brightly coloured icons painted on glass and aged lime wood. Many of the artists work as curators and restorers at the nearby National Museum (p122).

Vinil Klub MUSIC

(Map p112; vul Brativ Rohatyntsiv 24; 10am-7pm Mon-Sat, 11am-4pm Sun) Lviv's first post-digital vinyl shop is a cool place with racks of used LPs from both abroad and the ex-USSR, Ukrainian CDs and a cellar where you can lounge around on beanbags listening to Lviv rock or Bob Marley.

Gorgany.com SPORTS & OUTDOORS

(Map p118; vul Hnatyuka 13; 10am-8pm Mon-Sat, noon-6pm Sun) Outdoor gear store with international brands.

Terra Incognita SPORTS & OUTDOORS

(Map p118; vul Pekarska 28; 10am-8pm Mon-Fri, to 6pm Sat & Sun) Outdoor-gear shop selling good-quality essentials you might need for a hike into the Carpathians. Also stocks hiking maps.

Arsen FOOD & DRINKS

(Арсен; Map p112; pl Soborna 14, Roksolana mall; 24hr) Lviv's best central supermarket is this round-the-clock affair buried deep under the embarrassingly upmarket Roksolana shopping mall. For a cheap and healthy picnic meal try their huge range of ready-made food priced per 100g.

Dim Knyhy BOOKS
(Дім книги; Map p112; pl Mitskevycha 8; ⏲10am-7pm Mon-Fri, 11am-4pm Sun) The 'House of Books' is a reliable stop-off if you are sourcing maps of the Carpathians, postcards, books in English and publications on Lviv and Ukraine.

Shos Tsikave ARTS & CRAFTS
(Щось Цікаве; Map p112; pl Rynok 13; ⏲10am-8pm) This tiny emporium is the antidote to Ukraine's souvenir industry and offers one-of-a-kind handmade crafts, some produced by disabled children. It's buried deep behind the facades on pl Rynok's southern flank – enter along the alleyway next to Lvivski Plyatsky (p128). Also has a tranquil **courtyard cafe**.

Fanat SPORTS & OUTDOORS
(Фанат; Map p112; vul Voronoho 3; ⏲10am-8pm Mon-Fri, 11am-7pm Sat & Sun) The local football team is FK Karpaty Lviv who play in the highest Ukrainian league. This is where you can pick up the team paraphernalia and there's also a small **museum** dedicated to western Ukraine's most successful club.

Ravlyk GIFTS & SOUVENIRS
(Равлик; Map p112; pr Svobody 15; ⏲10am-6pm) Located in the Museum of Ethnography, Arts & Crafts (p120), the quality of the souvenirs at Ravlyk is high, particularly the *pysanky*.

Information

The glossy English-language lifestyle and list ings magazine, *Lviv Today* (www.lvivtoday.com.ua), is available at many hotels.

Central Post Office (Map p118; vul Slovatskoho 1; ⏲9am-8pm Mon-Fri, to 4pm Sat, to 3pm Sun)

Post Office pl Rynok (Map p112; pl Rynok 2, Palazzo Bandinelli; ⏲8am-7pm Mon-Fri, to 4pm Sat, 11am-4pm Sun)

Tourist Information Centre (Map p112; ☎032-254 6079; www.lviv.travel; pl Rynok 1, Ratusha; ⏲9am-8pm May-Sep, 10am-6pm Oct-Apr) Ukraine's best tourist information centre. Branches at the airport (☎067 673 9194; ⏲open depending on flight schedule) and the train station (Map p118; ☎032 226 2005; ticket hall; ⏲9am-6pm).

Getting There & Away

There are many ways of reaching Lviv from both inside and outside Ukraine. New direct trains to/from Przemyśl and possible Ryanair flights will link the city to the outside world. There are now extra bus services to Poland, Slovakia and the Czech Republic and other airlines are taking an interest in the city. Within Ukraine Lviv is linked well by train to points east, not so well by bus.

AIR

Lviv International Airport (Danylo Halytsky International Airport; ☎032 229 8112; www.lwo.aero; vul Lyubinska 168) lies 7km west of the city centre. UIA operates flights to Boryspil airport in Kyiv (one hour, two daily). Motor Sich has a daily flight to Kyiv, too.

Lviv attracts a good number of international flights. There are currently services to/from Vienna, Munich, Warsaw, Poznań, Wrocław, Minsk, Baku, Tel Aviv, Bologna and Istanbul. In summer many seasonal flights leave for Turkey and Egypt. The possible arrival of Ryanair will expand this list substantially and may include a direct service to London Stansted.

The best central place to buy plane tickets is **Aviakasy** (Авіакаси; Map p112; vul Nalyvayka 3; ⏲9am-7pm, closed 1-2pm).

BUS

The extremely inconveniently located **main bus station** (vul Stryska 109) is a whopping 7km south of the city centre. To reach the centre take trolleybus 5 (3uah, 20 minutes). Confusing **bus station No. 8** (Map p118; pl Dvirtseva 1), in front of the main train station, is the place to pick up a quick *marshrutka* (minibus) if you miss your train or there are no tickets; it also handles a few services to western and southern destinations and is the departure point for the Shehyni border *marshrutka* (fixed-price minibus). **Bus station No. 2** (vul Bohdana Khmelnytskoho) is 3km north of the city centre (take bus 1A from pr Svobody) but is only good for services to Zhovkva (14uah, 35 minutes, several hourly), Pochayiv (102uah, 3½ hours, five daily), Olesko (42uah, 1½ hours, at least hourly) and Kremenets (115uah, 3½ hours, five daily).

From the main bus station, buses serve most major cities, including the following.

DESTINATION	COST (UAH)	TIME (HR)	FREQUENCY
Chernivtsi	173	8½	at least hourly
Ivano-Frankivsk	104	4	many daily
Kamyanets-Podilsky	200	5	7 daily
Kolomyya	100	5-6	many daily
Kyiv	370	9	5 daily
Lutsk	110	3½	13 daily
Ternopil	75	3	many daily

There are many international coach services from the main bus station. The selection of destinations by and large reflects the number of Ukrainian *gastarbeiter* (guest or foreign workers) a country has, hence the numerous connections to the Czech Republic, Italy, Spain and Germany. Buy tickets at the **International Bus Ticket Office** (Міжнародна автобусна каса; vul Stryyska 109; 9am-8pm) inside the main bus station.

TRAIN

Lviv's main train station is 2km west of the city centre, connected to town by trams 1, 9 and 10 (3uah, 30 minutes).

The quickest way to Kyiv is on the Intercity express trains (289uah, five to six hours). There are also at least 10 regular trains per day, some of them overnight services (170 to 250uah, six to 13 hours).

Other connections from Lviv:

DESTINATION	COST (UAH)	TIME (HR)	FREQUENCY (DAILY)
Chernivtsi	116	6	2
Chop	183	5½-7	2
Ivano-Frankivsk	150	2-3	up to 9
Kolomyya	150	4	2
Odesa	195	12	4
Rakhiv	115	8	1
Ternopil	110	2	12
Ternopil (*elektrychka*)	14	3	4
Uzhhorod	120-300	6-9	up to 6
Vinnytsya	150-250	4½-7	8

Slow daily international trains serve Bratislava, Budapest, Prague and a handful of destinations in Poland. The new cross-border Intercity service to Przemyśl leaves at 11.17am and takes two hours 20 minutes to reach its destination. It leaves Przemyśl at 3.42pm. There's no change of wheels at the border. A through service to Kraków is planned.

The most painless way to acquire a train ticket is to use the Soviet-era but centrally located **Train Ticket Office** (Залізничні квиткові каси; Map p118; vul Hnatyuka 20; 8am-2pm & 3-8pm Mon-Sat, to 6pm Sun).

Getting Around

Lviv is riddled with tramlines and trolleybus wires, and *marshrutky* (minibuses) dart across the cobbles and into spaces between other vehicles that sometimes turn out to be too small. The Tourist Information Centre (p133) has comprehensive maps of the entire network (unthinkable in other Ukrainian cities). Useful tram 7 trundles from the NTON hotel to the Lychakivsky Cemetery via vul Pidvalna and the Museum of Folk Architecture and Life.

There's a **bike-rental centre** (Map p112; 050 388 2701; www.veliki.ua; pl Rynok; per hour/day from 50/200uah) right on pl Rynok. Take your passport or a 1500uah deposit.

TERNOPIL REGION

Ternopil Тернопіль

0352 / POP 218,600

Arrive in Ternopil on the right day, and this town – which lends its name to the wider region – has a laid-back, leafy, almost European feel, rather like an anonymous piece of Poland or the Czech Republic. Its signature feature is a huge artificial lake that's pleasant enough to stroll around of an evening, and the tiny Old Town centre has been appealingly renovated, but that's about it. For those with time, the town could be a low-key stop-off between Chernivtsi or Kamyanets-Podilsky and Lviv. Most snore through it on a sleeper train in the early hours.

Sights

★Museum of Political Prisoners MUSEUM
(Музей політичних в'язнів; vul Kopernyka 1; donation requested; 10am-5pm Tue & Thu-Sun) FREE A block back from bul Shevchenka, this former KGB prison is where several prominent members of UPA and OUN were held, tortured and shot in the years of Soviet repression following WWII. The prison only closed in 1986 and became a museum in the mid-1990s. The dank cells and other spaces contain various chilling exhibitions but have been left in their original state complete with crumbling plaster and barred cellar windows. Access is from the back of the building.

One cell contains an interesting shrine-like exhibition on Stepan Bandera himself, others have displays on the Soviet Union and one a mock up of an UPA underground hideout. Enthusiastic guides are on hand with heaps of detail.

Ternopil Lake LAKE
(Тернопільський став) Summer in Ternopil is all about the town's lake, actually a reservoir that started life as part of a defence system for the now all-but-defunct castle.

WORTH A TRIP

TRUSKAVETS

Truskavets is an old-fashioned spa town that in another country and another time might have given the Czech Republic's celebrated Karlovy Vary a run for its money. Unfortunately, that sort of rivalry is a long way off, but the town still makes a fun day trip from Lviv. Its heart is the mineral water *buvyet* (Бювет мінеральних вод; spring) in the central park, where locals supposedly once came to drink from the fountain of good health.

Two 'cures' are on tap. Sodova water is reputedly good for the digestive tract; Naftusya for kidney, urinary tract and liver ailments. The springs only run at certain hours and you're supposed to drink the water at a certain temperature, but you can find extensive instructions posted in several languages, including English. Oddly shaped spa cups are used here, with a long spout for sucking. They are so designed because the mineral-rich water is allegedly good for other bodily parts, but not the teeth. You can buy yourself a cup in one of the park kiosks.

Truskavets has thousands of beds in all price ranges but hotels tend to be much of a sameness, a grid of unappetising concrete sanatoria with names like Dnipro, Mir and Moldova. However, one hillside hotel stands out if you fancy an overnight stay. The **Rixos-Prikarpatye** (032 477 1111; www.rixos.ua; vul Horodyshche 8, Truskavets; d/tw from 2600uah;) is an oasis of luxury with a professional medical centre, trendy modern spa treatments, German patients and Ukrainian oligarchs. It even has its own supply of Sodova and Naftusya – drunk elegantly through straws up here.

The simplest way to reach Truskavets is by bus (53uah, two hours, at least two hourly). Services leave from Lviv's bus station No. 8 (p133), in front of the train station.

Once plagued by scruffy beer tents and dubious cafes, the city side of the lake has been sanitised in recent years, an 'I Love Ternopil' selfie point installed and general order introduced. There are boat trips across water in summer, skating in winter and an easy-going mood whatever time of year you show up.

Dominican Church CHURCH

(vul Hetmana Sahaydachnoho) At the western end of vul Hetmana Sahaydachnoho, where it opens up into maydan Voli, the dirty-cream-and-grey Dominican Church and monastery complex hoists the city's finest silhouette. Built in the mid-18th century, its symmetrical twin towers rise from a baroque facade. Pop inside to see the oval nave capped with a delicately painted trompe l'oeil dome.

Outside the church stands a bronze model of early-20th-century Ternopil complete with huge Catholic church at the end of bul Shevchenka, where the TsUM department store stands today.

Bul Tarasa Shevchenka STREET

The town's verdant showpiece, complete with landscaping, fountains and mature trees, is a popular hang-out and a pleasant spot for an evening corso. Heading north you cannot fail to notice the neoclassical **Shevchenko Theatre**, one of the region's grandest neo-Classical edifices. The square in front, maydan Teatralny, is remarkable as it must be the only sizeable piazza in all Europe not to have a single cafe table or brewery-sponsored sun shade occupying its expanse.

Rizdva Khrystovoho Church CHURCH

(vul Ruska) Ternopil's most attractive ecclesiastical interior belongs to the 17th-century Church of the Nativity. Inside this oasis of calm, the nave explodes in gilded colour, musty murals and polished-brass incense burners. Outside stands a very visible monument to the 1932–33 famine (many in Ukraine are hidden in obscure locations).

Sleeping

Though tourists are few and far between, bed supply is limited in Ternopil so prices are high. A few new hotels have eased the pressure a bit but booking ahead here is still a good idea.

★ **Avalon Palace** BUSINESS HOTEL $$

(098 822 4128; www.avalon.te.ua; vul Stepana Bandery 2; s/d from 600/740uah;) Immaculate, 21st-century multistorey hotel near the train station and just 600m on foot from the city centre. Rooms are tastefully decorated, sheets are crisp and bathrooms studies

in contemporary plumbing. A rare buffet breakfast is taken in the ground-floor restaurant, staff speak English and some rooms even have balconies with station views.

Hotel Ternopil HOTEL **$$**
(☎0352 524 263; www.hotelternopil.com; vul Zamkova 14; s/d from 690/780uah; 📶) Conveniently located between the lake and the Dominican Church, the Ternopil is a renovated former Intourist wedge with a restaurant and fitness centre. Rooms are OK but still have little Soviet features such as transparent curtains and nylon bedspreads.

Eating

The 'eating out' concept has finally arrived in Ternopil after decades in the casual dining wilderness. An explosion of cafes and restaurants means there is no longer any need to fall back on the town's supermarkets for provisions. Bul Shevchenka and around the lake are the best places to head when hunger strikes.

Dva Husya CAFETERIA **$**
(3rd fl of TsUM, bul Shevchenka 12; mains 20-40uah; ⏰9am-8pm daily; ❄📶) A very convenient place to eat is this self-service canteen on the 3rd floor of the TsUM department store, right in the centre of town. Point and hope at the array of pancakes, meatballs, *borshch* and buckwheat, order a coffee or beer and install yourself in one of the red leatherette cubicles. There's good wi-fi for long hot afternoons.

Stary Mlyn UKRAINIAN **$$**
(Старий Млин; ☎0352 519 555; vul Brodivska 1A; mains 50-120uah; ⏰11am-11pm daily; 📶) This restaurant 750m north of the train station has gone the whole hog when it comes to theme dining. The traditionally done-out interior, complete with embroidered towels, ceramics, wagon wheels and twisted wood, competes with the exterior for rural zaniness. The food is straight from the village kitchen and pretty well executed, and the service is efficient.

Information

Tourist Office (☎0352 520 720; www.visit.ternopil.ua; vul Hrushevskoho; ⏰24hr daily) Ternopil's tiny tourist office is open non-stop and is staffed by a saunter of hipsters who don't speak much English. However they do have free maps and can point you in the right direction in most matters.

Getting There & Away

BUS

Ternopil's frantic bus station, 1km south of the town centre, lives up to its role as a regional hub. Connections include the following:

Ivano-Frankivsk 87uah, 2¾ hours, at least hourly

Kamyanets-Podilsky 59uah, 3½ to 4½ hours, around seven daily

Kremenets 50uah, 1½ hours, at least hourly

Lutsk 104uah, 3½ hours, 11 daily

Lviv 75uah, three hours, many daily

Pochayiv 39uah, 1½ hours, 13 daily

TRAIN

The train station stands two blocks east of bul Shevchenka. Connections to/from Ternopil:

Chernivtsi 182uah, 7½ hours, daily

Kyiv 213uah, 5½ to 7½ hours, around five daily

Lviv 110uah, two hours, 12 daily plus four slower *elektrychka* (14uah)

Getting Around

Trolleybuses 5, 8 and 9 (2uah) will get you from the bus station to the train station and the town centre.

Kremenets Кременець

☎03546 / POP 22,000

For many Ukrainian pilgrims, Kremenets is simply the jumping-off point for Pochayiv monastery, but with its historical buildings and eerie hilltop Cossack cemetery it does hold interest for the foreign traveller. However, as there are few decent hotels or places to eat, the town is best tackled as a day trip from Lutsk 96km to the north or Ternopil 70km to the south.

Sights

Kremenets Fortress CASTLE
(www.kremdiaz.com; Zamkova Hora; 10uah; ⏰24hrs) The remains of this hilltop fortress are easily breeched by individual hikers and day trippers. Dating from at least the 12th century, and possibly earlier, the *zamok* (castle) lies in ruins, with only a ring of walls and a gate tower remaining. However, it's a surprisingly pleasant spot for longer-term travellers in Ukraine to while away a few hours and the views from the hill are magnificent (see if you can spot Pochayiv glistening in the distance).

Pyatnystke Cemetery CEMETERY

(vul Kozatska) FREE Some 100 or so of the Cossacks who died in the skirmishes during the Khmelnytsky uprising against Poland in 1648 are buried in the remarkable Pyatnytske Kladovyshche (Pyatnystke Cemetery), where stubby stone crosses stand lost in the long grass. It's a tranquil spot at any time of day but get up here at dawn or dusk for a bit of Ukrainian magic.

To reach the Cossack cemetery, look for the town market, with the word ринок across an arch. Heading from here back north to the bus station, take the next right opposite a small car park. Bear left, then left again where the road forks, and walk about 10 minutes uphill.

Jesuit Collegium NOTABLE BUILDING

(vul Shevchenka) When the Poles regained control of Kremenets, they sealed their victory by building another of the town's main sights, the Jesuit Collegium (1731–43), on the main drag. In turn, the Soviets sealed their triumph in WWII by plonking a bombastic war monument right in front of the complex. The baroque church is the only part of the building you can visit.

Regional Museum MUSEUM

(vul Shevchenka 90; 10uah; ⏲8.30am-5pm Thu-Tue) The obscure Regional Museum is worth a spin for its back-to-the-1980s exhibition and light-switch monitors. Highlights include some interesting Cossack and Kyivan

WORTH A TRIP

POCHAYIV MONASTERY

Its ornate golden domes rising up from the surrounding plain, **Pochayiv Monastery** (Pochayivska Lavra; ⏲grounds 24hr, excursion bureau 11am-4pm) FREE is a beacon of Ukrainian Orthodoxy (Moscow Patriarchate) on the edge of a largely Ukrainian Catholic region. Indeed, it's the country's second largest Orthodox complex after Kyiv's Kyevo-Pecherska Lavra and was founded by monks fleeing that mother ship when the Mongols sacked Kyiv in 1240.

Visitors will find the monastery's ornate golden dome and church interiors beautiful and its mystical aura intriguing. The atmosphere is much more devout than at the *lavra* (senior monastery) in Kyiv.

Pochayiv is frequently packed, but tourists are still outnumbered by pilgrims visiting the Mother of God icon (1597) or the 'footprint of the Virgin Mary'. The busiest religious festivals are the Feast of the Assumption on 28 August and the Feast of St Iov, a 17th-century Pochayiv abbot and the *lavra*'s most important monk, on 10 September.

Both of the monastery's famous religious relics are found in the baroque Uspensky Cathedral (1771–83), whose entrance is straight ahead and to your left, on the crest of the hill after you enter the main gate. The famed footprint of Mary, reportedly left after the Virgin appeared to a local monk and a shepherd, has a holy spring with purportedly healing waters. The Mother of God icon is imbued with the power to work any miracle. Both are to the right of the central aisle.

The 65m-tall baroque bell tower (1861–71) is worth climbing for the view, if you can sneak in with a tour group or monk. Its central knocker weighs over 315kg.

On the far side of the Uspensky Cathedral is a building with a door leading down to the Cave Church. Pilgrims come here to pay their respects to the relics (ie remains) of St Iov.

Because this is an Orthodox place of worship, men aren't allowed to wear hats or shorts, and women must cover their head, knees and hands (no trousers, shorts or skirts above the knee, but six-inch heels seem to be fine). This applies to the churches and the grounds. Trouser-clad women can borrow a wraparound skirt from the excursion bureau. The souvenir stalls on the way up to the monastery do a roaring trade in headscarves. No photography is allowed anywhere once through the gates, but a snap of the views from the monastery ramparts is possibly worth a ticking-off from a monk.

Tourists almost always visit Pochayiv as a day trip, either from Ternopil, Kremenets, Dubno or even, if they have a car, from Lviv. Little white *marshrutky* shuttle back and forth almost constantly to and from Kremenets (15uah, 30 minutes), from where you can pick up services on the main Lutsk–Ternopil or Rivne–Ternopil routes. They drop off and then wait to fill up at the bottom of the hill below the monastery.

Rus–era finds, some surprisingly modest folk costumes and photos of prewar Kremenets.

Sleeping & Eating

Kremenets has a few cafes but nothing to write home about. You are likely to end up self-catering, buying supplies from one of the town's supermarkets such as **Vopak** (vul Dubenska 132; ⏲8am-10pm).

Hotel Kalyna HOTEL $

(Готель Калина; ☎03546 252 15; vul Dubenska 175B; s/d from 150/300;) Cheap, cheerful and brand new, the well-kept Kalyna is just about the best place in Kremenets to zip open your pack. Rooms are surprisingly well furnished, if a touch spartan, and the staff are friendly. There's even a decent **restaurant** on the premises. Located very near the train station, so noise from passing night trains could be an issue.

Getting There & Away

Kremenets has the following bus connections to surrounding towns:

Dubno 26uah, 45 minutes, at least twice hourly

Lutsk 70uah, two hours, hourly

Pochayiv 15uah, 30 minutes, many daily

Ternopil 50uah, 1½ hours, at least hourly

Getting Around

The Old Town centre and hilltop fortress both lie 2.5km south of the bus station along the main artery, vul Shevchenka. Turn right when exiting the bus station or bus station office, and walk 30 to 40 minutes to the town, which is strung out along the road. To climb the hill, keep going to just past the edge of the town until you reach a turn-off marked with a yellow sign bearing the words Замкова гора. The entire walk from the bus station to the summit takes roughly 1¼ hours. Alternatively, take one of the many buses or *marshrutky* from the bus station to the town centre to halve your journey on foot.

VOLYN & RIVNE REGIONS

Lutsk Луцьк

☎0332 / POP 217,100

Volyn's chief settlement, historically fascinating Lutsk is a rare thing in Ukraine – a place that takes tourism seriously. It provides visitors with the genuine Ukrainian experience and gives them a free map to help them on their way.

Like many western Ukrainian towns, Lutsk has a split personality. The modern town is a relatively successful example of Soviet architecture, with broad boulevards and monumental squares creating a feeling of freedom and space. But the real jewel in Lutsk's crown is its historic conservation area and castle. This small, slowly refurbishing enclave of cobbled streets is lined with architecture from centuries past, harking back to Lutsk's Lithuanian, Polish and Russian history.

Sights

Lutsk Castle CASTLE

(Луцький замок; vul Kafedralna 1; 20uah; ⏲10am-7pm daily May-Sep, to 5pm Oct-Apr) Lutsk's 14th-century castle stands surrounded by ornate 17th-century churches and homes and is in fairly decent shape for a Ukrainian fortress. Known as Lubart's Castle after the Lithuanian prince who ordered it built, it has sturdy 13m-high ramparts topped with three tall towers, one containing a **bell museum**. There are also the archaeological remains of a 12th-century church and 14th-century palace, a small dungeon, and various tiny museums dedicated to books, bells and local artworks.

The castle's entrance tower features on the 200uah note if you want to get a sneak preview before visiting.

Trinity Church CHURCH

(maydan Teatralny) The main Orthodox church in Lutsk dates from 1752 and is a much more atmospheric affair than the Sts Peter's and Paul's Cathedral, not having been stripped of its gilding and icons by the Soviets. The interior is perfumed with beeswax candles and infused with 260 years of worship.

The rose garden outside is an oasis of peace. The shrine in the church to the Nebesna Sotnya (those killed in Kyiv during the Maidan revolution) and those who have died fighting the Russians in the Donbas is a more recent reminder of the turbulent times Ukraine is passing through.

Museum of the Volyn Icon MUSEUM

(Музей Волинської ікони; www.volyn-ikona.at.ua; vul Yaroshchuka 5; 20uah; ⏲10am-6pm, to 5pm Sun, closed Wed & Sat) Displaying over 100 painted icons, this museum provides an overview of the celebrated Volyn school of icon painting from the 16th to the 18th century. The highlight is the 'Chelm icon of the Blessed Virgin', which attracts processions of pilgrims to the museum.

Sts Peter's and Paul's Cathedral CATHEDRAL
(vul Kafedralna) The Jesuit complex on vul Kafedralna was designed in the early to mid-17th century by Italian architect Giacomo Briano. The stately, newly renovated facade of this Catholic cathedral dates from 1640; the understated interior is painted in pink and yellow tones and contains several Polish tombs. Closed following WWII, the building served as a museum of atheism in the 1970s.

St Bridget's Convent CONVENT
(Монастир бригідок; vul Kafedralna 14) In the 18th century the nuns at this working convent (no access inside) were so strict about their 'no-male-on-the-premises' rule that they didn't allow firefighters in when the building was ablaze. The result was a huge fire that destroyed much of the original timber town. The most interesting feature today is the memorial outside to the 3000 people shot here by the NKVD in 1941 as the Nazis approached Lutsk.

Festivals & Events

Artjazz Festival MUSIC
(www.artjazz.info; late Jul) Organised by the Lutsk Jazz Club, this is one of Ukraine's best jazz festivals and takes place at Lutsk Castle and in the city of Rivne.

Polessian Summer Folk Festival CULTURAL
(www.visitlutsk.com; Jul-Aug) This festival of folk dance and music takes place throughout summer at various venues around Lutsk, including Lutsk Castle.

Bandershtat MUSIC, ART
(www.bandershtat.org.ua; early Aug) Alternative music festival with a nationalist twist held just outside Lutsk. Attracts some of the biggest names in Ukrainian rock.

City Day & Independence Day FIESTA
(late Aug) Lutsk City Day falls in the third week in August, around the time of Ukrainian Independence Day, making this a great time to be in town.

Salo Festival FOOD & DRINK
(www.visitlutsk.com; Oct) Ukraine's number-one food festival is dedicated to the locals' love of *salo* (cured lard). Held in Lesya Ukrayinka Park.

Sleeping

There's no lack of beds in Lutsk though few are in the centre. Prices are low but make sure you book ahead if your visit coincides with a big festival such as Bandershtat.

Station Resting Rooms HOTEL $
(Кімнати відпочинку; Lutsk train station, 3rd fl; dm/tw 100/200uah) The rooms at Lutsk's immaculately renovated train station would put some midrange hotels to shame, though showers and toilets are shared. A mere 100uah gets you a bed in a twin, so pay double to avoid having a random stranger tumble into your room at 3am. Check-in is at the information (ДОВІДКА) window in the main station hall downstairs.

Some rooms overlook the platform – a trainspotter's dream.

Corner House GUESTHOUSE $$
(095 502 1999; www.cornerhouse.lutsk.ua; vul Ohiyenka 15; r 500-650uah;) These new, stylishly fitted-out rooms in a quiet location are incredibly good value for money. There's a pool and *banya*, the manager is friendly and helpful (but speaks no English) and a simple breakfast is served in the kitchen for 70uah extra. Only the location is a bit tricky – take trolleybus 2 to pl Peremohy then walk for 10 minutes along vul Ohiyenka.

OFF THE BEATEN TRACK

SHATSKY NATIONAL NATURE PARK

The Shatsky National Nature Park lies 160km northwest of Lutsk in the corner between Belarus and Poland, and has some 200 lakes, rivers and streams. However, while fascinating to scientists, Ukraine's wild 'Lake District' and its deep Lake Svityaz are a long way from appealing to all but the most adventurous of (camping and rafting) tourists.

If you are interested in heading to this park, catch one of the frequent buses to Kovel from Lviv and change for the village of Shatsk. At least six buses a day also go direct to Shatsk from Lutsk (108uah, 3½ hours). Don't even consider heading this way without lashings of mosquito repellent.

SCULPTOR'S HOUSE

In a quiet spot by the Styr River, sculptor Mykola Golovan is in the process of covering his otherwise modest house with his own flowing works, creating a surreal piece of Gaudi-esque theatre in the most unexpected of locations. It's certainly one of Ukraine's zaniest dwellings and its creator is often around to show visitors his opus. To find it, head along vul Kafedralna from Lutsk Castle to the neo-Gothic, yellow-brick Lutheran church – short vul Lyuteranska starts to the left of here.

Sribni Leleky HOTEL **$$**
(Срібні лелеки; ☎0332 757 989; www.leleky.com.ua; vul Chornovola 17; r from 600uah; ❄📶) The 'sliver storks' may have a bit of awkward location (1.5km south of the bus and train stations next to a busy road), but this well-designed 'recreation complex' with 68 rooms is staffed by friendly and helpful Lutskites, and rooms are fresh and clean. Rates include breakfast.

Hotel Ukraina HOTEL **$$**
(Готель Україна; ☎0332 788 100; www.hotel-lutsk.com; vul Slovatskoho 2; s/d from 550/830uah; 📶) Thehotel of choice in Lutsk, with its central location overlooking maydan Teatralny, has 128 modern rooms, good standards and reasonable prices. Rooms are simply furnished, there's a decent restaurant, staff are pleasant enough and there's even a spa. Rates include a buffet breakfast and parking.

Eating

Following its burst of tourism enthusiasm a few years ago, Lutsk has slightly scaled back its restaurant offering. However, you can still eat well here, prices are lower than in Lviv and service is friendly.

Teatralne Kafe UKRAINIAN **$**
(Театральне Кафе; vul Lesi Ukrainky 67; mains per 100g 20-30uah; ⏲8am-10pm) The Theatre Cafe is a cheap 'n' cheerful self-service canteen where chirpy dinner ladies plate up Ukrainian comfort food plus the odd foreign invader such as pizza. There's also good coffee, a dessert section and beer on tap, the last in the list making this a lively spot for an evening pint.

Korona Vitovta UKRAINIAN **$$**
(Корона Вітовта; www.kvrestoran.com; pl Zamkova; mains 100-250uah; ⏲noon-midnight; ❄) The idea behind Lutsk's grandest restaurant came from a recipe book – unearthed during an archaeological dig – that belonged to the cook of King Vitovta of Lithuania. The current chef remains as faithful as possible to those 15th-century recipes (though a few tomatoes and potatoes have crept in somewhere) and the menu is as meat heavy as feasting medieval royals would have demanded.

The wall in the entrance hall is hung with photos of the rich and good who have dined here, including Viktor Yushchenko (before he was president).

Brave Schweyk PUB FOOD **$$**
(Бравий Швейк; vul Lesi Ukrainky 56; mains 100-200uah; ⏲10am-11pm) Named for the famous fictional Czech soldier Švejk (Schweik in German) in *Good Soldier Švejk* by Jaroslav Hašek, this place harks back to the novel's Austro-Hungarian era with its mix of sausages, goulash, pigs' knuckles, milk veal and similar specialities. The atmosphere is that of a small beer hall, where you'll find German and Czech-style lagers on tap and lively vibe come sundown.

Drinking & Nightlife

Lutsk has plenty of places for a relaxing evening drink. Just wander down vul Lesi Ukrayinky and somewhere is bound to take your fancy.

Maydan PUB
(Майдан; vul Boyka 2; ⏲9am-2am) The best, most atmospheric watering hole in town boasts a dark tavern-like hall with long benches and a stage for local weekend strummers to perform, two quieter seating areas for daytime imbibing, and a beer menu populated by brews from Western Europe, Russia and Ukraine. The food menu is overambitious so stick to Ukrainian staples.

Information

Tourist Office (☎099 644 7779, 0332 723 419; www.visitlutsk.com; cnr vul Lesi Ukrainky & vul Senatorky Levchanivskoy; ⏲9am-6pm daily Apr-Oct, to 5pm Nov-Mar; 📶) Arguably Ukraine's best tourist office offering a booking service, heaps of information and free wi-fi, tea and coffee in the office. Lutsk is also well endowed with English-language maps positioned at strategic points around town.

Getting There & Away

BUS

Lutsk's large, shabby but functional bus station (watch out for beggars and pickpockets here) is 2km northeast of the city centre, next to a huge market; trolleybus 5 (2uah, 20 minutes), plus numerous *marshrutky*, link it to central maydan Teatralny (look for signs like центр or цум).

Scheduled bus connections:

Dubno 50uah, 1½ hours, at least hourly
Kremenets 70uah, two hours, hourly
Lviv 110uah, 3½ hours, 13 daily
Ternopil 104uah, 3½ hours, 11 daily

TRAIN

The train station is just a little south of the bus station, and also northeast of the city centre. Trolleybuses 4 and 7, plus numerous *marshrutky*, shuttle between here and maydan Teatralny. There are two trains to and from Kyiv (174 to 206uah, 6½ to 7½ hours); the best of these is the overnight express leaving Lutsk at 11.28pm.

Dubno Дубно

03656 / POP 38,000

Some 50km southeast of Lutsk, Dubno is one of several towns in the region with a castle, making it a relatively interesting stopover. It's conveniently located only 41km from Kremenets and 66km from Pochayiv (p137), meaning you could in theory visit all three in one day.

Sights

Castle CASTLE

(www.zamokdubno.com.ua; vul Zamkova 7A; 35uah; 8am-noon & 1-6pm daily) Dubno castle is where Andry, the son of Cossack Taras Bulba, falls in love with a Polish princess in Gogol's famous story, *Taras Bulba*, and crosses over to join the princess and her fellow Poles. At the same time, his Cossack brothers are busy trying to starve these enemies into submission. The main attraction here is the **museum** in the Lyubomyrsky Palace which has displays of local costume, weapons and local history.

The views of the sluggish Ikva River from the ramparts are also worth getting the camera out.

Church of St Nicholas CHURCH

(vul D Halytskoho) Apart from the castle, Dubno's only other attraction is the recently renovated Church of St Nicholas (1630), whose telltale plain interior suggests it was used for secular purposes during the decades of Soviet communism.

Festivals & Events

Taras Bulba Festival MUSIC

(www.tarasbulba-fest.kiev.ua; mid-Jul) Every July, Dubno hosts the large, popular Taras Bulba Festival, a rock-music bash held at the local football stadium.

Sleeping

Hotel Dubno HOTEL $

(03656 418 02; vul D Halytskoho 9; s/d from 150/180uah;) The unimaginatively renovated but hopelessly post-communist Hotel Dubno, offering very reasonably priced accommodation, is good for a one-nighter and it does have a cafe-restaurant on the premises (when not booked for a wedding do).

Antique House GUESTHOUSE $$

(050 579 5905; vul Zamkova 17; s/d 460/630uah;) The five-room, antique-filled, hunting-themed Antique House is an astonishingly well-appointed guesthouse for rural Ukraine and the location at the gates of the castle is superb.

Getting There & Away

BUS

Dubno has bus connections to Lutsk (50uah, 1½ hours, at least hourly), Ternopil (70uah, two hours, at least hourly) and Kremenets (25uah, 45 minutes, twice hourly), from where you can change onto *marshrutky* for Pochayiv. The vast majority of services leave from the bus station on the main drag heading east, though some 'through' buses to Lutsk pick up outside the castle.

TRAIN

Slow *elektrichky* (electric trains) call at Dubno on their way to Lviv (three hours, three daily).

The Carpathians
Карпати

POP 3.5 MILLION

Includes ➡

Best Places to Eat

- Reflection (p158)
- Manufactura (p146)
- Kukhnya (p163)
- Hutsulshchyna (p150)
- Familia (p146)

Best Places to Stay

- On the Corner (p151)
- Smerekova Hata (p154)
- Good Morning B&B (p151)
- Pid Templem (p146)
- Old Continent (p162)

Why Go?

Clipping the country's southwest corner, the Carpathian arc has endowed Ukraine with a crinkled region of forested hills and fast-flowing rivers that feel a continent away from the flatness of the steppe. This is the land of the Hutsuls, whose colourful folk culture is laced through thin villages stretching languidly along wide valley floors. It's also rural Ukraine at its best, where tiered wooden churches dot hillsides, horse-drawn carts clip-clop along potholed roads, *babushkas* shoo geese, and *marshrutka* passengers cross themselves as they whizz past roadside chapels.

The 'Hutsulshchyna' may be Ukraine's epicentre of rural folk culture, but this is also a leading holiday spot. The local peaks have been a long-term hit with Ukrainian hikers and skiers; the Carpathian National Nature Park, the country's biggest, lies in this region; and within the park's boundaries rises Mt Hoverla – Ukraine's highest peak at 2061m. It's also home to Bukovel, Ukraine's glitziest ski resort.

When to Go

Ivano-Frankivsk

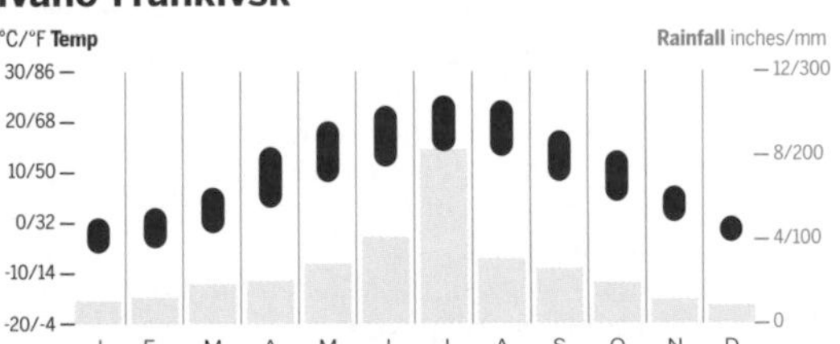

Jul Picnic on flower-filled *polonyna* (summer pastures) as you listen to the tinkle of cow bells.

Sep–Nov Watch local vintners bringing in the grape harvest in the Transcarpathia region.

Dec Enjoy some hearty Hutsul après-ski during the Carpathian ski season.

The Carpathians Highlights

1. **Kolomyya** (p150) Setting up base camp to visit its museums and arrange hikes into the hills.
2. **Uzhhorod** (p160) Soaking up the relaxed atmosphere of this border town on the frontier with Slovakia.
3. **Ivano-Frankivsk** (p144) Wandering the pastel-coloured heart of this pleasant gateway to the mountains.
4. **Mt Hoverla** (p147) Making an easy-going ascent of Ukraine's highest peak.
5. **Kosiv souvenir market** (p153) Bargaining hard for Hutsul souvenirs at this amazing craft market.
6. **Bukovel Ski Resort** (p148) Snapping on skis for a bit of downhill fun at Ukraine's ritziest ski resort.
7. **Chernivtsi University** (p156) Joining Bukovyna's student population at this trippy uni building, one of Eastern Europe's most mind-boggling places of learning.

History

Formed some 50 million years ago, during the same geological upheavals that produced the Alps, the crescent-shaped Carpathians were the cradle of Hutsul civilisation and are still home to this hardy mountain tribe.

A natural barrier between the Slavic countries and Romanised Dacia (Romania), the Carpathians have always provided a refuge from conquest and authority. When the Mongols sacked Kyiv in 1240, many of the city's citizens fled here, and when Poland and Lithuania invaded in the 14th century it's questionable how much control they exercised in the region's higher altitudes. The Poles' lengthy struggles to capture the 'Ukrainian Robin Hood' Oleska Dovbush suggest it was very little.

Signs of 19th-century Austro-Hungarian culture haven't penetrated any deeper than Ivano-Frankivsk and Chernivtsi. And when the Soviets rolled up after WWII, locals didn't exactly get out the salt and bread. The Ukrainian Insurgent Army (UPA) survived as guerrillas in the Carpathians well into the 1950s, using the mountains as a stronghold from which to launch attacks on the authorities (the UPA is a controversial entity because of its probable, but unquantified, role in the extermination of Ukrainian Jews during WWII). However, even ordinary Carpathian villagers resisted Russian rule.

The Soviets weren't initially keen on the Hutsuls' folklore and pagan traditions, but came to see their culture as a tourist attraction and largely let them be. However, the Hutsuls have long been integrated into mainstream western Ukrainian culture. Their arts, crafts, cuisine and farming lifestyle all survive, but they reserve their traditional dress, music and dancing for celebrations, ceremonies and other special occasions.

IVANO-FRANKIVSK

ІВАНО-ФРАНКІВСЬК

☎0342 / POP 231,000

A closed Soviet city until 1991, Ivano-Frankivsk is for many just a gateway to the Carpathians and a popular jumping-off point for the northern peaks. But this once grand city, sometimes dubbed 'little Lviv', is very much worth a day of exploration in its own right. With some decent places to stay, surprisingly sophisticated places to eat and a wonderful atmosphere on summer evenings, you're not likely to regret an overnight stay either.

Ivano-Frankivsk is a city that long ago embraced tourism – it was one of the first in the country to have a tourist office and now has signposting and street names in English.

Sights

★Cathedral of the Holy Resurrection CATHEDRAL

(Кафедральний собор Святого Воскресіння; maydan Sheptytskoho 22) The city's punctiliously renovated Greek Catholic cathedral is a fine example of baroque symmetry crafted in the mid-18th century. Huge bronzes of St Volodymyr and Princess Olga stand by the entrance, solemnly ushering the faithful into the beautiful, dimly lit and mustily aromatic interior.

★Former Armenian Church CHURCH

(vul Virmenska 6) A few steps off pl Rynok stands this eye-pleasingly symmetrical baroque church built by the Armenian community in 1762. Beyond the golden doors the interior is a typically fragrant affair busy with headscarved *babushkas* lighting beeswax candles and praying before gilt icons.

Ratusha NOTABLE BUILDING

(pl Rynok; 20uah; ⏲10am-1pm & 1.30-8pm Tue-Sun) In addition to housing the tourist office and the museum, Frankivsk's art-deco town hall, the only one built in this style in the country, is an attraction in itself. Sitting right in the middle of the Rynok, you can now climb the 122 steps of the building's octagonal tower for quite impressive views of all of the city's sights. Look out for the huge, circular, Soviet-era market building to the north.

Main Fountain FOUNTAIN

(maydan Vichevy) The dominating feature on maydan Vichevy is the fountain, a popular meeting spot. If you descend the steps below the fountain's main 'bowl', you can stand beneath the cascading water without getting wet – a little factoid of which locals are inordinately proud, especially those posing for wedding photos.

Taras Shevchenko Park PARK

(vul Shevchenka) Around 1.6km south of the Rynok, the city's main stretch of green is a great place to shake out the picnic blanket, hire a rowboat on the lake or chill with an ice cream, people-watching on a balmy eve. The approaches to the park are lined with refurbished Austro-Hungarian mansions and the grounds have been beautifully landscaped thanks to EU handouts.

Regional Museum MUSEUM
(Краєзнавчий музей; www.museum.if.ua; Town Hall, pl Rynok; 20uah; ⏲10am-5.30pm Tue-Sun) Within the town hall lurks the Soviet-era Regional Museum, which has displays on various archaeological digs in the region, a worthwhile room of folk art from the Carpathians, exhibitions relating to the history of Ivano-Frankivsk and a whole wing of goggle-eyed taxidermy.

Precarpathian Art Museum MUSEUM
(Музей мистецтв Прикарпаття; maydan Sheptytskoho 8; 15uah; ⏲10am-5pm Tue-Sun) Ensconced in the 17th-century Church of the Blessed Virgin Mary, the city's oldest building, this museum is packed with a jumble of religious sculptures and paintings from around central Europe.

Regional Administration Building NOTABLE BUILDING
(Обласна державна адміністрація; vul Hrushevskoho) Nicknamed the 'White House', this Soviet-realist hulk is worth seeing for its

Ivano-Frankivsk

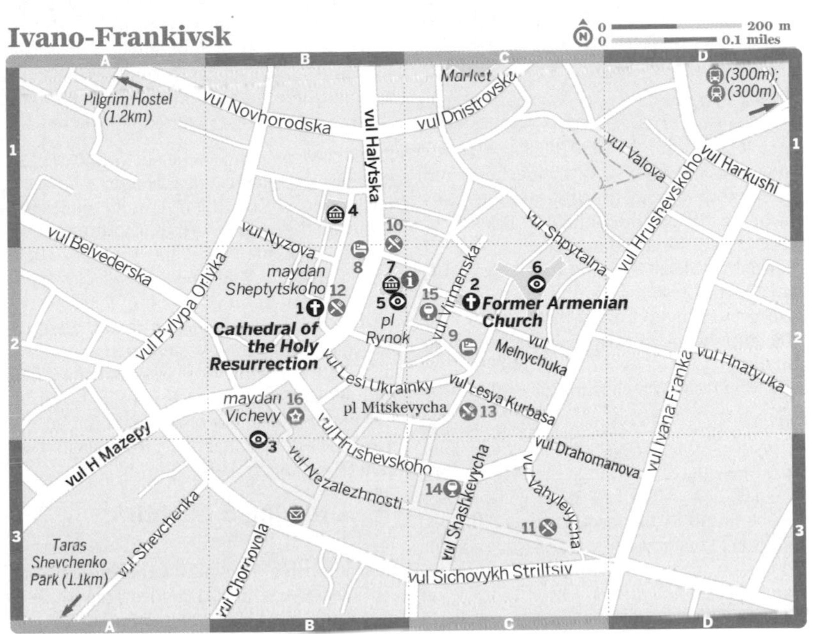

sheer size and bombast. The two traditional Ukrainian musician statues that guard the entrance are particularly impressive. The complex is not really open for visitors and there's little of interest inside anyway.

Sleeping

Pilgrim Hostel HOSTEL $

(0342 511 476, 098 606 4545; www.pilgrim-hostel.com; vul Naberezhna 28B; dm 150uah;) Though located 1.7km northwest of the city centre, this hostel has maintained its reputation as the city's best despite stiff competition. Facilities are crisp and clean and the welcome is hearty. Ask staff to pick you up at the bus or train station as it's a toughie to track down yourself.

★ **Pid Templem** HOTEL $$

(Під Темплем; 0342 595 333; www.tempel.if.ua; vul Strachenykh 7A; s 600uah d 870uah;) Just a few metres separate this 11-room hotel from the synagogue from which it takes its name (meaning 'Below the Temple'). Rooms are woody, there's free tea and coffee, a cooked-to-order breakfast is served in the cosy lobby bar and professionally minded anglophone staff are on hand. Throw in a central location, speedy wi-fi and Jewish-themed museum displays in the public areas and you have I-F's top place to catch some Zs.

Atrium HOTEL $$

(Атріум; 0342 557 879; www.atriumhotel.com.ua; vul Halytska 31; incl. breakfast, s 440uah, tw & d from 600uah;) I-F's most central beds can be found in this soothingly well-heeled minihotel looking out across pl Rynok. Rooms are studies in leathery luxury, bathrooms dazzle and staff are keen to show off their well-tuned English. Guests receive a 10% discount in the hotel's first-rate **restaurant**. Breakfast is taken in an adjoining cafe.

Eating

★ **Manufactura** HEALTH FOOD $

(vul Mytskevicha 6; dishes around 50uah; 9am-11pm Mon-Fri, 10am-11pm Sat & Sun;) Floating cloth lamps, simple timber furniture and a jolly soundtrack greet you at this cosy, family-friendly place. The menu is a simple affair of rare delights in regional Ukraine – carrot and ginger soup with bacon, baked trout in white wine sauce, lentil bake, freshly squeezed juices and sweet and savoury waffles, all made with organic ingredients as much as possible. Staff speak English and there are handmade souvenirs on sale.

Delikates CAFETERIA $

(cnr vul Halytska & pl Rynok; mains 15-20uah; 8am-10pm daily) Vaguely reminiscent of a US diner, this spacious, handily central self-service canteen plates up delicious Ukrainian food priced per 100g. There's Lviv beer on tap and a special coffee-and-cake counter, and the staff are superfriendly.

★ **Familia** UKRAINIAN $$

(vul Nezalezhnosti 31; mains 50-150uah; 9am-9pm daily;) A recent addition to Ivano-Frankivsk's dining and drinking scene, this fresh, casual bistro is incredibly progressive for Ukraine. Enjoy meat, pasta, salads and eastern Slavic favourites such as *borshch* and Carpathian trout amid blonde wood and to a funky soundtrack. Our only criticism is for the 'gourmet' portion sizes, but the long drinks menu almost makes up for those.

Franko UKRAINIAN $$

(Франко; www.franko.if.ua; vul Halytska 9A; mains 60-200uah; 10am-11pm) Franko plates up some of the best gourmet Ukrainian food in the Carpathians and has the door stickers to prove it. The finely tuned *varenyky* (dumplings), *ukha* (fish soup), *deruny* (potato pancakes) and *kotlety* (meatballs) are a world away from their canteen cousins, but there's lots of more sophisticated fare on the extensive menu if you've had your fill of Slavic edibles. The various dining spaces are done out with panache, the cellar Lower Hall (Нижній зал) being our favourite.

Drinking & Nightlife

Beer Club 10 MICROBREWERY

(Пивний клуб Десятка; www.beerclub10.if.ua; vul Shashkevycha 4; 11am-10pm Mon-Sat, from noon Sun) Good for a light lunch or a night on the house-brewed Klubne beer, this central European–style warren of brick cellars decorated with an assortment of international beer paraphernalia has proved so popular it's even subsumed a couple of adjacent eateries. Sit yourself down at one of the hefty wooden tables, wait for your golden ale to arrive, then choose from the thirst-inducing menu. Service is unusually brisk, and the crowd gets more good-natured as the night progresses.

Bochka PUB

(Бочка; vul Sheremety; mains 18-40uah; 11am-11pm) Seems every post-Soviet city has a pub called 'The Barrel', but they're not always as pleasant as this atmospheric little wood-and-stone faux-medieval cellar on pl Rynok.

Enter through the barrel-shaped facade or take a summertime seat by the town hall for a pint or two and some cheap soak-up grub.

★ Entertainment

Pasage Gartenberg CONCERT VENUE
(☎0342 725 101; www.pasage-gartenberg.com; vul Nezalezhnosti 3; 👪) Multipurpose entertainment centre in an early 20th-century former shopping gallery slap-bang in the middle of the city with 5D cinema, nightclub, pizzeria, bar, restaurant, kids room and live music. Some of the biggest names in Ukrainian music perform here so it's worth checking out the program.

ℹ Information

Post Office (vul Sichovykh Striltsiv 13A; ⏰7.30am-8pm Mon-Fri, 8am-7pm Sat, 9am-4pm Sun)

Tourist Office (☎0342 541 510; www.rtic.if.ua; Town Hall, pl Rynok; ⏰9am-7pm Mon-Fri, 10am-4pm Sat & Sun) Issues free audio guides and maps.

ℹ Getting There & Away

BUS

The bus station building is next to the train station on ramshackle pl Pryvokzalna. Only services to Ternopil leave from inconveniently located bus station No. 2 (AC-2) which can be reached by bus 22 from outside the train station. The following services run into the Carpathians and other destinations:

DESTINATION	COST (UAH)	TIME (HR)	FREQUENCY
Chernivtsi	96	3	at least hourly
Kolomyya	45	1¼	many daily
Kyiv	325	12	3 daily (2 overnight)
Lviv	104	4	many daily
Rakhiv	104	2½-4	at least hourly
Ternopil	87	2¾	at least hourly
Yaremche	42	1½	many daily

TRAIN

Ivano-Frankivsk has the following train services:

Kolomyya 13uah, 2½ hours, three daily

Kyiv 660uah, 8 to 13 hours, up to six daily

Lviv 150uah, two to three hours, up to nine daily

Rakhiv 106uah, 4¾ hours, daily

CARPATHIAN NATIONAL NATURE PARK & AROUND

КАРПАТСЬКИЙ НАЦІОНАЛЬНИЙ ПРИРОДНІЙ ПАРК

Ukraine's largest national park, **Carpathian National Nature Park** (CNNP; www.cnnp.if.ua; 20uah) is the heart of the Carpathians. However, it's a very different sort of national park – industrial logging occurs here, for example. Only about a quarter of the area is completely protected, but that hasn't detracted too much from the natural beauty of the place. Founded in 1980, the park covers 503 sq km of wooded mountains and hills. Parts of it shelter small numbers of animals and the alpine meadows are carpeted with species of flora. Realistically, however, hiking and possibly skiing are the main reasons to head this way. The adjoining Carpathian Biosphere Reserve (p153) stands a little apart from the main CNNP.

Chornohora Mountains

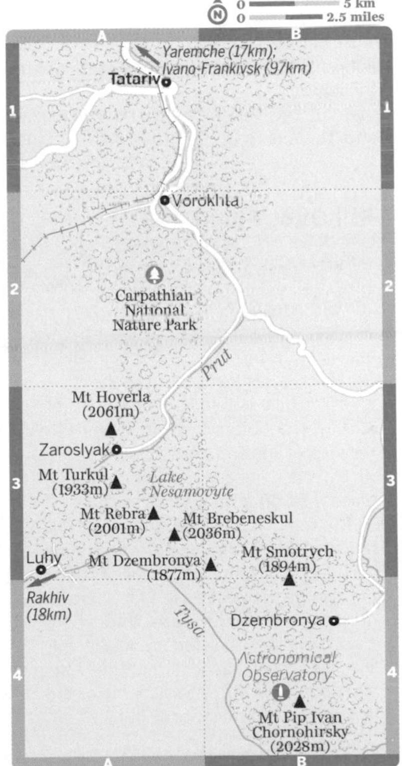

Activities

Hiking Mount Hoverla

It's hardly the most remote trail in the Carpathians, but the popular ascent to Ukraine's highest peak is relatively easy to achieve. On a clear day, the expansive views from Mt Hoverla are also breathtaking. Initially, the trail follows the Yaremche–Vorokhta–Zaroslyak road, so how much of the way you want to hike and how much you want to cover by *marshrutka* (which go as far as Vorokhta) or taxi is up to you.

About 7km south of Vorokhta you will need to take the right fork in the road, heading west. En route, you will cross the CNNP (p147) boundary and pay the entrance fee. From Zaroslyak (20km from Vorokhta) it's about 3.5km to the summit of Mt Hoverla, which is marked with a big iron cross and a huge Ukrainian national flag (which has now been joined by an equally large EU flag).

Along the Chornohora Ridge

The southern Chornohora peak of **Mt Pip Ivan Chornohirsky** (2028m) is well known for the abandoned astronomical observatory atop it. The Poles completed this observatory just before WWII, and anything of value has been looted, but the place stills retains atmosphere.

One of the easiest routes to Pip Ivan is along the crest of the Chornohora ridge from Mt Hoverla via Lake Nesamovyte. It's hard to get lost this way, as your views are unimpeded, and the route follows the former interwar border between Poland and Czechoslovakia, passing the old boundary markers. At more than 40km return, the hike will take at least three days.

Other routes to Pip Ivan include coming from the village of Verkhovyna via Dzembronya and over Mt Smotrych (requiring at least one night's camping). Alternatively, you can approach the mountain from Rakhiv.

BUKOVEL SKI RESORT

Hardcore regional skiers were sceptical when the ritzy **Bukovel resort** (☎0342 595 546; www.bukovel.com) opened in 2003-4 and immediately began attracting oligarchs from Kyiv and other 'new Ukrainian' guests. However, as the country's first fully planned ski area, Bukovel soon won doubters over with its sensible network of lifts and trails, printed trail maps, orderly queues, snowmaking machines and after-dark skiing sessions.

The resort has over 60km of runs ranging from 900m to 1370m in altitude, including 16 lifts, making it one of Eastern Europe's largest ski resorts. A brand-new road (H09) now passes through the area, cutting journey times considerably. Bukovel is best reached from Yaremche and Kolomyya, but special ski buses are laid on from Lviv and Ivano-Frankivsk at the height of the season.

Information

The **CNNP headquarters** (☎03434 227 31; www.cnnp.if.ua; vul Stusa 6; ⏲8am-5pm Mon-Fri) are in Yaremche but have little real information on hiking trails etc. The office is worth seeking out for its EU-funded exhibition on the flora and fauna of the local mountains. There are models of the peaks, a mock-up of a Hutsul dwelling and an interactive map showing short hikes. Otherwise there are no bona fide tourist offices in the region.

Getting There & Away

Bus is the most common way of reaching the access villages for the peaks. Regular services from western Ukraine's regional centres pull into places such as Yaremche and Rakhiv. From there smaller buses and minibuses continue deeper into the ranges. In summer all buses are crowded and unbearably hot. The only improvements in recent years are the new road surfaces.

The train line between Rakhiv and Kolomyya/Ivano-Frankivsk would be a superb way to access the Carpathians were there more than one train a day in any direction. Services are inconveniently timed but incredibly cheap. They are also slow, but the scenery on the other side of the windows is so wonderful that this matters little to most.

Yaremche — Яремче

☎03434 / POP 8200

Stretching for around 10km along the valley of the Prut River, Yaremche (also sometimes known as Yaremcha) is the tourist epicentre of the Carpathians. Along with a blitz of Hutsul souvenir markets and low-grade eateries, Yaremche also offers more accommodation, excursions, hikes and bike rides than any other valley community in the region. The town is an easily reachable staging point for an ascent of Mt Hoverla (join a group or catch a bus to Vorokhta) and is also one of the best places in the Ukrainian Carpathi-

THE HUTSULS

Fiercely independent and individualistic, the Carpathian-dwelling Hutsuls are a mainstay of Ukrainian national identity. They were first identified as a separate ethnic group at the end of the 18th century. According to some accounts, the 'Hutsul' encompass several tribes – including Boiki, Lemi and Pokuttian – so who and what they are is open to interpretation.

Ethnographers describe Hutsul life as dominated by herding sheep from *polonyny* (high mountain pastures) to lowland fields, with a little agriculture and forestry thrown in. They point to a dialect incomprehensible to other Ukrainians, a canon of pre-Christian, pagan legends and a diet based on mountain ingredients, including mushrooms, berries, *brynza* (a crumbly cow- or goat-milk cheese tasting like feta) and corn-based *mamalyha* (like polenta).

Wooden architecture, particularly churches, and a host of handicrafts, from decorated ceramics and embroidered shirts to woollen rugs and embossed leather, are also totems of Hutsul culture.

But whereas a traditional Hutsul would dress colourfully, carry an ornate *toporet* (hatchet) and play the *trembita* (a long alpine horn), most modern Hutsuls don't bother much with any of these. The few occasions on which they are likely to dust off their folk costumes include dances and weddings. For the former, men wear baggy trousers and women floral hair arrangements. For the latter, guests deck trees with paper flowers and ribbons, eat special flatbreads and consume lots of vodka.

Hutsul souvenirs are touted throughout the region, particularly in Yaremche. Quality ranges from mass-produced to individually crafted by local artists. Some vintage pieces are now finding their way onto the market – some local stallholders can source these, but they are more readily available in Lviv.

ans to strike out on two knobbly wheels – it boasts more bike-rental places than Kyiv. The town itself has few attractions as such, but Yaremche is all about getting out into the natural environment that surrounds it.

Activities

Dovbush Cliffs HIKING
(Скелі Довбуша) A popular activity in Yaremche (second only to souvenir shopping) is a hike to the nearby Dovbush Cliffs. To get there, take the well-signposted, not-too taxing trail that rises at the far southern end of town, 2.5km south of the train station. The caves are actually a series of boulders, which were pushed off a cliff to form shelters that outlaws once used as hideouts. With several looped trails around here, you could spend anything from half an hour to three hours walking.

Sleeping

Yaremche has no lack of bed, with everything from full-service hotels to cheap homestays to choose from. Many locals rent out rooms for as little as 120uah per person and more savvy individuals are even listing these on booking websites.

Yaremche is huge so make sure your accommodation is near the stations and easy to find (many streets lack names and house numbers). Organising a station pick-up can save you lots of legwork.

Mriya B&B $$
(Мрія; 067 902 1718; vul Hnata Hotkevych 8A; r from 500uah;) The nine rooms at this very friendly timber guesthouse are furnished jumble-sale style, but bathrooms are post-Soviet and things are pretty spacious, especially in the loft. There's a guest kitchen in the basement, and the guesthouse has its own riverside pavilion and semi-private stretch of beach. To reach Mriya, follow the signposts from the war memorial near the Vopak supermarket.

Tsvit Paporoti HOTEL $$
(Цвіт Папороті; 220 52; vul Pidskelna 10; r from 700uah;) This very well-appointed, 22-room hotel has the advantage of being easy to find with a location close to the stations. Well-proportioned rooms are a touch plasticky with synthetic fabrics, nylon carpets and faux-veneer furniture, but everything is spotless and functional and all have balconies with evergreen forest views.

Take the first left (vul Pidskelna) after the Vopak supermarket (heading from the bus station) – it's a short walk away on the right. Breakfast is 75uah extra.

YAREMCHE'S SOUVENIR MARKET

You haven't seen a Ukrainian souvenir market until you've visited the Yaremche's **market** (vul Petrasha; 9am-dusk), surely western Ukraine's largest. Now reaching absurd dimensions, it's centred around a beauty spot where a footbridge crosses the tumbling River Prut. The rocks below the bridge are still a pretty place to picnic, mainly because you can't see the market from there. On busy days tourists whizz across the river on zip lines, though most choose just to cool off in the fast-flowing water.

Krasna Sadyba HOTEL $$
(Красна садиба; 03434 212 75; www.krasnasadyba.if.ua; vul Ivasyuka 6; r 550-900uah;) In a secluded corner yet just minutes from the town centre, this red-brick hotel on the river looks like something from 'Hansel and Gretel'. Most of the 15 rooms are spacious and well furnished, and the few more basic rooms are good bargains.

Eating

For self-caterers there's a **Vopak Supermarket** (Вопак; vul Svobody 257; 8am-10pm) between the bus and train stations.

★**Hutsulshchyna** UKRAINIAN $$
(Гуцульщина; vul Svobody; mains 60-250uah; 11am-10pm daily;) Quite understandably the backdrop to many souvenir photos, this large, ornate log cabin built in the 1950s serves pretty decent food, including river fish, forest mushrooms, polenta, pancakes and all sorts of other authentically prepared regional fare. The interior is Yaremche's most tasteful, featuring real Hutsul fabrics, wood carving and ceramics – don't sit outside or you'll miss it.

It's located next to the souvenir market, around 1.5km south of the train station.

Kolyba Krasna Sadyba UKRAINIAN $$
(vul Ivasyuka 6; mains 50-150uah; 11am-midnight Tue-Sun, from 2pm Mon) Krasna Sadyba's *kolyba* (wooden hut) is one of the best eating spots in Yaremche, serving sumptuous spit-roasted pork, beef *shashlyk* (shish kebab), chicken wings or salmon on a terrace overlooking the river or in the understated Hutsul dining room. *Borshch,* forest-mushroom soup, carp, trout *and banosh* (a kind of Carpathian polenta) are other options. Beware – the interior seriously overheats in summer.

Information

Surprisingly, Yaremche has no proper tourist office.

Getting There & Away

BUS

The slightly disorganised bus station lies at the northern end of town. There are scheduled services to/from Ivano-Frankivsk (38uah, 1¼ hours, many daily) and Kolomyya (32uah, 70 minutes, 10 daily). Yaremche also lies on most routes in and out of Rakhiv (47uah, 2¼ hours, at least hourly). Nearby *marshrutka* destinations include Bukovel and Vorokhta. Be aware that journey times may now shorten due to the new road being laid along the valley at the time of research.

TRAIN

All trains between Kolomyya and Rakhiv, Lviv and Rakhiv and Ivano-Frankivsk and Rakhiv (all one each way daily) stop at Yaremche.

Kolomyya Коломия

03433 / POP 61,200

Despite being more than 50km east of the main part of the Chornohora range, pretty Kolomyya is one of the best bases for foreigners looking to discover the Carpathians. English-speaking assistance and relatively good transport links to the rest of the region make getting out into the forested peaks straightforward. It's also a centre of Hutsul culture, meaning lots of authentic souvenir material for low prices.

Spruced up in the early noughties, the town has a whiff of central Europe in places, with streets of faded fin-de-siècle architecture. This, plus two great museums, including the famous Pysanky Museum housed in a monster Easter egg, make Kolomyya a worthwhile halt on any tour of the west.

Sights

★**Museum of Hutsul Folk Art** MUSEUM
(Музей народного мистецтва Гуцульщини; 03433 239 12; http://hutsul.museum; vul Teatralna 25; 40uah; 10am-6pm Tue-Sun) This well-curated exhibition of Hutsul artefacts is probably the best of its kind in Ukraine. Decorated stove tiles and other ceramics, musical instruments, carved wooden tools, boxes, furniture, traditional and embroidered folk dress, woven wall hangings and an interesting collection of traditional Hut-

sul axes fill the museum's grand neoclassical home, which started life in the dying days of the Austro-Hungarian Empire as a Ukrainian cultural institute. Most of the wall texts have been translated into sound English but employing a guide (ask at the town's guesthouses) puts a considerable amount of meat on the exhibition's bones.

★Pysanky Museum MUSEUM
(Музей Писанки; ☎03433-278 91; vul Chornovola 39; 25uah; ⊙10am-6pm Tue-Sun) Kolomyya's most eye-catching attraction is a monster concrete Easter egg, which sits rather self-consciously on the town's main square. Inside in an adjoining building you'll discover a museum dedicated to the traditional art of egg decorating, with examples from across Ukraine as well as Romania, the Czech Republic and as far afield as India, China and Canada. Kolomyya's most photographed building also houses eggs signed by famous Ukrainians and a *pysanka* dating from 16th-century Lviv.

Sleeping & Eating

★On the Corner GUESTHOUSE $
(☎067 980 3326; vul Hetmanska 47A; dm/s/d 100/160/360uah; @🛜) The extended Pavliuk family continue to wow guests with their legendary hospitality, making this not only the best place to stay in Kolomyya, but one of the best in all Ukraine. This six-room B&B has a great range of extras such as cable TV, wi-fi, laundry and bike hire.

With outstanding cooking and coffee, a multitude of hikes and tours on offer, and assistance and advice provided in English, German, Ukrainian, Russian and Italian, comments praising 'the best place I stayed in Ukraine' just keep on filling up the guestbook.

Good Morning B&B GUESTHOUSE $
(Садиба Добрий ранок; ☎03433 547 97, 066 162 9870; www.ranok.kolomyya.org; vul Rankova 4; s/d 150/300uah; @🛜) You'll know you're on the right track to this superb B&B as the street is signposted in English from around 200m away. Charming hosts, Maria and Yuriy, speak English after having lived in the US for years, and can help with tours, travel and anything else you can think of.

The Hutsul-themed room is the most striking of the four immaculate bedrooms, the breakfast menu includes real porridge and they'll pick you up for free from the stations.

Kolomyya

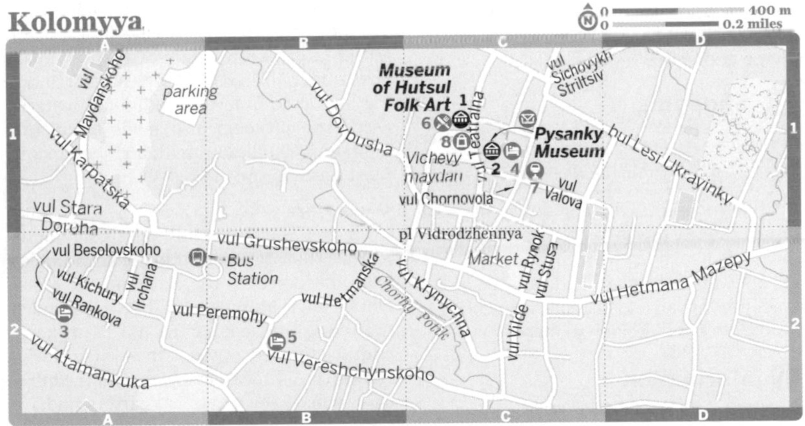

Kolomyya

Top Sights
1 Museum of Hutsul Folk Art C1
2 Pysanky Museum C1

Sleeping
3 Good Morning B&B A2
4 Hotel Pysanka C1
5 On the Corner B2

Eating
6 Kafe Elina C1

Drinking & Nightlife
7 Dzhem C1

Shopping
8 Skrynya C1

Hotel Pysanka HOTEL $
(Готель Писанка; ☎03433 203 56; www.pysanka-hotel.com; vul Chornovola 41; r 380-600uah; ❄📶) Dull but friendly and supercentral, it's strange to think the Hotel Pysanka was once the only show in town. The 22 rooms are cheaply furnished and have ageing bathrooms but some host pleasingly high ceilings. Ask for corner room 11, which has a balcony extending out towards the Pysanky Museum (p151). Breakfast is an extra 80uah.

Kafe Elina CAFE $
(Кафе Еліна; vul Shevchenka; mains 30-50uah; ⏰11am-11pm) This cafe behind the Museum of Hutsul Folk Art (p150) is a typical Hutsul *kolyba* (mountain inn) arrangement with tables and knick-knacks in a wooden hut serving large portions of Ukrainian favourites. In summer the set-up is reminiscent of a Bavarian beer garden with tables and little fairy-lit gazebos and pavilions nestling under mature trees. Service is efficient and polite.

Drinking & Nightlife

Dzhem BAR
(Джем; vul Chornovola 24; ⏰noon-midnight; 📶) Small central bar hang-out that manages to squeeze two cosy levels into its tiny interior as well as sporting a covered terrace in summer. Lots of Ukrainian beers, a vague sports theme and loud FM radio.

Shopping

Skrynya GIFTS & SOUVENIRS
(Скриня; vul Teatralna 23; ⏰9.30am-5pm Mon-Sat) If a tour of the Museum of Hutsul Folk Art has got you craving for something local to take home, this great little junk-antique-souvenir shop, hung with all kinds of ceramics, art, leather, blankets and assorted bric-a-brac (new, Soviet and prewar), is the place to head. Also stocks Kolomyya maps.

Information

Post Office (vul Chornovola 47; ⏰8am-6.30pm Mon-Fri, to 5.30 Sat)

Getting There & Away

BUS

Kolomyya's **bus station** (vul Grushevskovo) is a scruffy but functional affair. Kolomyya is linked to the following towns by bus:

Chernivtsi 56uah, two hours, at least hourly
Ivano-Frankivsk 45uah, 1¼ hours, many daily
Kosiv 26uah, one hour, many daily
Rakhiv 84uah, 3½ to four hours, seven daily
Yaremche 33uah, 70 minutes, many daily

TRAIN

Local trains go to and from Rakhiv (four hours, one daily), Ivano-Frankivsk (three hours, four daily) and Chernivtsi (two hours, four daily).

Kolomyya is linked to Lviv (280uah, five daily, three to four hours) by a variety of trains.

Kosiv Косів

☎03478 / POP 8600

Straggling along the valley of the River Rybnytsya, the ramshackle town of Kosiv is synonymous with serious, high-quality Hutsul crafts. They're sold at its well-known craft market and produced in the surrounding hills. The market and a worthwhile Hutsul-themed museum are the only real reasons to come here and most do so on a day trip from Kolomyya.

Sights

Museum of Hutsul Folk Art & Life MUSEUM
(vul Nezalezhnosti 55, 1st fl; 25uah; ⏰10am-6pm Tue-Sun) For those not seeking craft bargains, the main reason to vist Kosiv is to visit the Museum of Hutsul Folk Art and Life. It's worth visiting for a wide overview of the Hutsuls' artistic skills. It maintains a well-presented display of beautiful 19th- and 20th-century Kosiv ceramics, carpets, inlaid boxes and embossed leather, each room taking its theme from the traditional material used. The museum also holds fascinating temporary exhibitions with a Hutsul theme. Most captions are in English.

Miska Hora AREA
Kosiv is a minor Hasidic pilgrimage destination, though almost all the town's Jews were murdered by the Nazis on the Miska Hora (Town Mountain), a hill rising above the town. One side of the hill is peppered with the toppled graves of the former Jewish cemetery. Ask locals living around the hill to show you, as the graves are hard to find.

Sleeping & Eating

Stary Kosiv HOTEL $
(Старий Косів; ☎03478 528 26; vul Lesi Ukrayinky 62; d 450uah; ❄📶) Kosiv's most popular place to sleep is this sparklingly new palace-hotel around 2km east of the town centre. The hotel sits in its own slightly OTT grounds, resplendent with fake-baroque cherub statues and pergolas, but inside the staff are friendly and English-speaking,

OFF THE BEATEN TRACK

OLEKSA DOVBUSH MUSEUM

Few would brave the potholes to the sprawling Carpathian village of Kosmach, 35km to the southwest of Kolomyya, were it not for the privately run **Oleksa Dovbush Museum** (03478 576 17; vul Dovbusha 17, Kosmach; open on request) FREE. Run by the inimitable Mykhailo Didyshyn, this must be one of the oddest sights you'll find among the peaks of Europe's east. Didyshyn claims the garden hut housing his small museum is the one in which the 'Ukrainian Robin Hood' was killed and he even shows you Dovbush's very own hat, belt, axe and bag.

The rest of the one-room museum is mostly taken up with the strange figures Didyshyn has carved from tree roots, as well as assorted Carpathian junk with a tall story behind every piece. Outside stands Didyshyn's 1988 Dovbush monument, but the museum's most fascinating exhibit is the grandly mustachioed owner himself, an artist and photographer persecuted by the KGB for his Dovbush obsession. Take an interpreter along to hear some of the most colourful tales between Prague and Kyiv. Allow several hours for a visit if Didyshyn is in the mood to talk!

Substandard roads are keeping some tour guides away from Kosmach these days, which is a shame. Combined with Sheshory, it makes an interesting day out from Kolomyya, the best place to pick up a guide/interpreter, but be prepared for a rough ride. Public buses do head this way from Kolomyya but a little local help will save you lots of hassle.

rooms are spotless and well-designed, and the restaurant serves up decent food.

Garden INTERNATIONAL $
(vul Nezalezhnosti 2A; mains 30-90uah; 11am-11pm;) A much-needed addition to Kosiv's calamitous dining scene, the funky Garden feels completely out of place on Kosiv's scruffy streets. The urbane, faux-cosmo design, all lime greens, grey fabrics and chunky wood, sets the scene for the commendable attempts at pizza, salads and meat dishes. Some dishes contain rare ingredients such as pomegranate seeds; coffee comes with hot milk. There's a kid's playground outside, a jazzy soundtrack as background and Lviv beer on tap. The wi-fi and air-con make this a cool, wired hideaway on scalding afternoons.

Shopping

Craft Market MARKET
(off Highway P24; Sat) Kosiv's high-quality Hutsul crafts are sold at its well-known weekly craft market. It attracts sellers from across western Ukraine and from as far away as Moldova. Anything you buy here is guaranteed to be the real, homemade deal. It takes place on Saturday mornings, 2km southeast of the centre, across the river and just off the main P24 highway through town.

Getting There & Away

Buses run between Kosiv and Kolomyya (26uah, one hour, at least hourly). The **bus station** (vul Nebeskoyi Sotni) is in the centre of town.

Rakhiv Рахів

03132 / POP 15,400

An international band of brightly clad hikers slurping *borshch* with weather-beaten Hutsuls; mountain bikers competing with horse-drawn carts and clapped-out Ladas for pothole space; wooded mountainsides hoisting a beautiful backdrop as the fast-flowing Tysa River gurgles beneath precariously hung footbridges – this is Rakhiv, chaotically post-Soviet and crudely rural, but the best base from which to explore the southern Carpathians.

While Rakhiv's derelict state in places is shocking even by Ukrainian standards, the place has a raw energy that draws adventurous foreigners and Ukrainians alike. Some outsiders have settled here to farm and carry on the traditional ways of the Hutsuls. Peace Corps volunteers posted here love the place.

Rakhiv is good for a couple of days to organise supplies, have a chuckle visiting a 'geographical centre of Europe' that's really not, and enjoy a little hiking.

Sights

Carpathian Biosphere Reserve NATURE RESERVE
(http://cbr.nature.org.ua; Krasne Pleso 77) Declared a Unesco Biosphere Reserve in 1992, this protected area is made up of six separate locations, four of which can be found around Rakhiv. Some 90% of the reserve is made up of virgin forest, home to rare flora

UKRAINE'S ROBIN HOOD

All around the Carpathians you'll discover cliffs, rocks, trees and caves bearing the name 'Dovbush'. Legend has it that these are spots where the 'Robin Hood of the Carpathians', Oleksa Dovbush, and his band of merry Hutsuls slept while on the run.

Like his Sherwood Forest–dwelling counterpart, Dovbush robbed from wealthy merchants, travellers and nobles and distributed the loot to the poor – in his case Ruthenian peasants and poor Hutsul villagers. Born in 1700 near Kolomyya, he joined and later led a band of *opryshki* (outlaws). Many other bandits operated in the region, but Dovbush's particular generosity to the highlanders led to his legendary status.

Despite the best efforts of a hapless Polish army, which sent thousands of troops into the mountains after him, he eluded the authorities for years. In the end it was his mistress who betrayed him in 1741 to her husband, a Polish official. Arrested in the village of Kosmach he was executed without trial and his body parts displayed in villages around the Carpathians as a warning to other outlaws.

Western Ukraine continued to have a reputation for banditry until the 20th century. This dubious 'tradition' was even revived for several years in the early 1990s when whole convoys of trucks would mysteriously vanish from the region's highways.

and fauna. About 5km southwest of Rakhiv the main road leads to the **Carpathian Biosphere Reserve headquarters**, which isn't so much of interest for itself as for what's surrounding it.

Museum of Mountain Ecology MUSEUM
(Музей екології гір; ☎03132 229 14; Krasne Pleso 77; ⌚8am-5pm) FREE This old-school museum stands on the hill behind the Carpathian Biosphere Reserve headquarters building. The exhibition is surprisingly informative, rich and colourful as well as slightly kitsch, so in between sniggers at the odd moth-bitten, taxidermied sheep, you'll learn a bit from the handy Carpathian Mountains relief map, and the dioramas of forest landscapes and Hutsul festivals. Not always open when it should be, so call ahead before setting off from Rakhiv.

Geographical Centre of Europe MONUMENT
(Kruhly, Highway H09) FREE Fifteen kilometres southwest of Rakhiv lies what Ukraine contends is Europe's geographical centre, just before the village of Dilove. Ukraine is not the only country to declare itself the continent's centre: Germany, Lithuania, Poland and Slovakia have all staked rival claims. Furthermore, Austrian experts claim the pillar erected by Austro-Hungarian geographers in 1887, in what is now back-country Ukraine, was never intended to mark Europe's middle; its Latin inscription was mistranslated. None of this has dented official Ukrainian aspirations to the honour, although some locals are more sceptical. A Soviet-era spire joined the Austro-Hungarian pillar at the 'geographical centre of Europe' in the 1980s – a restaurant complex and souvenir stalls are more recent additions.

Festivals & Events

Bryndza Festival FOOD & DRINK
(⌚1st Sun Sep) The biggest annual bash in Rakhiv is the *bryndza* cheese festival that takes place at the amphitheatre above the town. Running for almost two decades it attracts *bryndz a* producers from across the Carpathian Mountains. A whopping seven tons of cheese change hands during the event.

Sleeping & Eating

★ **Smerekova Khata** GUESTHOUSE $
(Смерекова хата; ☎096 964 7603; www.smerekovahata.com.ua; vul Shevchenka 8; per person 130-170uah; 📶) This superb B&B near the market maintains its position as one of the Carpathians' most traveller-friendly halts. Rooms are fragrant with pinewood and combine traditional Hutsul bedspreads with ultramodern showers. Owners Vasyl and Anna can arrange all manner of tours and excursions, and even run Hutsul cookery classes (Vasyl is involved in Ukraine's embryonic Slow Food movement). The garden between the two buildings is a lovely spot to relax after a hike.

Dream Hostel HOSTEL $
(☎0682 525 825; www.dream-hostels.com; vul Karpatska 8a; dm from 80uah, d 290-550uah; 📶) Located near the stations, this branch of a professionally run national chain is the best place in the Carpathians to sleep on the

cheap and meet other travellers. Dorms are crisply furnished, all bunks have their own reading lights and the bathrooms are kept spotless. A kitchen and small cafe will keep you fed and there are pretty river views from strategic spots. The hostel is also a good starting point if you are in search of a guide or local tourist information.

Sadyba U Erika GUESTHOUSE $
(☎632 081 576; erwin75@mail.ru; vul Bohdana Khmelnytskoho 86; per person 120uah; P 📶) This welcoming, informal guesthouse has ageing rooms, good wi-fi and shared bathrooms. There's also a large garden to enjoy and bike hire. The owners are reliable sources of local information. It's 1.6km from the stations – take the first right just before the bridge and keep going to No. 86.

Olenka INTERNATIONAL $$
(Оленка; vul Myru 48; mains 50-100uah; ⏲8am-11pm) Rakhiv's fanciest dining option is a tranquil island of style and efficient service, and a fine place to grab some post-hike grub (but lose the muddy hiking boots first). Most items on the long menu, from local Hutsul fare to spaghetti Bolognese, were available when we visited, though food arrives micro-waved to the temperature of molten lava.

Olenka has a breakfast menu and opens early enough for it to be relevant.

Drinking & Nightlife

★Tsypa CRAFT BEER
(Ципа; www.tsypa.com.ua; cnr vuls Myru & Tykha; ⏲10am-11pm; 📶) Astoundingly out of character with the rest of Rakhiv, this excellent, colourful, egg-themed cellar pub has some of best food in Rakhiv and incredibly good, award-winning Carpathian craft beers including light Hoverla, blonde ale and an Alpine-style *rauchbier* (smoked beer) as well as its own *kvas*. Everything on the menu is available and service is pleasant.

The Tsypa brewery is based in the village of Kvasy, 15km north of Rakhiv.

Information

Rakhiv has no tourist information centre, but the small **kiosk** (vul Bohdana Khmelnytskoho) marked with a green 'i' next to the bridge (which once did serve as a centre but is now a souvenir shop) is worth a stab for basic info and maps. Otherwise the owners of Smerekova Khata and Dream Hostel are the best contacts in town when looking for a guide or tour.

Getting There & Away

BUS

Rakhiv's quaintly old-fashioned **station building** (vul Privokzalna) is open 24 hours a day and some services leave at ungodly hours. Buses winding over the mountains connect Rakhiv with the following destinations:

DESTINATION	FARE (UAH)	TIME (HRS)	FREQUENCY
Chernivtsi	144	5	6 daily
Ivano-Frankivsk	104	2½-4	at least hourly
Kolomyya	77	3½-4	8 daily
Mukacheve	117	3-4	at least hourly
Uzhhorod	144	5	around 15 daily
Yaremche	47	2¼	at least hourly

A daily overnight service runs to Prague (1150uah, 21 hours); see www.regabus.cz.

TRAIN

A handful of daily trains operate to and from Rakhiv's recently renovated terminus, one each way from Ivano-Frankivsk (five hours), one overnight service each to Lviv (115uah, eight hours) and Kyiv (283uah, 18 hours) and one service to Kolomyya (4½ hours). All of these pass through Yaremche.

Getting Around

Reaching the Museum of Mountain Ecology and the 'Geographical Centre of Europe' is a pain. Locals advise boarding any bus heading south but make sure the driver knows where you want to get off. Hitchhiking is also an option or arrange transport through your accommodation.

Heading north, there are *marshrutky* to Bohdan (11uah, at least hourly), which will bring you towards the start of the hiking trail to Mt Hoverla. Six services continue to Luhy (17uah, 1¼ hours), even closer to the trail.

Note that hitching is never entirely safe, and we don't recommend it. Travellers who hitch should understand that they are taking a small but potentially serious risk.

BUKOVYNA

Chernivtsi Чернівці

☎0372 / POP 266,300

Like many cities in the west of Ukraine, energetic Chernivtsi displays the hallmarks of a more elegant past, most obviously in the shape of its star attraction, the phantasmagorical university building. Shabby, leafy and slightly chaotic, this Ukrainian city has a somewhat non-Slavic flavour, possibly the residue of centuries of Romanian/Moldovan influence. Renovators are still busy with the stucco and whitewash in the city centre, and some of the old Austro-Hungarian tenements are looking pretty dapper, but in general Chernivtsi remains a slightly ramshackle place with a local student population keeping things lively. Just over six centuries old, Chernivtsi was once the chief city of Bukovyna (Beech Tree Land) in old Moldavia (now Moldova). It belonged to the Habsburg Empire in the 19th century, when much of the city's ornate architecture was built, and after WWI was temporarily drawn into Romania. Today the city remains the 'capital' of the unofficial Bukovyna region.

Sights

★Chernivtsi University NOTABLE BUILDING
(www.chnu.cv.ua; vul Kotsyubynskoho; tours 35uah; ⏲10am-5pm; 🚎2) University buildings are often called 'dreaming spires', but Chernivtsi's is more like an acid trip. This fantastic, Unesco-listed red-brick ensemble, with coloured tiles decorating its pseudo-Byzantine, pseudo-Moorish and pseudo-Hanseatic wings, is the last thing you'd expect here. The architect responsible was Czech Josef Hlavka, who was also behind Chernivtsi's Former Armenian Cathedral (p157), as well as large chunks of Vienna. He completed the university in 1882 for the Metropolitans (Orthodox Church leaders) of Bukovyna as their official residence. The Soviets moved the university here.

The wings surround a landscaped court. To the left as you pass the gatehouse is the **Seminarska Church** (Семінарська церква), reconsecrated in 1991 after four decades as a food store – students can get married here for free. Straight ahead stands the former main palace residence of the **Metropolitans** (Палац-резиденція метрополітів), housing two remarkable staircases and a fantastic, 1st-floor **Marmurovy Zal** (Мармуровий зал;

Chernivtsi

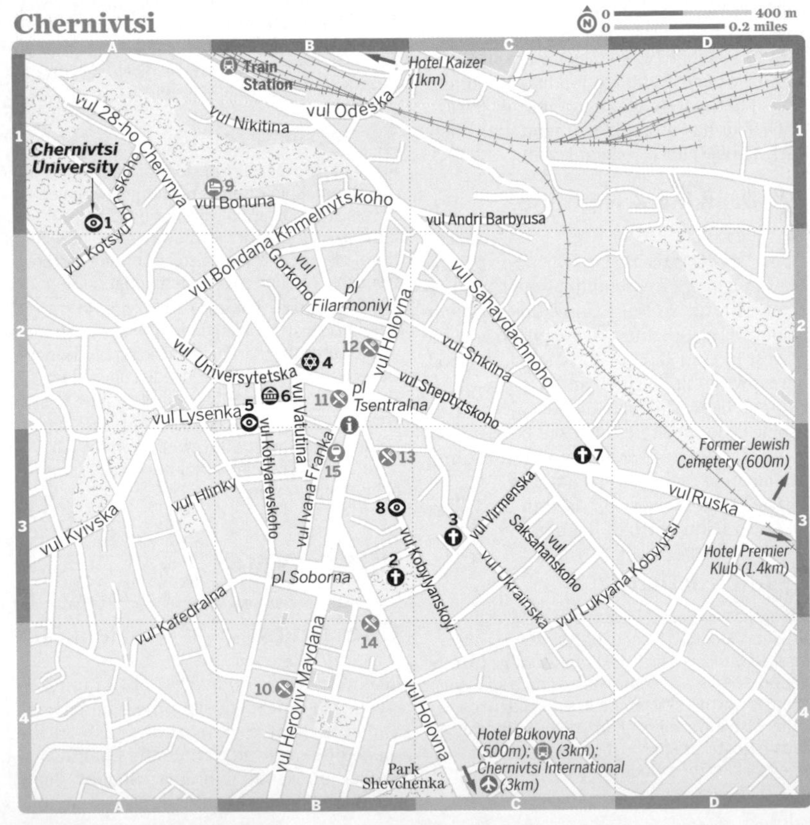

Marble Hall). Other highlights include the **Red Hall** (Червона зала) and the extensive dendropark behind the building.

As a public facility you can wander the buildings at will but the best rooms are usually locked. Best is to join a tour – official guides put together groups at the gates – but if there's no one around, the guides' office is in the church.

The university is about 1.5km northwest of the city centre.

Vul Kobylyanskoyi STREET

When you've had enough of Chernivtsi's barmy traffic, head for the tranquillity of vul Kobylyanskoyi, a pedestrianised street running between vuls Holovna and Shevchenka. It's certainly the city's most attractive thoroughfare hemmed with beautiful art nouveau facades containing music schools, a couple of minimuseums, bookshops, Lviv chain cafes, pizza places and some local government offices. Retro copies of 19th-century gas lamps, freshly planted trees and lots of benches make this the ideal venue for the evening corso and proves that Ukraine can do 'pleasant' when it puts its mind to it.

Kobylyanska Theatre NOTABLE BUILDING

(Театр ім. О. Кобилянської; www.dramtheater.cv.ua; pl Teatralna 1) Set on the exquisitely central European pl Teatralna, Chernivtsi's main drama and music theatre is a beautiful art nouveau confection that wouldn't look out of place in Prague or Paris. The ticket office is across the street at vul Lysenka 2.

Cathedral of the Holy Spirit CATHEDRAL

(Кафедральний собор Святого Духа; www.chernivtsi-sob.church.ua; vul Holovna 85) Painted a garish Disney-princess pink, the huge, mid-19th-century Orthodox cathedral that straddles gated parkland between vuls Holovna and Kobylyanskoyi is worth dipping into for its monster chandeliers, giant frescoes and high dome. It has incredible acoustics, as you'll find out if you happen to catch a wedding or christening here.

St Nicholas Cathedral CATHEDRAL

(Собор Св Миколи; vul Ruska 35) Chernivtsi's cathedral is nicknamed the 'drunken church', because of the four twisted turrets surrounding its cupola – painted blue with golden stars, these turrets create an optical illusion. The cathedral is a 1930s copy of a 14th-century royal church in Curtea de Arges (Romania).

Kalynivsky Market MARKET

(Калинівський ринок; just off P62, 3km north of city centre; ⌚8am-late) With its own police station, bus station and dedicated bank branches, this 33-hectare bazaar is like a town unto itself. As a conduit into Ukraine for goods from neighbouring countries, it attracts tens of thousands of shoppers a day and is a frenetic, intriguing phenomenon.

It's around 3km north of the city centre – take any of the numerous *marshrutky* to Калинівський ринок; many leave from in front of the train station.

Former Armenian Cathedral CHURCH

(vul Ukrainska 30; ⌚vary) In addition to Chernivtsi's fabulous university building, Josef Hlavka was also the architect responsible for the **Former Armenian Cathedral**.

Sleeping

Hotel Premier Klub HOTEL $

(Готель Прем'єр клуб; ☎554 698; vul Zhasmina 4D; d from 370uah; ❄📶) This decent, semi-budget option has a restful location around 2.5km east of the centre. Nine rooms have private bathrooms; the three more basic Ekonom class rooms share two showers and two toilets. Staff are friendly enough and the place is well maintained. Take trolleybus 2

Chernivtsi

Top Sights

1 Chernivtsi University ... A1

Sights

2 Cathedral of the Holy Spirit ... B3
3 Former Armenian Cathedral ... C3
4 Former Synagogue ... B2
5 Kobylyanska Theatre ... B2
6 Museum of Bukovinian Jews ... B2
7 St Nicholas Cathedral ... C3
8 Vul Kobylyanskoyi ... B3

Sleeping

9 Georg Palace ... B1

Eating

10 Hopachok ... B4
11 Jidalnya ... B2
12 Knaus ... B2
13 Panska Huralnya ... B3
14 Reflection ... B4

Drinking & Nightlife

15 Pub 34 ... B3

JEWISH CHERNIVTSI

One of Chernivtsi's most famous sons was leading 20th-century poet Paul Celan (1920–70), who was born into a German-speaking Jewish family at **vul Saksahansko-ho 5** (formerly Wassilkogasse), when 'Cernăuţi' was part of Romania. His parents died in Nazi concentration camps during WWII and Celan himself survived one to write his most famous 1948 poem 'Todesfuge' (Death Fugue). He later drowned himself in Paris' River Seine. There's also a **Celan monument** (Пам'ятник Паулю Целану) on vul Holovna.

Chernivtsi's **former synagogue** (cnr vul Universytetska & vul Zankovetskoyi) was once famous for its exotic African/Middle Eastern style, but was turned into a cinema in 1954. The **Museum of Bukovinian Jews** (www.muzejew.org.ua; pl Teatralna 5; admission 12uah, audio guide 10uah; ⏲10am-5pm Tue-Fri, to 2pm Sat, to 1pm Sun) brings to life the now virtually extinct Jewish culture of Bukovyna focusing on the period between 1774 and 1941.

The **former Jewish cemetery** (vul Zelena) is a melancholic jumble of leaning, overgrown headstones. To get there, follow vul Ruska (or catch trolleybus 2) until you cross the railway line. Take the first left, vul Zelena, and continue 500m.

along vul Ruska to the Zhytomyrska stop then walk along vul Zhasmina until you see the signposts. No breakfast.

Georg Palace HOTEL $$
(☎050 023 7177; www.georgpalace.com.ua; vul Bohuna 24; d from 700uah; ❄📶) New, purpose-built and professionally run, this superb hotel in a quiet street just north of the city centre is arguably Chernivtsi's best option for a night's sleep. Rooms come immaculately presented with vaguely Japanese-style furniture, pristine bathrooms and powerful air-con. Breakfast is an extra 100uah and is taken in the hotel restaurant.

Hotel Bukovyna HOTEL $$
(☎0372 585 625; www.bukovyna-hotel.com; vul Holovna 141; r from 1000uah; ❄📶) Once the only show in town, this jolly Soviet giant has renovated slowly over the last decade, though a whiff of the communist hospitality can still be felt here and there. Rooms range from 'Economy', where the post-Soviet renovation is skin-deep, to 'VIP', which comes with air-con and luxury furniture from this century. The unexpectedly good buffet breakfast spread is normally included in the price.

Hotel Kaizer HOTEL $$
(Готель Кайзер; ☎0372 585 275; www.kaiser-hotel.com.ua; vul Haharina 51; d from 600uah; ❄📶) Kyiv, Moscow, New York, Berlin, Rome, Warsaw, Istanbul: the world clocks tick loudly at the Hotel Kaizer, which offers some of Chernivtsi's nicest rooms featuring an appealing mix of new and retro furniture. They, and the lovely grill restaurant (complete with wooden windmill), are wildly underused though – probably because of the slightly out-of-the-way location on the wrong side of the train station.

Eating

Jidalnya CAFETERIA $
(Їдальня; vul Universytetska 1; mains 15-25uah; ⏲8am-7.30pm Mon-Fri, to 6pm Sat; ❄) Brightly painted no-frills, no-smiles basement feeding spot with grim dinner ladies ladling out buckwheat, pasta, fried fish and other Ukrainian staples as well as coffees and desserts. It's cheap as chips, and they have those, too.

★**Reflection** INTERNATIONAL $$
(Рефлекшн; vul Holovna 66; mains 100-160uah; ⏲9am-11pm; ❄📶) Tea, porridge, real English breakfasts – if you're from Blighty you'll love this tranquil retreat with its boutique interior, impeccably polite, English-speaking waiters and a quite un-Ukrainian atmosphere of calm and unobtrusiveness. And if you're from anywhere else, the Caesar salad, fried porcini appetisers, Black Forest gateau, pork in chilli sauce, panacotta and handmade chocolates remind you of the culinary world you left behind.

Surely one of the region's finest eateries and Chernivtsi's best since the start of the millennium.

Panska Huralnya UKRAINIAN $$
(www.huralnia.com.ua; vul Kobylyanskoyi 5; 60-300uah; ⏲11am-10pm Mon, from 10am Tue-Sun; ❄📶) Ask anyone in Chernivtsi where you should eat and most will recommend this 21st-century restaurant at the top end of vul Kobylyanskoyi. Don't be fooled by the

faux-noble entrance and uniformed waiters, inside things get quite urban with exposed brick arches, chesterfield-style booths and industrial lighting. The menu is a well-prepared mixed bag of local and international dishes.

Hopachok UKRAINIAN **$$**
(vul Heroyiv Maydanu 36A; mains 40-150uah; 10am-11pm daily;) Named after a famous Ukrainian dance, this rural-themed restaurant – all sunflowers, traditional carpets and stacked wood – has a menu that high-kicks its way through Chernivtsi's multicultural history with Jewish, Ukrainian, Moldovan and Bukovinian food all making the cut. Homemade pickles, compot, made-on-premises spirits and craft beer put this place way ahead of similar spots.

Knaus INTERNATIONAL **$$**
(www.knaus.com.ua; vul Holovna 26A; mains 60-150uah; noon-4am) Indoors this place teleports you to a kind of Ukrainian Bavaria, but summer is the best time to visit Knaus when you can sit out with a Bavarian beer in the courtyard beer garden. The menu is a mixed bag of Ukrainian staples, German pork knuckle and dumplings, and more exotic dishes such as pumpkin soup with curry.

The owners also rent out an **apartment** on the same courtyard and run a **travel company**.

Drinking & Nightlife

Pub 34 PUB
(vul Holovna 34; 11am-3am daily) Keeping to a post-Soviet tradition of naming your business after its building number, this brick cellar pub-club spins cool tracks as you kick back on leather sofas and enjoy the meat-heavy meals and beer. Live music evenings and regular DJ nights.

Information

Tourist Information Centre (0372 553 684; www.chernivtsy.eu; Tsentralna pl 1; 9am-6pm Mon-Thu, to 5pm Fri-Sun) Free audio guides available (300uah deposit or passport) and staff can arrange guides to the university.

WORTH A TRIP

KHOTYN

Ask any Ukrainian which is the country's finest castle and many will say **Khotyn Fortress** (25uah; 8am-8pm). Eastern European filmmakers love to use this massive fort overlooking the Dnister River as a location; for instance it served as Warsaw Castle in the highly controversial Russian-language blockbuster movie *Taras Bulba* (2009). With walls up to 40m high and 6m thick, today's stone fortress was built in the 15th century, replacing an earlier wooden structure. Its location safeguarded river trade routes, making it a sought-after prize.

The defining moment in its history came in 1621, with a threatened Turkish invasion. The incumbent Poles enlisted the help of 40,000 Cossacks and managed to rout a 250,000-strong Turkish army. This improbable victory made a hero of Cossack leader Petro Sahaydachny, whose huge statue greets you near the fortress entrance. However, any notion of the fortress' impregnability was dispelled in 1711 when the Turks finally nabbed it. The Russians took over in the 19th century.

Inside the fortress walls there ain't a whole lot to see, but it's really the large riverfront grounds that make the place. Some of the outer fortification walls remain and you can clamber precariously over these. In one far corner, locals even pose for pictures where it appears they're jumping over the fortress. But whatever you do, don't forget to bring a picnic.

You might first pass Khotyn on the way from Chernivtsi, but it's closer to Kamyanets-Podilsky and best visited as a day trip from there. There are regular buses and marshrutky making the 30km journey between Kamyanets-Podilsky and Khotyn (19uah, around 45 minutes) and every Kamyanets-Podilsky–Chernivtsi bus stops en route. The fortress is about 2.5km north of Khotyn town centre and the best strategy is to get off the bus when locals alight near the market (not at the far-flung bus station). Head along the road through the market and you'll pass a blue church on your right and a Soviet war memorial on your left. Stay on this road for a further 20 minutes until you see an old flaking sign marked Фортеця. Take a right here and you'll soon see the ticket office.

Getting There & Away

AIR

Chernivtsi International Airport (☎03722 432 21; http://airportchernivtsi.cv.ua; vul Chkalova 30) has two flights a day to Kyiv but bears the grand title 'international' thanks to a Sunday service to Bergamo and summer charters to Turkey.

BUS

The bus station is 3km southeast of the city centre. Coming from Kolomyya, get off the bus at the roundabout where around half the passengers alight. If you don't, you'll probably end up at the Kalynivsky Market (p157), from where you'll have to haul you luggage through the busy rows of stalls and jam it into a *marshrutka* to get to the city centre. Buses to Kolomyya leave from the same roundabout (but start at the market's bus station).

Services leave the bus station for the following destinations:

DESTINATION	COST (UAH)	TIME (HR)	FREQUENCY
Ivano-Frankivsk	96	3	at least hourly
Kamyanets-Podilsky	58	2½	at least hourly
Khotyn	49	2	30-60min
Kolomyya	56	2	at least hourly
Kyiv	334	16	6 daily (2 overnight)
Lviv	173	8½	at least hourly
Suceava	200	4	2-4 daily

TRAIN

Rail connections from Chernivtsi:

DESTINATION	COST (UAH)	TIME (HR)	FREQUENCY (DAILY)
Ivano-Frankivsk	100	2½	2
Kolomyya	12	2-2½	4
Kyiv	345	12	1
Lviv	116	6	2
Odesa	305	18	1

Getting Around

Trolleybuses 3 and 5, plus a whole host of *marshrutky*, run between the bus station and the train station. Trolleybus 2 trundles from the university to the city centre then along vul Ruska.

TRANSCARPATHIA

Most travellers are only likely to pass this way if entering or leaving Ukraine via neighbouring Hungary or Slovakia. This is a pity, as this corner of the world, where the Soviet Union faded away and Europe took over, is a melting pot of Hungarian, Slovak, Ukrainian and Roma cultures. It's also home to Ukraine's finest red wines, best-known mini spas and most impenetrable dialects. Transcarpathia is so far west that some old locals still set their clocks to Kyiv time minus one hour, and it's this undependent spirit that makes even Lviv seem a long way away beyond the high Carpathians.

Uzhhorod Ужгород

☎0132 / POP 115,100

Formerly known as Ungvar, this border town and main conduit for road traffic into and out of Slovakia and Hungary is a pleasant, if rather atypical, introduction to Ukraine. With its interwar villas, faded Hungarian shop signs, a whole neighbourhood of 1920s Czech-built administrative edifices, pedestrianised streets, a lively vibe and even the odd foreign tourist, it's as if central Europe has forgotten to end at the border, spilling over into the former USSR. With its large Hungarian and Romanian minorities and lots of cross-border wheeling and dealing, this is by far Ukraine's most cosmopolitan regional capital. Kyiv feels a long way away from here in every way, and war-torn Donetsk and occupied Crimea feel like a different continent.

Sights

★**Uzhhorod Castle** CASTLE

(vul Kapitalna; 35uah; ⏰10am-6pm Tue-Sun) On the hill overlooking the town stands the 15th-century castle with massive walls and beefy bastions built to withstand Turkish assaults. The main palace is home to the **Transcarpathian Museum of Local Lore** (Закарпатський краєзнавчий музей), which has a good collection of *pysanky* (patterned eggs), regional folk costume, some Hutsul musical instruments including nine *tremibity* (the Carpathian didgeridoo), a section on interwar Transcarpathia, a collection of antique clocks and several other themed rooms. On the ground floor the old-fashioned exhibition examines the nature of Transcarpathia.

The tranquil grounds are also fun to wander and the bastion in the northeast corner provides views across Uzhhorod. Wine tastings (p162) take place in the cellars and there's a decent restaurant (p163) in the castle. There's quite a lot to see here so allow at least two hours for a visit.

Cheshsky Kvartal AREA

(Czech Quarter) A short walk west of the immediate city centre, hemmed by the Uzh River on its southern flank, lies the Czech Quarter, an unexpected neighbourhood of 1920s Czech admin buildings and tenements, a treat for architecture fans. The assertive interwar functionalist style, so ubiquitous in Prague and other large Czech and Slovak cities, dominates, the most striking example being the Regional Assembly building. Along the river extends Europe's longest alley of lime trees, a pleasant way to wander into the area.

Folk Architecture & Life Museum MUSEUM

(Закарпатський музей народної архітектури та побуту; vul Kapitalna; 35uah; ⌚10am-6pm Wed-Mon) Next door to Uzhhorod Castle, this is one of the tidiest open-air museums in the

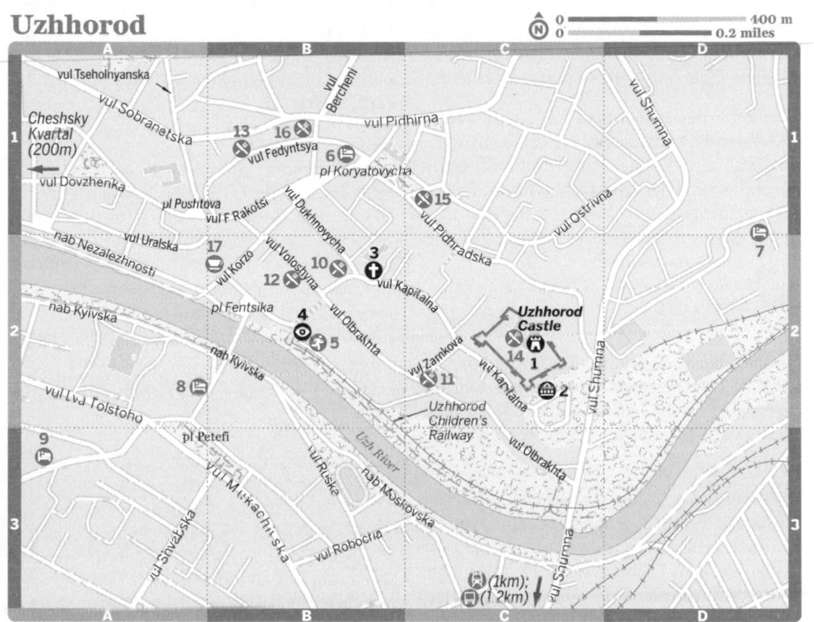

Uzhhorod

Top Sights
1 Uzhhorod Castle C2

Sights
2 Folk Architecture & Life Museum C2
3 Greek Catholic Church B2
4 Philharmonia B2

Activities, Courses & Tours
5 Uzhhorod Children's Railway B2
Wine Cellars .... (see 14)

Sleeping
6 Hotel Atlant B1
7 Hotel Ungvarskiy D1
8 Old Continent A2
9 Ungweiser A3

Eating
10 Cafe Mir B2
11 Cafe-Muzey Pid Zamkom C2
12 Eat Me B2
13 Kukhnya B1
14 Uzhhorodsky Zamok C2
15 Vopak C1
16 Yidalnya na Fedyntsya B1

Drinking & Nightlife
17 Kaktus Kafe B2
Ungweiser .... (see 9)

country, albeit small. Highlights include several Hutsul cottages with their bench-lined walls, a complete timber school and the timber 18th-century **Mykhaylivska Church** (St Michael's Church), rescued from the village of Shelestovo near Mukacheve in 1974 and still a working place of worship (services 10am Sundays).

Philharmonia NOTABLE BUILDING
(Філармонія; www.philarmonia.uz.ua; pl Teatralna) Built in 1911, it's pretty obvious at first glance that this beautiful concert venue began life as a synagogue. Its intricately carved terracota facade makes this Uzhhorod's most impressive edifice. To the left of the entrance is a small plaque to the 85,000 Transcarpathian Jews who died in the Holocaust. It's accessible only during performances.

Greek Catholic Church CHURCH
(pl Andreya Bachynskoho; 6.30am-9pm) Monumental, recently renovated and built in the neoclassical style, this 18th-century former Jesuit church is worth a peek inside for its huge iconostasis, striking ceiling frescoes and stained-glass windows.

Activities

Wine Cellars WINERY
(7 wines 75uah; 10am-6pm) If you have an urge to try the local plonk, wine tastings take place in the castle's atmospheric brick cellars with friendly sommeliers on hand.

Uzhhorod Children's Railway RAIL
(Ужгородська дитяча залізниця; adult/child 20/10uah; 11am-3pm daily May-Sep) Over the summer a narrow-gauge railway operates from near the Philharmonia building. The seven-minute ride takes you along the river to an aquapark. The line was purpose-built for children in the late 1940s and has run intermittently ever since.

Sleeping

Ungweiser PENSION $
(066 415 9287; vul Kapushanka 20; d 450uah;) The rooms above the Ungweiser microbrewery are new, immaculately maintained and air-conned to fridge-freezer levels, but a touch small for some. No noise or smell from the downstairs pub. The footbridge across the River Uzh to the centre is a mere 500m away.

Hotel Atlant HOTEL $$
(Атлант; 0312 614 095; www.atlant-hotel.com.ua; pl Koryatovycha 27; s 495uah, d from 545uah;) The 26 European-style rooms are great value, especially the singles, which are on the top floor (no lift) and have skylights and sloping ceilings. As Uzhhorod's best deal it's popular (especially on booking websites), so call ahead if you can.

Hotel Ungvarskiy HOTEL $$
(Готель Унгварський; 0312 631 515; www.ungvarskiy-hotel.com.ua; vul Elektrozavodska 2; r from 595uah;) With a miserable location on the edge of Uzhhorod's abandoned industrial zone, this plasticky hotel doesn't promise much, but inside rooms are generously cut, clean and well maintained. There's a spa, fitness centre and restaurant, where the high-quality but miserly breakfast is served by burly waiters. Lack of air-con and transparent curtains make for some superheated early starts.

★ **Old Continent** HOTEL $$$
(0312 669 366; www.hotel-oldcontinent.com; pl Petefi 4-6; s 1650-1990 d 2400-3900uah;) At Uzhhorod's finest digs the choice between 21st-century predictability, baroque opulence or swish art deco may be a difficult call, as all the rooms here are immaculate, very well maintained and sumptuously cosy. English-speaking staff are courteous, the location is bull's-eye central and there's a very good, multitasking **restaurant**.

Eating

For self-caterers, the only centrally located supermarket is **Vopak** (Вопак; vul Yarotska 2).

★ **Cafe-Muzey Pid Zamkom** EUROPEAN $
(Кафе-музей Під Замком; vul Olbrakhta 3; mains 30-70uah; 8am-11pm Mon-Fri, from 9am Sat) Wistfully celebrating Ungvar's all-too-short decades in the lap of Czechoslovak affluence, this great pub and nostalgia museum rolled into one is packed with chipped enamel signs, radios, typewriters and other assorted interwar junk. Benches are tightly packed, the Czech-style lager flows freely, and the hand-scrawled menu is a mixed bag of Ukrainian, Czech, Slovak and Hungarian fare.

Eat Me CAFE $
(vul Voloshyna 22; mains 45-85uah; 9am-10pm daily;) With colourful splashes of decor standing out against white walls, friendly service and liberally strewn design magazines, this is Uzhhorod's coolest place to take a break. Avoid the waffle menu and go for the sandwiches, coffee and cakes instead –

the lavender-and-blackcurrant latte is our own favourite. No wi-fi – to encourage conversation (according to the staff).

Cafe Mir CAFE $
(Кафе Мір; vul Kapitalna 5; pizzas 30-70uah; ⌚8am-9pm; 📶) This funky little oasis serves pizzas, cakes and drinks as you surf the web on chequered sofas. Tibetan prayer flags drape the interior and there's Mizhhirske beer on tap.

Yidalnya na Fedyntsya CAFETERIA $
(Rio Plaza mall, vul Fedyntsya; mains 15-30uah; ⌚9am-7pm Mon-Fri, to 4pm Sat; ❄) Basic self-service canteen dolloping out cheap groats for budget travellers and office workers. It's on the 1st floor of the Rio Plaza shopping mall.

★**Kukhnya** INTERNATIONAL $$
(Кухня; vul Fedyntsya 19; mains 175-240uah; ⌚noon-11pm daily; ❄📶) 'The Kitchen' serves high-quality European food in a jazzy, contemporary dining room from where you can watch chefs prepping your meal. A few traditional Carpathian dishes make it onto the menu (eel, boar) but international favourites made using top-quality ingredients rule here. There are 45 types of wine to choose from and a huge selection of whisky for postprandial chill-out time.

Uzhhorodsky Zamok UKRAINIAN $$
(Ужгородський Замок; Uzhhorod Castle; mains 30-150uah; ⌚8am-midnight) This is a cosy, old-fashioned restaurant at the castle (p160) if you happen to finish a tour at feeding time. Polite waiters keep you supplied with hearty, meaty, spice-filled dishes as you enjoy the slightly upmarket feel of what would in some countries be a touristy rip-off.

Drinking & Nightlife

Ungweiser MICROBREWERY
(www.ungweiser.com; vul Kapushanka 20; ⌚10am-midnight Sun-Thu, to 2am Fri, noon-2am Sat; 📶) Uzhhorod's top tavern is this microbrewery south of the river where large copper brewing cauldrons supply drinkers with four types of excellent beer. They also serve lots of soak-up material and guarantee a lively atmosphere in the evenings. Ask staff to show you the unusual **communism museum** hidden upstairs.

Kaktus Kafe CAFE
(vul Korzo 7; ⌚10am-10pm; 📶) The vaguely Wild West/Aztec theme may sit incongruously with the Hutsul/Transcarpathian cuisine (try the *kremzliki* – fried pork with potato pancakes in mushroom sauce) but this central joint is a long-established spot for international beer on tap, and the atmosphere is welcoming.

Information

Uzhhorod no longer has a tourist information centre but the website www.zakarpattyatourism.info has a lot of info on the city and the wider region.

Getting There & Away

BUS

There are long-distance buses to Lviv (186uah, five hours, up to 6 daily). Services also run to Rakhiv (144uah, around five hours, around 15 daily) and Mukacheve (28uah, one hour, every 15 to 20 minutes).

Marshrutky go to Chop (19uah, 50 minutes, around every 15 minutes) from the side of the **bus station** (vul Zaliznychna 2) facing the train station. Cross-border buses link Uzhhorod most usefully with Košice (201uah, 2½ hours, six daily) in Slovakia. **Regabus** (www.regabus.cz) operates a daily overnight service to Prague (950uah, 12 hours).

TRAIN

Trains to and from central Europe don't stop in Uzhhorod; you must go to nearby Chop.

Domestic trains go to and from Lviv (120-300uah, six to nine hours, up to six daily) and Kyiv (200uah, 12 to 14½ hours, four daily). Other services include slow-but-scenic *elektrychky* (electric trains) to Mukacheve (14uah, 2½ hours, six daily) via Chop.

Mukacheve Мукачево

☎03131 / POP 86,300

Echoes of Austro-Hungary, some fine interwar Czechoslovak architecture, rustic horse-drawn carts competing for cobble space and one of Ukraine's most dramatic castles make Mukacheve a worthwhile stop-off. The town can also serve as an easily reachable, low-key introduction to Ukraine if you're heading into the country by train.

Sights

★**Palanok Castle** CASTLE
(www.palanok.org.ua; prov Kurutsiv; 40uah; ⌚9am-6pm; 🚌3) Built atop a 68m-tall volcano, Mukacheve's highlight is this dramatic castle that pops up from the surrounding plain west of town, like something in a

fairy-tale fantasy. This 14th-century fortress, famous as the site where Croatian-Hungarian princess Ilona Zrini held off the Austrian Emperor's army for three years before finally capitulating in 1688, is also popular among Hungarians for its association with Sándor Petőfi (1823-49), the Hungarian national poet, who was held here during the century the building served as an Austrian prison.

A couple of ageing exhibits (folk costumes, archaeological finds) with English explanations provide minor distraction, unlike the views, which are wonderful. The scruffy souvenir stalls that once plagued the main courtyard have been cleared and once derelict spaces filled with exhibits. Half of the fun here, however, is scrambling through the different wings, getting lost on the various levels of arcading as you go.

To get here, board any bus 3 in front of the church on vul Pushkina or take any *marshrutka* heading to Тімірязєва.

Ploshcha Kyryla ta Mefodiya SQUARE

(pl Kyryla ta Mefodiya) Mukacheve's attractive main square, more a wide boulevard than a classic piazza, extends southeast from the town hall. At its northern end stands a monument to the 'Slavic apostles', Cyril and Methodius, down the middle runs a series of flower beds but the main attractions here are the rows of shops and cafes on both sides, ideal for idle ambling with an ice cream.

Town Hall NOTABLE BUILDING

(vul Pushkina) Castle aside, Mukacheve's most impressive chunk of architecture is its mint-green secessionist/neo-Gothic town hall, an unusual find in rural Ukraine. It houses various offices and businesses but sadly not a tourist office.

Sleeping & Eating

Hotel Star HOTEL $$

(☎03131 320 08; www.star-hotel.phnr.com; pl Kyryla i Mefodiya 10-12; s/d from 550/790uah; ❄📶🏊) Mukacheve's top address stands in neoclassical grandeur opposite the town hall and is by far the number one place to stay. The rug-lined, flagstaff halls and dark wooden doors lead to spotless rooms with minibar and international satellite TV. The hotel also has a rather ostentatious **restaurant** and **brews its own beer**.

Breakfast is usually included and economy room rates are low for this standard of accommodation.

Tonal HOTEL $$

(☎050 939 1542; vul Vokzalna 3; d 500uah; 📶) Just 150m from the train station, this sparklingly new minihotel is the best choice for late arrivals. Rooms are large, bathrooms clean and there's a **cafe** downstairs. Despite the hotel's sonic name, noise from the tracks out back is not an issue.

Bohrach UKRAINIAN $

(Бограч; pl Kyryla i Mefodiya 12; mains 60-90uah; ⏲7am-10am & noon-midnight) Mukacheve's top place for local rations is Bohrach, a rural-themed tavern just off the main square. The hearty Transcarpathian food comes heavily spiced and includes such local delicacies as brain stew and 'scars' in cream sauce (turns out to be tripe). The cosy interior is complimented in summer by a new, modern covered courtyard; some diners complain of long waits for food.

Getting There & Away

BUS

Services leave every 15 to 20 minutes for Uzhhorod (28uah, one hour) from the bus station, 1.5km east of the town centre. Services leave at least hourly for Rakhiv (117uah, three to four hours).

TRAIN

The train station is on vul Yaroslava Mudroho, 1.5km southwest of the town centre. Heading eastwards from Mukacheve, up to six trains a day go to Lviv (113uah, 3¾ to five hours) and up to five to Kyiv (190uah, 10½ to 14¼ hours). Heading west, there are at least six daily *elektrychka* (14uah, two hours) and mainline trains to Uzhhorod via Chop (where you can pick up international services originating in Chop).

Ukrainian Gems

Ukraine may be Europe's biggest country, but that doesn't mean its highlights are thin on the ground. Whether it be man-made gems such as the country's mammoth Soviet monuments, or nature's grand Carpathian opus, there's a lot to point your camera at in Ukraine.

Contents

Above: *Pysanky* (Easter eggs; p250)

Cultural Tapestry

Invasion, occupation and settlement from outside have bequeathed Ukraine a patchwork of cultures, from the woolly Hutsul traditions of the Carpathians to the exotic Middle Eastern world of the Crimean Tatars and the colourful Orthodox customs of the Slavic majority.

Pysanky

1 With their flashes of colour, intricate designs and pleasing shape, Ukraine's decorated eggs are an iconic symbol of traditional Slavic folk crafts. Kolomyya's Pysanky Museum (p151), itself housed in a monster egg, is the place to go to admire the egg-decorator's skill.

Bandura Players

2 Hey, Mr Bandura Man. *Kobzary* (minstrel-like bards; p252) were the keepers of Ukrainian folklore, travelling from village to village reciting epic poems across the steppe while strumming the 65-string *bandura*. Stalin had them all shot, but the tradition is making a slow comeback.

Slavic Knees-Up

3 Whether it's the on-the-spot jitter of a Hutsul hop, a boot-slapping Russian shindig, the swirling veils and curling hands of Crimean Tatars or the drama of Cossack acrobatics, dance is at the heart of all Ukraine's cultures.

Taras Shevchenko Statues

4 Chiselled in classic stone, set in 19th-century bronze and moulded in Art Deco concrete, old and young, moustachioed and clean-shaven, statues of the national poet Taras Shevchenko (p253) can be found in almost every city across Ukraine.

Jewish Ukraine

5 Jewish communities were virtually wiped out in the Holocaust and depleted further by post-independence emigration, but remnants of Ukraine's Jewish past can be seen in Berdychiv, Uman, Bratslav and Lviv.

Clockwise from top
1. Painting *pysanky* (Easter eggs; p250) **2.** *Bandura* player (p252), Kyiv **3.** Traditional dancers, Odesa

1

3

CAROL WILEY / GETTY IMAGES ©

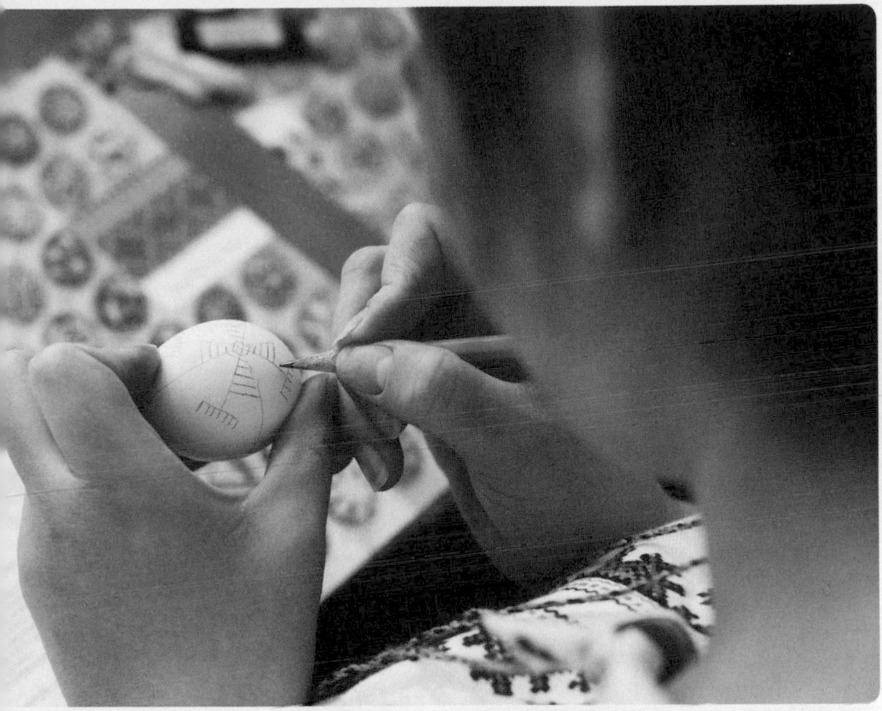

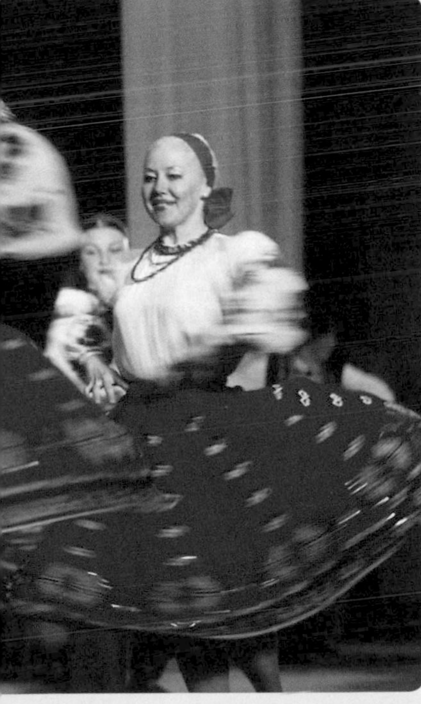

2

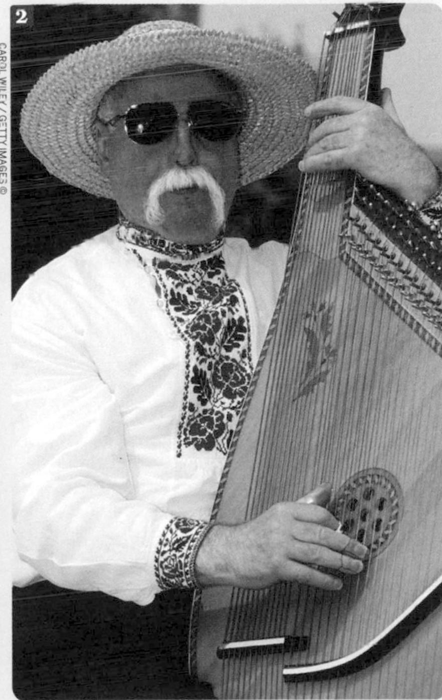

Great Outdoors

The Ukrainian steppe, traversed by mighty rivers, rolls on to far-flung horizons. The Carpathians, in the country's west, and the Crimean peninsula, jutting into the Black Sea in the south, provide striking landscapes and show-stopping vistas.

Kara-Dah Nature Reserve

1 Eerie volcanic rock formations on Crimea's east coast (p203) create an otherworldly landscape.

Black Sea Coast

2 A balmy Black Sea slaps its tepid waves against almost 2800km of coastline, much of which is hemmed with golden sand or shingle. Odesa (p174) is where most bucket-and-spade fun is to be had.

Snow Fun

3 Popular with Ukraine's steppe dwellers, and enjoying a relatively long winter season, the Carpathian ski resorts are slowly getting their act together. The most developed winter sports centre at Bukovel (p148), which has 60km of slopes and may one day host the Winter Olympics.

Summer in the Carpathians

4 With soothingly forested peaks and broad valleys, western Ukraine's Carpathian Mountains (p142) are the best place to head for some warm-weather hiking and mountain biking. Trails are faint or unmarked, but locals are working on them.

Mount Hoverla

5 At a mere 2061m, Ukraine's highest peak (p148) hardly has the Himalayas quaking with fear, but it makes up for its modest altitude with some soothing Carpathian vistas. The trails to the top are easy, but get busy in summer.

WIN-INITIATIVE / GETTY IMAGES ©

1

4

YEVGEN TIMASHOV / GETTY IMAGES ©

Clockwise from top left

1. Kara-Dah Nature Reserve (p203) **2.** Otrada Beach on the Route of Health (p178), Odesa **3.** Snowboarders in the Carpathians (p142) **4.** Hiking (p148) in the Carpathians

SASHA MASLOV / GETTY IMAGES ©

3

Religious Artistry

A highlight of Ukraine is its churches: from the golden domes of Orthodox monasteries to the Gothic arches of western Ukraine and the timber spires of the Carpathians, there's certainly nothing austere about its places of worship.

Inside an Orthodox Church

1 Featuring elaborately carved iconostases, riotously frescoed walls and neck-stiffening high domes, Ukrainian churches will impress you with their colour, atmosphere and scent.

Underground Monks

2 Kyiv's famous Kyevo-Pecherska Lavra cave complex (p56), final resting place of medieval monks, is one of Orthodox Christianity's most scared places. A tour is a memorable, if rather creepy experience, accompanied by pilgrims from across Eastern Europe.

Carpathian Timber Churches

3 If there's one commodity the Carpathians have in ample supply, it's wood! Locals have been cobbling together timber churches since at least the 16th century, and although fire and woodworm have destroyed many, a surprising number still dot the landscape.

Onion-Domed Beauty

4 The sight of the gilt onion domes of an Orthodox cathedral or monastery catching the fiery rays of a Ukrainian sunset is one of the strongest images travellers take home from these parts.

Temple Fatigue in Lviv

5 Lviv is said to have over 100 churches – not bad for a city of just over 700,000. The most interesting examples hoist their spires above the city centre, where it's easy to overdose on beautiful church interiors.

Clockwise from top

1. Bernardine Church and Monastery (p119), Lviv **2.** Kyevo-Pecherska Lavra (p56), Kyiv **3.** Mykhaylivska Church (p162), Uzhhorod

Soviet Relics

Ukraine may be shaking off the last vestiges of the Soviet Union, but some mammoth reminders of the USSR are here to stay. Lenin may have gone, but Stalinist metro stations, war memorials and giant sword-wielding women will be harder to remove.

Kyiv's Ornate Metro

1 Blasted deep into the rock below the city, Kyiv's metro system (p86) is a time-warped subterranean realm of ornate Stalinist-era stations, brave-new-world frescoes and socialist-realist reliefs.

Kharkiv's Derzhprom Building

2 Proof that big can be quite clever, Kharkiv's mammoth Derzhprom (House of State Industry; p214) used pioneering construction techniques when it was built in the 1920s. Now in a bit of a state, its granite and concrete hulk still dominates the world's second-largest city square.

Rodina Mat

3 There are red stars atop towers, plinthed tanks and brutish Red Army conscripts seemingly emerging from the bedrock, but the queen of Soviet relics must be Kyiv's sword-wielding Rodina Mat (Defence of the Motherland; p56).

Where's Lenin?

4 A post-Maidan phenomenon was the Leninopad – a play on words that sounds like *listopad*, the time of falling leaves – saw many a taxi-hailing Lenin tumble unceremoniously onto the cobbles across Ukraine, leaving many an empty plinth behind. He was replaced in Kyiv by a golden toilet.

Nuclear Missile Museum

5 The Cold War is long over and much of Ukraine's military infrastructure has been left to crumble into the steppe. But the fascinating Museum of Strategic Missile Forces (p172) near Pervomaysk is a real missile base preserved in the middle of the Ukrainian countryside.

RAINER LESNIEWSKI / SHUTTERSTOCK ©
1

2
SERGBOB / GETTY IMAGES ©

Right
1. Arsenala metro station (p57), Kyiv **2.** Derzhprom (p214), Kharkiv

Southern Ukraine
Південна Україна

POP 4.7 MILLION

Includes ➡

Best Places to Eat

- ➡ City Food Market (p183)
- ➡ Tavernetta (p184)
- ➡ Klarabara (p185)
- ➡ Bernardazzi (p185)
- ➡ Dacha (p184)

Best Places to Stay

- ➡ Hotel Londonskaya (p181)
- ➡ Frederic Koklen (p183)
- ➡ Mozart Hotel (p183)
- ➡ Dunayskaya Usadba (p192)
- ➡ Babushka Grand Hostel (p181)

Why Go?

This region feels much more New World than Europe. The flat steppe between the deltas of the Dnipro and the Danube was only properly colonised after Russian empress Catherine the Great wrested it from the Turks.

It was indeed touted as the Russian California when immigrants from all over Europe poured in to cultivate virgin lands and build the port of Odesa. Greek, Yiddish, Italian and German were all spoken here along with Russian and Ukrainian.

Although less multicultural today, Odesa is still permeated with *porto franco* spirit, displaying Jewish humour and French conviviality, along with crumbling mansion houses, which line the streets named after settlers' ethnicities.

To the west, colonist heritage lingers next to the birding paradise of the Danube Delta. In the east, swathes of virgin steppe are preserved on Dzharylhach island and in Askaniya Nova Reserve, which an eccentric German aristocrat populated with wildebeest and zebras.

When to Go

Odesa

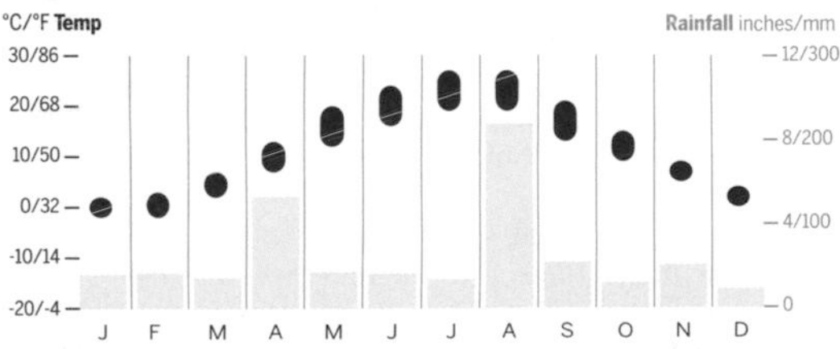

May Smell blooming lilacs and join the vanguard of Odesa's beach-bum army.

Jul Gorge on delicious fruit and watch silent movies on the Potemkin Steps.

Oct Arrive in time for the bird migration in the impressive Danube Delta.

Southern Ukraine Highlights

1. **City Food Market** (p183) Join Odesa foodies on a revolutionary assault.
2. **Askaniya Nova Reserve** (p182) Spot a zebra on a steppe safari through a vast wildlife reserve.
3. **Potemkin Steps** (p175) Relive the most poignant of cinematographic dramas at this Odesa landmark.
4. **Akkerman Fortress** (p189) Look down at the Dniester Estuary as if you own it.
5. **Dunayskaya Usadba** (p192) Overnight at a boatman's house before venturing into the Danube Delta.
6. **Vul Derybasivska** (p177) Mingle with the merriest of ex-USSR crowds in Odesa.
7. **Shabo Winery** (p190) Sample the produce of Ukraine's most progressive vineyard.
8. **Museum of Odesa Modern Art** (p178) See how artists reflect on Ukraine's tumultuous politics.

ODESA ОДЕСА

☎048 / POP 1 MILLION

Odesa is a city straight from literature – an energetic, decadent boom town. Its famous Potemkin Steps sweep down to the Black Sea and Ukraine's biggest commercial port. Behind them, a cosmopolitan cast of characters makes merry among neoclassical pastel buildings lining a geometric grid of leafy streets.

Immigrants from all over Europe were invited to make their fortune here when Odesa was founded in the late 18th century by Russia's Catherine the Great. These new inhabitants, particularly Jews, gave Russia's southern window on the world a singular, subversive nature.

Having weathered recent political storms, Odesa is booming again – it now substitutes for Crimea as the main domestic holiday destination. It's a golden age for local businesses, but it puts a strain on the already crowded sandy beaches.

History

Catherine the Great imagined Odesa as the St Petersburg of the south. Her lover, General Grygory Potemkin, laid the groundwork for her dream in 1789 by capturing the Turkish fortress of Hadjibey, which previously stood here. However, Potemkin died before work began on the city in 1794 and his senior commanders oversaw its construction instead. The Spanish-Neapolitan general José de Ribas, after whom the main street, vul Derybasivska, is named, built the harbour. The Duc de Richelieu (Armand Emmanuel du Plessis), an aristocrat fleeing the French Revolution, became the first governor, overseeing the city's affairs from 1803 to 1814.

In 1815, when the city became a duty-free port, things really began to boom. Its huge appetite for more labour meant the city became a refuge – 'Odesa Mama' – for runaway serfs, criminals, renegades and dissidents; many were fleeing the persecution of Christians in the Ottoman empire. By the 1880s it was the second-biggest Russian port, with grain the main export, and an important industrial base.

It was the crucible of the early 1905 workers' revolution, with a local uprising and the mutiny on the battleship *Potemkin Tavrichesky*. Then, between 1941 and 1944, Odesa sealed its reputation as one of the 'hero' cities when partisans sheltering in the city's catacombs during WWII put up a legendary fight against the occupying Romanian troops (allies of the Nazis). Around 100,000 Jews in the Odesa region were shot or burnt alive by the Romanians implementing the Nazi racial purification doctrine.

Odesa became a very Jewish city in the 1920s after many rural Jews moved in here while Russian bourgeoisie and intellectuals were fleeing the Bolshevik revolution. But the Holocaust and emigration fuelled by Soviet anti-Semitism reduced the Jewish minority to almost a shadow. Many Jews moved to New York's Brighton Beach, now nicknamed 'Little Odessa'.

As an almost entirely Russian-speaking city, with local identity by far prevailing over national loyalties, Odesa has always been skeptical about Ukraine's independence. But when local pro-Russian forces attempted a coup in the heady days of the Maidan revolution in 2014, residents didn't rush to support them. A stand-off with pro-Maidan Odessites ended in tragedy when a blaze killed dozens of pro-Russian activists in a trade union building they had seized.

As a result of that incident, the situation calmed down, and the city has since replaced Crimea as the number-one destination for domestic tourists. In a peculiar twist, the former president of Georgia, Mikheil Saakashvili, was appointed the governor of Odesa region. But after a promising a start, he didn't achieve much progress, fell out with Kyiv and resigned.

Sights

Odesa may lack the must-see sights of Kyiv or Lviv, but it still packs plenty of charm with its splendid architecture, eye-popping panoramas and quirky monuments. The city centre's shaded avenues are tailor-made for strolling, so lace up your best walking shoes. Most of Odesa's attractions are overhead in the form of intricate turn-of-the-20th-century facade details, onion-domed church spires and towering statues.

★Potemkin Steps — LANDMARK

(Потьомкінські сходи) A woman yells at a tidy line of soldiers as they take aim. An officer commands: 'Fire!' It takes many painful seconds for her to collapse and release a pram with a baby inside, which starts slowly tumbling down the steps – these very steps. All of that never happened during the real battleship *Potemkin* mutiny, but the genius film director Sergei Eisenstein made the world believe it did in his film *Battleship Potemkin*.

The steps lead down from bul Prymorsky to the sea port. Pause at the top to admire the sweeping views of the harbour. You can avoid climbing back up by taking a **funicular railway** (bul Primorsky; 3uah; ⏲8am-11pm) that runs parallel. Or, having walked halfway up, you can sneak into a passage that now connects the steps with the reconstructed **Istanbul Park**.

★Prymorsky Boulevard — STREET

(Приморський бульвар) Odesa's elegant facade, this tree-lined, clifftop promenade was designed to enchant the passengers of arriving boats with the neoclassical opulence of its architecture and old-worldish civility, unexpected in these parts at the time of construction in the early 19th century. Imperial architects also transformed the cliff face into terraced gardens descending to the port, divided by the famous Potemkin Steps – the **Istanbul Park** lies east of the steps and the **Greek Park** west of them.

At the boulevard's eastern end, you'll spot the pink-and-white colonnaded **City Hall**, which originally served as the stock exchange. The cannon here is a war trophy captured from the British during the Crimean War. In the square in front of City Hall is Odesa's most photographed monument, the **Pushkin statue**. The plaque reads 'To Pushkin – from the Citizens of Odesa'.

Continuing along the boulevard, at the top of the Potemkin Steps you'll reach the **statue of Duc de Richelieu** (Пам'ятник Рішельє), Odesa's first governor, looking like a Roman in a toga.

Odesa

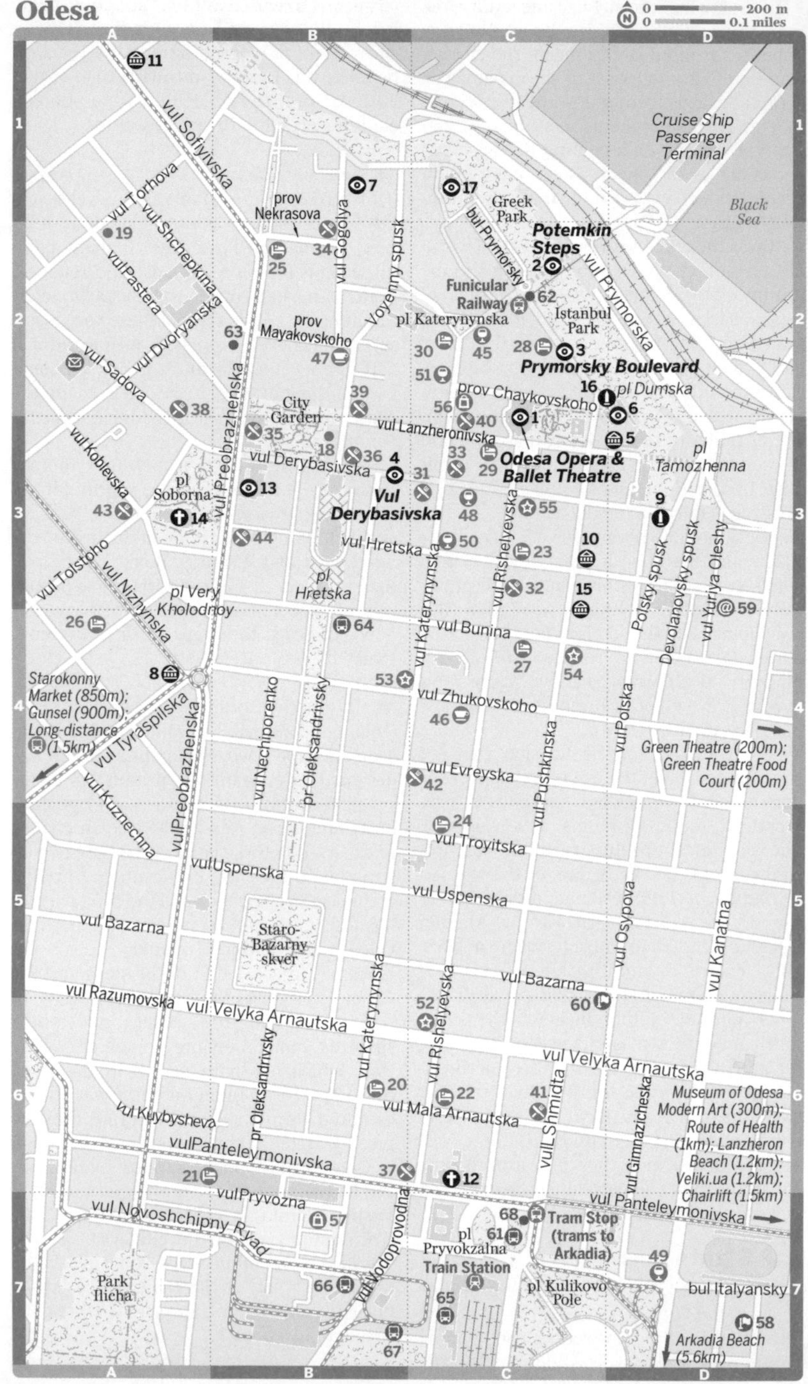

Cruise Ship Passenger Terminal
Black Sea
Potemkin Steps
Greek Park
Funicular Railway
pl Katerynynska
Istanbul Park
Prymorsky Boulevard
pl Dumska
City Garden
Odesa Opera & Ballet Theatre
pl Tamozhenna
Vul Derybasivska
pl Soborna
pl Hretska
pl Very Kholodnoy
Starokonny Market (850m); Gunsel (900m); Long-distance (1.5km)
Green Theatre (200m); Green Theatre Food Court (200m)
Staro-Bazarny skver
Museum of Odesa Modern Art (300m); Route of Health (1km); Lanzheron Beach (1.2km); Veliki.ua (1.2km); Chairlift (1.5km)
Tram Stop (trams to Arkadia)
pl Pryvokzalna
Train Station
pl Kulikovo Pole
Park Ilicha
bul Italyansky
Arkadia Beach (5.6km)

Underneath the eastern section of the boulevard, the Istanbul park was reopened with much pomp in 2017 after a thorough Turkish-funded reconstruction that turned it into a rather manicured patch with welcoming benches, sunbeds and an impressive sandstone grotto looming in the middle of a fountain.

At the western end of bul Prymorsky stands the semiderelict **Vorontsov Palace**. This was the residence of the city's third governor, built in 1826 in a classical style with interior Arabic detailing. The Greek-style colonnade behind the palace offers brilliant views over Odesa's bustling port. Both were under reconstruction at the time of research, along with the Greek Park underneath the western section of the boulevard.

★Vul Derybasivska STREET

(Дерибасівська вулиця) Odesa's main commercial street, pedestrian vul Derybasivska, is jam-packed with restaurants, bars and, in the summer high season, tourists. At its

Odesa

Top Sights
1 Odesa Opera & Ballet Theatre C3
2 Potemkin Steps C2
3 Prymorsky Boulevard C2
4 Vul Derybasivska B3

Sights
5 Archaeology Museum D3
6 City Hall D2
7 Falz-Fein House B1
8 History of Odesa Jews Museum A4
9 José de Ribas Statue D3
10 Museum of Western & Eastern Art C3
11 Odesa Fine Arts Museum A1
12 Panteleymonivska Church C6
13 Passazh B3
14 Preobrazhensky Cathedral A3
15 Pushkin Museum C3
16 Pushkin Statue C2
17 Vorontsov Palace C1

Activities, Courses & Tours
18 Freetours Odessa B3
19 Salix A2

Sleeping
20 Babushka Grand Hostel B6
21 Black Sea Panteleymonivska A6
22 Black Sea Rishelyevskaya C6
23 Consul Hotel C3
24 Frapolli 21 .... C5
25 Frederic Koklen B2
26 Hostel Hipstel A4
27 Hotel Ayvazovsky C4
28 Hotel Londonskaya C2
29 Mozart Hotel C3
30 Yekaterina II C2

Eating
Bernardazzi .... (see 54)
31 Bratya Grill C3
32 City Food Market C3
33 Dva Karla C3
34 Gogol Mogol B2
35 Klarabara B3
36 Kompot B3
37 Kompot B6
38 Kotelok Mussels Bar A2
39 Kumanets B2
40 Maman C3
41 Rozmarin C6
42 Tavernetta C4
43 Tyulka A3
44 Zharyu Paryu B3

Drinking & Nightlife
45 Dizyngoff C2
46 Foundation Roasters C4
Friends and Beer .... (see 55)
47 Kofeynya ZheTo B2
48 Mick O'Neill's Irish Bar C3
49 Palladium D7
50 Shkaf C3
51 The Fitz C2

Entertainment
52 Libertin C6
53 Morgan Club B4
Odesa Opera & Ballet Theatre .... (see 1)
54 Odessa Philharmonic Hall C4
55 Teatralna Kasa C3

Shopping
56 Benya&Zubrik C2
57 Privoz Market B7

Information
58 Georgian Consulate D7
59 Impact Hub D3
60 Romanian Consulate C6

Transport
61 Buses to City Centre C7
62 Funicular Railway C2
63 Kiy Avia B2
64 Pl Hretska Bus Stop (Buses to Airport) B4
65 Privokzalna bus station C7
66 Privoz Bus Station B7
67 Starosinna Bus Station B7
68 Tram Stop (Trams to Arkadia) C7

quieter eastern end you'll discover **the statue of José de Ribas**, the Spanish-Neapolitan general who built Odesa's harbour and also has a central street named after him. At the western end of the thoroughfare is the pleasant and beautifully renovated **City Garden**, surrounded by several restaurants.

A large wrought-iron arbour in the centre of the gardens serves as a stage for live jazz and classical concerts during weekends. Nearby, ex-Soviet tourists line up to get photographed with bronze sculptures, one of which is simply a chair – a reference to the satirical Soviet novel *The Twelve Chairs*. The other one is that of Odesa-born 1930s jazz singer Leonid Utyosov. Across the street, the opulent art nouveau edifice of **Bolshaya Moskovskaya Hotel**, designed by Lev Vlodek in 1901, stands locked, waiting for a long overdue reconstruction.

★Museum of Odesa Modern Art MUSEUM

(048-777 1250; www.msio.com.ua; vul Leontovycha (Belinskoho) 5; 60uah; 12pm-7pm Wed-Sat, till 6pm Sun) The war in the east and regular political strife give Ukrainian artists a lot of here-and-now material to reflect on, and the result is often brilliant, to which the exhibitions in this great establishment attest. Located in a stately imperial doctor's manor house, the museum is the main base of Odesa biennale. The awkwardly constructed official name abbreviates as MOMA. Because, Odesa.

★Odesa Opera & Ballet Theatre THEATRE

(Одеський театр опери та балету; www.opera.odessa.ua; prov Chaykovskoho 1) The jewel in Odesa's architectural crown was designed in the 1880s by the architects who also designed the famous Vienna State Opera, namely Ferdinand Fellner and Herman Helmer. You can take a Russian-language tour of the theatre (150uah), starting at 5pm on Friday and Saturday or, better yet, buy yourself a night at the opera.

Odesa Fine Arts Museum MUSEUM

(Одеський художній музей; www.ofam.od.ua; vul Sofiyivska 5A; main exhibition 50uah; 10.30am-4.30pm Wed-Mon) Located in the former palace of Count Pototsky, this museum has an impressive collection of Russian and Ukrainian art, including a few seascapes by master talent Ayvazovsky and some Soviet realist paintings.

José de Ribas Statue STATUE

(vul Derybasivska) José de Ribas, the half-Catalan, half-Irish illustrious gentleman who built Odesa's harbour, is honoured with a statue placed at the eastern end of vul Derybasivska.

Falz-Fein House ARCHITECTURE

(vul Gogolya 5-7) City tours inevitably stop near this portly art nouveau house with two atlantes holding a sphere dotted with stars, a depiction of the universe as if seen from the outside. Built by Odesa's most celebrated architect, Lev Wlodek, the house belonged to baron Friedrich von Falz-Fein. He was the eccentric German aristocrat who bred zebras and wildebeest at his steppe estate of Askaniya Nova (p182), where he was born in 1863. Or maybe he was only eccentric by the standards of his time, since these days he is remembered as a pioneer of environmental protection, cage-less zoos and, indeed, safari parks.

This is a residential house, so it's not possible to enter unless you befriend someone who lives there.

Lanzheron Beach BEACH

(Пляж Ланжерон) Perhaps to copy Brighton Beach, New York – where half of Odesa seems to have emigrated – the authorities built a boardwalk at the beach closest to the city centre. It looks modern and attractive, but it is small and hence often crowded. Reachable by foot via Shevchenko Park in the city centre, Lanzheron is the first beach on the Route of Health, a seaside promenade that goes all the way to Arkadia Beach (p179).

Passazh ARCHITECTURE

(vul Preobrazhenska 34) The opulently decorated Passazh shopping arcade is the best-preserved example of the neorenaissance architectural style that permeated Odesa in the late 19th century. Its interior walls are festooned with gods, goblins, lions and nymphs. Commissioned in 1899, the building is sadly underused, with the main occupant being a rather mediocre hotel. But the shops inside the arcade are worth browsing.

Route of Health BEACH

(Траса здоров'я) The dystopian Soviet name has stuck to this 5.5km stretch of sandy, rocky and concrete beaches that form the city's recreational belt. Packed like a sardine can and filled with noise and barbecue smells, the beaches are anything but idyllic, yet this is a great place for mingling with Ukrainian holidaymakers in their element. Starting at Lanzheron Beach (p178), which boasts a wooden boardwalk, the route ends at Arkadia, the newly renovated nightlife hot spot, filled with clubs and fancy resorts.

The route is great for both walking and cycling or there is a park train running frequently from one side to the other. You can also rent a bicycle at Veliki.ua (p180) on Lanzheron Beach. The Route of Health can be accessed in the middle via an antiquated Soviet-era **chairlift** (Канатна дорога до пляжу Отрада; kanatnaya doroga; one way 40uah) that connects bul Frantsuzsky with Otrada Beach underneath.

History of Odesa Jews Museum MUSEUM
(Музей історії євреїв Одеси; ☎048-728 9743; www.migdal.org.ua/migdal/museum/; vul Nizhynska 66; recommended donation 100uah, tour 200uah; ⏱1pm-7pm Mon-Thu, 10am-4pm Sun) Less than 2% of people call themselves Jewish in today's Odesa – against 44% in the early 1920s – but the resilient and humorous Jewish spirit still permeates every aspect of local life. Hidden inside a typical rundown courtyard with clothes drying on a rope and a rusty carcass of a prehistoric car, this modest but lovingly curated exhibition consists of items donated by Odessite families, many of whom have long emigrated to America or Israel.

Perhaps most touching is the photo of steamship *Ruslan* carrying the first Zionist settlers to Palestine in 1919, along with their immense hopes and terrible fears, both of which would soon materialise. English-language tours are available, but need to be arranged in advance.

Pushkin Museum MUSEUM
(Музей Пушкіна; http://museum-literature.odessa.ua; vul Pushkinska 13; adult/child & student 35/20uah; ⏱10am-5pm Tue-Sun) This is where Russia's greatest poet, Alexander Pushkin, spent his first weeks in Odesa after being exiled from St Petersburg in 1823 by the tsar for mischievous epigrams. Governor Vorontsov subsequently humiliated the writer with petty administrative jobs and it took only 13 months, an affair with Vorontsov's wife, a simultaneous affair with someone else's wife and more epigrams for Pushkin to be thrown out of Odesa too.

Somehow, he still found time while in town to finish the poem 'The Bakhchysaray Fountain', write the first chapter of *Eugene Onegin*, and scribble the notes and moaning letters found in this humble museum, along with Freemason artefacts and pictures of women Pushkin charmed during his Odesa stint.

City Hall NOTABLE BUILDING
(bul Prymorsky) Located at the eastern end of bul Prymorsky, the pink-and-white colonnaded City Hall originally served as the stock exchange. The cannon here is a war trophy captured from the British during the Crimean War. In the square in front of City Hall is Odesa's most photographed monument, the Pushkin statue.

Vorontsov Palace NOTABLE BUILDING
(bul Prymorsky) The semiderelict Vorontsov Palace, at the western end of bul Prymorsky, was the residence of the city's third governor. It was built in 1826 in a classical style with interior Arabic detailing. The Greek-style colonnade behind the palace offers great views over Odesa's port.

Pushkin Statue STATUE
(Пам'ятник Пушкіну; pl Dumska) Odesa's most photographed monument, the statue of Alexander Pushkin, stands in front of the City Hall on pl Dumska. The plaque reads 'To Pushkin – from the Citizens of Odesa'.

Arkadia Beach BEACH
(Пляж Аркадія) Reconstructed to resemble the glitzy resorts across the sea in Turkey, Odesa's main fun zone shines like a mini Las Vegas and remains crowded with revelers till the wee hours. A wide promenade lined with cafes and bars leads towards the seafront, which is jam packed with beach clubs that double as nightlife venues after dark. Arkadia can be reached by walking, cycling or riding a park train along the Route of Health from Lanzheron Beach.

Travelling from the centre, take tram 5 from the **tram stop** (pl Pryvokazlna) near the train station, in front of the McDonald's on vul Panteleymonivska, to the end of the line via the lovely tree-lined bul Frantsuzsky, where the crème de la crème of Odesa's aristocracy lived in tsarist times. Enjoy the views of the old mansions and sanatoriums along the way. Public transport to Arkadia gets extremely crowded in summer, so consider taking a taxi (around 70uah).

Panteleymonivska Church CHURCH
(Пантелеймонівська церква; vul Panteleymonivska 66) Near the train station you can't

help but spy the five silver onion domes of this Russian Orthodox church, built by Greek monks with stone from Constantinople in the late 19th century. According to legend, every time the Soviets painted over the church's elaborate frescoes, they would miraculously reappear. While the Soviets eventually succeeded in covering them up, many of the frescoes are once again visible thanks to vigorous restoration efforts.

Archaeology Museum MUSEUM

(Музей археології; vul Lanzheronivska 4; 70uah; ⏲10am-5pm Tue-Sun) Occupying a purpose-built, neoclassical edifice in the historical heart of the city, this half-renovated museum contains a fairly rich collection of archaeological finds, both sculpture and gold, from ancient Greek colonies in the northern Black Sea region and Skythian burial mounds. A separate hall in the underground floor displays Egyptian artefacts and mummies. There are signs in English.

Museum of Western & Eastern Art GALLERY

(Музей західного та східного мистецтва; www.oweamuseum.odessa.ua/; vul Pushkinska 9; adult/child & student 40/25uah; ⏲10.30am-5.30pm Thu-Tue Apr-Sep, 10am-4.30pm Thu-Tue Oct-Mar) This mid-19th-century palace houses a collection that's both rich and eclectic – apt for a cosmopolitan port city like Odesa. Classical Italian and Dutch art comes together with Asian treasures from as far away as Tibet and Indonesia, while temporary exhibitions showcase great examples of modern Ukrainian art.

Preobrazhensky Cathedral CATHEDRAL

(Преображенский собор; pl Soborna) Leafy pl Soborna is the site of the gigantic, newly rebuilt Preobrazhensky (Transfiguration) Cathedral, which was Odesa's most famous and important church until Stalin had it blown up in the 1930s.

Activities

Veliki.ua CYCLING

(☎050-388 84 12; www.veliki.ua; Nemo Dolphinarium, Lanzheron Beach; per hour/day 60/200uah; ⏲10am-8pm) Conveniently located at Lanzheron Beach, this rental shop allows you to explore the rest of the Route of Health by bicycle. You can book in advance on the website.

Tours

Odessa Walks TOURS

(☎063 814 6373; www.odessawalks.com; tours from 450uah) Inexpensive English-language themed walks around Odesa. You can trace the history of early settlers, stars of the 1920s criminal underworld or simply join a pub walk.

Salix TOURS

(☎048-728 9737; www.salix.od.ua; vul Torhova 14) A rare, authentically 'green' Ukrainian travel agency, with responsible tours to Vylkovo and the Danube Delta. Known for their bird-watching tours, they can also tailor a

NERUBAYSKE CATACOMB

The limestone on which Odesa stands is riddled with some 2000km of tunnels, which have always played an important part in the city's history. Quarried out for building in the 19th century, they were first used to hide smuggled goods. During WWII they sheltered a group of local partisans who waged a war of attrition against the occupying Romanians and forced the Nazis to keep greater troop numbers in the area.

Most of the catacomb network lies well outside Odesa's city centre. The only tunnels that can be visited, the **Nerubayske Catacomb** (☎067 292 3055; tours 200uah; ⏲9am-4pm Tue-Sun), are in the suburb of Nerubayske, about 15km north of central Odesa. Here, a resident speleologist offers 45-minute catacomb tours that wend through what was the headquarters of Odesa's WWII partisan movement. Tours are in Russian, so you may wish to bring a translator along, although you don't necessarily need a translator to enjoy the catacombs. Tours exit into the musty Partisan Museum (accessible only via a tour).

Marshrutka 84 to Nerubayske leaves every 10 minutes from Odesa's Privoz bus station (35 minutes). Ask the driver to let you off at the 'Katakomby' stop, easily identifiable by the hulking Soviet realist statue depicting five defiant partisans. Tour agencies in Odesa run tours out here for about 1200uah per group.

trip for those interested in Bessarabia's fascinating ethnography.

Freetours Odessa TOURS
(☎048-725 0024; www.infocenter.odessa.ua/en; vul Havanna 10) Freetours runs a small bureau where you can arrange a tour, including to the catacombs, or rent a bicycle. Enter through the City Garden.

Festivals & Events

Odesa Film Festival FILM
(http://oiff.com.ua; ⏲Jul) Odesa Film Festival is the main summer event that culminates in a silent film show on Potemkin Steps accompanied by a live musical performance by leading international musicians and orchestras.

Tzimes Market FOOD & DRINK
(www.facebook.com/tzimesodessa) A rather massive street-food event held in various locations a few times a year, with stalls and field kitchens set up by city's leading restaurants and Ukrainian microbreweries.

Carnival Humorina CARNIVAL
(⏲1 Apr) Odesa's annual Carnival Humorina, celebrated on 1 April, is no joke. The festival fills the streets with carnival floats, music and drunks, and is the biggest party of the year for most Odessites.

Odesa City Day FIESTA
(⏲2 Sep) Held annually on 2 September with parades, concerts and every other form of entertainment on bul Primorsky and all around the city, this is a frivolous celebration, its quality depending on who the current mayor is.

Sleeping

Odesa gets absolutely packed in the summer months, but new hotels open all the time and hundreds of apartments are available for rent on booking websites. The city's hostel situation is in constant flux, so it may be a good idea to check whether specific hostels are still operating before turning up at 4am unannounced.

Hostel Hipstel HOSTEL $
(☎068-101 3330; http://hipstel.com.ua; vul Spyrydonivska 8; dm 150uah, family r 600uah; 🛜) By investing in a competent designer, this establishment, located on the 1st floor of a stately 19th-century house, has put itself head and shoulders above other apartment hostels in Odesa. Dorms come in different sizes (some are a little cramped), but all bunk beds come with orthopedic mattresses and curtains. A reasonable shower/guest ratio prevents morning queues.

Babushka Grand Hostel HOSTEL $
(☎063 070 5535; www.babushkagrand.com; vul Mala Arnautska 60; dm/d from 150/620uah; ❄🛜) While Odesa's other hostels are decidedly for the young, day-sleeping crowd, the wonderfully named Grand Babushka, occupying a palatial apartment near the train station, has a more laid-back, traveller vibe. The stuccoed interiors and crystal chandeliers are stunning, the staff fun and occasionally a real Ukrainian *babushka* arrives to cook up a feast.

Hotel Londonskaya HOTEL $$
(Готель Лондонская; ☎738 0110; http://londonskaya-hotel.com.ua; bul Prymorsky 11; s/d from 1155/1365uah; ⊖❄🛜≋) A grand old dame chilling out on Odesa's main promenade, Londonskaya has hosted such dignitaries as Robert Louis Stevenson and Anton Chekhov in the imperial times, and remains the lodgings of choice for the modern-day smart set. With iron-lace balustrades, stained-glass windows, parquet flooring and an inner courtyard, the place still oozes Regency charm.

Curiously, the 'English' name was invented by the hotel's French founder in 1846.

Frapolli 21 HOTEL $$
(☎048-789 2292; http://frapolli-hotel.com/frapolli21; vul Troyitska 34; d incl breakfast from 900uah; ❄🛜) Escaping from Odesa's humid heat and urban decay into this small but sparkling clean ultramodern space, with very comfy beds and 21st century bathrooms, is a blessing. Thin walls are not, so a pair of earplugs may come in handy. Buffet breakfast meets the highest of Ukrainian standards and there is a nice bar with relaxing armchairs in the lobby.

Consul Hotel HOTEL $$
(☎098-988 7936; http://hotel-consul.od.ua; vul Hretska 22; d from 1100uah; ❄🛜) Not a conventional hotel, but rather a collection of large and very well-appointed rooms above a tiny reception area. In addition to comfy beds, rooms are furnished with couches, study desks and tables. Breakfast is not available, but the area is packed with restaurants. Each room is equipped with a kettle, fridge and kitchenware.

WORTH A TRIP

UKRAINIAN STEPPE SAFARI

Kherson region in continental Ukraine's far south is often neglected, especially now that Crimea is off the international tourist trail.

Meanwhile, herds of buffalo, wildebeest and zebras are roaming in the vicinity. Zebras? This isn't Africa! But this is the reality inside the 2300-hectare **Askaniya Nova Reserve** (☎055-386 1286; http://ascania-nova.com; vul Falts-Feyna 13, Askaniya Nova; adult/child 55/40uah; ⏲8am-5pm 1 Apr-10 Nov) – the brainchild of a 19th-century Odesa German, baron Friedrich von Falz-Fein, who acted on his slightly mad idea of importing animals from different continents to this unique natural steppe.

In addition to the above-mentioned species, the reserve boasts Przewalski horses from Mongolia, camels, Central Asian saiga antelopes and all manner of birds, from pink flamingos to rare steppe eagles. But perhaps the main attraction here is the virgin steppe – flat as a skating rink and preserved in the same shape as it was at the time of Attila the Hun.

As in Africa, the best way to see the animals is on a safari. Alas, that's easier said than done. Apart from its zoo and gardens, the reserve is closed for visitors for most of summer because of (very real) steppe fire danger. So late spring and early autumn are the best times to take a safari (150uah per person) in a horse-drawn cart (which is fun in itself).

Yet, if you are around during a cooler and wetter summer, it's still worth inquiring about visiting. It's a long journey to get here, so to avoid disappointment, arrange for a Russian speaker to book for you by phone. There are a couple of hotels in Askaniya Nova, the best one being **Kanna** (☎05538-61337; vul Soborna (Krasnoarmeyska) 22, Askaniya Nova; d from 570uah; ❄).

Another large chunk of virgin steppe that you can admire is actually out in the Black Sea. **Dzharylhach** is separated from the mainland by a narrow strait. It is also teeming with all kinds of wildlife – though, admittedly not African, which makes it all the more authentic. You can reach it by boat from the pier in the resort town of Skadovsk.

Dzharylhach is a wild and melancholic place, popular with campers who walk many miles away from the landing point to improve their chances of spotting the wild horses or deers inhabiting the island. Note that camping is not officially allowed, though in practice everyone gets away with a small unofficial fee to the rangers – if they ever bother to approach.

If you come on a day trip, definitely board one of the military trucks that meet larger boats. It takes people across the island to a beautiful sandy beach on the outer side. Riding the truck with other tourists is fun and you might be lucky to spot some wildlife.

Both Askaniya Nova and Skadovsk can be reached from the regional capital Kherson – a quaint, Greek-influenced, but otherwise unremarkable town sitting at the mouth of the Dnipro. From the local bus stations, buses depart for Odesa every half an hour or so (170uah, three to four hours). There are five buses a day for Askaniya Nova (130uah, three hours). Buses for Skadovsk are more frequent (80uah, 2½ hours, half-hourly).

Gagarinn HOTEL **$$**
(☎048-774 4477; http://gagarinn.com; vul Haharinske plato 5B; d from 1100uah; ❄📶) Towering above Arkadia beach, this slick 21st-century mammoth has seized the market niche once controlled by Soviet Intourist dinosaurs. Busy like an anthill, it has the expected bland-but-comfortable rooms, good sound isolation and splendid sea views. Seldom fully booked, it's a fairly safe option if you need to find a room with short notice.

Black Sea Rishelyevskaya HOTEL **$$**
(Чорне море Рішельєвська; ☎230 0911; http://blacksea-hotels.com; vul Rishelyevska 59; r from 600uah; 📶🏊) Size matters when it comes to value for money in Odesa. This 1970s glass-and-concrete tower might be an eyesore, but it shelters a multitude of spacious and mostly renovated – if rather bland – rooms, which go for a price you simply won't find anywhere else in the centre without compromising on comfort. Breakfast is extra.

Rates offered on international booking sites tend to be considerably lower than on the hotel's own site.

Black Sea Panteleymonivska HOTEL $$
(Чорне море Пантелеймонівська; ☎048-710 10-10; http://blacksea-hotels.com/; vul Panteleymonivska 25; s/d from 750/850uah;) Although in a slightly dodgy area, this hotel stretches your hryvnya a long way at the midrange level. While the decor is hit or miss, the generous size of the rooms, professional service and overall modernity of this 100-room high-rise make up for it. Note that rates on popular international booking sites are often lower than the hotel's own site.

Hotel Ayvazovsky HOTEL $$$
(Готель Айвазовський; ☎048-728 9777; www.ayvazovsky.com.ua; vul Bunina 19; s/d from 1400/2000uah;) From the Chesterfield sofas in the foyer to the spacious, European-standard bedrooms with high ceilings to the design-magazine-perfect bathrooms, this soothing, 27-room hotel in the heart of the city centre is worth every hryvnya. Continental breakfast is delivered to your room every morning and staff can book tours and countless other services.

Frederic Koklen BOUTIQUE HOTEL $$$
(Фредерік Коклен; ☎048-737 5553; www.koklenhotel.com; prov Nekrasova 7; s/d from 2400/2900uah;) Odesa's most sumptuous boutique hotel has guests gushing about the exceptional service, the luxurious period ambience and the great location. Rooms in this renovated mansion are studies in 18th- and 19th-century Imperial-era style, and the attention to detail, quality of materials and standard of maintenance are exceptional for Ukraine.

Mozart Hotel HOTEL $$$
(Готель Моцарт; ☎048-237 7777; http://mozart-hotel.com; vul Lanzheronivska 13; s/d from 1400/2500uah;) As the name suggests, this place epitomises European luxury, with elegant furnishings and a calm, light-filled interior tucked behind its refurbished neoclassical facade. The 40 rooms are individually decorated and the location, across from the Opera & Ballet Theatre, is perfect. Note, however, that the cheapest singles have no windows. Buffet breakfast is an extra 200uah.

Yekaterina II HOTEL $$$
(☎048-705 45-07; www.hotel-ekaterina.com/ekaterina2; pl Katerynynska 7; r from 1500uah;) Tucked away in a quiet courtyard right in the epicentre of Odesa's sightseeing and nightlife, this hotel occupies the upper floors of a residential building. Rooms face a ballet school, behind which you can just make out a thin line of the sea. The interior design is a little bland, but rooms have balconies and air-con.

Eating

Odesa's restaurant scene easily rivals Kyiv's thanks to a new phenomenon that time has come to call – loud and clear – Odesa cuisine. It's a magic stew of Russian, Ukrainian, Jewish and Moldovan cuisines cooked up in Soviet communal kitchens and fishermen's huts. Its main virtue is that it takes full advantage of the region's abundance in vegetables, fruit and seafood.

★ **City Food Market** FOOD HALL $
(Городской рынок еды; ☎048-702 1913; www.facebook.com/odessa.cityfood.market; Rishelyevska 9A; mains 50-120uah; 11am-2am;) Once an itinerant tribe, congregating here and there for irregular jamborees, Odesa foodies now have a rather palatial indoors base. The two-storey building is divided between shops, each with its own kitchen dedicated to a particular product – from the Vietnamese *pho* soup and Greek pita *gyros*, to grilled ribs and oysters.

Vegetarians are not forgotten, with a dedicated shop called Vegan Hooligano and another one specialising in hummus. The venue is often used for live concerts or film screenings.

Dva Karla MOLDOVAN $
(Bodega 2K; ☎096-524 1601; www.facebook.com/bodega2k; vul Hretska 22; mains 80-100uah; 10am-11pm) This envoy from nearby Moldova occupies a super-quaint courtyard covered with a vine canopy in summer and pleasant cellar premises in winter. Come here to try *mamalyga* (a version of polenta with *brynza* goat cheese or fried lard), paprika stuffed with rice and chopped meat, as well as juicy *mitityay* (kebabs).

Touting itself as a bodega, 2K also treats visitors to excellent Moldovan and (more experimental) Ukrainian wine. It's also a great breakfast option.

Green Theatre Food Court FAST FOOD $

(Shevchenko Park; mains 50-100uah; ⌚dawn-dusk) Another haunt for Odesa foodies, the food court inside the revived Green Theatre at Shevchenko Park is a smattering of kiosks and trailers churning out gourmet street food. One of the more unusual things to try here is *langos* – a pizza-like, Hungarian flatbread dish.

Tyulka UKRAINIAN $

(Тюлька; ☎048-233 3231; www.tulka.od.ua; vul Koblevska 46; snacks 30-50uah; ⌚10am-11pm) A clever take on Soviet nostalgia (no Lenins or red banners in sight), this cafe recreates the ambience of a 1970s working-class eatery, complete with authentic tablecloths, beer mugs and salads served in tall glasses. Food is an assortment of classic Odesa snacks, from the namesake *tyulka* (small fish, served fried or salted) to *cheburek* (meat pastry).

Zharyu Paryu CAFETERIA $

(Жарю Парю; vul Hretska 45; mains 30-40uah; ⌚8am-10pm) When lunchtime strikes, going where the local student and office-worker population find nourishment usually makes sense. This clinical self-service canteen of the factory or school variety is such a place, and with cheap and cheerful Ukrainian favourites on the menu board it's ideal for cash-strapped nomads.

Kompot EASTERN EUROPEAN $$

(☎345 145; www.kompot.ua; vul Panteleymonivska 70; mains 85-150uah; ⌚8am-11pm) This outlet of Odesa's best-known restaurant, famous for its unpretentious home-style fare (lavishly peppered with Soviet nostalgia), is conveniently located across the square from the train station and Privoz bus station. Great place for an unhurried lunch or dinner before a long journey.

Dacha RUSSIAN $$

(Дача; ☎714 3119; www.dacha.com.ua; bul Frantsuzsky 85, korpus 15; mains 120-250uah; 📶) *Dacha* (family summer cottage) is a dreamworld of happy childhood memories for locals. This Odesa institution, perched on a plateau above Arkadia inside Chkalov sanatorium, masterfully re-creates the atmosphere – on a slightly exaggerated scale. Food is homey, Odesa-style, with generous portions. You can choose between dining in the garden or inside the house, which looks very much like a *dacha*.

House policy: guests are encouraged to dress down to their underwear as Soviet-era dacha owners often did in their tiny but private gardens. We haven't seen anyone try it.

Tavernetta ITALIAN $$

(Тавернетта; ☎096-234 4621; www.tavernetta.ua; vul Katerynynska 45; mains 125-200 uah; ⌚9am-12pm; 📶) You'd need to hire an army of culinary detectives to find better pasta between here and Italy, but your chances would still be low. The restaurant occupies a large wooden terrace with an open kitchen, which churns out platefuls of magic – try spaghetti with local sardines. Waiters are humorous and if you understand Russian, you'll appreciate their Jewish-influenced 'Odesa speak'.

Warning: they'll attempt to put a hilarious paper napkin on your neck, which makes serious people look like toddlers.

Kompot EASTERN EUROPEAN $$

(Компот; www.kompot.ua; vul Derybasivska 20; mains 85-150uah; ⌚8am-11pm; 📶) Odesa's most celebrated restaurateur, Savely Libkin, conjured this place from his childhood memories, setting a trend for what is becoming known as Odesa cuisine. The simplest dishes are the best – try cutlets with potato puree and water them down with one of the eponymous *kompoty,* fruity drinks that housewives preserve in jars to consume in winter.

Rozmarin JEWISH $$

(Розмарин; ☎048-518 7030; www.rozmarin.od.ua; vul Uspenskaya 5; mains 80-180uah; ⌚10am-11pm) A lovingly re-created early 20th-century flat, with oak closets and rugs on the wall, this place is all about Jewish food as they made it in a *shtetl* during the same era. Definitely try gefilte fish (cold fish cutlets) and *latkes* (potatoes with pike roe). There is a small shop selling kosher food in the premises. Closed on Saturdays.

Maman FUSION $$

(Маман; ☎711 7035; vul Lanzheronivska 18; mains 90-170uah; ⌚noon-midnight; 📶) This Odesa mum is a worldly woman who absorbs Asian, Middle Eastern and French influences in her culinary adventures. But it's still local home food she is best at, so pay attention to the *kotlety* (meatballs) section the menu. Maman's best-kept secret is the pleasant outdoor sitting area in the Palais Royal gardens, unseen from the street.

Gogol Mogol EUROPEAN $$
(Гоголь-Моголь; www.seatandeat.com.ua; prov Nekrasova 2; mains 120-280uah; 9am-midnight;) From the multihued old bicycles and rainbow park benches bolted to the pavement outside to the jumble-sale decor of the quirky interior, this art cafe is a colourful chapter in the alternative city-centre story. They do a mean cappuccino and it's also a popular evening meeting spot. The short menu doubles up as a visitors book.

As elsewhere in Odesa, slow service can be an issue.

Kumanets UKRAINIAN $$
(Куманець; 048-237 6946; http://kumanets.com.ua; vul Havanna 7; mains 100-170uah; noon-midnight) A kitsch little Ukrainian island in Russian Odesa, Kumanets produces affordable *holubtsy* (cabbage rolls), *varenyky* (dumplings) and *deruny* (potato pancakes) in addition to pricier mains.

★**Bernardazzi** EUROPEAN $$$
(Бернардацци; 048-785 5585; www.bernardazzi.com; Odessa Philharmonic Hall, vul Bunina 15; mains 280-400uah; noon-midnight;) Few Ukrainian restaurants have truly authentic settings, but the art nouveau dining room of this Italianesque palazzo (once a stock exchange, now the Philharmonic Hall) is the real deal. In addition to well-crafted south and east European fare, there's an award-winning wine list, occasional live music and a secluded courtyard for summer time chilling. It's named after the architect who designed the building.

Kotelok Mussels Bar SEAFOOD $$$
(048-736 6030; www.facebook.com/kotelokodessa; vul Sadova 17; mains 250-300uah; 9am-11pm) This may not be obvious, but mussels are as much a part of Odesa food culture as aubergine 'caviar' (cold vegetable stew). Furnished like a bar, with a row of seats facing an open kitchen, Kotelok is all about Black Sea mussels served with a variety of dips, including the quintessentially local mixture of paprika and *brynza* goat cheese.

The non-maritime 'caviar' features in the list of delicious appetizers, along with *forshmak* (minced herring).

Bratya Grill EUROPEAN $$$
(Братья Гриль; 067-599 3399; www.facebook.com/bratiagrill; vul Derybasivska 17; mains 150-300uah; 11am-12am;) Not a rootless cosmopolitan like generic steakhouses, this place marries Odesa cuisine with American steak-and-burger culture. The home side is represented by seafood appetisers, notably rapana shellfish stewed with porcini mushrooms, and veggie snacks, including Odesa's trademark aubergine 'caviar'. Juicy steaks are among the best in Odesa.

Klarabara INTERNATIONAL $$$
(Кларабара; 048-701 5495; City Garden; mains 200-300uah; 9am-midnight) Tucked away in a quiet corner of the City Garden, this classy, cosy, ivy-covered place is awash with antique furniture and fine art. The menu is inspired by the food people make at home in the broader Black Sea region. That means local fish, delicious vegetable stews and various kinds of *khachapuri* (Georgian cheese pastry). We loved the charcoal-grilled mussels.

Drinking & Nightlife

Just about anywhere along vul Derybasivska is a good place for a drink.

Odesa's raucous club scene has two seasons: summer (June to August) and the rest of the year. In summer, the action is at Arkadia Beach, whose two huge, Ibiza-style nightclubs produce heightened levels of madness seven days a week.

★**Shkaf** BAR
(Шкаф; 048-232 5017; www.shkaff.od.ua; vul Hretska 32; 6pm-5am) It feels like entering a *shkaf* (wardrobe) from the outside, but what you find inside is a heaving basement bar-club, a surefire antidote to Odesa's trendy beach-club scene and pick-up bars. The inconspicuous, unmarked entrance is always surrounded by smoking/chilling-out patrons, so you won't miss it.

★**Dizyngoff** BAR
(050 542 4216; www.facebook.com/dizyngoff; pl Katerynynska 5; 9am-4am) Each of the three young owners here throw something into the mix: Israeli cultural influence, French culinary education and really good musical taste. That makes this place a bit like one of its famous cocktails: singular, intense and enchanting.

The Fitz BAR
(068-810 2070; www.facebook.com/TheFitzCocktailBar; vul Katerynynska 6; 3pm-3am) Doubling as a barbershop by day, this little bar has an edgy, decadent feel enhanced by aged walls and a magnificent

chandelier that bedazzles incoming customers. Some of the latter occupy barbers' work stations, complete with sinks and mirrors, which adds to the overall surreality. Mostly rum-based cocktails include all-time favourites, as well as those you've likely never tried.

Foundation Roasters COFFEE
(☎073-700 0330; www.facebook.com/foundation-coffeeroasters/; Zhukovskoho 19; ⏰8am-9pm; 📶) Designed in a cool retro-industrial style, this coffee shop is run by bearded lumberjack hipsters who approach the brewing process with a near-academic seriousness and excel in it in a big way. If there were a Nobel prize for coffee-making, we'd probably nominate them.

Friends and Beer BAR
(Друзі та пиво; vul Derybasivska 9; ⏰11am-11pm; 📶) This charming re-created USSR-era living room littered with photos of Russian film stars is proof that 'retro Soviet' doesn't have to mean political posters and Constructivist art. The huge TV screen is possibly not authentic for the period, but it's great for sports. Craft ales and lagers are as un-Soviet as it gets.

Plyazhnik CLUB
(Пляжник; ☎700 5522; http://plagenick.com; 13th station of Fontanskaya Doroga; ⏰summer) As often happens, you need to walk an extra mile to find something smarter than the clubs on Arkadia. This one attracts a crowd of goatee-bearded Vespa drivers and showcases Russian/Ukrainian musicians beloved by the young intelligentsia. By day, it is one of the nicest beach clubs on the coast.

Plyazhnik can be accessed by stairs from the lower carpark of the bigger Riviera Club, located under Bolshoy Fontan's 13th station. If that doesn't make sense – take a taxi.

Kofeynya ZheTo COFFEE
(Кофейня ЖеТо; prov Mayakovskoho 1; ⏰8.30am-11pm) If one dessert can save the world, then it is Kyiv-style cake produced in this tiny coffee shop that looks like a slightly cramped dollhouse. But the main emphasis here is on quality brews and refreshing lemonade. It comes with a beautifully arranged streetside seating area.

Itaka CLUB
(Ітака; www.itaka-club.com.ua; Arkadia Beach; ⏰summer) It's slightly more downmarket than other clubs in Arkadia and consequently often rowdier (in a good way). The Greek columns and statues are a tad much, but you'll hardly care when it's 5am after a big night out. Like Ibiza, it also draws big regional pop acts.

Mick O'Neill's Irish Bar IRISH PUB
(vul Derybasivska 13; ⏰24hr) This longstanding Irish pub is a great place to start an evening and an even better place to finish it, as it's the only outdoor patio on vul Derybasivska that's open round the clock.

Palladium CLUB
(Паладіум; www.palladium.com.ua; bul Italyansky 4; ⏰Sep-May) The winter headquarters of Itaka (p186) takes up the slack downtown when Itaka shuts down in September. There's a nightly show at around 11pm, followed by general debauchery.

Ibiza CLUB
(Ібіца; www.ibiza.ua; Arkadia Beach; ⏰summer) This white, open, cave-like structure is Arkadia's most upmarket and most expensive club. European DJs and big-ticket Russian and Ukrainian pop bands often play here. Ticket prices can be high when a big act is in town.

☆ Entertainment

Theatre, concert and opera tickets can be purchased at the venues or at a Teatralna Kasa (p188). There's one on the corner of vul Derybasivska and vul Rishelyevska. The most compehensive listings of events is available at www.today.od.ua (in Russian). You can also buy tickets there.

Green Theatre ARTS CENTRE
(Зелений театр; ☎048-796 8635; www.green theat.re; Shevchenko Park; ⏰9am-11pm) A child of the Maidan revolution, the revived open-air stage at Shevchenko Park has become a magnet for Odesa intellectuals who flock here for Ukrainian and Russian bands, film screenings and literary evenings. With sunbeds and a food court, this is also a nice place to while away a summer day.

Libertin DANCE
(☎067-252 0404; http://libertin-club.com; vul Rishelyevska 60; ⏰10pm-6am) Odesa's gay hot spot, Libertin is an easygoing place with great resident DJs and drag-queen shows.

Odesa Opera & Ballet Theatre THEATRE
(Одеський театр опери та балету; www.opera.odessa.ua; prov Chaykovskoho 1) In addition to being architecturally magnificent, Odesa's

MELTING POT ON THE DANUBE

Not too many Westerners venture into the fertile wedge of Ukraine that lies between the Danube and Dnister rivers. That's too bad because, in addition to being beautiful in spots, it's also one of Ukraine's most culturally peculiar regions.

Its history is equally peculiar. From the late 15th century until Russia's victory in the Russo-Turkish War of 1806–12, this region was part of the Ottoman Empire. The Turks named it 'Bessarabia' after the Wallachian family – the Basarabs – who controlled the area during the late medieval period. When the Russians took over, they expanded Bessarabia to include most of present-day Moldova (plus a small slice of Carpathian Ukraine). The section of Bessarabia lying south of the Moldovan border in present-day Ukraine was dubbed Southern Bessarabia, or Budzhak. Between the world wars it was part of Romania before the Soviets annexed it in 1940 and made it part of Ukraine.

Bessarabia has spent the better part of the past half-millennium getting tossed around like a hot potato by various regional powers. As a result of shifting borders, Moldovans, Romanians, Russians, Turks, Germans and Ukrainians have all called this region home, as have several more obscure groups.

Lipovans

One such group is the Lipovans, Russian 'Old Believers', who were exiled from Russia in the 18th century for refusing to comply with Russian Orthodox Church reforms instituted by Peter the Great. Most of them settled near the Danube Delta, where they still continue to live and practice Old Believer traditions, such as crossing themselves with two fingers, and not shaving. Lipovan churches – one example is the St Nicholas Church in Vylkove – are built in the shape of a boat instead of a cross, have two spires as well as separate entrances for men and women. The interior walls are completely devoid of frescoes.

Gagauz

Next up are the Gagauz, an Orthodox-Christianised Turkish group, originally from Bulgaria, who ended up in Bessarabia when the Russians annexed the area from the Turks after the Russo-Turkish War of 1806–12. Today most Gagauz live in Moldova (where they have their own autonomous republic, Gagauzia), but you'll find Gagauz communities throughout Southern Bessarabia, including an active one in Vylkove. The Gagauz language, Gagauzi, is a Turkish dialect influenced by Russian via the Russian Orthodox Church

Zaporizhsky Cossacks

From a Ukrainian perspective, the most significant group to settle in this area was the Zaporizhsky Cossacks, who founded the Danube Sich (a fortified camp) just south of the Danube (in present-day Romania) after being driven out of Zaporizhzhya by Catherine the Great in 1775. Its loyalties split by the Russo-Turkish Wars, the *sich* collapsed in 1828 and most of its inhabitants migrated back east. A few thousand Cossacks, however, remained in the area, ensuring that a dash of hearty Cossack blood would forever be ingrained in the populations of Southern Bessarabia and northern Romania (where a strong Ukrainian community persists to this day).

theatre is also known for its marvellous acoustics. Unfortunately, the local opera company does not do justice to the theatre's impressive physical attributes, but performances are eminently affordable and the Odessa Philharmonic Orchestra performs here from time to time.

Odessa Philharmonic Hall LIVE MUSIC
(Одеська філармонія; www.odessaphilharmonic.org; vul Bunina 15; ⏲Sep-Jun) Housed in Odesa's beautiful former stock exchange building. Unfortunately, the original inhabitants (traders) asked the architects for a building with subdued acoustics, so that their business discussions couldn't be overheard. This is a pain, but not an insurmountable obstacle for the **Odessa Philharmonic Orchestra**, led by charismatic American conductor Hobart Earle, a former student of Leonard Bernstein.

This orchestra accounts for half the symphonies performed here. Jazz and rock is often played here, too, and it's the venue of the Odessa Jazz Festival.

Teatralna Kasa BOOKING SERVICE
(Theatre Kiosk; cnr vul Derybasivska & vul Rishelyevska; 9am-5pm) Theatre, concert and opera tickets can be purchased at the venues or any Teatralna Kasa. There are several of them in the city centre.

Morgan Club DANCE
(vul Zhukovskoho 30; 24hr;) By day Morgan is a pretty benign breakfast or lunch spot or early-evening drinks stop, but at night capable DJs spin till the wee hours and there's a funky downstairs lounge. The crowd of expats, local heavies/beauties and sex tourists never fails to generate a colourful atmosphere.

Shopping

Benya&Zubrik CLOTHING
(093-141 4724; https://benyaizubrik.com; vul Katerynynska 7; 10am-9pm) Attractive, bright T-shirts with signs and pictures making fun of international fashion brands.

Starokonny Market MARKET
(Старокінний ринок; vul Rizovska & vul Serova) It's like the grungy old-school uncle of European flea markets – there is nothing neat or touristy about Starokonny. It seems like every semi-intact item Odessites throw in the rubbish ends up here. There are heaps of junk – if you patiently shuffle through it you may find some gems. The market sprawls around a large neighbourhood near the long-distance bus station.

There are no stalls – all merchandise is laid out on the ground. If something catches your eye, pretend you are barely interested, then start bargaining.

Privoz Market MARKET
(Ринок Привіз; vul Pryvozna) Odesa is home to two of Southern Ukraine's largest and most famous markets. This centrally located market is possibly the largest farmers market in the country and a must-visit for *rynok* (market) lovers. On hot days you may want to breathe through your mouth in the overheated halls. Whatever you buy – always bargain, you'll upset them if you don't.

Information

Central Post Office (vul Sadova 10)

Impact Hub (https://impacthub.odessa.ua/; vul Hretska 1a) This co-working space for freelancers is a pleasant environment where you can browse the internet (using your own gadget) and enjoy free coffee.

Getting There & Away

AIR

The old and the new terminals of **Odesa International Airport** (www.odessa.aero) stand 200m apart. The old one, a shabby Soviet affair, was still handling departures at the time of research. The slick new terminal only processed arrivals.

The airport is about 12km southwest of the city centre, off Ovidiopilska doroha. Trolleybus 14 connects it with the train station. The infrequent bus 117 goes to the centre, stopping at **Pl Hretska Bus Stop** (pl Hretska, vul Bunina side).

Odesa is better linked to Europe than any other Ukrainian city, with the exception of Kyiv. Austrian Airlines, LOT, Air Baltic, Czech Airlines and Turkish Airlines all have regular flights to Odesa, and various regional carriers fly to former Soviet countries. The Ukrainian airline UIA (MAU) has flights from Odesa to Istanbul and Tel Aviv.

UIA and Motor Sich fly between Odesa and Kyiv at least four times daily. **Kiy Avia** (www.kiyavia.com; vul Preobrazhenska 15; 8am-8pm) can sort you out with tickets and timetables. Sadly, there are no flights elsewhere around Ukraine.

BOAT

Ferry services to and from Odesa are notoriously unreliable, with destinations changing every summer and services ceasing for months on end without any explanation. The only regular service available at the time of writing linked the port terminal at Chernomorsk/Ilyichevsk (30km south of Odesa) with the Georgian ports of Batumi and Poti (from 3500uah, 80 hours, every two to three days). Tickets are available on ukrferry-tour.com.

BUS

Most intercity buses you might need in Odesa leave from the three poorly organised bus stations located within a few hundred metres of each other in the area between the railway station and Privoz Market.

Gunsel (048-702 2831; www.gunsel.ua; vul Kolontayevska 21; 24hr) buses for Kiev (350uah to 440uah, six to seven hours, five daily) depart from the new slick, but not particularly user-friendly, **Starosinna bus station** (pl Starosinna). Across the road, **Privokzalna bus station** (vul Starosennaya 1) handles frequent buses for Bilhorod-Dnistrovsky (70uah, 2½ hours) via Zatoka and Shabo.

Closer to the market, the slightly chaotic **Privoz bus station** (vul Vodoprovodna) is primarily useful for Vylkove (160uah, three to four hours, four daily). Here you can also catch the daily bus to Reni on the Moldovan/Romanian border (320uah, seven hours, three daily) and Chişinău in Moldova (200uah to 260uah, five to seven hours, many daily). Note that many of the latter pass through Tiraspol (120uah, three hours) in the breakaway territory of Transnistria. If you want to avoid that, ask for a bus going via Palanka.

Buses for Chornomorsk depart from both Privoz and Starosinna bus stations (26uah, one hour, every 15 minutes).

Note that small bus operators migrate between all three central stations, so if there is no convenient bus to your destination at one of them, check at the others.

Most international and long-haul domestic buses leave from the **long-distance bus station** (vul Kolontayivska 58), 3km west of the train station. Apart from Kyiv, there are services to most large cities in Ukraine, including Kherson (130uah to 170uah, three to four hours, hourly), Lviv (670uah, 15 hours, three daily), Dnipro (430uah, 9½ hours, five daily) and Chernivtsi (450uah, 13 hours, two daily) via Kamyanets-Podilsky.

There is at least one daily bus to Bucharest in Romania (700uah, 12 hours) and Sofia in Bulgaria (1200uah, 22 hours).

TRAIN

A daily Intercity+ train (330uah, seven hours) and a couple of daily overnight trains (470uah, 9½ to 13 hours) connect Odesa with Kyiv. There are also services to Lviv (260uah, 12 hours, four daily), Dnipro (185uah to 260uah, 11 hours, two daily) and Kharkiv (290uah, 14½ hours, daily).

International destinations include Chişinău (350uah, five hours, daily), Moscow (4000uah, 24 hours, daily) and Minsk (2200uah, 22 hours, daily).

Getting Around

To get to the city centre from the train station (about a 20-minute walk), go to the stop near the McDonald's (Pryvokzalna pl) and take any *marshrutka* (minibus) saying 'Площа Грецка' (pl Hretska), such as bus 148. Trolleybuses 4 and 10 trundle up vul Pushkinska before curving around to vul Prymorska, past the sea port and the foot of the Potemkin Steps.

From the airport, trolleybus 14 goes to the train station, while the infrequent bus 117 trundles all the way into the centre, stopping at Pl Hretska Bus Stop (pl Hretska, vul Bunina side).

Tram 5 goes from the train station to the long-distance bus station. If you're going from the Privoz bus station to pl Hretska, take bus 220.

A typical taxi with Uber costs 30uah to 40uah in the centre, 70uah to 80uah from the centre to Arkadia.

Rental cars are especially useful for exploring Bessarabia or the Kherson area. Try Europcar in the Black Sea Rishelyevskaya (p182). Most international car-rental companies are well represented in the airport.

DNISTER ESTUARY
ДНІСТРОВСЬКИЙ ЛИМАН

The bulging estuaries formed by rivers flowing into the Black Sea, known locally as *limany*, are easily the most noticeable geographical feature of the Odesa region. The largest one is formed by the Dnister, which originates in the Carpathians and flows through Moldova for much of its 1350km route. For centuries, the Dnister *liman* was controlled by the mighty Akkerman fortress, which remains intact in the town of Bilhorod Dnistrovsky. Both banks are covered in vineyards, with one of Ukraine's most famous wineries located in the former Swiss village of Shabo. White-sand beaches in the mouth of the river lure hordes of domestic holidaymakers, as well as unscrupulous real estate developers – a bad combination with disastrous consequences for the area's natural beauty.

Sights

A simple day trip from Odesa, Bilhorod-Dnistrovsky would be an ordinary industrial port if not for the impressive **Akkerman fortress** (☎225 96; vul Pushkina 19, Bilhorod-Dnistrovsky; adult/child 50/25uah; ⌚9am-6pm) (built by Moldavians, Genoese and Turks in the 13th to 15th centuries). Today the castle is among Ukraine's largest and best preserved. You can walk along most of the walls, which stretch nearly 2km in total, and admire the views of the Dnister estuary. Various 'medieval' activities, like bow shooting, are on offer. In summer, you'll also find a few makeshift cafes inside and around the fortress.

To reach the fortress from the train station, walk along vul Vokzalna and, after the park, turn right onto vul Izmailska (Dzerzhinskoho). From here, the fortress is a 1.5km walk.

The villages of Karolino-Buhaz and Zatoka occupy both sides of a sand bar that all but blocks the mouth of the Dnister. They have been transformed by the recent tourist boom into an enormous sprawl of holiday accommodation. Unconstrained development coupled with decaying infrastructure makes the area look like a cross between a Mediterranean sea resort and a third-world slum. But the fairly clean, white-sand beach invites for a much-needed break.

Halfway between Zatoka and Odesa, but slightly off the main route, the tidy but architecturally Soviet Chornomorsk is relevant for three reasons. One is the wide and regularly cleaned white-sand beach, arguably the best in the region and easily accessible from Odesa. The second is the port terminal that serves the notoriously unstable ferry routes (p188) that link Ukraine to other Black Sea countries, most notably Georgia. Third, it now hosts one of Ukraine's two main jazz festivals, **Koktebel Jazz** (http://koktebel.info; various locations, Chornomorsk; ⌚end of Aug), which had to find a new location following the Russian occupation of Crimea.

If either the festival schedule or your desire to spend time on the beach mandate that you overnight in Chornomorsk, head to **Fontan** (Фонтан; ☎048-686 5549; pr Myru 20/1, Chornomorsk; r 1100uah; ❄📶) – a slightly kitschy, but perfectly comfortable hotel in the town centre.

Still better known under its Soviet name of Ilyichevsk, Chornomorsk obtained its new post-Maidan moniker from a fictional seaside town described in *The Golden Calf*, a 1920s Soviet satirical book by Ilya Ilf and Yevgeny Petrov.

ℹ Getting There & Away

If you plan to see the fortress in Bilhorod-Dnistrovsky and then spend some time on the beach, it would be wise to take a morning train from Odesa railway station (20uah, 2½ hours, four daily) and return by bus. Bilhorod-Dnistrovsky is also served by minibuses departing from both Privoz and Privokzalna bus stations in Odesa (57uah, two hours, frequent). These pass through Karolino-Buhaz, Zatoka and Shabo.

Chornomorsk minibuses (20uah, every 15 minutes) depart from the same bus stations in Odesa and bring you into the town centre. Heading to Chornomorsk from Bilhorod-Dnistrovsky, you need to get off at Velykodolynske (better known as Bolshaya Dolina) where you can change for Chornomorsk-bound buses.

Shabo is 9km from Bilhorod-Dnistrovsky. Buses stop around 500m from the winery.

Vylkove Вилкове

☎04843 / POP 9300

A network of navigable canals has earned Vylkove the nickname 'the Venice of Ukraine'. Frankly, the comparison is preposterous. This sleepy fishing village feels light years removed from Venice – or any other form of civilisation. And while the canals – along which many villagers live – are interesting, you won't spend much time on them unless you take a special tour. But Vylkove does have one thing going for it that Venice lacks: the heavenly Danube Delta Biosphere Reserve.

SHABO

In 1822 a few dozen Francophone Swiss families from Vevey canton, led by botanist Louis Tardane, packed their belongings into horse-driven carts and drove across Europe to the Odesa region, which was touted at the time as Russian California. Taking over old Turkish vineyards in the estuary of the Dnister River, they set up a colony of wine-makers. It ceased to exist 120 years later, with the Soviet occupation of Bessarabia in WWII, when the descendants of the settlers packed up again and moved back to Switzerland.

Today the newly revived **Shabo winery** (Винзавод Шабо; http://shabo.ua; vul Dzerzhinskoho 10, Shabo; tour & tasting 240uah) is a slick modern operation, but its owners – Georgians from Odesa – are absolutely obsessed with the place's Swiss heritage. Although conducted in Russian, tours of the winery are interesting and fun. You'll see 200-year-old cellars (look out for the Romanian king's autograph on the wall), an entertaining museum that contains objects from Bessarabian-Swiss households, and a great silent movie taking viewers through all stages of wine production.

It all culminates in a wine-tasting session, which is when you can build camaraderie with Ukrainian and Russian tourists by giving thoughtful looks before and sharing opinions after each emptied glass. Across the road from the winery there is **Shabsky Dvorik** (vul Shveytsarska 21, Shabo; mains 100-150uah) – a Georgian restaurant, to which you can repair (be carried to by new friends) afterwards.

DANUBE DELTA BIOSPHERE RESERVE

The lion's share of the marshy, bird-laden **Danube Delta Biosphere Reserve** (www.dbr.org.ua), Europe's largest wetlands, lies in Romania. Few tourists enter from the Ukrainian side, but those who do are rewarded with extremely affordable half- to full-day boat tours through the delta's unique waterways. You can visit the Danube's terminus – dubbed the '0km mark' – or take a bird-watching tour.

Guides can drop you off on small islands populated by thousands of terns and their just-hatched chicks. On other islands, flocks of cormorants and white pelicans roost (the reserve is home to 70% of the world's white pelicans).

In the centre of the town of Vylkove you'll find the Biosphere Reserve office, with an on-site museum and informational videos (in German and Russian). The staff speaks some English and can set you up with a local tour operator to take you into the reserve by boat.

Vylkove's canals, built by the town's original Lipovan settlers, are the other main attraction. The villagers who live along the canals still use traditional, narrow fishing boats known as *chaika* (seagull) to fish and get around. Locals say there are 3000 such boats in Vylkove, compared with only 600 cars. While touring the canals, drop by a local's house and purchase a bottle of the local wine, known as *novak*.

Sights

Artist Aleksandr Sharonov's Exhibition MUSEUM

(067-153 4127; vul Rizdvziana (Lenina) 11; 30uah; 8am-1pm) A local lore museum in all but name, this impressive collection assembled by a local artist occupies a large building of the Soviet-era House of Culture. Exhibits include Lipovan household items and photos, religious books and icons, fishing equipment, ancient coins and other artefacts unearthed by the owner in the area. A large *chaika* boat proudly stands in the middle. The owner is around most of the time, if you wish to chat (in Russian).

Tours

Booking tours in advance is a good idea, particularly on weekends. Prices vary wildly, depending on the size of the group and the distance (fuel makes up a lion's share of expenses for boat operators). It makes lots of sense to find travel companions and share the cost. Expect to pay anything between 200uah and 800uah for a tour of the village, and 400uah to 1800uah for a half-day trip to the delta. English-speaking guides are available at extra charge.

Odesa travel agencies offer Vylkove as a day trip, but it is far more rewarding to spend a night in Vylkove and use the extra time to absorb some local flavour. In Odesa, we recommend Salix (p180) travel agency. In Vylkove, you'll find people touting tours by the bus and river stations.

Pelikan Tour TOURS

(Пеликан Тур; www.pelican-danube-tour.com.ua) Half-day tours to the Danube Delta cost 150uah to 200uah per person depending on the number of people in the boat. English-speaking guides cost around 100uah per hour (much more per hour for a professional ornithologist who speaks English). A half-day should be enough time to visit both the reserve and the canals. A one-hour canal tour costs about 65uah.

Sleeping

Pelikan City GUESTHOUSE, COTTAGES $

(067 483 5207; vul Bohdana Khmelnitskoho 54; guesthouse s/d/cottage from 245/395/670uah) Pelikan Tour (p191) runs a homey, 14-bed guesthouse on the banks of the Danube, a short walk from the city centre. The company has also built four comfortable timber cottages in a tranquil spot on the riverbank. The cottages have large glazed verandahs for bird spotting and to let the river views flood in.

You'll have to resist the urge to take up duck hunting when awakened by the loudly frolicking, nocturnal waterfowl in the small marina.

Venetslya HOTEL $

(Венеція; 68355-31374; http://vilkovo-venecia.at.ua; vul Rizdvyana (Lenina) 19A; s/d from 350/450uah;) On the main drag, this hotel has big, bright, comfy rooms and fluffy rugs. Most rooms share pristine bathrooms and there's also a restaurant.

★**Dunayskaya Usadba** GUESTHOUSE **$$**
(☎067 968-5207; www.facebook.com/dusadba.com.ua/; vul Ukrainskikh Prikordonnikov 2D; r 650uah; 📶) Owner Ivan Kozma rents out three rooms in a typical Vylkove house – made of reed and clay, with a Russian-style brick oven in the centre and layers of seashells in the foundation to absorb floodwater. The garden is criss-crossed by canals, where Ivan keeps his boats, and the Danube is metres away, accessed via a small bridge.

Ivan's wife, Larissa, cooks delicious Bessarabian food and Ivan runs tours of the village and the delta. Each tour involves visits to private households and gardens on islands that form a part of Vylkove. Expect to consume lots of *novak* wine.

Kuba-Daleko GUESTHOUSE **$$**
(Куба-далеко; ☎066 731 0850, 050 391 0678; www.brynzarnya.com; vul Prikordonnaya (Pogranichaya) 2, Primorske; d without bathroom 550-650uah) A fun place to stay, this *brynza* (goat cheese) farm comes with a little museum of Lipovan Old Believer culture on the premises and a hotel, bizarrely themed on a Soviet song about Cuba. The place is on the seaside in Primorske – otherwise known as Vylkove beach, 10km from town. Book well in advance.

Delta HOTEL **$$**
(☎098-78 73 588; http://deltahotel.net.ua; vul Tatarbunarskoho Povstannya 164; d 700uah) The only fully fledged hotel in town is a comfortable place to overnight. It's also a wonderful display of post-Soviet nouveau riche tastes, with a church and a religious-themed monument in the manicured grounds and near-pornographic art in otherwise perfectly standard hotel rooms. It is 200m away from the supermarket on the town's edge. Most Odesa buses stop here.

ℹ Getting There & Away

Buses to Vylkove leave from Odesa's Privoz bus station (p188; 170uah, three to four hours, four daily). Note that they pass through a short section of Moldovan territory soon after Odesa, but border guards only count heads so no one gets in on the way. Two services a day go to Izmayil (80uah, two hours), from where you can continue to Reni (one hour) on the Romanian/Moldovan border.

Crimea

Includes ➡

Fast Facts

Population: 2.3 million

Area: 26,200 sq km

Administrative regions: 2 (Republic of Crimea & Sevastopol)

Capital (Republic of Crimea): Simferopol

Average day temperature (July): 26–28 degrees Celsius

Highest point: Mt Ay-Petri (1234m)

Longest river: Salhir (204km)

Crimea Explained

Shaped like a diamond, this tiny subtropical gem has always been an eye-catcher for imperial rulers – from Romans to Russians. The latest invasion, albeit a largely peaceful one, took place in March 2014, when the peninsula was annexed by and once again incorporated into Russia after 23 years as part of independent Ukraine. Although this takeover has not been recognised by the international community, Crimea is now firmly controlled by Moscow, which applies the same rules to foreign visitors as in Russia proper.

In Crimea's south, mountains rise like a sail as if trying to carry it away into open sea. Protected from northern winds, the coast is covered in lush subtropical vegetation. This is where Russian royals built summer palaces, later transformed into sanatoriums for workers.

The mountains are the heartland of Crimean Tatars – a nation of survivors, who brought back from a 50-year exile their traditions of hospitality and excellent food. They live surrounded by limestone plateaus – a magnet for trekkers and cyclists who come here for great vistas and to explore ancient cave cities.

Crimea Coverage

As the UK Foreign and Commonwealth Office and the US State Department advise against all travel to Crimea, we have not visited the peninsula to update our coverage and we have provided no practical information or advice for visitors. Instead, we present an overview of its history and main destinations, as well as the implications of Russia's takeover of Crimea for travellers.

Crimea Highlights

1 **Cave cities** (p198 & p199) Ancient Crimeans carved dwellings out of limestone atop high plateaus: highlights include Mangup-Kale and Chufut-Kale.

2 **Bakhchysaray** (p198) The capital of the peninsula's largest minority, the Crimean Tatars.

3 **Sevastopol** (p200) This very pleasant and historically important city has a stunning bay filled with Russian warships. The Balaklava fjord nearby was the base of British troops during the allied invasion of Crimea in 1854.

4 **Yalta** (p197) Attractions here include writer Anton Chekhov's House-Museum and the Livadia Palace, where Soviet and Anglo-British allies carved up post-WWII Europe.

5 **Sudak's fortress** (p202) A fort built by medieval Genovese traders, who came here to link up with caravans bringing silk and spices from the Orient.

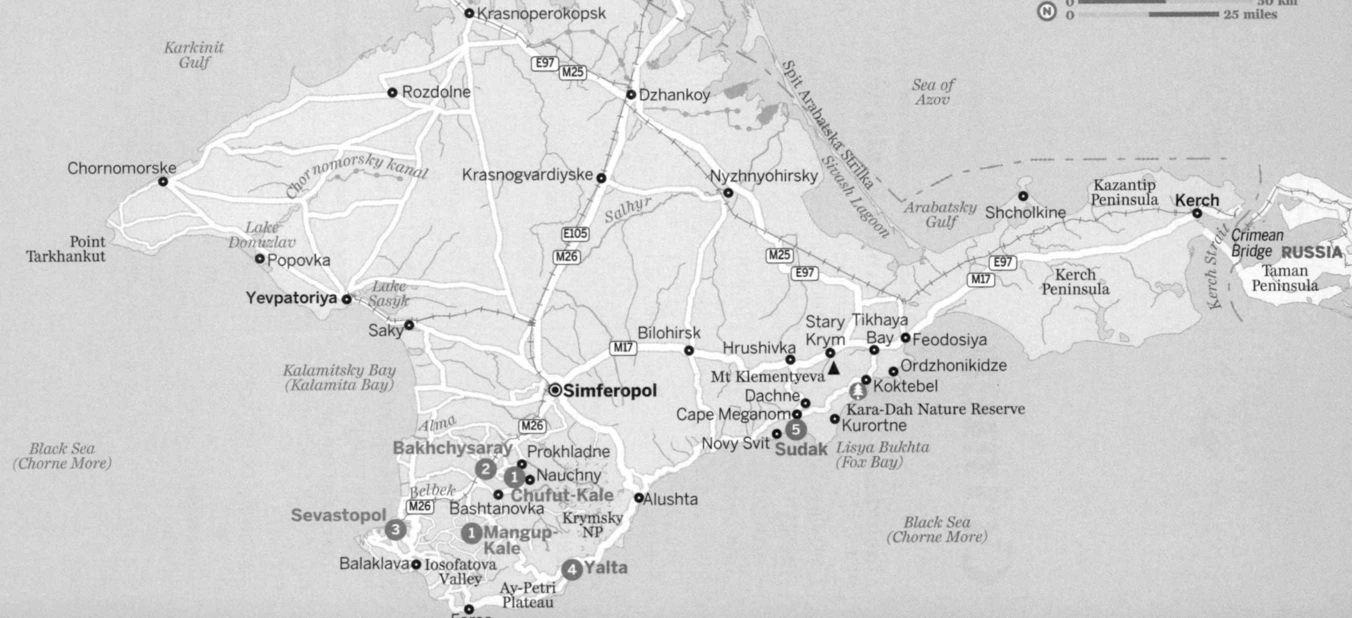

History

The stage is littered with cameo appearances, from ancient Greeks who built Chersonesus (now Khersones) to the 15th-century Genoese merchants behind the impressive Sudak fortress, as well as Cimmerians, Scythians, Sarmatians and Jews. However, the central theme of Crimean history revolves around the struggle between the Turkic and Slavic peoples for control of the peninsula.

This began in 1240, when Mongols conquered Crimea. Two centuries later control passed to their descendants, the Tatars, who held it for centuries. The Crimean Khanate became an independent political entity under Hacı I Giray in 1428, and after the 1475 invasion was a vassal state of the Ottoman Empire. Although advanced in culture and arts, its main economic activity was trading in slaves, captured during raids into the territory of modern Ukraine, Russia and Poland.

While a Turkish vassal state, Crimea enjoyed much autonomy. The same was not true when the Russians arrived in 1783 and began a campaign of assimilation. Three-quarters of Crimean Tatars fled to Turkey, while Russians, Ukrainians, Bulgarians, Germans and even some French were invited to resettle Crimea.

Such Russian expansionism soon began to worry the great powers, Britain and France. As Russia tried to encroach into the lands of the decaying Ottoman Empire, the Crimean War erupted in 1854.

With close ties to the monarchy, Crimea was one of the last White bastions during the Russian revolution, holding out till November 1920. It was occupied by German troops for three years during WWII and lost nearly half its population. In the war's aftermath, Stalin deported all remaining Crimean Tatars and most other ethnic minorities.

In 1954 Soviet leader Nikita Khrushchev, a self-styled Ukrainian, created the Autonomous Crimean Soviet Socialist Republic and transferred legislative control to the Ukrainian SSR from the Russian Federation.

This is how Crimea ended up inside independent Ukraine after the collapse of the USSR in 1991. Although never enthused by Ukrainian independence, the ethnic Russian majority didn't make any significant attempts to change the status quo. However, Russia secured the right to maintain a navy base in Sevastopol, which later proved to be a Trojan horse.

The early 1990s also saw the return of Crimean Tatars from exile in Central Asia, where Stalin sent the entire people in 1944, having accused them of collaboration with the Nazis. They tended to be overwhelmingly pro-Ukrainian.

A sudden change came in March 2014 when, following the collapse of Yanukovych government in Kyiv, Sevastopol-based Russian marines and special forces took over Crimea in a matter of days. Ukrainian military, policemen and security agents switched sides en masse, and those who didn't were peacefully squeezed out of the peninsula.

After a hastily conducted 'referendum', Russia proclaimed Crimea its territory in a move that was rejected by the international community. The war in the east of Ukraine has further exacerbated the situation, although by triggering it (as well as subsequently intervening in Syria) the Kremlin has succeeded in diverting attention from Crimea.

In the years that followed the occupation, Moscow was busily integrating the peninsula into its political system and investing into large-scale infrastructural projects, the main one being a gigantic bridge across the straits of Kerch, which will connect Crimea to the Russian mainland. The project was nearly finished at the time of writing. On the political front, security services were severely persecuting Crimean Tatar and Ukrainian activists. Yet, the popularity of pro-Ukrainian forces in Crimea is low, and the majority of the population remains visibly pro-Russian.

In the meantime, Ukraine cut off power and fresh water supplies to Crimea to impose additional costs on Russian occupants, while Western countries imposed Crimea-specific sanctions, which punish those who do business in Crimea and make it impossible to use international payment cards on the peninsula. As a result, even the largest Russian banks, airlines and retail companies refrained from operating in Crimea.

Crimea Under Russian Rule: What Has Changed for Travellers

From the standpoint of the international community, Crimea remains a part of Ukraine. Not even Moscow's closest allies, Belarus and Kazakhstan, have accepted the annexation. Yet the gloomy new reality of a heavily fortified border – which has emerged between the Russian-controlled Crimea and Ukraine proper – presents a set of challenges for travellers.

Crossing the Border

The main dilemma for foreign travellers to Crimea is posed by the conflict of legality and practicality, since the easiest method of entering Ukraine is technically illegal.

It's not that the Crimean border is completely impenetrable – Ukrainian nationals are allowed to cross by car, although train services from the mainland have been discontinued.

But Ukraine has adopted a 'law on occupied territories', which stipulates that holders of foreign passports can only travel between Crimea and Ukraine proper with a special permission from the Ukrainian government. These permits are issued by the Migration Service of Ukraine on no other grounds than the presence of close relatives in Crimea, journalistic and religious activities, or participation in the work of the Crimean Tatar Mejlis, an organisation outlawed in Russia. So basically it's a no-go for tourists.

By contrast, it's very easy to enter Crimea from the Russian side. That involves flying into Moscow or St Petersburg on a valid Russian visa – or without it, if you are a citizen of Israel, Turkey and most South American countries – then taking an onward domestic flight into Simferopol. The Kerch bridge, due to be opened in 2018, will simplify travel for motorists and re-establish the railway connection between Crimea and mainland Russia. Until it's open, ferries carry passengers and cars across the straits.

There are no borders checks and no additional stamps in your passport if you enter Crimea via Russia. But from the Ukrainian point of view, doing that is tantamount to illegal border crossing. Ukraine has indeed punished a large number of Russian cultural figures and a much smaller number of Western politicians for entering Crimea from the Russian side. They have all been declared persona non grata and barred from entering Ukraine.

INFO ON CRIMEA

Books

Crimea: The Last Crusade (Orlando Figes, 2010)

The Island of Crimea (Vassily Aksyonov, 1979)

The Crimean Tatars: From Soviet Genocide to Putin's Conquest (Brian Glyn Williams, 2015)

The Innocents Abroad (Mark Twain, 1869)

Online

Human Rights in Ukraine (www.khpg.org/en)

Mejlis of the Crimean Tatar People (www.qtmm.org/en)

Crimea Human Rights Portal (www.crimeahr.org/en)

Crimea Bridge (www.most.life)

Documentaries

Russian Roulette dispatches by Simon Ostrovsky (Vice News)

Ethical Dilemmas

Since almost no government in the world has recognised the Russian takeover of Crimea, there are also ethical dilemmas regarding travel there. Although Ukrainians are free to travel to the peninsula, most of them won't do so for political reasons (that said, many Ukrainians won't care whether Western travellers go to Crimea or not).

The idea of a travel boycott is also popular among liberal Russians who oppose the annexation. But it's not only the Russian state that gets 'punished' – the boycott also affects the locals, who are largely involved in the peninsula's travel industry. Many, if not most, Crimeans supported the Russian takeover – in Sevastopol in particular, the level of support is absolutely overwhelming.

However, owners of small and medium businesses, such as guesthouses and restaurants, often belong to the minority that opposes changes. Importantly, prior to the occupation, much of the travel industry in

A LA TATAR

When in Crimea, foreigners may often find themselves staring at a menu with a 'what the hell is it?' expression on their face. Most problematic are Crimean Tatar and Black Sea fish restaurants where people find nothing but endemic Crimean dishes they've never heard of.

Crimean Tatar cuisine is similar to the Turkish, but half a century in Central Asian exile left a significant imprint. Here is the list of the most ubiquitous eats:

Cherub (Чебурек) – a fried turnover filled with minced meat and onions

Plov (Плов) – a variation of the Asian pilaf rice dish, usually with pieces of mutton, carrots and raisins

Qashiq ash (Кашик Аш) – small, ravioli-style, meat-filled dumplings, usually served in broth

Manty (Манти) – large Central Asian dumplings filled with minced mutton

Sarma (Сарма) – grapevine leaves stuffed with minced meat

Dolma (Долма) – green paprika stuffed with a mixture of minced meat and rice

Studying the menu at a Crimean fish restaurant, a visitor is confronted by two questions: which fish to choose and how it should be cooked. For the latter, you can have your fish grilled, fried or cooked in the Greek-Jewish *shkara* style, where fish and vegetables are boiled in a frying pan until most of the liquid evaporates. For the former, here are the most common types of fish.

Barabulka/sultanka (Барабулька, Султанка) – surmullet, small fish that locals often swallow whole, although the fillet is easy to separate from the bones

Sargan (Сарган) – garfish, small needle-shaped fish that roll itself into neat-looking rings when fried

Lufar (Луфарь) – bluefish, medium-sized fish

Kefal (Кефаль) – mullet, the best known Black Sea fish, mentioned in classical Odesa songs

Katran (Катран) – a small (and totally harmless!) Black Sea shark

Kambala (Камбала) – sole

Crimea was controlled by Crimean Tatars – the largest ethnic minority, which remains staunchly pro-Ukrainian. Some of them are indeed in favour of all forms of boycott, even if it affects their incomes, but others are not that radical.

One last thing to keep in mind is that Western travellers' contribution to Crimean travel industry's revenues has always been modest if not insignificant.

What Has Changed

Those who have been to Crimea before might be surprised by how little has changed – at least on the surface. The main change for travellers is that now they can't use international payment cards like Visa due to Western sanctions specifically targeting Crimea.

Other changes mostly concerned locals. The Russian rouble has replaced the Ukrainian hryvnya as the only legal currency, which led to an increase in retail prices, though for Crimeans that was compensated by higher Russian salaries. It did, however, hit Russian tourists who benefited from cheap Ukrainian prices prior to 2014.

Ukrainian products gradually disappeared from supermarkets, replaced by Russian equivalents, sometimes of inferior quality. Severed power supplies from the Ukrainian mainland led to a series of blackouts, although the Russians have managed to alleviate that situation by providing additional capacities. The termination of fresh water supplies by the Ukrainians has badly affected the agriculture in Crimea's north.

Predictably, the Russian takeover hit the local travel industry, but only to an extent. Russian officials claim 5.5 million tourists visited Crimea in 2016, compared with 6.1 million in 2012 when Ukraine still controlled the peninsula. Ukrainian officials claim that Russian figures are grossly exaggerated. On the ground, beaches do look emptier than prior to 2014, but the real decrease is hard to assess.

Yalta

Yalta's air – an invigorating blend of sea and pine forest sprinkled with mountain chill – has always been its main asset. Back in the 19th century, doctors in St Petersburg had one remedy for poor-lunged aristocrats: Yalta. That's how the Russian royal family and other dignitaries, such as playwright Anton Chekhov, ended up here.

The **Chekhov House-Museum** is sort of *The Cherry Orchard* incarnate. Not only did Chekhov pen that classic play here, the lush garden would appeal to the most horticulturally challenged audience. A long-term tuberculosis sufferer, the great Russian dramatist spent much of his last five years in Yalta. He designed the white dacha (holiday home) and garden himself, and when he wasn't producing plays like *Three Sisters* and *The Cherry Orchard,* he was a legendary host and bon vivant, welcoming the Russian singer Feodor Chaliapin, composer Rachmaninov, and writers Maxim Gorky and Leo Tolstoy. At the dacha, all nine rooms are pretty much as Chekhov left them upon his departure from Yalta for Germany in May 1904.

Old parts of Yalta are still full of modest and not-so-modest former dachas of the tsarist-era intelligentsia, while the coast around the city is dotted with the luxurious palaces of the aristocracy. But back in 1913 a Russian travel guide remarked that Yalta was a long way from the Riviera in terms of comforts and civilisation. The latest Russian takeover of Crimea has made that gap even wider, but a very happy-looking granite Lenin seems pleased when *babushkas* gather at sunset to dance the waltz and polka on the plaza that still bears his name.

Just west of the city, **Livadia Palace** reverberates with history. It's the site of the 1945 Yalta Conference, where dying US president Franklin Roosevelt and heat-allergic British prime minister Winston Churchill turned up to be bullied by Soviet leader Josef Stalin. While here, Churchill declared Crimea 'the Riviera of Hades'. No wonder, given the company he was keeping. Stalin's insistent demands to keep Poland and other swathes of Eastern Europe shaped the face of postwar Europe.

In the enormous White Hall, the 'Big Three' and their staff met to tacitly agree that the USSR would wield the biggest influence in Eastern Europe, in exchange for keeping out of the Mediterranean. The crucial documents, dividing Germany and ceding parts of Poland to the USSR, were signed on 11 February in the English billiard room. The most famous Yalta photograph of Churchill, Roosevelt and Stalin is hung on a wall, along with the awkward out-takes, which bring history to life.

It's upstairs, however, that Livadia's other ghosts genuinely move even complete anti-monarchists. This Italian Renaissance–style building was designed as a summer residence for Russian Tsar Nicholas II in 1911. But he and his family spent just four seasons here before their arrest by Bolshevik troops in 1917 and execution in Yekaterinburg the following year. Photos and some poignant mementos of the doomed Romanovs are still in their private apartments.

Bakhchysaray

More a village than a town, the former capital of Crimean Tatar khans is cradled in a narrow valley squeezed between two limestone escarpments. Its name means 'garden palace', and it's a garden that needs a lot of tilling after 50 years of neglect, during which its owners lived in exile. Now the Crimean Tatars are back and, although lacking resources, they have already orchestrated a minor renaissance.

Sadly, the Russian annexation has once again turned Crimean Tatars into a persecuted minority, though not on a Soviet scale. Hence, some of the little hotels and restaurants that we used to love are now closed, their owners having fled to Kyiv. But Bakhchysaray is still an enchanting place full of remnants of past civilizations.

Rising 200m, the long and bluff plateau of **Chufut-Kale** houses a honeycomb of caves and structures where people took refuge for centuries. The burial chambers and casemates with large open 'windows' in the vertiginous northern cliff are truly breathtaking, as is the view into the valley below.

First appearing in historical records as Kyrk-Or (Forty Fortifications), the city was settled sometime between the 6th and 12th centuries by Christianised descendants of

CRIMEAN TATAR DEPORTATIONS

There's a plaque on the train station building in Bakhchysaray which commemorates Crimean Tatars who were herded here on 18 May 1944, forced into cattle cars and sent on an arduous journey to Central Asia. Stalin had decided to punish a whole people for collaboration with German occupiers, ignoring the fact that 9000 Crimean Tatars fought in the Soviet army and thousands more joined Soviet partisans.

A total of 180,000 Crimean Tatar were deported from Crimea, followed by 37,000 members of smaller minorities – Greeks from Balaklava, Italians from Kerch, Bulgarians from Koktebel, Armenians from Feodosiya and all ethnic Germans. They were usually given only a few minutes to take vital belongings and very few of them lived to see their homes again.

Sarmatian tribes. The last powerful ruler of the Golden Horde, Tokhtamysh, sheltered here after defeat in the 1390s, and the first Crimean khanate was established at Chufut-Kale in the 15th century, before moving to nearby Bakhchysaray. After the Tatars left, Turkic-Jewish Karaites occupied the city until the mid-19th century, which won the mountain its current name of 'Jewish Fortress'.

When Catherine the Great ordered the mass destruction of Bakhchysaray's mosques in the 18th and early 19th centuries, she decided to spare the **Khans' Palace**. Her decision was reportedly based on the building being 'romantic', and it is sweet. While it lacks the imposing grandeur of Islamic structures in, say, Istanbul, this is a major landmark of Crimean culture and history. Erected in the 16th century under the direction of Persian, Ottoman and Italian architects, it was rebuilt a few times, but the structure still resembles the original.

Passing through the back of the finely carved, Venetian Renaissance Demir Qapi Portal (also called Portal Alevizo after its Italian designer, who also authored parts of Moscow's Kremlin), one enters the west wing and the dimly lit Divan Hall. This was the seat of government, where the khan and his nobles discussed laws and wars.

Through the hall lies the inner courtyard, containing two fountains. With its white marble ornately inscribed with gold leaf, the Golden Fountain (1733) is probably the more beautiful. However, the neighbouring Fountain of Tears (1764) is more famous, thanks to Alexander Pushkin. It's tradition that two roses – one red for love and one yellow for chagrin – are placed atop the fountain; Pushkin was the first to do this. Behind the palace is the only surviving harem of the four that were traditionally attached to the palace and belonged to the khans' wives. Across the yard is the Falcon Tower. The Khans' Cemetery is beside the mosque, and way back in the grounds' southeast corner is the mausoleum of Dilara Bikez, who may or may not be the Polish beauty who bewitched the khan.

Located 22km south of Bakhchysaray, the remote plateau of **Mangup-Kale** is the peninsula's most spectacular cave city, in the shape of a hand with four fingers. Formerly the ancient capital of Feodoro, the principality of the 6th-century Ellinised Goths and Alans, this was an excellent fortress due to its sheer cliffs. It was finally abandoned in the 15th century.

Balaklava

From bloodthirsty pirates featuring in Homer's *Odyssey* to the Soviet nuclear submarine fleet – everyone used this beautiful curving fjord, invisible from the sea, as a secret hideout.

The 2500-year-old settlement became a Genoese trading post in the medieval period. In 1475 it fell to the conquering Turks who gave Balaklava its current name, which means Fish's Nest. After the Russian takeover of Crimea, the area was settled by Greek refugees escaping Ottoman rule.

The British army wintered here during the Crimean War when a storm destroyed many supply ships moored outside the bay. Reading about it in *The Times*, concerned women back home began knitting full-cover woolly caps for the freezing sailors. These garments became known as 'balaclava helmets' or simply 'balaclavas'.

During the war Florence Nightingale ran a field hospital on one of the plateaus above the village, and the infamous charge of the ill-fated Light Brigade took place in a valley north of the city.

Stalin deported Balaklava Greeks to Central Asia in 1944. Few of them returned to their hometown, which was turned into a top-secret Soviet submarine base.

Today the bay's turquoise waters, surrounded by arid, scrub-covered hills, shelter an armada of yachts and – as a sign of a new volatile epoch – Russian military vessels.

Simferopol

With its odd mixture of the Levantine and the Soviet, the Crimean capital is not an unpleasant city, but everything else on the peninsula is much more exciting. The Crimean capital was the scene of dramatic though largely bloodless events during the Russian seizure of the peninsula. Now it's the seat of the Russian-imposed government and the entry gate for Russian holidaymakers flying into Simferopol airport with myriad little-known airlines that don't care about potential Western sanctions. Meanwhile, the graceful train station stays largely empty because of the Ukrainian railway blockade.

Sevastopol

It's easy to understand why the Russians were keen to reclaim this town more than any other chunk of their lost empire. Orderly and clean as the deck of a ship, with whitewashed neoclassical buildings surrounding a cerulean bay, it has everything most Russian cities lack.

Even when it was controlled by Ukraine, most locals were linked to the navy in some respect and maintained a strong allegiance to Moscow. This resulted in a peculiar cultural microclimate, similar to Gibraltar's. It was no surprise that the locals were at the forefront of what they call 'the Russian spring' and the rest of the world calls 'the annexation of Crimea'.

Sevastopol has much to say about the irony of fate. Purpose-built as an impregnable sea fortress to shelter the imperial fleet, it fell three times after being attacked from land. Anglo-Franco-Turkish allies were the first to lay siege and capture it during the Crimean War. In 1920 the city became the last stronghold of the retreating White Russian army. It saw steamships carrying away the cream

CHARGE OF THE LIGHT BRIGADE

Unquestioning loyalty, bravery and inexplicable blunders leading to tragedy – these ingredients turned an engagement lasting just minutes into one of the most renowned battles in military history. The action in question is the ill-fated charge of the Light Brigade, which occurred during a Russian attempt to cut British supply lines from Balaklava to Sevastopol during the Crimean War.

The battle began northeast of Balaklava early on 25 October 1854. Russian forces based on the east–west Fedioukine Hills wrested control of Allied (Turkish-held) gun positions lining the parallel southern ridge of Causeway Heights. Then they moved towards Balaklava itself.

Initially the Russians were blocked by the 'thin red line' of the British 93rd Highlanders, and repulsed by Lord Lucan's Heavy Cavalry Brigade. But four hours later, they appeared to be regrouping at the eastern end of the valley between the Fedioukine Hills and Causeway Heights. British army commander Lord Raglan sent an order for the cavalry 'to try and prevent the enemy carrying away the guns'.

The order was vague – which guns exactly? – and misinterpreted. The Earl of Cardigan headed off down the wrong valley, leading his Light Cavalry Brigade into a cul-de-sac controlled on three sides by the enemy. The numbers are disputed, but nearly 200 of 673 soldiers were killed.

'C'est magnifique, mais ce n'est pas la guerre,' exclaimed a watching French general. ('It's magnificent, but it's not war.') Later, romantic poet Lord Alfred Tennyson would lionise the 'noble six hundred' who rode into 'the valley of death'. His poem 'The Charge of the Light Brigade' did more than anything to mythologise the event for posterity. On its 150th anniversary, the charge was even re-created in front of British dignitaries, including Prince Philip.

The 'Valley of Death' is now a vineyard, just north of the road from Sevastopol to Yalta.

of Russian society into a lifelong exile rather than surrender to the Bolsheviks.

History repeated itself in 1942, when the Germans captured Sevastopol after a devastating 250-day siege. There was hardly a building left standing when they entered. But very soon Sevastopol was rebuilt by the Soviets with an atypical regard for its historic outlook.

A favourite playground for fans of military history, Sevastopol is also attractive to those with no interest in weapons and uniforms. Simply put, it is the most pleasant Crimean city – civilised and easy-going, but largely bypassed by the recreational mayhem of Crimea's southern coast.

The ruins of the ancient Greek city founded in 422 BC are of great significance to local visitors. This is the place where Volodymyr the Great was famously baptised into Christianity in AD 988, launching what would become the Russian Orthodox Church. Earlier that year, he sacked the city, helping the Byzantine emperor to put down a local rebellion.

In the last weekend of July the city celebrates Russian Navy Day with an impressive show of battleships manoeuvring in the bay, planes flying overhead and marines landing on Grafskaya Pristan.

Feodosiya

Neighbourhood names like Chumka (Plague) and Quarantine aren't romantic, but they hark back to the city's past. Founded by the Greeks in the 6th century BC under its current name, Feodosiya was rebranded Kaffa by the Genoese, who took over in the 13th century, turning the city into a meeting point for caravans from the Orient and European merchants. This brought together people of all nationalities, notably Armenians, who left a significant imprint on the city.

Kaffa's fortress, still partly intact, protected it from plundering nomad armies but not the biological weapon used by the Mongols during one siege: they catapulted in the bodies of people in their camp who had died from the plague. It is believed that the fleeing Genoese subsequently brought the disease to Europe.

Imperial Russians built opulent sea-facing palazzos in the town, and some still soar above the present-day city's souvenir stands and fast-food joints.

Gurzuf

Gurzuf's steep, winding streets and old wooden houses, backed by Mt Roman-Kosh (1543m), were traditionally a magnet for artists and writers. Russia's greatest poet, Alexander Pushkin, frolicked in Gurzuf's subtropical gardens after being exiled from depressing St Petersburg, and writer Anton Chekhov cured his tuberculosis and misanthropy on these shores. The village, 18km northeast of Yalta, is built around a picturesque bay with the rocky Genoese Cliff (Skala Dzhenevez) at its eastern end. Mt Ayu-Dag (Bear Mountain, Gora Medved; 565m) looms along the coast to the east, protruding into the sea.

Tired of being a local celebrity in Yalta, Chekhov sought refuge in a little Tatar farmhouse tucked in a solitary cove under the Genoese Cliff. The melancholy of this place inspired him to create one of his best plays – *The Three Sisters*. Chekhov's dacha was turned into a museum but there is nothing much to see apart from the original furniture and photos of actors playing *The Seagull* and *Uncle Vanya*.

Two local recreational dinosaurs, sanatoriums Gurzufsky and Pushkino, occupy what used to be the dacha of the Duc de Richelieu, governor of Odesa (1803–14). The word dacha is a serious understatement, especially if compared with Chekhov's modest dwelling in Gurzuf. It really is a large coastal estate with a vast subtropical park and palatial buildings, including the one which now houses the 'Pushkin in Crimea' Museum. The exiled Russian poet stayed here after being rescued by governor Rayevsky from the life of misery in what is now Dnipro. By all accounts, he had a great time trekking in the mountains and courting all three of his host's daughters.

Kerch

The Russian annexation of Crimea has transformed Kerch, once a seldom visited backwater, in a big way, and will transform it even further once the bridge over the straits of Kerch is fully operational.

Kerch is, in fact, Crimea's oldest city. As the ancient Greek colony of Panticapaeum it was the capital of the Bosporan Kingdom from the 5th to 2nd centuries BC. It used to have a strong Italian community until WWII, but that community left with the retreating

Axis troops. In more recent times Kerch became a mecca for archaeologists, who would arrive in droves each year hoping to unearth Greek and Scythian treasures.

Catacombs in the Kerch suburb of Adzhimushkay (Аджимушкай) have been a source of construction material for the city from time immemorial. Early Christians held their clandestine services here in the 2nd century AD. When the Germans sacked Kerch in May 1942, 10,000 Soviet troops and civilians (many of them Jewish) descended into the catacombs and held them for 170 days until all of them were gassed or captured.

Not far from the Adzhimushkay Defence Museum, there is a monument from a completely different epoch. The empty, grass-covered 4th-century-BC burial mound is thought to be the grave of a Bosporan king. Its exterior is Scythian, but its symmetrical interior was built by the Greeks. Inside, there are small crosses and the name *Kosmae* left on the walls by the 2nd-century AD Christians.

Novy Svit

Its name meaning New World, the beautiful bay of Novy Svit used to be the realm of Prince Lev Golitsyn, an idealistic aristocrat turned winemaker. Obsessed with changing Russian drinking culture, he spent all his fortune selling wine and champagne at cheaper prices than vodka. This was a noble but rather hopeless cause – innovative drinkers soon realised they could achieve stunning results by mixing champagne with vodka. The resulting killer cocktail became known as Northern Lights. Financially broke, Golitsyn was rescued by Tsar Nicholas II, who appointed him the royal winemaker and commissioned him to build the Massandra winery.

Sudak

As an important stop on the Silk Route from China, Sudak was a major and well-defended trading centre run by the Genoese. Its central claim to fame is the fortress that survives from that era; a few kilometres away lie the popular beaches of Novy Svit.

The vertiginous location is one of the major appeals of Sudak's **fortress**. This once-impregnable complex is perched on a massive seaside cliff and in true Ukrainian fashion you're allowed to clamber all over it, at times perhaps unsafely. Built during the 14th and 15th centuries, the fortress still cuts a magnificent silhouette. The remains of its crenellated walls (6m high and 2m thick) extend for 2km, encircling more than 30 hectares of dry sloping terrain. Ten

CRIMEAN KARAITES

At the height of WWII, the Nazis summoned three Jewish professors who were imprisoned in the Warsaw and Vilnius ghettoes and told them to voice their opinion on the subject they had studied all their lives. The question was – are Crimean Karaites Jewish or not? In a series of debates with leading scholars, all of them independently gave a negative answer, which largely contradicted everything they said before in their long scholarly careers. Their names were Meyer Balaban, Yitzhak Schiper and Zelig Kalmanovich. None of them survived the Holocaust. But the Karaites did – following the debate, the Nazis classified them as 'impure' but not warranting extermination. They even reopened the *kenassa* (temple) in Yevpatoriya, which had been closed by the Bolsheviks, allowing services in Hebrew! All Crimean Jews captured by the Nazis were killed.

Today the Karaites number about 2000, with 650 living in Crimea, mostly in Yevpatoriya and Feodosiya. Although their leaders deny it – perhaps a legacy of their survival tactics – the name of the people probably derives from the ancient Hebrew word for 'reader'. Initially, it was an early medieval Jewish sect in Baghdad, which rejected the Talmud, believing the Old Testament to be the only source of holy wisdom. No one is sure how this teaching spread to Crimea, but by the Medieval Ages it became the second most important religion for the Turkic population of Crimea after Islam. It mixed with shamanism and the pagan beliefs of the ancient Turks. To this day the Karaites worship sacred oak groves and call their god Tengri, as did their pre-Judaist ancestors. Speaking a pure version of ancient Turkic, the Karaites even donated 330 words to the modern Turkish language when Kemal Ataturk was getting rid of Arabisms in the 1920s.

original towers remain, most of them bearing the grand-sounding names of Genoese nobles who ruled the city: Francesco di Camilla or Cigallo Corrado, for instance. The sea-facing 13th-century temple, originally a mosque, was at different times used by Italian Catholics, German Lutherans and Russian Orthodox Christians.

Kara-Dah Nature Reserve

The Kara-Dah Nature Reserve is a true Jurassic Park. Its dramatic landscape is the work of an extinct volcano (Kara-Dah; 'Black Mountain' in Tatar) that spewed lava and debris over land and sea during the Jurassic period. Over millennia the elements have moulded the volcanic rocks into striking shapes, with names like 'The Devil's Finger', 'The King and the Earth' and – the most striking – 'Golden Gate' (Zolotye Vorota), a freestanding arch in the sea. These all circle craggy, 575m Mt Kara-Dah; the friends of poet Maximilian Voloshin (who lived in nearby Koktebel) used to tell him he looked like it.

Yevpatoriya

Of all Crimean towns, underrated Yevpatoriya is the only one that has preserved an Ottoman-era **medina** in its centre, filled with traces of the ethnic and religious groups that once inhabited it.

At the time when the peninsula was controlled by the Crimean Tatars and the Turks, it was the largest centre where slave traders exchanged Slavs captured in the north for goods from Europe and the Orient. It was repeatedly raided by Zaporizhsky Cossacks, who robbed it of all goods, with the noble excuse of freeing Christian slaves. Legend says that in one of those raids they invented what became known as Cossack submarines by upturning their small boats and using reeds to breathe under water. This way they approached the harbour unnoticed and then wreaked havoc all over the town. Allied forces landed here at the start of the Crimean War before moving on to besiege Sevastopol.

Left intact despite decades of Communism, the medina contains Muslim, Christian and – most intriguingly – Karaite Jewish places of worship. The rest of the town is a dense grid of sanatoria, built in the Soviet period when the town was proclaimed the USSR's main resort for children.

Built in 1552, the landmark **Dzhuma-Dzhami Mosque** is attributed to Mimar Sinan, the architect of Istanbul's famous Blue Mosque. Although not in Bakhchysaray, it was considered the main mosque of Ottoman-ruled Crimea. It served as a venue for enthroning Crimean khans, who disembarked in Yevpatoriya after an obligatory inauguration visit to Istanbul.

The beautiful whitewashed colonnaded **Karaite Kenassas** complex became the main place of worship for Karaites in the aftermath of the Russian takeover of Crimea, when they were allowed to abandon cave cities and live where they pleased. Tsar Alexander I inaugurated the main *kenassa* (temple) in 1807. Staunch monarchists, the Karaites later erected his statue on the premises. During the Crimean War, the allies converted the *kenassas* into stables, which were targeted by Russian artillery.

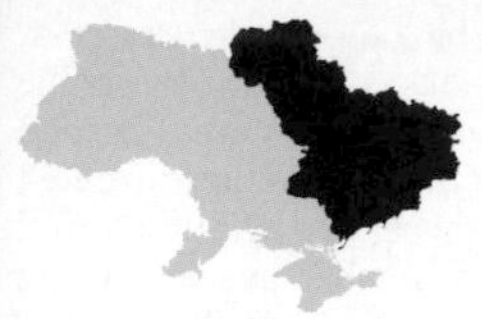

Eastern Ukraine
Східна Україна

POP 19.6 MILLION

Includes ➡

Best Places to Eat

- ➡ Puri Chveni (p221)
- ➡ Khryak (p207)
- ➡ Café Myshi Blyakhera (p221)
- ➡ Plasticine Crow (p216)
- ➡ Komora (p212)

Best Places to Stay

- ➡ Villa Otte (p208)
- ➡ Hotel 19 (p216)
- ➡ Hotel Cosmopolit (p215)
- ➡ Dream Hostel (p211)

Why Go?

In many ways a continent away from the folkloric west of Ukraine, the predominantly Russian-speaking territory east of the Dnipro River is often dismissed as 'not Ukrainian enough'. But, from an economic and political standpoint, this vast region is the country's power source.

The region was hit hardest by the crisis precipitated by the 2014 revolution. A part of it (fortunately not a very big one) has been occupied by Russian-backed rebels who proclaimed two 'people's republics', putting Donetsk and Luhansk on the front line of a simmering conflict. We can't overemphasise the danger of coming anywhere close to rebel-held areas. That said, the rest of eastern Ukraine is safe to travel in, provided that you watch the news. The area includes places that are key to understanding Ukraine, such as the Zaporizhska Sich, Gogol's Poltava region and Unesco-listed Chernihiv. Kharkiv and Dnipro are large industrial cities with intriguing cultural dynamics.

When to Go

Kharkiv

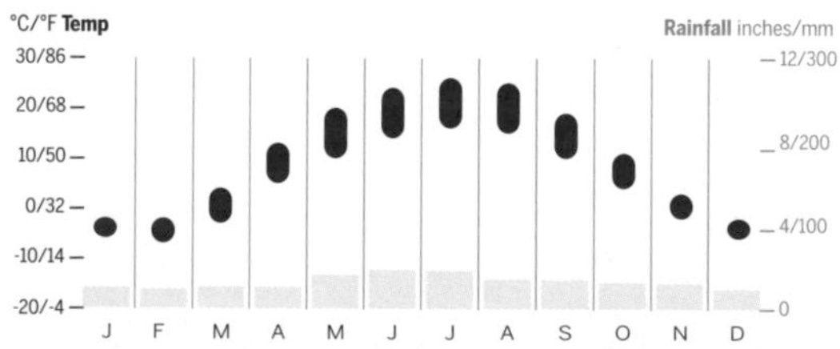

May The region is aflame with blooming lilacs and fruit trees.

Jul Heat builds in the countryside of Ukraine's east. Pumpkins ripen and sunflowers bloom.

Aug Shop at the annual Sorochynsky Yarmarok, made famous by local writer Gogol.

Eastern Ukraine Highlights

1 **Fabrika** (p217) Eating, drinking, dancing and learning at Kharkiv's antiquated plants turned arts and education centres.

2 **Dytynets** (p206) Hopping on a time machine in the historic core of Chernihiv.

3 **Khortitsa Equestrian Theatre** (p226) Confronting Ukrainian Cossack cavalry in the middle of the Dnipro River.

4 **Phaeton Museum of Machinery** (p223) Finding your dream Zaporozhets, Lada or Moskvich model in this extensive collection of vehicles, and military hardware.

5 **Museum-Preserve of Ukrainian Pottery** (p210) Mingling with Gogol-esque characters and taking pottery classes in the old potters' village of Opishnya.

Chernihiv Чернігів

☎0462 / POP 294,000

Modestly receding into provincial obscurity for the past millennium, Chernihiv, Ukraine's most northerly city, was once a Kyivan Rus he avyweight frequented by 11th-century royalty. The residue of those glory days is a tight cluster of churches on a green bluff in the city's historical core, now a Unesco-listed site and one of the highlights of Polissya. Otherwise this northern outpost has a slow provincial charm, the inert Desna River seemingly having given up on ever meeting the Dnipro, the population still deeming foreigners worthy of a stare on the dusty streets. The town makes for an easy day trip from the capital, or book ahead for a night out in the sticks and some deeper exploration of this seldom-visited corner of rural Ukraine.

Sights

Dytynets FORT

(Дитинець; enter from vul Preobrazhenska; 24hr) FREE From Krasna pl it's a three-minute walk southeast along pr Myru to the old historic core, known as the Dytynets ('citadel' in old Russian). Today it's an informal park dotted with domed churches overlooking the Desna River. The highlight is the 12th-century **Boryso-Hlibsky Cathedral** (Dytynets park; 15uah; 10am-6pm, 9am-5pm winter), which contains a worthwhile museum where the star attraction is the pair of intricate silver **Royal Doors**, commissioned by the famous Cossack leader Ivan Mazepa.

The building next to the cathedral is the 18th-century **collegium** (Коллегиум; vul Preobrazhenska 1; 15uah; 10am-6pm), built in a style known as Cossack baroque. It houses an exhibition of Ukrainian village icons.

Nearby is the **Spaso-Preobrazhensky Cathedral** (Transfiguration of the Saviour; 1017), with its two distinctive missile-like corner bell towers. Within its dark interior are the tombs of several members of the Kyivan Rus royalty, including the younger brother of Yaroslav the Wise. Lining the southwestern edge of the Dytynets is a row of 18th-century cannons, from where you get a prime view of the five sparkling golden domes of **St Catherine's Church** in the immediate foreground.

At the southern tip of the Dytynets stands a Shevchenko monument, or should that be 'sits' – this one has an unusually young Shevvy chilling gloomily on a park bench, momentarily distracted from his view of the sluggish river below.

Antoniy Caves CAVE

(vul Illinska 29; church & caves 10uah; 9am-5pm Sat-Thu, 9am-4pm Fri) These caves, Chernihiv's answer to Kyiv's Kyevo-Pecherska Lavra, lurk beneath the ground a short walk north of the Trinity Monastery, under the early 11th-century **Illinska Church**. The caves consist of 315m of passageways, galleries and chapels constructed from the 11th to 13th centuries. These are very different from those in Kyiv in that they lack both dead mummies and, for the most part, live tourists. Conditions here were too cold and humid to support mummification. Instead, the bones of monks killed during the Mongol invasion are preserved in a windowed sarcophagus; touching the sarcophagus is considered good luck. The cave's benefactor and namesake, St Antony of Pechersk, also helped burrow the Lavra caves.

To get to the church, get off trolleybus 8 at the stop before the Trinity Monastery bell tower and follow the dirt path downhill through the park across the street from the bus stop.

Tarnovsky History Museum MUSEUM

(462-647 738; vul Honcha 4; adults/students 20/10uah; 9am-4.30pm Fri-Wed) The charmingly old-fashioned museum traces local material history from paleolithic bones to the post-apocalyptic self-made shields and helmets of Maidan revolutionaries. In between, there are pictures of local celebrities, Cossack paraphernalia, period furniture and ancient books. The permanent exhibition is located on 2nd and 3rd floors, while the 1st floor is reserved for temporary exhibitions.

Trinity Monastery MONASTERY

(http://chernihiv-sob.church.ua; vul Tolstoho; bell tower 5uah; bell tower 10am-7.30pm) About 2km southwest of St Catherine's Church you'll spot the 58m bell tower of the **Troyitsko-Illynsky Monastery** (Trinity Monastery). It's worth climbing the **bell tower**, which looks right down on the 17th-century **Trinity Church**, an important pilgrimage site that is often mobbed with worshippers. It's about a 3km walk to the monastery from the Dytynets, or you can jump on trolleybus 8.

Krasna Ploshcha SQUARE

Life in Chernihiv revolves around the huge Krasna pl (Red Sq). As with its Moscow namesake, there is nothing remotely bolshie in the word 'red', which simply meant 'beautiful' in old Slavonic. In the park extending southeast of the square along vul Shevchenka rises the **St Paraskevy Pyatnytsi Church**, named after the patroness of the large outdoor market that once occupied Krasna pl. Despite its sturdy, fortress-like appearance, only about one-third of the church survived WWII. With its imposing brick wall and slender single cupola, it reflects the style popular when it was built in the 12th century.

Sleeping & Eating

Park Hotel Chernihiv HOTEL $$

(0462-646-464; www.park-hotel.cn.ua; vul Shevchenka 103A; s/d from 560/840uah; P ❄ 令) Chernihiv's most adequate hotel is located in a riverside park zone, a five-minute taxi ride from the centre. It's a business-like affair with well-appointed rooms and a good buffet breakfast (150uah). Guests get a discount in the nearby **beach club** and **restaurant**.

WORTH A TRIP

NOVHOROD-SIVERSKY

Life in this sleepy town, which hides in the deep forest in Ukraine's extreme north, may seem uneventful, but back in the Kyivan Rus times it was a happening place. It was from here that Prince Igor set out on his ill-fated expedition against the Polovtsy, an event immortalised in *The Tale of Igor's Campaign*, the 12th-century epic later made into an opera by Alexander Borodin.

Dating back to Prince Igor's era (but rebuilt several times since) is the idyllic **Spaso-Preobrazhensky Monastery** (Novhorod-Siversky; dawn-dusk) FREE, a complex of white stone buildings with wood-shingled roofs and golden-domed churches perched over the leafy banks of the Desna River. Strolling around the quiet grounds, you'll definitely feel like you're in another era. A wooden walkway atop the monastery fence provides prime views of the forested Desna valley, and it's an easy walk down to the river bank should you care for a swim or a picnic.

Picturesque as it is, Novhorod-Siversky would be receiving crowds of tourists if not for its remote location on the border with Belarus and Russia, which makes getting there quite an ordeal.

There is a daily early-morning bus from Kyiv's main bus station (160uah, five hours). From Chernihiv buses depart every couple of hours (65uah, three hours).

Overnight is inevitable, and you are presented with a choice between a perfectly commendable budget hotel **Pasvirda** (046 582 1225; vul Karla Marksa 3, Novhorod-Siversky; r from 240uah) and a more luxurious **Hotel Slovyansky** (04658-31551; http://ns-hotel.com.ua/; vul Lunacharskoho 2, Novhorod-Siversky; d from 500uah; P) , built for a summit of Ukrainian, Russian and Belarusian leaders.

Hotel Ukraina HOTEL $$
(Готель Україна; 046 265 1400; http://hotel-ukraina.com.ua/eng/; pr Myra 33; s/d 470/580uah;) The lurid fabrics draped through the rooms at Chernihiv's best digs would be hotel-style hara-kiri in many other countries but represent a great leap forward in rural Ukraine. Big, relatively well furnished and sound of plumbing, the rooms are a pretty good deal and there are even smiles at reception if you wait long enough.

★ **Khryak** EASTERN EUROPEAN $$
(Хряк; 063-100 4005; www.facebook.com/pg/hryak; vul Kyivska 12; mains 130-280uah) One level smarter than other restaurants in Chernihiv, this cosy establishment specialises in grilled meat and specifically in pork – think steak and *shashlyk*. The atmosphere is homey if a tad macabre, what with the flower-pot chandeliers and copper basins hanging from the ceiling. A pianist entertains patrons with Soviet film tunes in the evening.

Sharlotka/Varenichna Baluvana Halya CAFE $
(Шарлотка/Варенична Балувана Галя; pr Myru 21; mains 40-60uah; 10am-11pm) Sharlotka is a laid-back coffeehouse, good for snacks and light lunches; adjoining **Varenichna** is an unexpectedly sophisticated but inexpensive cafe serving a refreshingly limited menu of Ukrainian dishes in a dining room decorated in red plates and flashes of traditional style.The staff in both establishments cut new ground for Chernihiv in friendly service.

Falvarek EUROPEAN $
(Фальварек; pr Myru 20; mains 60-90uah; noon-midnight Sun-Thu, to 1am Fri & Sat;) A vaguely central European cellar pub with chatty waiters who like to show their proficiency in foreign languages (mostly German). Meat in all shapes dominates the menu. Just off Krasna pl.

Information

A rather comprehensive English- and Russian-language tourist website dedicated to the Chernihiv region is http://siver.org.ua.

Getting There & Away

The train and bus stations are right next to each other, 2km west of pl Krasna, on pl Vokzalna. Take trolleybus 3 or 11 or just about any *marshrutka* to the 'Hotel Ukraina' stop in the city centre.

BUS

The best way here from Kyiv is on a *marshrutka* from Lisova metro station (100uah, two hours, around every 30 minutes), which drop off outside McDonald's (on pr Pobedy). Buses for

Novhorod-Siversky leave hourly from Chernihiv's Central bus station (65uah, three hours), located near the train station.

TRAIN

The train station comes in handy if you are heading to Belarus, with at least one daily train to Minsk (690uah, 8½ hours) via Gomel (460uah, 3½ hours).

Myrhorod МИРГОРОД

05355 / POP 40,000

The relaxing spa town of Myrhorod is the place most closely associated with the writer Gogol and a major halt on the Kyiv–Kharkiv railway line. It makes for an easygoing base from which to explore the surrounding countryside, immortalised in works by the region's most famous literary son.

Sights

Near the church lies the town's famous 'puddle', a rather tidy pond which is here to remind about the 'eternal' dirty puddle in Myrhorod's city square used by Gogol as a metaphor for bureaucratic impotence in his satirical works. Bronzes of some of Gogol's characters (Taras Bulba, the two Ivans) ring the pond and the man himself looks out across the main road named in his honour.

Assumption Church CHURCH
(vul Gogolya 112) From the river you'll have views of the Assumption Church with its golden domes dusted with blue stars. If you find it open, come in to see locals and holidaymakers from the Myrhorod spa lighting up candles for the health of the living and peace of the dead.

Guramishvili Museum MUSEUM
(0 5355 52178; vul Nezalezhnosti 5; 5uah; 9am-5pm Wed-Mon) A small neoclassical building contains a museum dedicated to the 18th-century Georgian poet David Guramishvili, who was made a major local landowner for his valour as an officer in the Imperial Russian Army. Living here for 32 years after resigning from service, Guramishvili pretty much reinvented Georgian poetry as well as revolutionised local agriculture by introducing Georgian-style watermills.

Regional Museum MUSEUM
(Миргородський краєзнавчий музей; vul Nezalezhnosti 2; 5uah; 8.30-am-4.30pm Thu-Tue) With just two rooms, this quaint museum has an interesting collection of antiques and locally produced porcelain. Note the portraits of Myrhorod celebs – Danilo Apostol, who served as the Cossack Hetman from 1727 to 1734, and his 19th-century descendant, Matvey Muravyov-Apostol, a prominent participant in the Decembrist uprising in St Petersburg.

Activities

Byuvet SPA
(Mineral-water tap room; Myrhorod-kurort; 6.30am-10.30am, 11.30am-3.30pm & 4.30-8pm) FREE Rows of taps where you can fill your plastic bottle with potassium-rich water.

Therapeutic Beach BEACH
(Myrhorod-kurort; 35uah; 9am-6pm) A very tidy white-sand beach on the bank of the Khorol River.

Kurort SPA
(Myrhorod-kurort) FREE A vast expanse of parkland that contains Soviet-era water and mud spas, along with many sanatorium buildings that accommodate holidaymakers.

Sleeping & Eating

As in all Soviet spa towns, locals often rent out rooms to those taking the waters – the best street to try is vul Troitska at the back gates of the *kurort* where beds can be had for as little as 100uah a night (look out for кімната and житло signs).

Hotel Myrhorod HOTEL $
(525 61; www.hotelmirgorod.com.ua; vul Gogolya 102; s/d from 410/520uah;) Hotel Myrhorod, just along from the gates of the spa, is the obvious place to snooze, though it receives mixed reviews, especially with regard to the quality of service.

★**Villa Otte** RESORT $$
(05355 50604, 067 144 1441; www.otte-hotel.com.ua; vul Borovykovskoho 2; d from 1300uah;) This really is a villa with exquisitely designed rooms (think huge beds, comfy armchairs, many useful lamps and whole array of designer toiletries) that face a green lawn descending to the river – a great spot for watching sunset as well as for fishing. There is a little swimming pool and sauna in the premises, and bicycles are available for rent. One of the night guards doubles as a taxi driver. A full Gogol Circuit (p210) costs around 800uah.

Stare Misto EASTERN EUROPEAN $
(vul Gogolya 110; mains 50-110uah; 10am-12am) Right by the entrance to Myrhorod-Kurort,

THE WORLD OF NIKOLAI GOGOL

Although Taras Shevchenko is the greatest literary figure within Ukraine, one of the best-known Ukrainian writers outside the country's borders must be Nikolai Gogol. He was born in 1809 to impoverished parents in the Cossack village of Sorochyntsi near Poltava. It was here, in deepest rural Ukraine, that Gogol spent his formative years before leaving for St Petersburg in 1828.

Often claimed as a great Russian writer, Gogol was Ukrainian through and through. Many of his stories set in Ukraine are inspired by the supernatural world and the rural superstitions and folk tales of his youth in the Poltavshchina. His tales are set in a land of sun-drenched fields and blue skies, where faded nobles nap in the afternoon heat, Cossacks gulp down bowls of *borshch*, kitchen gardens overflow with tobacco and sunflowers, and shy Ukrainian beauties fall in love under star-dusted skies. Gogol's short novel *Taras Bulba* is a rollicking Cossack tale flush with romantic nationalism, adventure and derring-do.

During his years in St Petersburg, where he was employed in the civil service, Gogol's mood changed and his later stories such as 'The Nose', 'Nevsky Prospekt' and 'The Inspector General' are darker, gloomier, and riddled with ill health, crime and vice. In fact, the capital had such a bad effect on Gogol that he died in 1852 after burning the second half of his last novel, *Dead Souls*, in a fit of madness.

Gogol is an inspirational companion to pack into your rucksack on long train journeys across the snowbound steppe or midsummer bus trips through Ukraine's endless landscapes.

this cellar place serving Ukrainian and East European standards is bland and reliable. *Varenyky* with sour cherry are pretty outstanding.

Festivals & Events

Sorochynsky Yarmarok FAIR

(Velyki Sorochyntsi; end of Aug) Farmers and tourists from all over Ukraine gather for five days of festivities that accompany a famous village fair, vividly described by none other than Nikolai Gogol. Apart from many folksy musical acts and a few top Ukrainian politicians (often the president), this is the place to admire the country's fattest pumpkins, sweetest watermelons and tenderest *salo* (cured lard).

Getting There & Away

Myrhorod's train station lies 2.5km south of the town centre. The Intercity+ express is by far the best service for Kyiv (140uah, two hours), Kharkiv (160uah, 2½ hours) and Poltava (150uah, one hour). It runs around four to five times a day in each direction.

Buses to Poltava (70uah, 1½ hours, hourly), Velyky Sorochyntsy (7uah, around 10 daily) and Opishnya (40uah, three daily) leave from the central bus station across the street from the spa gates.

Poltava Полтава

0532 / POP 290,000

Quaint, leafy Poltava is all about one particular turning point in history. Had Russian tsar Peter I lost a decisive battle on the town's outskirts in 1709, he wouldn't have become Peter the Great and Ukraine could have celebrated the 300th anniversary of its independence in 2009. But the Russians defeated a joint Swedish-and-Cossack force, marking the event a century later by rebuilding the city's centre as a mini St Petersburg. As if avenging the lost battle and the architecture imposed from the north, Poltava became a centre of Ukrainian cultural renaissance in the 19th century. The battlefield lures throngs of war history buffs into the city, which is dotted with monuments dedicated to seemingly every regiment that took part in the faithful battle. Besides imperial architecture, Poltava boasts a few imposing Cossack-baroque cathedrals and enchanting views from a bluff at the far end of the main pedestrian drag.

Sights

Korpusny Park PARK

The focal point of the city centre is the circular Korpusny Park, laid out in the early 19th century in an attempt to emulate the grand planning ideals of St Petersburg. Eight

WORTH A TRIP

THE GOGOL CIRCUIT

North of Poltava lies Gogol-land: textbook Ukrainian countryside where writer Nikolai Gogol (1809–52) – who authored *Dead Souls* and 'The Nose' – lived and which he populated with his characters. Witty, humorous, imaginative and very laid-back, locals still have very much in common with Gogol's contemporaries.

Travelling with them in overcrowded village buses is part of the fun if you are doing the circuit of Gogol-related sites. However, this method is exhausting and time-consuming – you'll need at least two days to see everything. One day is probably enough if you charter a taxi (800uah to 1500uah, depending on your luck and bargaining skills, for the entire loop) or rent a car. All crucial turns are marked with English-language signs with the writer's trademark long-nosed profile.

To fully appreciate the trip, you may procure Gogol's *Evenings on a Farm near Dikanka* – a collection of funny and surreal stories inspired by the customs and superstitions of local villagers.

Dikanka

In *Evenings on a Farm near Dikanka*, the red-haired beekeeper Panko starts narrating his macabre tales to a group of eager listeners whiling away a summer evening at a farm near this large village, 30km north of Poltava. Once in the town centre, look out for signs pointing to **Troitska Church**. If we are to believe Gogol, its frescoes were authored by the local smith Vakula, who underwent a hair-raising trial while guarding a coffin of a beautiful witch inside this church. Troitska Church is tucked in a small lane diagonally across the square from the **Regional Museum** (vul Nezalezhnosti (Lenina) 68, Dikanka; 10uah; ⌚9am-5pm Tue-Sun).

Opishnya

Not directly related to Gogol, this potters' village, 20km north of Dikanka, has an excellent interactive **Museum-Preserve of Ukrainian Pottery** (☎05353-42416; www.opishne-museum.gov.ua; vul Vasilya Krichevskoho (Partizanska) 102, Opishnya; 60uah; ⌚8am-6pm, to 5pm Fri & Sun). It incorporates many potters' households where you can learn some secrets of the craft and see rural Ukrainians in their element. From Opishnya, road P42 goes west towards Velyki Sorochyntsi and Myrhorod.

Hoholeve

Away from the main roads and reachable from Poltava via Dikanka or from Myrhorod/Velyki Sorochyntsi, Gogol's family estate is surrounded by a tranquil park with a pond, and houses a lovingly curated, old-fashioned **museum** (http://muzey-gogolya.at.ua; Hoholeve, Shyshaky district; adult/student 20/10uah; ⌚8.30am-4.30pm Tue-Sun).

Velyki Sorochyntsi

This sleepy village comes to life in August during the annual Sorochynsky Yarmarok (p209) – the end-of-harvest farmers' fair, masterfully described by Gogol in *Evenings on a Farm near Dikanka*. The writer himself was born here in 1809. Outside the fair period, the main sight is the **Spaso-Preobrazhenska Church**, with its unique seven-tier wooden iconostasis. There is also a **regional museum** (vul Hoholya 28, Velyki Sorochyntsi; 20uah; ⌚9am-6pm Thu-Tue), which has sadly lost much of its appeal after a rather devastating 'reconstruction'.

Myrhorod

The circuit's main halt (or starting point, if you prefer).

streets radiate off the plaza, and in its centre rises the **Iron Column of Glory**, topped by a golden eagle. Southeast of Korpusny Park, the city's main pedestrian drag – **ul Sobornosti** – leads down to verdant **Soniachny Park**.

Poltava Museum of Local Lore MUSEUM
(www.pkm.poltava.ua; vul Konstytutsiyi 2; adult/student 15/5uah; ⌚9am-5pm Tue & Thu-Sun, Mon from 10am) Located on the southeast edge of Zhovtnevy Park, the museum exhibits random archaeological and cultural artefacts, its

collection almost overshadowed by its gorgeous art nouveau building (1903), adorned with the ceramic crests of each district capital in the Poltava *oblast*. Outside stands an impressive cubist Shevchenko monument, which has the national poet emerging from angular blocks of grey concrete.

Maidan Soborny SQUARE
(Cathedral Sq) Vul Zhovtneva terminates on a bluff at Cathedral Sq, the prettiest little spot in Poltava, with sweeping views of Khrestovozdvyzhensky Monastery across the valley to the northeast. The square is dominated by the rebuilt **Uspenska Church**. A footpath leads to the dramatic neoclassical **Friendship Rotunda** on the edge of the bluff, a great place for photographs. On the way to the rotunda look out for the *halushky* monument on the left, which pays due homage to the tasty local dumplings.

Kotlyarevsky Museum MUSEUM
(pl Soborny Maidan 3; 20uah; ⏲10am-6pm) Just behind Uspenska Church, surrounded by a lovely flower garden, this is the lovingly restored former home of Ivan Kotlyarevsky (1739–1838), one of the fathers of Ukrainian literature. The museum provides a glimpse into traditional Ukrainian life in the early 19th century.

Spaska Church CHURCH
(vul Sobornosti 10) A block northwest of maydan Soborny up vul Parizskoyi Komuny is the quaint Spaska Church (1705), with its rebuilt bell tower. It's faced by an odd monument to Tsar Peter I (Peter the Great) across the street on vul Pylypa Orlyka (Parizskoyi Komuny).

Poltava Battlefield HISTORIC SITE
(www.battle-poltava.org; vul Shvedskaya mohyla; ⏲24hr) FREE The famous battle was fought over a large area around what's now vul Zinkivska, about 7km north of the city centre. The best starting point is the **Poltava Battle Museum** (Shvedska mohyla 32; 20uah; ⏲9am-5pm Tue-Sun) by the Peter I statue. Inside are displays relating to the battle, including maps, paintings and Peter I's original uniform. Aside from the museum, the battlefield contains numerous monuments and various redoubts of the old fortress, many of which have been restored. Bus 4 from outside the Kyivsky shopping centre (near Avtovokzal 3) runs to the museum, which stands next to Shvedska Mohyla station, one stop away from Poltava's Kyivska station. A taxi should cost around 30uah one way from the city centre.

Khrestovozdvyzhensky Monastery MONASTERY
(Хрестовоздвиженський монастир; Paisiia Velychkovskoho St 2A) About 3km east of Korpusny Park is the early 18th-century Khrestovozdvyzhensky Monastery (Elevation of the Cross). The main cathedral is one of only two in the country with seven cupolas, rather than five (the other is St Michael's Monastery in Kyiv; p52). The complex is a 3km straight walk east on vul Monastyrska from Korpusny Park.

Sleeping

Dream Hostel HOSTEL $
(☎068 404 2255; http://dream-hostels.com/Hostels/Poltava/dreamhostelpoltava; vul Yevropeyska 5; dm from 150uah, d with/without bathroom 700/350uah; ❄📶) Regular hostel dwellers will rejoice at finding this sparkling new establishment in a location that can't be more central. Large enough to play mini-football, the common area is filled with comfy couches and tables encouraging spontaneous socialising and joint planning of sightseeing expeditions or pub crawls. Dorms are equally commendable.

Mini-Hotel Sinay GUESTHOUSE $
(Міні-готель Сінай; ☎0532-508 313; http://sinai.com.ua; vul Zinkivska 11/31; s/d from 180/300uah; ❄📶) Six-room guesthouse 500 metres from Kyivsky train station offering small, European standard rooms for Ukrainian countryside prices. Rooms are kept sparkling, breakfast costs extra and bathrooms are shared.

Reikartz Galereya HOTEL $$
(Готель Галерея; ☎561 697; http://galery.com.ua; vul Yevropeyska 7; s/d from 540/620uah; ❄📶) Slap bang in the city centre, it's not just the location that makes this friendly sleepery worth checking out. Rooms are of a recent ilk, perfectly dust free and modestly furnished. Bathrooms are large and some even have bidets, objects which must have a few members of Ukraine's nouveau riche scratching their heads. Breakfast can be taken in bed and is included – there's even an English menu.

Palazzo Hotel HOTEL $$
(☎0532 611 205; www.palazzo.com.ua; vul Gogolya 33; s/d from 900/1150uah; P🚭❄📶) This is the place for people travelling on a medium-range budget to enjoy four-star

luxury (well, almost). The attractive king-size beds have firm mattresses that will have your back feeling like butter after a lengthy snooze. That and the suave, tawny-toned design almost make up for the small size of the allegedly smoke-free rooms.

Eating

For self-caterers, the best supermarket in the city centre is **Brusnichka** (Брусничка; vul Sobornosti 43; ⏲9am-10pm), located on the left as you head from Korpusny Park towards Kyivsky train station.

★**Komora** UKRAINIAN $
(Комора; ☎0532-612 227; http://komora.kitchen; vul Pylypa Orlyka (Paryzskoi Kommuny) 29; mains 30-90uah; ⏲9am-9pm; ❄📶) *Halushky* are inverted dumplings – cubes of baked dough mixed with whatever is used as a filling in conventional dumplings. Come here to sample the famous Poltava variety, served with chicken meat or liver, as well as *halushky*'s overseas cousins from as far as China and Italy. East Asian–influenced set-meal trays work neatly with this most Ukrainian of staples. *Halushky* are essentially dumplings for lazy cooks. In one of Nikolai Gogol's short stories, they were rising from the plate and flying into the mouth of a Poltava Cossack character who couldn't be bothered to reach out for them with a spoon.

Sto Dorih PUB FOOD $
(Сто Доріг; vul Parizkoy Komuny 18; snacks & mains 20-50uah; ⏲10am-10pm) Studenty watering hole and live-music venue, with weekend rock bands, a long beer menu, and a big and busy summer beer garden.

Kozachka UKRAINIAN $$
(☎5325 695 36; vul Nebesnoi Sotni 34A; meals 70-150uah; ⏲12pm-11pm) Resembling a Ukrainian *khutor* (a traditional farmstead) with lots of outdoor seating in a lush garden, this folksy restaurant is the place to go if you need an introduction to Ukrainian cuisine. All major staples, from *borshch* to *varenyky* (dumplings), are represented on the extensive menu and most importantly – very competently cooked.

Drinking & Nightlife

Kavun COFFEE
(Кавун; vul Stritenska (Komsomolska) 34; ⏲7.30am-10pm; 📶) Brought here by the winds of the global coffee revolution, this tiny coffee shop employs chatty baristas who know how to make a mean brew and love to explain nuances of their craft. It's a comfortable little space with modern art on the walls that attracts a smart studenty crowd. Nice cakes, too.

Koffishka COFFEE
(Коффишка; vul Sobornosti (Zhovtneva) 34; ⏲24hr) Tiny but chirpy coffeehouse at the top of the main drag (near the entrance to the underpass leading to Korpusny Park) fashioned in the shape of a coffee-bean mill. Open round the clock for those who require Arabica at 3am.

Poltavske Pivo PUB
(vul Sobornosti (Zhovtneva) 26; ⏲8am-10pm) Fresh local brews, snacks and outdoor seating on the main drag, ideal for a spot of Poltavan watching. The service here can be rotten.

Shopping

Ukrainian Souvenir GIFTS & SOUVENIRS
(Український сувенір; www.vushuvanka.pl.ua/en_main.php; vul Stritenska (Komsomolska) 19; ⏲10am-6pm) Excellent souvenir shop offering beautifully embroidered traditional shirts, blouses and tablecloths, all handmade by villagers from the Poltava region.

Information

The official tourism website is www.tourism.poltava.ua/eng.

Getting There & Away

BUS

Buses go pretty much everywhere from distant **Avtovokzal 1** (Bus station 1; vul Velikotyrnivska), about 5.5km east of the city centre reached by any bus or *marshrutka* marked кільцевий. The most useful are to Myrhorod (100uah to 120uah, two hours, at least hourly), Kharkiv (140uah to 220uah, 2½ to three hours, many daily) and Dnipro (230uah to 290uah, four hours, hourly). Avtolyux and many other operators run buses to Kyiv (290uah to 350uah, six hours, at least twice hourly).

Avtovokzal 3 (Bus station No 3; vul Zhinkinvska 6B), just outside Kyivsky shopping mall and close to Kyivsky train station, has services to the nearest point on the Gogol Circuit – Dikanka (30uah, at least hourly).

New fast *marshrutky* leave when full from outside Kyivsky train station for Kharkiv (150uah).

TRAIN

Poltava has two train stations – Kyivsky Vokzal and Pyvdenniy Vokzal – the duo conveniently located on complete opposite sides of the city around 6.5km apart.

Kyivsky Vokzal is a stop on the Intercity+ service between Kyiv (100uah to 170uah, three hours, five daily) and Kharkiv (170uah, 1½ hours, three daily). Myrhorod is on the same line (50uah to 110uah, one hour, five daily).

Until the connection with Donetsk is resumed, Pyvdenniy Vokzal is only useful for Odesa (260uah, 12 hours, daily).

Trolleybus 1 links the two stations via the city centre. Trolleybuses 2, 4, 6 and 11 run from Pivdenniy Vokzal to the city centre (ticket 3uah).

Kharkiv

☎057 / POP 1.43 MILLION

Kharkiv (Kharkov in Russian) is one of those ex-Soviet cities that has much to say about itself but fairly little to show. Wars and Soviet development have reduced its historical centre, boasting some pretty fin de siècle buildings, to a narrow triangle between vuls Sumska and Pushkinska. The rest is Soviet monumentalism in all its glory, including one of the world's widest squares. The square lost Lenin's monument in the tumult of 2014, when Kharkiv narrowly escaped the fate of Donetsk, now controlled by pro-Russian rebels.

Just 40km from the Russian border, Kharkiv is home to Russian-speaking intelligentsia – scientists and engineers who turned it into the brain centre of the Soviet defence industry in the 1960s. Their grandchildren are now reinventing it as a hub of Ukraine's fledgling IT industry, with an active rock-music scene and a sprouting hipster culture.

Sights

★Kharkiv Art Museum MUSEUM

(Харківський художній музей; http://artmuseum.kh.ua/ru; permanent collection vul Zhon Myronosyts (Radnarkomivska) 11; per bldg 10uah; ⏲10am-6pm Wed-Sun; Ⓜ Arkhitektora Beketova) Kharkiv's most famous museum owns one of many versions of Ilya Repin's *Zaporizhsky Cossacks Writing a Letter to the Turkish Sultan*, which is found in a room full of Repin paintings in the museum's permanent collection. The entire collection of romantic paintings here is of a high standard for Ukraine, but the neighbouring exhibit hall is hit or miss.

★Ploshcha Svobody SQUARE

(Площа Свободи; Ⓜ Derzhprom) Locals claim that this enormous expanse of cobbles is the second largest in the world after Beijing's Tiananmen Sq. At 750m long it's indisputably huge and is certainly Kharkiv's most unique sight. Planned as an ensemble of Ukrainian government buildings when Kharkiv was the republican capital, it was laid out between 1925 and 1935. A Lenin statue, which stood in the middle, was toppled by the revolutionary mob in 2014, leaving a comically lonely granite shoe on the podium.

The area was obscured from view at the time of research due to ongoing reconstruction. At the western end of the square, a geometric series of concrete and glass blocks and bridges, the late-1920s Derzhprom building (p214) is an example of early Soviet-era constructivist architecture. On the southern side, the Karazin university (early 1930s), formerly the Ministry of Planning, displays classic Soviet aesthetics.

Kharkiv History Museum MUSEUM

(Харківський історичний музей; ☎731 1348; www.museum.kh.ua; pl Konstytutsiyi; 60uah; ⏲9.30am-5pm Tue-Sun; Ⓜ Istorychny Muzey) The city's history museum found itself encased in a giant glassy structure as the result of an unfinished reconstruction, which hasn't touched upon the building itself. But the changing wind of history can be felt in the musty halls, where exhibitions have been updated to reflect the Maidan revolution and the war in the east.

Outside the museum, which looms over the vast pl Konstitutsiyi, you'll find a rare British WW1 tank which took part in the Russian Civil War (1918–21). On the other side of the building, a winged statue officially known as *Flying Ukraine* has replaced a Soviet-era revolutionary monument, which tongue-in-cheek Kharkivites used to call 'five men carrying a fridge'.

Shevchenko Park PARK

(btwn vuls Sumska & Klochkovska; 👪🐾; Ⓜ Universytet) Central Shevchenko Park is one of those post-Soviet parks where you can sit for hours watching families boarding the kiddie train, listening to some remarkably talented buskers, and pondering the shortness of some skirts and height of most heels. Not sure what the national poet might have made of all that flesh on show – from the expression on the face of the Taras Shevchenko statue (p215) it doesn't look as though he approves.

Blahoveshchensky Cathedral CATHEDRAL

(Благовещенський собор; pl Blahoveshchenska (pl Karla Marksa); Ⓜ Tsentralny Rynok) The park across the street from Uspensky Cathedral offers the best vantage point of the striking red-and-cream striped cathedral down in the valley, built 1881–1901. Based on Istanbul's Hagia Sophia, it has a beautifully proportioned bell tower resembling a stick of candy.

Derzhprom NOTABLE BUILDING
(Держпром; pl Svobody 5/1) At the western end of pl Svobody, this late-1920s building is an example of early Soviet-era constructivist architecture: a geometric series of concrete and glass blocks and bridges. The building is not accessible for tourists, except for a smallish and low-key **museum of local government** located in the premises.

Pokrovsky Monastery NOTABLE BUILDING
(Intercession of the Virgin; vul Klochkovska) Just west of pl Konstytutsiyi, the gleaming domes of the Pokrovsky Monastery (Intercession of the Virgin) are visible from miles away. The predictably peaceful grounds (enter from pl Konstytutsiyi) have two attractive churches. The smaller and more important of the two is the blue, three-domed **Pokrovska Church** (1689). As in all Orthodox churches, the altar is under the east-pointing dome, and there's another altar hidden in the basement, which the attendant may show you if you ask. The church is almost always open

Central Kharkiv

for services. The yellow church next to it is the **Ozeyansky Church**.

Taras Shevchenko Statue MONUMENT
(vul Sumska; Ⓜ Universytet) Locals are perhaps overly proud of this statue. Yes, it's big and it does portray the heroic poet surrounded by 16 peasants, Cossacks and other Ukrainians representing the national history. However, it's also rather brutalist and is only softened by Shevchenko Park.

Uspensky Cathedral CATHEDRAL
(Успенський собор | Assumption Cathedral; vul Universytetskaya; Ⓜ Radyanska) This cathedral with its landmark mid-19th-century bell tower (89.5m tall) is now used only as a concert hall. The ticket office in the entrance is open in the afternoons only. Schedules available at http://filarmonia.kh.ua.

Sleeping

If you don't fancy bagging a bunk in one of the city's itinerant hostels, budget beds are hard to come by in business-oriented Kharkiv.

As is the case elsewhere in Ukraine, apartments often represent a better deal than cheap 'n' fusty hotel rooms.

Hotel Kharkiv HOTEL $
(Готель Харків; ☎758 0153; www.hotel.kharkov.com; pl Svobody 7; s/d from 700/850uah; 📶; Ⓜ Derzhprom, Universytet) Kharkiv's textbook Soviet behemoth looms over pl Svobody, providing adequately equipped, though unremarkable, rooms in the heart of the city. It's really the cheaper, barely renovated rooms that those on a budget will be interested in. If you've hryvnya to squander, there are more characterful sleeps in town.

Hotel De Gaulle HOTEL $$
(☎057 754 5154; http://degaulle.com.ua; pl Zakhysnykiv Ukrainy (Povstannya) 17A; d incl breakfast from 760uah; Ⓜ Zakhysnykiv Ukrainy & Sportyvna) Never mind drab surroundings (a football stadium, a bus station and a market), this insular compound succeeds in teleporting its guests from Kharkiv's post-Soviet reality into a Parisian dream, complete with flowery wallpaper, elegant faux-antique furniture and art-deco bathtubs. And yes – you get a proper croissant for breakfast. Two metro stations are both a short walk away.

Hotel Cosmopolit LUXURY HOTEL $$
(☎057-754 6886; www.cosmopolit-hotel.com; vul Akademika Proskury 1; s/d incl breakfast from 1100/1250uah; 🚭❄@) This sets the standard for contemporary design in Kharkiv, with flatscreen TVs and loads of extras like plush robes and 24-hour room service. The theme is Italian, and breakfast in swanky **Da Vinci restaurant** is divine. The huge 'king' rooms are worth the splurge (1500uah). If you're here on business, this is your top choice even if it is a short taxi ride from the city centre.

AN-2 HOTEL $$
(☎057-732 4954; www.antwo-hotel.com.ua; vul Plekhanivska 8; s/d from 700/900uah; ❄📶; Ⓜ Prospekt Gagarina) This very reasonably priced hotel, a short walk from both the main bus station and Prospekt Gagarina metro station, is named after a famous Soviet-era aircraft

Central Kharkiv

Top Sights
1 Kharkiv Art Museum ... C3
2 Ploshcha Svobody ... B1

Sights
3 Blahoveshchensky Cathedral ... A5
4 Derzhprom ... B1
5 Kharkiv History Museum ... B4
6 Pokrovsky Monastery ... B4
7 Shevchenko Park ... B2
8 Taras Shevchenko Statue ... C2
9 Uspensky Cathedral ... B5

Sleeping
10 Chichikov Hotel ... C3
11 Hostinny Dvir ... B3
12 Hotel 19 ... B3
13 Hotel Kharkiv ... C1

Eating
14 Dedushka s Tatuirovkoy Drakona ... D1
15 Plasticine Crow ... C3
16 Puzata Khata ... B4
17 Shoti ... C2
18 The Varenik ... B4

Drinking & Nightlife
19 Fabrika ... A5
20 Irish Pub ... C1
21 Pivobar ... D2

Entertainment
22 Jazzter ... C4

Shopping
23 Ye ... B5

Information
Fabrika Co-working ... (see 19)

VANGUARD OF THE PROLETARI-ART

The profusion of derelict factories gives post-Soviet architects and developers wonderful material to play with. Ukraine has only recently jumped on the gentrification bandwagon, with Kharkiv in the lead. The city now has two old factories transformed into excellent multipurpose spaces, which work as arts, education, nightlife and gastronomy hotspots.

Once a seed-selection plant, the centrally located Fabrika has a large dining area on the 1st floor, with an entire wall made of old drawers poached from some bureaucratic institution and a huge Soviet-era still-life painting by the entrance.

With a bar in the middle, it gets filled with patrons coming to enjoy wonderful fusion food, cocktails and an occasional live music act. Upper floors are used for lectures and conferences (many of them dedicated to IT, a fledgling industry in Kharkiv). The top floor is occupied by a very comfortable co-working space, which you can use for work or simply to browse the web.

Although not in the centre, Mekhanika Arts Factory is also a happening place with live concerts, DJ parties and food festivals taking place all the time. But it only opened for specific events at the time of writing; the schedule is available on its website.

but won't have you heading for the emergency exit. The 34 contemporary, box-ticking rooms are spotless and well designed, the staff speak English and the rates include Ukrainian-style breakfast on the 7th floor.

★**Hotel 19** BOUTIQUE HOTEL **$$$**
(☎095 868 3232; http://hotel19.ua; vul Sumska 19; s/d from 1200/1900uah; ❄📶; Ⓜ Istorychny Muzey) This freshly minted, extravagantly fashioned boutique hotel hides away on a tranquil courtyard just off traffic-plagued vul Sumska. The 24 rooms are a soothing antidote to the remnants of the proletarian utopia outside, all done out in wistful 19th-century antique-style furniture and boasting stuccoed ceilings and libraries (books are in Russian, so just nice to look at for most).

Guests can swim for free at the 19's sister hotel **Nasha Dacha**, located outside the city centre. Ask the extremely professional staff how to get there.

Hostinny Dvir BOUTIQUE HOTEL **$$$**
(Гостинний двір; ☎057 705 6086; www.hotel-gd.com.ua; vul Rymarska 28; s/d from 1000/1300uah; ❄@; Ⓜ Arkhitektora Beketova) This pretty little hotel set in a courtyard behind the posh Chateau restaurant only really becomes boutique as you summit the room scale at junior suite and suite level. Otherwise quarters are business standard, very comfortable, and boast minibars and soundproof windows.

Chichikov Hotel LUXURY HOTEL **$$$**
(Готель Чічіков; ☎057-752 2300; www.chichikov-hotel.com.ua; vul Gogolya 6/8; s/d from 1400/1600uah; ❄📶; Ⓜ Arkhitektora Beketova) You may feel you'd like a bit more space in the rooms for the prices this relatively new (2006) epicentral hotel charges, but overall this is a commendable place to kip. Rooms are elegantly furnished, kitted out with all those things you never use and bathrooms are spotless.

Eating

A restaurant row of sorts runs along vul Yaroslava Mudroho (formerly vul Petrovskoho) where you'll find the best variety of cuisines in the city.

The Varenik UKRAINIAN **$**
(☎050 186 2872; http://thevarenik.ua; vul Sumska 1; mains 30uah; ⏲10am-10pm) *Varenyky* (triangular-shaped dumplings) are the chubby Zeus of the Ukrainian culinary pantheon. Here is the place not only to gorge on them, experimenting with various fillings – from liver to sweet cherries – but also to see them made by hand in an open kitchen. Fruity *nalyvky* liquors make up a large part of the drinks menu.

Puzata Khata UKRAINIAN **$**
(Пузата хата; cnr vuls Sumska & Konstytutsiyi; mains 40-60uah; ⏲8am-11pm; Ⓜ Istorychny Muzey) This city-centre branch of Ukraine's most celebrated fast-food chain is incongruously styled as a warren of thatched cottages bedecked in bucolic knick-knackery, but the food is cheap as you like and it can be elbow-to-elbow at feeding time.

★**Plasticine Crow** UKRAINIAN **$$**
(Пластилиновая ворона; ☎066 557 5922; http://artvorona.com.ua; vul Sumska 17; mains

80-170uah; ❄📶) If you've been to Lviv, this is one of those – 'emotional restaurants' – again. Hungry? Get some theatre for starters. To come in, you'll first have to confront a 'janitor' character who will be helping you to guess the 'secret password'. Having succeeded, you'll be treated to excellent west Ukrainian food, including goulash and *banosh* (like polenta).

There is no sign, but the white door featuring number 17 is hard to miss. Just walk down and ring the bell. Now what about the 'plasticine crow'? That's the name of an excellent Soviet plasticine cartoon, which features a janitor and a crow. The walls of the restaurant are covered with signs and pictures made with plasticine, and you'll be invited to leave your own legacy. In case you still don't find the experience exceedingly eclectic, a cover band comes to play Soviet pop songs in the evening.

Stargorod CZECH **$$**
(Старгород; ☎700 9030; www.stargorod.net/kh; vul Lermontovska 7; mains 100-220uah; ⏲24hr; Ⓜ Pushkinska) Rivers of beer cut through mountains of meat to the sound of oompah-pah music in this Kharkivite version of a Czech pub. There is a microbrewery on the premises pumping out fresh lager and ale, which contributes to the overall happy party atmosphere and triggers wild, table-crushing dances slightly more often than you need.

A full-sized sheep or pig is grilled on an open fire each Saturday and Sunday.

Dedushka s Tatuirovkoy Drakona INTERNATIONAL **$$**
(Дедушка с татуировкой дракона; ☎067 572 0902; www.facebook.com/dedwithtattoo; vul Yaroslava Mudroho (Petrovskoho) 22; mains 90-130uah; ⏲9am-2am; 📶; Ⓜ Pushkinska) With an inviting terrace that lures a smart youngish crowd on hot summer evenings, the Grandad with Dragon Tattoo (a play on words from Stieg Larsson's book) specialises in gourmet burgers and other meat dishes, complemented with Ukrainian and international beers.

Shoti CAUCASIAN, UKRAINIAN **$$**
(Шоті; vul Myronosytska 12; mains 80-200uah; ⏲10am-11pm Mon-Thu & Sun, to midnight Fri & Sat; Ⓜ Universytet) Don't be fooled by the plain, though pleasant, interior of this place – here the focus is firmly on well-crafted food from Ukraine and the Caucasus with a menu of *khachapuri* (Georgian cheese-filled bread), grilled meats and syrupy desserts infused with authentic flavour. Takeaway dishes (from the counter in the entrance) are 20% cheaper.

Drinking & Nightlife

The bar scene is low-key and very fluid, but the gentrification of old factories is helping to improve the situation. Many restaurants also double as drinking venues.

★**Fabrika** BAR
(☎068-100 1155; https://fabrika.space; vul Blagoveshchenska (Karla Marksa) 1; mains 100-150uah; ⏲10am-12am, to 3am Fri, Sat; 📶) A former seed-selection factory now disseminates the seeds of cultured drinking in a place prone to wild drinking habits. The extensive bar menu lists out sours, tikis, fizzes and spritzes, as well as craft beer and sangria. The kitchen churns out excellent fusion food.

Pivobar PUB
(vul Bagaliya (Frunze) 3; ⏲11am-11pm; Ⓜ Pushkinska) Beloved English ales like Owd Rodger and Riggwelter, as well as its own numbered beers and an encyclopaedic food menu.

Irish Pub PUB
(Ірландський Паб; vul Myronosytska 46; ⏲1-11pm; Ⓜ Derzhprom, Universytet) Offers exactly what you'd expect: plenty of beer (fine imports and inexpensive domestic lagers), sports on TV, a few strange Irish dishes and the chance to hobnob with Kharkiv expats.

Entertainment

Jazzter LIVE MUSIC
(www.jazzter.com.ua; prov Teatralny 11/13; 30-100uah; ⏲11am-11pm; Ⓜ Istorychny Muzey) Surprisingly sophisticated bar and lounge for backstreet Kharkiv with smooth local acts and a foot-tapping, tie-loosening after-work crowd.

Mekhanika Arts Factory ARTS CENTRE
(Арт-завод Механіка; ☎095 775 3721; www.facebook.com/artzavodmechanica; vul Plekhanovska 126M; Ⓜ Zavod imeni Malysheva) A happening place with live concerts, DJ parties and food festivals taking place all the time. It only opened for specific events at the time of writing; the schedule is available on its website.

Shopping

Barabashova Market MARKET
(www.barabashka.com; vul Amurska; Ⓜ Akademika Barabashova) For the ultimate post-Soviet bazaar experience, cheap jeans and Vietnamese food, head to this market, which rivals similar bazaars in Odesa for the 'biggest in Europe' title. It's really a mind-bogglingly huge affair, run by Africans and Vietnamese who sell cheap Chinese clothes and all sorts of ripped-off junk.

Ye BOOKS
(vul Sumska 3; ⌚9am-9pm; Ⓜ Radyanska) This modern bookshop, on a seemingly hopeless crusade to Ukrainianise a Russian-speaking city, serves as a club for Kharkiv's Ukrainian speakers and cosmopolitans. English speakers are welcome to participate in regular meetings with students of the language, a great way to find local friends.

Information

Fabrika Co-working (☎099-100 1177; https://fabrika.space; vul Blagoveshchenska 1; per hour/day 90/180uah) A vast and comfortable co-working space on the top floor of a gentrified factory. Pay for time and fiddle with your gadget making use of fast wi-fi and free coffee in the common kitchen. Check out the balcony with splendid views of the city.

Post Office (pl Pryvokzalna; ⌚7.30am-9pm; Ⓜ Pivdenny Vokzal) Also provides internet access.

Getting There & Away

AIR

Kharkiv's **Osnova airport** (☎657, 090 031 6571; www.hrk.aero) handles international flights to/from Warsaw, Istanbul, Minsk in Belarus and Kutaisi in Georgia, as well as two daily flights to/from Kyiv.

The airport is 8km south of the city centre, off pr Gagarina – take trolleybus 5 and *marshrutka* 115E (4uah, 15 min) from the Prospekt Gagarina metro stop.

BUS

The most useful services from the **Central bus station** (☎732 6502; pr Gagarina 22; Ⓜ Prospekt Gagarina) are to Poltava (125uah, 2½ hours, hourly) and Dnipro (300uah, 4½ hours, hourly).

There is also plenty of buses for Moscow in Russia (1300uah to 1700uah, 13 hours, every couple of hours). More of these leave from the parking lot by Pivdenny Vokzal.

Autolux (www.autolux.ua) and **Günsel** (www.gunsel.com.ua) run several buses a day to Kyiv (from 225uah, seven hours) including some overnight services.

Kharkiv Metro

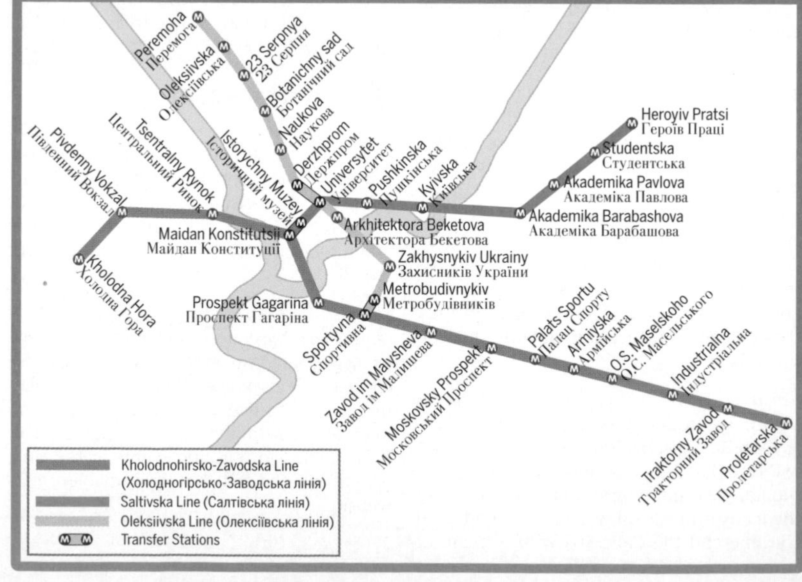

TRAIN

The main station is **Pivdenny Vokzal** (M Pivdenny Vokzal). By far the fastest way to get to/from Kyiv is aboard the Intercity+ service (320uah, 4½ hours, four daily), which stop in Poltava (80uah to 135uah, 1½ hours) and Myrhorod (90uah to 150uah, 2½ hours).

Other connections from Kharkiv:

Odesa 180uah, 15 hours, daily

Dnipro 170uah, four hours, daily

Moscow (Russia) 1500uah, 12½ to 14½ hours, two to three daily

Getting Around

The three interconnected metro lines cover most of the centre. The train station has its own metro stop, 'Pivdenny Vokzal'. Single-trip metro tokens cost 4uah. There are no cashiers selling tokens – only machines that don't accept notes with denominations higher than 10uah.

Dnipro Дніпро

056 / POP 979,000

Ukraine's latest revolution has guillotined this city's name: with a Bolshevik hero's moniker chopped off, what used to be known as Dnipropetrovsk is now called 'Dnipro', like the river it stands on. With portly 19th-century houses, trams trundling along leafy boulevards and beautiful river vistas, the city has every chance to become an attractive place. But unfortunately its fathers (and godfathers) are too busy opening boutiques and shopping emporiums – heritage buildings are crumbling away and whole blocks are being bulldozed to make way for yet another glassy rectangle. A major airspace-industry hub, Dnipro is also famous for its Jewish heritage, now represented by a fortress-like community centre that looms over the city.

Sights

★Menorah Center JEWISH SITE

(050 452 2163; http://menorah-center.com; vul Sholom-Aleykhema 4/26; museum 10am-7pm Tue, Thu & Sun) FREE Vaguely reminiscent of MI6 headquarters in Vauxhall, this giant structure looming over the remains of the Old Town is the slick new heart of the city's Jewish community. It was built over the city's old synagogue, of which only the original facade remains – the interior is completely new. The compound also contains a shopping arcade, two hotels and the main attraction – the **Museum of Jewish Heritage and Holocaust in Ukraine**.

The 1st floor of the museum covers the history of Ukrainian Jews till WWII. The 2nd floor is all about the Shoah. Around 70% of Jews who lived in Ukraine before the war were shot, gassed, burnt alive or thrown into coal mines as the Nazis prepared Lebensraum for 'pure-blood' settlers from Germany.

Rocket Park PARK

(Парк ракет; 24hr) Every city has a symbol of its might, but few of these symbols are so straightforwardly phallic as Dnipro's. Space rockets produced at the local Yuzhmash plant were its raison d'être in the Soviet times and, to an extent, continue to be now. Three of these decorate this manicured park, which also features two poignant memorials – one to the victims of the Chornobyl catastrophe and another to the soldiers who have fallen in the ongoing war in the Donbas region.

An interactive **science and information centre** called Space Hub, located next to the rockets, was waiting to be inaugurated at the time of research.

History Museum & Diorama MUSEUM

(Історичний музей; http://museum.dp.ua; pr Dmytro Yavornitskoho (Karla Marksa) 16; adult/student 20/10uah, diorama adult/student 10/5uah; 10am-4pm Tue-Sun) A lovingly curated establishment, the museum has visually attractive rooms dedicated to the Cossacks, the Russian empire, the Civil War and Holodomor. Adjoining the museum is a **diorama**, an 840-sq-metre painted canvas depicting the WWII Battle of the Dnipro, which was fought near here. The space between the two is occupied by the **ATO museum** – an open-air exhibition dedicated to the war under way in the nearby Donbas region and displaying burned-down military hardware and bullet-riddled road signs.

Preobrazhensky Cathedral CATHEDRAL

(Спасо-Преображенський кафедральний собор; pl Soborna 1) With its glistening gold spire and dome, Preobrazhensky Cathedral is a classical structure dating from 1830 to 1835. This is Dnipro's holiest church, so don't barge in wearing beach clothes.

Activities

Sentosa Cable Park WATER SPORTS

(068 794 7953; http://sentosacablepark.com; nab Pobedy 37B; 1hr ride 230uah; 1pm-8pm, from 11am on weekends) A slick new establishment

for the fans of wakeboarding and water skiing, this is a cable loop, essentially a carousel, with skiers/wakeboarders pulled along a succession of jumping ramps.

Sleeping

Hostel CapsularHouse HOSTEL $
(☎093-004 8632, 068-400 0189; www.facebook.com/Hostel-CapsularHouse-353288738369289/; vul Yevropeyskaya (Mironova) 13A; dm from 120uah)

Dnipro

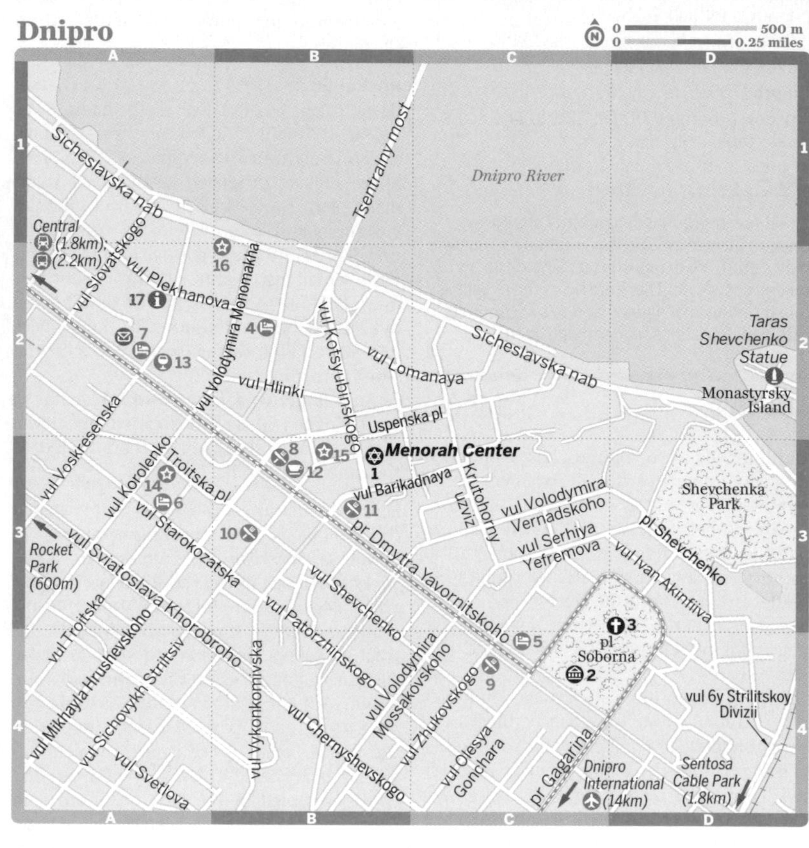

Dnipro

Top Sights
1 Menorah Center ... B3

Sights
2 History Museum & Diorama ... C4
3 Preobrazhensky Cathedral ... D3

Sleeping
4 Hostel CapsularHouse ... B2
5 Hotel Academy ... C4
6 Litera ... A3
Menorah Hotel ... (see 1)
7 Mystay.org ... A2

Eating
8 Café Myshi Blyakhera ... B3
9 Papa Karla ... C4
10 Puri Chveni ... B3
11 Reporter ... B3

Drinking & Nightlife
12 DoubleDecker Cake & Co ... B3
13 Zavodnaya Obezyana ... A2

Entertainment
14 Art-Kvartira ... A3
15 Labyrinth ... B3
16 Neizvestny Petrovsky ... B2

Information
17 Fish Andriy ... A2

The most convenient and professionally run apartment hostel at the time of writing. We just hope it lingers for some years, as many such establishments in Dnipro compete with fruit flies for shortest life span.

Litera HOTEL $$
(☎095-604 6200, 056-230 0600; http://hotellitera.com; vul Troitska 8; d from 1000uah; ❄📶) On a quieter street in the very centre, this smallish hotel has classically designed rooms that are perfectly comfortable and well equipped.

Hotel Academy HOTEL $$
(Готель Академія; ☎056-370 0505; www.academyhotel.com.ua; pr Dmytra Yavornytskoho (Karla Marksa) 20; s/d incl breakfast from 700/1000uah; ❄) Fans of Soviet-realist art need look no further than this museum-like hotel. The walls in the lobby and corridors are covered in brilliant paintings epitomising the best of the genre. While the service is outstanding, the rooms (which, curiously, bear Cézanne prints) are simply average. Breakfast in the **Deja Vu restaurant** downstairs is a highlight.

Mystay.org ACCOMMODATION SERVICES $$
(☎067 563 5906; www.mystay.org; pr Dmytra Yavornytskoho (Karla Marksa) 60/16; apt from 500uah) An apartment rental agency used to working with foreign travellers.

Menorah Hotel HOTEL $$$
(☎056-717 7001; http://menorahotel.com; vul Sholom-Aleykhema 4/26; s/d from 1270/1560uah; 📶) The fortress-like skyscraper of the Jewish Menorah Center looks so formidable that no besieging army can possibly disturb your sleep in its in-house hotel, which sports large comfortable rooms modelled on those you'll find in a typical four-star chain hotel. Nice views of the city come as a bonus.

Eating

Papa Karla EASTERN EUROPEAN $
(pr Dmytro Yavornitskoho (Karla Marksa) 27A; mains 60-110uah; ⏲8am-11pm) An ubercute 20th-century nostalgia place without hammers and sickles – think visiting a Soviet granny back in the 1970s. Savour your beetroot and prune salad or steamed cutlets made of pike to the soundtrack of Soviet pop divas, like Alla Pugacheva and Sofia Rotaru.

★ **Café Myshi Blyakhera** UKRAINIAN $$
(Кафе Мыши Бляхера; ☎377 3377; pr Dmytra Yavornitskoho (Karla Marksa) 46; mains 110-210uah; ⏲8am-11pm) There is an overcomplicated pun in the name involving mice and a retired Jewish gangster who allegedly left a handwritten book of recipes in this cellar place. If we are to believe the legend, this hardened man had a soft spot for Italian pasta, Azov Sea fish and Danubian frogs. A cool place full of old books and local bohemians. To find the entrance, look out for a blue door on the side of the block.

Puri Chveni GEORGIAN $$
(☎066 844 5664; vul Sichovykh Striltsiv (Artyoma) 4; mains 100-200uah; ⏲11am-11pm) Dark stone, aged wood and the smell of baking *khachapuri* (cheese pastry) – that's a combination which instantly carries one across the Caucasus range into Georgia's gastronomical Eden. A very modern take on the bimillennial culinary tradition, this stylish establishment makes exemplary *lobio* and *pkhali* (veggie snacks) and lamb *shashlyk*. Plenty of Georgian wine on the bar menu.

Reporter EUROPEAN $$
(Репортёр; ☎056 233 7575; cnr pr Dmytro Yavornitskoho (Karla Marksa) & vul Barikadnaya; mains 90-260uah; ⏲24hr) Reporter has three wings: a ground-floor coffeehouse serving breakfasts and possibly the plumpest, tastiest homemade *varenyky* (stuffed, ravioli-like dumplings) in the land; a chichi restaurant upstairs; and a superb basement 'warm-up bar' with a great in-house DJ getting the city's hipsters fired up for a night on the town. You'll find at least one wing open, day or night.

Drinking & Nightlife

DoubleDecker Cake & Co CAFE
(pr Dmytro Yavornitskoho (Karla Marksa) 46; ⏲8am-10pm) It looks tiny when you enter, but the upper floor (or deck, rather) has a spacious sitting area with comfy armchairs and a large common table invitingly fitted with plugs for your gadgets. Tastiest brew and best desserts we've tried in the region.

Zavodnaya Obezyana BAR
(Clockwork Monkey; ☎068-398 6869; www.facebook.com/zavodnaya.bar/; vul Voskresenska (Lenina) 11; ⏲12pm-12am) Lacquered wood, faux-antique furniture and comfy couches makes this cosy bar an agreeable place to spend a quiet evening over a cocktail, except the evening is no longer quiet when the DJ sets the room in motion and wild dancing ensues in the tiny area before the counter.

A bunch of sculpted monkeys observe the scrum approvingly from cabinet shelves.

☆ Entertainment

Art-Kvartira ARTS CENTRE
(http://artkvartira.dp.ua; pl Krasnaya 3/1; ⏰Wed-Sun) A modern arts centre hosting theatre performances, concerts, dancing and yoga classes.

Neizvestny Petrovsky CLUB
(Unknown Petrovsky; http://np.dp.ua/; Sicheslavska nab 15A; 70uah; ⏰24hr) Run by the same people as Fish Andriy, this is a place where young Bohemians meet for a beer, inexpensive food and some jazz or alternative live music.

Labyrinth CLUB
(Лабіринт; cnr vul Kharkivskaya & vul Mahdeburzhskoho Prava; 100-200uah; ⏰10pm till dawn) True to its name, this is an underground maze of corridors and halls, each with its own bar and soundtrack. Don't buy the full ticket unless you are desperate to see a striptease show in the upstairs 'VIP' lounges.

ℹ Information

Check out http://gorod.dp.ua for the latest hotel, restaurant and club news.

Fish Andriy (Риба Андрій; http://ryba.dp.ua/; vul Volodymira Velykoho (Plekhanova) 13A; internet per hr 40uah; ⏰24hr) A pay-for-time 'anti-cafe', like those in Kyiv, this is primarily a comfortable environment to fire up your gadget and Skype away with friends. Help yourself to free coffee and lemonade. Even more usefully for travellers, they run tours of old Soviet plants and old Cossack villages in the vicinity of Dnipro. There is a smallish hostel in the premises. At the time of writing, the travel outfit of Fish Andriy was due to move to the Space Hub in the Rocket Park (p219). By all means, you can still inquire about tours at the original location.

Post Office (Почтамт; pr Karla Marksa 62; internet per hr 6uah; ⏰8am-8pm Mon-Fri, 8am-7pm Sat) Handle both your snail-mail and email needs here.

ℹ Getting There & Away

AIR

About 15km southeast of the city towards Zaporizhzhya (and also convenient for that city), **Dnipro International Airport** (☎395 209; http://dnk.aero) has daily flights to Vienna (Austrian Airlines) and four flights a day to Tel Aviv (MAU). There are also at least eight flights a day to both airports in Kyiv.

BUS

Dnipro has the country's largest **bus station** (☎778 4090; www.dopas.dp.ua; vul Kurchatova 10), located west of the city centre, 700 metres away from the train station.

Buses for the nearby Zaporizhzhya leave every 15 minutes (54uah, 1½ hours, every 15 minutes). 'Luxury' bus operators **Autolux** (☎371 0353; www.autolux.ua) and **Günsel** (☎778 3935; www.gunsel.com.ua) have overnight trips to Kyiv (260uah to 320uah, seven to eight hours), and you'll find plenty of buses to Poltava, Kharkiv and Odesa.

TRAIN

From the **Central train station** (☎005 395 209; pr Dmytra Yavornytskoho 108) there are three fast Intercity trains daily to Kyiv (320uah, six hours). Some of them continue to the nearby Zaporizhzhya, providing a comfortable alternative for minibuses. Kyiv is also served by a bunch of slower trains that mostly go at night.

Trains also rumble to Odesa (185uah, 11½ hours, daily), Lviv (300uah, 16 to 17 hours, three-four weekly), Kharkiv (200uah, 4½ hours, a couple daily) and other major cities.

ℹ Getting Around

Tram 1 runs the length of pr Dmytra Yavornitskoho, originating at the train station. The metro line currently connects the train station with outlying districts. It will become more useful for travellers once the construction of two stations is completed in the city centre (yes, there are signs of them working on it again!).

A typical taxi ride with Uber in the centre costs 30uah to 40uah.

Zaporizhzhya Запоріжжя

☎0612 / POP 767,000

So, so Soviet! Yes, they've knocked down Lenin's statue in the wake of the 2014 revolution, but the Stalinesque grandeur of the former Lenin avenue is still very much there. Now called pr Sobornosti, it runs from Avtozaz, the birthplace of the Zaporozhets (remembered as the USSR's most ridiculed car model), to the 1920s industrial icon Dniproges power station. But Zaporizhzhya's mummified Sovietness is not the main reason to visit the city. Tourists flock here to see Khortytsya, a rocky, forested island where Cossacks set up their all-male free-rule republic, which prospered from raids on neighbouring empires and duties levied on anyone who used the river trade route. Today it is the place to learn about Cossack culture and history, admire beautiful river vistas and spend a day hiking or bicycling.

Sights

Khortytsya Island HISTORIC SITE

(Острів Хортиця; http://hortica.zp.ua; Khortisya island) The Zaporizhska Sich on Khortytsya Island was the cradle of Ukrainian Cossackdom, where Hetman (chieftain) Dmytro Baida united disparate groups of Cossacks in the construction of a *sich* (fort) in 1553–54. Today the island houses the **Historical Museum of Zaporizhsky Cossacks**, closed for renovation at the time of writing, as well as the **Sich Reconstruction** (adult/child & student 24/12uah; 9.30am-4.30pm Tue-Sun) – a wooden fortress, complete with churches and about a dozen thatched-roof *khaty* (dwellings), built for the epic movie *Taras Bulba* in 2007.

The rocky island made a perfect base for an army camp: strategically located below the Dnipro rapids and beyond the control of Polish or Russian authority. Any man could come to join the Cossack brotherhood, irrespective of social background or indeed criminal record. But no women were allowed entry.

At the height of its power the community numbered some 20,000 fighters, under the authority of one *hetman*. On the battlefield they were formidable opponents; off it, formidable vodka drinkers. The *sich* was eventually destroyed in 1775, on the order of Russian empress Catherine the Great.

With its network of forest paths and tarmac roads, Khortytsya Island is a haven for hikers and bicyclists. You can usually find a bicycle-rental stand near the parking lot. Khortytsya is also the best spot to admire the Dniproges dam from.

No public transport goes all the way to the main sights on Khortytsya, so it's better to take a taxi or rent a bike. Some *marshrutka* buses (e.g. 55, and 56), which go along pr Soborny from the train station, stop on the Khortytsya side of the bridge that connects the island to the centre. From here, it is a 3km hike to the museum and Sich Reconstruction.

Phaeton Museum of Machinery MUSEUM

(Музей техники Фаэтон; 099-905 2702; http://faeton.zp.ua/; vul Vyborzka 8; 50uah; 9am-5pm) A huge hangar in the gritty industrial part of city, 3.5km from pr Soborny (Lenina), contains a lovingly arranged exhibition of civilian and military vehicles. Highlights include Soviet government limousines (such as ZIL and Chaika) facing their American prototypes in the main hall, and the full range of Zaporozhets – USSR's most ridiculed (and beloved) mini produced in Zaporizhzhya.

Marshrutka 54 (4uah, 10 minutes) goes that way from McDonald's on pr Soborny.

Dniproges Dam DAM

At 760m – two and a half times longer than the famous Hoover Dam – the wall of the USSR's first dam certainly represented a monumental engineering feat when constructed under US supervision between 1927 and 1932. It's still impressive, although stained by years of local pollution. It is best viewed from the Historical Museum of Zaporizhsky Cossacks.

Activities

Bity Obod CYCLING

(http://obod.com.ua; bul Shevchenka 27; bike rental per hour/day from 30/180uah) Bicycles are the best way to experience Khortytsya Island. You can rent them at this centrally located shop.

Sleeping

Teatralny Hotel HOTEL $$

(061-228 8000; http://teatr-hotel.com; vul Troitska 23; s/d from 700/950uah;) The proximity to a theatre, which supposedly contributes to its brisk business, has prompted the owners to decorate the walls of this cavernous establishment with black-and-white photos of Hollywood actors. Rooms are comfortable and well equipped, but businesslike rather than theatrical. Food is available around the clock in the lobby bar.

Venetsia HOTEL $$

(Венеція; 0610289 4512; http://venecia-hotel.com.ua; vul Nizhnedneprovskaya 1B; d incl breakfast from 700uah) Right by the river, Venetsia has rooms with faux-Victorian furniture, unexpectedly luxurious for the price. Annoyingly you need to order breakfast the night before and tell staff exactly when you want it. A sandy beach is across the road and there is a great sauna inside the hotel.

Khortitsa Palace HOTEL $$$

(061-766 0031; www.khortitsa-palace.com; bul Shevchenka 71A; d from 2200uah) Located in newly built twin towers with splendid river views but no longer a part of the Sheraton franchise, this properly business hotel provides comforts unrivalled in Zaporizhzhya. Most rooms come with floor-to-ceiling windows and balconies.

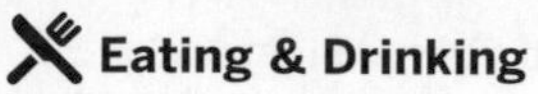

Eating & Drinking

Pechki-Lavochki RUSSIAN $
(☎050 775-2457; vul Peremohy 16; mains 30-50uah; ⊙9am-7pm Mon-Fri) This unassuming tiny cafe sets the golden standard for

FLAMES IN THE EAST

The military conflict in Ukraine's region of Donbas is something to be aware of if travelling in the east. The conflict zone comprises 2.5% of Ukrainian territory in the far eastern corner of the country, and spans a good 1300km from its western border with the EU. The rest of Ukraine is peaceful and reasonably safe. In fact, you're unlikely to see any signs of war, apart from the inevitable propaganda, unless you come really close to the area, which we strongly advise against. Be attentive to the latest news and alerts while planning your trip and travelling in the east of the country. Most Western governments have issued travel warnings against visiting the entire Donetsk and Luhansk regions, including parts controlled by Ukraine.

What Happened

A popular antiwar comics meme shows the first cosmonaut Yury Gagarin phoning into our time from 1961, when he had just returned from space to be greeted by the Soviet leader Nikita Khrushchev, a self-styled Ukrainian.

'Hello guys', says Gagarin wearing the trademark Gagarin smile in image 1. 'How are things in the 21st century? Have you made it to Mars?'

In image 2, a dismayed Gagarin asks: 'A war with whom?'.

A war between Russia and Ukraine felt unthinkable even when Russian troops were occupying Crimea in a response to the victory of Maidan revolution in Kyiv in February 2014. That annexation went peacefully, but a few weeks later a band of military veterans assembled in Crimea by the rogue Russian security agent Igor Girkin took over the town of Sloviansk in the eastern Ukrainian region of Donbas. Meanwhile, pro-Russian activists started seizing administrative power in major cities of eastern and southern Ukraine. In some of them, namely Kharkiv and Dnipro, the uprising was quelled without bloodshed by the local authorities. But the two regional centres in Donbas, Donetsk and Luhansk, found themselves under the control of a heavily armed rebel force assisted by the Russians. The rebels set up two entities, called 'people's republics', with capitals in Donetsk and Luhansk.

Having lost Crimea largely due to inaction, the new government in Kyiv decided it was time to send troops. In no time the standoff degraded into a full-out war. At first, it felt like the Ukrainians were taking the upper hand. They pushed Girkin out of Sloviansk and were advancing on the key cities of Donetsk and Luhansk. International sympathy shifted decisively to the Ukrainian side after a Malaysian airliner was shot down by a missile widely believed to have been fired from the rebel positions. Thousands of Ukrainians joined privately funded volunteer battalions or organisations procuring supplies for the army, boosting morale among the professional military. But in August of that year Russia tipped the balance by assisting the rebels with artillery support, hardware supplies and manpower. By February 2015, the Ukrainian army had suffered a series of defeats that allowed Moscow to stabilise the frontline and force Kyiv into negotiations, which became known as the Minsk process, after the Belarusian capital that had been chosen as a venue for peace talks.

With heavy artillery removed from the frontline, the conflict continued as low-intensity trench warfare, with neither side respecting repeatedly renewed armistice agreements. The office of the UN high commissioner for human rights put the number of casualties since the start of the war at 10,225, of whom 2803 are civilians. More than two million people were displaced by the conflict, according to the UN, with 1.6 million remaining in other parts of Ukraine and others fleeing to Russia and other countries.

What is the Donbas?

The densely populated coal- and iron-rich area known as Donbas (an acronym, which stands for Donets river basin) largely overlaps with Ukraine's easternmost regions of Donetsk and Luhansk. Populated by nomads until the end of the 17th century, the area was *pelmeni* (Russian meat-filled dumplings) and their triangular-shaped Ukrainian cousins, *varenyki*. All dumplings are made by hand in front of you and you can buy them frozen, if you want to cook at home.

Bosfor TURKISH $
(Босфор; vul Yakova Novitskoho 3; mains 70-90uah; ⏲10am-11pm;) Turkish expats run this pleasant eatery just off pr Lenina. The convenient picture menu features lots of *shashlyks* and appetising Turkish snacks.

colonised by Ukranian peasants, followed by Christian refugees from the Ottoman empire (notably Greeks) as well as Russian, German and Jewish colonists. With one of the largest salt deposits in Europe near Bakhmut, it became a major centre of salt production.

The coal rush began in the second part of the 19th century, when entrepreneur John Hughes built a metallurgy plant and numerous coal mines in what is now Donetsk. Thousands of predominantly Russian-speaking migrants poured in searching for work, changing the ethnic composition of the region. Russian became the dominant language during Soviet times, especially when the region was essentially repopulated after the devastation brought by WWII.

The first decade after Ukraine gained independence in 1991 was mired by turf wars between local gangsters fighting for control of local industries. But eventually the region's riches were consolidated in the hands of a few oligarchs, notably Rinat Akhmetov, who became the richest man in Ukraine. Donbas elites grew political muscle promoting a pro-Russian agenda and nostalgia for the USSR. They eventually succeeded in getting their nominee and Donbas native, Viktor Yanukovych, elected as president, but his corruption and incompetence precipitated their demise, since these issues were the primary cause of Ukraine's 2014 revolution.

As with many other regions in Ukraine, Donbas has developed its own identity, which largely trumps national loyalty. The pro-Russian orientation has traditionally been strong, but not nearly as strong as in Crimea. A very sizeable number of locals fiercely opposed what they saw as the Russian occupation of the region, fled to territories controlled by Kyiv and joined the Ukrainian army. But the central government is unpopular, as exemplified by elections in the parts of Donbas now controlled by Ukraine, where the old, Russia-leaning elites have pretty easily secured majorities in local legislatures.

The Situation Now

Officially known in Ukraine as Special Districts of Donetsk and Luhansk regions, the occupied areas of Donbas are now ruled by gangster-ridden governments of 'people's republics', which have made lawlessness and violence a new normal, though their Moscow supervisors are gradually pushing them to improve the governance. The area is not impenetrable – thousands of people travel back and forth across the frontline daily, many of them local pensioners who can only access their accounts on the territory controlled by Ukraine. Minibuses headed for Donetsk and Luhansk are advertised at Kharkiv's railway station. The fast Intercity+ train goes daily from Kyiv to the Kostiantivka, near the frontline and 70km from the rebel-held Donetsk.

Some foreign nationals, mostly journalists and Organization for Security and Co-operation in Europe (OSCE) observers, also travel into the 'republics', securing permits and accreditations from both the rebel governments and the Ukrainian authorities. Issued by the Ukrainian Security Service (SBU; www.ssu.gov.ua), the basic permit to visit is required not only for crossing the rebel-controlled zone, but for entering the adjacent areas controlled by the Ukrainian military. Roadblocks, where you'll be asked to present the document, begin dozens of kilometres away from the frontline. It would be extremely unwise to turn up at a checkpoint without a permit – you'll be scolded and sent away at best. Risks of travelling into the rebel-controlled zone are high, as a number of foreign nationals have been subject to illegal detentions, outright kidnappings, torture and other forms of violence during the conflict.

The areas of Donbas controlled by Ukraine are technically visitable, and places like Sloviansk and Kramatorsk now have an expat population, mostly involved with humanitarian aid and development organisations. Kramatorsk is also the place where journalists get accreditations to work in the conflict zone (on top of basic permits). But Ukrainian security services are understandably suspicious about foreigners popping up near the conflict zone, as some Westerners have previously joined the rebels. You may get into a rough situation if your reason for being in the area is not immediately clear.

Patrons smoke *shisha* on an open-air terrace.

Fishcafe UKRAINIAN $$
(pr Soborny (Lenina) 107; mains 100-200uah; ⏲11am-11pm) This lovely restaurant, with a wood-filled interior and many multicoloured fish-shaped objects adorning the walls, could have easily become our favourite in a more sophisticated city than Zaporizhzhya. The main speciality is Black Sea fish, but there are more intriguing dishes inspired by Ukrainian cuisine. Try *svekolnik* – a cold beetroot soup.

Pub Tyrlo GRILL $$
(Pub Tyrlo; ☎061-220 5662; pr Soborny 186A; mains 100-180uah; ⏲1pm-12am; ❄📶) With bare concrete walls, this cellar place underneath a Stalin-era apartment block could have been a nuclear bunker, but now it is a lively restaurant that specialises in two products that some find essential for their well-being – meat and beer. Both fail to disappoint, which can't be said about the sluggish service.

Cholla & Joshua COFFEE
(www.facebook.com/cholla.joshua; pr Soborny 200; ⏲8am-10pm; 📶) A tiny coffee shop with comfy arm chairs, super-attentive service and desserts (fruit parfait and pavlova) to die for.

☆ Entertainment

Khortitsa Equestrian Theatre CIRCUS
(☎701 2481; http://zp-kazaki.com/; Khortytsya Island; adults/students 100/70uah) Standing on top of a horse, attached to the side of a horse, hanging upside down on a horse – Cossacks defy fear and forces of gravitation in this captivating (and humorous) show. The venue resembles a Ukrainian village, complete with an inn and shops selling crafts. It is unreachable by public transport, so arrange a taxi from your hotel.

Performances typically take place at 12pm on Saturday, but check the website, sadly Ukrainian-only, or inquire at your hotel reception.

ℹ Information

Just about every service you need is found around pl Festyvalna – many inside **Hotel Intourist-Zaporizhzhya** (pr Soborny 132), which has a travel agency among myriad other services.

Post Office (pr Lenina 133; ⏲post office 7.30am-8pm, telephone centre 8am-9pm) Besides postal services, an internet and telephone centre, there is also an ATM.

ℹ Getting There & Away

AIR

The locally based airline **Motor Sich** operates a fleet of old Antonov-24 planes that fly to Kyiv's Zhulyany airport.

Turkish Airlines connect the ramshackle affair that goes by the name of **Zaporizhzhya International Airport** (☎061-227 0579; www.avia.zp.ua; Donetske shosse) with Istanbul.

BUS

Buses for Dnipro (54uah, 2 hours, every 20 minutes) leave from the **bus station** (☎642 657; pr Leninaya 20), located near Zaporizhzhya-1 train station.

TRAIN

Zaporizhzhya-1 train station (☎224 4060; pr Leninaya 2) is at the southeastern end of pr Soborny. Three daily Intercity+ are best for Kyiv (360uah, seven hours). All of them pass through nearby Dnipro. Southbound trains stop here on the way to Novooleksiivka (75 to 240 uah, three hours, five daily) on the border with Russian-controlled Crimea.

ℹ Getting Around

The main street, pr Soborny (Lenina), stretches for 10km from Zaporizhzhya-1 train station at its southeastern end to pl Zaporizhka (Lenina) overlooking the Dniproges Dam. Most trolleybuses and *marshrutky* run the length of pr Soborny between Zaporizhzhya-1 train station and pl Lenina, but you can bank on trolleybus 3.

Khortytsya Island lies in the Dnipro, 2km southwest of the Dniproges Dam wall. To get there, take a *marshrutka* marked Хортиця (eg 87 or 58), leaving from the corner of pr Lenina and pr Metallurgov, and get off after it crosses Khortytsya's southern bridge. The trip takes 15 minutes and costs 5uah. From there, it is a 3km hike north to the museum.

Understand Ukraine

Ukraine Today

So far, so close. The simmering conflict in Ukraine's far east feels eons away as you sip your *kava* (coffee) in a Lviv cafe or frolic on a beach in Odesa, yet it's the inescapable reality that affects millions. Ukraine may feel extraordinarily normal given its predicament, but talk to people and you'll sense the tension and fatigue. On the upside, the conflict has precipitated a visible tectonic shift – Ukraine is no longer the same divided nation it was before 2014.

Best In Print

Evenings on a Farm near Dikanka Nikolai Gogol's stories, mostly set in his native Poltava region.

Borderland Anna Reid's journey through Ukrainian history.

Death and the Penguin Andrey Kurkov's Kafkaesque tale set in the troubled early 1990s.

Everything is Illuminated Jonathan Safran Foer searches for the lost west Ukrainian *shtetl* of Trachimbrod.

The Gates of Europe Serhiy Plohiy has penned the most readable and balanced account of Ukraine's history.

The White Guard Bulgakov's portrait of Kyiv during the Russian Civil War.

Best On Film

Shadows of Forgotten Ancestors (1964) Shaggy Hutsul customs and symbolism.

Za Dvumya Zaytsami (Chasing Two Hares; 1961) Diverting romp through early-20th-century Kyiv.

The Battle of Chernobyl (2006) Detailed documentary on the Chornobyl disaster and its aftermath.

Close Relations (2007) Vitaly Mansky's story of his own family divided by the war in Ukraine.

Evenings on a Farm near Dikanka (1961) Technicolor film version of Gogol's Ukrainian tales.

Challenges Ahead

Elected months after the 2014 revolution, Ukrainian president Petro Poroshenko is facing re-election in 2019. He can boast a few tangible achievements in implementing much-needed reforms, like the new noncorrupt and efficient patrol police, but most of his accomplishments can only be appreciated by macroeconomists. For ordinary people, reforms meant skyrocketing prices for winter heating and electricity, with monthly payments often exceeding their incomes. Ukraine is the poorest country in Europe, with the average net salary equalling US$200. With the unashamedly populist opposition leader Yulia Tymoshenko breathing down his neck, Poroshenko is facing an uphill struggle to continue unpopular but necessary reforms while simultaneously running an election campaign.

Goodbye, Russia

For almost 20 years, Ukrainian politics was determined by the divide between pro-Western and pro-Russian forces. To a large extent, it ran along existing geographic, linguistic and generational barriers. Russian-speakers in southeastern parts of Ukraine, as much of the older Communist-era generation, naturally leant towards Moscow, while most Ukrainian speakers in the West and a substantial part of the younger generation were oriented towards the West.

Three key issues served as markers of geopolitical leanings: the status of Russian language, views on Ukrainian history and the Euro-Atlantic integration. All of that changed after Russia occupied Crimea and triggered the war in eastern Ukraine in what felt like a punitive action in response to the victory of the Maidan revolution in 2014. The shock of a blatant aggression by a nation they genuinely perceived as brotherly demoralised the Russia-leaning party and turned many Russian speakers into fervent Ukrainian patriots, practically overnight.

The markers of the old divide no longer matter as much as they did and most of the population is in support of Ukraine joining NATO. A reform of education phasing out Russian-language schooling is causing few protests. Meanwhile, the Ukrainian insurgents who fought against the Soviets in WWII are broadly recognised as national heroes. That shift also shows in elections, with pro-Western parties firmly holding sway. Ever so prone to dark humour, some Ukrainians call Russian leader Vladimir Putin the true father of the new Ukrainian nation. Well, it's only a half-joke.

No Turning Back?

Ukrainian leaders like boasting about the 'civilisational choice' the country made by decisively breaking up with Russia. It would be easier to believe if they – just as decisively – broke up with their old habits. Although considerably reshuffled, the old oligarchic elites remain at the forefront of the Ukrainian politics, gradually chipping away at the achievements of the 2014 revolution. Anticorruption activists and investigative journalists are finding themselves under increased pressure from the mafia state – an unholy alliance of corrupt politicians, security agents, gangsters and ultra-nationalist paramilitaries. Bringing down the mafia state was the main goal of the Maidan revolution, but it's creeping back in the guise of patriotism and nationalist zeal. Ukrainian politics is mired by circus-like populism, which discredits the democratic form of governance in the eyes of ordinary people.

By 2017, polls were showing that all major political institutions – the presidency, the government and the parliament – were trusted by an ever-diminishing minority of Ukrainians. The army, however, remained popular, betraying the nostalgia for a strong hand. But there's another institution that also retains a great deal of public trust and serves as a bulwark against reactionary forces. Known to Ukrainians as the 'volunteer movement', it's broadly speaking what they call civil society in the West. This is what makes Ukraine stand out among other ex-Soviet countries and gives hope that the revolution will deliver on its promise.

Should I Go?

Ukraine is going through a tumultuous period, but it remains a reasonably safe and thoroughly enjoyable place to travel. On top of that, it really wants and needs to be heard and seen. Politics aside, there is a peaceful revolution under way that improves the urban environment, brings about new public spaces and art projects, encourages people to experiment and pursue their dreams. Bursting with youthful energy, Ukraine is a place to seek inspiration and feel the wind change.

HELLO: **DOBRY DEN | DOBRY DEN | UKRAINIAN**

UNEMPLOYMENT: **9.5% (OFFICIAL)**

POPULATION: **42.5 MILLION**

if Ukraine were 100 people

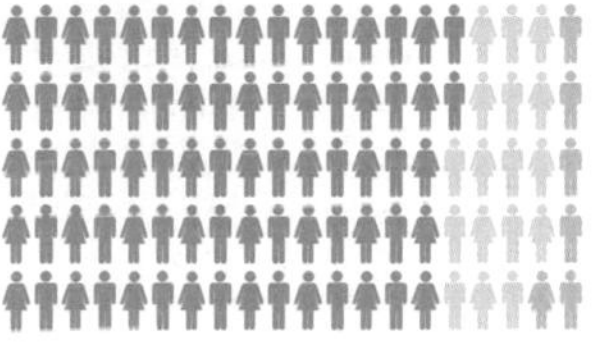

77 would be Ukrainian
17 would be Russian
6 would be Others

belief systems

(% of population)

population per sq km

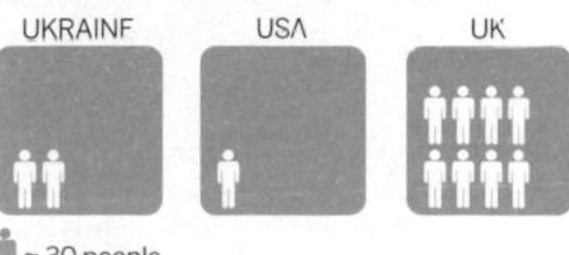

History

Kyiv is the cradle of not only the Ukrainian nationhood, but also those of Russia and Belarus as well. This has created a range of highly politicised interpretations and heated arguments about what came first: Ukraine or Russia? The irony, though, is that the original east Slavic state was actually founded in the 9th century by the Vikings who gave the name of their tribe to the country, which thus became known as Kyivan Rus.

Cimmerians to Khazars

Before Kyivan Rus, Ukraine's prehistory is tribal. First came the Cimmerians in the 12th century BC. Then, fierce warrior Scythians from Central Asia settled the steppe in the 7th century BC, while Greeks from western Asia Minor established city-states around the Black Sea. The two groups formed a symbiotic relationship. The famous gold work found in Scythian tombs is believed to have been commissioned from Greek artisans; a fine collection is found in Kyiv's Kyevo-Pecherska Lavra.

Successive waves of nomadic invaders (Sarmatians from the east, Germanic Ostrogoths from northern Poland and Huns from Mongolia) continued to sweep into Ukraine. However, the Slavs, thought to originate from near the borders of present-day Poland, Belarus and northwestern Ukraine, remained untouched by these invasions. Turkic-Iranian Khazars from the Caucasus were probably the first to bring the Slavs under subjugation, in the 8th century AD.

Orest Subtelny's 700-page *Ukraine, A History* is widely considered the definitive work on the subject, narrowly edging out Paul Magosci's equally long *History of Ukraine*. However, the most readable and up-to-date account of Ukraine's history is Serhiy Plohiy's *The Gates of Europe*, which neatly divides events into digestible chunks.

Kyivan Rus

Meanwhile, Scandinavians – known as Varangians – had been exploring, trading and setting up small states east of the Baltic since the 6th century AD. Travelling south from their Novgorod power centre (near today's St Petersburg) in 879, King Oleh stopped just long enough to declare himself ruler of Kyiv. The city handily lay between Novgorod and Constantinople on the Dnipro River, and under Oleh's urging it became capital of a huge, unified state. At its largest, under the rule of Volodymyr the Great (978–1015), this empire stretched from the Volga to the Danube and to the Baltic, its prosperity based on trade along the Dnipro.

TIMELINE

Date unknown

One of Eastern Europe's oldest settlements, Kyiv's origins aren't crystal clear. Legend has it that Slavic brothers Kiy, Shchek and Khoriv and their sister Lybid founded it.

879

Nordic King Oleh travels to Kyiv. Taken by its strategic position on the Dnipro River between Scandinavia and Constantinople, he wrests it from his own emissaries Askold and Dir – by murdering them.

989

With Kyivan Rus now established as the first Eastern Slavic state, Volodymyr the Great adopts Orthodox Christianity. A mass baptism in the Dnipro River seals this early pro-European decision.

As well as consolidating Rus territory, Volodymyr firmly established Orthodox Christianity as the pre-eminent religion. By accepting baptism in 989 and marrying the Byzantine emperor's daughter (at Khersones outside Sevastopol), he opened the door to Byzantine artistic influences and cast Kyivan Rus as a European state. St Sofia's Cathedral in Kyiv is still testament to Kyivan Rus's greatness and the importance of Orthodox Christianity within the state.

After the death of Kyivan Rus's last great ruler, Yaroslav the Wise, in 1054, the empire began disintegrating into separate princedoms. When Mongol warriors sacked Kyiv in 1240, it largely ceased to exist. The centres of power then simply shifted north and west, with the Muscovite kingdom evolving from the northern princedom of Vladimir-Suzdal to eventually transform in what is now known as Russia. Another stronghold of Eastern Slavic statehood continued to evolve as the Princedom of Halych in the part of western Ukraine, currently known as Halychyina or Galicia.

Mongols, Tatars & Turks

The Mongol invasion that sounded the death knell for Kyivan Rus in 1240 was led by Genghis Khan's grandson Batu. A large swath of the Rus empire was subsumed into the so-called Golden Horde ('horde' meaning region) of the Mongol empire. This encompassed much of eastern and southern Ukraine, along with parts of European Russia and Siberia, with the now vanished city of Sarai, on the Volga, its capital.

WEB RESOURCES

Federation of East European Family History Societies (www.feefhs.org)

JewishGen (www.jewishgen.org)

Ukraine Geneaology Forum (http://genforum.genealogy.com/ukraine/)

East European Genealogical Society (www.eegsociety.org)

State Archives Geneaology Section (www.archives.gov.ua/Eng/genealogia.php)

Routes to Roots Foundation (www.rtrfoundation.org)

Memory Book (www.memory-book.com.ua)

Jewish Galicia and Bukovina (http://jgaliciabukovina.net)

Geneology of Italychyna/Eastern Galacia (www.halgal.com)

Ukrainian Genealogical and Historical Society (http://ukrainiangenealogist.tripod.com)

1199

West of Kyiv, Prince Roman Mstyslavych merges the regions of Galicia and Volynia into one Grand Duchy. Although landowners continue to rebel against his rule, a thriving agricultural society emerges.

1240

A pivotal moment in Kyivan Rus history is reached, as Mongols sack the capital. The already fragmented empire's eastern regions are absorbed into the Mongolian Golden Horde. Many Kyivans flee west.

1349

Ukraine comes under attack from the opposite direction, as Poland overruns Galicia and its capital Lviv. Nearly 40 years later, Poland teams up with Lithuania as both states look east.

1475

The Crimean Khanate, which succeeded the Mongolian Golden Horde in 1428, becomes a client state of the Ottoman Empire, remaining so until 1772. Crimean Tatars frequently take slaves from mainland Ukraine.

Over time, Mongol leaders were gradually replaced by their Tatar colleagues and descendants, and when the horde began to disintegrate in the 15th century, it divided into several smaller *khanates*.

One of these – the Crimean Khanate – eventually became a client state of the Ottoman Turk Empire in 1475. The Crimean Tatars, as the people of the *khanate* were known, made frequent slave raids into Ukrainian, Russian and Polish territories until the 18th century. When Russia overran Crimea in 1783, large numbers of the Tatars fled to the Ottoman empire and they gradually turned into a minority. Reminders of their once-powerful civilisation can be seen in the old capital of Bakhchysaray.

For an easy-to-absorb, chronological listing of Ukrainian events from the 9th to the 20th centuries, set alongside those in the rest of the world, head to www.brama.com/ukraine/history.

Galicia-Volynia

Meanwhile, from 1199 under the rule of Prince Roman Mstyslavych, the region of Galicia-Volynia (most of present-day western, central and northern Ukraine, plus parts of northeastern Poland and southern Belarus) became one of the most powerful within Kyivan Rus. This enclave's geography differentiated it from the rest of the empire. It was far enough west to avoid conquest by eastern invaders like the Mongols and more likely to fall prey to its Catholic neighbours Hungary and Poland – or, later, Lithuania.

Until 1340 Galicia-Volynia enjoyed independent rule under Roman, his son Danylo, grandson Lev and descendants, who kept the Mongols at bay and helped Lviv and other cities flourish. Political control was wrested from this local dynasty by the Poles and Lithuanians in the 1340s, who split the kingdom between them and used it as a base to expand eastwards. However, its brief period of early self-determination seems to have left Galicia-Volynia with a particularly strong taste for Ukrainian nationalism, still evident today.

Roxelana, the powerful wife of Ottoman emperor Suleyman the Magnificent, is believed to have been a Ukrainian slave, who was sold at Kaffa (today's Feodosiya) and taken to 16th-century Turkey.

Cossacks

Later lionised by nationalist writers such as Taras Shevchenko and Ivan Franko, the Cossacks are central to Ukraine's identity. They arose out of the steppe in the country's sparsely populated mid-south. In the mid-15th century, this area was a kind of no-man's-land separating the Polish-Lithuanian settlements in the northwest from Crimea's Tatars.

However, the steppe offered abundant natural wealth, and poorer individuals in Polish-Lithuanian society began making longer forays south to hunt for food. The area also attracted runaway serfs, criminals, bandits and Orthodox refugees. Along with a few semi-independent Tatar bands, the hard-drinking inhabitants formed self-governing militaristic communities and became known as *kozaky* (Cossacks in English), from a Turkic word meaning 'outlaw, adventurer or free person'. The people elected the ruling chieftain *(hetman)*. The most famous group of Cos-

1554

Some 60 years after Cossacks first appear in the historical record, the fiercest and most famous band of warriors – the Zaporizhzhya Sich – sets up on an island in the Dnipro River.

1569

The Union of Lublin builds on existing links to establish the Polish-Lithuanian Commonwealth. This monarchical democracy includes parts of today's Belarus, Estonia, Latvia, Russia and Ukraine.

1648

Central Ukrainian Cossacks become weary of foreign rule and, under the leadership of Bohdan Khmelnytsky, rebel against the Poles.

1654

Cossacks enter into a military alliance with Russia against Poland. The Cossacks form their own fledgling state – whose initial success is shortlived – called a Hetmanate.

sacks was based below the rapids *(za porohamy)* on the lower Dnipro, in a fortified island community called the Zaporizhya Sich.

Although they were officially under Polish-Lithuanian rule from 1569, and sometimes joined the commonwealth army as mercenaries, the Cossacks were mostly left to their own devices. They waged a number of successful campaigns against the Turks and Tatars, twice assaulting Istanbul (in 1615 and 1620), and sacking the Black Sea cities of Varna (in today's Bulgaria) and Kaffa (modern-day Feodosiya).

As Poland tried to tighten its control in the 17th century, there were Cossack-led uprisings to try to win greater autonomy. In 1654 the Cossacks formed their own so-called Hetmanate to assert the concept of Ukrainian self-determination. While initially successful, ultimately the Cossacks' military uprisings only led to a change of overlord – from Polish to Russian.

Terry Brighton's *Hell Riders: The True Story of the Charge of the Light Brigade* interweaves participants' accounts and factual reports to unravel the Crimean War's greatest blunder.

Russian Control

It's safe to say that without Ukraine and its abundant natural wealth, Russia would never have become such a powerful nation. Ukraine also offered access to the Black Sea, so after a series of wars with the Turks in the 18th century, Russia was keen to expand into southern Ukraine. At the same time, the Western-educated Cossack nobility, now firmly incorporated into the Russian ruling class, was at the forefront of empire building, modernising the state and reforming the Orthodox Church.

Under Russian rule, Ukraine saw an economic boom which made thousands of peasants flee poverty and religious persecution in the Polish-controlled lands. The growth was largely precipitated by the empire expanding into the sparsely populated steppe in the east and south. Ukrainian peasants and Cossacks were the largest group of colonists, followed by Jews, Germans, Greeks and Bulgarians, invited by the crown to cultivate the phenomenally productive land, which soon became known as the 'bread basket of Europe'.

Neal Ascherson's *Black Sea* is a fascinating tale of the civilisations – and barbarians – that jostled for supremacy around this coast, from prehistory's Scythians to multicultural Odesa's 19th-century founders.

This came at a price for the Ukrainian national idea, when in 1775 Catherine the Great ordered to destroy its last stronghold, the Zaporizhska Sich. The newly acquired lands in Ukraine's southeast became the imperial province of Novorossia (New Russia), a term that was recycled in 2014, when Moscow set up puppet statelets in parts of the same territory. The first governor of Novorossia, Catherine's lieutenant (and lover) Grygory Potemkin, embarked on establishing new cities, such as Yekaterinoslav (now Dnipro), Sevastopol and Simferopol, but died before Odesa was completed.

In 1772 powerful Prussia, Austria and Russia decided to carve up Poland. Under the resulting Partitions of Poland (1772–95), most of western Ukraine was handed to Russia, but the far west around Lviv went to

1709

Cossacks seize another chance to throw off the colonial yoke, by joining Sweden in its 'Northern War' with Russia. But the Battle of Poltava doesn't go their way and victorious Tsarist forces execute them.

1772

During the three Partitions of Poland, Russia, Prussia and Habsburg Austria divvy up the weakened Polish-Lithuanian Commonwealth.

1775

As her army moves south, and her lover Grygory Potemkin follows, blithely building film-set villages, Catherine the Great orders the destruction of the Zaporizhzhya Sich.

1783

Russia establishes its sovereignty over Crimea by demolishing mosques. Many Crimean Tatars flee. The Khans' Palace at Bakhchysaray survives because Empress Catherine finds it 'romantic'.

the Habsburg empire. The Ukrainian nationalist movement was born in Kyiv in the 1840s, but when the tsarist authorities there banned the Ukrainian language from official use in 1876, the movement's focus shifted to Austrian-controlled Lviv.

Mikhail Bulgakov's novel *The White Guard* brings to life the confusion reigning in Kyiv during the 1918 Civil War – and better explains the competing factions than most history books do.

Civil War

Following WWI and the collapse of the tsarist monarchy, Ukraine had a shot at independence, but the international community was unsupportive. In Kyiv, the first autonomous Ukrainian National Republic (UNR) was proclaimed in 1918 under president Mykhailo Hrushevsky. Meanwhile, Russian Bolsheviks set up a rival Congress of Soviets in Kharkiv. Civil war broke out, with five different armies – Red (Bolshevik), White, Polish, Ukrainian and Allied – vying for power, while various anarchist bands of Cossacks roamed the land. Author Mikhail Bulgakov estimated that Kyiv changed hands 14 times in 18 months.

EUROPE'S HIDDEN FAMINE

Between 1932 and 1933, some three to five million citizens of Ukraine – 'Europe's breadbasket' – died of starvation while surrounded by fields of wheat and locked government storehouses full of food. How did this happen? Stalin collectivised Soviet farms and ordered the production of unrealistic quotas of grain, which was then confiscated.

Ukraine now officially regards this famine as a genocidal act aimed at destroying Ukrainians as an ethnic group. This radical approach causes a lot of controversy, especially since large swaths of Russia experienced similar man-made famines, orchestrated by the collectivising Bolsheviks. However, historians note, Ukraine was particularly hard hit, and documents released in 2006 suggest that Ukrainians were deliberately targeted in the 'Great Hunger'.

An estimated seven to 10 million people died throughout the USSR. Yet the true scale of the disaster it caused has rarely been appreciated in the West.

As Soviet collectivisation began in the 1930s, combining individual farms into huge state-run communes, wealthier peasants (*kulaks,* or *kurkuli* in Ukrainian) who resisted were deported or starved into submission. By 1932 Communist Party activists were seizing grain and produce from collectives and houses. Watchtowers were erected above fields. Anyone caught stealing was executed or deported. As entire villages starved, people committed suicide and even resorted to cannibalism.

At the time Soviet authorities denied the famine's existence, but damning facts have emerged since Ukrainian independence. In 2003 Kyiv designated the Holodomor (Ukrainian famine) as genocide, and a handful of other governments followed suit. In 2005 president Viktor Yushchenko declared 26 November as official Holodomor Remembrance Day, and called on the international community to recognise the famine as genocide.

1825

Many of the Decembrists behind a doomed St Petersburg coup hail from Ukraine. The most famous of the Decembrist wives, Maria Volkonskaya, also has close links to the country.

1854

France and England have watched Russia's moves south with unease and decide to put a stop to it. The Crimea War sees Sevastopol come under 349 days' siege.

1861

Tsar Aleksander II abolishes serfdom across the Russian Empire. That same year the first railway on Ukrainian soil is opened between Lviv and Przemysl (in today's Poland).

1876

With a new Ukrainian nationalist movement bubbling up since the 1840s, Tsar Aleksander II issues a decree banning the use of the Ukrainian language in public.

Just as any UNR victories in Kyiv proved short-lived, so too did the West Ukrainian National Republic (ZUNR) in Lviv. Proclaimed in October 1918, it was overrun by Polish troops the following summer. Under the 1919 Treaty of Versailles negotiated after WWI and the following Treaty of Riga in 1921, Poland, Romania and Czechoslovakia took portions of western Ukraine, while Soviet forces were given control of the rest. Nationalist leader Semyon Petlyura set up a government in exile, but was assassinated in Paris in 1926.

It's generally agreed that Winston Churchill was saved from execution during the Boer War by Ukrainian writer and journalist Yury Budyak, though neither man mentions the incident in their memoirs.

Soviet Power

Thus handed to the Soviets, Ukraine was at the founding of the USSR in 1922. Behind Russia, it was the second largest and second most powerful republic in the union, with its own autonomous Communist Party, which initially conducted the policy of 'ukrainisation', encouraging the expansion of Ukrainian language into political and cultural spheres. That ended with Stalin starting to stamp out what he called 'bourgeois nationalism' and eventually precipitating a famine. The official Kyiv line nowadays describes this as a deliberate genocidal policy aimed at destroying Ukrainians as an ethnic group, even though similar man-made famines had been orchestrated by the Bolsheviks in Russia. Executions and deportations of intellectuals and political 'dissidents' followed. During the great purges of 1937–39, an estimated one million people in the USSR were executed and a further three to 12 million (the numbers are difficult to quantify) sent to labour camps, many of them from Ukraine.

While the east industrialised, in western Ukraine became controlled by Poland. Liberal nationalists there were losing ground to radicals inspired by Mussolini's fascism and were adopting tactics of terror against the Polish authorities and Ukrainian moderates. Pro-Moscow Communists were also very strong, especially in the Zakarpattia region, then Czechoslovakia.

WWII

Even by the standards of Ukrainian history, WWII was a particularly bloody and fratricidal period. Caught between Soviet Russia, Nazi Germany and an ongoing struggle for independence, some six to eight million Ukrainians, at least 1.6 million of them Jews, were killed. Entire cities were levelled. The Red Army rolled into Polish Ukraine in September 1939, the Germans attacked in 1941, and the Nazis and their Romanian allies occupied most of the country for more than two years. Two million Ukrainians were conscripted into the Soviet army and fought on the Soviet side. However, some nationalists hoped the Nazis would back Ukrainian independence and collaborated with Germany. These are often accused of playing a role in the Holocaust and of massacring ethnic Poles.

1918

In the chaotic aftermath of WWI, Ukrainians try to form an independent republic but are hamstrung by internecine fighting. Fourteen different factions control Kyiv in 18 months.

1917–34

The capital of the Ukrainian SSR is moved to Kharkiv by the Soviets. The city is still often referred to as Ukraine's 'first capital'.

1928

Stalin's first Five Year Plan sees rapid and brutal industrialisation and massive immigration from the countryside into cities across Ukraine. Industrial output subsequently increases fourfold.

1932–33

Millions of Ukrainians die in a famine caused by Stalin's farm collectivisation. Some historians believe that other grain-grabbing, border closing measures deliberately targeted its people.

All of this is a source of much postwar recrimination (and a very ill-informed 'debate' still occasionally flares up today when it suits the political aims of one group or another), but many partisans in the Ukrainian Insurgent Army (UPA) fought both German and Soviet troops in a bid for independence.

In the end the Soviet army prevailed. In 1943 it retook Kharkiv and Kyiv before launching a massive offensive in early 1944 that pushed back German forces. In the process, any hopes for an independent Ukraine were obliterated. Soviet leader Stalin also saw fit to deport thousands of Ukrainians or send them to Siberia for supposed 'disloyalty or collaboration'. This included the entire population of Crimean Tatars in May 1944.

New York Times journalist Walter Duranty is a very controversial Pulitzer Prize winner because of his denial of the Ukrainian famine when reporting from the 1930s USSR.

Towards the war's end, in February 1945, Stalin met with British and US leaders Churchill and Roosevelt at Yalta's Livadia Palace to discuss the administration of postwar Europe. The fact that the Red Army occupied so much of Eastern Europe at the end of WWII helped the USSR hold onto it in the postwar period.

Postwar Period

For most, WWII ended in 1945. However, the Ukrainian Insurgent Army (UPA) continued a guerrilla existence well into the 1950s, taking pot shots at the Soviet authorities, especially in the Carpathian region. A government in exile was led by former partisan Stepan Bandera, until he was assassinated in Munich in 1959.

Ukraine acquired strategic technological and military importance during this era, and at least one Ukrainian rose to become a Soviet leader. Leonid Brezhnev graduated from metallurgy engineer to Communist Party General Secretary from 1964 to 1982. Brezhnev's predecessor, Nikita Khrushchev (Soviet leader from 1953 to 1964) was born just outside Ukraine but lived there from adolescence and styled himself as a Ukrainian. Khrushchev's post-Stalin reformist agenda led him to create the Autonomous Crimean Soviet Socialist Republic in 1954, and transfer legislative control over Crimea to the Ukrainian Soviet Socialist Republic.

Despite that, the process of 'Russification', which involved squeezing Ukrainian language out of the public sphere, rapidly accelerated under Volodymir Shcherbitsky who led the Ukrainian Communist Party from 1972 till 1989.

Nationalism Reappears

The rotten underbelly of Soviet high-tech was cruelly exposed by the nuclear disaster at the power plant Chornobyl on 26 April 1986. Ukrainians weren't just killed and injured by the radioactive material that spewed over their countryside, but also appalled by the way the authorities attempted to cover up the accident. The first Kremlin announcement

1941

During WWII Ukraine becomes a blood-soaked battleground for opposing Nazi, Soviet and nationalist forces and some six million locals perish. The death toll includes almost all of Ukraine's Jews.

1943

The Red Army liberates Kyiv from the Nazis on 6 November. Earlier, retreating Soviets had blown up buildings along the main street of Khreshchatyk; these were replaced post-war with Stalinist structures.

1944

Stalin deports the entire 250,000-strong Crimean Tatar population in just a few days, beginning 18 May. He accuses them of 'Nazi collaboration'. Thousands die during this genocidal journey of 'Sürgün'.

1945

Winston Churchill and an ailing Franklin Roosevelt travel to 'the Riviera of Hades' so Stalin can bully them. At the Yalta Conference, the Soviet leader demands chunks of Eastern Europe.

wasn't made until two days after the event – and only then at the prompting of Swedish authorities, who detected abnormal radiation levels over their own country. However, by then Kyiv was awash with rumours that something was afoot and many promptly decamped to the Carpathians and Crimea as fast as they could.

As more information came to light, discontent over Moscow's handling of the Chornobyl disaster revived nationalist feeling. Ukrainian independence had become a minority interest, mainly confined to the country's west, but slowly, the hardcore in the west started to take the rest of Ukraine with them.

Leading 20th-century artist Joseph Beuys was rescued by Crimean Tatars when he crash landed on the peninsula during WWII, and his oeuvre of sleds, felt and honey recalls their healing methods.

Independent Ukraine

With the nationalist movement snowballing and the USSR disintegrating, many politicians within the Communist Party of Ukraine (CPU) saw the writing on the wall. After the Soviet countercoup in Moscow in August 1991 failed, they decided that if they didn't take their country to independence, the opposition would. So, on 24 August 1991, the Verkhovna Rada (Supreme Council) met, with speaker Stanyslav Hurenko's wonderfully pithy announcement recorded by the *Economist* for posterity: 'Today we will vote for Ukrainian independence, because if we don't we're in the shit.' In December some 84% of the population voted in a referendum to back that pragmatic decision, and former CPU chairman Leonid Kravchuk was elected president.

As the new republic found its feet, there were more than the usual separation traumas from Russia. Disagreements and tensions arose, particularly over ownership of the Black Sea Fleet in Sevastopol. These were only resolved in 1999 by offering Russia a lease until 2017, controversially extended by the new government in 2010 to 2042.

Economic crisis forced Kravchuk's government to resign in September 1992. Leonid Kuchma, a Soviet-styled rocket factory manager, came to power in July 1994 and stayed for 10 years. He abstained from applying shock therapy reforms, like the liberals in charge of the Russian government, which earned him respect from much of the population that lingers today.

During Kuchma's tenure, the economy gradually improved. The hryvnya was introduced and inflation was lowered from a spiralling 10,000% in 1993 to 5.2% in 2004, by which time GDP was growing at a rate of 9%. Kuchma's reign is also remembered for its extreme cronyism. Foreign investors complained that companies being privatised were often sold to Ukrainian ventures with presidential connections, sometimes for well under market value, and international watchdog Transparency International named Ukraine the world's third most corrupt country.

1959

Stepan Bandera, the exiled Ukrainian Insurgent Army (UPA) leader, is killed in Munich by the KGB. Ukrainian partisans had continued ambushing Soviet police until the mid-1950s.

1986

Reactor No 4 at the Chornobyl nuclear power plant explodes, after a failed safety test. More than 90 Hiroshimas are spewed out over the Ukrainian and Belarusian countryside.

1991

President Gorbachev is held prisoner at his country retreat in Crimea while a coup led by hardliners takes place in Moscow.

1991

As the Soviet Union falters, Ukraine's parliament votes for independence. Some 90% of the population figures that's about right and backs the decision in a referendum.

The Orange Revolution

Former central banker Viktor Yushchenko had proved too reformist and pro-European for his masters when he was Leonid Kuchma's prime minister from 1998 to 2001. However, in 2004, as Kuchma prepared to stand down, Yushchenko re-emerged as a strong presidential contender.

Kuchma's anointed successor, the Kremlin-friendly Viktor Yanukovych, had expected an easy victory but the popularity of Yushchenko's Nasha Ukraina (Our Ukraine) party looked threatening. During an increasingly bitter campaign, and seven weeks before the scheduled 31 October election, Yushchenko underwent a remarkable physical transformation – disfiguration that Austrian doctors later confirmed was the result of dioxin poisoning.

The Battle for Chernobyl is an in-depth documentary that tells the story of the world's worst nuclear accident and the truth about the clear up.

After an inconclusive first round, a second vote was held on 21 November. A day later amid widespread claims of vote rigging by electoral observers, Yanukovych was declared winner.

Over the next few days and weeks Yushchenko supporters staged a show of people power unlike any Ukraine had ever seen. Despite freezing temperatures they took to the streets, brandishing banners and clothes in the opposition's trademark orange. They assembled to listen to Yushchenko and his powerful political ally Yulia Tymoshenko at mass rallies in Kyiv's maydan Nezalezhnosti (Independence Sq). They surrounded parliament and established a demonstrators' tent city along Kyiv's main Khreshchatyk boulevard to keep up pressure on the authorities.

The Yanukovych camp refused to respond to a parliamentary vote of no confidence in the election result and his eastern Ukrainian supporters threatened to secede if Yushchenko was declared president. Despite this, on 3 December the Supreme Court annulled the first election result, and the way was paved for a second poll on 26 December, which Yushchenko won. The tent city was dismantled just in time for Yushchenko's swearing in on 3 January 2005.

The Orange Glow Fades

Alas, the course of true reform never did run smoothly in Ukraine – less than a year after they had stood shoulder to shoulder on the Maidan, the Orange Revolution's heroes had fallen out.

Anyone able to follow the ins and outs of Ukraine's political scene after the Orange Revolution probably should have got out more. In the late noughties, the blonde-braided Yulia Tymoshenko, a weak president Yushchenko and a resurgent Viktor Yanukovych engaged in an absurd political soap opera featuring snap elections, drawn-out coalition deals, fisticuffs in parliament and musical chairs in the prime minister's office.

1994

Former rocket scientist Leonid Kuchma becomes president. With inflation running at 10,000%, he moves to reform the economy, but his popularity wanes when he's implicated in a series of corruption scandals.

2000

After opposition journalist Georgiy Gongadze is murdered, a recording emerges of President Kuchma asking his staff to 'deal with' the journalist. Kuchma later claims the tape has been selectively edited.

2004

Thousands take to the freezing streets to protest that vote rigging has robbed Viktor Yushchenko of the presidency. The 'Orange Revolution' leads to a fairer second election, which Yushchenko wins.

2006

Russia cuts off gas supplies on 1 January. Kyiv suspects punishment for becoming more pro-European. Moscow says it just wants a fair price – nearly five times the existing level.

Promises of stamping out corruption were never delivered – cronyism flourished, only with new actors.

Russia turned off the gas at opportune moments and the West got bored and moved on. The upshot was disillusionment with the Orange Revolution and Viktor Yanukovych's victory in the April 2010 presidential elections.

Yanukovych & the Maidan

Many feared that upon coming to power Yanukovych and his oligarch-backed, east-based Party of the Regions – allegedly behind the electoral fraud that sparked the Orange Revolution – would begin to gnaw away at democracy, press freedom and human rights. The new president confirmed everyone's misgivings in 2011 when Yulia Tymoshenko was put on trial for abuse of office (basically for signing a 2009 gas deal with Russia that annoyed a few wealthy regime string pullers). This was seen in the West and by most commentators as nothing short of a political show trial and a successful attempt by the new regime to rid itself of any meaningful opposition. Intimidation of critical journalists, provocative language laws sceptically brought to parliament just two days after the Euro 2012 final (ensuring the country didn't stay united for too long), jailing of other members of the previous government, inaction on corruption and a whole list of controversial laws and provocative campaigns followed.

A highly individual, entertaining and quite moving short photo essay, www.theorangerevolution.com looks back at the false dawn of 2004.

In late 2013, president Yanukovych's refusal to sign an Association Agreement with the European Union (EU) led to huge protests in Kyiv and Lviv, which became known as the Maidan. In the course of winter, the protests grew into urban warfare between riot police and hired thugs on the government side and a ragtag urban guerrilla army on the other. More than a hundred people died in clashes which eventually forced president Yanukovych to flee. Tymoshenko's allies Oleksandr Turchynov and Arseniy Yatsenyuk were appointed acting president and prime minister respectively.

Annexation of Crimea

Before Ukraine could take a breath, Russian special troops aided by local riot policemen started taking over government buildings and military facilities in Crimea. Locals, the majority of whom were ethnic Russians, either hailed the developments or remained apathetic. Only Crimean Tatars and a handful of Ukrainian activists attempted to voice their disagreement.

In the blink of an eye, Crimea had a new, Russia-backed government, which conducted a hastily organised 'referendum' on 16 March 2014. The new leaders claimed that 97% of the participants voted for the region to

2007

Some 100 people die in the worst mining accident in Ukraine's history. The disaster at Zasyadko, eastern Donetsk, highlights safety concerns about all of the country's ageing coalmines.

2007

The Ukraine-Poland bid to host the Euro 2012 football (soccer) championships is successful. Immediately, doubts about Ukraine's ability to hold the event are voiced.

2009

Russia once again turns off the gas on 1 January as Moscow claims Kyiv has failed to pay its bills. This time the EU steps in to resolve the dispute.

2010

Despite allegations of a fraudulent election in 2004, Viktor Yanukovych becomes president in a closely fought February poll. Many Ukrainians fear press freedom and democracy will suffer under his rule.

join Russia. A few days later Moscow formally incorporated Crimea into the Russian Federation. This largely peaceful takeover drew comparisons with Hitler's annexation of the Sudetenlands in 1938.

War in the East

Towards the end of March 2014, groups of militants and pro-Russian activists started attacking government buildings in various places across Ukraine's predominantly Russian-speaking southeast. In most places – most notably in Kharkiv – the government, aided by powerful members of business elites and nationalist paramilitaries, managed to quell the unrest. But events took a particularly nasty turn in the Donbas region, where a heavily armed band led by Russian officer Igor Girkin seized the town of Slovyansk, which became the capital of an armed rebellion that instantly spread in much of the Donetsk and Luhansk regions. The rebels proclaimed 'people's republics' in these regions, which became a magnet for Ukrainian anti-Maidan paramilitaries and Russian irrendentists.

The 'Ukrainian Katyn' (mass grave) was revealed globally in 2007, when authorities reburied 2000 victims of the Soviet Secret Police (NKVD). The deaths at Bykovyna, near Kyiv, occurred in the 1930s and '40s.

In response, the Kyiv government moved troops into the region, launching what it called an antiterrorist operation that soon degraded into a full-on war.

In May 2014, the confectionery magnate and moderately pro-Maidan politician Petro Poroshenko was elected Ukrainian president. He campaigned on the promise of ending the conflict with Russia – Moscow had other plans.

In summer, the government efforts to revitalise the badly underfunded and demoralised army bore fruit. It started advancing on the rebels and seized Slovyansk. In July, a rocket widely believed to have been shot from a rebel position destroyed a Malaysian airliner, killing all passengers on board. The tragedy alerted Western governments to the situation in Ukraine and encouraged them to increase pressure on Russia.

But Moscow responded by beefing up the rebel force with modern hardware and sending whole units of professional soldiers (barely disguised as volunteers), thus inflicting a series of humiliating defeats on the Ukrainian army and forcing Ukraine to engage in peace talks that became known as the Minsk process.

The armistice agreements achieved in Minsk never succeeded in stopping the hostilities, but they turned the conflict into a low-intensity trench warfare, which still claims lives of both soldiers and civilians. More than 10,000 people died in the war, with no end on the horizon at the time of writing.

2011

Opposition leader Yulia Tymoshenko is jailed for abuse of office while prime minister. Many see this as a political trial and a sign that president Yanukovych is pushing the country towards dictatorship.

2012

In partnership with Poland, Ukraine hosts the Euro 2012 Cup, the largest sporting event the country has ever witnessed. However, matches are boycotted by EU governments over the Tymoshenko affair.

2013

Protests erupt when president Yanukovych refuses to sign an Association Agreement with the EU. Kyiv's Maidan protests endure brutal police attacks and sub-zero temperatures.

2014

Yanukovych is deposed after a fierce gun battle in the centre of Kyiv that killed over 100 people. Russia annexes Crimea and triggers a conflict in Donbas. Petro Poroshenko gets elected as Ukraine's new president.

The People

From the Tatars of Crimea to the miners of the Donbas to the hipsters of Lviv, Ukraine is arguably Eastern Europe's most diverse country. Poverty, heartfelt hospitality and a love of nature are the few things they share, but little else really unites this country of 42 million people. Only sport sees the nation genuinely come together, as it did whenever Klytschko pulled on his boxing gloves, and still does when the national football team takes to the pitch.

The National Psyche

Having endured centuries of different foreign rulers, Ukrainians are a long-suffering people. They're nothing if not survivors (historically they've had to be), but after suffering a kind of identity theft during centuries of Russian rule in particular, this ancient nation that 'suddenly' emerged almost three decades ago is well on the road to forging a new personality. The recent war with Russia has focused minds even more on Ukrainian identity – the debate is still raging as to what exactly it means to be a Ukrainian.

Traditionally, many patriots would unite behind a vague sense of free-spirited Cossack culture and the national poet Taras Shevchenko. This is a religious society, a superstitious society and one in which traditional gender roles, strong family and community ties still bind. It's a culture where people are friendly and sometimes more generous than they can really afford to be. Paradoxically, it's also one in which remnants of the Soviet mentality – of unofficial unhelpfulness and fear of saying too much – remain. As in Russia, many people lead a kind of double life – snarling, elbowing *homo sovieticus* outside the house, but generous, kind and hospitable Europeans around their kitchen tables. This is particularly true in the east and south, less so in Ukraine's west.

Ukraine is also a patchwork nation – city dwellers and peasants, east and west, young and old, Russian-speaking and Ukrainian-speaking, Hutsul and Tatar have very different attitudes. Broadly speaking, Russian-speaking easterners still hark back to the days of the Soviet Union, while Ukrainian-speaking westerners gaze hopefully towards a future in Europe. But for every rule, there's an exception too.

In *The Ukrainians: Unexpected Nation*, academic Andrew Wilson examines Ukraine's founding myths, how its history and culture have shaped its national identity and what it all means for this ancient but young nation.

Lifestyle

Just as there is no one 'typical' Ukrainian, so there is no single average lifestyle. This is still a relatively poor, second-world country, and the 2008 financial crisis and Donbas war have only made things more difficult. Even in relatively prosperous Kyiv, the average wage is only around 7000uah (€230) a month, outside the capital around 5000uah (€160). Pensions can be as little as 1000uah (€30) and with prices of some goods nearing European levels, life is hard for many, especially the old.

Throughout Ukraine's troubled independence, most middle-class Ukrainians have had ways of getting by, holding down several jobs, pursuing a number of money-making schemes and looking out for each other. Outside big cities, it's also been common for people to grow food in

Buying produce such as milk, honey and vegetables from old ladies on the street means you are contributing directly to the local economy, and not funding a minigarch supermarket-owner's lifestyle in the Bahamas.

their back garden and for extended families to share domestic duties. *Baba* (grandma) is frequently a respected household member, very often in charge of the kids while parents go off to work.

Old Soviet apartments are quite compact and old-fashioned, but most have undergone some *remont* (refurbishment) since 1991. Despite low earnings, Ukrainians always seem to have a new washing machine and the latest flat-screen TV – the average family enjoys few other luxuries. Those with a little extra cash have tentatively started taking foreign holidays, no longer needing a visa to travel to Greece or Bulgaria, though cheaper Turkey and Egypt remain the favourites.

There are an estimated 1.4 million internally displaced people in Ukraine, around 60,000 from Crimea, the rest from the Donbas.

Amid the old housing stock and creaking public transport infrastructure, young Ukrainians are avid users of new technology. A smartphone is a must and social media is as popular as it is in the West. Wi-fi is ubiquitous – even in the most rundown bus station you might catch an open signal.

Mind the Gap

Even after three decades of stop-start 'reforms', there's still a mammoth gap between average Ukrainians and the super-rich elite. It's the country's minigarchs (semirich businesspeople), corrupt officials and 'new Ukrainian' businesspeople you see driving the luxury cars and shopping in Kyiv's designer boutiques (oligarchs do their shopping in London and Paris).

At the lower end of the scale are the elderly and other pensioners who somehow survive despite minute pensions and rising prices. Due to losses in WWII, industrial accidents, deadly roads, vodka and general bad health among males, many of the elderly are women. They can often be seen selling their surplus home-grown produce on the street.

The challenge for post-Maidan is to narrow this gap and make Ukrainian society a fairer deal for all – some believe Maidan mark III is an inevitability otherwise. A little progress has been made, but the perception of most is that not much has really changed since the 2014 revolution.

Population

As a crossroads between Europe and Central Asia, Ukraine has been settled by numerous ethnic groups throughout history and has a fascinating underlying mix. However, most people still describe themselves as Ukrainians and, hence, of Slavic origin. However, this is not reflected in the language people speak; many claiming to be Ukrainian use Russian as their first language. In 1970s and '80s USSR, many Ukrainian-speaking parents were forced to send their children to Russian schools, hence the high numbers of Russian speakers. But since the Russian invasion, the trend has begun to head the other way – all schools teach in Ukrainian and hundreds of thousands of previously Russian-speaking Ukrainians are now rediscovering the language of their early childhood, making sure their offspring speak the national language. In rural central Ukraine, some people speak *Surzhyk,* a clumsy, uneducated-sounding sludge of both languages mixed together. Мова (language) is still one of the hottest topics in Ukraine and will remain so for some time to come.

Former Israeli prime minister Golda Meir and film star Milla Jovovich were both born in Kyiv, Bolshevik Leon Trotsky hailed from outside Odesa, and both Dustin Hoffman and Sylvester Stallone have Ukrainian roots.

Minorities

Ukraine's ethnic minority groups include, in order of size, Belarusians, Moldovans, Tatars, Bulgarians, Hungarians, Romanians, Poles and Jews. Ukraine has around a quarter of a million Crimean Tatars, most of whom have remained in Crimea, despite the Russian occupation. No one measures the size of western Ukrainian Hutsul communities, which in any case are seamlessly integrated into the wider community.

Dying Nation

Since independence, Ukraine's population has fallen dramatically. The number of citizens plummeted from 52.2 million in 1993 to around 42.5 million in 2016, as birth rates and life expectancy dropped concomitantly. Also, due to the bureaucratic system of registering citizens at a specific address, population figures include a huge chunk of the nation that has emigrated in search of a better life, but still officially resides in Ukraine on paper for legal reasons. This means the actual population figure may be as low as 32 million.

A large Ukrainian diaspora of around 2.5 million people exists; many live in North America, particularly Canada.

War & Occupation

As you may have gathered, Ukraine is fighting a war with Russia in parts of the eastern provinces of Donetsk and Luhansk. This has had a profound effect on Ukrainian society with almost 3000 soldiers killed, millions displaced and many young men either bravely volunteering for the front or desperately trying to dodge the draft. Those trapped in the so-called People's Republics of Donetsk and Luhansk are subject to a barrage of anti-Ukrainian propaganda and a return to purely Soviet practices, which will be difficult to deal with if and when these areas are liberated.

Only around 20 countries in the world have a lower birth rate than Ukraine, with 2016 estimates putting the average number of children born per 1000 people at just 10.5.

Crimea

Crimea is under Russian occupation, but it has never seen armed conflict like the Donbas. Here the situation is much better than in Ukraine's east with the population enjoying wage and pension rises, but also price hikes and instability around infrastructure, banking and basics such as food, electricity and water. The Crimean Tatars – not exactly best of chums with Moscow after Stalin's 1944 deportations – have suffered most with arrests, kidnappings, disappearances and general harrassment the norm. Inside Ukraine, the small Tatar minority is striving to keep its traditions and language alive.

Religion

As the sheer number of churches in Ukraine attests, religion in this country is pivotal. It has provided comfort during many hard times and even shaped Ukrainian identity; by accepting Orthodox Christianity in AD 989, Volodymyr the Great cast Kyivan Rus as a European, rather than Islamic Asian, state. According to 2016 figures, some 91% of people in western Ukraine identify as adhering to one religion or another, a very high number for Europe. This drops to 55% in the east.

TEMPLE DOS AND DON'TS

Religious Ukrainians are a pretty tolerant lot, but women should cover their heads when entering Orthodox churches. There's an even stricter dress code (no above-knee skirts for women and no hats for men) when visiting particularly holy sites such as the Kyevo-Pecherska Lavra and Pochayiv Monastery. Taking photos during a service, touching the icons and affectionate hand-holding may incur the wrath of the church's elderly custodians.

Feel free to buy a candle and do as the Ukrainians do – light it, place it in a holder in front of an icon and make a wish. In Catholic churches, taking a seat in a pew after a long day's sightseeing is perfectly acceptable. In Orthodox churches there are no seats – congregations stand.

Ukraine's Many Churches

Today the country's sizeable Christian population is confusingly splintered into three Orthodox churches and one major form of Catholicism. Some 65% of Ukrainians belong to one of the Orthodox congregations.

According to local superstition, women should never sit down on steps, walls or anything concrete, lest their ovaries freeze and they can't bear children.

In the 17th century, when Ukraine came under Russian rule, so did its Orthodox Church. Even now, almost three decades after independence, the largest Orthodox congregation in the country belongs to the Ukrainian Orthodox Church, the former Ukrainian section of the Russian Orthodox Church that still pays allegiance to the Moscow Patriarch. There are also two smaller, breakaway Orthodox churches, which are both more 'Ukrainian' in nature. Another Ukrainian Orthodox Church was formed in 1992 after independence to pay allegiance to a local Kyiv Patriarch. Meanwhile, the Ukrainian Autocephalous Orthodox Church, formed during the 19th century in western Ukraine and suppressed by the Soviets, has bounced back since independence.

To complicate matters, another five to six million Ukrainians follow another brand of Christianity entirely. In 1596 the Union of Brest established the Uniate Church (often called the Greek Catholic Church). Mixing Orthodox Christian practices with allegiance to the Pope, this essentially Catholic church was, and is, popular in the western part of the country once under Polish and Austrian rule.

Religious Rivalry

The two main Orthodox churches – Moscow Patriarchate and Kyiv Patriarchate – have had territorial disputes in the past. The Ukrainian government's 1995 refusal to allow Kyiv Patriarch Volodymyr Romanyuk to be buried inside Kyiv's St Sophia's Cathedral, for fear of reprisals from Moscow, is a good example. The recent conflicts and invasions have only made things worse, though all-out war between the two has yet to break out. Naturally the Moscow-backed church has lost many adherents in recent years as it is closely aligned with the Russian regime. All other denominations welcome stronger Western ties.

Other Faiths

Minority faiths include Roman Catholicism, Judaism and, among Crimean Tatars, Sunni Islam. Ukraine's religious freedom means Evangelical, Buddhist, Jehovah's Witness and neopagan communities have also emerged since independence from the atheist USSR. Many young people in big cities are turning away from religion altogether.

Sport

Every Ukrainian will tell you his or her country is sports mad, but as with most ex-USSR countries, you'll hardly ever see anyone actually engaging in sporting activities, especially outside the big cities.

Football

Football is Ukraine's national sport and has few real rivals among sports fans. Dynamo Kyiv is no longer the only well-known Ukrainian team, with the rather more successful Shakhtar Donetsk now regularly appearing in European competitions (Shakhtar won the UEFA Cup in 2009 – it is currrently forced to host matches in Odesa due to the war). Both play in the Ukrainian Premier League along with 10 other clubs. The most famous player in the postindependence era is Andriy Shevchenko who netted goals for the likes of Chelsea and AC Milan plus the national team before becoming the national coach in 2016.

In 2012 Ukraine successfully cohosted the Euro 2012 football championships with Poland. The final between Spain and Italy was played at Kyiv's Olympic Stadium and watched by over 63,000 spectators.

Other Sports

Ukraine is known in the international boxing world due to the brothers Vitaly and Volodymyr Klytschko. After netting $80 million in the ring, Vitaly went into politics and is now mayor of Kyiv. Volodymyr only retired from the sport in 2017 at the age of 41.

Tennis has also gained huge popularity since independence, and Ukraine now has two men and two women in the Association of Tennis Professionals (ATP) and Women's Tennis Association (WTP) top 100 rankings. The top Ukrainian female player is Elina Svitolina, ranked number 4 in the world at the time of writing.

Ukraine also enjoys ice hockey (though the national team brings little joy) and regularly wins medals in gymnastics, athletics and the biathlon. Though some may not regard it as a sport, a big name in the chess world is Lviv-born Kateryna Lagno, the youngest ever female grandmaster.

Some Crimean Tatars have moved to other parts of Ukraine to escape the Russian occupation, bringing their delicious oriental cuisine with them.

Women in Ukraine

Cynically speaking, women have been one of independent Ukraine's biggest tourist attractions. Combine their legendary beauty, devotion to personal grooming and sometimes outrageous, sexualised fashion sense with a relatively impoverished society and you were always going to have fertile ground for online 'dating agencies', 'marriage agencies' and straight-out sex tourism. Sex trafficking of Ukrainian women remains a serious problem, too.

Gender Roles & Discrimination

Traditional gender roles are quite entrenched in Ukraine's paternalistic society. Even the country's many young career women unashamedly place much greater emphasis on their looks than their Western counterparts would. Ukrainian women face job discrimination, with age, appearance and family circumstances often excluding them from roles they are professionally qualified for.

A MIDSUMMER NIGHT'S DREAM

It involves fire, water, dancing, fortune-telling and strong overtones of sex. No wonder the Soviets tried to quash the festival of Ivan Kupala, a pagan midsummer celebration Indeed, leaders since the Middle Ages – including Cossack *hetmans* (chieftains) – have tried to outlaw it, but all without success. The festival is still marked across Ukraine and beyond.

To ancient pre-Christians, Kupala was the god of love and fertility, and young people would choose a marriage partner on this eve. Today's rituals vary, but typically begin with folk singing and a maypole-style dance performed by young women wearing white gowns and flower wreaths in their hair. After this, the women float their wreaths (symbolising virginity) down the requisite nearby river or other body of water. A wreath that sinks indicates bad fortune in love for its owner.

Later a bonfire is lit, around which young couples dance. Couples will also jump over small fires, holding hands, to test whether – if they maintain their grip – their love will last.

After Kyivan Rus adopted Christianity, the festival became mixed up with the birthday of John the Baptist. This not only means the festival has largely been shifted from the summer solstice on 22 June to 7 July, it sometimes means people walk in the fire or jump in the river as a 'cleansing' act. A good spot to join Kupala celebrations is Pyrohovo in Kyiv, or head to the countryside for more traditional rituals.

Sextremism: The Femen Phenomenon

Founded in 2008 in Kyiv by former economist Anna Hutsol and a group of student activists, the Femen movement is now known by many as Ukraine's most controversial political export. This group of radical feminists engages in topless protests, an approach that certainly caused much tabloid sensation on the streets of Kyiv in the late noughties and early teenies. Early targets for their naked wrath included Euro 2012, the Orthodox Church, Party of the Regions MPs, prostitution, people trafficking and sex tourists.

There are over 3½ million more women in Ukraine than there are men, despite slightly more boys being born on average than girls.

In 2012 Femen went international, opening loosely affiliated branches in several countries and a European headquarters in Paris (established by group member Inna Shevchenko, who was forced to seek asylum in France after death threats in Kyiv). The group stripped off at Davos, protested against the imprisonment of Pussy Riot, got very close to President Putin, went topless against Belarus president Lukashenko (which nearly ended very badly for some members of the group) and prepared a bare-breasted welcome at Boryspil International Airport for Russian Patriarch Kirill. Since the Maidan revolution some members have returned to Ukraine but the movement has gone truly global, with nude attacks on everything from European football matches to the Turkish regime. Femen members are often put on trial and ocassionally imprisoned for their activities, especially in more conservative countries.

For more information on the group's activities and fate of its members visit www.femen.org. An award-winning documentary called *Ukraine is not a Brothel,* by Australian filmmaker Kitty Green, was shown at the Venice International Film Festival in 2013.

The Ukrainian Table

Ukrainians admit theirs is a cuisine of comfort – full of hearty, mild dishes designed for fierce winters – rather than one of gastronomic zing. And yet, while it has suffered from negative stereotypes of Soviet-style cabbage slop and pernicious pickles, Ukrainian cooking is vastly improved these days. In recent years chefs have rediscovered the wholesome appeal of the national cuisine, and plenty of Ukrainian restaurants now offer the chance to sample homestyle cooking that may surprise many with its strong flavours.

Staples & Specialities

Many of the country's specialities originated as down-to-earth peasant dishes based on grains and staple vegetables like potatoes, cabbage, beets or mushrooms, seasoned with garlic and dill.

Borshch Locals would have you know that *borshch* (борщ) is Ukrainian – not Russian, not Polish, but Ukrainian – and there's nothing better than a steaming bowlful in winter. A typical version of the national soup is made with beetroot, pork fat and herbs, but there's also an aromatic 'green' variety, based on sorrel. There sometimes seem to be as many recipes for *borshch* as there are Ukrainian cooks, but all add a dollop of soured cream before serving.

Bread Dark and white varieties of *khlib* (хліб) are available every day, including the white *pampushky* (soft rolls rubbed with garlic and oil and then fried) occasionally served with *borshch*. Bread is often used in religious ceremonies and on special occasions. Visitors are traditionally greeted with bread and salt.

Cabbage Rolls *Holubtsy* (голубці) are cabbage rolls stuffed with seasoned rice and meat and stewed in a tomato and soured cream sauce.

Kasha Pretty much any grain is called *kasha* (каша) in Ukrainian, and while the word might be used to describe what Westerners would call porridge, more commonly it turns out to be buckwheat. The latter appears as a side dish, as stuffing or as an unusual but filling breakfast gruel.

Pancakes Two types of pancake might land on your plate. *Deruny* (деруни) are potato pancakes, and are served with soured cream and vegetables or meat. *Mlyntsy* (млинці) are thicker and smaller, like Russian *blyny*.

Varenyky Similar to Polish *pierogi*, *varenyky* (вареники) are to Ukraine what dim sum is to China and filled pasta is to Italy. These small half-moon-shaped dumplings have more than 50 different traditional vegetarian and meat fillings. They're usually served with yes, you guessed it, soured cream.

You can learn how to cook everything from different types of *borshch* to delicious *medovyky* (honey cakes) with *Best of Ukrainian Cuisine* (1998) by Bohdan Zahny.

Okroshka is a kind of Slavic gazpacho. Eaten cold in summer, it's a thick concoction of cucumbers, spring onions, boiled eggs, meat and herbs, diluted with *kvas* (ginger beer).

Drinks

At markets in summer, you might see small kiosks selling *kvas* (квас), a gingery, beerlike soft drink, which is made from sugar and old black bread and is mildly alcoholic. *Kvas* is proffered in plastic beakers, the communal mug on a chain having mostly disappeared. In winter you can buy *kvas* in plastic bottles at the supermarket, but it's over-carbonated and lacks that zingy 'live' taste.

The situation with Ukrainian wine is not very rosé, with production still suffering after Gorbachev's 'dry law' saw many vines pulled up in the late 1980s. Crimea still produces wines, but most of them are sugary dessert wines akin to Madeira or sherry, and are now difficult to get due to the ban on produce from the occupied peninsula. Wines are also produced in the Transcarpathian region, but sadly, the best wines available in Ukraine still come from neighbouring Moldova or the EU.

Visit www.ukrainiansoulfood.ca for Raisa Marika Stohyn's lifetime collection of recipes and stories from the old country.

Surveys show that Ukrainians are off their vodka, though you wouldn't think so walking around your average supermarket. Though it's cheap, getting smashed on vodka is definitely out of fashion, with most young people turning to beer for their ethanol consumption.

Ukraine produces some very quaffable beers, most more than able to compete with international brands. The beer market is booming and one new arrival on the scene is craft beer, which you will find across the land in almost every town. Conventional breweries produce various light, dark, unfiltered and flavoured lagers; there are at least 40 different domestic varieties, the leading brands being Chernihivske, Lvivske and Obolon. Those lagers with German-sounding names you've never heard are definitely brewed in Ukraine, as are almost all Czech beer brands.

The former Soviet Union is not a place many associate with good coffee, but Ukraine is the shining exception. Excellent lattes, cappucinos and espressos are now the norm, especially in Lviv which has a whole central European coffee and cafe culture of its own.

Celebrations

Ukrainian food truly comes into its own during Christmas, Easter and wedding celebrations. Marta Pisetska Farley's *Festive Ukrainian Cooking* (1990) has the low-down.

At Easter, certain foods are taken to church in a covered basket to be blessed. These usually include hard-boiled eggs, baked cheese and Easter breads like round *paska* (паска; decorated with crosses) or tall, cylindrical *babka* (бабка; a sweet egg bread).

Even if you are a fan of soured cream, there's simply too much of the stuff on dishes for most. 'Bez smetany, bud laska' (no soured cream for me, please) is a very useful phrase to know.

On their wedding day, the bride and groom break a spectacular round bread called a *korovay* (Коровай) – whoever gets the bigger half will be the dominant partner in the marriage.

Where to Eat & Drink

Restaurant (ресторан) and cafe (кафе) sound similar in English and Ukrainian. Some Ukrainian restaurants specialise in a particular dish, such as a *varenychna* (варенична), which serves only *varenyky* (stuffed dumplings). A *stolova* (столова) is a Russian-style self-service canteen. Theme restaurants aren't as popular as they once were.

When eating out, be aware that prices for many meat and fish dishes are listed on the menu by weight. For example, the *shashlyk* (shish ke-

FAT OF THE LAND

Eating raw pig fat (*salo* in Ukrainian; сало in Russian) is a centuries-old tradition that runs deep and thick, quite literally, in the Ukrainian blood. Songs and poems are even dedicated to this product, which long provided a cheaper and more preservable alternative to meat. Some Ukrainian doctors even recommend 30g each morning for a long and healthy life! You'll find it on most menus, flavoured with garlic and salt and sometimes smoked. Occasionally you'll even alight on the 'Ukrainian Snickers bar' – *salo* in chocolate.

bab) that looks good value at 30uah might actually be 30uah per 100g, so read the menu carefully.

Tipping is virtually unheard of except in big-city places where waiters have become used to foreigners adding something to the bill. Out in rural areas a tip may even be returned – the staff believing you've overpaid by accident.

Once and for all – chicken Kiev is not from Kyiv! It originated in Paris and was brought to 19th-century Russia by aristocrats obsessed with Gallic cuisine.

Quick Eats

Food kiosks selling drinks and snacks sprout up at markets and around train, metro and bus stations. These sell pastries or warm snacks, including hamburgers and hot dogs as well as Soviet favourites such as *shashlyky* (шашлик) and *perepichky* (перепічки, fairground-style frankfurters deep-fried in dough) and *chebureky* (чебуреки, fried meat turnovers). The bottles on the shelves range from water and soft drinks to beer, which is also considered a soft drink by most Ukrainians but is now illegal to drink in most public places.

If you're self-catering, head to the local *rynok* (market), which always provides a colourful experience. Even small towns in Ukraine now have well-stocked, Western-style supermarkets.

Vegetarians & Vegans

While most Ukrainians are carnivores by nature, vegetarians won't find eating out too trying, especially in the larger cities where pizza joints and international restaurants abound. Even Ukrainian cuisine can be meat-free if you stick to a fairly bland diet of *deruny* (potato pancakes) or potato-and-mushroom *varenyky*. However, it's always a good idea to specify that you want a meat-free salad and *borshch* is, sadly, best avoided if you're strict about your diet. Even 'vegetarian' versions are often made using beef stock.

The website www.foodukraine.com is an excellent database of popular Ukrainian recipes.

Vegans are much worse off. In a land obsessed with *smetana* (soured cream), dining out will prove a trial. While most Ukrainians have heard of vegetarianism, veganism is an unknown concept.

Art & Architecture

Not many people would associate Ukraine with the arts and architecture, but as anyone who's been to the country will tell you, Ukrainian museums and galleries showcase exquisite local art and traditional crafts, much of it with a folksy rural theme, and its architecture is not all about USSR-era concrete blocks and Stalinist pomp.

Some of Kyiv's most impressive Soviet architecture can be found underground in the shape of its ornate metro stations.

Painting & Sculpture

Ukraine's galleries are packed with an eclectic mix of local and foreign art, though few Ukrainian artists have ever made a name for themselves outside the country. Where Ukraine is strong is in folk art – glass painting and egg decoration from the Carpathians and beyond are two obvious examples. Icon art is another genre where local painters once excelled.

Icons

Icons are small holy images painted on a lime-wood panel with a mix of tempera, egg yolk and hot wax. Brought to Ukraine from Constantinople by Volodymyr the Great in the 10th century and remaining the key religious art until the 17th century, icons were attributed with healing and spiritual powers. Icon painters – mostly monks – rarely signed works, and depicted only Christ, the Virgin, angels and saints. Many of the oldest examples can be seen in museums, the best being Lviv's National Museum and Lutsk's Museum of the Volyn Icon.

Pysanky

Pysanky (painted Easter eggs) is an ancient Slavic art found across Eastern Europe. A traditional way of decorating eggs sees designs drawn in wax on the eggshell (hollowed out beforehand), which is then dyed one colour; the process is continually repeated until a complex pattern is built up. Other methods include painting and adorning the shell with various other materials. Different symbols represent varying natural forces – a circle with a dot in the middle is the sun and so on – but each Ukrainian region has its own traditions. The place to go to view them is Kolomyya's Pysanky Museum.

Ukraine's most celebrated sculptor is Oleksandr Arkhipenko (1887–1964), who was born in Kyiv but spent most of his life abroad. His works are scattered across many galleries, mostly in the US.

Romanticism

The first break from religious art occurred during the Cossack Hetmanate. A secular, romantic trend of folk painting slowly developed, common themes being the Kozak Mamay (a Cossack playing the lute-like *bandura* or *kobza*), country life and folk traditions. Few of these paintings gained widespread recognition, but Ukrainian-born Ilya Repin gained international fame. His famous *Zaporizhsky Cossacks Writing a Letter to the Turkish Sultan* and other Romantic paintings are found in the Kharkiv Art Museum (p213).

Ivan Ayvazovsky is regarded as one of the world's best seascape painters. Ethnically Armenian, he was born and lived in Feodosiya, Crimea, where hundreds of his works populate the Ayvazovsky Gallery.

Soviet Era & Beyond

Socialist realism propagated Soviet ideals – the industrialised peasant, the muscular worker and the heroic soldier. Take, as an example, the sculptural reliefs near Kyiv's Great Patriotic War Museum (p57). Ukrainian nationalism asserted itself through the age-old tradition of folk art, leading the Soviet authorities to take a dim view of folk embroidery.

After independence, Ukrainian art enjoyed a reawakening, with art schools in Kyiv producing new stars, like painter Maxim Mamsikov (b 1968), sculptor Zhana Khadyrova (b 1981) and multimedia artist Kyril Protsenko (b 1967). One of the most important artists to emerge at this time was the Ukrainian photographer Boris Mikhailov (b 1938).

Since 2006, art lovers in Kyiv have been making a beeline to the PinchukArtCentre (p47). This gallery not only has major international exhibitions and pieces by the likes of Damien Hirst, Anthony Gormley and Andreas Gursky, it's also a good place to see works by leading local artists.

An artistic phenomenon since the Maidan revolution has been the appearance of giant murals painted on the sides of multi-storey buildings. Some of these are so impressive that they have become tourist attractions. Kyiv's JC Travel (p64) can show you the best examples.

Polish noble Wladyslaw Horodecki is responsible for some of Kyiv's most striking early-20th-century buildings including the House of the Chimeras, and the Karaite Kenesa.

Architecture

Church design has wrought a vast influence on Ukrainian architecture. Byzantine layout has at various times been merged with traditional wooden Hutsul churches (colonnaded porches and freestanding belfries) and 17th-century baroque to produce unique styles. 'Ukrainian baroque', with its trademark green, helmet-shaped dome, is typified by Kyiv's St Andrew's Church (p52).

Otherwise, various styles have come in and out of vogue. After St Petersburg proved such a success in Russia, its planned layout and neoclassical architecture was copied in Odesa and Poltava. In the 19th century there were revivals of Byzantine design (as seen in St Volodymyr's Cathedral (p46) in Kyiv) and Renaissance style merged with baroque – for example, in the opera houses in Kyiv, Odesa and Lviv. A modern Ukrainian style based on Art Nouveau features in the Regional Museum in Poltava and the eclectic Metropolitan Palace, now the university, in Chernivtsi.

One of the finest renovation projects in Kyiv since independence must be the main train station, which received an opulent makeover in 2001.

The Soviets had a penchant for pompous 'monumental classicism', with enormous state edifices. Extensively rebuilt after WWII, Kyiv is full of such buildings. The Soviets were also responsible for the most widespread architectural style seen in Ukraine's big cities – the apartment block. Even these can be divided into periods, starting with the so-called Khrushchyovka, normally a five-storey brick or concrete tenement built in the 1960s during Khrushchev's tenure at the Kremlin. However, most of Kyiv and Kharkiv's housing stock was erected in the 1970s and '80s. The acres of shabby blocks that ring the capital are made of prefabricated concrete panels that could be locked together in a matter of weeks. Despite their dilapidated appearance, most Ukrainian apartments are very comfortable inside and warm in winter, but not terribly cool in summer.

Music & Literature

From whooping folk ensembles to cable TV chick-pop, dreamy Soviet masters of the chanson to post-Soviet rock, music in all its forms flows in every Ukrainian's blood. They're also a well-read nation, though most might know more about French and English literature than their own.

Music

Folk Music

Bandura 'buskers' can often be seen strumming in Kyiv and Lviv for the tourists. Lviv's pl Rynok and the surrounding streets are favourite spots.

Ukrainian folk music developed as a form of storytelling. The guardians of Ukrainian folklore, *kobzary* were highly respected wandering minstrels who travelled from town to town spreading news through an extensive repertoire of songs. These included *bylyny,* epic narrative poems relating the courageous deeds of the heroes of Kyivan Rus, and *dumy,* lyrical ballads glorifying the exploits of the Cossacks.

Traditionally, *kobzary* were required to be blind and they used the lute-like *kobza* to accompany their historical narratives. In the 18th century the *kobza* was replaced by the *bandura,* a larger instrument with up to 65 strings. Popular *bandura* choirs accompanied Ukrainian national songs and folk dances, and this unparalleled instrument soon became a national symbol.

Traditional *kobzary* themselves suffered the all-too-familiar and miserable fate of many who lived under Stalin. During the Soviet era, they kept Ukrainians apprised of collectivisation, famine and repression. When Stalin heard about them, he immediately ordered a national *kobzary* conference, feigning great interest – and then had all the attendees shot.

Classical Music & Opera

The most notable local composer remains Mykola Lysenko (1842–1912). The 'father of Ukrainian national music' applied the logic of Ukrainian folk songs to piano-based classical music. Ukrainian operettas combine more acting and dancing than typical operas.

Contemporary Music

Online music shop www.umka.com.ua has an international shipping service and offers anything from Transcarpathian folk to the latest Dnipro hip-hop.

Ukraine's active rock scene provides a welcome antidote to tinny home-grown and Russian pop. Broadly, the scene can be split into four categories: the legends, the nationalists, mainstream alt rock and hip-hop.

The legends are Vopli Vidopliasova (VV) and Okean Elzy. Both have been going since the 1990s and have charismatic frontmen – Oleh Skrypka and Svyatoslav Vakarchuk, respectively – who seek to promote the Ukrainian identity through music. The nationalists, from Lviv and the west, are defenders of Ukrainian heritage. This category, including Plach Yeremiyi, Mertvy Piven and Mandry, might also fit into the category of folksy alt rock, alongside the edgier Druha Rika.

Next up are popular hip-hop acts, like TNMK, Tartak, Boombox and Vova z Lvova. Acoustic reggae duo 5'nizza and ska band Haydamaky boast large followings thanks to their often exceptional arrangements.

Ukrainian chick-pop follows the tried-and-tested formula of scantily clad singers belting out studio-driven hits. Ukraine's Eurovision entries

SOFIA ROTARU

The most famous Ukrainian songstress of the last 40 years, bar none, is Sofia Rotaru (b 1947), an ethnic Moldovan born near Chernivtsi. Dubbed the 'Nightingale of Bukovyna', her voice is as familiar to Ukrainians as it is to music followers in Riga, Irkutsk or Vladivostok. Indeed, across the ex-USSR, only the immovable Alla Pugacheva comes anywhere near her profile. Rotaru began her career in the early 1970s, gaining many 'People's Artist of...' and 'Hero of...' titles before making a successful transition to the new order of the 1990s. Singing in three languages (Russian, Ukrainian and Romanian), she still has huge appeal among the over 40s.

– including Tina Karol (2006) and even 2004 winner Ruslana – tend to hail from this group, as does high-profile video star Ani Lorak. Russian pop that once dominated Ukrainian MTV has mostly been replaced by local 'talent' but it's still the same kind of porno-pop highlighting the physical attributes of female singers more than anything else.

Many Russian performers who condoned the occupation of Crimea have been banned from Ukraine and are firmly out of favour with the public. There's definitely less music from across the border around than there once was.

Eurovision is followed with a passion in Ukraine and the 2016 victory, which saw Jamala's song about the Crimean Tatars fate under Stalin pip Russia's entry to victory at the last gasp, must rate as the most enjoyable moment of national celebration so far, post-Maidan. Ukraine's 2007 Eurovision entry and the overall runner-up – cross-dressing comedian/singer Verka Serduchka – occupies a category all of his/her own in the weird-and-wonderful world of post-Soviet entertainment. The 2004 winner, Ruslana, was a prominent figure in the Maidan revolution.

Another colourful outfit is NYC gypsy punk outfit Gogol Bordello, whose eccentric singer, Eugene Hutz, is originally from Boyarka near Kyiv. An outstanding mainstream group is Vremya i Steklo, a duo hailing from Simferopol and Kyiv whose exciting electro-pop receives millions of views on YouTube.

Literature

Taras Shevchenko is *the* figure towering over all Ukrainian literature. Literally: statues of Shevchenko now stand on pedestals vacated by Lenin across the entire west of the country. Shevchenko (1814–61) embodied and stirred the national consciousness, while achieving literary respectability for a Ukrainian language then suppressed under tsarist Russian rule. Born a serf and orphaned as a teenager, Shevchenko studied painting at the Academy of Arts in St Petersburg, where in 1840 he published his first work, *Kobzar* (The Bard), a book of eight romantic poems. It was a great success and his epic poem *Haidamaky* (1841) and ballad *Hamaliia* (1844) followed soon afterwards. Later works, such as *Son* (The Dream), *Kavkas* (Caucasus) and *Velyky Lokh* (The Great Dungeon), were not immediately published but are now held in great affection.

Alexander Pushkin spent some of his scandal-filled 20s in Ukraine, most notably in Odesa and Crimea. He was also friends with Gogol and some of the Ukraine-based Decembrists.

Through Shevchenko's prolific work, Ukrainian was elevated from a peasant tongue to a vehicle of eloquent and poetic expression. Combining vernacular expressions and colloquial dialects with Church Slavonic, he formed a unique voice. He passionately preached social justice, in universal terms as well as to the downtrodden peasant and to the Ukrainian nation, referring to 'this land of ours that is not our own'. A staunch antitsarist, the poet was banished to Siberia for 10 years, which led to his premature death in 1861. In 1876 Tsar Alexander II banned all Ukrainian books and publishing, but Shevchenko's message remained. He was, and is, a Ukrainian hero.

Anton Chekhov spent a lot of time in Crimea, where he wrote *Three Sisters* and *The Cherry Orchard* – his *dacha* in Yalta is now the House Museum.

In addition to Shevchenko there are three other Ukrainian writers who rate a mention. Ivan Franko (1856–1916) is another hero who promoted the Ukrainian language. His better-known writings include *The Turnip Farmer, The Converted Sinner* and *During Work;* he was also a prolific poet. Equally distinguished was Larysa Kosach (1871–1913), known by her pen name, Lesia Ukrainka. Her frail health inspired her to compose deeply moving poetry expressing inner strength and inspiration – symbolic beatitudes for the Ukrainian people. Her *Forest Song* inspired a ballet, an opera and a film.

Greatly influenced by Taras Shevchenko, Mikhailo Kotsyubinsky (1864–1913) was probably the finest Ukrainian literary talent around the turn of the century. His novels are a snapshot of Ukrainian life in the late 19th and early 20th centuries and some, including the famous *Shadows of Forgotten Ancestors,* were made into films during the Soviet era.

There are several other proudly Ukrainian authors, but none are translated into English. On the other hand, two internationally renowned authors usually claimed by Russia are Ukrainian-born. Mikhail Bulgakov's (1891–1940) first novel, *The White Guard,* is set in his native Kyiv. Nikolai Gogol's (1809–52) novels *Evenings on a Farm near Dikanka* and *Dead Souls* and short story 'Taras Bulba' (about a Cossack hero and included in the collection *Mirgorod,* in Ukrainian *Myrhorod*) all have links to his country of birth. Odesa-born Isaac Babel (1894–1939) was the most famous chronicler of that city.

Contemporary Writers

As far as contemporary writers go, Kyiv-based author Andrey Kurkov (b 1961) has been called Bulgakov's heir. That might be taking things a bit far, but Kurkov is widely known abroad and his *Death and the Penguin, Penguin Lost* and *The President's Last Love* do indulge in the same flights of fancy as Bulgakov's classic *The Master and Margarita.* In *Death and the Penguin,* for example, would-be novelist Viktor is eking out a miserable existence with his pet penguin Misha, when suddenly he gets a great gig writing stock obituaries for still-living prominent people. Then suddenly, one by one, the subjects of his profiles all start dying.

The star of the Ukrainian contemporary literature scene, Andrey Kurkov has had his works translated from Russian into no less than 25 languages – including Ukrainian.

More for the Ukrainian cognoscenti are the works of Yuri Andrukhovych (b 1960), a western Ukrainian and cofounder of the Bu-Ba-Bu (loosely 'burlesque, side-show, buffoonery') poetry group. Andrukhovych's *Recreations* is a burlesque retelling of four poets' time at a pagan festival of excess, while *Perverzion* presents a twist on *Death in Venice.*

Oksana Zabuzhko (b 1960) is another major contemporary name, best known for her 1990s Ukrainian-language novel *Field Research on Ukrainian Sex.*

TOP 10 READS

- *The White Guard* (1925) by Mikhail Bulgakov
- *Street of Crocodiles* (1934) by Bruno Schulz
- *Taras Bulba* (1835) by Nikolai Gogol
- *Dead Souls* (1842) by Nikolai Gogol
- *Death and the Penguin* (1996) by Andrey Kurkov
- *Borderland* (1998) by Anna Reid
- *Recreations* (1998) by Yuri Andrukhovych
- *Everything Is Illuminated* (2002) by Jonathan Safran Foer
- *Complete Works* (reissued 2005) by Isaac Babel
- *A Short History of Tractors in Ukrainian* (2005) by Marina Lewycka

Survival Guide

Directory A-Z

Accommodation

Booking a bed a long time ahead is only necessary during the summer in Lviv and Odesa and across the country in early January and early May. The Carpathians are normally busy at the height of summer and to a lesser extent during the ski season.

Sleeping Price Ranges

The following price ranges refer to a double room in high season. Unless otherwise stated, breakfast is included in the price.

$ less than 500uah

$$ 500–1500uah

$$$ more than 1500uah

Climate

Ukraine has an extreme continental climate with temperatures dipping down to -30°C in winter and +40°C in summer. These can be extremely uncomfortable times to travel, especially the hotter months. The Black Sea and the altitude of the Carpathians take the edge off the sweltering temperatures, but only slightly.

Customs Regulations

You are allowed to carry up to €10,000 when entering Ukraine without having to sign any documentation. You are also permitted to bring in the following items duty-free:

- 1L of spirits
- 2L of wine
- 200 cigarettes or 250g of tobacco
- €50 worth of food

If you exceed these limits, you'll have to sign a *deklaratsiya* (customs declaration). Be careful not to lose this completed form – you will need to present it when departing the country. See www.iatatravelcentre.com/UA-Ukraine-customs-currency-airport-tax-regulations-details.htm for information in English.

It's prohibited to export antiques (including icons), works of art or cultural/historical treasures without special written permission from the **Ministry of Culture** (http://mincult.kmu.gov.ua; vul Ivana Franka 19; ⌚9am-6pm Mon-Thu, to 4.45pm Fri).

Discount Cards

The only discount card in Ukraine is the new Kyiv City Card (https://citycard.travel/kiev-en/), which gives discounts on museums and restaurants and will, it is hoped, also include public transport in the future.

Electricity

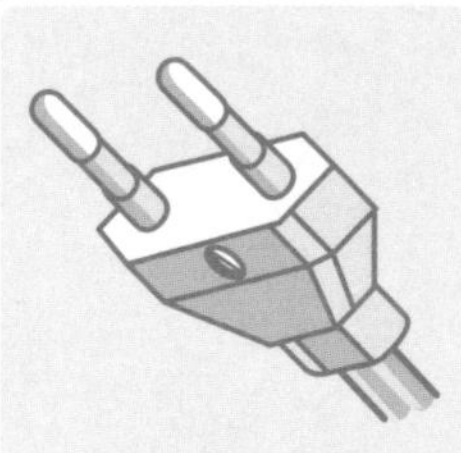

Type C
220V/50Hz

BOOK YOUR STAY ONLINE

For more accommodation reviews by Lonely Planet authors, check out http://lonelyplanet.com/hotels/. You'll find independent reviews, as well as recommendations on the best places to stay. Best of all, you can book online.

Embassies & Consulates

The following are located in Kyiv unless otherwise noted. Call your embassy if you need emergency help. Consulates issue visas and can help their own citizens if there is no embassy.

Australian Consulate (044-290 6400; http://ukraine.embassy.gov.au; vul Kostyolna 13A; M Maydan Nezalezhnosti)

Belarusian Embassy (044-537 5200; vul Mykhayla Kotsyubynskoho 3; M Boryspilska)

Canadian Embassy (044-590 3100; www.canadainternational.gc.ca/ukraine; vul Kostyolna 13A; M Maydan Nezalezhnosti)

Dutch Embassy (044-490 8200; www.netherlandsandyou.nl; pl Kontraktova 7; M Kontraktova pl)

French Embassy (044-590 3600; www.ambafrance-ua.org; vul Reytarska 39; M Zoloti Vorota)

Georgian Embassy (044-220 0340; http://ukraine.mfa.gov.ge; bul Tarasa Shevchenka 25; M Lukyanivska); Consulate (0402 728 4727; Mariinska 4, Odesa)

German Embassy (044-247 6800; www.kiew.diplo.de; vul Bohdana Khmelnytskoho 25; M Zoloti Vorota)

Hungarian Embassy (044-230 8000; vul Reytarska 33; M Zoloti Vorota)

Moldovan Embassy (044-521 2280; www.ucraina.mfa.md; vul Yagotinska 2; M Lybidska)

Polish Embassy (044-230 0700; http://kijow.msz.gov.pl/uk; vul Yaroslaviv Val 12; M Zoloti Vorota)

Romanian Embassy (044-234 5261; http://kiev.mae.ro; vul Mykhayla Kotsyubynskoho 8; M Universytet); Consulate (048 725 0399; http://odessa.mae.ro; vul Bazarna 31, Odesa)

Russian Embassy (044-244 0961; https://ukraine.mid.ru; pr Povitroflotsky 27; 9.30am-5pm Mon-Fri; M Vokzalna); **Consulate** (048 784 1542; Gagarinskoe Plato 14, Odesa)

UK Embassy (044-490 3660; http://ukinukraine.fco.gov.uk/en; vul Desyatynna 9; M Maydan Nezalezhnosti)

US Embassy (044-521 5000; https://ua.usembassy.gov; vul Sikorskoho 4; M Beresteiska)

EATING PRICE RANGES

The following price ranges refer to a main course.

$ less than 100uah

$$ 100–200uah

$$$ more than 200uah

Gay & Lesbian Travellers

Ukraine lags behind most of Europe on gay rights, but pride marches do take place, heavily guarded by police and threatened by right-wing thugs. Ukrainian ultranationalists in the west and their pro-Russian foes in the east of the country have both been engaged in homophobic rhetoric and attacks on gays. Kyiv appears to have the most enlightened approach to the issue, while Lviv and Kharkiv have shown signs of institutional homophobia.

- Homosexuality is legal in Ukraine.
- Few people are very out here and attitudes vary – what's acceptable in large cities may not be in smaller communities.
- Ukraine's gay scene is largely underground, but gay clubs do exist in big cities.
- Displays of affection between two men (and perhaps two women) in public could create hostility.
- The biggest scene is in Kyiv, but Kharkiv and Odesa have one or two clubs.

The following are useful gay websites.

- www.gayua.com
- www.gay.org.ua

Health

Ukraine's health system is under-resourced and decidedly primitive by Western European standards, so it's important to come prepared. State hospitals and clinics are very basic affairs with limited supplies and facilities. Patients are expected to supply everything from food to syringes, and doctors expect (unofficial) payment for every stage of treatment. Avoid admittance to this type of hospital if you can by contacting **American Medical Centers** (032 253 7000; www.amcenters.com; vul Dohomoltsa 3; 24hr), where Western standards of care are maintained.

Recommended Vaccinations

No jabs are mandatory to enter Ukraine, but the following are recommended:

- diphtheria
- hepatitis A
- measles
- polio
- rabies
- tetanus
- tick-borne encephalitis (if hiking in summer)
- typhoid

Health Insurance

Ukraine has reciprocal agreements with most countries (not the UK), which in theory guarantee foreign citizens free emergency care. However, heading to Ukraine without medical insurance would be foolhardy indeed.

HIV & AIDS

- Ukraine is the site of Europe's worst HIV epidemic.
- The country is thought to have 360,000 people living with HIV, far more than any other European state.
- The virus continues to spread faster here than elsewhere on the continent.
- The worst-hit areas are Crimea, Dnipro, Donetsk, Odesa, Mykolayiv and Kyiv.
- The message is clear: always practise safe sex.

Tap Water

Drinking tap water is not recommended anywhere in Ukraine. Bottled water is cheap and comes both still and fizzy.

Insurance

Make sure you are fully insured before heading to Ukraine. Worldwide travel insurance is available at www.lonelyplanet.com/bookings. You can buy, extend and claim online anytime – even if you're already on the road.

Private health insurance is an absolute must for Ukraine. If you need to see a doctor, approaching a private medical clinic is vastly preferable to entering the third-world state health system. Neither are free. Brits should be aware that in 2016 the UK government quietly scrapped reciprocal agreements with most former Soviet republics, meaning UK citizens are not covered for emergencies as they once were.

If you're staying longer than 90 days in the country (and therefore will need a visa), you might also be asked to show you have appropriate health insurance, as decided by the Department of Citizenship, Passport & Immigration.

MEDICAL CHECKLIST

Pharmacists in Ukraine are the first port of call for many people suffering minor complaints, and they will usually perform a diagnosis if you can explain or point to the problem. It's always a good idea to bring extra supplies of any medication you are taking and familiarise yourself with the Latin name if it's not on the label. In Ukraine this is often written in the Roman alphabet alongside any medicine's local name. Most common medicines are available, but it might be handy to bring at least some of the following:

- adhesive tape
- antibacterial ointment (for cuts and abrasions)
- antidiarrhoeal drugs (eg Loperamide)
- antihistamine (for hay fever and allergic reactions)
- anti-inflammatory drugs (eg Ibuprofen)
- aspirin or paracetamol
- bandages, gauze rolls
- DEET-based insect repellent for the skin
- tick removal kit
- eye drops
- insect spray containing pyrethrin, for clothing, tents and bed nets
- oral rehydration salts
- scissors, safety pins, tweezers
- sunscreen
- thermometer

Internet Access

Internet service in Ukraine has improved immensely in recent years.

- Free wi-fi internet access is the norm in hotels, cafes and restaurants across the country, with or without a password.
- Bus stations, train stations and airports often have free wi-fi.
- Most cities have free wi-fi hotspots.
- Wi-fi is available on Intercity trains and on some long-distance coaches.
- Upmarket hotels often have a business centre with a couple of terminals hooked up to the internet.
- Internet cafes are uncommon these days; many of them have devolved into dodgy gaming centres.

Legal Matters

- Carry your passport with you at all times; if stopped by the police, you are obliged to show it.
- If you are stopped by the police, ask to see their ID immediately.
- The police must return your documents at once.
- Do not get involved with drugs; penalties can be severe and the process leading up to them labyrinthine.
- The US embassy in Kyiv maintains a list of English-speaking lawyers.

Maps

Accurate city *plan mista* (maps) are widely available for all reasonably sized cities. They're available from bookshops and news kiosks.

Easyway (www.eway.in.ua) Detailed online maps of Ukrainian cities, including public transport.

Freytag & Berndt (www.freytagberndt.at) Austrian company producing a comprehensive Ukraine-Moldova (1:1,000,000) map. Order online.

GPS Server (www.navigation.com.ua) Download very detailed maps of the Carpathians and other parts of Ukraine to your Garmin GPS device.

Kartohrafiya (www.ukrmap.com.ua) The most widely available local maps covering the entire country. Particularly good for the Carpathians.

Stanfords (www.stanfords.co.uk) This UK travel bookshop sells a wide range of Ukraine road atlases and city maps. Everything can be ordered online.

Money

- The Ukrainian hryvnya (uah) is divided into 100 kopecks.
- Coins come in denominations of one, five, 10, 25 and 50 kopecks and one hryvnya.
- Notes come in one, two, five, 10, 20, 50, 100, 200 and 500 hryvnya.
- Kopecks have become virtually worthless and prices are often rounded up or down.
- There is a chronic shortage of change throughout the country – try to give the correct money whenever you can.
- In Russian-speaking regions, people may still quote prices in roubles instead of hryvnya from force of habit.
- It's virtually impossible to buy any hryvnya before you get to Ukraine and it doesn't make a lot of sense to do so.

ATMs

- Cash machines/ATMs are more common than in some Western countries and can be found in the same sorts of places.
- ATMs limit withdrawal amounts depending on which bank they belong to. This can be as low as 2000uah.
- The best way to manage your money here is to take it out of your account in hryvnya.
- Cirrus, Plus, Visa, MasterCard/EuroCard and other global networks are all recognised.
- ATMs are often slow and clunky. The English translations of the instructions can be unclear.
- Your own bank will charge you a small fee for taking out foreign currency.
- Some ATMs also distribute euros and US dollars.
- When possible, try to avoid street ATMs and use those inside bank offices to avoid card-number theft.

Bargaining

Haggling is not common in Ukraine and probably shouldn't be attempted. The only time we would recommend it is if you know you are being overcharged at a market.

Cash

Exchanging currency is still very much a part of everyday life for many locals. Hoarding hard currency is still common. Rip-off rates are unusual.

- US dollars, euros and Russian roubles are the easiest currencies to exchange.
- The British pound is harder to exchange, except in Kyiv.
- In western Ukraine, Polish zloty and Hungarian forints are widely accepted.
- Banks and currency exchange offices will not accept old, tatty notes with rips or tears.
- US dollar bills issued before 1990 cannot be exchanged.

Some hotels have an exchange office and there are numerous exchange kiosks (обмін валют) scattered along main streets and within markets (though not as many as there once were). Rates vary very little and none charge commission.

Credit Cards & International Transfers

Credit cards are accepted by most restaurants and shops, but much of the Ukrainian economy is still cash only. Also, be alert to possible credit-card fraud.

With so many ATMs, asking a bank for an advance is unnecessary unless you've forgotten your PIN. The process can be long and rather bureaucratic.

Western Union and many similar services will receive money wired from anywhere in the world.

Tipping

Tipping is rare in Ukraine. Round up the price to the nearest 10uah or 50uah if you want to give a little extra. Leaving 10% of the bill would surprise many waiters and your money might be returned in the belief you had inadvertently overpaid!

Opening Hours

Opening hours are consistent throughout the year with very few seasonal variations. Lunch breaks (1pm to 2pm or 2pm to 3pm) are an all-too-common throwback to Soviet days. Sunday closing is rare.

Banks 9am–5pm Monday to Friday

Restaurants 11am–11pm

Cafes 9am–10pm

Bars and Clubs 10pm–3am

Shops 9am–9pm daily

Sights 9am–5pm or 6pm, closed at least one day a week

Post

The national postal service is run by Ukrposhta (www.ukrposhta.ua). However, many now use the privately owned Nova Poshta (www.novaposhta.ua), an efficient branch-to-branch alternative to the state-run service.

➡ Sending a postcard or a letter of up to 20g costs 18uah to anywhere outside Ukraine.

➡ Major post offices (*poshta* or *poshtamt*) are open from around 8am to 9pm weekdays, and 9am to 7pm on Saturday.

➡ Smaller post offices close earlier and are not open on Saturday.

➡ Outward mail is fairly reliable, but you should always send things *avia* (airmail).

➡ Mail takes about a week or less to reach Europe, and two to three weeks to the USA or Australia.

➡ Take packages to the post office unwrapped, so their contents can be verified.

➡ The state-run International Express Mail (EMS) is available at most main post offices.

➡ Incoming post is not very reliable.

➡ DHL and FedEx have offices throughout Ukraine.

Addressing Mail

➡ Traditionally, addresses were written in reverse order (eg Ukraina, Kyiv 252091, vul Franko 26/8, kv 12, Yuri Orestovich Vesolovsky), but the continental European fashion (Yuri Orestovich Vesolovsky, vul Franko 26/8, kv 12, Kyiv 252091, Ukraina) is now common.

➡ The return address is written in smaller print in the top left-hand corner on the front of the envelope (not on the back).

➡ When addressing outgoing mail, repeat the country destination in Cyrillic if you can. Incoming mail addressed in Cyrillic, rather than Roman, characters will reach its destination sooner.

THE MEDIA

Newspapers

Newspapers include *Fakti i Kommentarii* (www.fakty.ua), *Segodnya* (www.segodnya.ua), *Ukrayina Moloda* (www.umoloda.kiev.ua), *Holos Ukrayiny* (www.golos.com.ua) and *Vysoky Zamok* (www.wz.lviv.ua). News weeklies include *Korrespondent* (http://korrespondent.net) and English-language *Kyiv Post* (www.kyivpost.com). UNIAN (www.unian.info) is the Ukrainian news agency and has an English-language website.

Radio

Hundreds of FM radio stations broadcast in Ukrainian and Russian; BBC World Service (www.bbc.co.uk) and Radio Liberty (www.rferl.org) broadcast in English.

TV

Channels include Inter TV (www.inter.ua), Hromadske (www.hromadske.ua), 1+1 (www.1plus1.ua), 5 Kanal (www.5.ua), state-run UT-1 (www.1tv.com.ua), and pop-music channels M1 (http://m1.tv/ua/) and MTV.

➡ Be aware that many streets have changed their names since 2014.

Public Holidays

Currently the main public holidays in Ukraine are the following.

New Year's Day 1 January

Orthodox Christmas 7 January

International Women's Day 8 March

Orthodox Easter (Paskha) April/May

Labour Day 1–2 May

Victory Day (1945) 9 May

Constitution Day 28 June

Independence Day (1991) 24 August

Defender of Ukraine Day 14 October

Safe Travel

With Ukraine in the news for all the wrong reasons, safety is a major concern for travellers these days. However, Ukraine is no more dangerous than it ever was – in fact, with better policing and improving roads, the country may actually be safer than it was pre-Maidan.

Crime

Ukraine is normally as safe as most Western European countries; however, petty theft is a serious problem.

THEFT

Avoiding becoming a victim of theft is a matter of common sense:

➡ Don't flash your money around.

➡ Watch your wallet and belongings, particularly on public transport and in crowded situations.

➡ Stay low-key in appearance and have more than one place on your body where you stash your cash.

➡ Avoid being alone at night in parks or secluded places.

HAZARDOUS HIGHWAYS

You don't need to travel very long in Ukraine to realise that it has some of the most perilous driving conditions in Europe. The country's mix of poorly lit, potholed roads, an often idiotically aggressive driving style and the poor state of many (seatbelt-less) vehicles is a lethal cocktail indeed.

In a bid to stop the carnage and stimulate at least a basic instinct for self-preservation in local drivers, Ukrainian TV channels broadcast daily and weekly programs featuring dashcam footage of horrific road accidents, most of which are caused by mind-boggling stupidity and/or drunkenness.

- In hostels, stash your gear away in lockers – traveller-on-traveller crime is all too common.
- Lock your compartment door on overnight trains.

CREDIT-CARD FRAUD

Credit-card fraud is a fairly recent but increasingly common phenomenon. Be particularly careful when using ATMs and only use cards in reputable locations if possible. Take all the usual precautions to make sure no one sees or copies your PIN.

Government Travel Advice

The following government websites offer travel advisories and information on current hot spots. Note that all of them advise against any travel to Crimea or to the Donetsk and Luhansk regions of eastern Ukraine.

Australian Department of Foreign Affairs and Trade (www.smartraveller.gov.au)

Foreign Affairs and International Trade Canada (www.dfait-maeci.gc.ca)

UK Foreign and Commonwealth Office (www.fco.gov.uk)

US State Department (http://travel.state.gov)

Racism

Ukraine has tended to be more welcoming to people of African, Asian and Caribbean appearance than neighbouring Russia, though that's not saying a lot. There have been attacks on non-Europeans, but the situation is nowhere near as bad as it is in, say, St Petersburg or Moscow. If you're black, Asian or Middle Eastern, stay alert and exercise extreme caution if going out alone at night.

War & Crimea

The war with Russia affects a small part of the far southeast of Ukraine and has little direct impact on the rest of the country. Do not be tempted to visit Donetsk – as a foreigner you are a prime target for kidnapping or accusations of spying.

The situation in Crimea is not as acute, but from the Ukrainian point of view, entering the peninsula via Russia is tantamount to illegal border crossing, and holders of foreign passports can only travel between Crimea and Ukraine proper with special permission from the Ukrainian government.

Smoking

Smoking (including vaping) is officially banned in all indoor public places, including public transport. Vaping has yet to take off in Ukraine.

Taxes & Refunds

Ukraine's VAT rate is 205uah and is included in all prices. Global Blue (www.globalblue.com) handles tax refunds for non-EU citizens.

Telephone

All numbers now start with 0, that zero being a part of the national code. If you see a number starting with 8, this is the old intercity and mobile prefix and should be left off.

Mobile Phones

Local SIM cards can be used in European and Australian phones. US and other phones aren't compatible; consider a cheap Ukrainian mobile.

European GSM phones usually work in Ukraine; double check with your provider before leaving. However, if you're going to be making a few calls, it's more economical to get a prepaid SIM card costing as little as 10uah. Top up credit using vouchers available from mobile-phone shops and news kiosks, or use the special touch screen terminals found in busy places such as bus stations, markets and shopping centres.

Mobile numbers start with 050, 067, 066 or similar three-digit prefixes.

The main pay-as-you-go mobile providers:

Vodafone (www.vodafone.ua)

Life:) (www.life.ua)

Kyiv Star (www.mts.com.ua)

Ukraine does plan to join the EU's roaming tariff zone at some point, meaning that, with an EU SIM card, you would pay as much as you do at home.

Codes

- Ukraine's country code is +380, but the zero is always included in local codes and numbers, so you only need to add +38 when calling from outside Ukraine. For instance, to call Kyiv (code 044) from London, dial 00 38 044 and the subscriber number.

- There's no need to dial the city code if dialling within that city, unless you're calling from a mobile.
- To call internationally, dial 0, wait for a second tone, then dial 0 again, followed by the country code, city code and number.

Time

Ukraine is located in one time zone – GMT plus two hours. During daylight-saving time, from the last Sunday in March until the last Sunday in October, it's GMT plus three hours.

When it's noon in Kyiv, it's 5am in New York, 10am in London, 11am in Paris, 1pm in Moscow and 8pm in Sydney.

Ukraine generally uses the 24-hour clock (for instance 8pm is 20:00).

Toilets

A women's toilet *(tualet)* is marked with an upwards-facing triangle or ж (for *zhinochy*); men's are marked with a downwards facing triangle, ч or м (for *cholovichy* or *muzhcheny*).

Tourist Information

Reliable tourist information is not as hard to come by as it once was.

Ukraine has no tourist offices abroad, and the information stocked by its consulates and embassies is very general and basic.

Local Tourist Information

You can obtain tourist information in several ways:

Hostels Hostel staff and owners are sometimes very up to date on what's going on locally, and they speak English.

Hotel receptions Due to the lack of tourist offices, reception staff have become used to fielding travellers' queries.

Internet There's a lot of information on the net if you know where to look. Sadly, much of it is out of date.

Tourist information offices Most large towns in the west of the country have tourist offices; the east lags way behind.

Travellers with Disabilities

Even Kyiv, the best-equipped Ukrainian city, isn't that friendly to people with disabilities. The rest of the country is worse. Uneven pavements, steep drops off curbs, holes in the road, lack of disabled access to public transport and very few wheelchair-accessible hotel rooms mean the only way to have an enjoyable time would be to come on a tour catering specifically for disabled travellers – and these don't exist.

The following companies and organisations can give advice on travel for those with disabilities, though their knowledge of facilities in Ukraine will be very limited.

Access Travel (www.access-travel.co.uk)

Holiday Care Services (www.holidaycare.org.uk)

Lonely Planet (http://lptravel.to/AccessibleTravel) Free Accessible Travel guide available for download.

Society for the Advancement of Travelers with Handicaps (www.sath.org)

Visas

Generally, visas are not needed for stays of up to 90 days.

Citizens of the EU, Canada, the USA and many other nations can stay without visas for up to 90 days. Australian citizens still need a visa, as does anyone intending to work, study, take up permanent residency or stay for more than 90 days. Some visa-on-arrival arrangements for tourists are available at major airports and sea ports. Check before departure.

For other matters related to visas:

CALL OF NATURE

Ukraine simply doesn't do public conveniences – one visit to a vile, stinky, clogged hole with foot markers on either side at a rural bus station will convince you of that. Toilets in cities are better, but sometimes not by much. A tree or bush is always preferable, where possible.

Where it's not feasible to consult nature, you'll invariably have to pay. At pay toilets an attendant will demand 5uah and proffer an absurdly small amount of toilet paper in exchange. The toilets at newly renovated train stations are quite acceptable, if a bit smelly. Avoid free blue Portaloos, which often stand unemptied for days and can be categorically vile. Cafes and restaurants can often be touchy about noncustomers using their loos.

The bathrooms on the trains are another mucky subject. By the end of a journey, they are usually awash in liquid – but be consoled that it's usually nothing but water that's been splashed around from the tap.

Toilet paper in Ukraine is no longer so bad or so rare that you need to carry a major stash. That said, it's a good idea to always keep a little on hand.

SOLO TRAVELLERS

More independent travellers are making their way to Ukraine, and though the rest of the country still doesn't exactly cater to their needs, the growing network of hostels does. Apart from a few well-trodden international train routes (eg Przemysl, Poland to Lviv), these are the only places you can really bank on meeting other travellers.

However, if you're moving around, rather than staying in one city, you'll never feel alone in Ukraine. Whether pressed against local people on a crowded, long-distance bus seat or sharing a train compartment with them, they will often want to chat – regardless of your respective language skills. It's a good incentive to learn at least a little Ukrainian or Russian.

Similarly, you won't feel particularly alone in restaurants. With eating out considered such a treat here, almost no local would do so alone; everyone will immediately realise you're foreign and chalk your solitude up to that.

Ministry of Foreign Affairs of Ukraine (www.mfa.gov.ua) Offers a complete list of embassies.

Letters of invitation These are technically needed for all visas, although this is more of a formality these days.

Validity Single- and double-entry visas can be bought for one to six months. Multiple-entry visas are valid for three to 12 months.

Visa types Business, tourist and private, with single, double and multiple entries available.

In theory you can extend your visa at the **DMS Main Department** (www.dmsu.gov.ua) office, but the process is a bureaucratic ordeal that's best avoided if at all possible. Take a friend or helper along if you don't speak Russian or Ukrainian.

Many foreigners who reach the end of their 90-day visa-free limit simply make a 'border run', leaving the country then immediately entering again, giving them another 90 days in the country.

Volunteering

Volunteers for the US Peace Corps and Soros Foundation have a long history with the country, as do religious missionaries.

Life2Orphans (www.life2orphans.org) Volunteers are sorely needed in Ukraine's desperately underfunded orphanages.

Svit Ukraine (www.svit-ukraine.org) This NGO organises various volunteer camps and placements for young people with the aim of promoting issues such as sustainable development, human rights and democracy.

Volunteer in Ukraine (www.volunteerinukraine.com) NGO dispatching volunteers to orphanages, children's hospitals and disabled children's homes.

Ukraine Relief (www.ukrainerelief.org) Occasionally requires volunteers to take aid out to areas of Ukraine affected by war.

Weights & Measures

The metric system is used throughout the country.

Women Travellers

- Old-fashioned attitudes towards women of all ages still reign in Ukraine.
- The likelihood of being harassed in public is pretty slim.
- Local men tend to be either wary of or protective towards foreign women.
- Young Ukrainian women dress to kill and deflect most sexual attention away from travellers.
- If you're very cautious, always travel 2nd class on trains. Sharing the compartment with three other passengers, rather than just one, offers safety in numbers.
- Pregnant women get reduced fares on some public transport, but you'll probably need more than just a big bump to prove you are with child.

Work

Since independence, English teachers and a few adventurous entrepreneurs have been attracted to Ukraine to work and do business. Kafkaesque bureaucracy puts many off registering legally. To get a work permit you have to show that a Ukrainian could not do the job you're being hired for.

Online jobs are advertised on the following websites:

Cicerone (www.cicerone.com.ua) Kyiv language school.

Go2Kiev (www.go2kiev.com/view/jobs.html) Jobs and work permit info in English.

Jobcast (www.jobcast.com.ua) Type 'English' or 'Teacher' into the search field.

Rabota (www.rabota.ua) Lists a limited number of jobs for English speakers.

Transport

GETTING THERE & AWAY

The majority of visitors fly to Ukraine – generally to Kyiv. The possible entry of Ryanair into the Ukrainian market means this number will increase. Some new direct train services to/from Poland have appeared and, as it has across Europe, international bus travel has made a big comeback.

Flights, cars and tours can be booked online at lonelyplanet.com/bookings.

Entering Ukraine

- Your passport must be valid for the duration of your intended stay in Ukraine (obviously). It must be stamped with a visa if you need one.
- Entry is usually trouble-free and border officials ask few questions these days.

Air

Ukraine's international airports:

Boryspil International Airport (044-364 4505; www.kbp.aero) Most international flights use Kyiv's main airport (p84), 30km southeast of the city centre.

Lviv International Airport (032 229 8112; www.lwo.aero; vul Lyubinska 168) The fastest-growing airport in the country (p133) – handles a few domestic flights plus services to some European destinations and holiday flights to the sun.

Odesa International Airport (www.odessa.aero) Ukraine's third airport (p188) handles a few domestic services plus flights to a handful of big European cities.

Ukraine's main international operator is **Ukraine International Airlines** (UIA; www.flyuia.com). It's essentially a no-frills, low-cost airline that flies to all major destinations in Europe and beyond from major Ukrainian airports. It's always worth checking its ratings against those of your country's national carrier. UIA is the only Ukrainian airline to fly direct to the US.

All flights to Russia have been suspended in the wake of the conflict; connect with Moscow via Minsk or Riga.

Land

Bicycle

You should have no problems bringing your bicycle into Ukraine. Travelling this way puts you at an advantage as you can push to the front of the vehicle queue.

Border Crossings

- Crossing the border into Ukraine is a fairly straightforward, if slightly drawn out, affair.

CLIMATE CHANGE & TRAVEL

Every form of transport that relies on carbon-based fuel generates CO_2, the main cause of human-induced climate change. Modern travel is dependent on aeroplanes, which might use less fuel per kilometre per person than most cars but travel much greater distances. The altitude at which aircraft emit gases (including CO_2) and particles also contributes to their climate change impact. Many websites offer 'carbon calculators' that allow people to estimate the carbon emissions generated by their journey and, for those who wish to do so, to offset the impact of the greenhouse gases emitted with contributions to portfolios of climate-friendly initiatives throughout the world. Lonely Planet offsets the carbon footprint of all staff and author travel.

- Expect customs personnel to scrutinise your papers and search your vehicle.
- Be prepared for delays heading out of Ukraine into the EU and Schengen zone.
- The Poland–Ukraine and Romania–Ukraine borders are popular smuggling routes, hence the thorough customs checks.
- When heading for Belarus or Russia, ensure you have the right visa.
- Despite the conflict, it is still possible to cross into Russia when travelling by train, bus or car from Kyiv or Kharkiv.
- It is possible to cross into Russian-occupied Crimea, provided you get a Russian visa and obtain a permit from the Ukrainian State Migration Service. You must return to Ukraine via the same route rather than continuing into Russia, otherwise you risk being charged with illegal crossing next time you enter the country.
- Entering Crimea or rebel-held territory in the east of Ukraine from Russia is a criminal offence under Ukrainian law.
- You might need special medical insurance for Belarus, purchasable at the border.
- In the unlikely event you are hitchhiking into Ukraine, it may be a good idea to take a local bus or train across the border, as drivers are generally reluctant to take hitchhikers over the line.
- You are permitted to walk across the country's borders.

Bus

Bus operator Regabus (www.regabus.cz) has services from several (mostly western) Ukrainian towns to Prague and other locations in the Czech Republic. Ecolines (www.ecolines.net) travels between a handful of Ukrainian cities and many Eastern and Western European destinations. Leo Express (www.le.cz) is a useful service connecting Lviv and Uzhhorod with key hubs in Poland, the Czech Republic and Austria.

Car & Motorcycle

To bring your own vehicle into the country, you'll need:

- your original registration papers (photocopies are not accepted) and a certificate of motor insurance
- a 'Green Card' International Motor Insurance Certificate (a must)
- an international vehicle registration sticker (GB for the UK, D for Germany etc), even if your car has European number plates
- warning triangle
- fire extinguisher
- first-aid kit

Your registration number will be noted, and you'll have to explain why you're leaving the country without your vehicle if you attempt to do so.

Hitching

Hitching into Ukraine is tricky as drivers are reluctant to take hitchhikers over the line. Getting a bus or taxi across the border then continuing on the other side is the best way to go. You could always walk across the border, too.

Train

HUNGARY

Chop, 22km southwest of Uzhhorod, is the international junction for trains between Ukraine and Hungary. Because the two countries use different rail gauges, services have a long stop while the carriage bogies are changed to a different gauge. A local train connects Chop to its Hungarian sister town Zahony (18 minutes, seven daily), where you can change for Hungarian trains; check www.mavcsoport.hu for timetables. Long-distance connections include:

Kyiv–Budapest 24 hours, one daily

Chop–Budapest six hours, one daily

Lviv–Budapest 14 hours, one daily

MOLDOVA

There are around three trains a day from Kyiv to Chişinău (14 to 17 hours), all of which originate in Russia. One evening train a day makes the Odesa–Chişinău run (five hours).

POLAND

Poland has an online train timetable (www.rozklad.pkp.pl) in English. The following is a list of direct connections between Poland and Ukraine, but there are plenty of other services if you are prepared to change.

Kyiv–Warsaw Wschodnia 18 hours, one daily

Lviv–Przemyśl 2½ hours, one daily

Lviv–Kraków 8½ hours, one daily

SLOVAKIA

Chop is the gateway to/from Slovakia. Carriage bogies are changed there, which takes a couple of hours.

Kyiv–Bratislava 29 hours, daily

Chop–Bratislava 10 hours, daily

Lviv–Bratislava 18 hours, daily

RUSSIA

Russian, Ukrainian and Moldovan trains still connect main Ukrainian cities with Moscow.

Kyiv–Moscow 14 to 16 hours, seven daily

Lviv– Moscow 24 hours, daily

DEPARTURE TAX

Departure tax is included in the price of the ticket.

Odesa–Moscow 23 hours, daily

Kharkiv–Moscow 11 to 13 hours, two daily

Sea

Cruise and cargo ships are the main users of Ukrainian ports, but some useful scheduled ferry services do exist. As across the ex-USSR, boat services are erratic to say the least, and if the cost of docking and fuel rises, sailings are cancelled without notice. Basing your travel plans around sea or river travel is probably not advisable.

To/From Chornomorsk

Ukrferry (www.ukrferry.com) is the main operator from Ilychevsk, outside Odesa to Poti and Batumi (Georgia), Derince (Turkey), Varna (Bulgaria) and Constanța (Romania). Be aware that services are regularly cancelled for months on end without explanation. Check its website for the latest sailing times and days (if there are any).

To/From Odesa

London Sky Travel (www.lstravel.com.ua) sells tickets for summer ferries and cruise ships from Odesa and Ilyichevsk.

GETTING AROUND

Air

The network is very centralised, so more often than not you need to change flights in Kyiv when travelling between the southeast and the west. The number of domestic flights and carriers has fallen considerably in recent years.

Airlines in Ukraine

Dniproavia (www.dniproavia.com) Domestic airline based at Dnipro Airport. Serves an increasing number of domestic destinations.

Motor Sich (www.flymotorsich.com) Based in Zaporizhzhya. Serves Zaporizhzhya, Kyiv, Odesa and Lviv.

Ukraine International Airlines (www.flyuia.com) Essentially an international airline based at Boryspil International Airport in Kyiv, UIA is also now the country's largest domestic carrier. Links Kyiv, Kharkiv, Lviv, Odesa, Dnipro and Ivano-Frankivsk.

Tickets

Kiyavia Travel (www.kiyavia.com) This useful company has branches across the country. You can buy tickets online for printout or pick them up at a branch.

Bicycle

Although you have to keep an eye out for crazy drivers and keep to the road's shoulder, cycling is a great way to see the real Ukraine. The Carpathians are particularly pleasant cycling country.

➡ Markets everywhere sell lots of spare parts.

➡ Rental is rare except in Kyiv and the Carpathians.

➡ To transport your bike on a mainline train, you must remove the wheels, wrap the bike in plastic and place it in the luggage niche above the top bunks.

➡ On local *electrychky* trains, buy an outsized luggage ticket from the conductor (in the rare event that you are asked to do so).

Boat

Chervona Ruta (Червона Рута; ☎044-253 6909; www.ruta-cruise.com; vul Lyuteranska 24; Ⓜ Khreshchatyk) is your only port of call if you're interested in Dnipro River and Black Sea cruises. The standard cruise is one week along the Kyiv–Odesa route calling at seven cities along the way. Some cruises go into the Danube delta.

Although unreliable, Ukrferry (www.ukrferry.com) offers sporadic Black Sea cruises. Contact London Sky Travel (www.lstravel.com.ua) for details.

Bus

Buses serve every city and small town, but they're best for short trips (three hours or less), as vehicles can often be small, old and overcrowded. However, luxury bus services run by big companies provide a good alternative to trains. Some bus stations have become quite orderly, others remain chaotic.

Stations & Companies

There are literally thousands of tiny transport companies operating services across Ukraine. However, on the main intercity routes the two large operators, Gunsel (www.gunsel.ua) and Autolux (www.autolux.ua), use Western-standard coaches. Opt for their not-so-expensive 'VIP' services if you want more comfort as well as on-board wi-fi. German operator Flixbus (www.flixbus.com) has just entered the Ukrainian market and is set to expand its network.

Bus stations are called *avtovokzal* or *avtostantsiya*. Some of Ukraine's larger cities have several stations – a main one for long-distance routes and smaller stations that serve local destinations. Stations are real traveller hubs with lots of services available, such as food, toilets, news-stands, waiting rooms and even dorm beds.

Information

You'll save yourself a lot of hassle at crowded terminals if you check timetables online before coming to the station. The caveat, though, is that these are in Ukrainian/Russian only. Gunsel and Autolux, however, have English-language interface on their sites. Tourist offices can sometimes look up timetables for you.

Timetables Reliable timetables are displayed near the ticket windows and onboard; Soviet-era route maps are unreliable.

Service Information There might be an information window (*dovidkove byuro*; довідкове бюро), but you can usually ask at any window.

Platforms Platforms are numbered and destinations are usually signposted.

Tickets

➡ Buy tickets online, if you can, using www.busfor.ua or the major bus companies' websites.

➡ Tickets resembling shop receipts are sold at the bus station right up to departure.

➡ Your destination, seat number (*meestseh*; місце) and time of travel are clearly marked.

➡ Tickets from the bus station are valid only for one service. Having bought a ticket, you can't suddenly decide to take a later bus without paying again.

➡ If a bus is passing through a town or village without a bus station, the fare can only be paid to the driver. No tickets are issued.

Car & Motorcycle

Travelling by car in Ukraine can be a rewarding if nerve-racking experience. However, road conditions are improving and drivers may even be becoming a little more disciplined.

Driving Licence

An International Driving Permit is required, and you may get yourself into trouble if you don't have one.

Insurance

Third-party insurance is compulsory. This will normally be covered by a 'Green Card' International Motor Insurance Certificate, which should be obtained before you enter Ukraine in your own car. Hire companies provide their own vehicle insurance.

Fuel & Spare Parts

Petrol stations are very common and frequent on main roads. Innovative, shoestring repairs are widely available, but head to official dealers you want genuine spare parts.

Road Conditions

Major roads between Kyiv and regional centres tend to be in fairly good condition, but some routes linking towns and cities in the regions, especially in the west, have deteriorated almost to the point of nonexistence. Soviet-era bridges are also beginning to fail, especially across the Dnister River, causing chaos and long diversions. A programme of road building is ongoing but progress is slow.

Traffic Police

Notoriously corrupt traffic cops used to be the main

SURVIVING UKRAINE'S BUSES

For the uninitiated, Ukrainian bus travel can be a bemusing and uncomfortable ordeal. Here are our survival tips.

➡ 'Bus' can mean anything from a lumbering 60-seater to a 1980s Hungarian coach to a luxury Mercedes minibus.

➡ On-board toilets are uncommon even on luxury services.

➡ Your ticket has a seat number printed on it, but on small buses passengers generally just sit where they like (but not always!).

➡ Don't sit in a seat that has something on it. This means someone else has 'reserved' it while they go shopping/visit the toilet/call on relatives across town.

➡ Yes, the bleary-eyed guy stumbling towards the bus – one dose of *salo* (raw pig fat) away from a coronary – is your driver. His job is to drive, not answer questions.

➡ Luggage should be stored in the luggage space *(bagazhnyk)* under the bus. It's normally free to do so.

➡ Even if the mercury is pushing 40°C (95°F), all windows will be slammed shut as soon as the bus moves off. The roof hatch may be left open.

➡ Buses often stop at stations for between five minutes and half an hour, giving people a chance to use the toilet and buy snacks. Make sure you know how long the break is, as drivers rarely check if everyone is back on board.

➡ Buses act as an unofficial postal system, with anything from punnets of strawberries to large car parts transported between towns for a small fee.

road hazard in Ukraine until the 2014 revolution changed this. You will hardly see a traffic officer these days and a combination of relatively good salaries, Western training and the threat of severe punishment for taking bribes has reduced corruption in a big way.

Road Rules

- Drive on the right.
- Unless otherwise indicated, speed limits are 60km/h in towns, 90km/h on major roads and 110km/h on dual carriageways.
- There's a zero-tolerance policy on drink driving.
- Believe it or not, it's a criminal offence not to wear a seat belt (although everybody ignores this rule).
- Traffic cops have the power to stop you but not to issue on-the-spot fines.

Hitching

Hitching is never entirely safe anywhere and it's probably best avoided in Ukraine for no other reason than the roads are so dangerous.

A fancy form of hitchhiking, the Blablacar (www.blablacar.com.ua) ride-sharing service has made inroads in Ukraine in recent years, but of course few drivers speak English.

Local Transport

Ukrainian cities are navigable by trolleybus, tram, bus and (in Kyiv, Kharkiv and Dnipro) metro. Urban public-transport systems are usually overworked and overcrowded. There's no room for being shy or squeamish – learn to assert yourself quickly.

- A ticket *(kvytok* or *bilyet)* for one ride by bus/tram/trolleybus costs 2uah to 5uah.
- There are virtually no return, transfer, timed or day tickets available anywhere.
- It's always simplest to pay the driver or conductor.
- Tickets have to be punched on board (or ripped by the conductor).
- Unclipped or untorn tickets warrant an on-the-spot fine should you be caught.
- For the metros you need a plastic token *(zheton)*, sold at the counters inside the stations. Top-up cards are now also available in Kyiv.
- Metros run from around 5.30am to midnight.

Taxi

Travelling by taxi anywhere in the ex-USSR can be a decidedly unpleasant experience for foreigners, so if there's a bus or tram going to your destination, take it. Uber is now making inroads in Ukraine, starting with Kyiv. This will hopefully make life easier.

- There are virtually no regular taxis that you can flag down in the street these days; everyone books by phone.
- To order by phone you need to speak some Ukrainian-Russian and know exact pickup and destination addresses. Asking to drop you 'somewhere near Maidan' won't work. You also need a Ukrainian SIM card on your phone, so they can call you back. You'll typically receive a text message with arrival time and car registration once you have placed your order.
- If possible, have your hostel or hotel call a cab for you – they generally use trustworthy companies with set fares.
- Avoid taxis that tout for business outside airports and stations as these operators are very likely to rip you off.
- Never travel in a cab that already has passengers in it.
- Seatbelts are optional extras in taxis. Child seats are unheard of.

Train

For long journeys, train is the preferred method of travel in Ukraine. Carriages are old and the network in need of updating, but services are mostly punctual.

Train Types

There are basically three types of train:

Express trains The Intercity express trains between Kyiv and major cities have airplane-style seats, a cafe, functional air-con and pleasant staff. They make few stops between the capital and regional centres.

Pasazhyrsky poyizd (also known as *poyizd, skory poyizd* or *shvydky poyizd)* These are mainline services travelling long distances between cities, often overnight. They usually have compartments with individual berths for each passenger.

Elektrychka *(prymisky poyizd; prigorodny poyezd* in Russian) These are slow electric trains running between cities and rural areas. They're often used by locals to reach summer cottages and gardens. *Elektrychky* sometimes leave from a dedicated part of a station set aside for local trains. They are extremely slow and stop at every station. No air-con and toilets are a hole in the floor.

Carriage Classes

All classes have assigned places. Your carriage *(vahon)* and bunk *(mesto)* numbers are printed on your ticket.

SV *Spalny vahon* (SV, sometimes called *Lyux*) is a 1st-class couchette (sleeper) compartment for two people. It's perfect for couples, but if you're travelling alone, sharing with a stranger can be awkward. Not available on many routes and books up immediately despite costing two to three times more than *kupe*.

Kupe *Kupe* or *kupeyny* is a 2nd-class sleeper compartment for four people. The most popular class and also the safest and most fun. Sharing the compartment with two or three others is less awkward than sharing with one other (as in 1st class) and there's safety in numbers. *Kupe* is about twice as costly as *platskart*. Unless otherwise noted, train prices are for *kupe*.

Platskart *Platskart* is a 3rd-class sleeper. The entire carriage is open (no separate compartments), with groups of four bunks in each alcove, along with two others in the aisle.

Zahalny vahon (*obshchy* in Russian) Fourth-class travel means an upright bench seat for the entire journey. This class of carriage is now rare on intercity trains, but most *elektrychky* (slow electric trains) have this kind of seating.

1st/2nd Class (C1/C2) Carriages on the Intercity services have seating divided into two classes (there's little difference between them).

Tickets

- To avoid hassle, buy tickets online at the official Ukrainian railways site (www.uz.gov.ua) or via other similar services if you can. You can then pick tickets up from the station without waiting in a queue.
- Tickets are still relatively cheap.
- Ticket clerks don't speak English, so get a local to write down what you need.
- When buying tickets you need to know your destination, number of tickets required, class of carriage and date of travel.
- You are supposed to show your passport when buying tickets.
- Several cities, such as Kyiv and Lviv, have advance ticket offices in the city centres.
- 'Service centres' are comfortable, Western-style ticket offices found at big-city stations. Tickets cost slightly more here, but there's no queue.
- Never ever buy tickets from touts.
- You cannot pay for international tickets using a credit or debit card – cash only.

Information

ONLINE

Ukrainian Railways (www.uz.gov.ua) The official Ukrainian Railway website is now also in English.

Poezda.net (www.poezda.net) This online timetable for the entire ex-USSR is available in English. The search facility uses some perverse spellings for town names but is still pretty good.

Seat 61 (www.seat61.com/Ukraine.htm) Worth checking out, especially if you're planning to enter Ukraine by rail.

AT THE STATION

- Strictly Russian- or Ukrainian-speaking attendants in information booths (*dovidkove byuro;* довідкове бюро) are frequently surly and uncooperative.

GIVE ME A SIGN

There are so many varying classifications of desk across Ukraine's non-English-speaking train stations that it's impossible to list them all. However, the following are a few major signs to watch out for and words to know.

Довідкове бюро Information desk

інформація Information

Добова каса/каса квиткова Добова Tickets for today (for departures within the next 24 hours)

Продаж квитків Ticket booking/advance tickets

інвалідів та учасників війни Avoid windows with this on the glass, unless you have a disability or are a war veteran

сервісний центр Service centre, where you may or may not be sent if you hold a foreign passport

міжнародні квитки International tickets

приміський вокзал Station for local or suburban trains (usually part of, or adjoining, the main train station)

приміська каса Local or suburban ticket desk

камера схову/камера зберігання/камера хранення Left-luggage room and/or lockers

Кімнати відпочинку 'Resting' rooms, or rooms for overnight stays, ie train-station hotel

розклад Timetable

прибуття Arrivals

відправлення Departures

➡ There's a small charge for any information that staff write down.

➡ Schedules are posted on the wall – once you have mastered some basic words, they're simple to decipher.

➡ You may find railway timetables in business catalogues, posted in hotels and occasionally at bus stations.

Left Luggage

Every train station *(zal-iznychny vokzal* or just *vokzal)* has a left-luggage counter, which usually goes by the Russian name *kamera khranyeninya* (камера хранения) or *kamera zberihannaya* (камера зберігання) in Ukrainian. Many are open 24 hours except for signposted short breaks. You usually pay when you deposit your luggage and retrieve it with the receipt or metal tag you are given.

On the Journey

➡ Intercity trains are like any similar train in Western countries and the same rules apply, except you need to show your passport when tickets are checked.

➡ In older trains, each carriage has an attendant called a *provodnik* (male) or *provodnitsa* (female), who collects your ticket, distributes sheets, makes morning wake-up calls and serves cups of tea.

➡ Dining cars rarely sell anything more than sandwiches, snacks and drinks, so bring supplies.

➡ Toilets are often locked some 30 minutes either side of a station. Bring your own paper.

➡ Don't drink the water from the tap.

Language

The official language of Ukraine is Ukrainian, which belongs to the Slavic language family and is most closely related to Russian and Belarusian. It has about 50 million speakers worldwide, including significant Ukrainian-speaking communities in Eastern Europe, Central Asia and North America.

Many Ukrainians speak Russian as their first language and many more know it as a second language; it's predominantly spoken in the east and the south (apart from Crimean Tatar in Crimea). In many places, including Kyiv, you'll hear Russian and Ukrainian intermingled to create a dialect commonly known as *surzhyk*. However, many locals – particularly those in the west who overwhelmingly speak Ukrainian – still see Russian as the language of an oppressor and it's often more politically correct not to use it.

Ukrainian is written in the Cyrillic alphabet (see the following page), and it's well worth the effort familiarising yourself with it so that you can read maps, menus, timetables and street signs. Otherwise, you can simply read the coloured pronunciation guides given next to each Ukrainian phrase in this chapter as if they were English, and you'll be understood. Most sounds are the same as those found in English, and the few differences in pronunciation are explained in the alphabet table. Note that the stressed syllables are indicated with italics.

WANT MORE?

For in-depth language information and handy phrases, check out Lonely Planet's *Ukrainian Phrasebook*. You'll find it at **shop.lonelyplanet.com**, or you can buy Lonely Planet's iPhone phrasebooks at the Apple App Store.

BASICS

Hello.	Добрий день.	*do*·bry den'
Goodbye.	До побачення.	do po·*ba*·chen·nya
How are you?	Як справи?	yak *spra*·vy
Fine, thanks.	Добре, дякую.	*do*·bro *dya*·ku·yu
Please.	Прошу.	*pro*·shu
Thank you.	Дякую.	*dya*·ku·yu
You're welcome.	Добро пожалувати.	do·*bro* po·*zha*·lu·va·ty
Yes./No.	Так./Ні.	tak/ni
Excuse me.	Вибачте.	*vy*·bach·te
I'm sorry.	Перепрошую.	pe·re·*pro*·shu·yu
What's your name?	Як вас звати?	yak vas *zva*·ty
My name is ...	Мене звати …	me·*ne* zva·ty ...

Do you speak English?
Ви розмовляєте англійською мовою? vy roz·mow·*lya*·ye·te an·*hllys'*·ko·yu *mo*·vo·yu

I don't understand (you).
Я (вас) не розумію. ya (vas) ne ro·zu·*mi*·yu

ACCOMMODATION

Do you have any rooms available?
У вас є вільні номери? u vas ye *vil'*·ni no·me·*ry*

How much is it per night/person?
Скільки коштує номер за ніч/особу? *skil'*·ky *ko*·shtu·ye *no*·mer za nich/o·*so*·bu

Is breakfast included?
Чи це включає вартість сніданку? chy tse wklyu·*cha*·ye *var*·tist' sni·*dan*·ku

campsite	кемпінг	*kem*·pinh
hotel	готель	ho·*tel'*
youth hostel	молодіжний гуртожиток	mo·lo·*dizh*·ny hur·*to*·zhy·tok

bathroom	ванна	van·na
double room	номер на двох	*no*·mer na dvokh
shared room	місце	*mis*·tse
single room	номер на одного	*no*·mer na o·dno·*ho*
window	вікно	*vik*·no

DIRECTIONS

Where is ...?
Де ...? de ...

What's the address?
Яка адреса? ya·*ka* a·*dre*·sa

Could you write it down, please?
Могли б ви записати, будь ласка? *moh*·lu b vy za·py·*sa*·ty bud' *la*·ska

Can you show me (on the map)?
Ви можете показати, мени (на карти)? vy *mo*·zhe·te po·ka·*za*·ty me·*ni* (na *kar*·ti)

Go straight ahead.
Ідіть прямо. i·*dit' prya*·mo

Turn left.
Поверніть ліворуч. po·ver·*nit'* li·*vo*·ruch

Turn right.
Поверніть праворуч. po·ver·*nit'* pra·*vo*·ruch

at the corner	на розі	na *ro*·zi
at the traffic lights	біля світлофора	*bi*·lya svi·tlo·*fo*·ra
behind	ззаду	z·*za*·du
in front of	спереду	*spe*·re·du
near (to)	біля	*bi*·lya
opposite	протилежний	pro·ty·*le*·zhny

EATING & DRINKING

Do you have any free tables?
У Вас є вільні столи? u vas ye *vil'*·ni *sto*·ly

Can I see the menu?
Можна подивитися на меню? *mo*·zhna po·dy·*vy*·ty·sya na me·*nyu*

Do you have a menu in English?
У Вас є меню англійською мовою? u vas ye me·*nyu* an·*hliys'*·ko·yu *mo*·vo·yu

I'm a vegetarian.
Я вегетаріанець/вегетаріанка. ya ve·he·ta·ri·*a*·nets'/ve·he·ta·ri·*an*·ka (m/f)

What do you recommend?
Що Ви порадите? shcho vy po·*ra*·dy·te

I'd like ...
Я візьму ... ya viz'·*mu* ...

Bon appetit!
Смачного! smach·*no*·ho

CYRILLIC ALPHABET

Cyrillic	Sound	
А, а	a	as in 'father'
Б, б	b	as in 'but'
В, в	v	as in 'van' (before a vowel);
	w	as in 'wood' (before a consonant or at the end of a syllable)
Г, г	h	as in 'hat'
Ґ, ґ	g	as in 'good'
Д, д	d	as in 'dog'
Е, е	e	as in 'end'
Є, є	ye	as in 'yet'
Ж, ж	zh	as the 's' in 'measure'
З, з	z	as in 'zoo'
И, и	y	as the 'ir' in 'birch', but short
І, і	i	as in 'pit'
Ї, ї	yi	as in 'yip'
Й, й	y	as in 'yell'; usually precedes or follows a vowel
К, к	k	as in 'kind'
Л, л	l	as in 'lamp'
М, м	m	as in 'mad'
Н, н	n	as in 'not'
О, о	o	as in 'pot' but with jaws more closed and lips more pursed
П, п	p	as in 'pig'
Р, р	r	as in 'rub' (trilled)
С, с	s	as in 'sing'
Т, т	t	as in 'ten'
У, у	u	as in 'put'
Ф, ф	f	as in 'fan'
Х, х	kh	as the 'ch' in the Scottish *loch*
Ц, ц	ts	as in 'bits'
Ч, ч	ch	as in 'chin'
Ш, ш	sh	as in 'shop'
Щ, щ	shch	as 'sh-ch' in 'fresh chips'
Ю, ю	yu	as the 'u' in 'use'
Я, я	ya	as in 'yard' (when stressed);
	ye	as in 'yearn' (when unstressed)
Ь, ь	'	'soft sign'; softens the preceding consonant (like a faint 'y' sound)

Cheers!
Будьмо! *bud'*·mo

I don't drink (alcohol).
Я не п'ю. ya ne pyu

Can we have the bill?
Можна рахунок? *mo*·zhna ra·*khu*·nok

The meal was delicious!
Було дуже смачно! bu·*lo duz*·he *smach*·no

Signs

Вхід	Entrance
Вихід	Exit
Відчинено	Open
Зачинено	Closed
Інформація	Information
Заборонено	Prohibited
Туалет	Toilets
Чоловічий	Men
Жіночий	Women

Key Words

bar	бар	bar
bottle	пляшка	*plyash*·ka
breakfast	сніданок	sni·*da*·nok
cafe	кафе/ кав'ярня	ka·*fe*/ ka·*vyar*·nya
cold	холодний	kho·*lod*·ny
cup	чашка	*chash*·ka
dinner	вечеря	ve·*che*·rya
food	їжа	*yi*·zha
fork	виделка	vy·*del*·ka
glass	склянка	*sklyan*·ka
hot (warm)	гарячий	ha·*rya*·chy
knife	ніж	nizh
lunch	обід	o·*bid*
market	ринок	*ry*·nok
menu	меню	me·*nyu*
plate	тарілка	ta·*ril*·ka
restaurant	ресторан	re·sto·*ran*
salad	салат	sa·*lat*
soup	суп	sup
sour	кислий	*ky*·sly
spicy	гострий	*ho*·stry
spoon	ложка	*lozh*·ka
sweet	солодкий	so·*lod*·ky
with/without	з/без	z/bez

Meat & Fish

beef	яловичина	*ya*·lo·vy·chy·na
carp	короп	*ko*·rop
caviar	ікра	i·*kra*
chicken	курка	*kur*·ka
crabs	краби	*kra*·by
duck	качка	*kach*·ka
ham	шинка	*shyn*·ka
herring	оселедець	o·se·*le*·dets'
lamb	баранина	ba·*ra*·ny·na
pork	свинина	svy·*ny*·na
salami	салямі	sa·*lya*·mi
salmon	лосось	lo·*sos'*
sturgeon	осетрина	o·se·*try*·na
trout	форель	fo·*rel*
tuna	тунець	tu·*nets*
turkey	індик	in·*dyk*
veal	телятина	te·*lya*·ty·na

Fruit & Vegetables

apple	яблуко	*ya*·blu·ko
banana	банан	ba·*nan*
beetroot	буряк	bu·*ryak*
cabbage	капуста	ka·*pu*·sta
capsicum	перець	*pe*·rets
carrot	морква	*mor*·kva
corn	кукуруза	ku·ku·*ru*·za
grapes	виноград	vy·no·*hrad*
kiwi fruit	ківі	*ki*·vi
mushroom	гриб	hryb
olives	маслини	ma·*sly*·ny
onion	цибуля	tsy·*bu*·lya
orange	помаранча	po·ma·*ran*·cha
pineapple	ананас	a·na·*nas*
pomegranate	гранат	hra·*nat*
potato	картопля	kar·*to*·plya
raspberry	малина	ma·*ly*·na
tomatoes	помідори	po·mi·*do*·ri
watermelon	кавун	ka·*vun*

Other

biscuits	печення	pe·*chen*·nya
bread	хліб	khlib
butter	масло	*ma*·slo
cake	торт	tort
cheese	сир	syr
chips	чіпси	*cheep*·si
chocolate	шоколад	sho·ko·*lad*
egg	яйце	*yay*·tse
honey	мед	med
horseradish	хрін	khrin
ice cream	морозиво	mo·*ro*·zy·vo
jam	варення	va·*ryen*·nya
mayonnaise	майонез	ma·yo·*nez*
mustard	гірчиця	hir·*chu*·tsya

oil	олія	o·*li*·ya
pepper	перець	*pe*·rets
salt	сіль	sil'
sour cream	сметана	sme·*ta*·na
sugar	цукор	*tsu*·kor
tatar sauce	соус татарський	*so*·us ta·*tar*·sky
tomato sauce	кетчуп	*ket*·chup
vinegar	оцет	o·*tset*

Drinks

beer	пиво	*py*·vo
coffee	кава	*ka*·va
juice	сік	sik
milk	молоко	mo·lo·*ko*
red/white wine	вино червоне/біле	vy·*no* cher·*vo*·ne/*bi*·le
tea	чай	chai
vodka	горілка	ho·*ril*·ka
(mineral) water	(мінеральна) вода	(mi·ne·*ral'*·na) vo·*da*
yoghurt	кефір	ke·*fir*

EMERGENCIES

Help!
Допоможіть! — do·po·mo·*zhit'*

Go away!
Іди/Ідіть звідси! — i·*dy*/i·*dit' zvid*·sy (pol/inf)

I'm lost.
Я заблукав/заблукала. — ya za·blu·*kaw*/za·blu·*ka*·la (m/f)

There's been an accident.
Там був нещасний випадок. — tam buw ne·*shcha*·sny vy·padok

Call a doctor!
Викличте лікаря! — *vy*·klych·te *li*·ka·rya

Call the police!
Викличте поліцію! — *vy*·kly·chit' pol-li-tsi-yu

I'm ill.
Мені погано. — me·*ni* po·*ha*·no

It hurts here.
У мене болить тут. — u *me*·ne bo·*lyt'* tut

Question Words

How?	Як?	yak
What?	Що?	shcho
When?	Коли?	ko·*ly*
Where?	Де?	de
Which?	Котрий?	ko·*try*
Who?	Хто?	khto

I'm allergic to (antibiotics).
У мене алергія на (антибіотики). — u *me*·ne a·ler·*hi*·ya na (an·ty·bi·*o*·ty·ky)

SHOPPING & SERVICES

I'd like to buy ...
Я б хотів/хотіла купити ... — ya b kho·*tiw*/kho·*ti*·la ku·*py*·ty ... (m/f)

I'm just looking.
Я лише дивюся. — ya ly·*she* dy·*wlyu*·sya

Please show me ...
Покажіть мені, будь ласка ... — po·ka·*zhit'* me·*ni* bud' *la*·ska ...

I don't like it.
Мені не подобається. — me·*ni* ne po·*do*·ba·yet'·sya

How much is it?
Скільки це (він/вона) коштує? — *skil'*·ky tse (vin/vo·*na*) *ko*·shtu·ye? (m/f)

That's too expensive.
Це надто дорого. — tse *nad*·to *do*·ro·ho

Can you make me a better price?
А дешевше не буде? — a de·*she*·wshe ne *bu*·de

ATM	банкомат	ban·ko·*mat*
credit card	кредитна картка	kre·*dy*·tna *kar*·tka
internet cafe	інтернетове кафе	in·ter·*ne*·to·ve ka·*fe*
post office	пошта	*po*·shta
tourist office	туристичне бюро	tu·ry·*stych*·ne byu·*ro*

TIME & DATES

What time is it?
Котра година? — ko·*tra* ho·*dy*·na

It's (eight) o'clock.
(Восьма) година. — (*vos'*·ma) ho·*dy*·na

in the morning	вранці	*wran*·tsi
in the afternoon	вдень	w·*den'*
in the evening	у вечері	u·ve·che·ri
yesterday	вчора	*wcho*·ra
today	сьогодні	s'o·*ho*·dni
tomorrow	завтра	*zaw*·tra

Monday	понеділок	po·ne·*di*·lok
Tuesday	вівторок	vi·*wto*·rok
Wednesday	середа	se·re·*da*
Thursday	четвер	che·*tver*
Friday	п'ятниця	*pya*·tny·tsya
Saturday	субота	su·*bo*·ta
Sunday	неділя	ne·*di*·lya

Numbers

1	один	o·*dyn*
2	два	dva
3	три	try
4	чотири	cho·*ty*·ry
5	п'ять	pyat'
6	шість	shist'
7	сім	sim
8	вісім	*vi*·sim
9	дев'ять	*de*·vyat'
10	десять	*de*·syat'
20	двадцять	*dva*·tsyat'
30	тридцять	*try*·tsyat'
40	сорок	*so*·rok
50	п'ятдесят	pya·de·*syat*
60	шістдесят	shis·de·*syat*
70	сімдесят	sim·de·*syat*
80	вісімдесят	vi·sim·de·*syat*
90	дев'яносто	de·vya·*no*·sto
100	сто	sto
1000	тисяча	*ty*·sya·cha

January	січень	*si*·chen'
February	лютий	*lyu*·ty
March	березень	*be*·re·zen'
April	квітень	*kvi*·ten'
May	травень	*tra*·ven'
June	червень	*che*·rven'
July	липень	*ly*·pen'
August	серпень	*ser*·pen'
September	вересень	*ve*·re·sen'
October	жовтень	*zhow*·ten'
November	листопад	ly·sto·*pad*
December	грудень	*hru*·den'

TRANSPORT

Public Transport

I want to go to ...
Мені треба їхати до … — me·*ni* *tre*·ba *yi*·kha·ty do ...

At what time does the ... leave?
Коли відправляється …? — ko·*ly* vid·pra·*wlya*·yet'·sya ...

At what time does the ... arrive?
Коли … прибуває? — ko·*ly* ... pry·bu·*va*·ye

Can you tell me when we get to ...?
Ви можете мени казати, коли ми доїдемо до …? — vy *mo*·zhe·te me·*ni* ska·*za*·ty ko·*ly* my do·*yi*·de·mo do ...

boat	пароплав	pa·ro·*plaw*
bus	автобус	aw·*to*·bus
metro	метро	me·*tro*
plane	літак	li·*tak*
taxi	таксі	tak·*si*
train	поїзд	*po*·yizd
tram	трамвай	tram·*vai*
trolleybus	тролейбус	tro·*ley*·bus
one-way ticket	квиток в один бік	kvy·*tok* v o·*dyn* bik
return ticket	зворотний квиток	zvo·*ro*·tny kvy·*tok*
first	перший	*per*·shy
next	наступний	na·*stup*·ny
last	останній	o·*stan*·niy
platform	платформа	plat·*for*·ma
ticket office	квиткові каси	kvy·*tko*·vi *ka*·sy
timetable	розклад	*roz*·klad
train station	залізнична станція	za·li·*znych*·na *stant*·si·ya

Driving & Cycling

I'd like to hire a ...	Я хочу взяти на прокат …	ya *kho*·chu *vzya*·tu na pro·*kat* ...
4WD	чотирьох привідну машину	cho·ty·*ryokh* pry·vid·*nu* ma·*shy*·nu
bicycle	велосипед	ve·lo·sy·*ped*
car	машину	ma·*shy*·nu
motorcycle	мотоцикл	mo·to·*tsykl*

Is this the road to ...?
Це дорога до …? — tse do·*ro*·ha do ...

I have a flat tyre.
В мене спустила шина. — w *me*·ne spu·*sty*·la *shy*·na

I've run out of petrol.
У мене закінчився бензин. — u *me*·ne za·kin·*chy*·wsya ben·*zyn*

My car has broken down.
У мене поламалася машина. — u *me*·ne po·la·*ma*·la·sya ma·*shy*·na

diesel	дізель	*di*·zel
helmet	шолом	sho·*lom*
petrol/gas	бензин	ben·*zyn*
pump	насос	na·*sos*
service station	заправка	za·*praw*·ka
unleaded	очищений	o·*chy*·shche·ny

Behind the Scenes

SEND US YOUR FEEDBACK

We love to hear from travellers – your comments keep us on our toes and help make our books better. Our well-travelled team reads every word on what you loved or loathed about this book. Although we cannot reply individually to your submissions, we always guarantee that your feedback goes straight to the appropriate authors, in time for the next edition. Each person who sends us information is thanked in the next edition – the most useful submissions are rewarded with a selection of digital PDF chapters.

Visit **lonelyplanet.com/contact** to submit your updates and suggestions or to ask for help. Our award-winning website also features inspirational travel stories, news and discussions.

Note: We may edit, reproduce and incorporate your comments in Lonely Planet products such as guidebooks, websites and digital products, so let us know if you don't want your comments reproduced or your name acknowledged. For a copy of our privacy policy visit lonelyplanet.com/privacy.

OUR READERS

Many thanks to the travellers who used the last edition and wrote to us with helpful hints, useful advice and interesting anecdotes:
Andrii Moroz, Brian Fackler, Charly Amannsberger, Chris den Engelsman, Chris Wensink, David Toppin, Erland Sommarskog, Fabian Froehlich, Hakan Yilmaztürk, Jerry Salem, Kyrylo Shevchenko, Larissa Abramiuk, Leo Martinez, Osamu Okamura, Peter Rozo, Rob Charlton, Terry Rafferty, Todd Wells, Yuryy Granovsky

AUTHOR THANKS

Marc Di Duca

A huge *dyakuyu* (thanks) go to Kyiv parents-in-law for looking after the kiddies while we were on the road. Also thanks to Yulia and Alexandr in Kyiv, Markiyan in Lviv, staff at the On the Corner Guesthouse in Kolomiyya, Vasyl in Rakhiv and all the enthusiastic staff at tourist offices around the country. A big thank you also to my wife Tanya for accompanying me through the long and sweltering Ukrainian summer.

Greg Bloom

Thanks to pop for tagging along one more time and helping out with restaurant and bar (and bowling!) research. Thanks to Mandy for all the helpful Kyiv tips and restaurant intel. Thanks to various old Kyiv hands for the advice, especially Vitaly, Misha, Vita, and nightlife wingman Yury. On the home front, thanks to Windi as always for doing double duty in my absence, and to Callie and Anna for regular smiles and sanity checks.

Leonid Ragozin

I'd like to thank Dmytro Yegorenkov in Kharkiv for all the tips and great *shashlyk* night at his dacha; Volodymir Chaplin for a few great ideas in Odesa; Ivan Kozma in Vylkove for the village tour, great food and lots of novak wine; Kirll 'Volunteer' for his help in Dnipro. Finally, I want to thank my wife Masha Makeeva for enduring a particularly enormous LP stint this year.

ACKNOWLEDGEMENTS

Climate map data adapted from Peel MC, Finlayson BL & McMahon TA (2007) 'Updated World Map of the Köppen-Geiger Climate Classification', Hydrology and Earth System Sciences, 11, 163344.

Cover photograph: Easter egg, Kyiv, orhancam/Getty ©

THIS BOOK

This 5th edition of Lonely Planet's *Ukraine* guidebook was researched and written by Marc Di Duca, Greg Bloom and Leonid Ragozin. This guidebook was produced by the following:

Destination Editor Brana Vladisavljevic

Product Editors Kate James, Ronan Abayawickrema, Anne Mason

Senior Cartographer Valentina Kremenchutskaya

Book Designer Nicholas Colicchia

Assisting Editors Melanie Dankel, Jodie Martire, Sarah Stewart, Maya Vatrić

Cover Researcher Naomi Parker

Thanks to Pavlo Fedykovych, Claire Naylor, Karyn Noble, Lauren O'Connell, Alison Ridgway

Index

Map Pages **000**
Photo Pages **000**

Map Pages **000**
Photo Pages 000

N

O

P

Map Pages **000**
Photo Pages **000**

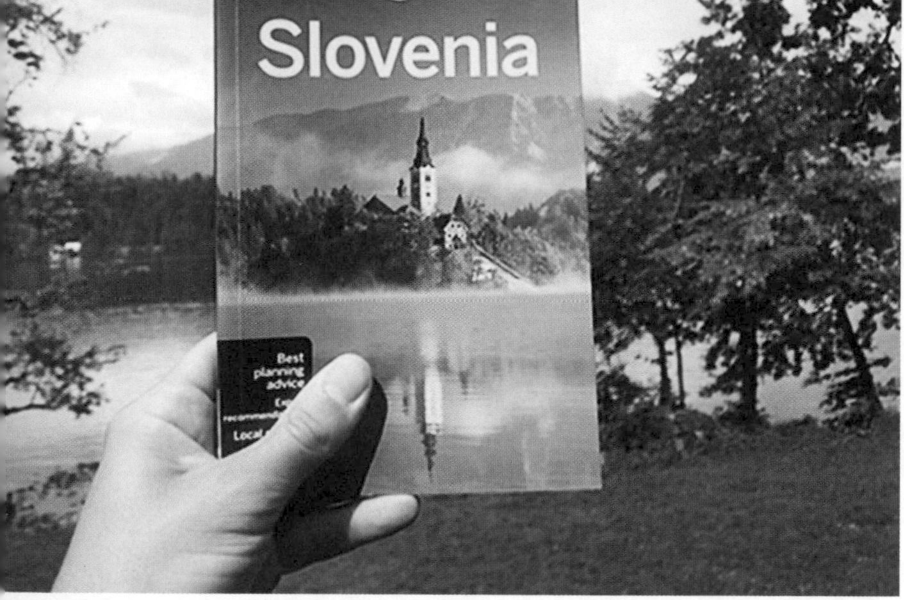

Map Legend

Sights

- Beach
- Bird Sanctuary
- Buddhist
- Castle/Palace
- Christian
- Confucian
- Hindu
- Islamic
- Jain
- Jewish
- Monument
- Museum/Gallery/Historic Building
- Ruin
- Shinto
- Sikh
- Taoist
- Winery/Vineyard
- Zoo/Wildlife Sanctuary
- Other Sight

Activities, Courses & Tours

- Bodysurfing
- Diving
- Canoeing/Kayaking
- Course/Tour
- Sento Hot Baths/Onsen
- Skiing
- Snorkelling
- Surfing
- Swimming/Pool
- Walking
- Windsurfing
- Other Activity

Sleeping

- Sleeping
- Camping
- Hut/Shelter

Eating

- Eating

Drinking & Nightlife

- Drinking & Nightlife
- Cafe

Entertainment

- Entertainment

Shopping

- Shopping

Information

- Bank
- Embassy/Consulate
- Hospital/Medical
- Internet
- Police
- Post Office
- Telephone
- Toilet
- Tourist Information
- Other Information

Geographic

- Beach
- Gate
- Hut/Shelter
- Lighthouse
- Lookout
- Mountain/Volcano
- Oasis
- Park
- Pass
- Picnic Area
- Waterfall

Population

- Capital (National)
- Capital (State/Province)
- City/Large Town
- Town/Village

Transport

- Airport
- Border crossing
- Bus
- Cable car/Funicular
- Cycling
- Ferry
- Metro station
- Monorail
- Parking
- Petrol station
- S-Bahn/Subway station
- Taxi
- T-bane/Tunnelbana station
- Train station/Railway
- Tram
- Tube station
- U-Bahn/Underground station
- Other Transport

Routes

- Tollway
- Freeway
- Primary
- Secondary
- Tertiary
- Lane
- Unsealed road
- Road under construction
- Plaza/Mall
- Steps
- Tunnel
- Pedestrian overpass
- Walking Tour
- Walking Tour detour
- Path/Walking Trail

Boundaries

- International
- State/Province
- Disputed
- Regional/Suburb
- Marine Park
- Cliff
- Wall

Hydrography

- River, Creek
- Intermittent River
- Canal
- Water
- Dry/Salt/Intermittent Lake
- Reef

Areas

- Airport/Runway
- Beach/Desert
- Cemetery (Christian)
- Cemetery (Other)
- Glacier
- Mudflat
- Park/Forest
- Sight (Building)
- Sportsground
- Swamp/Mangrove

Note: Not all symbols displayed above appear on the maps in this book

OUR STORY

A beat-up old car, a few dollars in the pocket and a sense of adventure. In 1972 that's all Tony and Maureen Wheeler needed for the trip of a lifetime – across Europe and Asia overland to Australia. It took several months, and at the end – broke but inspired – they sat at their kitchen table writing and stapling together their first travel guide, *Across Asia on the Cheap*. Within a week they'd sold 1500 copies. Lonely Planet was born.

Today, Lonely Planet has offices in Franklin, London, Melbourne, Oakland, Dublin, Beijing and Delhi, with more than 600 staff and writers. We share Tony's belief that 'a great guidebook should do three things: inform, educate and amuse'.

OUR WRITERS

Marc Di Duca

Lviv & Western Ukraine, The Carpathians A travel author for the last decade, Marc has worked for Lonely Planet in Siberia, Slovakia, Bavaria, England, Ukraine, Austria, Poland, Croatia, Portugal, Madeira and on the Trans-Siberian Railway, as well as writing and updating many other guides for other publishers. When not on the road, Marc lives between Sandwich, Kent and Mariánské Lázně in the Czech Republic with his wife and two sons.

Greg Bloom

Kyiv, Central Ukraine Greg is a freelance writer, tour operator and travel planner based out of Siem Reap, Cambodia, and Manila, Philippines. Greg began his writing career in the late '90s in Ukraine, working as a journalist and later editor-in-chief of the *Kyiv Post*. He has contributed to some 35 Lonely Planet titles, mostly in Eastern Europe and Asia. Born in California and raised in the northeast United States, Greg graduated from university with a degree in international development, but it was journalism that would ultimately lure him overseas. Greg's travel articles have been published in the *Sydney Morning Herald*, the *South China Morning Post*, BBC.com and the *Toronto Globe & Mail*, among many other publications.

Leonid Ragozin

Southern Ukraine, Crimea, Eastern Ukraine Leonid Ragozin studied beach dynamics at Moscow State University, but for want of decent beaches in Russia, he switched to journalism and spent 12 years voyaging through different parts of the BBC, with a break for a four-year stint as a foreign correspondent for the Russian *Newsweek*. Leonid is currently a freelance journalist focusing largely on the conflict between Russia and Ukraine (both his Lonely Planet destinations), which prompted him to leave Moscow and find a new home in Rīga.

Published by Lonely Planet Global Limited
CRN 554153
5th edition – Jul 2018
ISBN 978 1 78657 571 5

10 9 8 7 6 5 4 3 2 1
Printed in China